U. S. Foreign Policy in Asia

U. S. Foreign Policy in Asia:
An Appraisal

Edited by
YUNG-HWAN JO

ABC-Clio, Inc.

Santa Barbara, California
Oxford, England

Library of Congress Cataloging in Publication Data
Main entry under title:

U. S. foreign policy in Asia.

   Includes index.
   1. Asia—Foreign relations—United States—
Addresses, essays, lectures. 2. United States—
Foreign relations—Asia—Addresses, essays, lectures.
I. Jo, Yung-hwan, 1932–
DS33.4.U6U55   327.73'05   77-19128
ISBN 0-87436-268-7

American Bibliographical Center—Clio Press
2040 Alameda Padre Serra
Santa Barbara, California 93103

European Bibliographical Centre—Clio Press, Ltd.
Woodside House, Hinksey Hill
Oxford OX1 5BE, England

1 2 3 4 5 6 7 8 9

Manufactured in the United States of America

Contents

v

Introduction

Yung-hwan Jo

A reassessment of American foreign policy was started by Richard Nixon and Henry Kissinger in 1969, when the fall of Saigon was feared, and when America's role as the world's policeman was seriously questioned. The Vietnam frustration produced a mood of neo-isolationism, and the concept of the United States as an Asian power was replaced with the assumption that it was rather a Pacific and Atlantic power.

American foreign policy heretofore was criticized for paying greater attention to foreign heads of state than to American mayors and governors, to images abroad rather than to domestic resources, and to military expenditures rather than to unemployment. Priorities and issues of values versus number were debated. The narrow definition of national security was challenged as well as the question of overloading the American system and the "military-industrial-congressional complex."

Carter came to the White House convinced that the ability to formulate foreign policy depends on popular support. After a week-long seminar at the U.S. Department of State in June 1977, I am convinced that the administration intends to give U.S. foreign policy a popular basis and to "democratize" the process of decision-making in foreign policy. But does Ambassador Young's style of "open-mouth" diplomacy represent any change in the substance of foreign policy? At least Kissinger's secret diplomacy, based on Spenglerian pessimism and superpower rivalry, will be replaced by what Brzezinski, Carter's National Security Adviser, calls "cooperative activism," combining "power realism" with "planetary humanism." By "activism" the Carter staff seems to mean willingness to work with problems, thereby reversing neo-isolationistic trends. By "humanism" they probably mean empathy for the problem of the poor nations and helpless individuals, with commitment to a non-violent solution to them. Is it in the context of such idealism that the search for peace rather than war has

1

been translated into troop withdrawal from Korea, and the search for human rights is being extended to such an ally as South Korea and such an adversary as the U.S.S.R.? Hardly anyone of the nearly thirty officials I contacted in the Department of State failed to relate the human rights aspect to their respective area or functional specialty. Focus on such issues was unprecedented in U.S. diplomacy.

It is ironic today that the Socialist Republic of Vietnam indicates readiness for friendship with the U.S. due to probable fear of trading Chinese domination for Russian control. It might become the "Yugoslavia of East Asia." Yet it is from its ally South Korea that the United States is witnessing a blatant violation of the human rights approach to diplomacy. Those critics of Seoul, such as Professor Edwin Reischauer, Gregory Henderson, and Congressman Frazer, cite the repressive nature and improper activities in Washington as warranting our military withdrawal, and lament the insufficient difference between North and South Korea. Supporters or friendly critics of the South such as Professor Robert A. Scalapino point to an important difference between the two in that Park represses his opponents while Kim allows none to exist.

Since "human rights" is ill-defined and universally inapplicable, the degree of its violation must be related to the degree of a country's socioeconomic development and the intensity of the external threat that it faces. South Korea is facing a threat from the North although its intensity is often exaggerated, but it is in the stage of miraculous economic development with a high literacy level. Hence the conditions in South Korea hardly warrant crude violations of human rights. Officials in Seoul like to point out that their domestic stability takes precedence over the alliance with the U.S., yet forget in so stating that Carter is even more concerned with the domestic support of his policy toward Korea.

Historically, both Vietnam and Korea were a part of the Sinic cultural tradition. French colonialism was imposed on Vietnam, and American involvement in the Vietnam War (the longest war in U.S. history) grew inexorably after the failure of France's efforts to regain possession of its Indochinese colony after World War II. In the case of Korea, it was Japan—not a Western power—that imposed colonialism, and our involvement began by filling the vacuum following the defeat of Japan in 1945, with a total commitment resulting from the Korean War in 1950.

As background information, here is a chronology of major events in U.S. relations with Vietnam and Korea, giving historical antecedents of our massive involvement.

For twenty years, successive American administrations rejected the abundant evidence provided by intelligence sources of endemic political weakness in Saigon. Yet most of our policy-makers in the

TABLE I: A COMPARATIVE HISTORY OF U.S. INVOLVEMENT

Year	Vietnam	Year	Korea
1862	French colonized Vietnam.	1882	The first treaty with a Western power was signed with the U.S. which was drawn up in China.
1930	Formation of the Indochinese Communist Party.		
1941–1945	Vichy French ran Indochinese under Japanese control and Japan occupied it just before the end of World War II (1945).	1905	The U.S. closed its legation in Seoul and thereafter conducted all diplomatic business regarding Korea in Tokyo.
1946–1952	Civil war broke out when the French attempted to restore the colonial regime in 1946. U.S. support for France came to bolster it against the Soviet threat in Europe.	1910	Japan annexed Korea in 1910.
		1941–1945	The advent of war against Japan removed the restraints on U.S. extending assistance to the Korean nationalist movement. At Cairo, Yalta and Potsdam Conferences the Allied leaders committed to ultimate independence for Korea.
1953–1960	After French defeat and division of Vietnam, the U.S. deemed Indochina as a cold war battleground, sponsored SEATO and gave more aid and advisers to South Vietnam.		
1961–1963	Increase of military advisers to 16,500 by 1963 and the 1962 Laos agreement did not improve South Vietnam situation. The divided Kennedy administration fell out with Diem over his dictatorial rule.	1945–1946	Division of Korea at the 38th parallel north degree and establishment of an American military government in South Korea followed by that of the Provisional People's Committee in the North.
		1948	Establishment of the Republic of Korea in the South and the Democratic People's Republic of Korea in the North.
1963–1968	Johnson increased U.S. ground forces to 541,000 and launched bombing of the North but failed to ease a chaotic political situation in Saigon. He renounced reelection and halted bombing while opening talks with Hanoi at Paris.	1948–1949	Withdrawal of Soviet and American troops from Korea.
		1950–1953	The North invaded the South and the U.S. reintroduced its troops to the South with intense confrontation against the Communist bloc.
1969–1973	Nixon pursued "Vietnamization" and withdrawal of all but a few thousand of the U.S. forces in Vietnam. The U.S. invaded Cambodia, Laos, resumed bombing the North and mined its harbors. After summit meetings at Peking and Moscow, reached peace negotiations through Kissinger.	1960	Syngman Rhee was overthrown by students.
		1960–1961	New government was more democratic but political instability and chaos resulted.
1975	Fall of Saigon and the end of U.S. involvement with refugees coming to the U.S.	1961	Military Coup d'Etat by General Park Chung-hee who continues on as President.
1976	United Vietnam officially proclaimed as the Socialist Republic of Vietnam.	1965–1969	Korean troops dispatched to Vietnam.
1977	Carter Commission's trip to Vietnam and Laos discussed Americans missing in action, normalization of relations and economic and humanitarian assistance to Hanoi. Admission to the U.N. and the U.S. no longer opposes.	1969–1971	Nixon proclaimed disengagement plan and visited Peking.
		1972	North-South dialogue begun.
		1977	Negotiations and consultations begun to implement Carter's plan to withdraw U.S. ground forces from Korea in 4 to 5 years.

postwar era have felt that appeasement of Stalin, Mao, Kim and Ho invited war, since they were socialized in the hard lessons learned from appeasement at the Munich Conference of 1938 leading to World War II.

Both the Korean and Vietnam Wars have revolutionized the direction of American foreign policy in different ways. The former reinforced the policy of containment and helped accelerate the process of alliance-making while the Vietnam War weakened the containment policy among the allies. In 1969, Nixon adopted a disengagement policy instead. As the "monolithic" unity of international communism was polycentralized, our strategic doctrine of "massive retaliation" was replaced by "flexible response."

Following World War II, Korea's strategic importance was so undervalued that it was placed outside the defense zone of the U.S. But the communist victory in China and the Korean War with Chinese participation enhanced the need for total commitment to Korea against China. On Vietnam, Johnson used to say that "behind Vietnam is [hostile] China." Today, in view of the dramatic improvement with the People's Republic of China, has not the official policy for keeping U.S. forces in South Korea been weakened? (See the comments of Michael Pillsbury, a noted advocate of closer ties between the U.S. and the PRC.)

Because of its close relations to Japan—the major U.S. ally—Korea has been regarded by the U.S. as more important than Vietnam. Yet the Vietnam fiasco strengthens the arguments of not repeating the mistakes made there. This in turn means to some that Korea represents a potential Vietnam, hence early withdrawal of U.S. forces if not the commitment itself. Yet many in the executive and security communities feel uncertain about Kim Il-sung's intention, and fear the impact of Carter's withdrawal plan from Korea. Will the withdrawal plan have effect on Japan's confidence in the U.S. security commitment to Japan? Will it force Japan to increase its conventional military strength? Some even fear that it might make Japan less willing to support the South Korean economy through her investments. However, very recently (July 1977), Japanese Premier Fukuda showed some inclination towards assuming a military and political role greater than before, in part because of his party's better-than-anticipated performance in the Senatorial election, and also in part because of increasing demands of such roles by the ASEAN nations. (See the comments of John K. Emmerson of Stanford University.)

What about the impact of U.S. withdrawal on two Koreas? Would not that be as important as the weaponry possessed by the two sides in determining the conflictual behavior? Would not the effects on the likelihood of conflict be greater than the effects on South Korean domestic politics? The South Korean opposition is just as much concerned about U.S. withdrawal as is the regime in power, since it could reduce U.S. influence on Korean politics. Others fear that withdrawal might accelerate the arms race in both North and South Korea.

Whatever might have been the anticipated impacts, Nixon once planned troop withdrawal, with 1970 as the target date. Because of Kissinger's opposition, Nixon then changed the date to 1975. The Carter administration has announced a plan to withdraw our ground troops from Korea by 1981 or 1982. The U.S. says this does not represent a strategic change but a tactical one. Both Seoul and Washington realize the U.S. presence is a symbol of deterrence, but the U.S. appears to be unwilling to assure Seoul with an automatic and instantaneous response in case of Northern attack, a condition the South demands in place of the withdrawal.

The U.S. is often reminded by South Korea and its supporters about what happened to the South in 1950 and the consequence of U.S. withdrawal. The latter ignores what the U.S. did when the North attacked and the hard lessons which Pyongyang must have learned, which seemed to have diminished the likelihood of taking another major risk against the South. Several discussions I had with North Korean leaders in 1974 have led me to conjecture in this direction in contradistinction to the assessment of North Korea made by General John Singlaub.

In view of the clear-cut open invasion launched by the North in 1950, any events like the 1969 Pearl River incident (the last nationalist-communist Chinese military encounter occurred when the nationalist Chinese dispatched several attack boats on a mission up to the Pearl River), or the Tonkin Gulf incident might either make the outside world suspect the North or be unable to say with certainty who attacked whom.

Under these circumstances, why is the Carter administration considering new approaches to Asia on such issues as phased withdrawal of U.S. ground forces from Korea, normalization of relations with the Socialist Republic of Vietnam and the People's Republic of China, and more effective ways to improve observance of human rights, especially when the troop withdrawal does not save American tax payers money anyway? Although Richard C. Holbrooke, Assistant Secretary of State for East Asian and Pacific Affairs, did tell us at the State Department Seminar that (1) there is no major conflict in the area, (2) all major powers favor the status quo in the area, and (3) economic prospects are better for Asia than any other time before, does not the "new" approach mean "retreat from Asia" to return to a "Europe first" strategy? The philosophy of the Trilateral Commission once managed by Brzezinski appears to have contributed to this type of approach. Accordingly, America's vital interests in Asia have shifted to be limited essentially to the security of Japan. Japan can best be protected by an offshore strategy built around island-based air and naval powers and also by improving relations with the People's Republic of China. With more troops in Europe, is not the U.S. more willing to fight a land war in Europe but not in Asia? Is it merely a coincidence that NATO is being strengthened when SEATO is being buried (on June 30, 1977), even though the latter had been ill for all of its life?

In terms of a cost-and-benefit analysis, America has paid dearly in the two major wars in postwar Asia. For this reason alone, a reassessment is long overdue, and to do that requires a comparative analysis of the costs involved in terms of American material and human resources. Even if one discounts the figure of $676 billion as our total war costs in Vietnam (set by economist Tom Riddell in *Progressive*, October 1975), there appears to be little doubt that South Vietnam has received more U.S. aid funds than any other government in the world. Since 1945, 17.5 percent of all U.S. aid grants went to Vietnam, whose population is only .8 percent of those countries receiving U.S. aid. (See the figures provided by the Indochinese Resource Center in the Congressional Record, cited in Figure II.)

TABLE II: A COMPARATIVE COST OF U.S. INVOLVEMENT

Items		Korea		Vietnam
1. Number of U.S. soldiers during the war.		5,764,143		8,744,000
2. Battle deaths.		33,629		46,498
3. Other deaths.		20,617		10,388
4. Wounded.		103,284		153,329
5. Direct military cost during the war.	5a.	$164,000 million [116,784 million]	5b.	$352,000 million [350,350 million]
6. Percentage of GNP.		5a. = 11–12%		5b. = 8–9%
7. Aid grants.		$4,400 million (1945–1975)		4,883.5 million (1968–1974)
			7b.	[Sino-Soviet aid to North Vietnam = $5,325 million (1968–1974)]
8. Arms training.		$6,500 million		$14,249 million
	8a.	[Sino-Soviet aid to North Korea = $2,000 million]	8b.	[Sino-Soviet aid to North Vietnam = $3,950 million]

Sources: 1, 2, 3, and 4 are from *The World Almanac 1977*, pp. 330–333; 5 is from *Statistical Abstracts of the U.S., 1971*, p. 243; 5a and 5b and 6 are from Colonel Michael Eiland of the United States Department of State; 7 (Vietnam), 7b, 8 (Vietnam), and 8b are from *Congressional Record-Senate* (S8156), May 14, 1975; 8 (Korea), and 8a are from Gregory Henderson of Tufts University.

II.

If the fall of Saigon was avoided in 1975, and the Thieu regime hangs on at a great expense of military and economic aid from the U.S., could the Carter administration be able to tell the American public that survival of the Vietnamese government is worth our costs in spite of the domestic needs? If Carter could not defend our commitment to Saigon, will he do it differently regarding Seoul? If so, how and why is the U.S. commitment to Seoul any different from the commitment the U.S. has with forty-three countries formally and a dozen informally? Is Korea too complex and important to dismiss it with just a comparison with Vietnam?

Against these backgrounds, questions, and an uncertain future in mind, the Center for Asian Studies at Arizona State University decided through symposiums to examine the Korean question from the unfortunate past of Vietnam in order to reassess America's role in Asia as a means of commemorating the Bicentennial event. The first and the major part of the symposiums was held on our campus on February 6 and 7, 1976. Thirty scholars and experts on Vietnam and Korea participated, including several well-known critics of the South Korean government, and Seoul's Ambassador to the U.S. as well as an *informal* representative of North Korea. A former political consultant to the South Vietnamese Embassy in Washington was included, as was a long-time adviser to the South Korean President. America's two best-known specialists on Vietnam—a leading supporter of the U.S. policy in Vietnam (U.S. Department of State), and a leading opponent of the policy—were also there, as well as a scholar from East Germany informally representing the Socialist bloc of East Europe and the U.S.S.R. An effort was made to include specialists on security policy, including some members of the U.S. security and defense community.

On February 8, 1976, Ambassador Hahm of South Korea was to meet again Professor Gregory Henderson of Tufts University, a former foreign service officer in Korea and a leading critic of the Seoul-Washington ties. This was to take place at the University of Southern California, and the debate was expected to be joined by a dozen Asian specialists of the southern California area. The Ambassador made a last-minute decision to return to Washington a few hours before the event was to take place. His paper was distributed and examined by Professor Henderson and other discussants, some of whom also participated in the Arizona meeting the day before. One of the discussants informally represented the Ambassador and thus the latter was adequately substituted. In spite of his excuse, the Ambassador's last minute cancellation of the commitment points to the degree of sensitivity of the Korean issue and the awkward situation in which he found himself. At that time, even the U.S. State Department had to renege on the early offer to send us a specialist on Korean politics.

Instead, they wanted us to accept a specialist on Korean economics or commerce. A specialist on Vietnamese politics was available and invited, but the State Department appeared to be unwilling to allow their specialist on Korean politics to attend our meeting.

A year later another symposium was held at the University of Southern California, which was the last of the series of three meetings on "A Reassessment of America's Role in Asia with Focus on Korea." This time, Professor Robert A. Scalapino was asked to deliver a major paper on U.S. policy toward two Koreas. The paper by this leading authority on Asia was debated by contending specialists of China, Japan, and the Soviet Union and Korea. The date was April 2, 1977, the time when the South Korean scandal at the U.S. Congress was revealed and even labelled as "Koreagate." The discussions at this meeting updated the previous discussions and also enlarged the scope of the issues.

In selecting participants for these symposiums, a special effort was made to have balanced and representative viewpoints, as was the intention of our previous symposium volume, *Taiwan's Future?* (Hong Kong: Union Institute, 1974). Compared to *Taiwan's Future?*, this volume represents viewpoints perhaps more critical of the establishment policy, in part because the objective of the symposiums was a "reassessment" of our policy.

Part I of the text starts with "Conception of America's Involvement in Asia." Soon S. Cho traces the genesis of the tragedy of the two Asian wars to the careless division of Korea and Vietnam, about which most Americans had never heard before 1945. American policy toward these countries was based on placating European powers, and without detailed plans, the U.S. overlooked the aspiration of the people and the danger of division. To Gareth Porter, U.S. policy originated from anticommunist-encouraged military spending and consumption and discouraged development of modern industry, and it was doomed to failure due to its contradiction with the needs of the Vietnamese people. He argues that the rights of any country to intervene in another for strategic reasons without regard for the people must be rejected in the future. But Robert T. Oliver, who advised Syngman Rhee even during World War II, would probably believe in "rightful" intervention in that the desires of the people are not easy to define. He also wants to correct the popular conception that Syngman Rhee was a stooge for the American government.

The second section of Part I contains papers of five Vietnam experts dealing with "Past Failures and Future Challenges in Vietnam." To Douglas Pike, an eminent expert on Vietnam in the Department of State, the U.S. and Vietnam have little in common in either a positive or negative sense. He suggests we look at those factors which influence our national policy from the vantage of Washington policy-makers. Yet Phan Thien Chau, one-time official of the South Vietnamese government, appeals to the U.S. to abet the development of Vietnam independence from the PRC and the U.S.S.R., since Vietnam silently welcomes the U.S. armed presence in the Pacific basin. Jayne Werner sees no way that Vietnam can stand directly to threaten the U.S., but that Vietnam might seek a policy of non-alignment. Thus the major obstacle to the improvement of relations with Vietnam is an inordinate amount of bitterness held by the American leadership and especially by Congress toward Vietnam.

How have events in Southeast Asia dictated a reassessment of our strategic theories in reference to Korea and elsewhere? Scott McNall argues that our Vietnam experiences have failed to prove or disprove the theories of limited war, and that neither will our détente with the U.S.S.R. prove our nuclear policy. On the other hand, to Donald E. Weatherbee, of the U.S. Army War College, the Vietnam fiasco rejects the domino theory not *in toto,* although it does reject a security strategy relying on American *military presence.*

The question and scope of American military presence with regard to Korea's security is dealt with in Part II, "U.S. Policy: Whither Korea?" For Gregory Henderson, the policies and attitudes shown in Korea will set the tone and temper of our future in post-Vietnam Asia. Our military aid, which is more than three times that of the Sino-Soviet aid to North Korea, should be reversed to defuse the volatile situation in Korea which has more arms per square mile than elsewhere. He is critical of the military culture permeating the life of two Koreas; the military has been more of an advocate of the belligerent status quo in Korea. T. C. Rhee opines that deterioration in South Korea, such as political repression and defraudation of the state, combined with positive changes in North Korea over the past few years, has nullified the original American premises for being in Korea. He calls for retooling our policy to fit the future and to benefit the American interests at first through equidistance policy toward two Koreas and demobilization of the military.

According to Anthony Kahng, a review of the circumstances surrounding Vietnam and our involvement there should aid us in avoiding a second catastrophe of that nature in Korea. Like Henderson, T. C. Rhee also regards reunification as the key solution of Korea. But Fred Carrier goes a little further and advocates a position practically identical to that of North Korea. As co-chairman of the American-Korean Friendship and Information Center, about the only organization with close affiliation—though not official affiliation—with the North Korean government, he was an excellent substitute for a North Korean delegate. Both of them would argue that the U.S. persistence in its present two-Korea policy is increasing the likelihood of Korea becoming a second Vietnam.

A contrasting view to the preceding discussion is presented by the South Korean Ambassador, Pyong-Choon Hahm, in the second section of Part II, "Seoul's View and American Reaction." According to him, one of the best-trained spokesmen for Seoul, U.S. involvement is necessary for strategic reasons and for regional stability. To him, real ideological détente is impossible since peaceful coexistence does not preclude "revolutionary struggle." In the context of South Korea's top priority being for war prevention, U.S. presence is needed for the South's security, which in turn facilitates economic growth in South Korea and Japan. Critical and contradicting points of view were presented by Gregory Henderson and George O. Totten of Southern California. Added also were the perspectives of Japan presented by Hans Bearwald of UCLA; of foreign policy by a specialist in comparative communism, Peter Berton of University of Southern California; of security policy by a Southeast Asian expert, Guy Pauker of Rand Corporation.

In an attempt to make this book more comprehensive and broad in scope, a section was added for comparative purposes. Part III, "Other Asian Sides' Perceptions of America's Role," deals with America's role as perceived by other Asian nations. Japan is approaching an equidistance policy towards two Koreas while the U.S. is still taking a one-sided policy for Seoul. Yet Carter's shift of Ford's agreement on the long-term stationing of U.S. troops in Korea is reluctantly tolerated by Tokyo. (See Yung H. Park on Japan.) In spite of diplomatic setbacks and the U.S. approach to normalization with the PRC, Taiwan is convinced of its natural viability and has a higher confidence level than South Korea. (See Douglas Mendel on Taiwan.) The Philippines is striving toward a greater independence in foreign policy than Taiwan and South Korea. This is so in spite of its increasing economic dependence on the U.S., and despite decreasing American support for Marcos. To Robert Youngblood the U.S. cannot, therefore, continue to ride roughshod over the growing nationalism there.

Turning to the perspectives of the socialist giants, Bernd Kaufmann of East Germany makes a good defense of the Soviet position which is well contrasted by Thomas Robinson, a China specialist of the University of Washington. Viewing détente as the prerequisite to multilateral cooperation, Kaufmann argues that only the U.S.S.R. has made concrete efforts in this direction by way of handling regional problems as an all-Asian problem. The only country that is reluctant to accept recent historical trends is the PRC, which believes that another world war is inevitable and promotes a clash between the U.S. and the U.S.S.R. Kaufmann warns that the United States cannot expect to occupy a privileged position between the U.S.S.R. and the PRC, for the latter attempts to press the U.S. into assuming a more anti-U.S.S.R. position. Robinson rightly argues that much of the Chinese perception

of America's role in Asia is conditioned by its disputes with the
U.S.S.R., just as much of Russian perception is influenced by its relations with China. While Donald Weatherbee chides the U.S.S.R. for
lack of success in the regional security system, Robinson calls for an
equal treatment of Russia and China, which requires further improvement of relations with the PRC to the level of U.S.-U.S.S.R. relations.

Last but not least is the paper recently delivered by Robert A.
Scalapino of the University of California at Berkeley. Compared to the
other specialists' views in Part II, his views represent a moderately
conservative position, though shared by many in the policy-making
community. From the vantage point of seasoned scholarship and expertise, he warns that U.S. strategic withdrawal does increase suspicion
of U.S. intention, although it does not weaken South Korean security.
Besides, it could force Seoul to tighten its internal control, opting for
more anti-liberal measures. Our troops numbering 33,000 in South
Korea is a small fraction in comparison with the 300,000 U.S. soldiers
in West Europe. Scalapino's opinions are critiqued and analyzed by
Michael Pillsbury, a Sinologist; Seung Kwon Synn, a Sovietologist;
John K. Emmerson, a Japanologist; and by James B. Palais, a
Koreanologist.

III.

In order to understand U.S.-South Korea relations as a part of the
regional—if not the world—system, it is essential to include, though
briefly, North-South relations as well as North Korea itself and its
relations with its allies.

According to Henderson and Rhee, a four-power conference leading to neutrality, confederation, and gradual reunification of two
Koreas on the Austrian or Finnish model is advantageous to peace and
to the U.S. To Rhee, even if reunification results in North Korean
control, this is a better solution in the long-run. With this view both
Henderson and Hahm would probably disagree, for both believe in the
continuation of the ideological war. For some, like Ambassador Hahm,
the U.S. commitment to Seoul must continue for ideological reasons,
while others like Henderson argue for reduction or elimination of our
commitment due to lack of democracy in the South. To many critics,
without the ideal of democracy and freedom, opposing communism
would have little hope in Korea, Taiwan, and elsewhere. In spite of
heavy reliance on foreign capital—especially Japanese—it would be
difficult to restrict benefits to the masses of South Korean economic
growth, which is twice that of the North and which is projected to have
a GNP seven times larger than that of the North by 1981. The question
is, will the openness and growth in the economy lead to parallel development in the political sphere? Having invested so much in South

Korea's development, does not the U.S. have a sufficient stake to help avoid a regressive trend in political development?

In terms of suggesting a new approach to the Korean problem, it may be worth turning attention to the experiences and solution soon to be found in connection with China, in addition to the Vietnam parallel. A conscious effort to fully implement the Shanghai Communiqué would effectively negate the 1954 Mutual Defense Treaty with Taiwan, and vice versa. Eventually, a solution might be attempted to provide Taiwan with a practical means of defending the security and independence of the island without the treaty benefits. A series of Chinese-American talks, analysis, and probing took place before Kissinger's secret visit to Peking. Why cannot the U.S. do something similar with regard to North Korea? Pyongyang's insistence on dealing directly with Washington, thereby by-passing Seoul, is unrealistic, but when compared with their past demands to solve the Korean issues by the Koreans themselves, this overture to the U.S. is worth some response or probing. Cannot the U.S. have bilateral talks with North Korea on procedural matters and on a preliminary basis, and then insist inclusion of Seoul's participation for subsequent and substantial matters? We should not equate blunt talks as aggressiveness. After all, most of the bellicose talk and inflammatory action has come as much, if not more, from Taipei as from Peking. Slow economic development and precariousness in grooming Kim Il-sung's unqualified son to succeed him are likely helping to build up tension in North Korea but probably not in the preparation to attack the South. The only time the North seriously considered such a risk was probably during the American preoccupation with the Vietnam War but not afterwards.

Efforts and means must be provided to promote a Seoul/Pyongyang dialogue. The best way to facilitate this is by a U.S./Japan dialogue with the U.S.S.R. and China or North Korea, because Washington and/or Tokyo relations with Moscow and/or Peking is far better than that between Pyongyang and Seoul. Hence, efforts in this direction of diplomacy and four-power talks are more effective means to stabilize the Korean peninsula rather than by calculating comparative capabilities of two Koreas. Nevertheless, comparative figures of these two might still be of some use as a reference.

In conclusion, there is no way the world's greatest power, with a half-of-the-world economy, can ignore Asia with a half-of-the-world population just because of its uncertain future and revolutionary potential. Geostrategically, it is Asia—not Europe—where all the major powers converge. Hence the world future will depend as much on the cross-Pacific relations as on cross-Atlantic traffic, if not more. Much American failure in Asia could have been avoided if Americans had not dismissed Asia with a narrow and parochial view. If American knowl-

TABLE III: CAPABILITY COMPARISON OF TWO KOREAS

	South Korea	North Korea
Population (1976)	34.8 million	16.3 million
GNP (1976)	$25.02 billion	$5.81 billion
Total Forces	625,000 (+ 1,128,000 reserves)	467,000 (+ 290,000 reserves)
Defense Budget Percentage of GNP	6%	15%
Foreign Troops	33,000 (U.S.)	None
Tactical Nuclear Weapons	698	0
Combat Aircraft (1975)	220+ U.S.	590
Tanks	1,000	1,300
Navy (1975)	78,000 tons + U.S.	44,000 tons
Foreign Arms and Training So Far	$6.5 to 7 billion	$2 billion
Diplomatic Recognition	96 nations + 46 international organizations	91 nations + 10 international organizations
Per Population	The largest CIA	The largest Communist Party

Sources: U.S. Army Command and General Staff College, *Pacific Assessment: Professional Development Course* (R7302) (St. Leavenworth, Kansas, 1975), pp. 1–64, pp. 1–73; Gregory Henderson of Tufts University; and my own.

edge of Asia and its potential was nearly as great as its understanding of Europe, American tax payers could have saved much in material and human resources. For that reason, past failures in Vietnam should serve as the source of success on future American relations with Korea and the rest of Asia. It is hoped that this book will make a contribution, however small, to that successful future, even though it could not offer definitive conclusions or solutions.

IV.

Writing a book from the proceedings of symposiums creates organizational problems of redundancy and of coherence. This required a considerable amount of siphoning off certain portions of the papers, if not entire parts of the discussion and/or papers. Our sincere apologies are extended to those who became victims of the editorial butchery when faults were not of their own making. Thanks are due to the nearly fifty participants of the seminars as well as to our Center staff who took part in organizing these seminars, including Donna Collins, Pat Conge, Ralph Marshall, Jackie Parnell, Chen-Ming Yang, and Pat Johnson for proofreading. But we owe our special thanks to the Center secretary, Sarah Veblen, for the painstaking job of retyping the entire manuscript while making editorial improvement here and there. For whatever defects of this volume, however, responsibilities go to this Editor. Additionally, we wish to acknowledge our debts to the support given by the central administration of our University; the University of Southern California for providing facilities; the Japan Seminar of Los Angeles for co-sponsoring the February 8, 1976, seminar; the UCLA-USC Joint Program in East Asian Studies for subsidy for the April 2, 1977, conference through the Association for Korean Studies; and finally to Dr. Eun Sik Yang, the President of the Association for Korean Studies, for his dedication and support for all of these seminars.

Part I

CONCEPTION OF AMERICA'S INVOLVEMENT IN ASIA

The Genesis of Tragedy:
Division of Korea and Vietnam

Soon S. Cho

Within two decades of the end of World War II, the United States fought two tragic wars on the fringe area of the Asian continent. These two wars were fought in hills, valleys and towns so remote that most Americans never heard of their names. There, almost 100,000 American youths lost their lives. American soldiers, in both wars, fought gallantly and shed their blood thinking that the sacrifice of their lives could save these lands from the spread of communism and maintain the honor and prestige of the American flag. The first of the post-World War involvements took place in Korea for the purpose of containing communism, specifically to arrest North Korean aggression. The war cost over 142,000 human casualties (including over 35,000 deaths) and over 20 billion dollars. Ten years after the end of the Korean War the United States once again committed its soldiers in Asia to stop the spread of communism—this time to stop communist North Vietnam from dominating "democratic" South Vietnam. In this venture, the United States negotiated its "peace with honor" in 1972 after wasting 150 billion dollars and losing more than 50,000 American lives.

The Korean War was fought at the apex of American power. In 1950, the United States held a nuclear monopoly and its economic strength accounted for no less than 50 percent of the world's entire output of goods and services. The United States was in an abnormal condition, one of near omnipotence. Even with this awesome industrial strength and its advanced military technology, it took American forces three long years of hard fighting to repel the North Korean aggressors. The war stalemated and ended near the place where it had started—along the 38th parallel.

The outcome of the war was so indecisive that both sides claimed the victory. Certainly there was no "roll back" of the communist iron curtain. The war boosted the prestige and further solidified the new

17

North Korean communist regime. To the Third World this war was the first sign of the decline of postwar American dominance. In Korea, the United States clearly lost prestige. But it was the Koreans (North and South) who lost the most and paid most dearly for the three years of futile war. North Korea was devastated by the relentless bombardment of American air power that turned most of North Korea's industrial centers and cities into mounds of ashes. North Korea alone sustained half a million deaths in its armed forces and lost one million civilians. For South Korea the effect of the war was equally devastating. Its military casualties mounted to more than 300,000, and at least one million civilians lost their lives. In July 1953, when the war officially ended, there were 2.5 million refugees in the streets of Korean cities, and another five million people living on relief. The total number of dead Korean civilians has never been accurately calculated.[1] However, it has been estimated that three to four million lives were lost, roughly one-sixth of the total Korean population. The damages and casualties of this three year war certainly surpassed those caused by any prior wars in Korean history, including the Mongolian and Japanese invasions of the 13th and 16th centuries. In terms of physical and spiritual destruction and sufferings on the part of the Korean people, it was a tragedy unprecedented in Korean history. In hindsight it was an unnecessary and meaningless war, and if the involved leaders had more foresight, tolerance and warmer hearts for their own brothers and sisters, much of the tragedy could have been averted. Because of the ambitions of a few leaders, millions of innocent men perished and millions of Koreans suffered severe economic, physical, geographical, and cultural dislocation.

In August 1964, the first "tit-for-tat" American air assaults on North Vietnam were ordered by President Johnson in retaliation for attacks by North Vietnamese torpedo boats on U.S. destroyers in the Gulf of Tonkin. Then, in May 1965, the first American combat troops landed in South Vietnam and thus started the longest "war" in American history. In this war, more than a half million well-armed American combat troops fought against the poorly armed guerrilla forces of South Vietnam. It can be clearly stated that America lost more than it gained in the South Vietnam incursion. After the war had dragged on for three years, the American home front was nearly torn apart due to domestic unrest over the war. It turned out to be one of the most costly wars in American history, with 57,000 American lives lost, and 150 billion dollars allocated toward a lost cause. By 1974, it had become quite clear that the United States had, in fact, lost the war. The last remnants of American forces fled from Saigon in disarray just one step ahead of the victorious communist troops. To many Asians, the United States had become an unreliable ally. The United States was no longer the omnipotent "policeman" of the free world. With its economy so weakened by the Vietnamese conflict, the United States G.N.P. in 1974 was only 27 percent of the world G.N.P., and its military power was equalled by that of the Soviet Union.

South Vietnam was also destroyed physically and spiritually by the war. Millions of South Vietnamese were displaced; their families were separated, forcing more than 100,000 to take refuge in the United States.

If one analyzes the Korean and Vietnam tragedies in light of the modern history of Asia, the analysis will reveal stark similarities between the two wars—origins, developments and outcomes. Similar origins can be seen by the fact that both Korea and Vietnam were artificially divided by big power diplomacy near the end of World War II.

In short, one can argue that the United States was at least partially responsible for the conflicts that would later destroy American honor and prestige. Shortsightedness and indecisiveness of American leaders at the diplomatic conference tables at the end of World War II would haunt the American peoples for decades thereafter. Thus, the central thesis of this study is that the United States' policy regarding the postwar status of Korea and Vietnam was a major contributing factor for the Korean and Vietnam Wars. This paper will argue that the genesis of the tragedies can be traced to the American policy that allowed Korea to be divided at the 38th parallel and Vietnam at the 16th parallel (later at the 17th parallel after the Geneva settlement in 1954). If there had been no division, there would have been no war in these two countries; at least no fratricidal war of the attained magnitude.

II.

Korea and Vietnam provided the theaters for the only two major international wars since 1945. From 1945 on, these two countries would constitute one of the most volatile areas of contention between the Chinese and American ambitions and their separate spheres of influence. In fact, throughout modern times, the international environment has had a peculiarly powerful impact on Korean and Vietnamese affairs.

But these two nations have much more in common than their recent international experience. Even though each was deeply influenced by the Chinese culture, both ultimately attained independence from the "Celestial Empire," with each bearing the brunt of Western colonialism. Thus the invitation to compare their patterns of internal and external development is a tempting one, especially from the standpoint of their relationships with the U.S. Nevertheless, before the start of World War II, the United States government had very little knowledge or interest in these two countries.

Since 1905, the United States recognized Japan's predominant interest in Korea and treated Korea as an integral part of the Japanese Empire. From its birth in 1919, the Korean Government in Exile (the Provisional Government) strenuously sought official recognition by the Chinese and American governments. At times, its efforts won the sympathy of many Chinese and American leaders who had some knowledge of Korea. In April 1942, the Chinese government proposed to "extend such recognition without delay" and sought the American government's support for this overture. However, the United States opposed the accordance of the recognition to any one Korean group, pointing out such factors as: (1) the lack of unity existing among diverse Korean groups; and (2) the exiled leadership group existing outside of Korea had little association with the indigenous Korean population.[2] Subsequently, the Chinese government also withheld recognition. The failure of attaining this official recognition at that point in time proved to be fatal for the realization of a Korean dream, i.e., the establishment of a unified independent nation that would become effective upon the surrender of Japan.

Since the Manchurian crisis of 1931, the United States had strenuously opposed Japan's encroachment of Chinese sovereignty. The United States employed all available diplomatic means at its command, including a refusal to recognize Japan's acquisition of Manchuria. Public opinion in the United States also strongly supported the "Hoover-Stimson Doctrine" that advocated this non-recognition.[3] Nevertheless, the United States paid little attention to the appeals of leaders and showed little interest in the plight of Korea. Korea had virtually become a forgotten nation. During World War II, U.S. officials were absorbed with the more immediate problem of winning the war and paid little attention to the potential importance of Korea's strategic position and its key role in the future of Asian international relations. Thus the Korean problem never became an important issue to American leaders until the time of the Cairo Conference (1943).

Unlike the Korean situation, the United States paid careful attention to the problems of Vietnam during World War II. However, it was not until the start of World War II, when Japan occupied the French colony, that America became interested in Vietnam. American leaders worried about Vietnam's strategic importance in defense of the Philippines and, particularly, American economic interests in the area of Southeast Asia. In fact, the United States considered Vietnam of such strategic importance that this area played a major role in the subsequent war between the United States and Japan.[4]

Prior to World War II, the Japanese government had long been irritated by the supply traffic along the Haiphong-Hanoi-Kuming Railroad that ran between French Indochina and the Yunan Province of China. By cutting this supply route, the Japanese government sought to stop the continuous flow of American arms and supplies to Chiang

Kai-shek. Promoted by the outbreak of war in Europe, and given impetus by the speedy success of Germany's occupation of France, Japan decided to move into Southeast Asia in order to secure important raw materials and food stuffs for itself. In April 1940, Japan bombed the Hanoi-Kuming Railroad and forced France to agree to the suspension, transferring munitions and war supplies to China.[5] On June 18, 1940, one day after the defeated France requested an armistice with Germany, Japan demanded that France close down the Hanoi-Kuming Railroad completely and allow Japan to station its military observers in Tongking area. Under this pressure the powerless Vichy government signed on August 30, 1940, an agreement with Japan granting the Japanese army the right of passage through Indochina and the establishment of military bases in North Vietnam. Afterwards, the French were forced to make concession after concession, and finally on July 29, 1941, they allowed Japan to use military facilities throughout all of Vietnam. By the end of 1941, Japanese forces militarily controlled all of French Indochina and planned to move further south to Thailand and Malaysia.

However, we have to remember, the concessions made by France to Japan in this period were made not only because France was weak and helpless, but also because no support was forthcoming from the United States and Great Britain. The failure of British support was understandable because she was engaging in a life and death struggle against the Nazi attack on her homeland. The United States, however, was in a much better position to aid France in Indochina, but chose not to do so. Despite the urgent pleas of the Vichy government, the United States maintained that it could not give any aid because French forces in Indochina offered little resistance to the Japanese demands, and because the Vichy government failed to keep Washington informed on its concessions to Japan. However, the underlying reason for no aid was the American fear that military aid would inevitably draw the United States into war against Japan. Sumner Welles, Undersecretary of State, argued vehemently in July of 1941 that the United States should not enforce sanctions against Japan because of the risk of war, and because of American public opinion that was opposed to any such entanglement.[6] This indecisive American policy toward French Indochina certainly encouraged the Japanese war planners to move more boldly into the Southeast Asian area and to further threaten the sphere of interest of the United States.

Whether American military aid to French Indochina could have deterred Japanese occupation of this strategic peninsula is dubious, but America's indecisive policy certainly did not help the French and Vietnamese resistance movements there. The formulation of America's policy toward French Indochina was further complicated by the problem of deciding whether to deal with the Vichy regime under

Marshall Henri Petan or the French Committee of National Liberation under General Charles De Gaulle. Unlike Great Britain and the Soviet Union, the United States at this time decided not to support the De Gaulle "Free France" movement on the grounds that De Gaulle had no significant following, in or out of France.[7] Furthermore, the personality conflict and the mutual antipathy between Roosevelt and De Gaulle heavily influenced America's decision not to recognize De Gaulle's "Committee of Liberation." Roosevelt was greatly disturbed by De Gaulle's "decisions of Grandeur," while De Gaulle was incensed by Roosevelt's self-appointed posture as the savior of the colonial world and guardian of democracy.[8]

III.

As the war progressed, President Roosevelt's antipathy toward colonialism became increasingly dominant, and his idea of liberating the colonial world began to create serious conflict between the U.S. and Great Britain and France (with both the Vichy and De Gaulle groups). The Atlantic Charter of August 1941, which incorporated the basic principles for future peace agreed upon by Roosevelt and Churchill, clearly manifested the lofty idealism of President Roosevelt.[9] The third of the eight principles in the Atlantic Charter states: "they respect the right of all peoples to choose the form of government under which they live; and they wish to see sovereign rights and self-government might be attained." They specifically encouraged the Korean and Vietnamese people to look forward to the prospect of self-government and independence after the end of the Second World War. Just like Woodrow Wilson, President Roosevelt genuinely hoped that the war would end the colonial empire of the Western European nations. Colonialism was, after all, an anathema to the ideology of the "Founding Fathers" and remains diametrically opposed to American custom and tradition. On March 15, 1941, President Roosevelt declared:

> There has never been, there isn't now, and there never will be, any race of people on earth fit to serve as masters of their fellow men. . . . We believe that any nationality, no matter how small, has the inherent right to its own nationhood.[10]

No Asian leaders seriously doubted the sincerity of the published manifesto, nor the good intentions of the American President. To them, he was the only hope that they could achieve their independence and be free from the colonial yoke, which had long dehumanized them and mercilessly exploited them. Franklin D. Roosevelt was the embodiment of American idealism and the hope of colonial people. Hope is eternal; but, some of the older and more informed leaders in Korea and Vietnam must have remembered Wilson's idealism and how his words were never turned into action.

Roosevelt deplored French colonialism and steadfastly stood against the return of active French control of Indochina after the end of the war. Roosevelt felt that French misrule in Indochina had facilitated the easy Japanese takeover of the French colony. In February of 1943, on the way to the Casablanca Conference, the President expressed his feelings to his son:

> How do they belong to France . . .? Take Indochina. The Japanese control that colony now; why was it a cinch for the Japanese to conquer that land? The native indo-Chinese had been so flagrantly downtrodden that they thought to themselves: anything must be better than to live under French colonial rule! Should a land belong to France? By what logic and by what custom and by what historical rule . . .? Don't think for a moment . . . that Americans would be dying tonight if it had not been for the shortsighted greed of the French, British and Dutch.[11]

Roosevelt's anti-colonialist sentiments were shared by many other important Americans, both within and outside the government. Vice-President Henry Wallace and the 1940 republican candidate Wendell Wilkie expressed similar views toward colonialism. Wilkie strongly denounced the "white man's burden philosophy" that had been prevalent in the American and British attitudes toward Asia.[12]

American predilections of anti-colonialism greatly disturbed British and French leaders. British and French leaders were not ready to renounce their nations' colonies in order to fulfill the promise of the Atlantic Charter. The French people felt that through their empire they were rightly and honorably fulfilling their "mission civilisatrice." On this point the Vichy and De Gaulle groups shared a common attitude. De Gaulle had his own mission for France to fulfill and resented Roosevelt arbitrarily dictating what the future should be for France and the rest of the world.[13] Perhaps no Frenchman was more distressed by the possibility of France losing her Empire than was Charles De Gaulle. British leaders also felt that Roosevelt's ideas of self-government by the colonial people seriously threatened their holdings in India, Burma and in other parts of the world. As early as March 1942, in a letter to Churchill he urged the promotion of the idea of self-government for India. Churchill perceived Roosevelt's idea to be ridiculous, and declared that he was not going to be "the King's First Minister to preside over the liquidation of the British Empire."[14]

IV.

Despite repeated pronouncement by the United States government that Japanese occupation of South Vietnam seriously threatened American national interests in that part of Asia, the Japanese government on July 26, 1941, forced the Vichy government to accept a joint protectorate of Indochina and then quickly moved its troops into South Vietnam. On the same day, President Roosevelt acted by issuing an Executive Order to freeze Japanese assets in the United States and to stop completely the trade between the United States and Japan. The United States considered Japanese occupation of Indochina a serious threat to its own security, and further inaction or concessions would lead to complete domination of Southeast Asia by the Japanese. Americans feared that the Japanese wanted to extend their "Empire" so as to include the Philippine Islands. President Roosevelt's message to the Japanese Ambassador on December 2, 1941, stated that Japanese military occupation of Indochina "would seem to imply the utilization of these forces by Japan for the purpose of further aggression, since no such number of forces could possibly be required for the policing of that region."[15] The Japanese regarded this action as tantamount to encirclement. They perceived the American, the British, the Chinese and the Dutch as attempting to cut off the lifeline to Japan.[16] President Roosevelt's last ditch appeal of December 6, 1941, to the Emperor of Japan's reason and sense of humanity was not heeded. The next day Japan attacked Pearl Harbor and the Pacific War began. There is no doubt that the Japanese occupation of Indochina was a key issue in the conflict between the United States and Japan that eventually led into the total war.

In a time of war, moralism and idealism tend to give way to realism and expediency. The United States needed to support French authority in Indochina in order to encourage French and Vietnamese resistance to Japanese occupation. Thus, the United States gradually toned down its attack on the French colonialism. Furthermore, American officials indicated possible American support for the postwar preservation of French rule in Vietnam. On August 2, 1941, Secretary Cordell Hull hinted that the American government might support French efforts to preserve their Empire, depending on how effectively the French resisted the Axis powers—both within France (underground, allied forces) and in the French colonies. President Roosevelt's letter to Marshall Petan on December 7, 1941, implied a qualified American willingness to recognize the French Empire "as long as French sovereign control remains in reality purely French. . . ."[17] However, as Japanese control over Indochina became more extensive and more manifest, the sympathy of the American government for the restoration of French sovereignty over Vietnam diminished. Nevertheless, with no alternatives left, on November 2, 1942, the American government clearly indicated its support for the preservation of the French colony in Vietnam after the end of the war.[18] America's ambivalent position on the Indochina question not only worried the French, it also worried the Vietnamese leaders who wanted postwar independence. America's credibility was being questioned by the pro-colonialist French and the anti-colonialist Vietnamese.

To the Vietnamese and Korean leaders who were striving for their independence, American policy toward colonialism was less than clear. To them, America looked like a man trying to straddle a fence, but a man who would in the near future be forced to choose one side or the other.

V.

Immediately after the outbreak of the Pacific War, all exiled Korean groups applied to be recognized by the U.S. as the official Provisional Government, or at least for an official declaration recognizing the general independence of Korea. On December 11, 1941, three days after the American declaration of war, the Korean Provisional Government in exile also declared war against Japan.[19] In order to gain the support of the United States, the Provisional Government, through Dr. Syngman Rhee in Washington, offered the State Department the full support of Korean guerrillas and requested the recognition of the Provisional Government. Dr. Rhee suggested that U.S. recognition of the Provisional Government would make possible the effective organization of Korean guerrilla attacks upon the Japanese supply lines in Korea, and would eventually prevent a possible seizure of Korea by Russia in case the Soviet Union entered the Pacific War.[20]

The Provisional Government (P.G.) sent letters to Chinese Nationalist President Chiang Kai-shek, U.S. President Roosevelt, and British Prime Minister Churchill urging that recognition of the P.G. would best serve the war efforts of the allies. When Dr. Rhee presented the letter to Dr. Stanley Hornbeck, the Chief of the Office of Far Eastern Affairs in the U.S. State Department, Hornbeck accepted the letter with careful circumspection and he emphasized that "he was not accepting Dr. Rhee in any degree as the representative of either a nation or a people."[21] Later, Dr. Rhee's request for recognition was flatly refused and he was not given any sign of encouragement. At this time the Department of State had practically no information on the Provisional Government. Thus, on December 22, 1941, two weeks after the declaration of war against Japan, the State Department instructed its Ambassador to China to "make very discreet inquiries" of the Nationalist Government as to its perception and attitude about the Provisional Government of the Republic of Korea. But, Ambassador Gauss's subsequent reports on the inquiries were discouraging. He reported that the Korean Provisional Government was dominated by the moderate Korean Independence Party and had no support from the left-wing National Revolutionary Party, which had "a large following among Koreans in Manchuria." He also reported that the Chinese government position was "one of sympathy but hesitation to accord formal recognition" to any particular group in the face of obvious disunity among Korean expatriates and the inability of any one of the organizations to show that it had a real following among the Korean masses.[22]

Strangely enough, even after the declaration of war, the State Department seemed seriously concerned over harsh Japanese retaliations upon learning that the U.S. had granted recognition to the Korean Provisional Government. However, a more pressing reason for American reluctance to grant this recognition was the potential of Russian interference. When Dr. Rhee had a chance to talk about Korean problems with Mr. Alger Hiss, who served as a direct representative of Secretary Hull in the field of the Far Eastern Affairs, Mr. Hiss declared to Dr. Rhee that since his proposal involved a recognition of the Korean government, there was "little or nothing the United States could do" because the recognition could offend the Soviet Union, which traditionally had a great interest in Korea.[23]

The specific question of according some sort of recognition to the Korean Provisional Government and the more general question of Korean independence per se were informally discussed in early 1942 by members at the Pacific War Council. This Council agreed to postpone any positive action until it might be more useful in arousing a Korean revolt against Japan. It unanimously decided that recognition would be "premature and unwise."[24] It is, however, unknown whether their decisions were based upon humanitarian considerations or upon the portended actions by Russia and Japan. It is quite probable that at that time recognition would have frustrated Japanese intentions for an early settlement of the Pacific War. Even though Dr. Rhee continuously warned the State Department in subsequent letters that "the inevitable consequence of the rejection of the Government of the Republic of Korea would result in the creation of a communist state," the State Department paid little attention.[25]

In February 1942, a "Liberty Conference" was held at the La Fayette Hotel in Washington, D.C. for the purpose of showing solidarity of Korean groups within the United States and support strengthening diplomatic ties with the Korean P.G. But the show of solidarity among the Korean group at this meeting produced nothing more than an expression of sympathy and encouragement from various U.S. officials. Furthermore, in the latter part of 1942, Dr. Rhee was coldly informed by Hornbeck that "in the opinion of the State Department he was wholly unknown inside Korea and the Provisional Government was no more than a self-constituted club with limited membership among the exiled Korean people."[26] Thus, the State Department made it clear that it had no intention whatsoever of recognizing the Provisional Government as the legal government of the Korean people.

On the other hand, in April 1942, the Chinese government

proposed that the United States "extend such recognition without delay." In fact, some months previously, Dr. Quo Tai-chi, then Minister of Chinese Foreign Affairs, recommended recognition of the Korean independence movement. But President Chiang Kai-shek vetoed this recommendation and urged delay. This negative action aroused the suspicion of the Korean P.G. leaders with regard to future Chinese intentions on Korea. Thus, primary considerations in reaching this decision to accord "the recognition without delay" were that by recognition the Chinese would: (1) dispel any suspicions that China had any territorial ambitions, not only to Korea but also to Thailand and Burma; and (2) give evidence of China's adherence to the principles of the Atlantic Charter.[27]

The United States opposed the Chinese government's proposed recognition of any one Korean group based on such factors as: (1) the lack of unity existing among Korean groups; and (2) the possibility that the groups existing outside of Korea had little association with the Korean population in Korea.[28] Secretary of State Cordell Hull added another point to President Roosevelt's objections against recognition by the U.S. at this time. The Secretary perceived that if the Korean Provisional Government was recognized by the Chinese government, the Soviet Union might support some other Korean group associated ideologically with the Soviet Union. He thought the Chinese government might be motivated to grant recognition because of its "wish to nip in the bud the development of any Soviet supported Korean group." Thus the consideration of Soviet reaction was the paramount reason in opposing this recognition. Accordingly, the Chinese government withheld its recognition.

Judging from the above development in Korea and Vietnam, we have seen that lofty idealism abruptly gave way to pragmatism and expediency. The United States was more concerned about the attitudes of its wartime allies, Great Britain, France, and the Soviet Union, than it was with the propagation of idealistic policies such as anti-colonialism and representative democracy. Although in principle President Roosevelt was still opposed to colonialism by all the European powers, he had to soften his attitude and compromise with the more powerful allies. Since Roosevelt still thought that colonialism of any sort was despicable, he began to consider possible alternatives to postwar French rule in Vietnam. He came to the conclusion that the best answer was for Indochina and Korea to be placed under some form of "international trusteeship."

Early in 1943, the State Department developed this idea of a general trusteeship for dependent peoples. For several months the State Department was seriously considering the problems of dependent peoples in the colonial areas. In March 1943, under the guidance of Cordell Hull, Leo Pavolsky, Special Assistant to the Secretary of

State for International Organization and Security Affairs, formulated a plan of trusteeship with the help of Green Hackworth, Legal Advisor of the State Department, and Stanley Hornback, Advisor on Political Affairs. Their draft proposal was an effort "to implement the pledges contained in the Atlantic Charter." In this draft proposal they suggested that the peoples liberated from Japanese rule, who were unprepared for autonomy, should be placed under some form of international trusteeship representing a United Nations body that would be created at the end of the war. This draft proposal was submitted to President Roosevelt who, according to Hull, "enthusiastically" concurred with the proposal.[29]

The State Department was in fact formalizing an idea, a desire that had been present in the heart of President Roosevelt for some time. Using the American relationship with the Philippines as a paradigm, the President supported the idea that the liberated Asian colonial peoples should come under the tutelage of the Great Powers and be educated in democratic institutions. As early as 1942, the President expressed this idea of political tutelage.[30]

His trusteeship ideas were first put forth at a White House Conference with British Foreign Secretary, Anthony Eden, on March 27, 1943. At this meeting, Roosevelt suggested that Korea and Indochina be placed under an international trusteeship supervised by China, the United States, and one or two other countries. The British Foreign Secretary did not report the official British response to Roosevelt's trusteeship plan until the Quebec Conference in August 1943. When Roosevelt once again presented this idea, Eden expressed his reservation to the President's idea, because he "did not like the draft" and was especially troubled by the word "independence." He further expressed his preference of a national rather than international trusteeship.[31]

Despite a clear reluctance on the part of Great Britain and France, Roosevelt thereafter steadfastly pressed for the acceptance of the idea of an international trusteeship over the colonies that were not yet ready for independence. In October 1943, just before Secretary of State Hull left for the Moscow Foreign Ministers Conference, Roosevelt mentioned to him that Indochina and the Japanese mandate island might be placed under international trusteeships, along with security points in other parts of the world.[32]

When Roosevelt talked with President Chiang Kai-shek at the Cairo Conference, he again elaborated on his idea of an international trusteeship for Indochina. Roosevelt first asked Chiang "point blank" if he wanted Indochina. Chiang replied, "Under no circumstances! It's no help to us. We don't want it. They are not Chinese. They would not assimilate into the Chinese people."[33] Roosevelt then suggested to Chiang Kai-shek that Indochina be placed under a trusteeship that would be held by a "Frenchman, one or two Indo-Chinese, and a Chinese and a Russian because they are on the coast, and maybe a Philippino and an American—to educate them for self-government." It is interesting to infer as to why Roosevelt suddenly made an about face with regard to his espoused principle of independence for all colonial people. It is possible that Roosevelt's "trusteeship" suggestions were not made seriously; Bernard Fall has suggested, "Roosevelt may have offered Indochina to Chiang as a sop to keep China in the war."[34]

However, there was no official record of the Roosevelt-Chiang Kai-shek discussion at Cairo about the Korean trusteeship problem. However, at this conference, President Chiang publicly gave strong support for the independence of Korea immediately after the war. He did this even though the British objected to any reference to Korean independence in the conference communiqué. The subsequent communiqué declared that "the three great powers, mindful of the enslavement of the people of Korea, are determined that in due course Korea shall become free and independent."[35] By this statement, the three powers officially committed themselves to the independence of Korea after the war. However, the phrase "in due course" left some question as to the nature of this commitment. Although the phrase "in due course" had a distinctively British flavor, it is almost certain that the thinking behind it was Roosevelt's. The original draft of the Cairo Declaration, dictated by Harry Hopkins, used the phrase "at the earliest possible moment." However, this phrase was revised to read "at the proper moment," apparently at the insistence of Roosevelt. It seems probable that Churchill may have examined the revised draft and altered Roosevelt's phrase to finally read "in due course." The original British draft of the communiqué, which is virtually identical with the final version of the declaration, used the unfortunate phrase "in due course."[36] The Korean trusteeship may not have been discussed with Chiang Kai-shek because Roosevelt went to Cairo determined that "this conference should be a success from the Chinese point of view,"[37] and the Chinese demanded an immediate independence of Korea.[38]

From Cairo, Roosevelt and Churchill went to Teheran to meet with Stalin. There Roosevelt suggested to Stalin that Korea would need about forty years of apprenticeship before full independence might be granted. For Indochina he also suggested the possibility of a trusteeship "which would have the task of preparing the people for independence within a definite period of time, perhaps 20 to 30 years." Stalin completely agreed with this view. Winston Churchill, however, strongly opposed Roosevelt's trusteeship scheme for Indochina; when he objected, Roosevelt reportedly quipped, "Now look, Winston, you are out-voted three to one."[39]

Thirteen months after the Cairo-Teheran Conference, the United States, Great Britain, and the Soviet Union met once again at Yalta. The Yalta Conference opened on Sunday, February 4, 1945, amidst the rising tide of allied victories. The German counteroffensive in the West had been halted in the bloody battle of the Ardennes Forest, and the allies were preparing to launch their main drive across the Rhine. Nevertheless the military leaders of the United States felt that the participation of the Soviet army would be essential to win the Pacific War. Since Korea was not explicitly mentioned in the signed Yalta Declaration, we can assume that Stalin and Roosevelt made no definite agreement with regard to the future of Korea. They did, however, reach a mutual, albeit informal, oral understanding on at least two points: (1) that a multipower trusteeship should be established, vis-à-vis Korea, and (2) that no foreign troops would be permanently stationed in Korea. The State Department briefs clearly indicated that the State Department envisaged the establishment of the Four-Power Trusteeship rather than the recognition of the Provisional Government as the solution to the Korean problem. Roosevelt's only concern seemed to be the education of the Korean people for enlightened self-government based on the Philippine model. Thus, at Cairo he proposed forty years of tutelage and then at Yalta shortened this time span to "twenty to thirty years."[40]

After the Yalta Conference, the Korean Provisional Government became increasingly suspicious of American and Soviet intentions and pressed still harder for immediate recognition. Rhee once again expressed to the State Department his fear that Soviet Russia might advance into Korea and establish a pro-Soviet government in that region.

Subsequently, on March 8, 1945, Rhee requested the State Department to allow a Korean delegate to attend the upcoming San Francisco Conference. It seemed to be a reasonable request in view of the fact that Germany was at the time on the verge of collapse, the Japanese were virtually defeated, and the three allied powers—the United States, China, and Great Britain—had already pledged to the Koreans at Cairo independence "in due course." This request, however, was rejected with the qualification that participation was limited only to members of the United Nations.

By the time of the Yalta Conference, Roosevelt's initial idea of an international trusteeship for Indochina had been substantially modified into a different form. The United States' plan for dependent peoples presented at the Dumbarton Oaks Conference in 1944, contained no reference to the eventual independence of European colonies. According to this new plan, the trusteeship system set up under the auspices of the U.N. should apply to three categories of territories. They were: (1) territories then under mandates of the League of Nations, (2) territories taken from enemy states as a result of war, and (3) territories voluntarily placed under the system by states responsible for their administration.[41] Although this plan was not discussed extensively at Dumbarton Oaks, some of the proposals had been approved by the Big Three at Yalta and were finally adopted later at the San Francisco Conference in 1945. By this tentative plan, Korea would be grouped into the second category, and Indochina would be grouped into the third. Thus, Korea would automatically become a dependent nation under the international trusteeship system. However, if Indochina were to be placed under an international trusteeship, France would have to do this voluntarily. Judging from the past French and British positions on the subject, the possibility of an international or national trusteeship for Indochina seemed to be very remote. Apparently the U.S. government abandoned Roosevelt's earlier ideas of placing Indochina under international trusteeship.

The reasons for the U.S. abandonment of Roosevelt's ideas were not clear. However, it is probable that the U.S. had more immediate problems to face on the eve of the ending of World War II. With Japan's defeat in sight, the Joint Chiefs of Staff felt that the United States should have trusteeship over strategic Japanese islands in the Pacific for purposes of protecting the national security of the United States. If the United States wanted to be sole trustee over these strategic islands, then the United States could not insist that its own allies place their colonies under international trusteeship. In other words, the U.S. would have to compromise and decide on priorities. Meanwhile, De Gaulle, who had steadfastly opposed Roosevelt's idea for a trusteeship in Indochina, was now becoming an internationally popular leader; hence, his desires carried more weight. De Gaulle's visit to Washington in July 1944, apparently had a substantial impact on the formulation of the subsequent U.S. policy toward Indochina. In any case, after De Gaulle's visit it became increasingly difficult for Roosevelt to press for an international trusteeship over Indochina. At the San Francisco Conference of May 1945, the French foreign minister made it clear that any decision on trusteeship for Indochina would be made by France alone.[42] This French argument subsequently prevailed at that conference; France could retain her former colony. Roosevelt's earlier dream—the elimination of French colonialism in Indochina—was only a memory.

VI.

During the six months between the Yalta Conference and the Japanese surrender on August 14, 1945, international events developed quickly. The war was rapidly moving toward its conclusion, but the occupation plans of the allied powers were still on the drawing board. By the middle of March, the strategic island of Iwo Jima had been occupied by American Marines. On the European front, the American army had already crossed the Rhine at Remagen, and the entire German army was nearing collapse. Furthermore, during this vitally important time span, President Roosevelt suddenly died on April 12, 1945, less than two weeks before the opening ceremonies of the San Francisco Conference. To the Indochinese people, and to some degree to all the people of all the colonized areas of the world, Roosevelt's death was the loss of a concerned friend. After he died there was no leader amongst the Great Powers who would become an ardent supporter of anti-colonialism.

In the final stage of the war, France under De Gaulle became anxious to land its troops in Indochina to "liberate" their colony. De Gaulle believed that French blood shed on the soil of Indochina would provide France with a more valid claim to the area.[43] The French were afraid that the Chinese would liberate Indochina before they had a chance to return to their former colony. As early as November 1943, the French officially requested that Roosevelt intervene on their part and preclude any Chinese participation in the liberation of Indochina. However, in February of 1944, Roosevelt told Secretary of State Settinius that "no French troops whatever should be used for operations in Indochina," and that "the operation should be Anglo-American in character and should be followed by the establishment of international trusteeship over the French colony."[44] It was not until February 1945, that Roosevelt modified his position somewhat and agreed to aid the French underground in Indochina. But he did not forget to stipulate that the aid should be limited only to that which was necessary to defeat Japan. He further stipulated that the aid should not be construed as an official American recognition of French interests in Indochina. Meanwhile, on March 9, 1945, the Japanese occupation forces staged a coup in Indochina, which completely eliminated French administrative control there; the Japanese established the puppet government of Bao Dai. Nevertheless, Roosevelt's strong opposition to the return of French control over Indochina still held credence.

The sudden death of Roosevelt provided an excellent opportunity for France to reassert its interests in Indochina. Although the new American President swore he would continue his predecessor's policy, Truman found it very difficult to follow Roosevelt's comprehensive war policy, especially vis-à-vis Indochina. Truman did not have any hostile feelings toward De Gaulle, although he did not support colonialism in Indochina. With Roosevelt gone, there was a good chance that the United States could be convinced to reverse or modify its original plans for Indochina. De Gaulle himself had acknowledged that Roosevelt's death gave France an opportunity to return to Indochina.[45] As the European war was ending, Truman's major concern was how to meet the threat of Soviet communism. He did not want to create unnecessary dissension among the allies over the issue of colonialism. Truman welcomed French participation in the war against Japan and decided that Indochina would be placed under an international trusteeship only if France consented. And if there was to be a trusteeship, it would be under French supervision and control.[46] On paper, the Truman policy seemed basically a continuation of Roosevelt's, but in actuality there was a considerable change in tone, especially with regard to France.

The major impact of Truman's policy toward Indochina, however, did not come from his soft attitude toward French colonialism. Rather, it came from his decision to allow Indochina to be placed within the British military operation zone. American-British differences over Indochina had been present throughout the war, especially concerning theater placement and command. General Wedemeyer, the American Commander in the China theater, thought that his British counterpart, Mountbatten, had agreed not to undertake operations in Indochina until he (Wedemeyer) had approved them. Mountbatten intended to bomb Indochina in order to support French guerrilla troops. The Wedemeyer-Mountbatten dispute over command of operations in Indochina was finally resolved at the Potsdam Conference in favor of the British. There, the combined Chiefs of Staff allowed the British (SEAC) to occupy the part of Indochina situated south of the 16th parallel; they assigned the Chinese to occupy the area north of the 16th parallel.[47] This decision of operation had a most consequential impact upon the postwar development of Indochina, primarily because the British occupied southern Indochina with the intention of returning it to the French after the war. Thus, French colonialism would be allowed to return to Vietnam.

Another serious mistake in Truman's policy toward Indochina was his failure to recognize the increasing popularity of the indigenous political forces under the leadership of Ho Chi-minh. Since 1930, the major anti-French underground activity in Vietnam had been pursued by communist organizations. Three of these groups were united in 1930 into the Indochinese Communist Party by Ho Chi-minh. When World War II began in Europe, the Indochinese Communist Party organized a "United Front" with several non-communist nationalist forces, and in May of 1941, they formed the Vietnam Doc-Lap Dong Minh Hoi (Revolutionary League for Independence for Vietnam), popularly known as the Viet Minh.[48] This group was, in effect, a national front organization led primarily by the Indochinese Communist Party. In the short run its purpose was to defeat the Japanese; in the long run its purpose was to prevent the French from regaining control after the war. During the period of Japanese occupation in Indochina, the Viet Minh, under the leadership of Ho Chi-minh, had been allowed to operate in southern China and had cooperated with the Nationalist Chinese Government and American Intelligence Agency.

At the close of the war in August 1945, the Viet Minh emerged as the most important and best organized political force in Vietnam. As soon as the Japanese regime collapsed, they organized the Provisional Government of the Democratic Republic of Vietnam in Hanoi, and sought to gain the recognition of the United States and the allied powers. However, the official American policy was to have political non-involvement in Indochina; thus, the U.S. did not recognize the Viet Minh government. Since the United States had already decided to sanction the return of French colonialism to Indochina, Truman felt that recognition of the Viet Minh would foment greater trouble between the allied efforts to end the war. However, this attitude of indifference and neutrality not only disillusioned the Vietnamese people, it also created an image that the United States was an unreliable friend. This failure to recognize the power of Vietnamese indigenous political forces, and the concomitant failure to support Vietnamese independence, would return decades later to haunt the U.S.

VII.

The United States had no concrete policy toward Korea except for a vague plan that Korea should be placed under international trusteeship after the end of the war. However, the Japanese surrender came so quickly that the Truman Administration was totally unprepared for the occupation of Korea. In fact, President Truman did not have his own blueprint for Korean policy; he simply accepted the policy of Roosevelt. President Truman did not discuss the Korean problems with Stalin and Roosevelt at Potsdam.[49] Taking advantage of this situation, the Soviet Union declared war against Japan on August 9, 1945, and a large number of Soviet soldiers began to march into Korea. In order to stop the Soviet occupation of all Korea, the United States proposed to the Soviet Union to divide Korea at the 38th parallel for the purpose of the military operation.

Contrary to a widely held view that the division of Korea was a secret agreement made either at Yalta or Potsdam, the division appears to have originated in the War Department in Washington. As an "eye witness" to the birth of the 38th parallel, Secretary of State Dean Rusk stated as follows:

> The suddenness of the Japanese surrender forced emergency consideration by the Department of State and the armed services of the necessary orders to General MacArthur and the necessary arrangements with other allied governments about the Japanese surrender. For this purpose, SWNCC (Mr. Dunn for State, Mr. McCloy for Army, and Mr. Ralph Bard for Navy) held several long sessions during the period August 10–15. Dunn, McCloy and Bard held a meeting

in Mr. McCloy's office in the Pentagon on, I believe, the night of August 10–11, a meeting which lasted throughout most of the night. The subject was arrangements for the receipt of the Japanese surrender. The Department of State had suggested (through Mr. Byrnes) that U.S. forces received the surrender as far north as practicable. The military was faced with the scarcity of U.S. forces immediately available and time and space factors which would make it difficult to reach very far north before Soviet troops could enter the area.

The military view was that if our proposals for receiving the surrender greatly over-reached our probable military capabilities, there would be little likelihood of Soviet acceptance—and speed was the essence of the problem. Mr. McCloy asked Col. C. H. Bonesteel, III, and me (then a Colonel on the War Department General Staff) to retire to an adjoining room and come up with a proposal which would harmonize the political desire to have U.S. forces receive the surrender as far north as possible and the obvious limitations on the ability of the U.S. forces to reach the area.

We recommended the 38th parallel even though it was further north than could be realistically reached by U.S. forces in the event of Soviet disagreement, but we did so because we felt it important to include the capital of Korea in the area of responsibility of American troops. The 38th parallel became a part of the Army's recommendation to the Department of State and that line was subsequently agreed internationally. I remember at the time that I was somewhat surprised that the Soviet accepted the 38th parallel since I thought they might insist upon a line further south in view of our respective military position in the area.[50]

The idea of the 38th parallel being a dividing line in Korea had never been the subject of international discussion among the wartime leaders. This artificial division was destined to be the locus around which the Korean War was fought. It was intended to be purely a military demarcation of a temporary nature in order to accept the surrender of Japanese forces in Korea. It was proposed by the United States to stop the Soviet occupation of the whole of Korea. Thus the United States laid seed for a potential conflict that later became a major tragedy in Korean history.

With German surrender, the Korean nationalist leaders became so fearful that Soviet troops would enter the Korean area that on May 14, 1945, Dr. Rhee sent telegrams to President Truman, Senators Owen Brewster and Walter F. George, and Representative E. Hoffman, soliciting their support. These telegrams warned of Russian ambitions in Korea and appealed to their sense of American justice to exert their influence on the alleged secret agreement at Yalta. When they made no reply to this appeal, Rhee called a press conference and publicly stated his charge of a "secret deal." The Koreans were fearful that the Soviets were committed to attaining territory for themselves and that they were not interested in Korean independence.

In response, the State Department, on June 8, 1945, denied any such secret agreement and reaffirmed the American intention to fulfill its commitment made at the Cairo Conference. Acting Secretary of State Joseph C. Grew stated:

There has been no change in this government's intention to fulfill its commitment under the Cairo declaration. . . . The United Nations which are represented at the United Nations Conference on International Organization all have legally constituted governing authorities, whereas, the Korean Provisional Government, and other Korean organizations do not possess at the present time the qualifications requisite for obtaining recognition by the United States as governing authority. The Korean Provisional Government has never exercised administrative authority over any part of Korea, nor can it be regarded as representative of the Korean people of today. Due to geographical and other factors, its following, even among exiled Koreans, is inevitably limited. It is the policy of this government in dealing with groups such as the Korean Provisional Government to avoid taking action which might, when the victory of the United Nations is achieved, tend to compromise the right of the Korean people to choose the ultimate form and personnel of the government which they may wish to establish. It is principally for this reason that the American Government has not recognized the "Korean Provisional Government."[51]

It is apparent from this statement that the State Department seriously doubted the alleged representative character of the Provisional Government. Since many groups appealed for the independence of Korea, there seemed to be some confusion as to the nature of the Provisional Government among the policy planners at the State Department. Therefore, it seemed that the State Department had become extremely cautious not to commit itself to any one group.

As Secretary Cordell Hull mentioned, the ultimate goal of the United States' foreign policy during war time was "to defeat its enemy as quickly as possible." In determining their foreign policy, they must first see clearly what their true national interests are. It was a general consensus among the American leaders that the entry of the Soviet army into the Pacific War would serve the national interest of the United States. Faced with this situation, the United States could not possibly offend the Soviet Union by granting unilateral recognition to the Korean Provisional Government. It would first attain the consent of the Soviet Union.

The United States was fully aware of the existence and activities of the Korean Provisional Government at Chungking, not only through the repeated appeals of Korean leaders, but also through the Pacific War Council in which China was represented. Nevertheless, it carefully avoided tendering any official recognition, hence, bringing about much confusion. In the view of the State Department, there was hopeless factional rivalry among the Koreans, even those in the United States; before any recognition would be realized, there had to be an adjustment on the part of the Korean factions toward unity. Thus they concluded that the Provisional Government was no more than a self-constituted club with limited followers among the exiled Korean people. This line was also in accord with the general reluctance of the United States to commit its government to support for resistance forces, except for governments-in-exile recognized prior to the war.

But what the Provisional Government of Korea wanted was that they might be granted more provisional recognition contingent on the understanding that an election under allied supervision might be held as soon as Korea should be liberated. The Korean leaders were aware of the fact that the Provisional Government had been so long and so far removed from Korea that it no longer represented the people. But they did realize one fact, a fact that the United States government failed to realize—that the recognition of the exiled government alone would be "an effective means of blocking Soviet seizure of Korea." They worried about the distinct probability of a power-vacuum in Korea after the defeat of Japan. The experiences of their past pointed to the inevitability of Soviet influence in Korea after the Second World War.

VIII.

This paper has attempted to portray American policy toward Korea and Vietnam prior to, during, and after World War II. This paper has tried to present the idea that American policy, vis-à-vis Korea and Vietnam, was a policy based on placating the European colonialist powers and not a policy based upon the aspirations and needs of the Korean and Vietnamese people. American policy makers at this time were concerned with winning a worldwide war, and progress toward this basic goal took precedent over all other considerations. Korea and Vietnam were only minute problems compared with the problem of war in general—at least to the United States. The United States government, aside from a few individual officials, failed to concern itself seriously with the Korean and Indochinese questions until the end of 1943. Even after the commitment made at the Cairo Conference to guarantee the independence of Korea "in due course," it was revealed that the United States had no intention to assume responsibilities in the implementation of the commitment beyond that of ending Japanese control. The government of the United States was totally unprepared for the problem of transferring the authority held by the Japanese government to the Korean and Indochinese people. However, the primary factor in American non-recognition of Korean and Vietnamese sovereignty stemmed from the commitment on the part of the United States to instituting worldwide trusteeships for dependent nations. This idea, first espoused by Roosevelt, had a permanent bearing on the thinking of U.S. policy makers.

In retrospect, if United States leaders had not been so anxious to placate the European powers, if they had formulated detailed contingency plans vis-à-vis Korea and Vietnam, if they had even been more aware of the future political tides in those nations, and if they had been aware of the effects of dividing these nations, they might well have averted the tragedies of the Korean and Vietnam Wars.

In the Korean case, if the United States had recognized the Provisional Government in early 1942, and had been prepared to grant responsibility and power to this government, the division of Korea for the sake of military occupation would not have been necessary. Unfortunately, American policy planners at this time lacked clear vision as to the future of Korea and Vietnam.

Yet it is unfair to assign all the blame to the international situation; Koreans and Vietnamese should bear partial responsibility for their tragedies. Even though the Korean and Vietnamese problems were created by the major powers, it would have been theoretically possible for the Koreans and the Vietnamese themselves to create a national government, had they each been united for this purpose. Their failure to keep their houses in order figured importantly in perpetuating the division of their countries. The pathologically confused and chaotic situation that arose immediately following liberation was due to a lack of strong leadership and political experience, as well as to irresponsible political factionalism among parties. Because of this, they wasted many opportunities for presenting their ideas to the allied powers. Had they been firmly united in the struggle to achieve the goal of independence, united solidly either for or against trusteeship after World War II, the division of their countries might have been averted. Then there would not be the genesis of the later tragedies.

1. David Rees, *Korea, the Limited War* (New York, 1964), pp. 440–446.
2. U.S. Department of State, *Foreign Relations of the United States: Diplomatic Papers, 1942* (Washington, 1962), I:873–876.
3. H. S. Stimson, *The Far Eastern Crisis* (New York, 1936), p. 32.
4. Edward R. Drachman, *United States Policy toward Vietnam, 1940–1945* (Cranbury, New Jersey, 1970), p. 33.
5. Gaimusho (Japanese Ministry of Foreign Affairs), *Nihon Gaiko Hyakunen Shoshi* [One hundred year's history of Japanese diplomacy] (Tokyo, 1962), pp. 187–190.
6. Cordell Hull, *The Memoirs of Cordell Hull*, 2 vols. (New York, 1948) I:71.
7. Ibid., II:1193.
8. Charles De Gaulle, *The Complete Memoirs of Charles De Gaulle*, 3 vols. (New York, 1967), II:385.
9. Alexander De Conde, *A History of American Foreign Policy* (New York, 1971), pp. 599–601.
10. Cited by Samuel I. Roseman (ed.), *The Public Papers of FDR* (New York, 1950), X:69.
11. Elliot Roosevelt, *As He Saw It* (New York, 1945), pp. 114–116.
12. Wendell L. Willkie, *One World* (New York, 1945). His speech on 26 October 1942.
13. Charles De Gaulle, op. cit., II:385.
14. Churchill's famous speech at Lord Mayor's dinner at Mansion House. *New York Times*, 11 November 1942.
15. Department of State, *Peace and War: United States Foreign Policy: 1931–1941* (Washington, 1943), pp. 704–705.
16. Gaimusho, op. cit., p. 188.
17. U.S. State Department, *Foreign Relations of the United States: Diplomatic Papers, 1941* (Washington, 1959), p. 205.
18. Robert Murphy, *Diplomat Among Warriors* (New York, 1964), p. 39.
19. Tsuboe Senji, *Chosen Dokuritsu Undo Hishi* [Secret history of Korean people's independence movement] (Tokyo, 1959), p. 108.
20. See the text in Ko Kwon Sam, *Choson Chung Ch'i Sa* [Korean political history] (Seoul, Korea, 1948), pp. 233–234.
21. Robert T. Oliver, *Syngman Rhee* (New York, 1950), p. 176.
22. *Foreign Relations of the United States: 1942*, I:865–867.
23. Oliver, ibid., p. 178. For the independence movement of the Provisional Korean Government see Kuksa Pyonch'an Uiwon Hoe, *Hangkuk Tokryp Undong Sa* [History of Korean independence movement] 5 volumes, (Seoul, 1969).
24. George McCune and Arthur L. Grey, Jr., *Korea Today* (Cambridge, 1950), p. 41.
25. Dr. Rhee's letter to Cordell Hull. The text in Oliver, op. cit., p. 361.
26. Oliver, op. cit., p. 182. Oliver's book is one of the important sources for the study of Korean Independence Movement.
27. *Foreign Relations of the United States: 1942*, I:859–881.
28. Ibid., I:875–876.
29. Cordell Hull, op. cit., p. 1706.
30. Samuel Rosenbaum, op. cit., 1942 volumes, pp. 473–476.
31. Hull, op. cit., II:1237.
32. Ibid., II:1595–1596.

39

33. Theodore White (ed.), *The Stillwell Papers* (New York, 1948), p. 253. See also, Edward Stettinius, Jr., *Roosevelt and President* (New York, 1949), p. 258.

34. Bernard Fall, *The Two Vietnams* (New York, 1967), pp. 467 and 53. Henry Wallace also claims that before his trip to the Far East in early 1944, he was told by Roosevelt to inform Chiang that "He proposed to see that both Hong Kong and Indochina would be returned to China." See Henry Wallace, *Toward World Peace* (New York, 1948), p. 97.

35. U.S. Department of State, *In Quest of Peace and Security* (Washington, 1951), p. 10.

36. Soon Sung Cho, *Korea in World Politics* (Berkeley, 1967), pp. 19–20.

37. Sherwood, op. cit., p. 773.

38. Chang Chi-Yun, *Record of the Cairo Conference* (Taipei, 1953), pp. 4–10.

39. Stettinius, op. cit., p. 238.

40. Soon S. Cho, op. cit., pp. 25–34. U.S. Department of State, *Foreign Relations of the United States: Conference at Malta and Yalta*, p. 770.

41. *Documents of the United Nations Conference on International Organization, Vol. III: Dumbarton Oaks Proposals* (New York, 1947), pp. 607–608.

42. Ibid., Document 230, pp. 641–655.

43. Charles De Gaulle, *Memoirs*, I:160.

44. *Foreign Relations of the United States: 1945, The Near East, South Asia, Africa, the Far East* (Washington, 1965), p. 1206.

45. Phillipe Devillers, *Histoire du Vietnam de 1940 a 1952* (Paris, 1952), pp. 149–150

46. On 10 June 1945 the State Department cabled Ambassador Hurley in China about Truman's policy toward Indochina. Drachman, op. cit., p. 92.

47. *British Involvement in Indochinese Conflict*, pp. 47–52.

48. George M. Kahn and John W. Lewis, *The United States in Vietnam* (New York, 1967), p. 17.

49. Harry S. Truman, *Years of Trial and Hope* (New York, 1955), p. 317. See also, *Foreign Relations of the United States: Conference of Berlin*, II:253.

50. *Foreign Relations of the United States: 1945*, VI:1039.

51. *Department of State Bulletin*, 10 June 1945, pp. 1058–1059. See also, World Peace Foundation, *Documents on American Foreign Relations, 1944–45*, pp. 230–231.

United States Involvement in Asia: Syngman Rhee and the Establishment of the Republic of Korea

Robert T. Oliver

Recent revelations about the role of the C.I.A. in countries around the globe have heightened an ever-present uneasiness felt by the American public about the conduct of our foreign policy. Matters dealt with among governments are always complex. They are also only partly manageable. Other governments may change; the Congress and the public may demand changes on our part. Events are so interrelated that what happens in one part of the world profoundly affects other situations that appear to be quite separated from them. To the public, and sometimes even to the experts, foreign affairs seem very confusing.

This report is presented as a case study of the evolution and shift of American policy regarding the establishment of the Republic of Korea and more explicitly, in regard to the selection of Syngman Rhee as first president of that Republic.

The establishment of the Republic of Korea would seem to have been inevitable, since the nation had had an independent existence for some four thousand years, except for the thirty-five years of domination by Japan, from 1910 to 1945.

The fact is that the establishment of the Republic proved to be highly controversial. One reason was that the Korean nation was left divided, with both the northern and southern governments claiming jurisdiction over the entire peninsula. Another reason was the communist charge, widely repeated in the world press, that Syngman Rhee had been hand-picked for the presidency by the United States. Still another cause for controversy was the belief fostered among many Koreans that Dr. Rhee accepted the permanent division of the nation in order to satisfy his own ambition to become president of at least half the nation. Yet another factor in the controversy was the dislike felt by many Americans for an involvement by the U.S. government on the continent of Asia. Even after our involvement was an accomplished

41

fact, such notable spokesmen as Secretary of State Dean Acheson, Senator Tom Connally (Chairman of the Foreign Relations Committee), and General Douglas MacArthur all tried to define the Pacific defense perimeter as running down from the Aleutian Islands through Japan and Okinawa to the Philippines, leaving the entire Asian mainland outside the zone for which we accepted responsibility. The thinking of official Washington was not misrepresented by Owen Lattimore when he said, in the July 17, 1949, issue of the *New York Post* that, "The thing to do is to let South Korea fall [into communist control] but not to let it look as if we pushed it."

The question this report explores is the intertwined relationships between Syngman Rhee and the United States government, through seven successive stages, in the years from 1942 through 1948.

II.

Stage One covered the years from 1942 to late in 1945, with a setting focused in Washington, D.C. The essential characteristic of this stage was that Dr. Rhee made strenuous efforts to secure a guarantee of Korean independence that was rejected and largely ignored by the United States government.

The starting date is largely arbitrary, as must be true for most historical inquiries. Under the auspices of the Korean Commission, which he set up in Washington, Dr. Rhee had been seeking American recognition of the Provisional Republic of Korea in Exile, ever since the Mansei Revolution of March 1919. But an interesting and significant starting point occurred on January 22, 1942. On that day, Dr. Rhee, in company with John Staggers and Jay Jerome Williams, two of his friends, met with Alger Hiss in the State Department. Rhee argued earnestly that the outbreak of the war had ended any American obligation to recognize Japanese suzerainty over Korea. He urged that the United States recognize the Provisional Republic and extend lend-lease aid to it, following the practice already established of granting both recognition and aid to various exiled governments in Europe. He explained that Russia had for a century entertained ambitions to control Korea and warned that unless America extended its recognition of Korean independence, the Soviets would find means of entering into the peninsula. He added that if Russia gained a foothold in Korea this would be a disaster not only for the Korean people but a threat to the postwar stability of all northeast Asia. Then he concluded by pointing out that to extend recognition would be an easy thing for the United States to do, inasmuch as we were at war with Japan, Russia was not a party to that war, and Nationalist China would not object to such recognition. Alger Hiss at first objected that the U.S. could not recognize Dr. Rhee as President of the Republic for there was no way of knowing whether he was truly supported by the Korean people. Dr. Rhee replied that he did not want the United States to guarantee the presidency for him, beyond the fact that the exiled Republic would need a recognized head during the duration of the war. After Japan's defeat, he said, it would be proper and acceptable for the United States to supervise an election in Korea to insure that the people would have a government and a president of their own free choice. At this point Hiss shifted ground, asserting that the United States had no intention of taking any unilateral action in Korea without the approval of the Soviet Union and that most certainly we would not extend to Korea a recognition of independence which, as Rhee had said, was in direct opposition to Russian long-term interests. On this note the conference was concluded.

We do not know when President Franklin D. Roosevelt first conceived the notion of using Korea as an inducement for obtaining a Russian commitment to enter the war against Japan; nor do we know who put the idea in his head. We do know that by March 1943, Roosevelt was telling both Anthony Eden and Cordell Hull that he wanted to use the option of Russian entry into Korea as a price for getting Stalin to enter the Pacific War.[1] It is well known that at the Cairo Conference, when Chiang Kai-shek insisted that Roosevelt and Churchill join in a pledge of independence for Korea, Roosevelt contrived the insertion into the pledge of the escape clause, "in due course," which could mean indefinite postponement and opened the door to further manipulation. By the time of the Yalta Conference, in February 1945, President Roosevelt was determined that Russia must be accorded a coequal status with the United States in deciding the future of Korea—even if the Soviet Union continued to remain out of the Pacific War.[2]

A month later, in March 1945, Eleanor Roosevelt, who obviously knew nothing of what her husband had in mind for Korea, wrote in her syndicated newspaper column a paragraph of praise of the Provisional Republic of Korea. Dr. and Mrs. Rhee went to see her, and on March 9th Eleanor Roosevelt wrote me a letter saying she was exceedingly friendly and that she had promised to speak to President Roosevelt to urge the granting of lend-lease aid to the exiled Republic.

The following month Roosevelt died. On May 28, 1945, Harry Hopkins was in Moscow as an emissary of the new President, Harry Truman, where he and Stalin agreed that Korea should be placed under a Four-Power Trusteeship.[3] Months later, on December 17th of that year, the decision was formalized and made public in what was known as the Moscow Decision. Thus was the fate of Korea decided by the United States and Russia, without any Korean participation, and in flat rejection of the warnings and appeals presented to the State Department by Dr. Rhee.

While the fate of Korea was being decided behind the scenes and off the record, Dr. Rhee and his associates were far from idle. Acting through the Korean Commission, Colonel Ben Limb, Dr. Henry DeYoung, and several others were busily lobbying in the State Department and the Pentagon. John Staggers and Jay Jerome Williams were asking friendly senators and congressmen to use their influence to alter State Department policy. Syngman Rhee was trying to convince American officials that he was in fact the spokesman for the Korean independence cause, in contravention to claims by Youngjeung Kim and Kilsoo Han that they were more truly representatives of Korean nationalism. George McCune, at the Korea Desk in the State Department, was deeply troubled, as he told me, because he was unable to arouse interest among the policy-makers for undertaking plans for postwar freedom for Korea. Obviously, he was unaware of the decisions President Roosevelt had already made.

On May 14, 1945, from San Francisco, Dr. Rhee sent a telegram to friendly U.S. Senators, saying in part: "President Truman has been informed of a secret agreement at Yalta which turns Korea over to Russian domination. We are positive of our source of information on this agreement. . . ."

In San Francisco, the United Korean Committee was organized under Dr. Rhee's chairmanship, to present a united front of exiled Korean nationalists to the delegates who were in the process of organizing the United Nations. To Dr. Rhee's dismay, the U.K.C. voted to support the establishment in Korea of a coalition government in which communists would have full participation. This was not as shocking either to other Koreans or to the American and European public opinion as it was to Syngman Rhee. It was a time, and San Francisco was a place, of *accommodation* with world communism. The coalition pattern had been accepted by the Allies and imposed, without consulting the populations affected, upon the whole tier of nations in eastern Europe. Roosevelt's belief that concessions had to be made to secure harmonious and cooperative relations with Russia had become American policy and was widely supported by Congressional and public opinion. The end of the war in Europe had led to a great wave of euphoria and of hopefulness that through the United Nations a new era of peaceful competition—the détente of that day—was emerging. Dr. Syngman Rhee demonstrated what was already coming to be known as his "stubbornness" in refusing to agree to sponsor such an imposed coalition regime upon the Korean people. His critics, Korean and American, stormed against him. "Why couldn't Korea be treated like Romania, Czechoslovakia and Hungary?" they asked. Dr. Rhee broke up the United Korean Committee and abruptly left San Francisco for Washington, to continue his battle there for a guarantee of free elections to permit the Korean people to select their own leadership and a form of government of their own choice.

I flew down from Syracuse to add my own urging that Rhee must bow to the current of the time and accept coalition in Korea as part and parcel of the new spirit of cooperation that was going to create lasting peace. He listened to me while I argued that unless he did so he would be shunted aside and new leadership would be chosen under the coalition that then appeared inevitable. He told me that he would probably not have strength enough to prevent the coalition from being imposed. "But," he concluded, "I have fought all my life to free Korea from Japan. Now in my old age, I have no intention of seeking office for myself by turning Korea over to the Soviet Union." I left him, thinking he was making a mistake—for the euphoric expectations of Russian-American cooperation were exceedingly strong in the wake of the German and Italian defeat—but admiring his willingness to sacrifice his own ambitions for what he believed to be the welfare of Korea. In retrospect, we all must pay tribute to his judgment as well as his patriotism. Had it not been for his determined opposition, Korea would almost certainly have been treated as were the countries of eastern Europe.

III.

Stage Two in the unfolding drama leading to the establishment of the Republic of Korea commenced with Dr. Rhee's return to his homeland on October 16, 1945. Note that this was two months after the defeat of Japan. Russian and American forces had already occupied their respective zones, north and south of the 38th parallel. His return to Korea had encountered a series of delays. Neither the State or War Departments had been willing to complicate the problem of taking control of South Korea from Japan by admitting exiles claiming to represent a Korean government. On October 2nd, Dr. Rhee wrote to me that " . . . there are still many obstacles to be cleared. It may be cleared tomorrow or next month. However, the way will open sooner or later and I will go as soon as possible."

When he did arrive in Seoul, he was greeted as the outstanding hero of Korean nationalism. General John R. Hodge, commander of the U.S. Occupation Forces, flew to Tokyo to escort him to Seoul personally. He offered to recondition the Kyongbok Palace for Dr. Rhee to live in—which Rhee smilingly refused. On October 21st, at 5:30 A.M., sitting up in bed, Dr. Rhee wrote to me describing his reception:

> It seems the whole nation is agog since my arrival was announced. Hundreds of people gather around the hotel entrance and ask for a chance to see me.

General Hodge and I had agreed not to announce my arrival until we were ready, but the next morning the General came and said the American news reporters knew it and demanded an interview. So we rushed to the palace and entered the news conference, with General Hodge and General Arnold escorting me and I was introduced by the General. Then I spoke, both in English and in Korean. Since that time to this, crowds gathered in front of the outside gate and I could not find one minute for rest. . . .

We are planning to bring Kim Koo and several others from Chungking. With the exception of the Kongsan group, all parties and the people are solidly behind me. Lyuh Woon Heung and his brother say they will do anything I want them to do. . . .

This afternoon I will hold a conference with leaders of several parties and groups and I hope they will form a central committee. Funny part of it is that the Communist Party formed a Government with me at its head. I told them it is a high honor to be a Communist leader while Moscow condemned me as an anti-Communist. . . .

There were two reasons for the overwhelming rush by both the Americans and the Koreans to welcome Dr. Rhee as the outstanding nationalist leader. The first reason is that to the Korean populace, he was indeed the only Korean to be widely known and respected as the President of the Republic established by the 1919 Mansei Revolution. The second reason was that in view of his age—then sixty-eight—both the American authorities and the Korean party leaders who were then in Seoul believed that he could be pampered and flattered, heaped with honors, but rendered powerless and used as a mere front and figurehead, while the effective policy decisions would be implemented behind his back. This was a role Syngman Rhee refused to accept. Similarly, neither the Seoul politicians or the American authorities were willing to grant real power to him.

The general situation in Korea in the fall of 1945 was one of great confusion. The American hope that the 38th parallel division would be only partial and temporary was quashed when Russia began fortifying the line and clamped down along it the most impenetrable Iron Curtain in the world. Hur Hun, Secretary General of the Communist Party in the South, proclaimed the People's Republic to be the only legal government in Korea and commanded the populace to obey it. Kim Koo from Chungking issued a similar claim for the Provisional Republic. General Hodge was receiving little guidance from Washington beyond his original instructions to "prevent disease and unrest." On October 23rd, Dr. Rhee presided over a meeting of all the prominent political leaders in Seoul, in which a Central Committee for Korean Independence was organized. A resolution was adopted labelling as a "great insult" some remarks President Truman had made in September to the effect that independence for Korea was not contemplated.

Then, on December 17th came the proclamation of the Moscow Decision, that a Four-Power Trusteeship was to be imposed on Korea.

Up to this time, Dr. Rhee had been writing me assurances that "General Hodge is our best friend in Korea." But now the political climate in South Korea changed dramatically and suddenly. Stage Two, the period of celebration of Syngman Rhee's titular leadership and of general if superficial cooperation, was ended abruptly.

IV.

Stage Three, which was to last all through 1946, was a time in which Dr. Rhee became progressively isolated from both the American authorities and the other major Korean political leaders.

This stage may be said to have commenced with a three-day general strike in South Korea, during which Koreans refused to maintain the sanitation, janitorial and other service functions, to show their rejection of the trusteeship. Water pipes froze and burst in the government buildings, and garbage piled up in the streets. Major General Archibald V. Arnold, then serving as Military Governor of South Korea, called Dr. Rhee to his office and asked him to call off the strike —which Rhee did. Two new facts emerged as a result of the trusteeship announcement and the general strike reaction to it: (1) it became evident to everyone that Syngman Rhee's leadership position was not merely titular but had widespread popular support; and (2) the question of whether the American Occupation authorities and the Korean political leaders were cooperating for a common goal or were working at cross purposes for competing goals was brought sharply into focus.

Dr. Rhee started the New Year of 1946 by withdrawing from all the political parties that had offered him their chairmanship and announced formation of The Society for the Rapid Realization of Korean Independence—which, he explained, was not a political party but a union of the entire population with the aim of hastening creation of a free Korean government.

General Hodge countered by forming a Representative Democratic Council of South Korea, to which he named Dr. Rhee as chairman, Kimm Kiusic and Kim Koo as vice-chairmen, and Lyuh Woon Heung as a member. Hodge intended that this council would have two functions—only the first of which was openly described. It was to advise the American Military Government on purely domestic political matters; and it was to educate the Korean people to accept trusteeship as a merely transitional state leading to ultimate Korean sovereignty. The original adverse popular rejection of trusteeship, Hodge explained to the press, was the result of a clumsy translation of the term trusteeship, which led the Koreans to equate it with their subjection to Japan. How little the General understood the people he was trying to govern!

What the United States government envisioned for the trusteeship plan was a situation somewhat like that which was established in the Philippines in 1903, a period of tutelage leading gradually toward self-government and eventual independence. There were essential differences, however, that Washington apparently did not take into sufficient account. For one thing, the Korean nation had a character and a tradition far more sturdily independent than the Philippines had at the opening of the twentieth century. Even more significantly, unlike the unilateral rule of the United States over the Philippines, the plan announced for Korea was a Four-Power Trusteeship in which, Dr. Rhee was convinced, Russia would be the decisive force. China was far too distraught with its own internal troubles to be a significant factor. Great Britain, too, was going through the throes of liquidating its worldwide empire and of recovering from the grievous wounds of World War II. American public opinion had no taste for continuing direct involvement on the mainland of Asia and was uninformed about Korea. Russia, on the other hand, with a genuine need for all-year warm water sea ports opening to the Pacific, and with a century-old record of seeking a foothold in Korea, would surely pursue every opportunity to remain in and to control the peninsula. This was why Dr. Rhee was certain that the projected trusteeship (however the term might be translated) would lead surely and squarely to the communization and subjection of Korea. Beyond this, he did not accept the American belief that the Koreans were incapable of ruling themselves. These were the reasons why Syngman Rhee declined any further role as a symbol of Korean-American cooperation.

The position of the United States was also clear-cut and adamant. Trusteeship, whether right or wrong, had been agreed upon at Moscow (having been predetermined two or three years earlier by President Roosevelt), and as such it had become a key factor in U.S.-U.S.S.R. relations. The plan had the specific support of Atlee's England, which was the closest ally of the United States, and of Nehru's India, which was the emerging leader of the "Third World," that the United States felt it must woo. The North Koreans were all in favor of the plan. Even in South Korea, the only really effective opposition to trusteeship was coming from Syngman Rhee, along with his pesky and troublesome Washington lobby, which kept prodding the *New York Times,* the *Washington Post,* the *Christian Science Monitor,* and other influential organs and individuals to oppose it. General Hodge sought to end the matter by telling the Koreans bluntly that trusteeship was "immutable law."

For various reasons, trusteeship for Korea made good sense to Washington officialdom. The plan fitted precisely into the underlying assumption upon which the United Nations was created—namely, that conciliation and concessions to Russia were required to develop global cooperation for peace. Russia deserved this treatment because of its valiant defense against the Nazi invasion and also because of the generation-long worldwide renunciation of the 1917 Revolution. But deserving or not, Russia was the one power on earth that threatened to prevent a new era of peace, and its suspicion and dislike of the democracies had to be diverted. Moreover, it seemed evident to American officials that the Koreans were, in fact, unsuited for self-government without a preparatory period. After all, they had lived for forty centuries under an absolutist monarchy, and then for a generation under Japanese domination so complete that the use of their own language had been forbidden. Even so outstanding a Korean patriot as Philip Jaison, upon his return to Korea as Hodge's principal adviser in July 1946, remarked disdainfully that of course the Koreans could not rule themselves—"They couldn't even make a cake of soap." Among the Americans in Korea in 1946-47, it was simply a truism, often restated, that the Koreans were not ready to govern themselves. In the view of official Washington, trusteeship was a constructive program under which aid and guidance would be generously provided during an essential period of transition. There would be light, they were sure, at the end of the tunnel.

Most of the articulate Korean leaders were persuaded, however reluctantly, to accept this reasoning. Neither Kimm Kiusic nor Lyuh Woon Heung, who drifted into an uneasy alliance, shared Dr. Rhee's conviction that trusteeship with Soviet participation was a period of transition not toward freedom but into absolute Communist domination. After all, the lesson of eastern Europe was still to be learned—as was also the emerging fact of Russian intransigence in the United Nations. Kim Sung Soo, heading the Democratic Party, had an influential following of wealthy Koreans who had prospered under the Japanese and who believed their property would be safeguarded only through a transitory trusteeship program. Naturally, the communists in South Korea favored the trusteeship plan that Russia demanded. This left Kim Koo, who represented still another policy position. He strongly supported Dr. Rhee in renouncing trusteeship. But Kim Koo went further and insisted that the American Military Government should be disbanded and that governing power should be summarily assumed by the Provisional Republic of Korea, under his presidency. All these positions taken by the other leaders, Dr. Rhee rejected.

He did not accept the American view that the Russians would quietly and reasonably cooperate in a transitional period that would terminate in genuine Korean independence. He did not accept Kim Koo's view that the Americans, along with the Russians, should be openly defied. If conflict with the Americans should break out, he told Kim Koo, and if so much as a single American soldier should be killed by Korean patriots, American support would be withdrawn and the prospect of Korean independence would be forever lost. Neither could he "cooperate" with the American program, as Kimm Kiusic, Lyuh Woon Heung, and Kim Sung Soo were willing to do, on the hope that Washington would staunchly and benevolently continue to protect Korea against Russian designs on the peninsula.

What Syngman Rhee foresaw was a wholly different outcome. The policy he pursued was consistent with the career he had followed all his life. As a young man in his teens, he had gone to prison for opposing the repressive and absolutist rule of the Korean monarchy. In his prison-written book, *The Spirit of Independence,* he had developed a Confucian theory of democracy—one that stressed individual responsibility for the well-being of the state, rather than stressing individual rights and privileges. During his forty-year residence in the United States (while he earned an A.B. degree at George Washington University, an M.A. at Harvard, and a Ph.D. at Princeton, and later maintained the Korean Commission as a means of influencing American opinion to support Korean sovereignty), he had developed a faith that the American people, if they were informed and aroused, would insist that their government support justice and freedom for Korea.

In short, what Dr. Rhee tried hard to accomplish during 1946 was to maintain viable relations with the United States government, through the operations of the Representative Democratic Council, to obstruct the implementation of trusteeship, and to wage a public relations campaign to win the sympathy and support of the American public. Concurrently, he also had a major problem to solve in Korea —namely, to persuade the Korean populace to follow him in opposing the American basic policy of promulgating trusteeship yet at the same time to avoid drifting into opposition to the United States itself.

Both the correctness of Syngman Rhee's analysis and the effectiveness of his program have been strikingly attested by an American official who was uniquely in a position to know. General John R. Hilldring was Assistant Secretary of State for Occupied Countries (Germany and Korea) through the crucial years of 1946–47. In our Washington office, we found him unfailingly sympathetic with our efforts to win support for Rhee's views on Korea. Two years after his retirement from office, in the fall of 1949, Secretary Hilldring, from his retirement home in Phoenix, wrote to me a lengthy letter reviewing the struggle we had waged. Since this letter was based on Hilldring's detailed inside knowledge of what was happening, I shall quote from it at length:

> You and I both know that it wasn't many weeks after the Moscow Conference [he wrote] before everyone who had anything to do with the Korean Declaration deeply and honestly regretted it. But it is one thing to regret a mistake and quite another to come forward and recommend that an international agreement be renounced in order to correct the mistake. The cold war was already on, which further tightened the conviction of most officials, particularly the career diplo-

mats, that any abrogation by us of an agreement with Russia would have disastrous consequences. In any case, this was the dilemma of the U.S. Government.

I, of course, know this very well. I lived with it for many months. I recall vividly the indoctrination I received on this point when I entered the State Department in April, 1946. I was cautioned that I would be the target of dulcet importunities and of threats of dire consequences unless America renounced trusteeship for Korea. I was told that I must be prepared for this, and that I would be expected to stand up under it. Of course everyone wanted to help Korea, but I must understand that such assistance couldn't be given at the expense of an open rift with the Soviet Union, etc., etc. You know the story as well as I do.

It was in this diplomatic climate that the Korean Commission carried on its crusade in Washington, and it was the persistent and patient labors of Rhee, Oliver and Limb that converted first one and then another official and reporter to the view that to deal honestly with Korea—to declare openly and unequivocally that the trusteeship agreement was a mistake—was more important than to persist in the error for fear of displeasing Russia.

It was a great crusade, and even now my recollection of how the objections of the horrified dissenters were plowed under fills me with glee and delight. . . .

Hilldring's letter, we must remember, was written in 1949. In 1946, we could not foresee with confidence a favorable outcome. America was not won over quickly. In Seoul, General Hodge told a news conference that "Oliver should be hanged" because of our opposition to the policy of trusteeship. By this time the stalemate that marked Stage Three was ending and a new and even more difficult period was commencing.

V.

Stage Four, a period of open and bitter conflict between Dr. Rhee and General Hodge, commenced in November 1946.

General Hodge sought to sidetrack or ameliorate Dr. Rhee's opposition by holding an election for a Korean Representative Assembly. The aim was to provide a channel through which elected Korean representatives could add their advice and guidance in the development of internal domestic programs. To insure that the new assembly would not arrogate to itself power beyond this limited objective, General Hodge decided that to balance the forty-five elected assemblymen, he would himself appoint an additional forty-five. The election actually resulted in the choice of forty-four followers or adherents of Dr. Rhee, with one communist elected from the island province of Cheju-do. General Hodge then undertook to "rectify the balance" by appointing forty-five members—and he made his choices all from a list of names provided for him by Kimm Kiusic. The appointees favored close cooperation with the American program of gradualism, of a transitional trusteeship, and of seeking an accord with the communist regime that had been set up in the North. When the ninety members of the Assembly—half elected, half appointed—convened, they elected Kim Kiusic as their Chairman. General Hodge and Dr. Rhee held a meeting marked by bitter personal recriminations, after which Dr. Rhee left abruptly for Washington, D.C. to protest in person against what he felt was a farcical repudiation of democracy.

It was at this time that I left my teaching duties at Syracuse University to devote full time in Washington in the effort to secure a shift in American policy on the Korean question. Dr. Rhee found difficulties in getting back into Korea, for Hodge made serious efforts to keep him out. Had it not been for the combined support of Secretary John Hilldring, General Douglas MacArthur, and Chiang Kai-shek, it is dubious that Rhee could have returned. As it was, when he arrived in Seoul in April 1947, General Hodge placed him under virtual house arrest. He was forbidden to speak over the radio or to hold public meetings, the telephone was removed from his home, and visitors coming to see him were carefully screened. Of course the correspondence between him and our group in Washington was strictly censored.

Nevertheless, Dr. Rhee's political organization continued to build support among the Korean people and we in Washington continued to build support in American public opinion. The gross injustice of Hodge's appointments, which nullified the result of the Assembly election, was a powerful weapon for us to use. American public opinion and editorial influence swung toward Dr. Rhee. Meantime, the Russian domination of eastern Europe, its subjection of the various coalition governments there, and its active efforts to penetrate into Asia, Africa, and Latin America were all resulting in a surging anti-communist sentiment in America. The Moscow Decision on trusteeship was becoming increasingly distasteful. Moreover, the American public was deeply alarmed by communist successes in China—despite an intense campaign that represented Mao Tse-tung and his followers as no more than "agrarian liberals."

In reaction to all these factors, and confronting the failure of the U.S.-U.S.S.R. Joint Commission in Korea to reach any constructive agreements, in August 1947, Secretary of State George Marshall undertook to escape from the deadlock with Russia over the Korean problem by presenting it to the United Nations. In those days, which now seem so long ago, American influence in the U.N. was sufficiently strong so that our suggestion became its decision. In September, "the Korean question" was placed on the agenda of the General Assembly. Thus ended the Fourth Stage—the period of open conflict between Dr. Rhee and the American Military Government of South Korea.

VI.

The Fifth Stage in the progress toward establishment of the Republic of Korea was a messy period in which constructive cooperation was marred by the suspicion with which all the major participants regarded one another, and also by basic differences of opinion about what could be safely and should be wisely undertaken. Trusteeship was shelved and the Republic was going to be set up. But how to proceed toward that goal was a problem complicated by bitter disagreements. Looking back, we know what happened; but by that time, looking ahead, no one could be sure what would happen. There were uncertainties on all sides.

One of the major uncertainties was what the United Nations might do. Russia denied that the U.N. had any valid jurisdiction, claiming the Korean question had been predetermined by the Four-Power Conference held in Moscow in December 1945. When the General Assembly of the U.N. proceeded, in any event, to discuss the question and on November 14, 1947, voted to establish the United Nations Temporary Commission on Korea, charged with responsibility for holding an election which would result in formation of a Korean government, Russia flatly refused to permit the Commission to have any access to the northern part of the peninsula. The Russian stand posed serious problems for which no one had ready solutions.

The General Assembly appointed to the Temporary Commission representatives from Australia, Canada, China, El Salvador, France, India, the Philippines, Syria and the Ukraine. The Ukraine declined appointment. Chairmanship of the Commission was lodged in the Indian representative. The representatives of Australia, Canada and Syria were dubious about the wisdom of proceeding, after Russia refused the Commission access to the North. The French representative showed little interest in the proceedings and absented himself from some of the meetings. The General Assembly of the U.N. adjourned in December, but it established an Interim Committee known popularly as the "Little Assembly" to remain on call in New York to respond to any inquiries the Temporary Commission might address to it. Dr. Rhee and other Korean nationalists made earnest efforts to have some kind of South Korean representation at the United Nations, on the grounds that the fate of the Korean people ought not to be determined without their participation; but this request was rejected—as was a parallel request from the communist regime in the North.

In Seoul Dr. Rhee was demanding that the American Military

Government proceed immediately to hold an election that would result in selection by the Korean voters of officials with whom the U.N. Commission could consult. For this stand he was condemned in the world press for "obstructing" the United Nations program—whatever that program might turn out to be. On December 22, 1947, Dr. Rhee wrote to me, saying that, "My idea is to implement the U.N. Commission rather than to undermine it." Then he went on:

> When the U.N. Commission arrives, the Koreans will have no representative spokesman to speak for them. The result will be another failure and the U.N. Commission will ultimately make no showing whatever. The Korean situation will be presented to the world as most difficult of solution. If, on the other hand, we have a number of people chosen by the Korean people to represent them and to participate in the discussion of our problems, the U.N. cannot—even if it wants to—make the mistake the Four Powers made at Moscow without consulting the Koreans.

The Temporary Commission held its first meeting in Seoul on January 12, 1948. In an undated letter written about January 20th, Dr. Rhee described to me the chaotic condition of the Korean public's reaction: "The Commission members go around and any English speaking Korean is trying to get hold of them. They are already so confused that people get discouraged." Then he went on:

> I called on Ambassador Menon, the chairman, and had a very good talk. Dr. Djabi of the Syrian Delegation called on me. I tried to see Patterson, of Canada; he made the excuse that two weeks after his arrival he had not yet called on General Hodge and therefore could not see anyone. We are having the Chinese delegation for dinner on the 22nd and Menon, Nair, Djabi, Muhir and Chin on the 27th. They do not wish to be invited together with the others. At the official reception the French delegate was not there. I believe it was because the grandstand was so packed he could not get in. That was the story he told. I went to his hotel with the intention to apologize but was told that he had gone out hunting. He was not at the buffet dinner at the Changduk Palace, either. . . . Dr. Bunce [then serving as Hodge's principal State Department adviser] has placed all middle-roaders as translators and advisers to the U.N. Commission. He is working hard to promote Dr. Kimm Kiusic. . . .

General Hodge pleaded with the "big three" Korean leaders (Rhee, Kimm Kiusic, and Kim Koo) to present a unified front to the U.N. Commission, saying that if disunity prevailed, the Commission might decide that an election was impossible. On February 3rd, the usually reliable Gordon Walker sent a story to the *Christian Science Monitor* saying that Kimm Kiusic had been "slated by the American Military Government" to become the first President of the Republic of Korea. On February 11th, Dr. Rhee wrote me a very long letter in which he told of efforts he made to get together with Kim Koo and Kimm Kiusic to try to agree on a joint statement favoring the holding of an election. The two Kims insisted that they wanted no election to be held until after they had had another opportunity to persuade the

North Korean regime of Kim Il-sung to join with the South in an all-Korean union. On February 26th, the "Little Assembly" of the U.N. took the decisive step of authorizing an election "in such parts of Korea as are accessible to the Commission." By this vote the troublesome Fifth Stage in the march toward independence was ended. The troubles, however, continued.

VII.

Stage Six, lasting through March and April, was largely concerned with the controversy concerning a North-South Conference to be held in Pyongyang on the question of how to secure the reunification of Korea. Dr. Rhee agreed with Kim Koo and Kimm Kiusic that such a conference should be held—so long as it did not result in postponement of the election. This question was determined on February 28th, when the U.N. Commission voted that the election should be held no later than May 10th.

Were there any realistic prospects that the North Korean communist regime might be willing to engage in the establishment of an all-Korea government that would be both independent and democratic? Kim Koo and Kimm Kiusic thought the question should be explored. They accepted the invitation by Kim Il-sung to come to Pyongyang to talk about it. Dr. Rhee was not invited to the North-South Conference. He was very dubious about its advisability. He was convinced that the communists would not relinquish the control they already had over the North and that they would use the conference solely to accomplish their own aims. As a minimum, they would seek to delay the election in the South. They would seek to divide and disrupt the Korean people while consolidating and extending the communist influence in the southern part of the peninsula. Beyond this, their aim would be to inveigle the U.N. and the American Military Government into holding the election under conditions that would result in a coalition government which the communists would shortly control. All three of these leaders were undoubtedly sincere. But their views were widely divergent.

These differences among the Korean leaders, added to the deep-seated and worldwide uneasiness about the Soviet-American hostility toward one another, threatened to upset the plans for the election. On March 8th and 9th, the Indian, Syrian, Canadian and Australian delegates on the Commission—a majority of its membership—all expressed doubts about the wisdom of proceeding with plans for the May 10th election. Kim Koo and Kimm Kiusic both issued statements denouncing the election as a betrayal of Korea's hopes for reunification. The South Korean Interim Legislature (which was the one half-elected, half-appointed by Hodge in November 1946) voted forty to zero to support the election, but more than half its members were either absent or abstained from the vote.

The North-South Conference, called by Kim Il-sung, was to be held in Pyongyang on April 19–25. On April 5th, Dr. Rhee wrote to me about his expectations concerning it:

> The general belief is that Kim Koo and Kimm Kiusic will go north and that their participation will be played up very much up there. Already now the Communist press is praising them. They will make Kim Koo the vice-chairman and keep him there. Their propaganda is working hard to tell the northerners that Kim Koo is coming home to save the nation, etc., etc. It will go all right for awhile, but they will insist on pronouncing that their government is *the* Government of Korea and will move down. All the military preparations are pointing toward it. Kim Koo will demand the withdrawal of the Americans—he always clamoured for it—the Russians will move across the border [into Siberia] and watch to see how the Americans react. If the Americans pull out, too, you know the rest. Kimm Kiusic is too smart, and he still thinks he can outwit the Russians. The only thing for us to do is to go right ahead with our program in the South without any delay.

The situation throughout April continued to be confused. General Hodge added his warnings to those by Dr. Rhee, saying that the Pyongyang meeting would be dangerous and could not be helpful. In South Korea, spokesmen for the so-called "moderates" as well as the "leftists" insisted that they would boycott the election in protest against its being held to set up a separate South Korean government. These threats proved to be very empty; voter registration was extremely heavy, comprising well over 90 percent of all eligible voters.

On May 5th, Kim Koo and Kimm Kiusic returned from Pyongyang, assuring the public that the meeting had been a great success. Kim Il-sung had assured them, they reported, that a separate North Korean government would "never" be set up. He had promised that all problems "shall be successfully solved by frequent negotiations between North and South leaders." And he had declared that, "The problem of international cooperation shall be solved by the action of foreign countries." In short, the division of Korea should be left for settlement by Russia and the United States. Kim Koo and Kimm Kiusic added their own assurance that the flow of electric energy from the hydro-electric plants of the North would not be shut off and that the water reservoirs to the north of the 38th parallel would be opened for use by Kaesong and other towns and villages in the South.

Then Kim Koo and Kimm Kiusic gave their endorsement to the resolution with which the Pyongyang Conference had concluded: a resolution calling for the withdrawal of all foreign troops and the subsequent holding of an all-Korea election, without interference by the United Nations.

VIII.

The Seventh Stage was the establishment of the Republic—a process that was far from anti-climactic.

On May 10th, 94 percent of all eligible voters were registered, and 91 percent of all registrants voted. So much for the boycott. The American Military Government conducted the election and it was observed by staff members of the U.N. Commission. The A.M.G. reported that "comparatively little trouble occurred" and the U.N. Commission reported that there were no irregularities that might have affected the outcome of the election. The 198 Assemblymen who were elected set about accomplishing the establishment of the government —namely, the formation of a Constitution and the election of the Chief Executive.

Syngman Rhee was elected chairman of the Assembly, receiving 188 of the 198 votes. It was evident that he would become the first president of the Republic. It was also evident that the task of governing the new nation would be overwhelming. On May 14th, the *Kiplinger Newsletter* and the *U.S. News and World Affairs* both carried stories saying that the United States planned to "abandon" Korea to Russia. On May 17th, the *New York Times* carried a follow-up story reporting that American plans were maturing to allow the Soviet Union to take over control of all Korea.

Kim Koo and Kimm Kiusic met with the U.N. Temporary Commission to tell it that plans were developing for the reunification of the peninsula; they gave their personal assurance that there would be no invasion from the North. This assurance looked a bit shaky in view of the fact that the hydro-electric power flowing southward across the 38th parallel was promptly shut off, and the water reservoirs were kept closed to southern use.

Within the Assembly there was a wide diversity of views and of personalities. The average age of the members was forty-seven, with a range from twenty-eight to seventy-four. Kim Koo, Kim Sung Soo, and Shin Icki all had substantial groups of followers and held them under strict control, hoping they might be able to unite and form a majority party. A movement was started to promote Kim Koo for the vice-presidency. Another movement favored establishment of the English cabinet system of government, with either Kim Koo or Shin Icki to become the Prime Minister. South Korean newspapers criticized Dr. Rhee for his support of the American presidential system, charging that this was an effort on his part to "seize power." Once again, as had happened following his 1945 return to Korea, a movement was launched to render him powerless as a mere ceremonial Head of State.

On July 7th, sitting in his upstairs office in the Assembly building, Dr. Rhee wrote me a long explanation of the various proposals and counterproposals, which were reminiscent of the meetings of the Constitutional Delegates in Independence Hall in 1787. "The reading of the constitution," he wrote "was just as stormy as in the American Congress—debates, and ups and downs, as democratic as could be. It was wise to give everyone a chance to do the talking; otherwise, the chairman would have been denounced as a dictator, which they cannot say now."

On July 21st, the Constitution was adopted and the Assembly moved promptly to election of the executive officers of the new Republic. For President, Dr. Rhee received 180 votes, Kim Koo 13. For Vice-President, Yi Si Young (a compromise candidate) was elected with 133 votes, as against 62 for Kim Koo. In another compromise, the presidential system was adopted but there was also provision for a Prime Minister, whose appointment must be approved by the Assembly—and whose duties were left virtually undefined.

President Rhee and Vice-President Yi took their oaths of office on July 24th. The inauguration of the Republic of Korea was set for August 15th—the third anniversary of the defeat of Japan and the liberation of Korea from thirty-five years of Japanese rule. The three years of struggle over the question of whether there would be an independent government in Korea, and if so, by what means it should be set up, had left deep wounds that were slow to heal. Both the People's Republic of Korea, in Pyongyang, and the Republic of Korea, in Seoul, claimed jurisdiction over the entire nation. The United Nations Commission was charged to continue its efforts to secure reunification of the divided nation. There was to be turmoil and war ahead, but Stage Seven was concluded.

IX.

As a personal footnote to this account of the establishment of the Republic of Korea, I may add that General John R. Hodge, as one of his last acts as Commander of the United States Force of Occupation, refused me a military permit to enter Korea to attend the August 15th inaugural ceremonies. To make the matter very clear, I immediately entered a second request for clearance; on August 2, 1948, the Korean Commission in Washington received the following radiogram from Seoul:

> AMG AUTHORITIES ADVISE OLIVER SHOULD WAIT TILL GOVERNMENT IS SET UP TO REQUEST CLEARANCE.

General Hodge had the last word. At least it was abundantly clear that Syngman Rhee was not an American stooge selected by Washington as a puppet figurehead to conceal American imperialism in Korea. I think the record makes it equally clear that Dr. Rhee's insistence upon proceeding with the United Nation's plan to hold an election in South Korea, after Russia refused to permit it in the North, was not the result of personal ambition but of genuine patriotism. Dr. Rhee's own final word on this was contained in a letter he wrote to me on June 21, 1948, while Kimm Kiusic and Kim Koo were still demanding that inauguration of the Republic be postponed pending yet one more attempt to reach some kind of bargain for North-South reunification. "Any coalition government," Dr. Rhee wrote, "will make Korea another Czechoslovakia." All students of recent world history must conclude, I think, that this judgment was correct.

The end of this case study of American involvement in Korea must, of course, be inconclusive. The involvement itself continues. Some 42,000 American troops are still in Korea. We have implanted in South Korea strategic nuclear weapons and have announced officially that this is one area in which we shall not hesitate to use them in case of an enemy attack, not even if the enemy restricts his attack to conventional weapons of war. Many millions of American dollars are still committed annually to the Republic of Korea—some for military, some for economic purposes. United States policies declare unequivocally that in case the Republic of Korea should be attacked, the United States will "automatically" be in the war. No one can foresee where an involvement once begun may end, or on what terms.

Away back in 1942 or 1943—and perhaps earlier, perhaps even before Pearl Harbor—Franklin Roosevelt conceived the notion that the Korean Peninsula could be used as a pawn to help him achieve the "grand design" of securing Russian entry into the Pacific War and then, subsequently, of insuring Russian cooperation in maintaining world peace. If someone had informed him of how stubbornly the Korean people cling to their own idea of their own independence, he might have looked elsewhere for bait with which to entice the Russian bear. No one told him then. As Americans confront the always complex and difficult questions of how foreign relations may best be conducted, it is time they were told now. Involvement is a prickly thorn, to be taken up only with caution and with understanding. As Confucius warned, long ago, the time to think about the end of any endeavor is at its beginning.

1. U.S. Department of State, *Diplomatic Papers, 1943* (Washington, D.C. 1963), vol. III, p. 37.

2. Ibid., *Diplomatic Papers: The Conference at Malta and Yalta, 1945* (Washington, D.C., 1955), pp. 358–361.

3. Ibid., *Diplomatic Papers: The Conference of Berlin (Potsdam Conference), 1945* (Washington, D.C., 1960), vol. I, pp. 310–315.

The Costs of Counterrevolution: U.S. Intervention vs. Vietnamese Interests, 1954–1963

Gareth Porter

If a re-examination of U.S. intervention in Vietnam is not to stray into the intellectual and moral quicksand of speculation on what the U.S. might have done to change the outcome, it must address the most fundamental question of all: what were the objectives of that intervention and what policies did those objectives demand? Only by examining these American objectives and policies in the context of *Vietnamese* social and political realities can one appreciate fully why the U.S. failed.

It is the thesis of this paper that the American government pursued objectives in Vietnam which were essentially unattainable, because they put the U.S. at odds with the needs and desires of the South Vietnamese people. By 1954 the U.S. confronted in Vietnam a mature revolutionary movement which had, in its thirty-year history, absorbed the most fundamental aspirations of the Vietnamese nation. For the masses of poor workers and peasants, those aspirations included the building of a society in which the extremes of poverty and wealth would be eliminated, and which would advance toward a modern, industrialized economy. At the same time, most Vietnamese wanted an end to the dominant role of Western powers in Vietnamese society.

In aiming at the suppression of the communist-led revolution and the maintenance of an anti-communist regime in South Vietnam, the U.S. found itself opposing those aspirations, thus placing itself in the role of foreign oppressor which the French had occupied for so long. Whether or not the U.S. sympathized with the objectives of social progress, economic development and national independence, the definition of American interests which controlled the U.S. intervention required policies which were aimed at maintaining the status quo and which caused social and economic regression.

Washington threw its diplomatic and military power and its economic resources into Vietnam, not because of any positive interest in the advancement of the Vietnamese people, but because of a U.S. political-military interest in preventing any communist advance in Southeast Asia. In the absence of this anti-communist motivation, the U.S. would certainly not have been deeply involved in Vietnam. In basing American intervention exclusively on a geopolitical interest in maintaining the anti-communist regime in Saigon, U.S. policy-makers did not take into account the cost of pursuing those interests to the South Vietnamese people themselves.

A counterrevolutionary policy in a society which was already in the midst of revolution required two main features: first, a repressive apparatus had to be built up which was capable of rooting out and destroying the revolutionary political organization in the South. Second, because it was the wealthier strata of society—the landlords and the urban middle class—who were viewed as natural enemies of the communist revolution, the U.S. had to insure their political support for the Diem regime and their cooperation with its policies.

These two imperatives in turn shaped the U.S. assistance program in South Vietnam during the first decade of direct U.S. involvement. Because the Saigon regime could not muster the economic resources to sustain its military-paramilitary apparatus, the U.S. had to concentrate its economic aid heavily on subsidizing the security apparatus of its client state at the expense of assistance for economic and social development. Moreover, the U.S. aid was aimed especially at the economic interests of the middle class, which was considered the political base of the anti-communist regime, but also a possible source of political unrest. The economy had to be devoted, therefore, to a high level of consumption of imported goods, while sacrificing any possibility of economic growth. Meanwhile, the system of tenancy had to be maintained in order to preserve the existing village elite, which was considered indispensable to anti-communist programs in the countryside.

Beyond the geopolitical interests of U.S. policy loomed another kind of interest which also had a major impact on U.S. policy: the economic interest of American grain exporters in avoiding competition from developing nations in the world grain market. Their pressure prevented the U.S. from having any consistent or well-planned program for increasing rice production in South Vietnam, which was a rice-exporting nation. This aspect of U.S. policy, which actually conflicted with the political aims of Washington in South Vietnam, indicated that, above even geopolitical concerns in the structure of U.S. interests were the narrow interests of powerful sectors of the U.S. economy.

The real failure of the U.S. in Vietnam, then, was its unwillingness to take the needs and desires of the Vietnamese people as the basis of its policy there. A policy which began with an effort to determine what most Vietnamese wanted, rather than what the U.S. wanted in Vietnam, would have brought into focus the moral and political dangers of a policy of trying to maintain a conservative, anti-communist Saigon regime in a society which was in the midst of a revolution for national liberation and against social and economic backwardness.

The analysis which follows concentrates on two aspects of U.S. policy in South Vietnam: the American commercial aid program and U.S. policy toward agriculture and land tenure. Each of these aspects of U.S. policy impinged directly on the lives of millions of Vietnamese, determining to a large extent the structure of the economy and society of South Vietnam. The analysis will show how an obsession with U.S. power and pressures from powerful economic interests in the U.S., combined with an absence of positive commitment to improving the welfare of the people, made U.S. "aid" a form of oppression rather than of real assistance. And it was this character of the entire American involvement—not any specific failure in implementing policy—which insured that the U.S. could not prevail in Vietnam.

II.

The origins of U.S. involvement in Vietnam are too well-documented elsewhere to require recapitulation here. It need only be recalled here that the U.S. showed little public interest in Indochina—while privately expressing concern over the Viet Minh movement's communist orientation—until the end of 1949, when the Chinese communists gained control over the entire mainland. Then the U.S. began thinking in terms of containing communism in Asia as a counterpart to its containment policy elsewhere on the globe. By the time of the Geneva Agreement in 1954, the U.S. was providing 80 percent of the funding for the French war in Indochina. By January 1955, the U.S. became the direct paymaster to the Vietnamese military, thus ensuring that its officer corps would be responsive to American policy.[1] By taking over that role, the U.S. in effect replaced the French as the real sovereign power in South Vietnam, in spite of legal independence granted by France at the time of the Geneva Agreement.

Having signed the SEATO Treaty in September 1954, the State Department hoped that the threat of American military intervention would deter any move by the Vietnam People's Army to reunify Vietnam after the refusal of the U.S. and Diem to carry out the Geneva Agreement. That left the possibility of revolutionary activity within South Vietnam as the main concern for the U.S. Mission in Saigon. The first objective of U.S. policy, therefore, was to build up a military and paramilitary force which was strong enough to suppress any renewal of armed struggle and which could root out the remaining communist political organization in the South.

The controlling factor in deciding on the size and shape of U.S. aid to South Vietnam, therefore, was the decision on how large the armed forces should be. Since the Saigon government could not generate the resources needed to support a large enough army, the size of the armed forces was determined by the amount which the U.S. was willing to pay. As the U.S. economic aid chief at the time, Leland Barrows, explained, "After appropriate discussions between the representatives of the two governments, the United States agreed to support a military budget of a certain size, taking into account both military needs and the amount of money which Viet-Nam itself will be able to contribute."[2]

Saigon's contribution to its own military budget was minimal. During the 1955–1959 period, it provided only 10 percent of its military expenditures, which average about 47 percent of the total budget annually, for its own resources.[3] This did not take into account the $85 million worth of equipment shipped to the Saigon army under the U.S. military assistance program.[4] In order to pay for 90 percent of Saigon's military budget, the U.S. economic aid had to be concentrated heavily on that sector. During the same 1955 to 1959 period, 80 percent of U.S. budgetary subsidies were to pay military expenses, and except for 1958, the percent devoted to the military sector continued to increase each year.[5]

Looking at the entire U.S. aid effort in South Vietnam, moreover, the concentration of American resources on political stability and the security apparatus, to the detriment of development, is even more striking. From 1955 through 1961, Washington provided $3.162 billion in economic and military aid to the R.V.N., of which only $186.9 million was for development projects. But since all but $82.5 million of this subtotal was spent on highway construction (primarily for military purposes) and public administration, most of which went for development of the South Vietnamese police, only about 2 percent of all U.S. aid in South Vietnam was for social and economic development during these seven years.[6]

U.S. officials recognized from the beginning that they were not going to accomplish anything in South Vietnam except a lopsided security apparatus, as long as the threat of a communist takeover loomed in the country. Leland Barrows, in a later interview, said the U.S. Mission was "always . . . faced with the fact that until a settlement was reached, our resources would be consumed in the military effort."[7] The former chief of the Mission's Financial Division said in 1957, "The main purpose of our program thus far has been . . . supporting a very large army."[8]

It was in this context that the U.S. Commercial Import Program (C.I.P.) played a key role in U.S. policy in South Vietnam. Originally conceived as a means of subsidizing the military budget without causing inflation, the Commercial Import Program actually permitted the raising of living standards for some segments of the population while maintaining the Saigon armed forces at more than 200,000 men by 1957, and nearly 250,000 by 1959.[9] It was a program which made more palatable the absence of sufficient investment in expansion of production by keeping the level of consumer goods at an artificially high level. "What we were doing," Barrows recalled in a later interview, "was paying off the Vietnamese economy for diverting its resources into the military sector."[10] But the payoff was not in productive investment but in consumption, where it went primarily to the wealthier strata of society.

Under the Commercial Import Program, dollar credits were provided to the R.V.N. for the purchase of commodities jointly agreed on by both governments from American suppliers. The Saigon government would then sell the credits to local importers, in return for Vietnamese piasters at the official rate of exchange. The piasters thus acquired could be deposited in the government central bank in a "counterpart fund" along with the customs duties on the commodities when they arrived in the port of Saigon. The Vietnamese piasters in the counterpart fund were owned legally by the Vietnamese government, but they could be used only in ways previously agreed to by the two governments in bilateral aid agreements.

The commercial aid program permitted the client regime to continue the subsidized import economy which it had inherited from the French colonial period. Although South Vietnam's exports varied from a high of $84 million in 1960 to a low of only $34 million in 1956, it was able to import an average of about $226 million worth of goods every year, thanks to U.S. commercial aid.[11] This high level of commercial aid also translated into U.S. subsidization of the largest part of Saigon's revenues—about two-thirds of the total in 1959, according to the director of the U.S. Operations Mission, Arthur Z. Gardiner.[12]

This extreme dependence on U.S. aid to finance the Saigon government gave Washington a determining role in South Vietnamese political life, in spite of its nominal independence. The R.V.N. lacked sufficient internal political support to reduce its repressive apparatus to the point that it could be financed by South Vietnam's own revenues. Moreover, through the Commercial Import Program, the U.S. not only determined the structure of the government's budget, but the structure of the economy as well. How certain strata of the population would fare economically, whether and how much people would be asked to make sacrifices, and whether the economy would be oriented toward production or consumption—all these decisions were made primarily by the U.S. rather than by internal political forces in South Vietnam.

Moreover, these decisions were made by the U.S. on the basis of the single objective of maintaining the regime of Ngo Dinh Diem in power. This objective required both a powerful security apparatus and political stability. The U.S. was preoccupied, therefore, with that segment of the society which it felt would support U.S. anti-communist policy in Vietnam but which could also upset political stability by any opposition to the Diem regime. In order to consolidate Diem's position and head off any movement of opposition in the cities, the U.S. tried to use the Commercial Import Program to satisfy the immediate economic aspirations of the urban middle class of civil servants, intellectuals, professional, and business people.

The Commercial Import Program did not benefit all strata of the population equally. Studies of the Vietnamese economy supported the common sense observation that the poor could afford to buy few imported goods of any kind.[13] A survey of one Mekong Delta village, for example, showed that, of the 70 percent of the population whose incomes made them part of the "lower class," not a single household owned such imported consumer durables as a wristwatch, a motor bike or a radio.[14] Even fertilizer, which accounted for only a small fraction of the total program, was purchased mainly by the wealthier strata.[15] It was the urban middle class which purchased most of the imported goods. It was this class which not only maintained incomes for Western-style consumption, but also had been most exposed to European standards of consumption and had succumbed to the "demonstration" effect during the French occupation.[16]

Moreover, the individuals who profited most from the import program—the importers themselves—were also the most conspicuous consumers in the society. The Commercial Import Program made possible unprecedented incomes for thousands of Vietnamese, because the holder of the import license purchased the goods at only one-third their actual value. He obtained dollars at an artificially low exchange rate; the disparity between the official and real value of the piaster in exchange for the dollar made possible unearned profits.[17] Virtually the entire urban middle class joined the scramble to obtain a license—civil servants who quit their jobs, land owners whose land was not returning sufficient income, politicians, lawyers and doctors. Hardly any of them had any experience or interest in business and simply resold the license to a Chinese trader who knew something about markets and distribution and would actually do the work of importing.[18] A Vietnamese newspaper reported that "tremendous profits" were being made "just in the buying and selling of import licenses."[19]

For a time it seemed that most of the urban middle class would share in the C.I.P.'s bounty. By 1956 more than 20,000 people held import licenses. But this situation, which created an intolerable amount of paperwork for the Ministry of Economics, was soon brought to an end by a law requiring that the importer put up a 350,000-piaster bond ($5,000 U.S. at that time).[20] Only 1,373 import firms, most of them still speculators, had made their deposits in time for the August 15, 1956, deadline to qualify for an import license.[21] Although most of the actual importing was still done by ethnic Chinese businessmen, the Commercial Import Program still had the effect of redistributing the profits from import trade, once a near-monopoly of French companies, into the hands of Vietnamese.

One of the effects of the C.I.P. on the standard of living of the urban middle and upper class was that it allowed a dramatic increase in the consumption of luxury goods. The number of private automobiles registered during this period increased rapidly. In 1956, 3,652 new private cars were registered; in 1957, 3,593 more were registered; and in 1958, 5,460. The total number of private passenger cars in circulation, which had been only 10,000 in 1952, had increased to 38,000 by 1960.[22]

The Commercial Import Program, which at first brought into South Vietnam whatever the importers felt would sell, came under attack from American congressmen for its luxury imports, whereupon most were shifted to G.V.N.-financing. Since the G.V.N. had been able to hoard at least $225 million in foreign currency by 1960, because American commercial aid had met virtually all its import needs, it only had to maintain high levels of luxury imports.[23] Thus, the G.V.N.-financed import plan for calendar year 1961 included automobiles, deluxe fabrics, air conditioners, musical instruments, photographic equipment, Swiss watches selling for as much as $300, and German radio-phonographs selling for $700.[24] The Commercial Import Program, by permitting the G.V.N. to maintain huge foreign currency reserves, thus made possible the continued high levels of imported luxury goods by the G.V.N., even as the U.S. had to suspend this financing.

The most striking social consequence of the American aid program in Vietnam was that it not only maintained the artificial standard of living which the urban middle class had experienced during the French neo-colonial period, *but actually raised it.* At the same time, the evidence indicates clearly that it had no impact whatsoever on the masses of poor farmers who made up the majority of the population. The commercial attaché of the French Embassy in Saigon, in a report on American aid to South Vietnam, concluded that the Commercial Import Program did not permit "any real amelioration of the standard of living of the rural masses" but did permit "an urban minority to have a living standard very much above the real means of the country —and consequently artificial."[25]

American officials were keenly aware that the commercial aid program was responsible for a widening gap between rich and poor, but such a tilt toward the wealthier groups was deemed necessary for the sake of political stability. As one U.S. official observed, the Diem regime believed that the "extravagant standard of living" which the U.S. had made possible could not be "allowed to drop very much if the present hard-won anti-Communist political gains are to be preserved."[26] In regard to the officer corps, which Diem continued to view as the key to his regime's survival,[27] military pay scales were maintained, with U.S. approval, at the same levels established by the French in order to attract Vietnamese youth in the late 1940s. A South Vietnamese major earned more than twice as much per month in base pay and allowances as his Thai counterpart, thanks to this continuation of the neo-colonial compensation system.[28] The purpose of these pay scales was specifically to cement the political loyalties of the officer corps to Diem.[29]

American officials shared Diem's concern with the potential threat of political unrest from civil servants, army officials and intellectuals, and supported his strategy of neutralizing potential opposition elements by providing artificially high salaries and abundant imported goods at low prices. The U.S. view was that commercial aid was helping to tie the political strata in the cities to the regime. As Leland Barrows explained privately in 1958:

> Apart from their economic value as an anti-inflationary force commercial imports have served the political value of supplying the Vietnamese middle class with goods they wanted and could afford to buy. This provided a source of loyalty to Diem from the army, the civil servants and small professional people, who were able to obtain better clothes, better household furnishings and equipment than they had before.[30]

The Central Intelligence Agency's assessment was similar to Barrows'. In a 1959 report on the political situation in South Vietnam, the C.I.A. concluded that, despite some dissatisfaction among the educated elite and army officers, there had been little "identifiable public unrest," in large part because of the artificially high living standards in the cities. "The growth of dissatisfaction is inhibited by South Vietnam's continued high standard of living relative to that of its neighbors," it said. But it warned that "a significant cutback in the standard of living would probably create serious political problems for the government."[31]

The U.S. Commercial Import Program also served the short-term political interests of the Diem regime by providing an alternative to direct taxation. Since two-thirds of his budget was paid for by the C.I.P.-generated "counterpart funds," and the import revenues which imported goods brought in, Diem was under no pressure to establish a modern system of direct taxes which would have fallen most heavily on the wealthy.

Between 1955 and 1958, the contribution of income taxes to total tax revenues declined from about 20 percent to only 10 percent, even though the gross national product had increased by 10 percent in the same period.[32] In 1959, direct taxes constituted only 5 percent of all G.V.N. revenues, compared with 48 percent for U.S. aid and custom receipts, and 20 percent for indirect taxes. By 1963 the contribution of direct taxes had slipped to 4 percent of total revenues, while U.S.-generated counterpart funds and customs duties had increased to 52 percent. The contribution in indirect taxes and increases in money supply (another form of indirect and regressive taxation), increased to 23 percent in 1963.[33] This clear de-emphasis by the regime on direct taxes on personal income prompted an American tax analyst to observe that the South Vietnamese tax system places a "heavier burden on low . . . than on middle and higher income groups." As a result, he pointed out, "after taxes, the rich are richer and the poor are poorer."[34]

Commercial aid was also costly to the majority of poor Vietnamese in a more important way: its function was to maintain the status quo, and in so doing, it could not encourage economic development, without which more and more South Vietnamese would sink into unemployment and underemployment. Commercial aid not only failed to stimulate growth; it actively discouraged it. For one thing, U.S. officials intentionally kept the import of capital goods under the program to a minimum, because higher levels of imported machinery would have conflicted with the primary purpose of the commercial aid program: to offset the inflationary pressures generated by military expenditures.

While imports of investment goods would pay off in increased living standards in the long run, they would have to subtract from the overall level of consumer goods available to the public in the short run. Such equipment could not soak up excess purchasing power generated by counterpart funds, which was the economic advantage of consumer goods.[35] Moreover, the importation of capital goods was slow and cumbersome in comparison with consumer goods, so it did not satisfy the need for a fast, reliable source of counterpart funds and customs revenues.[36] American officials, whose responsibility was to ensure that there would be enough piasters in the bank when they were needed to cover the budget deficit, were wary of too much capital equipment in the Commercial Import Program. Leland Barrows explained in 1958 that those Vietnamese who complained that the U.S. was not providing for the building of new factories did not understand that such aid would "either slow military aid to the pace of project implementation, or it would bring about inflation."[37]

In this context, textiles were more important than industrial equipment; the import of $34 million in textiles in 1958, compared with $30 million in industrial machinery, reflected the economic and political priorities of American policy.[38] The percentage of capital goods in the commercial aid program never rose above 20 percent during the nine years of the Diem regime.[39] The fact that it did not constitute a greater part of the total U.S. import program was that the U.S. did not want it to go any higher.

The commercial aid program was certainly the most important single factor in shaping the character of the Vietnamese capitalist class after 1954. In 1960, Arthur Z. Gardiner spoke of the "importer and trader whose life blood commercial aid in Vietnam has so long nourished."[40] That aid insured that the South Vietnamese economy would be import-oriented. For the incentives it offered encouraged Vietnamese businessmen to channel their energy and capital into importing. As one spokesman for the Vietnamese capitalist class commented in 1959, "thanks to U.S. aid and thanks to a very favorable exchange rate, only in importing can one earn a large profit with a relatively small, rotating amount of capital. . . ."[41]

In fact, the Commercial Import Program not only ruled out an adequate level of investment for economic growth, but had adverse impact on the existing productive capacity of the country. Due to the massively overvalued piaster, imported goods were artificially cheap, thus driving local producers out of the market.

The local rubber, textile and sugar industries, for example, were severely hurt by the sudden onslaught of cheap imports, which forced prices down on those items. A rubber products plant which had employed 300 workers in 1951 reduced the number to sixty in 1957, when it was unable to compete with imported rubber products from the U.S. The Hiep Hoa sugar plant produced 10,000 tons of refined sugar before the war, but after 1955 it only functioned three to five months per year, and its annual production fell to only 1,111 tons, as South Vietnam began importing as much as 56,000 tons of refined sugar annually.[42]

Similarly, with American textiles and raw materials for textile manufacture being imported at artificially low prices, Vietnamese cotton and textiles were driven out of the market. The acreage planted with cotton declined from 3,340 hectares in 1955 to only 840 hectares in 1960.[43] Cotton production fell from 2,600 tons annually before the war to 500 tons in 1957, and then to 300 tons in 1961.[44] The Vietnamese textile handicrafts industry was hardest hit. Approximately two-thirds of the handicraftsmen, or 13,000, were idled by the loss of a market for their goods by 1958.[45]

Gardiner alluded to the adverse impact of the commercial aid program in local industry in his presentation to the Mission Directors' Conference in Hong Kong in 1959. In order to maintain the level of Vietnamese military forces established by U.S. military officials as necessary, he said, the U.S. had been forced to "resort to luxury imports and to destructive competition with local industry. . . ."[46] The Central Intelligence Agency also noted in a National Intelligence Estimate at that time that commercial aid had "tended to inhibit the development of local consumer goods industries. . . ."[47] One study in 1958 indicated that as much as one-half of South Vietnam's industrial capacity remained unused.[48]

The result of American economic policy was a creeping crisis of economic stagnation and unemployment which the facade of prosperity could not obscure. In 1962, one of Saigon's economists pointed out that South Vietnam needed $120 million dollars of additional investment each year just in order to keep up with its population increase, while actual investments were estimated at about $8 million per year.[49] The enormous gap between what was required and what was actually being done meant rising unemployment in the cities, and a general lowering of the living standards of the poor. A survey of Saigon in 1961 found that one-fourth of the working class was unemployed.[50] The urban poor were seen by foreign observers scavenging for food in the garbage cans of the rich.[51] When Charles Cooper, economist for the Agency for International Development, first visited South Vietnam in 1964, he got an "overwhelming . . . impression . . . of really massive unemployment in the cities and substantial unemployment in the rural areas."[52]

Since the South Vietnamese economy was oriented toward military spending and consumption, rather than investment, planning for economic development was nothing more than an empty gesture. While the Diem regime went through the motions of creating a "First Five-Year Plan," its declared aims could hardly be described as ambitious. It proposed an increase in national income by eighteen billion piasters in five years, a 12 percent increase from its 1955 level. But since population was increasing at an estimated 2.5 percent per year, this planned increase in income of 2.4 percent annually would have resulted in a net *decrease* in per capita income.[53] When the time for the second five year plan arrived, the staff of the planning organization was reduced to one person.[54]

In summary, the U.S. tried through its Commercial Import Program to maintain an army and police apparatus large enough to suppress any revolutionary challenge in South Vietnam, while at the same time maintaining and even raising the living standards of the urban middle class. But it had to sacrifice any hope of economic development; poverty and unemployment actually increased during the nine years of Diem's regime, even while the wealthier strata increased their standard of living, thanks to U.S.-financed imports. The result of U.S. policy was thus to increase the existing differences between rich and poor, rather than to narrow them through programs aimed at low-income groups.

III.

One of the central issues confronting the U.S. in its early intervention in South Vietnam was on which side the U.S. would throw its weight in the social conflict over land tenure rights in the Vietnamese countryside. The Viet Minh revolution had meant a retreat by the landlords in South and Central Vietnam from their positions of social and economic dominance in colonial Vietnam. The Viet Minh had reduced rents, imposed high agricultural taxes on the landlords and redistributed land to tenant farmers during the resistance.

With the Diem regime's takeover of former Viet Minh zones, the struggle of poor peasants against the old land tenure regime did not come to an end but continued in new forms. The communists counselled peasants to resist landowners who tried to reclaim land already redistributed by the Viet Minh and to demand the same rental levels which had prevailed during the resistance. While Diem's "rent control" ordinance fixed the rentals at 15 to 25 percent of the crop, the peasants demanded that 15 percent be the maximum rental, as it had been from 1946 to 1955.[55] The peasants did not drop the rhetoric of agrarian revolution in the presence of Saigon government officials. "When talking to the peasants," wrote U.S. land reform adviser J. Price Gittinger, "observers found they were unable to separate the farmers' own thoughts on tenure from a rote piece implanted during the years of Viet Minh indoctrination."[56]

For their part, landowners generally demanded that the tenants sign contracts establishing the rent at 25 percent of the crop, and if the tenant refused, evicted him in favor of a more pliable tenant. But they often went well beyond the 25 percent maximum under the Diem regime's rent-control law.[57] In 1957 the Saigon newspaper *Buoi Sang* (Morning) carried complaints by tenants that landlords were demanding rents from 35 to 40 percent of the crop.[58]

The Diem regime supported the rights of landlords over those of tenants, for Diem's basic attitude was that the communist revolution had to be defeated without a redistribution of wealth and power in the countryside. Diem's conception of what Vietnamese society should be like was essentially hierarchical, acquired from his landed family and an education which trained him in the elitist mandarin tradition.[59] He saw that the old hierarchy had been seriously undermined by revolutionary struggle, and the main problem for him was how to restore it. "Vietnam's priority is stability, central control, respect for authority and law and order," he declared to an American journalist.[60]

Diem's view of the landowner's role in this idealized Confucian social order was well defined. "Diem had no idea of destroying the influence of landowners," recalls one official in Diem's Land Reform Ministry, "because he was from Central Vietnam, where there is little land and many people and the position of the landowner was very strong."[61] As Gittinger recalled later, Diem held the "traditional Vietnamese view" that the village elite of landowners "have a reasonable claim to more resources."[62]

The landowner class was also an indispensable ally in the fight against the communist foe. For the resident landlords, most of whom owned from five to fifty hectares and had some education under the French, were the only ones in the villages on whom Diem could count to collaborate actively and loyally in the government's anti-communist programs. Gittinger explains that Diem was especially concerned about the "village elders, who had time to administer village affairs."[63] And an official of the Diem government said that Diem "wanted to stabilize society. He wanted to keep the landowners to protect the regime. They were allies in the anti-Communist struggle."[64] Arthur Z. Gardiner recalled that Diem "realized you need leadership . . . I recall we used to figure he wanted to allow a landowner $50,000 dollars worth of rice a year. He wanted to keep a middle class."[65]

Diem's policy clearly opposed any dramatic change in the land tenure system of South Vietnam. His only concession to "reform" was a program which permitted the big landlords to sell all the land they wanted, while permitting them to retain far more than the 100 hectares supposedly constituting the retention limit on holdings.

The landlords could increase the amount retained by 25 percent for the fourth and each succeeding child and also transfer 100 hectares to each of several relatives, including children, in order to avoid expropriation.[66]

The U.S. approach to land tenure, despite the differences in culture and ideology which separated the two governments, had far more in common with Diem's than it had in conflict with it. For the U.S. also accepted the existing rural class structure as the basis for its anti-communist strategy. The primary consideration in U.S. policy was what would contribute the most to the stability of the Diem regime and the building of an anti-communist apparatus. There was no interest in Vietnamese interests or aspirations, except insofar as they had to be taken into account as a threat to U.S. objectives.

In June 1956, Diem requested American financial assistance to compensate the landowners who would be confiscated under the proposed ordinance limiting landholdings to 100 hectares. The response of the U.S. Mission in Saigon was to suggest that the program was probably not necessary for the pursuit of U.S. interests in Vietnam. A memorandum on U.S. policy by the American land reform adviser, J. Price Gittinger, stated explicitly the question of land transfer would be examined "exclusively in terms of United States interests."[67] It pointed out that there were a number of general justifications for land transfers in Vietnam, including such arguments as "all peasants want land" and "broadening the base of the social pyramid." But such arguments were "too broad to be operative," the memorandum said, and "in a discussion of immediate United States interests may be discarded."

The only question relevant to the land transfer issue, according to Gittinger's memorandum, was whether or not the peasants of South Vietnam were so insistent on such a change as to make it a "pressing need"—presumably meaning necessary to stave off rebellion against the Saigon government. And Gittinger claimed that there was not sufficient evidence of such peasant demands to cause immediate concern.

In support of his contention that land transfer was not necessary in order to keep rural discontent under control, Gittinger cited the lack of interest in the issue on the part of the Diem government. The government, he wrote, did not really "consider the issue important," as indicated by its proposal for a retention limit of 100 hectares. "Surely, if land transfer was a pressing political move necessary to save this nation from chaos, the program would have to reach more than one fourth of the tenants," Gittinger argued.

In other words, as long as U.S. officials did not fear an immediate outbreak of insurgency, or felt that it could be controlled by military-police measures alone, they had no interest in pushing for land redistribution as such. They seem to have been perfectly willing to use an unjust and exploitative social and political system in order to repress a communist insurgency, as long as it appeared to be "working," and the use of land reform was only a last resort to be used when the status quo appeared to be failing as a basis for counter-insurgency.

In part, this policy toward land tenure grew out of the confidence that any insurgency which did arise could be kept within manageable bounds by a combination of military-police measures and political warfare efforts, while programs of social reform could be used for the longer-term stabilization of the situation. It had been the application of counterinsurgency techniques which had succeeded in getting the Huk rebellion under control in the Philippines in 1952 and 1953.[68] Land reform was thus seen as only one part of a total counterrevolutionary effort in which physical repression was counted on to play the main role.

In South Vietnam the very success of the Diem regime in restoring security in 1955 and 1956, which Gittinger cited as a probable cause of later peasant resentment against the government, was also a triumph for American counterinsurgency techniques. For the military sweeps of former Viet Minh zones and the campaign to hunt down

"Communist agents" were devised and planned by U.S. officials, led by Col. Edward Lansdale, who had been involved in the successful suppression of the Huk rebellion in the Philippines. It was Lansdale who worked out the program for sending "Civic Action" cadres into the old Viet Minh strongholds of Quang Ngai and Binh Dinh to carry out "anti-Communist denunciation" sessions among other activities— all in close coordination with U.S. officers.[69]

When the communists failed to respond militarily to Diem's repression of their cadres in the South, and the security situation continued to improve for the Saigon government, there was a further reduction in American interest in land reform. Gittinger, who had in 1956 regarded Diem's limited land transfer program as having little political significance in terms of peasant attitudes and had advised planning for an eventual program of limited land redistribution in case of tenant unrest, later began to hope that the 1956 program would be enough to insure social stability. "One reason Americans were not prepared to argue for land reform," he recalled later, "was that they hoped the 100 hectare limit would have a big and perhaps decisive impact."[70]

Moreover, from the viewpoint of U.S. officials in Saigon, a major restructuring of rural society would have been in conflict with the political interests of the Saigon regime. They agreed with the Diem regime that it could not afford to destroy its main source of political support in the countryside, the resident landlords who had taken an active interest in village affairs in the past. "When we talked about the retention limit," says Gittinger, "we never talked about 2 or 3 or even 5 hectares. We did not want to destroy the traditional village structure. The biggest support for the Diem government was the traditional village leadership strata. It seemed unwise politically."[71] I.C.A. Director in Vietnam Leland Barrows also had "personal doubts" about any further land transfer in South Vietnam. "Our emphasis on the peasants overlooked the fact that a free society has to have a bourgeoisie," he says. "While landlords aren't a good bourgeoisie, you have to distinguish between absentee landlords and resident landlords."[72] Confronted with the potential threat of agrarian revolution, the U.S., like Diem, fell back on the landowning class as the most reliable social base for its client regime.

This concern for preserving the village landlord class put sharp limits on the kind of land redistribution program which could be proposed. The majority of the tenant farmers were believed to be working land of proprietors of twenty-five hectares or less who were resident in the village.[73] So there was no way of reaching the majority of the landless peasants without also harming the village landlord class.[74]

Reinforcing the reluctance to push for any further land redistribution was yet another consideration: the fear that it would cause a significant reduction in the amount of rice available for export from South Vietnam. During the late 1950s, the technical desks in Washington had a strong influence on economic policies in Asia and Africa, and their concerns were the overall level of production and the ability of the country to improve its trade balance, rather than the distribution of socio-economic benefits within the society.[75] In South Vietnam, rice constituted from 25 to 30 percent of the country's exports between 1957 and 1960, second only to rubber.[76] If rice exports were to fall, South Vietnam would become increasingly dependent on American aid, with no prospects for becoming economically viable.

In this context, the conventional economists in Washington believed that land redistribution would have two harmful consequences: first, other land reforms had been followed by a reduction in overall production, presumably because large, well-managed farms had higher productivity than small individual plots. Second, it was feared that more rice would be consumed by the former tenants and less would be available for export. "The consensus was that peasants were eating more when liberated from the landlords, so that less was available for export," recalled Milton Esman, program director for the U.S. Mission from 1957 to 1959. "This tended to confirm that more rice would be available under the landlord system."[77] Gittinger remembers the same objections from Washington to any land distribution scheme: "The economists feared negative income elasticity of market surplus, which means that people would eat more," he says.[78] Thus, the same land tenure system which had served French colonial economic interests at the expense of adequate nutrition for the Vietnamese peasant was now viewed by the American managers of the Vietnamese economy as a necessary prop of South Vietnam's sagging export trade.

But South Vietnam's real problem was that the tenancy system was not producing enough to assure exports in the long run. Per capita food availability in South Vietnam had diminished by 30 percent since World War II.[79] And even with tenancy exploitation to maximize the share of the rice crop available for export, South Vietnam's prospects for rice exports were not very bright, given its low productivity and high population growth. By 1958, U.S. economists, projecting the estimates of land development and population growth which were likely under the policies then being pursued, believed that South Vietnam's exports of rice would probably decrease over a five-year period, even with the tenancy system intact.[80]

It was clear to U.S. officials in Vietnam that the problem was not how to continue to squeeze the landless peasant in order to keep a stagnant rice economy from losing all its export potential, but how to vastly increase the country's paddy yield, which in 1958 was estimated at from 1.1 to 1.3 metric tons per hectare, one of the lowest in Asia.[81]

But the constraints imposed on them from Washington prevented them from doing anything meaningful to assist Vietnamese peasants in increasing production.

Those constraints originated with American agricultural export interests, who did not want rice-growing countries to compete with American rice on the world markets. Because of the political pressures from these American agri-business interests, the International Cooperation Administration in Washington made a policy decision in April 1956 which forbade the use of any American funds for increasing production of crops "in world surplus."[82] This was simply a euphemism for those crops which the U.S. was exporting: rice, cotton, and citrus fruits. In fact, rice was not "in world surplus" at all, since South Vietnam could not fulfill all the requests for its rice. American policy ruled out U.S. assistance of any kind in raising production of rice in Vietnam, whether for irrigation, seed variety development, or fertilizer. "About all we agriculturalists can do under this policy is malaria control," said Gittinger in 1958. Since this policy directly threatened short-range American interests in South Vietnam, such as trying to stabilize the South Vietnamese economy, the U.S. Mission attempted to disguise a variety of activities which would increase production, calling a project for rice seed multiplication "crop improvement" and the building of irrigation dams "restoration of wartime damage."[83]

But more important was what could *not* be done due to policy restrictions. Hundreds of thousands of hectares which could have been double-cropped with adequate irrigation, remained single-cropped, while the importation of simple water pumps were held up in Washington in early 1958. Although a program to supply 140,000 tons of fertilizer annually could have increased rice exports by an amount estimated to be worth $45 million annually (thus increasing Vietnamese export earnings by about 40 percent), only $5 million worth of fertilizer was being imported per year—less than the amount spent to import private automobiles.[84] As late as 1961, only 10 percent of the cultivated land was properly fertilized.[85] Even a reasonable program of pest control could have increased rice production by approximately 300,000 tons of paddy annually, according to Taiwanese experts, but this too was forbidden. A real policy of development of rice production, it was estimated, could increase exports to 500,000 tons in five or six years.[86]

So U.S. policies toward land tenure and agriculture in South Vietnam, based on narrowly political U.S. interests and on domestic economic interests, left the poor and landless peasants of South Vietnam no better off than before independence. A land regime which squeezed the tenant to the profit of the landlord was an invitation to agricultural stagnation, and the lower per hectare yields registered in South Vietnam reflected that reality. Moreover, the absence of any policy for agricultural development, like the absence of an overall economic development plan, meant that the economic position of the Vietnamese peasant tended to decline rather than improve during the first decade of direct U.S. involvement in South Vietnam.

IV.

The foregoing analysis has suggested that the central difficulty of American intervention in Vietnam was that it was not on the side of any identifiable, positive objective insofar as the South Vietnamese people themselves were concerned. Whatever small benefit accrued to the population was more than outweighed by the high cost of the U.S. effort to maintain the Diem regime in power—in terms of the sacrifice of economic development, the preservation of a regressive landowning system, and the prolongation of economic dependence. The overarching issue of self-determination and national independence were, of course, inherent in the nature of U.S. intervention. And the negative consequences of U.S. policies only reinforced the charge that the U.S. role in South Vietnam was essentially "imperialist"—exercising control over the country's politics in order to pursue its own selfish interests in the region. Tragically, the U.S. never even questioned the legitimacy of doing precisely that.

This analysis leads, therefore, not to a search for an alternative set of policies which might have been more successful in defeating the communist revolution in Vietnam. A policy which was based on the primacy of economic development and social justice would not have prevented the communists from bringing about the early reunification of their country. Rather, it presents a challenge to the fundamental framework of more assumptions underlying U.S. policy. The notion that a great power has any right to intervene in another country, for the sake of geopolitical interests, as defined by a national security elite, and without regard for the aspirations and rights of the people in question, must be looked at honestly and rejected if the real lesson of Vietnam is to be learned.

1. The abruptness of the changeover from French to American sponsorship of the Vietnamese army was symbolized by the fact that the National Bank of the State of Vietnam was still tied to the French franc when the U.S. began paying the salaries of the army in January 1955. The Chief of the U.S. Operations Mission at that time, Leland Barrows, later recalled, "We took a 28-million dollar check into the Presidency and handed it to the Vietnamese, but it left the meeting in the pocket of the French financial adviser." Interview, Washington, D.C., 17 April 1972.

2. Leland Barrows, "American Economic Aid to Viet Nam," *Viet-My* (Saigon), vol. 1, no. 2, December 1956, p. 36.

3. Ibid; Pham Van Thuyet, "Government Finance and Economic Development in Viet Nam, with Special Reference to the Impact of U.S. Aid" (unpublished Ph.D. Thesis, University of Pennsylvania, 1967), p. 45.

4. Robert Scigliano, *South Vietnam: Nation Under Stress* (Boston: Houghton Mifflin, 1964), p. 114.

5. Davy Henderson McCall, "The Effects of Independence on the Economy of Viet-Nam" (unpublished Ph.D. Dissertation, Harvard University, 1969), p. 205.

6. John D. Montgomery, The Politics of Foreign Aid (New York: Praeger Books, 1962), table 4, appendix I-A, p. 84, and table 4, appendix I-B, p. 289. As Leland Barrows has pointed out, moreover, 60 percent of the funds for U.S. project aid in South Vietnam went for American personnel. Interview, 17 April 1972.

7. Interview, 17 April 1972.

8. Frank Schiff, Verbatim Transcript of the Conference on "The Economic Needs of Vietnam," sponsored by the American Friends of Vietnam, 15 March 1957, (mimeographed), p. 16.

9. William Henderson, "Background Paper on United States Economic Aid to Vietnam," Council on Foreign Relations Study Group on Indochina, Working Paper no. 5, 28 September 1957, p. 19; U.S. Department of Defense, *United States-Vietnam Relations, 1945–1967,* vol. 2, IV.A. 5, p. 24.

10. Interview, 17 April 1972.

11. Statement by Arthur Z. Gardiner to Mission Directors Conference, Hong Kong, December 1959. (Original copy provided to the author by Arthur Gardiner.)

12. Ibid.

13. As one economic specialist has stated, "The mass of the population do not consume large amounts of imports," McCall, op. cit., p. 306.

14. James Hendry, assisted by Nguyen Van Thuan, *The Study of a Vietnamese Community-Economic Activity* (Saigon: Michigan State University Advisory Group, 1959), p. 279.

15. Scigliano, op. cit., p. 121.

16. Trinh Thi Ngoc Uyen, "Vietnam Save and Survive," *The Times of Vietnam Magazine,* vol. 1, no. 31, 3 December 1959; McCall, op. cit., p. 249.

17. On the artificially-maintained exchange rate, see U.S. Senate, Special Committee to Study the Foreign Aid Program, *The Foreign Aid Program,* 85th Congress, 1st Session, p. 200.

18. Interview with industrialist Tran Quang Huy, Saigon, 31 August 1971; interview with Vu Quoc Thuc, Director of the National Bank under Diem, Saigon, 6 September 1971; interview with Nguyen Ngoc Diep, Viet-Nam Bank, 4 August 1971.

19. "The Ugliness of Monopoly," *The Times of Viet-Nam,* 19 May 1956.

20. *The Times of Viet-Nam,* 1 June 1957; interview with Nguyen Duc Cuong, Vice-Minister of Economics, Saigon, 11 January 1971.

21. McCall, op. cit., p. 201.

22. Comptroller General of the United States, *Review of Certain Problems Relating to the Technical Assistance Program for Viet-Nam, 1958–1962* (Washington, D.C., July 1964), p. 25.

23. In 1960, the National Bank indicated to an American economist that it had a reserve of $225 million U.S. Frank C. Child, "Economic Growth, Capital Formation, and Public Policy in Viet-Nam," Michigan State University, Viet-Nam Advisory Group, May 1961 (mimeographed), pp. 16–18. There were rumors that the actual size of the foreign currency hoard of the Diem regime was much larger than that figure.

24. *Review of Certain Problems,* p. 25.

25. "L'Aide Americaine au Vietnam," *Problemes Economiques,* La Documentation Francaise, no. 88, 5 January 1965, p. 24.

26. Lawrence Morrison, "Industrial Development Efforts," in *Viet-Nam, The First Five-Years, An International Symposium,* ed. Richard W. Lindholm (East Lansing, Michigan: Michigan State University, 1959), p. 215.

27. Interview by John D. Montgomery with unidentified U.S.O.M. official, 9 August 1958. (Papers of John D. Montgomery, Harvard University.)

28. For a table comparing pay scales in the three former French colonies of Indochina with those in Thailand, see Clement Johnson, Southeast Asia, *Report on U.S. Foreign Assistance Programs,* U.S. Senate, 85th Congress, 1st Session, 1957.

29. See *Use of Defense Support Funds for Economic and Political Purposes,* Hearings before a Subcommittee of the Committee on Government Operations, House of Representatives, 85th Congress, 2nd Session, 1958, p. 43.

30. Interview by John D. Montgomery with Barrows, 4 June 1958, Montgomery Papers.

31. "Prospects for North and South Vietnam," apparently a Central Intelligence Agency National Intelligence Estimate, dated 1959, *U.S.-Viet-Nam Relations, 1945–1967,* vol. 10, p. 1194.

32. For data on income taxes and local revenues, see Milton Taylor, *The Taxation of Income in Viet-Nam* (Saigon: Michigan State University Viet-Nam Advisory Group, 1969), p. 26. For Gross National Product for these years, see Pham Van Thuyet, op. cit., p. 185.

33. See United States Operations Mission to Vietnam, Economic and Financial Planning Division, *Annual Statistical Bulletin,* no. 8, 1965.

34. Taylor, *The Taxation of Income in Viet-Nam,* p. 82.

35. See Schiff, op. cit., pp. 16–17.

36. See McCall, op. cit., p. 310.

37. Montgomery interview with Barrows, 4 June 1958, Montgomery Papers.

38. Trent J. Bertrand, "An Evaluation of U.S. Economic Aid to Vietnam, 1955–1959," *France-Asie* 188 (Winter, 1966–67), p. 220. Pham Van Thuyet, op. cit., p. 239.

39. McCall, op. cit., p. 260. In contrast, the percentage of capital goods in North Vietnam's imports increased from 70 percent in 1958 to over 90 percent in 1960. See Yoshinoru Nakano "Economic Conditions in North Vietnam," *The Developing Economies,* vol. 1, no. 2, 1963, p. 94.

40. Arthur Z. Gardiner, "Aspects of Foreign Aid," speech delivered to the Rotary Club of Saigon, 22 September 1960. (Original manuscript provided by Mr. Gardiner.)

41. Phan Ba Thuc, "Huy Dong Von A Viet Nam," [Mobilizing Capital in Vietnam], speech to the first National Congress of Vietnamese Confederation of Merchants and Industrialists, 26 June 1959, *Tuan San Phong Thuong Mai,* October–December 1959, pp. 50–51.

42. Supplement, *Bulletin Economique de la Banque Nationale du Vietnam,* no. 1–2, 1958, p. 33.

43. McCall, loc. cit.

44. Tran Van Giau, *Mien Nam Giu Vung Thanh Dong* [The South Holds Firmly the Brass Fortress] (Hanoi: Nha Xua Ban Hhoa Hoc, 1964), vol. I (1954–1960), p. 234.

45. *Bulletin Economique de la Banque Nationale du Vietnam*, 15 September 1958, p. IX-1; Economic Research Service, U.S. Department of Agriculture, *Agriculture in the Vietnam Economy, A System for Economic Analysis*, FDD Field Report, no. 32, June 1973, p. 241, Appendix, Table F-1.

46. Statement of Arthur Z. Gardiner at Mission Directors' Conference. Gardiner also discussed this problem in an unpublished paper, "The Problem of Unutilized Aid," 6 January 1961; cited in Pham Van Thuyet, op. cit., p. 212.

47. "Prospects for North and South Vietnam," *United States-Vietnam Relations, 1945–1967*, vol. 10, p. 1194.

48. Child, "Economic Growth," p. 120.

49. Nguyen Huu Hanh, "Apres Cinq Annees de Privileges d'investissment," *Journal d'extreme Orient*, 23 June 1962.

50. Center for Vietnamese Studies, *Profile of the Vietnamese Population, The Saigon Pilot Study*, Preliminary Report (Saigon: April 1961). Cited in Scigliano, op. cit., p. 116.

51. Adrian Jaffe and Milton C. Taylor, "A Crumbling Bastion: Flattery and Lies Won't Save Vietnam," *The New Republic*, 19 June 1961, p. 18.

52. Testimony of Charles Cooper, unpublished transcript of hearings before the Subcommittee on Foreign Operations and Information, Committee on Government Operations, House of Representatives, July 1971, p. 74.

53. Pham Van Thuyet, op. cit., p. 69.

54. Ibid.

55. "Chinh Sach cua Dang Lao Dong Vietnam doi voi giai Cap Nong Dan," [Policy of the Vietnam Workers Party Toward the Peasants], no. 2 in the series "Cac Chinh Sach cua Dang" [Policies of the Party] dated 1957, Viet Cong Document 856 in Douglas Pike Collection.

56. See David Wurfel, "Agrarian Reform in the Republic of Vietnam," *Far Eastern Survey*, 26 (June 1957), p. 85; Gittinger op. cit., p. 130–131.

57. J. Price Gittinger, *Agrarian Reform Status Report*, vol II. *Studies in Land Tenure in Vietnam: Terminal Report* (Saigon: U.S. Opening to Vietnam, 1959), p. 111.

58. Vietnam News Agency, Hanoi Radio, 15 June 1957.

59. Diem was left by his father, a Minister of Rites and Chamberlain at the court of Hue, in the keeping of a high court official, and he was prepared for a career in the administration, along with his older brother, Khoi. Diem entered the French school of law and administration in Hanoi after finishing his studies at the French Lycee in Hue. He graduated in 1921 and was appointed district chief. He was governor of Ning Thuan Province when the revolutionary "high tide" of 1939–41 occurred. See Bernard Fall, *The Two Viet-Nams* (New York: Praeger, 1967), second revised edition, pp. 238–39; Denis Wearner, *The Last Confucian* (Baltimore: Penguin Books, 1964), pp. 88–89.

60. Marguerite Higgins, *Our Vietnam Nightmare* (New York: Harper and Row, 1965), pp. 166–167.

61. Interview with Tran Van Hoa, former land reform chief, Dinh Tuong Province, 17 September 1971.

62. Interview with J. Price Gittinger, Washington, 13 May 1972.

63. Interview with J. Price Gittinger.

64. Interview with Tran Van Hoa.

65. Interview with Arthur Z. Gardiner, 17 April 1972.

66. MacDonald, Salter, "Land Reform in South Vietnam," Agency for International Development Spring Review, Country Paper, June 1970, p. 63.

67. J. Price Gittinger, "Comments on Land Transfer from a United States Policy Viewpoint," (mimeographed, n.d.), in *Studies on Land Tenure in Vietnam: Terminal Report*.

68.   See Edward Geary Lansdale, *In the Midst of Wars* (New York: Harper and Row, 1972). Also, see Charles T. R. Bohanan and Napolean D. Valeriano, *Counter-Guerilla Operations: The Philippine Experience* (New York: Praeger, 1962).

69.   On the role of Lansdale and other C.I.A. officials in the Diem regime's repression of former Viet Minh, see Tran Van Don, *Tieng Noi Dan Toc,* 20, 24, and 25 May 1971; William Nighswonger, *Rural Pacification in Vietnam* (New York: Praeger, 1967), p. 36.

70.   Interview with Gittinger, 13 May 1972.

71.   Ibid.

72.   Interview with Leland Barrows, 17 April 1972.

73.   John Donnell, "Politics in South Vietnam: Doctrines of Authority in Conflict" (Ph.D. Dissertation, University of California, Berkeley, 1964), p. 176.

74.   Interview with Gittinger.

75.   Interview with Arthur Z. Gardiner, Washington, D.C., 1 June 1972.

76.   Fall, op. cit., Table 12, p. 296.

77.   Interview with Milton Esman, Ithaca, New York, 24 January 1972.

78.   Interview with Gittinger.

79.   Fall, op. cit., p. 292.

80.   Interview by John Montgomery with J. Fippin, Director, Agricultural Division of U.S.O.M., Saigon, 25 July 1958, Montgomery Papers.

81.   Ibid., Gittinger, "Statement on Draft H.C. 2102.1, I.C.A. Policy on Agricultural Activities Abroad," 21 August 1958, unclassified telegram, p. 4.

82.   Interview by John Montgomery with J. Price Gittinger, 25 and 26 June, 1958, Montgomery Papers.

83.   Ibid.

84.   Jaffee and Taylor, op. cit., p. 18.

85.   C. H. Zondag, "The Vietnam Fertilizer Story," AID Bureau for Vietnam, June 1969, p. 1. Very little of the fertilizer which was imported even went for rice land. Ibid., pp. 1–2.

86.   "Statement on Draft H.C. 2101.1," p. 4; Montgomery interview with Gittinger.

PAST FAILURES AND FUTURE CHALLENGES IN VIETNAM

Vietnamese-American Relations: Future Prospects

Douglas Pike

The point of view of the Washington policy-makers, begins with what I consider to be their four major overriding considerations. It is the aim of the national government leaders to concern themselves chiefly with these four external issues in the formulation of national policy.

The first is what comes under the code name "détente," or peaceful coexistence; mainly it involved strategic arms limitations. The basic problem here revolves around what kind of power relationship that is stable can exist and develop around the world—hopefully something beyond what we now have, which in essence is a balance of terror. This administration has a policy of détente with a number of peoples around the globe in various sectors.

The second, and these are not listed in any particular order of significance, are the so-called "flash areas." These are situations around the world that have the potential for escalation, for dragging in other powers and developing from a very local incident to something that is far more significant and dangerous in terms of confrontation. Angola, I suppose, is the current example of such a potentially dangerous area, although in many ways I would say that Cypress was an almost classic example. The U.S. generally seeks a policy that will dampen these situations.

The third concern relates to natural resource acquisition problems. This is not just a question of getting at the source but rather includes the whole dimension of the meaning of allocation of resources and the so-called Third World countries' perceptions of their fair share payment, in terms of reciprocal economic exchange. Population problems make this an extremely complicated issue. Last year I attended a conference at which economists discussed this issue of resource allocation; if I were to summarize my impressions from that meeting, it would be that if all the economists in the world were laid end-to-end they still could not reach a conclusion. But before we come down too hard on economists, perhaps we should note that it is equally difficult to obtain consensus among non-economists.

The fourth concern is nuclear proliferation. Although we do not hear much about this in laymen circles, among the officials at the upper levels it is in many ways the major concern. They are particularly worried over the proliferation of nuclear weapons manufacture, not by governments only, but by non-governmental groups. Beyond this is the problem of arms transfers, particularly of course the transfer of nuclear arms.

Let us now turn to the subject of this talk, American-Vietnamese relations. The victory by the Vietnamese communists in 1975 of course radically altered the basic U.S.-Vietnamese relationship, one which had existed since the days of World War II. Vietnamese communist's confrontation with the U.S., a proxy confrontation since the Paris Agreements, vanished almost overnight. There was a psychological recoil by the U.S., as well as a general refusal to think seriously about future Vietnamese relations. There was momentary loss of certitude on the part of the Vietnamese as to how to proceed.

Soon developed what could be called a tacit two-stage foreign policy relationship. Stage One was a let-the-dust-settle period. The paramount factor here was that both sides were to prevent relations from going into a deep freeze, as was the case with the U.S. and China after the Korean War. The stage was to be marked by mutual and measured responses, as indeed became the case: a steady liberalizing by the U.S. in defining private humanitarian aid, the return of a few MIAs—missing in action—by the Vietnamese.

At the appropriate time, and after a suitable period, would come Stage Two: the movement towards establishment of normal relations.

All of this however was to be—and is—dynamic, in that each side watches the behavior of the other. The U.S. carefully monitors Vietnamese actions in Thailand and elsewhere in Southeast Asia. The Vietnamese look for evidence of a roll-back effort in Indochina or U.S. attempts to create an anti-Vietnam alliance in Southeast Asia.

There are a number of specific issues relevant to the relationship between the U.S. and Vietnam. Let me just list a few of these.

We mentioned earlier the dynamics of the new international scene. Another important consideration in establishing a relationship is economics. It is quite obvious from an inspection of Vietnam now that economics is an overriding concern. When I lived in Hong Kong, I had a Red Guard cigarette lighter. It was red with a quotation from Mao Tse-tung, which freely translated read: "Politics is more important than economics. But not always." I think that this is now the case of Vietnam. Economic considerations are the predominant factor. There is a very strong need of economic assistance and outside input, from China, the U.S., Japan, etc. Any policy must keep in mind these considerations. Unfortunately, I do not think the prospects for assistance from the Congress is likely. Again we have to be wary of predictions, but all of my friends and contacts involved in analysis of Congressional behavior agree that the chance of getting economic aid through Congress will be exceedingly small. Most Congressmen feel that American money would be better spent in domestic programs in the U.S. But for whatever reasons they are generally opposed to financial aid.

Other considerations include trade, and the possibility of oil development. In fact, oil may be the thin entering wedge here; overtures are being made. This is difficult intelligence to pick up around Asia. We do know that there are some overtures, some kind of traffic back and forth, but at the moment that is all we know. There have also been conversations with the Soviets, French, Japanese, Italians and others. Apparently, technology is Hanoi's main interest at this point.

Although the MIA problem is small, it has wide ranging implications on Capitol Hill. It is a peculiar problem, in a way, because it is extremely sensitive. Any Congressman who appears hostile on the MIA issue is taking the risk of political suicide.

Other questions that must be dealt with are United Nations membership and disposition of arms.

But the central fact in all of this—and it should be underscored in discussing future relations—is that in truth and actuality the U.S. and Vietnam now have only a minimum sort of interest in each other. Neither can be very useful to the other. Neither at the moment appears to be a credible threat. What Vietnam wants chiefly from the U.S. it cannot get, and knows it cannot get—namely vast sums of money,. billions of dollars. Beyond this it wants assurance of security, assurance that the U.S. will not try to roll back communism in Indochina. It wants a U.S. stamp of approval on the new Vietnam, to help it legitimatize its takeover of the South. It wants technical assistance in key sectors of economic development. Perhaps it wants trade but less so than aid, since it has very little to sell now or in the foreseeable future. Oil revenues, even if ambitiously exploited, are nearly a decade away.

As a tentative listing, it would appear that these will be the major U.S. objectives with respect to Vietnam and Indochina:

1. To insure that relations do not sharply deteriorate or freeze into some form of permanent hostility.

2. To encourage Vietnamese restraint in Indochina and throughout Southeast Asia. Primarily this would mean making it in the Vietnamese interest not to fund lavishly various local insurgencies in the area.

3. To dilute Soviet influence in Indochina.

4. To prevent polarization of relations in Southeast Asia of

which Hanoi would be a party. This has been envisioned in various ways: a Jakarta-Hanoi polarization, an insular-mainland division, or Indochina vs. the rest of Southeast Asia.

5.   To develop mutually beneficial economic and commercial arrangements between the U.S. and Vietnam, and eventually to establish normal travel and diplomatic relations.

6.   To resolve the MIA issue as far as possible (recognizing that probably several hundred never will be accounted for because the Vietnamese simply are unable to do so).

7.   Not to block Vietnamese participation in international organization.

New Forces in Southeast Asia
The View from Hanoi

Jayne Werner

Following the fall of Saigon on April 30, 1975, and the U.S. withdrawal from Indochina, the countries of Southeast Asia have experienced a profound change in their relations with one another and outside forces. In the region as a whole the balance of power has shifted: the influence of the United States has substantially declined while a reunited Vietnam will undoubtedly become a dominant power in the area.

The implications of the post-Vietnam War change in the balance of power becomes clear when one considers that it will probably usher in a whole new era in Southeast Asian affairs. Western influence and colonialism in the region commenced with the intervention of the Portuguese during the sixteenth century and spanned a series of colonial wars and domination until 1954, when the French were finally driven from Vietnam. Subsequently the United States, seeking to control or contain the destiny of Vietnam, fought an interventionist war, which it finally was compelled to relinquish. It seems fairly certain, following the U.S. withdrawal from Indochina, that the possibility of Western interventionist wars in Southeast Asia is greatly diminished. It now appears that Southeast Asia will be free from the interventionist or gunboat style of Western diplomacy associated with its history for the past three centuries.

The transformation of regional politics will give Vietnam a major role in Southeast Asian affairs. U.S. policy, as well as the policies of China and the Soviet Union, will necessarily be shaped by that role and the new goals the Democratic Republic of Vietnam (DRV) is setting for itself. One matter for speculation is whether the DRV will favor an active or passive role in the region; furthermore, relations with China and the Soviet Union have also been under investigation. The type of relationship desired by the DRV with the United States has also been discussed. Now that nearly three years have passed since the fall of

91

Saigon, new trends in Southeast Asia are beginning to emerge. The United States has defined a new policy toward Asia and the Pacific. The pattern of Sino-Soviet competitive interests in Southeast Asia is beginning to emerge. The countries in the region have all taken steps in new directions. The DRV, fresh from its celebrations of victory, has given serious attention to the changed situation in regular and lengthy policy statements over the past two-and-a-half years in its major state and army newspapers.

The parameters of the new situation include: (1) DRV relations with its neighbors, its policy towards the Association of Southeast Asian Nations (ASEAN) and the "neutralization" of Southeast Asia, and its attitude toward the degree of support it will give to what it terms national liberation movements in Southeast Asia; (2) the yet to be defined DRV-United States relationship; and (3) the DRV attitude toward Chinese and Soviet strategic interests in Southeast Asia and Vietnam's relationship to increased Sino-Soviet competition in the region, as well as the DRV's conception of its responsibility towards "international proletarianism."

All of these considerations flow from a single strategic plan, however, rather than an ad hoc approach to foreign policy or as a reaction to international events as they occur. This is in keeping with the long-standing tradition of the Vietnamese communists in formulating long-term integrated strategic plans for domestic and international policy in the form of discrete and progressive stages. In the Vietnamese view, the new situation in Southeast Asia has ushered in a "new stage" with new problems and priorities. It might be well to determine what this new stage is in Hanoi's view before analyzing the first parameter of the new situation mentioned above.

II.

Following the liberation of Saigon, Vietnamese state and party leaders devoted considerable attention to the impact of the Indochina defeat on the United States. They concluded Indochina was America's greatest military and political defeat. They predicted that the United States would no longer be able to play the role of an "international gendarme" as previously was the case. Their main assessment, however, was that U.S. global strategy had been proven to be bankrupt and that revolutionary and progressive currents all over the world had been irreversibly strengthened.[1] The U.S. attempt to stem the rising tide of national liberation movements by taking a stand in Indochina was totally defeated. The recent dissolution of the SEATO pact represents, in Hanoi's view, the bankruptcy of U.S. strategy in the key area of Southeast Asia. To the Vietnamese, the Indochina peninsula was a strategic, while being the weakest, link in the U.S. global strategy or "defense line." Since Indochina was the "spearhead" of U.S. strategic interests, the war in Indochina represented a "historic confrontation" between world revolutionary forces and imperialism and reactionary forces led by the United States. The defeat of the United States showed that the forces of revolution are now stronger than those of reaction. Even U.S. attempts to "maintain a balance of forces among big powers" and thereby control developments in Southeast Asia were doomed to failure.[2] Also the U.S. defeat showed the "infeasibility of its vacuum-filling policy [in Southeast Asia]."[3] The U.S. debacle signalled the change in the world balance of forces "increasingly in favor of the Socialist, nationalist, democratic, and peace forces."[4]

In his victory celebration speech May 15, 1975, at the Hang Day Stadium in Hanoi, Party Secretary Le Duan maintained that not only did the Vietnamese victory create "new favorable conditions of the safeguarding of peace and national independence in Indochina and Southeast Asia" but that it was also a victory of "great international significance."[5] In a major three-part analysis in the party's theoretical journal, *Hop Tac,* a North Vietnamese military analyst, Hai Van, concluded that the Indochina defeat had driven the United States into a strategic impasse from which it will never recover.[6]

Consequently, as Le Duan put it, "the victory of Vietnam has opened a new stage of development."[7] This new stage is marked by a growing trend of independence, peace and neutrality among small capitalist and socialist states and the desire on the part of these states to free themselves from the U.S. orbit. Further, Vietnamese leaders feel this trend contributes to the strengthening of the "forces of world socialism" and the eventual collapse of world capitalism. The DRV's role in this strategic concept is obviously to help advance these progressive trends.

III.

The main concern, then, of the DRV toward its regional neighbors is their relationship with the United States. Vietnamese policy toward all the countries of Southeast Asia is now based on a desire to see their bilateral relationships with the United States terminated. The main theme in leading DRV newspapers over the past nine months has been "Southeast Asia for the Southeast Asians." In a major article in the state newspaper, *Nhan Dan* [The People], in June, Quang Thai reiterated that the United States could no longer play a hegemonic role in Southeast Asia. He condemned the Nixon doctrine for using Southeast Asians to fight Southeast Asians and creating division and hostility in the region. He emphasized that Southeast Asia could now embark on a road to independence and that "the imperialists must not interfere in this region."[8]

The DRV defined its policy toward the countries of Southeast Asia soon after the liberation of Saigon. Significantly this policy is based not on confrontation but on cooperation. Le Duan stated in his May 15th address that the Vietnamese people were determined to "develop friendly relations with all countries on the basis of equality, mutual respect, mutual benefit and peaceful co-existence."[9] That this included Southeast Asia was made clear in a subsequent remark in this address that the DRV would "persist in [its] policy of strengthening solidarity and friendship with [its] neighbors in Southeast Asia."[10] Premier Pham Van Dong also stated in his speech at the first session of the 1975 National Assembly that the DRV would persist in its policy "to strengthen relations of friendship and good neighborly relations with the Southeast Asian countries and develop relations of cooperation in various fields with these countries on the basis of respect for each other's independence and sovereignty, equality, mutual benefit and peaceful coexistence."[11]

These considerations have also been mentioned with regard to Vietnam's relations with Laos and Cambodia but obviously the three Indochinese countries, which share the same geographical and political frame of reference, will work closely together. They may form a "bloc" under Hanoi's guidance, but it is clear that Hanoi will be protective of their interests.

Vietnam has stated its desire on several occasions to establish diplomatic relations with those countries with which it has been on a hostile footing in the past: Thailand, the Philippines, and Malaysia. (Diplomatic relations were established with Burma on May 28th for the DRV and May 30th for the Provisional Revolutionary Government.) Vietnam does not seek regional isolation and seems committed to full participation for itself, Laos and Cambodia in Southeast Asia. The DRV has not insisted that the political regimes in these countries be compatible with its own before it will establish relations with them. Le Duan stated that relations with these countries would be based on their efforts to "maintain national independence, consolidate sovereignty and oppose all schemes and manoeuvres of imperialism and old and new colonialism."[12] It appears that the DRV hopes to draw the countries of Southeast Asia into its scheme of nonalignment and disassociation from the major powers.

The primary focus of Vietnamese efforts in the diplomatic arena since victory has been on the non-alignment issue. In August 1975, the DRV was the first socialist state to join the Organization of Non-Aligned Countries at its conference in Lima. (The PRG had been admitted at the Algiers conference of the non-aligned nations in September 1973.) Vietnam's interest in the non-aligned movement stems from its desire to promote the goals of political and economic independence from the United States which the non-aligned nations also support. The fact that none of these countries is socialist is less important to the Vietnamese than their common foreign and diplomatic interests. Fostering unity and independence from the United States in the third world has become an axiom of Vietnamese policy. The recent Vietnamese moves to join the United Nations should probably be interpreted as an effort to strengthen their ties with the Third World. DRV leaders do not feel their interest in the Third World is inconsistent with their membership in the socialist camp. They view the new non-aligned movement as a "qualitative and quantitative developmental step of the anti-imperialist movement,"[13] and therefore contributing to the forces of socialism.

The DRV's attitude toward the countries of Southeast Asia and ASEAN is likely to be shaped by these recent diplomatic policies. Schemes for the "neutralization" of Southeast Asia through ASEAN or other organizations may be supported if they fit into the DRV's overall strategic plan. It is noteworthy that the DRV, since victory, has not condemned the present structure of ASEAN, although it has attacked some of its individual members. DRV leaders seem to be adopting a wait-and-see attitude toward ASEAN and are reluctant to condemn an organization that could evolve in a favorable direction. In fact, when referring to a May 1975 ASEAN statement indicating ASEAN's desire to promote friendly relations with the new governments of Indochina, Quang Thai in *Nhan Dan* praised ASEAN "which formerly served U.S. policies" for talking "about peace, cooperation, and neutrality in this region."[14] Although it appears that the DRV's main interest in ASEAN may be diplomatic, the promotion of regional economic interests could also be attractive to a reunited Vietnam.

As for its current relations with individual Southeast Asian states, the establishment of peaceful relations with Thailand seems to head Vietnam's list. The DRV obviously hoped to be able to exchange ambassadors sooner than has happened. Normalization has been impeded by continuing acrimonious disputes over the return of what the DRV considers to be Vietnamese property to Vietnam, the status of Vietnamese residents in northern Thailand, and Thailand's continued hostility towards Laos and its closing of the Thai-Lao border. Thailand was bitterly condemned by the DRV for not returning the planes and other material taken to that country by the former officials of the Thieu regime. It appears that this material will not be returned since Thai Prime Minister Kukrit Pramoj has maintained that this issue should not be an obstacle for the establishment of diplomatic relations. On December 12, 1975, Kukrit admitted that negotiations with the DRV were at a deadlock because of this point.[15] The DRV feels that the return of this material "will be a touchstone—a concrete proof of the Thai administration's avowed policy of friendship with the neighboring countries and desire to improve . . . relations."[16]

Vietnam has also condemned Thailand for staging naval maneuvers with the United States, failing to make firm plans to close down all U.S. bases in Thailand (Thai authorities may keep the U-Taphao base open), permitting the United States to build an additional radar base in northern Thailand, allowing U-2 aircraft to carry out reconnaissance flights over North Vietnam and Laos, planning to maintain 300 U.S. advisors after U.S. troops have been withdrawn (scheduled for March 1976), and for sheltering reactionary elements. Also, Hanoi blames Thailand for the state of hostility and antagonism which exists between Laos and Thailand.[17] In September 1975, Vietnam stepped up its attacks on Thailand and accused it of harboring "an unfriendly attitude."[18] Progress on improved relations that had been made during DRV Deputy Prime Minister Phan Hien's visit to Bangkok in May 1975, and a visit of a PRG delegation that same month has since been stalled. The first sign of an opening has not appeared until January 1976, when Hanoi radio noted that Thailand had finally agreed to open the border with Laos.[19] A permanent closing of the border could have severe economic repercussions in Laos, which could only be harmed by being isolated from Thailand.

As for the Philippines, the main issue shaping future relations will also involve the continuation of U.S. bases in the Philippines and its bilateral treaty commitments with the United States.[20] A joint communiqué on diplomatic relations was signed between the DRV and a Filipino official in Hanoi on August 7, 1975, but Manila later disavowed the authority of the official, who has since resigned.[21] No progress has been made on the question subsequently. It appears that the DRV's condition for reduction of the U.S. presence in the Philippines is at present too stiff. However, Hanoi has favorably noted that since their victory, the Philippines has reassessed its relationship with the United States and has reviewed its bilateral defense commitments. The Philippines also quickly moved to establish diplomatic relations with the People's Republic of China after the fall of Saigon, as did Thailand (the former on June 5, 1975, and the latter on July 1, 1975).

The DRV could possibly find more of an identity of interests with Malaysia because of Malaysia's stand on non-alignment. No moves have yet been taken by either party toward establishing relations, however. Nonetheless, Malaysia was the first ASEAN country to send an ambassador to Peking and it also responded more favorably than any other member of ASEAN to the communist victory in Vietnam. Malaysia is the only country in ASEAN that Hanoi has not attacked in its news media since liberation, mainly because Malaysia does not have a military pact with the United States and has no U.S. bases. In fact, Quang Thai, cited above, favorably commented on the fact that the "king of Malaysia" came out in favor of establishing a peaceful, neutral, and independent zone in Southeast Asia following the communist victory.[22]

Singapore and Indonesia have been attacked for their continuing close ties to the United States. Lee Kwan Yew's comments that the communist victory in Indochina is a disaster have been strongly condemned as provocative.[23] But although Indonesia's ties with the United States do not appear to be under review at the present time, Hanoi has noted some recent statements to be indicative of the beginning of a change. According to an army article in May 1975, Indonesia called for "concord" following Vietnam's victory and stated that the Indochinese countries "could help small nations to struggle resolutely against the ambitions of great powers."[24] However, Indonesia's intervention in Timor has been condemned as a tactic serving U.S. strategic interests in the Pacific in the wake of its withdrawal from Indochina.[25]

IV.

The United States has yet to define its attitude toward the new Indochinese government but it seems fairly certain that prolonged silence will not last much longer. The DRV has let it be known that it wishes to establish diplomatic relations with the United States and does not appear to attach preconditions as such to them. However, it feels that a general improvement in relations will have to take into account the provisions in the Paris Accords obliging the United States to aid Vietnam in the healing of war wounds and reconstruction. The DRV, for its part, is willing to supply the United States with information on M.I.A.s and Hanoi recently received a U.S. Congressional delegation which took the remains of three U.S. pilots to the United States back home with them. The DRV has attached great significance to Article 21 of the Paris Accords (on the healing of war wounds and reconstruction) and it appears the United States will need to take steps toward fulfilling this provision if normalization of relations is to occur. However, in a June 1975 editorial, *Nhan Dan* indicated that the implementation of the *spirit* of Article 21 may be acceptable.[26] It is improbable that the United States would fully implement this provision since following the communist victory, U.S. officials have expressed the view that the Agreement is a dead letter as far as U.S. policy is concerned.

The DRV's official position vis-à-vis the United States remains the one included in a statement issued by the Foreign Ministry in August 1975:

> Regarding the United States, the policy of the Democratic Republic of Vietnam is to normalize the relations between the two sides in the spirit of Article 22 of the Paris Agreement on Vietnam and on the basis of a sincere respect on the part of the U.S. Government for Articles 1 and 4 on the fundamental national rights

of Vietnam, and the scrupulous implementation of Article 21 on its obligation to take part in the healing of the wounds of war in Vietnam.[27]

It may be, however, that the DRV would forego its desire for war reparations if the United States were willing to provide aid through other channels.

The trade embargo instituted by the United States against Vietnam and Cambodia in May 1975, would also have to be lifted. There are business, banking, and political pressures within the United States to reverse the senseless trade restrictions. The Vietnamese have openly discussed with Western reporters the possibilities of joint ventures with U.S. companies and are likely to grant off-shore drilling concessions to U.S. oil companies.[28] Following the liberation of Saigon, the off-shore oil rigs abandoned by U.S. companies were left intact by Vietnamese authorities, obviously with a view for future use by the same companies.

Aside from the M.I.A. issue which seems to be somewhat of a delaying tactic on the part of the United States, the real issue in DRV-U.S. relations will be the degree of U.S. presence on the Southeast Asia mainland. The United States may insist that the DRV accept a scaled-down U.S. presence in Thailand.[29] It also seems unlikely that the United States would move to establish diplomatic relations with Vietnam in the absence of normalization of ties between the DRV and Thailand.

Further, Vietnam has condemned the United States for its veto of the DRV and PRG applications to the United Nations, which the PRG has interpreted as a "hostile act" attempting to isolate Vietnam.[30] President Ford's new "Pacific Doctrine" announced December 7, 1975, has also been condemned. It is seen to represent no change in U.S. policy in Southeast Asia. The United States' "continuing stake in the stability and security of Southeast Asia" (one of the three parts of the Pacific Doctrine) is interpreted by Hanoi to mean the continuation of U.S. "aggressive and interventionist" policies. The DRV believes that the aim of the new U.S. policy is to consolidate the U.S. military alliance system in Asia, "to build reactionary forces . . . to counter socialist countries and the national liberation movement," and to sabotage the revolutionary movement in Southeast Asia.[31]

Hanoi contends that this doctrine is totally unrealistic given the seriously weakened U.S. position in Southeast Asia and the loss of confidence in the United States by formerly pro-U.S. forces.[32] Further, it now sees the main obstacle to peace in Southeast Asia to be continued U.S. policies of aggression, efforts by the Japanese to sabotage the economic independence of the countries of Southeast Asia, and pro-U.S. forces in Southeast Asia which favor the U.S. presence (notably the current Singapore and Indonesian leaderships).[33]

The structure of DRV-U.S. relations will necessarily be affected by the DRV's relations with its neighbors now that the Vietnamese have forced the West's strongest power to withdraw. If the forces for change in Southeast Asia move rapidly toward neutralization and disengagement from the United States military network, then the DRV's role in the region will be enhanced. The United States will be obliged to take cognizance of this if it wishes to retain influence in the area. That question, however, now appears to be a function of U.S. relations with China and the Soviet Union.

V.

Despite Ford's Pacific Doctrine, there is speculation that the United States plans a strategic withdrawal from Southeast Asia. It may be counting on its relationship with China to "continue its role as a stabilizing force" in the Southeast Asia region.[34] U.S. and Chinese rivalry with the Soviet Union may lead to a coincidence of U.S. and Chinese interests in Southeast Asia, the first dimension of which would be to exclude the U.S.S.R. from the region. Alternatively, increased Sino-Soviet rivalry in Southeast Asia following a total U.S. withdrawal from the Asian mainland could mean for Southeast Asia a diminished relationship with all the superpowers. That is, the level and intensity of regional interaction with the international strategic system could well subside.

The one exception to a diminished interaction with world politics could possibly be Hanoi's relations with or leadership of the non-aligned movement. If the Third World achieves a measure of unity and acquires more force in international politics (perhaps through united economic action) than it has to date, then possibly small countries in Southeast Asia along with countries in Latin America and Africa would begin to play an influential global role. This prospect seems dim at the present but Vietnam's attempt to break out of the present mold of world politics polarized around the triangular relationship between China, the Soviet Union, and the United States could be the beginning of a gradual readjustment in the present configuration. This may not necessarily be in conformity with Hanoi's present strategic conception of the forces of socialism moving ahead of the forces of capitalism but may lead to a greater complexity in world affairs than the tri-polar system now allows. On the other hand, Hanoi's ties to the non-aligned movement will enable it to circumvent the poisoned atmosphere of the Sino-Soviet dispute and continue the policy of independence it pursued during the long years of the war. Vietnam may well find the non-aligned movement to be its more natural element.

The immediate benefactor in Southeast Asia of the Vietnamese victory was not Vietnam strangely enough, but rather China. Although each country of Southeast Asia obviously will need to readjust its policies with Vietnam, accommodation with China was the first order of business following the U.S. withdrawal from Indochina. The Philippines and Thailand in quick succession sent ambassadors to Peking after the liberation of Saigon. New concerns and fears about Chinese-inspired insurgencies in these countries were again raised. Indeed the Vietnamese victory did not increase Southeast Asian countries' fears about external threats to their security but *internal* threats. As a result of Vietnam, the countries of Southeast Asia with conservative leadership face greater problems in containing challenges—both urban and rural (guerrilla)—to their rule. China, not Vietnam, is seen as the key to these domestic problems. The one exception is Thailand where Thai leaders judge the main support of the communist insurgency in northern Thailand to be North Vietnamese, not Chinese.[35] Even in Thailand, China's attitude toward the Thai Communist Party will be important.

Southeast Asian countries' new-found solicitude toward China (with the exception of Indonesia) may put the DRV in an awkward position. It appears that China subscribes to the view, like the United States, that there is a "vacuum" of power in Southeast Asia.[36] As the countries of Southeast Asia improve their relations with China, the DRV may come to feel this poses an obstacle to non-alignment in the region, particularly if the Chinese do not see U.S. interests in the region to be incompatible with their own objectives. There is evidence, for instance, that the Chinese may not press for a total U.S. withdrawal from Thailand, which is unlikely to earn them Hanoi's gratitude.[37] The People's Republic of China of course is adverse to the growing Soviet influence in Thai politics which was given a new impetus by the Vietnam victory.

Hanoi's strategic plan does not appear incompatible, however, with Moscow's ideas for the area. It is unlikely that over the long run the Soviet Union will be able to exercise much influence in Southeast Asia, which is not contiguous to its borders. Nevertheless, Vietnam has shown a preference for the Soviet Union and its policies over China perhaps because the countries are not geographic neighbors and also because the Soviet Union appears willing to grant Vietnam generous credits to finance its reconstruction. Soviet aid is so important to the Vietnamese that a top-level delegation, headed by Le Duan, visited the U.S.S.R. and Eastern Europe barely five months after victory to conclude aid agreements. An economic agreement was also signed in China in September 1975 (also a Le Duan-led delegation), but received far less attention in the Hanoi news media.

The Soviets proposed six years ago a collective security pact for Southeast Asia but it seems to have fallen on unwilling ears. Although Vietnam could conceivably be receptive to the plan, its standing with the non-aligned movement would undoubtedly be jeopardized if it joined. Also, its demands that the countries of Southeast Asia terminate their military alliances with the United States would be nothing more than hollow propaganda if Vietnam were to enter into a close military relationship with the Soviet Union. The Chinese have voiced fears that Vietnam may lease Cam Ranh Bay to the Soviets but this again seems unlikely for the same reasons.

1. "A Major American Strategy is Bankrupt; One of Its Major Defense Lines Collapses," *Nhan Dan* [The People], editorial, 8 May 1975, reported on Hanoi radio, Foreign Broadcast Information Service, hereafter referred to as FBIS, Asia and Pacific *Daily Report*, no. 90, 8 May 1975.

2. "Vietnam's Victory—A Victory of International Significance," *Quan Doi Nhan Dan* [People's Army], n.d., reported on Hanoi radio, FBIS, no. 102, 27 May 1975.

3. "New Era for Peoples of Indochina," *Nhan Dan*, 31 May 1975, reported on Hanoi radio, FBIS, no. 107, 3 June 1975.

4. "The United States Still Cherishes Grandiose Ambitions but Its Position and Strength have Considerably Declined," *Nhan Dan*, 28 July 1975, reported on Hanoi radio, FBIS, no. 149, 1 August 1975.

5. Le Duan, speech at the 15 May Mass Rally, reported on Hanoi radio, FBIS, no. 95, 15 May 1975.

6. Hai Van, "U. S. Global Strategy Has Been Upset and Is Facing a Serious Post-Vietnam Crisis," *Tap Chi Quan Doi Nhan Dan* [People's Army Review], no. 11 (1975), reported on Hanoi radio, pt. 1, 7 December 1975, FBIS, no. 238, 10 December 1975; pts. 2 and 3, 8 December 1975, FBIS, no. 240, 12 December 1975.

7. Le Duan, 15 May victory speech.

8. Quang Thai, "Southeast Asia Belongs to the Southeast Asian Peoples," *Nhan Dan*, 12 June 1975, reported on Hanoi radio, FBIS, no. 115, 13 June 1975.

9. Le Duan, 15 May victory speech.

10. Le Duan, 15 May victory speech.

11. As summarized by Quang Thai, "Southeast Asia Belongs to the Southeast Asian Peoples."

12. Le Duan, 15 May victory speech.

13. "The Combined Strength of the Three Revolutionary Currents," *Nhan Dan*, reported on Hanoi radio, FBIS, no. 2, 5 January 1976; and "New Development Step of the Nonaligned Countries Movement," *Hop Tac* [Study-Practice], September 1975, reported on Hanoi radio, FBIS, no. 205, 22 October 1975.

14. Quang Thai, "Southeast Asia Belongs to the Southeast Asian Peoples."

15. Kukrit Pramoj, interviewed by Denzil Peiris, *Far Eastern Economic Review*, hereafter referred to as *FEER*, 12 December 1975, pp. 20–22.

16. "The Thai Government Should Positively Respond to our People's Demand," radio commentary on Hanoi radio, 1 August 1975, FBIS, no. 150, 4 August 1975.

17. "Is the United States Really Withdrawing from Thailand," *Quan Doi Nhan Dan* [People's Army], 26 July 1975, reported on Hanoi radio, FBIS, no. 145, 28 July 1975; "Talking About Staying Before Leaving," *Quan Doi Nhan Dan*, 6 November 1975, reported on Hanoi radio, FBIS, no. 219, 12 November 1975; "The Unscrupulous Attitude of the Thai Government," *Nhan Dan*, 13 November 1975, reported on Hanoi radio, FBIS, no. 220, 13 November 1975; and Untitled commentary criticizing Thai hostility towards Laos, *Quan Doi Nhan Dan*, 21 October 1975, reported on Hanoi radio, FBIS, no. 205, 22 October 1975.

18. "Thailand Maintains an Unfriendly Attitude toward Vietnam," *Nhan Dan*, 24 September 1975, reported on Hanoi radio, FBIS, no. 186, 24 September 1975.

19. According to the Pathet Lao News Agency, the Thai Minister of Foreign Affairs announced to the Ambassador of the Lao People's Democratic Republic to Thailand on 29 December 1975 that Thailand would reopen the border as of 1 January 1976. Reported on Hanoi radio, 31 December 1975, FBIS, no. 1, 2 January 1976.

20. Deputy Prime Minister Phan Hien, interviewed by Malcolm Salmon, *FEER*, 10 October 1975.

21. According to *FEER,* 12 December 1975.

22. Quang Thai, "Southeast Asia Belongs to the Southeast Asian Peoples."

23. Untitled commentary attacking Lee Kwan Yew, *Quan Doi Nhan Dan,* 20 May 1975, reported on Hanoi radio, FBIS, no. 98, 20 May 1975; Station commentary, "The Outmoded, Slanted Arguments of the Singapore Prime Minister," Hanoi radio, 20 May 1975, FBIS, no. 99, 21 May 1975; and Untitled commentary "reaffirming Southeast Asia must belong to the Southeast Asians," Hanoi radio, 12 June 1975, FBIS, no. 114, 12 June 1975.

24. "Vietnam's Victory Has Greatly Inspired All Nations Struggling for Independence," *Quan Doi Nhan Dan,* 28 May 1975, reported on Hanoi radio, FBIS, no. 103, 28 May 1975.

25. "Old Reactionary Doctrine, New Weak Situation," *Quan Doi Nhan Dan,* 10 December 1975, reported on Hanoi radio, FBIS, no. 240, 12 December 1975.

26. "Erroneous Attitude of the United States," *Nhan Dan,* 11 June 1975, reported on Hanoi radio, FBIS, no. 113, 11 June 1975.

27. Statement of the DRV Foreign Ministry, 12 August 1975, reported on Hanoi radio, same date FBIS, vol. 157, 13 August 1975.

28. *FEER,* 12 December 1975.

29. In the view of Nayan Chanda, one of the most knowledgeable Western-publication reporters who has reported from Vietnam since the fall of Saigon. *FEER,* 26 December 1975.

30. PRG Station commentary, "The Responsibility Lies with the U.S. Side," PRG radio, 16 September 1975, FBIS, no. 186, 24 September 1975.

31. "Old Reactionary Doctrine, New Weak Situations."

32. Ibid.

33. Phrases from "Humiliating Bankruptcy of a Reactionary Strategy," *Nhan Dan,* 27 September 1975, reported on Hanoi radio, FBIS, no. 189, 29 September 1975. The DRV has *not* criticized China in this regard, only Southeast Asian countries which are maintaining this outlook. Bernd Kaufmann says that Chinese leaders have expressed the view to U.S. officials on several occasions, that they see the U.S. presence in Asia and the Pacific to be a "stabilizing factor." Kaufmann feels U.S. strategic goals in Asia have not been altered since Vietnam, however. Bernd Kaufmann, "Die Asienpolitik des USA —Imperialismus nach seiner niederlager in Indochina," *Horizont* (Berlin), no. 43 (1975).

34. "Humiliating Bankruptcy of a Reactionary Strategy."

35. Kukrit Pramoj, interviewed by Denzil Peiris.

36. According to a *FEER* correspondent in Moscow, the Soviets say that the Chinese frequently mention the "vacuum theory" with regard to Southeast Asia. Miles Hanley, *FEER,* 19 October 1975, p. 20.

37. According to "Intelligence," *FEER,* 19 December 1975, p. 5.

Image Maintenance:
U.S. Defense Policies Before and After Vietnam

Scott G. McNall

It seems unkind to raise, still again, the issue of why the United States became involved in Vietnam, and what the results of that adventure were for the American body politic. Yet the explanations are as many-sided as was that murky conflict. Depending on which school of thought you favor, America got involved because of the nature of capitalist society; because of a conspiracy of a limited number of men in the White House; because we were committed by our treaty obligations; because it was just a fluke; and so on. But at the risk of being the bore at the party, let me raise the issue again, though hopefully in a somewhat new light. It still is significant to understand the "why," for it bears directly on whether or not it will happen again. Have we already forgotten the Mayaguez incident?

Let me make my position clear at the outset and then re-examine some of the incidents of that war from that standpoint. The U.S. became involved, and stayed, because we were trying to demonstrate the credibility of a particular policy of defense. The fact that we were in Vietnam, or Indochina if you prefer, was the only fluke in that long involvement. Vietnam just happened to be the right country in which to demonstrate the policies that had evolved to that point. As the war progressed, it took on the character of a theater. Not just because it was our first live, television war; but because events were being staged there for an audience: not only the American public, but also our NATO allies, those in the Third World who had yet to make a commitment to one of the major military camps, and, of course, the Soviets and Chinese. Policies that had a seemingly irrational character because of their contradictory nature made sense—if one had the script.

Image maintenance suggests that the thing or event is not quite real—that a real self, or the essence of an event, is hidden behind the charade. It is important to remember that the president is the director of our collective drama. He often defines what is in the national interest, what U.S. foreign policy objectives will be, and what military doctrines and strategies we will adopt at a given point in history. Richard Nixon, like his predecessors, stood in the wings and directed the shadowy characters that occupied the national security stage. Nixon also understood that the reality of the war and its meaning were dependent on a number of linkages. All parts of the system must interconnect to support the image. One member of the audience crying that the emperor was without clothes would be sufficient to spoil the mood.

II.

The cause of any war is a complex and important issue, because the factors that are included often depend on which data is available for analysis. At the risk of omitting too much, let us begin at the end of the Second World War. The U.S. had the bomb, and was clearly the most important military and political power in the world. One element that is often overlooked in casting over this old history is that not only did the U.S. have atomic weapons, but we had demonstrated a willingness to use them in what was regarded by some other countries as an irrational manner. We did not, for instance, blow up an isolated island as many have suggested we ought to have done. We did not bomb one city and then wait until we got a *clear* response from the Japanese government. We dropped two bombs on civilians in two cities. The "should," or the "ought," is entirely beside the point for the moment. What is significant is that from the perspective of others we had shown what we would do. No other nation on the face of the earth has ever demonstrated so clearly their willingness to make diplomatic and military points in such an awesome fashion—partly, of course, because they did not have the wherewithal to do it.

The cold war has also been examined many times. Part of the way, however, in which others behaved was determined by the fact that the U.S. had atomic weapons. We were sometimes able to get our way in diplomatic struggles because of this fact, but for the most part we really did not press our military and political advantages. Our foreign policy after the war reflected our attitude of moral superiority. We continued to carry out the dictates of Wilsonian diplomacy, i.e., the willingness to go anywhere and pay any price, with the firm conviction that others should be glad of our interference, and if they were not it was probably because they were communist. Other countries, the Soviets in particular, were not convinced that the U.S. would behave in an upright fashion, and would not use atomic weapons. The Soviets, naturally, began preparations for their own nuclear arsenal. American allies felt that the U.S. would protect them.

Let us jump again, and come to De Gaulle, who provided the U.S. with its opportunity in Vietnam. De Gaulle was a problem for American policy-makers. He would not cooperate and his *force de frappe,* even if it did represent a free ride on U.S. nuclear superiority, contributed to a falling away of American influence. It did no good for policy analysts to point out that France's nuclear force was ineffective and that the French knew that if an attack were aimed at her, the U.S. would respond. It cost France nothing in security to pull out of NATO because she was protected by a buffer of NATO allies. She gained a great deal in terms of increased prestige with other small powers.

One of the reasons, then, for American involvement in Vietnam stemmed from the fact that American influence was on the wane; the U.S. needed a place to assert its authority. What better place than a country in which the French had failed? But this jumps too far ahead. Let us return for the moment to the defense policies that evolved prior to the Vietnam conflict.

Prior to Kennedy's election, the issue of how many missiles the U.S. had, as opposed to the Soviet Union, was never really discussed; nor was the issue of exactly what our strategic policy might be. It was simply assumed that we had nuclear supremacy, and that no other nation would be foolish enough to attack us, for fear that our retaliatory effort would decimate their country. The "missile gap" changed strategic thinking, or at least stimulated it. When McNamara assumed office as Secretary of Defense, the evolution of our doctrines began. The first thing with which McNamara was confronted was a messy picture.

> The air force had the mid-range Thor IRBM . . . ; the air force had no fewer than three competitive ICBM's, the monumental Atlas, the merely large Titan, and the small Minuteman. The navy, or rather Admiral Hyman Rickover's rebellious fiefdom within it, had already deployed the first Polaris boats after an astonishingly successful research-and-development program and was hard at work on follow-up missiles and boats. The army was in the anti-missile business, too, with a working prototype (Nike-Zeus) which it was eager to put into production. The missiles were stealing the limelight, but the bombers were still the largest element in the arsenal: the Strategic Air Command had 1,000 B-47's, 600 long range B-52's, and 30 B-58's in 1961, and it was eager to deploy yet more B-52's, and proceed with the supersonic B-58. SAC also wanted a great deal of money to develop the B-70.[1]

To the extent that the U.S. had a strategic doctrine, it simply emphasized survivability. A new doctrine needed to be articulated, partly, as Luttwak has indicated, to adjudicate among the rival service claims for development of nuclear weapons systems. Our announced strategic doctrine evolved through the early sixties by first emphasizing the ability to destroy the enemy's war making capabilities; then in 1963, we emphasized city avoidance, which meant that we could strike at both military and non-military targets, or we could strike the one first, and hold Soviet cities hostage so that the Russians would not strike back. In 1964, we stressed a damage limiting policy, which meant that we could destroy Soviet society even if they retaliated, and we could limit damage to U.S. cities by striking both Soviet cities and their unlaunched forces. Finally, we came, in 1965, to what has been called the M.A.D. (mutual assured destruction) strategy.[2] It was decided that it was not really possible, given the present state of technology, to completely protect U.S. cities from attack. But if we could not completely defend, we ought to be able to defer the attack. We must have sufficient weapons so that we could absorb the bulk of the Soviets' attack, and still counterattack. Figures were even published to indicate to the Soviets what we considered to be "sufficient" damage to them: the ability to destroy between one-fourth to one-third of their population, and at least two-thirds of their industrial capacity.[3] At the time, this seemed feasible, for our number of missiles and bombers was clearly superior to that of the Soviets, something they must have considered during the 1962 confrontation over Cuba.

The evolution of the M.A.D. Doctrine shaped American strategic thinking in a number of ways, and was one of the reasons we did not begin work on an ABM system during the early sixties. It was argued that an ABM system would destroy the credibility of the M.A.D. Doctrine because it would look as though we were not really willing to take a first strike, and then decimate the other side's forces. Accuracy was also not pushed because that too was destabilizing. M.A.D. suffered some setbacks. First, the Soviets proved to be obdurate pupils.

> In 1967 . . . the Russians added 160 ICBM's, in 1968 they added 340, thus virtually doubling their force in one year. By 1969, they had come level with the United States at the 1,050 mark. Even then, the M.A.D. theorists insisted that the Russians would now stop adding more weapons since *their* theory "proved" that additional weapons would merely be useless, given that the Russians now had enough for mutual assured destruction. . . . Worse still, McNamara and his theorists were distressed to see that the Russians had failed to understand the *technical* implications of the doctrine; instead of deploying neat little missiles like the Minuteman, cheap and reliable solid-fuel weapons good enough for "city-busting," they were producing a much larger standard missile (SS-11) and an exceedingly expensive extra-large missile (SS-9) that strangely enough had all the making of a counterforce weapon. . . .[4]

Another thing forgotten by the M.A.D. strategists was the political implications of force structure. The size of the defense budget and the size of the military machine were signals to our allies, as well as to our real and imagined enemies, that we would honor commitments and provide the necessary protection spelled out in various treaties.[5] Another point, of course, was that to the Soviets our strategy could have looked aggressive.

M.A.D., as Iklé clearly pointed out, contained some rather bizarre psychological assumptions. First, the role of victim and aggressor are reversed. The aggressor is supposed to be deterred because he will rationally calculate what losses he will sustain after he strikes first, and the victim will wait to absorb the first strike, and then respond with his entire arsenal, or what's left of it. Too, it ignores the fact that the Soviet Union seems to consider nuclear war a possibility, and their strategy also seems guided by the notion of a first strike capability. It is also a policy of disguised genocide.

> The common phrase, "deterring a potential aggressor," conveys a false simplicity about the processes that might lead to a nuclear attack, as if we had to worry about some ambitious despot who sits calculating whether or not to start a nuclear war. A moral perversity lies hidden behind the standard formula: in the event this "aggressor" attacks, we must "retaliate by knocking out *his* cities." Tomas de Torquemada, who burned 10,000 heretics at the stake, could claim principles more humane than our nuclear strategy; for his tribunals found all his victims guilty of having knowingly committed mortal sin.[6]

There were—and are—strategic, moral, and political problems with the M.A.D. Doctrine, but it dominated our thinking throughout the sixties, and still does so. Only one alternative policy has really been put forth, by Schlesinger while he was Secretary of Defense. Schlesinger felt that the Soviets were moving toward a counterforce strategy, and that the M.A.D. Doctrine tied our hands in a number of ways, e.g., it crippled new strategic thinking, and it also contributed to the Soviets' achieving dominance. Schlesinger, as we know, wanted to move to a counterforce-plus-deterrence strategy, but was defeated in his efforts. Nitze, too, feels ". . . that under the terms of the Salt agreements the Soviet Union will continue to pursue a nuclear superiority that is not merely quantitative but designed to produce a theoretical war-winning capability."[7] The M.A.D. strategy, which was fully accepted by Kissinger, has dominated the Salt I and II talks; but more of this later.

The essential point that we would like to draw from the above is that the M.A.D. strategy affected our doctrines before and after Vietnam in a variety of ways. First, the necessity of war itself, once begun, meant that monies were channeled from strategic arms to fighting the war, and M.A.D. was a cost-cutting move. Secondly, it made it necessary to demonstrate the credibility of our nuclear policy, and our willingness to use force. M.A.D., coupled with our doctrines of limited war, caused much of our confused military behavior.

III.

Under Eisenhower, Secretary Dulles had established the policy of massive retaliation, or brinkmanship. This meant that the U.S. must rush to the edge of the cliff each time its interests were threatened, scorning its foes, brandishing its weapons, and then draw back at the last moment, hoping that it had been scary enough. Kissinger was among the first to realize that this policy simply lacked credibility. It was unlikely that the Soviet Union would believe that we would use nuclear weapons, especially if the area threatened were not of strategic importance to the United States. In his 1957 work, *Nuclear Weapons and Foreign Policy,* Kissinger argued that nuclear war no longer had any real meaning. It was unthinkable, and could not be a meaningful instrument of U.S. policy. Nuclear weapons, therefore, immobilized those who held them. But there was a strategic problem, as he noted. "The dilemma of the nuclear period can, therefore, be defined as follows: the enormity of modern weapons makes the thought of war repugnant, but the refusal to run any risks would amount to giving the Soviet ruler a blank check."[8] One must stand firm, but how, and still demonstrate the credibility of U.S. foreign and military policy? A middle course was sighted—limited war. Kissinger dutifully identified three reasons for this type of war. "First, limited war represents the only means for preventing the Soviet bloc, at an acceptable cost, from overrunning the peripheral areas of Eurasia. Second, a wide range of military capabilities may spell the difference between defeat and victory even in an all-out war. Finally, intermediate applications of our power offer the best chance to bring about strategic changes favorable to our side."[9] We wanted to maintain a policy of containment, and assure that our nuclear deterrence would be taken seriously. How, but defensively and offensively, pursuing limited war in order to demonstrate credibility?

Though the psychological nature of the nuclear war has been referred to before, it is clear how the concept of limited war underscores it by emphasizing the ability to demonstrate resolve, will, power, determination, commitments, and so forth. Now, as Schell has aptly argued, this takes war, or strategy, into the arena of advertising.

> How to make demonstrations of credibility was, above all, a problem of public relations, since what counted was not the substance of America's strength or the actual state of its willingness but the *image of strength* and willingness. To put it more precisely, the substance of the nation's strength was useful only insofar as it enhanced the image of strength. In Kissinger's words, "Soviet reactions to what we do will depend not on what we intend but on what the Soviet leaders think we intend."[10]

If there was any area in which weakness could not be tolerated, it would be in the area of limited war, for this would undermine the credibility of our entire strategic doctrine. During the latter part of Eisenhower's tenure, and the beginning of Kennedy's, a theory of limited war began to develop, so that when Vietnam "occurred" it was an excellent place in which to put to test the theories that the President's advisors were so assiduously supporting.

IV.

When Kennedy sent the first large group of advisors to Vietnam to support Diem, the public was not much concerned, nor were they given any explanations other than the standard Cold War phrases: "We are protecting the interests of democracy; we are checking communist aggression; we are honoring our commitments," and so forth. Now it is instructive to remember that several events began to run together. The Cuban missile crisis of 1962 seemed to satisfy many of the national strategy managers that M.A.D. was a successful doctrine. But the Soviets began a crash program to catch up; by all accounts had achieved parity by 1969, and went on adding missiles into the 1970s. The U.S. also had a line that encouraged the full and vigorous pursuit of limited war. Where it was pursued was of little matter. So, multiple pressures evolved during the conflict that contributed to a growing need to demonstrate credibility.

Armed with theories as to how the scenario would unfold, the U.S. entered Vietnam with some confidence. First, we would test our theories on a limited scale, with a limited number of men, and should that fail to produce the desired results, we would increase pressure on the enemy. Recall in this war of science and rationalism the "ratchet" theory, which came from defense psychologists, who argued that the slow increase of pain, or negative reinforcement, would surely break a victim or country, because the person always believes you have stopped, and when he finds that you have gone on to a new level, his willingness to endure diminishes. Now, the question of why the enemy failed to be impressed with the logic of our theories can be held in abeyance for the moment. The issue we want to concentrate on is how the war was *presented.*

That the war was fought by the Executive Branch on two fronts —home and abroad—now seems clear to many. There was an agenda for U.S. allies and other interested parties, and one for the American public. Wars have always, at least since the time of Louis Napoleon, involved public relations work. We are, essentially, a democratic society, and people have to be convinced that a war is somehow in their interest before they want to fight. We also have to believe that, if our interests are only indirectly involved, we are at least backing the right side, and have a reasonable likelihood of winning the conflict. As *The Pentagon Papers* have demonstrated, a great deal of information was kept from the American public about the conflict and the direction of the war. Lyndon Johnson said we were not going to become involved, while plans were being laid down for involvement. Enemy strength was deliberately misrepresented, and official estimates of who was "winning" were grossly inadequate, as was the evaluation of the regime we were supporting.

And, should this point escape revisionists, *it is not a war that we could have been allowed to win.* The People's Republic of China could not have tolerated the Americans actually conquering North Vietnam. This does not mean that they had a direct political stake in the country, but simply that they could not permit the classic situation to develop in which they would ultimately be faced with two hostile fronts: on their northern border the Soviet Union, and one at their underbelly in Vietnam. On one other occasion the Chinese entered a modern war against the United States—when we began bombing, under General MacArthur's direction, dangerously close to their power plants in Manchuria. In that case they even sent their envoy, Chou En-lai, to warn us through our allies that they could not tolerate that situation. We had also been warned repeatedly that the Chinese would enter the war on the side of North Vietnam if their national security was threatened. If we could not win, i.e., dominate and occupy North Vietnam, which is what would have been required, then why did we bomb North Vietnam? The answer, to which we will return, is that the U.S. wanted to make a political point, not a military one.

That the reason for Vietnam was political seemed most clear during Richard Nixon's administration. In March 1969, the secret bombings began in Cambodia. As the later evidence has shown, even within the government itself, there was a set of procedures for keeping this war secret. Not because keeping it secret had specific military consequences, but because to have revealed that we were now expanding the war, rather than ending it as Nixon had promised, would have risked public alarm and demonstrations. These demonstrations did occur when, in his national speech on April 30, 1970, Nixon revealed that for thirteen months the U.S. had been conducting secret operations in Cambodia. The explanations offered by the President for this involvement centered around the need to destroy sanctuaries of the enemy, and to demonstrate our will. He was careful to distinguish, too, between military power, and the commitment to use that power. "It is not," he said, "our power but our will and character that is being tested tonight." The Cambodian crisis, like the Vietnam crisis, was a test of America's "real character." The enemy was as much within, as it was without. To the public relations experts explaining the war, then, the domestic crisis at home was as important as the fighting in the field. Demonstrators, though they did not know it at the time, really could undermine U.S. security in the way that it had been defined, because they called into question the ability of the President to conduct the war as he saw fit. In addition, sufficient domestic discord could be the catalyst to pull the U.S. out of the war. As Klaus Knorr has shown, a nation's military strength must also be measured by the public's willingness to support a conflict,[11] and in this sense the U.S. could be seen as not capable of supporting the strategic doctrines to which she had committed herself. The Executive Branch did make a considered effort to control dissent in the United States, and to defuse the anti-war movement. Kissinger, who was to become Nixon's factotum, writing in 1966, seemed particularly prophetic. "If the domestic structures are based on commensurable notions of what is just, a consensus about permissible aims and methods of foreign policy develops. If domestic structures are reasonably stable, temptations to use an adventurous foreign policy to achieve domestic cohesion are at a minimum."[12] Domestic and foreign policies quickly became mixed, with Nixon trying to demonstrate resolve both to those outside of the United States and to those within.

In order to show our resolve, the U.S. again began another major operation under a news blackout. On February 6, 1971, South Vietnamese forces under U.S. aircover began an invasion of Laos. A short time later these forces were routed. With the attempt to demonstrate resolve going badly at home and abroad, the type of situation to which Kissinger referred in 1966 became much more clear—foreign policy was being used for domestic purposes. Nixon went on television on July 15, 1971, to announce that he intended to visit the People's Republic of China, and that Dr. Kissinger had secretly arranged the visit. Two months later he announced his intended visit to the Soviet Union. I do not think it is stretching things too far to suggest that the President's campaign for re-election, the Vietnam conflict, the domestic discord that was experienced, the trips to visit our arch "enemies," and our strategic policies, were all linked.

In January of 1972, for instance, Nixon appeared on television and indicated that Kissinger had been carrying out secret talks with the North Vietnamese for about one year, thus partly defusing the anti-war issue for the Democrats. While trying to reach a peace agreement, though, the United States had been conducting intensive air raids. On each day between December 25, 1971, and January 1, 1972, the U.S. sent 350 planes to bomb North Vietnam. The reason for the bombing was essentially political. We were informing the North that we would indeed "bomb them back to the stone age." And we were signaling our resolve to other countries that, whatever the outcome of the negotiations, we were more than willing to continue non-military bombing. That the U.S. did not intend to invade the North, or cause it to capitulate, seemed to be made clear by Nixon's February 1972 trip to the People's Republic. Scenes of Nixon and Chinese leaders were beamed back to the U.S., and Nixon was hailed as the man of peace while bombs rained on Vietnam to the South.

A month after this trip, in March, the North Vietnamese began their invasion of the South, showing what the practical utility of the bombing had been. The U.S., partly because of domestic opposition to any more lives being lost, took the war to the air, and from that time, until the time we left Vietnam, the support we gave was primarily from the air.

The pullout of troops and the move to an air war had been underway for some time. It was part of the Nixon Doctrine that had been articulated as early as the Guam statement, when it became clear that sooner or later the U.S. would have to leave, but not before demonstrating our will.[13] The Nixon Doctrine, which became the cornerstone of Vietnamization, was most clearly expressed in Nixon's 1973 report to the Congress. Shared responsibility was now part of the key.

> The balance we seek abroad is crucial. We only compound insecurity if we modify our protective or development responsibilities without giving our friends the time and the means to adjust, materially and psychologically, to a new form of American participation in the world.[14]

We would be firm, but only when our national security called for it. Nixon also recognized, and once again emphasized, the need to have a stable domestic situation.

> Steadiness abroad required steadiness at home. But understanding and support for a responsible foreign policy were in serious jeopardy in 1969. Years of burden, Cold War tensions, and a difficult war threatened to undermine our constancy.
>
> While new policies were required to meet transferred conditions abroad, they were equally imperative because of the changing climate at home. Americans needed a new positive vision of the world and our place in it. While maintaining strong defenses, we also had to seek national security through negotiations with adversaries. And where American families were most directly affected, we had to gain a peace with honor to win domestic support of our new foreign policy as well as to make it seem credible abroad.[15]

That last sentence, perhaps better than any other, sums up the dual aims of policy at this period. For those at home, peace with honor could mean a number of things, but chiefly a managed withdrawal of U.S. troops. We were going home because we wanted to, not because we were being chased out, and because we had supplied the South Vietnamese, and it was now their war. If they failed, well, they did not have the will. This was the public position, but with Nixon's resignation it also became clear that one reason Thieu made concessions was that he clearly believed Nixon would and *could* deliver on his promise to prevent a takeover of the South by the North.

Another public relations event linked to peace with honor was the P.O.W. issue. In 1972, Nixon had indicated that the price for withdrawing all U.S. forces would be the release of American prisoners of war. Yet in no other war has the release of prisoners of war been problematic after withdrawal of troops. It was made a public issue in order to make it seem at home as though our peace with honor achieved something tangible. Their return home was also a staged event, and the military went to extreme efforts to prevent any dissension among the prisoners. They were to present a united front and they were *all* supposed to be heroes. This is why when some of the captives accused other P.O.W.s of being traitors, and contributing to their ill-treatment, they got no hearing. Americans were indeed mistreated in prison camps, and some of their conditions were made worse because of other Americans. But in this war, there could be no split in the ranks.

But let us return to Vietnam for a moment longer. The North Vietnamese were continuing to overrun South Vietnamese forces. At this time, prior to the President's trip to the Soviet Union, he accused the Russians of aiding the North, and urged in strong language that they stop. Détente was moving forward, but firmness was necessary. Then, on May 8, 1972, the U.S. mined the ports of North Vietnam, which could have been construed as an act of war by the Soviet Union. Yet, for food and trade, the Soviets ignored this, and on May 22, 1972, Nixon went to meet the Kremlin leaders. He had first, however, demonstrated his resolve. Now in a sense, these policies are good military strategy. After claiming to be within one inch of peace with a hostile party, then without explanation one of the heaviest bombing raids of the war is begun. Support for détente is indicated, and then harbors are mined and shipping cut off. This very element of irrationality makes an opponent seem dangerous. If one does not know when the opponent is really bluffing, then his nuclear strategy is taken more seriously.

That the purpose of the entire war had been to conduct a campaign to demonstrate credibility had been seen as early as 1966 by government officials. In a memo that sums it all up, the then Assistant Secretary of Defense, John McNaughton, said,

> *The present U.S. objective in Vietnam is to avoid humiliation.* The reasons why we *went into* Vietnam to the present depth are varied; but they are now largely academic. Why we have *not withdrawn* is, by all odds, *one* reason. (1) To preserve our reputation as a guarantor, and thus preserve our effectiveness in the rest of the world. We have not hung on (2) to save a friend, or (3) to deny the Communists the added acres and heads (because the dominoes don't fall for that reason in this case), or even (4) to prove that "wars of national liberation" won't work (except as our reputation is involved).[16]

V.

The collapse of Nixon's administration was followed by the crumbling of the last U.S. outposts.[17] It was all so sudden that people do not see where the U.S. ended up as a result of Vietnam, and what effect this entire framework of events has had on present American strategic policy. Let us briefly summarize what transpired during the course of the war, remembering that many of these actions were for the purpose of image maintenance.

First, the U.S. went into Vietnam to demonstrate the viability of the concept of limited war with the concomitant need to demonstrate the credibility of our nuclear policy, which was assured mutual destruction. In a sense, neither of these policies was affected by Vietnam. The theory of limited war has not been proved or disproved, we did not demonstrate the credibility of our nuclear policy, and we did not change it.

Second, as a result of the Vietnam conflict, the U.S. has the volunteer armed forces. Initially, in order to partly defuse the draft protest, we moved to a lottery system; then because of changing military needs, and again to curb civilian discontent, we moved to a volunteer force. This volunteer force is, of course, smaller than a draft army and it has slightly different strategic implications. The U.S. is developing a combat-ready guard and is moving to strike-oriented units that can fight in both conventional and limited wars. We have not given up on that idea. Our development efforts are concentrated partly around equipment and men that can be moved quickly to reach a wide number of areas in the world.

Third, Nixon's Guam statement still stands, in the sense that America will become involved when it is in our strategic interests— which are always broad—to do so. But our willingness, or ability, to honor treaty commitments as in the past has been seriously eroded. A number of our allies are looking to other alliances, or neutrality, as a means of guaranteeing their security. Some are probably considering developing their own nuclear forces. The integrity of NATO is being tried every day. Ravenal sees the collapse of South Vietnam as calling into question the whole of America's defense posture.

> The dilution of American guarantees makes it both more necessary and more feasible for allies, as the case may be, to seek the protection of the adversary, to accommodate the adversary, to strike a posture of neutrality, to attempt more equidistance between the great powers, or even to pursue self-reliance, perhaps to the point of acquiring a national nuclear force.[18]

The ability of the Executive Branch to wage war on its own authority has met with serious challenge. This is not to argue that this situation is not to prevail, but to point to the fact that our credibility, especially our nuclear credibility, depended on foreign leaders believing that the Executive had the power to mobilize politicians and the public to support issues defined as affecting the national security. There is, of course, a caveat that should be introduced here. American public opinion might well support action that was quick, forceful, and decisive.

A fourth major consequence of the Vietnam years was the evolution of détente, which was reflected in the Salt I and II talks. Détente and the arms limitation agreements stemmed, as we suggested above, from two sources: the desire to use foreign policy to manage discord, and also from a belief in the theoretical viability of the concept of M.A.D. Pachter believes that détente was a public relations campaign designed to cover up the loss in Vietnam, and other problems.

> I believe that there are domestic as well as diplomatic reasons for advertising this new philosophy. Whether America "won" or "lost" the Cold War, it is indisputable that the dominant conception with which this country conducted the Cold War has not emerged triumphant. The United States must now face further losses of prestige, influence, and power. We can no longer play the role of international policeman and expect other nations to accept our solutions quasi-automatically. But, rather than a new policy, we are offered a new word: "détente" —an ideology where we need concrete relations.[19]

What détente does, and does not, mean to each side, as well as what has been gained and lost, should be summarized. Optimists, such as Rosecrance, who have done an excellent job of providing a balance sheet, conclude that overall détente is positive because it ultimately provides for stability, and it makes the U.S.S.R. seem like a responsible world power. Let me use Rosecrance's own words:

> Today the Soviet Union faces the choice between crude power and responsible influence in world politics. The attempt to use the former will surely undermine the latter. Since this dilemma is coming to be understood in Moscow, there is reason to believe that Russia's "revolutionary" policy may well be nearing an end. Henceforth it seems likely that Russian gains will be sought through marginal increments in her own domestic political, economic and military position, and through ties with other nations that do not commit her to crisis intervention. If gains are not sought in this marginalist fashion, the ultimate achievement of modernity in the Soviet Union itself may be jeopardized.[20]

I am less optimistic, for a drive to modernization does not necessarily bring temperance, and I am by no means convinced that the Soviet Union is less imperialistic than the United States.

The U.S. litany against détente has been gone through before, but let us provide it again.[21] The U.S.S.R. did not restrain their clients in the case of the 1973 Middle East War, where they resupplied the Arabs as quickly as possible, and the U.S. did not involve itself until the Soviet effort was fully underway, and then it was almost too late. The Soviet Union wants high technological inputs from the U.S., but does not reciprocate in any meaningful way. The Soviets want access to U.S. food markets, but have not provided access to their raw material markets. And, finally, they have encouraged their militant Arab client states in their efforts to raise the price of oil.

Some argue that the Soviets have also found détente costly. The U.S., for instance, did not remain in a state of paralysis after Vietnam; we rebounded in the Middle East, and though we gave up advantages in the 1972 Salt proceedings, we are still the superior military power.[22] Now, I would argue that these are not parallel examples, and the issue of what has been given up in terms of nuclear superiority is still questionable. It might be worthwhile to remember that after the Salt I agreement it was noted that although we had given up numerical strength, this did not matter because our technology was far superior to that of the Soviets; and it probably was. But one year later, the Soviet Union had tested MIRV systems and began installing them on their missiles. But after MIRV, we had MARV (maneuverable, independently targetable re-entry vehicles). There was a failure to reach agreement on the number of MIRVed missiles in 1974, and no agreement is in sight for MARVed missiles. Again, the argument of the M.A.D. proponents is that it does not matter that the Soviets have more throw weight, for once they catch up technologically they will stop building missiles. There are those who believe that U.S. technology will continue to be superior, and hence differences in numbers of missiles is not relevant. The Salt agreements, of course, even encourage a race in technology. But can we be as optimistic as Rosecrance about the outcome?

> Any such competition will almost certainly underscore American advantages, not only putting some Soviet systems under constraint of pressure but also demonstrating American prowess before the rest of the world. Very accurate missiles, higher-yield warheads, maneuverable reentry vehicles are only some of the innovations that will follow from the reopening of the Pandora's box of American technological wizardry.[23]

There are some rather ethnocentric assumptions contained in this statement, as well as a failure to recognize that what one has, is not necessarily as important as what one is willing to use. The discussion of the use of nuclear weapons always seems as though it ought not to be conducted, because it is too unreal. Yet, as we noted above, Soviet leaders do consider nuclear war a possibility. Then, nuclear wars do not necessarily involve dropping all of one's bombs on another country, for we also have tactical nuclear weapons and "mini-nukes."

We have come to a point in the United States at which we are trying to effect détente and to limit arms, without really debating our defense strategies. We have gone to a different type of army, and we are developing new weapons. We need to demonstrate the credibility of these policies. But, don't the Soviet leaders, now that they have achieved parity in many areas, and superiority in others, also need to demonstrate their credibility? What about image management in the Soviet Union?

VI.

Let me summarize by drawing one analogy and sketching a scene for the future. First, Angola is the Soviet Union's Vietnam, not in the sense that it is a hopeless quagmire, but that their reasons for being there are the same as were ours in Vietnam—to demonstrate the credibility of their nuclear and related military policies. One can argue about who this is directed at—the U.S., the Chinese, or their Arab client states—but I suspect that is all. Angola is not really strategically important. Though Angola has some mineral resources, the Soviet Union has more untapped resources in Siberia. It is clear that détente has no meaning for the Soviets in terms of Angola, no more so than détente was effective in deterring us from mining the harbors of North Vietnam. Her use of Cuban troops has been much more effective than was our use of client troops in Vietnam.

I would like to be an optimist, but it is difficult to believe that there will be no more areas in the world in which the U.S. will not feel it incumbent to demonstrate its will and resolve. Nuclear weapons, as long as they exist, constrain those who have them to find other means to guarantee that their policies will be believed. Thus, arms control automatically poses a built-in problem. And the U.S. is one up on the Soviet Union because they have already used atomic weapons. Nor does total parity bring with it the guarantee that there will be no need for further conflict. Only the complete elimination of nuclear weapons, which at the time, with Third World states trying to get in the club, is unlikely, makes it unnecessary to demonstrate credibility in the way we have described above.

There are other ways, of course, of demonstrating resolve, and this is where our scene can be filled in. Consider a state of affairs in which the U.S. is being seriously challenged by the Soviets. After their success in Angola, the Soviets begin a series of intrusions into the American sphere of influence, Latin America and the Caribbean, using Castro's forces, backed up, of course, with Soviet supplies and equipment—for in these types of adventures, it is important that one's adversary realize the adventure is not solely that of the client state. The U.S. could threaten intervention—and probably would, supply advisors, and if the situation were serious enough to warrant it, American troops.

It is in such circumstances that the use of tactical nuclear weapons, or mini-nukes, becomes possible. Not by the U.S., but by a state that is clearly identified as one of our clients. It would be too serious a measure for either the U.S. or the Soviet Union to turn to the use of nuclear weapons. It would be not only preferable, but strategically necessary, to get someone else to use them.

There is one other geopolitical area in which use of nuclear weapons is both feasible, and possible. For some time now, Israel's Arab neighbors have been rearming themselves with Soviet assistance. One can envision a situation in which Israel is faced with being overrun by Arab forces and possible genocide. Then, Israel could only guarantee survival by the use of tactical nuclear weapons. A major dash across the Sinai by Arab troops, which threatened to completely destroy Israel, would do it. Or, if intelligence were sufficient, nuclear weapons could take the place of a pre-emptive air strike against Arab military bases. Once they had been used, there would indeed be a great cry and debate about limiting the use of all nuclear arms, and the morality of this act; but, they would have been used, and they would have demonstrated both credibility and will, which are the cornerstones of our defense policy.

1.   Edward N. Luttwak, "Nuclear Strategy: The New Debate," *Commentary*, Vol. 57 (April 1974), p. 54.

2.   For a discussion of the evolution of the policies as they relate to our weapons systems see: Graham T. Allison and Frederic A. Morris, "Armaments and Arms Control: Exploring the Determinants of Military Weapons," *Daedalus*, Vol. 104 (Summer 1975.).

3.   Ibid., p. 110.

4.   Luttwak, op. cit., p. 57.

5.   Barry M. Blechman and Edward R. Fried, "Controlling the Defense Budget," *Foreign Affairs*, Vol. 54 (January 1976), p. 238.

6.   Fred Charles Iklé, "Can Nuclear Deterrence Last Out the Century?" *Foreign Affairs*, Vol. 51 (January 1973), p. 281.

7.   Paul H. Nitze, "Assuring Strategic Stability in an Era of Détente," *Foreign Affairs*, Vol. 54 (January 1976), p. 207.

8.   Henry Kissinger, *Nuclear Weapons and Foreign Policy* (New York: Council on Foreign Relations, 1957).

9.   Ibid.

10.   Jonathan Schell, "Reflections," VI, *The New Yorker*, Vol. 51 (7 July 1975), p. 44. Emphases added.

11.   Klaus E. Knorr, *Military Power and Potential* (Lexington, Massachusetts: Heath-Lexington Books, 1970).

12.   Henry A. Kissinger, "Domestic Structure and Foreign Policy," *Daedalus*, Vol. 92 (Spring 1966), p. 503.

13.   *Nixon: The First Year of His Presidency* (Washington, D.C.: The Congressional Quarterly, 1970), pp. 55A and 96A.

14.   Richard M. Nixon, "U.S. Foreign Policy for the 1970s," Report to the Congress, 3 May 1973.

15.   Ibid.

16.   Cited in Schell, op. cit., p. 48. Emphases in the original.

17.   Taken from the title of Earl C. Ravenal's "Consequences of the End Game in Vietnam," *Foreign Affairs*, Vol. 53 (July 1975).

18.   Ravenal, ibid.

19.   Henry Pachter, "Détente—Reality and Myth," *Dissent*, Vol. 21 (Winter 1974), p. 28.

20.   Richard Rosecrance, "Detente or Entente?" *Foreign Affairs*, Vol. 54 (April 1975), p. 477.

21.   Joseph Clark, "Détente—Shadow or Substance," *Dissent*, Vol. 21 (Summer 1974).

22.   Rosecrance, op. cit., p. 470.

23.   Ibid., p. 471.

The Emergence of Communist Indochina and Its Impact on the Security of Southeast Asia: Some Preliminary Indicators

Donald E. Weatherbee

The sudden and surprisingly conventional military termination of the Indochinese wars has ushered in a more complex pattern of security interactions among the Southeast Asian states. The general framework of the political outcome had been anticipated by the non-communist states grouped together in the Association of Southeast Asian Nations (ASEAN—Indonesia, Malaysia, Philippines, Thailand, and Singapore). The Nixon Doctrine and the Paris Accords had impelled them to reappraise their own positions within the changing distribution of power. The notion of the "domino theory" conceived of as the sequential and automatic collapse of the non-communist states of the region as a result of an eventual communist triumph in Indochina was explicitly rejected. With it too went the security strategy of linking indigenous interest to American power presence in Southeast Asia in support of a policy of containment.

Since April 1975, the interrelated events in Indochina have given a new dimension of urgency and potential danger to the ASEAN efforts to vitalize a new, coherent strategy to meet the security requirements of the new international reality in Southeast Asia. Of signal importance was the abrupt violence and totality of the transfer of power in South Vietnam. This was followed by rapid progress towards unification, quickly underlining the ephemeral quality of the Provisional Revolutionary Government of South Vietnam. In Cambodia the precipitate collapse of the Khmer Republic was attended by the Khmer Rouge's savage uprooting of an entire population in a mobilization campaign unparalleled in communist history. Finally came the militant transformation of the Lao Provisional Government of National Union (PGNU) into the Laotian People's Democratic Republic (LPDR) against a background of physical intimidation and threatened military assault. This put to rest any lingering illusions that the PGNU could be a neutral buffer between the Democratic Republic of Vietnam (DRV) and Thailand.

The events in Indochina illuminate the first of five significant conditions that have emerged to shape the security environment of Southeast Asia. A substantial proportion of the population and resources of the region is now controlled and allocated by indigenous communist authorities, whose interests and capacity to act suggest a desire for power and influence in the wider, ASEAN sphere. An eventually unified Vietnam of 45 million people, led by a skilled and cohesive elite, backed by proven military power, supposes a new asymmetry in the power relationship between the ASEAN states and the communist actors. The triumph of communist power in the region has as its obverse the perception of American defeat and withdrawal. Concern about the U.S.'s continued role as a significant actor is compounded by what appears to be a systemic inability of the United States to respond coherently and in a sustained manner to international crisis and commitment. This defines the second condition of Southeast Asian security politics: the incredibility of repeated U.S. post-Vietnam pronouncements about active American engagement and maintenance of strength in Asia; for example the successor to the Nixon Doctrine, President Ford's "Pacific Doctrine."

The diminuation of the U.S.'s great power role in Southeast Asia has thrown into stark relief the Southeast Asian salient of the U.S.S.R.-PRC worldwide struggle for influence to the exclusion of the other. This describes the third condition: the conflictive interests and presence of the Soviet Union and the PRC in the region. Although the Vietnam watershed has not changed the strategic terms of the Sino-Soviet competition in Southeast Asia, the ending of the Indochina conflict did remove the restraints on the communist superpowers imposed by the situational needs for solidarity with the DRV in the war. The DRV in turn is exposed to more open pressures from both communist giants and may find that its ability to articulate policies for its own autonomous regional interests constrained.

For the non-communist states, the operation of the Sino-Soviet competition and the DRV's potentially powerful independent role exposes the fourth factor influencing external security relations: the tipping of the balance-of-power towards the communist actors. The absence of a credible American commitment only heightens this imbalance. The ASEAN perceptions of a shift in power explains their policy thrust towards accommodation in the framework of relations vaguely defined as "normalization." The process of "normalization" of relations, particularly with the communist states of Asia, has been accompanied by the acceleration of the process of self-distancing from the United States, hence accentuating the power imbalance. While moving towards a new international ordering in the region, the ASEAN states have also sought to create a generalized strategic framework to cushion the effect of the changed distribution of power on their own security. Regardless of whether or not the strategic concept is advanced as "neutralization" or "regional resilience," it supposes a high level of community of political interest within ASEAN. Although rhetorical peaks have been climbed in the manipulation of ASEAN symbols of cooperation and community, these have not been accompanied by meaningful actions in the political sphere. This marks the fifth condition: the lack of plausibility of the notion of a unified ASEAN political response to the common political/security challenge. Despite the fact that the ASEAN foreign ministers in the aftermath of Vietnam declared that the ASEAN structure was the logical framework for establishing peace, progress and stability in the region,[1] actual state behavior of the members proceeded from differentiated perceptions of interest and advantage, channelled through bilateral structures independent of any ASEAN community interest. The question of the future international security ordering in Southeast Asia will essentially be determined not so much by the capabilities of the ASEAN states to act jointly, but on the limits on those states who would threaten their future.

For nearly two decades security policy in Southeast Asia had been inextricably connected to the American definition of its military/political requirements in the area responding to the American perception of the regional aspect of the global strategic conflict.[2] Today, however, the Southeast Asian states are faced with the necessity of fashioning security policy resting on their own state capacity and directed realistically towards potential threats independently of the possible employment of U.S. power. The conditions of the post-Vietnam War order suggest that "security" for the independent non-communist states of Southeast Asia has to be considered in a more restricted, indigenous context than before, and that security policy is essentially based on individual responses rather than collective.

National security, although admittedly an ambiguous notion, is perceived in Southeast Asia explicitly in traditional terms—maintenance of sovereignty, territorial integrity of the state, administrative integration of the population. The implicit statement of security has increasingly come to mean the preservation of the political system and persistence of the regime. There is an underlying psychological identity between the incumbency of the elites, who after all are the makers of policy, and the indigenous definition of national security. To these elites the changed power structure in Southeast Asia does not necessarily mean that the environment is any less hostile or threatening. The rejection of the "domino theory" as a geopolitical justification for American policy should not obscure the fact of the interrelatedness of security events in the region. The emergence of communist states in Indochina will impinge on the security of the other Southeast Asian nations in terms of acts, perceptions, and reactions. The policy issues to be addressed turn on questions of the political level of security interactions and the vitality of the interests involved. The security implications of the changed environment can be examined at three levels of interaction: between the regional states and the great-power actors; between the ASEAN states and the Indochinese communist actors; and the level of internal challenge within the ASEAN states themselves. The problem of fashioning responsive policies is complicated by the fact of interrelationships among the levels. Changes in the patterns of response at one level tend to induce changes at other levels as well. Thailand's normalization of previously hostile relations with the People's Republic of China, for example, influences Thailand's orientation towards the DRV on the regional level as well as being internally relevant with respect to the Communist Party of Thailand's (CPT) "national liberation" struggle.

II.

Great power interests in the Southeast Asian region can be catalogued in the traditional categories—political, economic, social, cultural, historical, etc. As these interests, which are manifested in multiple bilateral and multilateral structures and connections, come to be linked to the great power's appreciation of its relative power position in terms of its strategic relationship with global adversaries, policy tends to focus on more specific, narrowly national security interests. Although the end of the Indochinese wars reduced the level of violence, Southeast Asia remains an area of great power conflict and hence security concern.

The salient contest is the Sino-Soviet confrontation.[3] Both the Soviet Union and China accuse the other of seeking global hegemony, with Southeast Asia a geopolitical key. The PRC places the U.S.S.R.'s aggressive, universalistic pretensions in the context of the "contending superpower" thesis. Of the two superpowers, the Soviet Union is the most dangerous; as impelled by the corrupt forces of social-imperialism it seeks to act as militaristic global overlord as U.S. power wanes. The U.S.S.R., on the other hand, warns of Maoist subjective nationalism aspiring to great power status, which in Southeast Asia can be interpreted in the framework of "great-Han chauvinism," the re-creation of the traditional structure of Chinese superiority over the states to the south and southwest. The policy reaction of the communist giants is to mobilize support in Southeast Asia for the exclusion of the other. In this competition the U.S.S.R. defines Chinese policy in Southeast Asia as "anti-Soviet," while the PRC defines reciprocal Russian policies as "anti-PRC." In this negatively symbolized rivalry, the targets of policy—the Southeast Asian states themselves—find political neutrality difficult to maintain.

The Russian strategy has been essentially that of containment of

China by forging countervailing links of its own to Southeast Asian states. Soviet political, economic, cultural, and social relations in Southeast Asia are stridently condemned by Peking as part of the Russian plot to penetrate and then dominate in an imperialist way the region. The major Soviet initiative has been its collective security proposal.[4] Although vague and ambiguous in detail, the proposal would have the effect of internationally sanctioning the growing Russian political-military presence in the region (resting in fact on a unilateral determination of Soviet national security requirements). The projected web of bilateral agreements (on the Indian model) and multilateral arrangements (on the Helsinki model) would pre-empt any PRC security alternative in Southeast Asia, undercut the PRC's political warfare against the Soviet Union, impede Sino-American rapprochement in its balance-of-power aspect, and perhaps forestall a nuclear Japan. Although ostensibly an all Asian proposal, including China, the Chinese containment end is unmistakable. Peking has no illusions and warns that the collective security scheme is a "sinister design" of the U.S.S.R. to contend for hegemony and to "disintegrate and control the Asian countries." The Chinese note approvingly that the Soviet system has enjoyed no favor in Southeast Asia, a hearkening perhaps to the maxim: "Guard against the tiger at the back door while repulsing the wolf at the gate."[5]

Southeast Asia's implicit rejection of the Soviet collective security system (Soviet claims to the contrary notwithstanding) is a function of the Southeast Asian elites' perception of the rather tenuous connection between the Soviets' inherent definition of security—i.e., the containment of China—and their own evaluation of the requirements of normalization of relations with the PRC. The U.S.S.R. has no significant indigenous Southeast Asian forces to deploy in support of its policy goals and its concerns are still viewed as being rather remote from the central interests of non-communist Southeast Asia. In its search for allies the Soviet Union has been singularly unsuccessful in exploiting the fluid and dynamic security environment. It has no real, immediately compelling sanctions—political, economic, or military— to forestall PRC engagement in the region.

The PRC's strategic response to the Soviet challenge has been the promotion, albeit indirectly and ambivalently, of a regional balance of power. This has involved three tactics in Southeast Asia. First, normalization of bilateral relations with the Southeast Asian states has the effect of denying them as possible allies of the Soviet Union. Specifically through the mutual PRC-Southeast Asian endorsement of the "anti-hegemony" clause, which is the principal symbolic weapon in Peking's anti-Soviet arsenal, the PRC seeks to make the Soviet presence in the region illegitimate, the pursuit of its state interests by definition social-imperialism. The statement itself seems on the surface innocuous: "The two Governments are also opposed to any attempt by any country or group of countries to establish hegemony or create spheres of influence in any part of the world."[6] Malaysia's then Prime Minister Razak, Thailand's Kukrit, and the Philippines' Marcos can blandly generalize the clause to any country including the PRC (and by extension the United States). Its true political significance is testified to, however, by the importance that Peking attaches to the adherence of states to the declaration and more particularly by the vehemence of the Soviet reaction. Peking's insistence on the inclusion of the "anti-hegemony" clause is decried from the Russian side as, "blatant anti-Sovietism and attempts to use the international contacts established ostensibly for the purpose of normalizing relations in order to involve other parties in intrigues against the Soviet Union."[7]

The willingness of three ASEAN members to associate themselves with an "anti-Soviet" posture represents their appraisal of their relative "security distance" from the U.S.S.R. as opposed to the PRC. The PRC's interests in Southeast Asia are viewed as a key to the development of an orderly security future in the region. Although the U.S.S.R. and the United States may articulate policies that are regional pendants of primary global interests, the ASEAN states have accepted the fact that their region is an important Chinese geostrategic sphere of primary interest. They are hastening to put their relationships with the PRC on correct and cooperative bases. In this process of normalization the PRC has at its disposal political, economic, and even military levers not available to the Soviet Union; oil, insurgency, and overseas Chinese give a different quality to the Sino-ASEAN connection. The PRC seeks to maximize its future influence through the tactic of dichotomous links: government to government and fraternal revolutionary party to revolutionary movement. In ranging themselves in the Peking shaped pattern of accommodation, the ASEAN states hope to make the former link more valuable to Peking in a *real politik* and economic sense than the latter's symbolic and ideological attractiveness.

As the ASEAN states grope for a relationship with the PRC that minimizes the real power differentials between them, they find, ironically, that in one sense it is through the PRC that continuity with the previous security regime in the region, connecting them to the American power presence, can be maintained. Sino-American rapprochement has, on the Chinese side at least, some of the characteristics of a latent strategic guarantee to the PRC in its contest with the Soviet Union. The Shanghai Communiqué contained the "anti-hegemony" clause. One Chinese interpretation of the consequences of American defeat in Indochina is that it permits the United States, given its weakness and strategic passivity in Southeast Asia, to redeploy to more appropriate and defensible positions from which to play its *necessary* security role. Peking's concerns about the destabilizing effects of an American precipitate retreat from Southeast Asia, opening the region to Soviet encroachment, explains its advice to Thailand and the Philippines about the continued utility of the American presence and Chinese acceptance of the implications of the "Pacific Doctrine."

Southeast Asian responses to the impingement of great power politics on the region are necessarily reactive. At this level of state interaction the capabilities of the indigenous actors are not such that they can induce through the application of power substantial alterations in the terms of great power competition. In the wake of the collapse of the U.S. security system the ASEAN states have sought to develop a regional strategy that would allow them to maintain extra-regional political-military connections on a bilateral basis while at the same time insulating Southeast Asia as a region from great power conflict. The significant political response on the regional level has been the so-called neutralization proposal. Lobbied for by Malaysia, the proposal was accepted by the ASEAN governments in 1971, when they agreed to exert the necessary efforts "to secure recognition of, and respect for, Southeast Asia as a Zone of Peace, Freedom, and Neutrality, free from any form or manner of interference by outside powers."[8] At the first summit meeting of the ASEAN heads of state in February 1976, the leaders noted with "satisfaction" the "efforts to draw up initially necessary steps to secure the recognition of and respect for the zone."[9] Between the lines the summit declaration acknowledged that progress towards fruition was largely rhetorical rather than substantive. In part this flows from the fact that as an operational security policy "neutralization" rests on two imperative premises, neither of which can be demonstrated as valid for the ASEAN region: (1) a community of political interests among the ASEAN states, and (2) a common interest among the great powers with respect to the future of Southeast Asia. As neutralization has come to be described, particularly in the exegitical Malaysian pronouncements, its implementation will require political-military equidistance of the ASEAN states in their posture towards the great powers. At the same time the great powers would have to make a self-denying guarantee of their intentions to respect the Southeast Asian zone of peace, freedom, and neutrality. Although all ASEAN states adhere to the neutralization proposal as a valued, ultimate end, its implementation cannot take priority over the immediate security requirements of maintaining logistical pipelines to the suppliers of hardware on credit, by assistance, or outright sales. This is particularly true of the Philippines and Indonesia; to a lesser extent of Thailand. An equidistance that would require the cutting of the American logistical tail is not perceived as enhancing security. This aspect of the great power political-military link is particularly salient as the ASEAN states must come to grips with the intransigence of revolutionary elites on the regional and domestic levels of security concerns.

A major consideration of the security elites in the Philippines, Thailand, and Indonesia has been to keep the material channel to the U.S. open. As they adjusted to the new U.S. posture, they were concerned that the lowered U.S. power profile in Southeast Asia would be accompanied by concomitant reductions in the assistance web. In the absence of a viable alternative these elites are not going to deny themselves this connection for the sake of a problematical equidistance.

The great power response to the neutralization proposal suggests that it has become part of the symbolic competition between the U.S.S.R. and PRC. Rather than insulating ASEAN from the Sino-Soviet rift, neutralization has entered the polemic. The PRC has embraced neutralization because it forecloses the Soviet's collective security option. The Soviet Union on the other hand, perhaps making the best of a bad thing, argues that the neutralization scheme is the first stage in the development of a collective security system. The United States seems to have adopted the position that neutralization will describe a condition of a regional balance-of-power.

The problem of nuetralizing Southeast Asia from great power politics cannot be separated from issues deriving from intra-regional conflict. The first question that must be asked is what part of Southeast Asia is to be covered by the "zone of neutrality"; only ASEAN, or all regional states including the DRV. Secondly, in order for neutralization to work, the neutralized states must evolve processes and structures for the peaceful resolution of disputes among them in order to forestall appeal to external powers. In this consideration the orientations of the communist states of Indochina towards ASEAN states will be a critical factor in determining progress irrespective of the scope of the neutralized zone.

III.

On a priori grounds the prospects for success in an undertaking such as neutralization or the pacific settlement of disputes, which as-

TABLE I: U.S MILITARY ASSISTANCE TO ASEAN STATES
($ thousands)

	Actual FY 74	Actual FY 75	Proposed FY 76
Indonesia	14,010	15,850	19,400
Malaysia	180	283	
Philippines	15,710	21,010	19,600
Thailand	32,498	30,126	28,300

Source: *Foreign Military Sales and Military Assistance Facts* (November 1975).[10]

sumes shared values and norms and a minimum level of political community, seems doomed to failure on an all-Southeast Asia basis. Even among the ASEAN states themselves, where for a decade the so-called "ASEAN spirit" has operated to dampen open international political division among the members, the fragile framework of consultation, cooperation, and occasionally coordination is still jeopardized by unilateral acts and symbols in the service of national (as opposed by community) interest. Even the draft "Treaty of Amity and Cooperation In Southeast Asia," which seeks to regularize political relations among the ASEAN states and is open to adherence by other Southeast Asian states, can only paper over the fact of division on the issue of community interest versus national interest when the two may diverge.[11] In the key chapter on the Pacific Settlement Disputes, the mechanisms for the regional processes of adjustment, negotiation and settlement do not become operational until all parties to the dispute agree in advance to their application.

The rudimentary framework of ASEAN political cooperation rests on the good intentions and will of the foreign policy elites in the ASEAN states. It results from a self-conscious realization of shared general problems of policy. All of the ASEAN elites are anti-communist in their domestic politics. In the prosecution of counter-insurgency they have evolved patterns of bilateral assistance and intelligence sharing. All of the ASEAN members pursue economic development strategies that welcome Western capital participation, public and private. To a large extent their domestic economies have become integrated into the international trading framework of the industrial capitalist economies, with 61 percent of ASEAN's exports going to the U.S., Japan, and the Common Market nations, and 54 percent of its imports coming from these areas. This trade, combined with the growing importance of intra-ASEAN commerce, accounts for the part of ASEAN's international trade. All of the ASEAN members have been linked to Western military and defense establishments including, with the exception of Indonesia, participation in a Western anchored mutual security structure. Of intangible importance in this

TABLE II: DIRECTION OF ASEAN EXPORT TRADE 1974 ($ millions)

	Indonesia	Malaysia	Philippines	Singapore	Thailand
World	7449.7	4235.9	2673.0	5484.6	2492.6
U.S.	1526.8	595.4	1133.1	776.2	188.2
Japan	3954.8	713.9	932.4	637.6	639.2
EEC	380.0	849.0	321.0	645.3	388.3
Total U.S., Japan, EEC	5861.6	2158.3	2386.5	2059.1	1215.7
Percentage of World	.79	.51	.89	.38	.49

Source: IMF-IBRD, *Directions of Trade, 1970–1974.*

regard is the political and technical orientations of the ASEAN officer corps that have had training and other contact with Western military institutions.

This functional definition of the ASEAN grouping is of critical relevance to questions of relations between ASEAN and Indochinese communist states, particularly if the problem is framed in terms of providing an integrative regional framework for an enlarged ASEAN. Arguments that rest on the identification of some kind of vague "Southeast Asianess" of the DRV, giving it a natural tie to the region (other than simple geographic contiguity), cannot be logically demonstrated. What can be demonstrated is that the functional lines of cooperation that give ASEAN its body are absent when the ASEAN concept is generalized to the wider region. Looking to the future one Indonesian security planner clearly put the issues:

> Whatever development Vietnam is going to experience in its political system, the fact remains that she has to live with neighboring nations. Southeast Asia will certainly welcome a friendly, cooperative and rehabilitated Vietnam in her midst. But, if on the contrary she should become an ambitious and expansive nation, dedicated to spreading her influence and ideology physically and subversively among neighboring people she would certainly have to expect resistance.[12]

The DRV does not feel itself in any supplicant position vis-à-vis ASEAN. Its attitude continues to be hostile. The DRV has rebuffed all attempts to engage it in an ASEAN dialogue. This is a natural reaction given its perception of ASEAN as a neocolonialist, anti-communist, reactionary structure serving the cause of imperialism.[13] The neutralization proposal too is an American inspired plot. The DRV's vision of Southeast Asia is not that of a peacefully integrating region in the post-Vietnam War period. For the DRV, Southeast Asia remains the principal anti-imperialist battle ground; the most important center of the world contradictions.[14] The future development of Southeast Asia will be decided by the strength of the revolutionary currents of the time, which are strong and on the offensive. The impact of the triumph of the revolutionary forces has been to decisively shift the regional

TABLE III: DIRECTION OF ASEAN IMPORT TRADE 1974 ($ millions)

	Indonesia	Malaysia	Philippines	Singapore	Thailand
World	3754.1	4156.2	3444.0	8592.8	3214.8
U.S.	600.7	397.3	828.8	1132.8	406.5
Japan	1139.2	915.5	923.9	1528.5	1009.8
EEC	723.3	873.2	421.9	1073.6	595.8
Total U.S., Japan, EEC	2463.2	2186.0	2174.6	3734.9	2012.1
Percentage of World	.66	.53	.63	.43	.63

Source: IMF-IBRD, *Directions of Trade, 1970–1974.*

balance of power to the favor of the progressives. In order to accommodate themselves to the "current of the times" and the new balance-of-forces, the DRV demands that non-communist Southeast Asian states must abandon their subordinate political, military, economic and cultural relations with the United States. Otherwise, Hanoi warns, the elites of ASEAN will meet the fate that befell the Thieu clique or the Lon Nol clique. Although the general foreign policy line of the DRV is based on the principles of peaceful coexistence, it is clear that these have come to be interpreted within the framework of the revolutionary struggles of the people and Hanoi's idiosyncratic definitions of "peace," "neutrality," "non-interference," "independence," etc., which have in common the requirement of expulsion of Western, primarily American, political influence. As its conditions for ASEAN, Hanoi wants to "escape from the influence of US imperialists, dismantle all US bases, abandon the policy of trailing after the US, and adopt a truly cooperative and friendly attitude."[15]

One can point to the continuity of hostility in the Thai-DRV connection as a possible indicator of the quality to be expected in the ASEAN-Vietnamese relationship. In this bilateral case the differences in political, social and economic identities are boldly underlined; historical antagonisms revived; and perceptions of mutual threat inform decision making. Despite initial Thai efforts to establish proper state to state dialogue on the basis of the givens of the post-April 1975 status quo, DRV insistence on the conditions of an alternative future order has meant diplomatic stand off. Although the Thais do not perceive an immediate military threat from communist armies in Indochina, they do have great concern about the changed strategic situation in north and northeast Thailand. For nearly three decades Thai security policy has rested on the existence of a compliant, dependent Lao buffer state in the trans-Mekong region, insulating Thailand from direct confrontation with the aggressively independent forces of the Pathet Lao and DRV. With the extension of communist authority to all of Laos, the old defense line has crumbled. The Lao border is now with a potential enemy having close political and military links to the new power of the DRV.

Although the Thais because of geographic proximity and past alliance have the most immediate adjustments to make in their relations with the Indochinese states, in the longer run, just as critical in determining the structure of intra-Southeast Asian relations will be the Indonesian perception of its security requirements. Already the DRV has identified Jakarta as the center of reactionary, counter-revolutionary Southeast Asian politics. DRV propaganda attacks on the character of the "fascist" Suharto regime again wave the bloody flag of the aftermath of the abortive 1965 coup. Jakarta is portrayed as the chief remaining prop of American imperialism in the region. Hanoi welcomed the representatives of the Fretilin government of East Timor, vigorously denouncing Indonesia's "naked aggression" and "barbaric massacres" there. The DRV posture has served to confirm the Indonesian leadership in the correctness of their suspicion of the ultimate regional political ends of the Vietnamese communist elite. Events since the end of the Indochina wars have been consistent with Indonesian suggestion that future political orientations in Southeast Asia will tend to cluster around two antagonistic poles: Jakarta and Hanoi. In fact, although an acceleration in the polarization process can be noted, the actual terms of the clustering cannot be explained by reference simply to an ASEAN-DRV dichotomy.

Indonesian security strategy is based on the doctrine of "national resilience" *(ketahanan nasional)*.[16] This places maximum emphasis on self-help and self-reliance, calling for the mobilization of material and moral resources of the nation in defense of the national interest. Although the doctrine eschews strategic dependence on an outside power, in its external manifestation—regional resilience—increasingly it encompasses explicit Indonesian military and other security ties with its ASEAN partners. As one influential Indonesian newspaper commented, it is only natural that the Southeast Asian states bordering on Indochina should adapt their defense and foreign policy orientations to Indonesia.[17] This is most clearly evident in the Indonesian-Malaysia security network where, after the Suharto-Razak talks in Medan in November 1975, it appears that a *de facto* mutual security arrangement exists. The Indonesian Defense Chief, General Panggabean, put it concisely: "Whatever problem Malaysia faces is considered to be a problem of Indonesia too and vice-versa."[18] On the Indonesian side it was hoped that the Malaysian-Indonesian security framework would become the model for a number of bilateral defense arrangements between ASEAN members.[19]

The suggestion of the possible militarization of relations within ASEAN aroused strongly negative reactions on the part of the DRV and the Soviet Union.[20] More importantly for the evolution of cooperation within the ASEAN sphere, the Indonesian tactic lays bare the differences in Thai and Indonesian perceptions of the appropriate response to the latent threat from the north. For the Indonesians "regional resilience" appears to be translated into oppositional solidarity. For Thailand, beset with a weak government and fragmented security decision-making structures, resilience has led to isolating accommodation. The Thai government has expressly rejected the concept of bilateral security agreements within ASEAN.[21] It has hastened the withdrawal of the American military from Thailand. Even the residual U.S. presence that might have given some reciprocal effect to whatever remains of the Thai-U.S. "alliance" has been sacrificed. The Thais have sought in their new relationship with the PRC to find a regional counterweight to the DRV.[22] A growing center and left domestic consensus in Thailand would have the government forebear from raising thorny political or security questions with the DRV in pursuit of "normalization." Within the framework of regional international relations Thailand appears to be moving towards a "Finlandized" position between the Indonesian "core area" and the DRV "core area."

Even on the Indochinese side of the emerging polarity in Southeast Asia there is no "bloc" cohesion. Although the LPDR-DRV relationship is viewed by both as a "special, pure, consistent, exemplary and rarely-to-be seen" one, forged in blood and common party history (the Indochinese Communist Party),[23] no parallel ties link Phnom Penh to Hanoi. On the contrary, Democratic Cambodia's efforts have been to isolate itself as much as possible from Hanoi's influence. Phnom Penh as well has embraced the PRC's case in the Sino-Soviet polemic. It is clear that the operation of the communist superpower rivalry in Southeast Asia will operate to prevent immediate consolidation of DRV hegemonic ascendency in Indochina.

Hanoi's view of Southeast Asia and its putative role as leader of the revolutionary forces in the region has meant that non-communist efforts to accommodate to the changed power relationships have taken place under certain tension in a psychological climate of unsubtle threat: "Vietnam's victory is eloquent proof of the offensive posture of the world revolutionary movement. *The offensive strategy has defeated the compromise and negative strategies.* "[24] (Emphasis added.) The symbols wielded by the Vietnamese elite indicate that the "offensive strategy" will be directed against non-communist Southeast Asia. The constraints on state action by the DRV to these ends are important in determining its capacity; its ability to bring real power to bear on the ASEAN targets. The internal restraints include the resource requirements of socialist reconstruction and development in the unified Vietnamese state. On the regional level there is the "resilience" of the ASEAN states themselves with which to contend. The DRV also has to take into account its position in the global contest, particularly its economic dependency on the Soviet Union. Although the Vietnamese state cannot be divorced from the Vietnamese revolution, it does not seem likely, at least on the basis of available evidence, that the DRV's promotion of revolution elsewhere in Southeast Asia is going to be accomplished by the external projection of state power in conventional military terms; at least not until the revolutionary process has reached a higher level.

IV.

The DRV's analysis of the Southeast Asian political environment concludes that the internal contradictions in the region have been heightened as a result of the Vietnamese triumph. Revolutionary movements are on the offensive; reactionaries are on the defensive. Even while the ASEAN heads-of-state, by definition reactionaries, were meeting in their Bali summit, Hanoi was boldly calling for an intensification of the peoples' struggles in Southeast Asia, postulating that the growing strength of the forces of revolutionary change and the weakness of the reactionaries was a trend compatible with the law of historic evolution and hence, irreversible. The DRV, together with the LPDR, has promised to support the "just and surely victorious struggle of the peoples," and has said it will actively contribute to the outcome.[25] (So much for the principles of peaceful coexistence.) The relevant question naturally is, "of what will the contribution consist?"

Psychologically the Vietnamese victory has had a morale stirring impact on the communist insurgencies of Southeast Asia. The CPT and fraternal analogues have impressive testimony of the fact that history is on their side; of the appropriateness of their strategy and tactics; of the value of their sacrifices. This positive, inspiring psychological lift on the insurgents' side has a negative, disheartening impact on the government's side. Two conflicting reactions can be discerned: making political concessions to the domestic left and hardening of the line against the domestic left. When these occur simultaneously from different elements in the incumbent elite, the result is, as was the case in Thailand, internal paralysis on security matters. This psychological transfer of power has been felt in Burma and Malaysia as well.

A second manner of contribution is more tangible and direct—weapons transfers. It has been feared that the large amount of small arms, rockets, etc., that was part of the Vietnamese booty would be used to re-equip communist forces outside of Indochina. Although reports of Vietnamese weapons transfers have been heard from Burma and Malaysia, only in Thailand does there seem to be hard evidence of logistic assistance to the CPT (as opposed to weapons purchases on the Hong Kong arms market). In north and northeast Thailand, DRV and Pathet Lao involvement in the building of a "peoples' war" in terms of training, communications, propaganda, support, supply, and perhaps even specialized cadres (sapper units, etc.) has been amply demonstrated. Although the DRV ritualistically denies interference in Thailand, it nevertheless makes fulsome promises of support to the just struggle of the "Thai patriots." The Thai apprehension is that the existent degree of foreign penetration will be escalated now that Laos is a sanctuary and base area for the CPT warriors.

The Thai concern about the linkage between the DRV victory and its own internal war situation has to be viewed against the background of governmental instability and confusion at the center. Not only have the insurgents been able to extend their infrastructure in the northeastern provinces, but in the disillusioned and angry mood of Thai democratic politics, the propaganda appeals of the CPT have relevance to the urbanized Thai. The Thai case, although the most extreme, illustrates the connection between the DRV's triumph and the internal security of the non-communist states of ASEAN. The DRV's success did not create a revolutionary situation in Thailand. It does, however, give a bright alternate model to the frustrated modernizers as well as the confirmed revolutionary. Certainly if the North Vietnamese are able in their reconstruction and development programs to demonstrate dynamic progress in circumstances not environmentally dissimilar from those of the rest of Southeast Asia, then the model will be even more attractive. As the DRV is able and willing to provide either directly or through proxies such as the LPDR assistance to communist movements in Southeast Asia, it will tend to supplant the PRC as the guiding center of the revolution.

The critical response to the challenge posed by the internal counter-elites is no different now than it was before the DRV emerged the winner in Indochina. The requirements of political, economic, and social investment in meaningful development is no less. The problem is that the time-frame has been shortened. Here a different kind of "domino theory" is at work. This is a "domino theory" as proposed by Hanoi! "The domino theory formulated by Washington amounts to an admission of the development of national independence movements in various countries—a development which the US has failed to check."[26] The dominoes will fall from the "inside, out." Given this, slogans and regulations designed to "discipline" the DRV's international relations in the Southeast Asian region do not apply realistic guidelines to the central political conflict in Southeast Asia, which at one and the same time transcends and is confined within state boundaries.

1. Press statement at conclusion of 8th ASEAN Foreign Ministers Meeting, Kuala Lumpur, 15 May 1975, as reported in Foreign Broadcast Information Service, *Daily Report-Asia and the Pacific,* 16 May 1975.

2. See my monograph, *Collective Defense, Neutralization, and the Balance of Power: Contending Security Policies in Southeast Asia,* U.S. Army War College, Strategic Studies Institute Military Issues Research Memorandum, September 1975.

3. In this section I draw on my paper, "The USSR-DRV-PRC Triangle in Southeast Asia," prepared for the U.S. Army War College, Strategic Studies Institute, Security Issues Symposium, March 1976.

4. In general see: Alexander O. Ghebhardt, "The Soviet System of Collective Security in Asia," *Asian Survey* (December 1972), pp.1075–1091; Arnold Horelick, "The Soviet Union's Collective Security Proposal: A Club in Search of Members," *Pacific Affairs* 47 (Fall 1974), pp. 269–287.

5. "Asian Countries and People—Guard Against Tiger At the Back Door While Repulsing Wolf At the Gate," *Peking Review,* 9 January 1976, p. 20.

6. The clause is embodied in the joint communiqués announcing normalization of relations signed between the PRC and Malaysia, PRC and Thailand, and PRC and the Philippines. The clause became a significant issue in the three cornered PRC-Japan-U.S.S.R. relationship.

7. Y. Lugovskoy, "Peking's Policy In Asia," *Soviet Military Review* (November 1975), p. 46.

8. For the neutralization proposal and its evolution see: Sheldon W. Simon, *Asian Neutralism and U.S. Policy* (Washington, D.C.: American Enterprise Institute for Public Policy Research, 1975); Dick Wilson, *The Neutralization of Southeast Asia* (New York: Praeger Publishers, 1975).

9. Joint press communiqué as reported by the Indonesian news service ANTARA, 25 February 1976.

10. U.S. Department of Defense, Security Assistance Agency, *Foreign Military Sales and Military Assistance Facts, November 1975,* Data Systems and Reports Division, Comptroller DSAA.

11. Text as given by *Agence France Presse,* Hong Kong, 24 May 1976.

12. Sayidiman Suryohadiprojo, "The Future Of Southeast Asia," *The Indonesian Quarterly* (January 1973), p. 47.

13. Hanoi's most scathing denunciations of ASEAN came during the ASEAN summit meeting of February 1976; see for example, commentary in *Quan Doi Nhan Dan,* February 26.

14. Hanoi's analysis of the post-April 1975, Southeast Asian scene is drawn from, *inter alia:* commentary, "A Great Change in Southeast Asia," *Quan Doi Nhan Dan,* 28 May 1975; Quang Thai, "Southeast Asia Belongs to the Southeast Asian People," *Nhan Dan,* 12 June 1975; Hai Van, "The New Pacific Doctrine—The US Counterrevolutionary strategy in Asia after Vietnam," *Quan Doi Nhan Dan,* 10 February 1976; Nguyen Cao Hien, "Southeast Asia After Vietnam," *Hoc Tap,* February 1976.

15. Hanoi radio, 26 May 1976, as reported in Foreign Broadcast Information Service, *Daily Report—Asia and the Pacific,* 27 May 1976.

16. A recent English language discussion of the doctrine is, Justus M. van der Kroef, "Indonesia's National Security: Problems and Strategy," *South-East Asian Spectrum* (July 1975), pp. 37–48; see also, Donald E. Weatherbee, *Indonesia's Role in Regional*

Southeast Asian Politics, paper delivered to Southeast Region Conference, Association for Asian Studies, January 1975.

17.   *Kompas,* as reported by *Agence France Presse,* 11 June 1976.

18.   As reported by *Agence France Presse,* 20 November 1975.

19.   Kuala Lumpur, domestic service, 19 November 1975, as reported in Foreign Broadcast Information Service, *Daily Report—Asia and the Pacific,* 20 November 1975.

20.   See for example the article by Yury Aninsky, "Dangerous Tendencies," *Pravda,* 31 August 1975.

21.   Interview given by Prime Minister Kukrit to Denzil Peires of the *Far Eastern Economic Review,* published in the Bangkok *Nation,* 9 December 1975, and the *Far Eastern Economic Review,* December 12.

22.   Weatherbee, "The USSR-DRV-PRC Triangle in Southeast Asia," op. cit.

23.   Text of a joint communiqué as given by *Vietnamese News Agency,* reported in Foreign Broadcast Information Service, *Daily Report—Asia and the Pacific,* 12 February 1975.

24.   "A Great Change in Southeast Asia," op. cit.

25.   DRV-LPDR joint communiqué, op. cit.

26.   Commentary, "Unprecedented Opportunity For Southeast Asian Nations," *Nhan Dan,* 28 February 1976.

The United States and Vietnam: The Road Ahead

Phan Thien Chau

The year 1976 is important internally for both the United States of America and for Vietnam. It also may prove to be an important year in the transition in the relations between the two countries from belligerence to mutual peaceful acceptance. This year of course marks the Bicentennial of the United States' struggle for national independence and self-determination. It is also a year for presidential and congressional elections when this national self-determination renews its vigor. For Vietnam, 1976 is a year of great historic importance. On April 25, an all-Vietnam election for a National Assembly is to take place in an unprecedented atmosphere of national independence, unity, sovereignty and territorial integrity. After centuries and, more recently, decades of struggle, the people of Vietnam finally are able to pursue their own destiny without foreign interference and intervention. Just as the republicans and the democrats in the United States will be going through the process of quadrennial party reinvigoration through caucuses, conventions, primary elections and the national presidential nominating conventions, Vietnam is expected to be in the process of calling for the Fourth National Congress of the ruling Vietnam Workers Party which starts at the local level. (If the comparison might seem forced and artificial, it could be said that genuine popular participation in the process of selecting party candidates in both systems has long been a valid subject of scholarly debate.)

Other dimensions need to be kept in mind. Vietnam has been undergoing a massive postwar reconstruction and rehabilitation project since early 1973 in the North and since May 1975 in the South. In all of this, the reminders of destruction by the United States have been omnipresent. In the United States, on the other hand, the national mood since the collapse of the Thieu regime has been to obliterate Vietnam from its collective consciousness. Thus, in any discussion of United States-Vietnam relations, there is an imbalance of interest

141

and urgency, with only Vietnam having made friendly overtures to the United States to date, and with the latter having responded mainly in the negative. [The Carter administration has changed this trend by sending the Leonard Woodcock mission to Hanoi, March 16–20, 1977, and also by subsequently holding talks between the representatives of the two countries. Editor's note.] These divergent attitudes arose from diametrically opposed views as to who was the aggressor in the Vietnam War and were perceptional divergences that could not be terminated because Vietnam exulted in victory while the United States would not concede defeat. The fact that the United States did not win the war in Indochina has embittered its leaders against Vietnam to a degree greater than they ever manifested towards its vanquished enemies Italy, Germany, and Japan after World War II.

Yet, in spite of these difficulties strewn in the path of Vietnam-United States relations, it may be useful to ask whether the road ahead needs to be dictated by pitfalls of the past. The answer perhaps could be collated from what has happened to the Cold War between the United States and the Soviet Union, which has turned into peaceful coexistence and détente, and from the strident United States-China invectives of the early 1950s to the Kissinger-Nixon-Ford pilgrimages to China twenty years later. In both cases, the mellowing of relations took over two decades. But could not the United States learn from these experiences and shorten that period considerably in its relations with Vietnam? If one considers the case of Cuba, the prospects are not encouraging. But could it not be that the case of Vietnam is drastically different from those of the Soviet Union, China, and Cuba since there is currently no basic conflict between Vietnam and the United States, either in terms of security or economics? As a matter of factual consideration, it may seem that the two nations' interests are complementary and could be made mutually self-sustaining. It is on this basis of mutual interest that we should explore possible future United States-Vietnam relations.

The United States has been and remains a major power in the Pacific basin, with its interests in this area stretching from the Bering Straits to the Straits of Malacca. Other Pacific powers are the Soviet Union, China, and Japan. The intricate web of bilateral and multilateral relationships between and among these countries dictates a delicate balancing process. None of the major actors would be likely to accept any drastic change in the overall Pacific power configuration since such a move might disrupt the tense stability of the region. Besides Korea and Taiwan, the natural candidates for regional competition are the countries of Southeast Asia, Vietnam being one of these. In such a setting, what are Vietnam's interests? Stated simply, Vietnam needs to consolidate its national independence and sovereignty, and needs to safeguard its territorial integrity while obtaining economic and technical assistance to help its reconstruction and development efforts. Vietnam needs and wants the help of all four major Pacific powers. In particular, it needs the United States in two specific matters. First, Vietnam is very wary of the perennial hostility between itself and China. The hostility was papered over during the war years but has burst out in the open with both countries' rival claims over the Hoang Sa (Paracel) islands off the Vietnamese coast; these islands bear important natural fertilizer deposits and sit amidst promising pools of petroleum. Second, Vietnam has no desire to be a Soviet satellite, even though it has entered into a *de facto* alliance with the Soviet Union in its maneuver to protect itself against Chinese encroachments. Thus, a unified and communist Vietnam only perfunctorily objects to, and in fact may silently welcome, the United States' armed presence in the Pacific basin as long as that armed presence does not constitute a threat against Vietnam, which has been the case in the past. Furthermore, a unified Vietnam will have perhaps one of the most cosmopolitan experiences with foreign assistance. That experience seems to indicate that in certain matters of economic development, the technical expertise and the financial capabilities of the United States, Japan, and Europe may indeed be preferred to those of the Soviet Union, China, and other communist countries.

What is at stake? It may seem ironical that a unified communist Vietnam has changed little in the United States' national security interests, even though from Truman to Ford, from Acheson to Kissinger, much ado was made over the necessity of keeping part of Vietnam from becoming communist on the grounds of national security. If we are to review the official American rhetoric on Vietnam from 1949 to early April 1975, everything seemed to be at stake in Vietnam; nay, the very survival of "the Free World" was at stake. Today, no American politician of any standing speaks of "the Free World," and most ignore Vietnam as if it has evaporated into oblivion. Yet, even though forgetting Vietnam is a psychological necessity for the American public, it may not be in the long-term interests of the United States as a Pacific power. As has been the case with former enemy nations, the United States should be guided in its relations with Vietnam by the well-known axiom that a country has no permanent friends nor permanent enemies, only permanent interests. The interests of the United States in Asia are many, but an undeniable one is the desire not to see Soviet power in the Pacific basin substantially increased at a time when American presence in mainland Asia is reduced to one stronghold in South Korea. This has to be done simultaneously with the policies of normalizing relations with China, of protecting bilateral relations with Japan, and of fostering stable relations among countries of South and Southeast Asia. In all of these rational aims of the United States, the role of Vietnam in inter-Asian affairs is hard to ignore because it has the largest concentration of battle-tired armed forces which are both well armed and experienced in unconventional warfare. Alone, the People's Army of Vietnam, with manpower reserves that could be quickly activated, presents a formidable force in mainland Southeast Asia. Together with Soviet air and naval armaments, it does pose as a formidable military power vis-à-vis insular Southeast Asia as well.

What are the United States' concerns regarding the new Vietnam? Certainly the United States is no longer interested in changing the development of the Vietnamese political and economic systems the way it has been attempting since the late 1940s. The United States' interests could be defined, in terms of security, as the need to contain Soviet and Chinese expansionism into Southeast Asia, Vietnam being the pivotal actor here. In terms of economics, the United States may stand to gain from a benevolent interest in Vietnam's burgeoning capabilities as both an importer of sophisticated industrial hardware and a potential supplier of raw materials, including petroleum, to Japan. In terms of humanitarian development, a non-hostile United States will help millions of Vietnamese enjoy a less austere economic life, which may induce a more relaxed political life. It eventually may be possible to negotiate for the reuniting of separated families, allowing the repatriation of thousands of refugees now living wretchedly in the United States, as well as for the emigration of Vietnamese who have the inclination and the resources to leave Vietnam. Overall, it may be in the United States' interest not to isolate Vietnam and thus exacerbate the wounds of the past, but rather to not interfere in Vietnam's internal affairs while helping it foster its independence in relation to both China and the Soviet Union. Thus assured, Vietnam may not feel the necessity of fighting for its own survival through expansionist drives in Southeast Asia. One needs to be reminded that after thirty years of war, the Vietnamese do not relish fighting further wars.

The challenge is before the United States, to face and tackle creatively. Instead of the burdens of the past, it should look at the future possibilities. The first steps are difficult as a certain amount of refocusing of America's national values is in order. To put it bluntly, if the United States claims to stand for national self-determination and peaceful relations among nations, then it should be ready to accept the startlingly simple facts that the Vietnamese have fought for their national self-determination rather than against America's self-determination, and that it was the United States that brought the destruction of war to Vietnam rather than the reverse.

These considerations having been made, what steps could the two countries take to gradually come to amicable relations? The first step would be for the United States not to veto a unified Vietnam application for admission to the United Nations. Next, preparations should be taken toward the establishment of diplomatic relations between the two countries. [The U.S. now seems to be prepared to take these two steps. Editor's note.] To prepare for such relations, various negotiating teams dealing with substantive and technical issues should be established. Among the issues are questions arising out of war, such as the accounting of persons missing in action and reconstruction assistance; the lifting of trade and travel embargo against Vietnam by the United States; the status of American assets in Vietnam and the Vietnamese government's assets in the United States; the reunion of separated members of families either through repatriation of refugees with amnesty or emigration of persons living in Vietnam who want to join their relatives in the United States or elsewhere. After relations are established, then such questions as exchange of students and scholars, tourism and state visits could be envisioned. In all of this, the biggest stumbling block may not be any segment of the American public as much as some die-hard elements from the fallen Diem-Ky-Thieu regimes who have taken refuge in this country.

The items listed above are matters for the agenda. Whether and when they would ever come about remains a question which only the political leaders of this country can tackle. A leadership with vision and willingness to face issues is all that counts. Experience has shown us that the American public needs little persuasion to go along with changes of United States foreign policy when such modifications are shown to be in the national interest. The war between Vietnam and the United States has long been over. The task ahead is to heal the wounds of war. Such wounds cannot truly heal until both former belligerents have come to accept each other, if not in friendship, at least in tolerance. Both countries have nothing to lose but a nightmarish past.

Discussion

PORTER: The topic of our relationship with Vietnam is something on which I have been spending most of my time for the last few months, and this includes serving as an advisor to the House Committee on MIAs in the House of Representatives—a relationship that I have just terminated because of differences of view on how that Committee should proceed.

The main point I wanted to make is that the U.S. has the incredible opportunity under present circumstances to build a new relationship with Vietnam very, very quickly in terms of resource material after the long relationship of conflict and war. The reasons are three-fold.

First, the Vietnamese perhaps more than any other people, are incredibly open and internationalistic in their view of other countries —even those countries with which they have had the most unpleasant of relationships in the past. This was true under French colonialism when the communist leaders themselves were able to relate on a personal level to the French people very easily and very comfortably. They are, of course, men who in many cases have traveled widely throughout the world and are quite cosmopolitan in this respect, and they have a great appreciation for foreign cultures and for what other countries have to offer them. The Vietnamese are open to us, they have not closed their minds and hearts to Americans. They hope for a very constructive relationship with us. It was for this reason that they went so far to personalize the bombings of the 1969–1973 period; they were very much linked with Nixon himself. If you have seen the movie "Hearts and Minds," you will recall a scene of a man who has seen his home destroyed by American bombing, his daughter killed, and he is destroyed emotionally. He does not blame the American people; the blame is all on Nixon. This was done very deliberately so that it would be easier, once the war was over, for Vietnamese to have rapprochement with the American people under new leadership.

Second, the Vietnamese need our technical help and our capital; they need this very urgently. I think that it is now known that the U.S. had offered, or that Nixon had offered, as part of the Paris Agreement, a secret agreement that was negotiated before the signing but not actually formalized in a policy paper until February 1973—he pledged 3.25 billion dollars in postwar reconstruction. The interesting thing about this is that compared with Soviet aid over a five year period, this would be far more massive than anything the Soviets have offered them. If this pledge had been carried out, the U.S. today would be three times more important to the future economic development of

147

North Vietnam than the Soviet Union. This therefore indicates the importance of any American technical and capital assistance in Vietnam's future development.

Finally, the Vietnamese are very urgently interested in diversifying their foreign contacts, their economic and diplomatic contacts. The reason is obvious. The Vietnamese are in a geographic and political situation where the more support they have from the U.S., and the better relationships they have with the U.S., the more flexibility they will have in their relations with the Soviet Union and China.

U.S. policy has been marked during this period by a refusal to even contemplate in any real terms the future of relations with Vietnam. There has been not only a refusal to extend trade and diplomatic relations with Vietnam, but also a refusal to negotiate without preconditions on these two problems of MIAs and reconstruction aid—preconditions that naturally and logically go together and that must be resolved before we can enter into a new relationship. Of course, the U.S. has also vetoed Vietnamese membership in the U.N. There has been a very clear pattern of holding up any sort of relationship with Vietnam to an indefinite future dictated by Secretary Henry Kissinger.

This is where I differ quite strongly from Mr. Pike, and I do not think the Paris Agreement is totally irrelevant. It is a document that we now know was not made totally public at the time. It was a secret agreement between Premier Dong and President Nixon that was formalized in the February 1, 1973, letter by Nixon, which was recently revealed. The U.S. offered to give postwar construction aid without political conditions. This aid was to be negotiated in detail in the joint economic commission and was not to be subject to complete renegotiation in terms of the overall amount. Six months after this secret agreement, the U.S., after having reached a point of agreement, was ready to sign an economic agreement with the Democratic Republic of Vietnam. The U.S. then said they would not sign the agreement unless the Vietnamese agreed to a series of political conditions. One of the political conditions was a guarantee of a cease fire in Cambodia —a point not even relevant to the Paris Agreements.

This raises the question of whether the U.S. had any legal or moral basis for refusing to go ahead with postwar economic assistance to the DRV at that time. This in turn raises the question of whether or not America wants to return to the negotiating table with the DRV, to find out if there is any way that the U.S. can help in the reconstruction of Vietnam in an effort to heal the wounds of war there as well as the wounds of war here at home. The U.S. does, in fact, have interests politically as well as economically in a fruitful interchange with Vietnam. Vietnam will certainly be one of the two major regional powers in Southeast Asia. It is shortsighted as well as immoral for the U.S. to walk away after ten years of warfare in Vietnam and from any obligations to help rebuild that country.

McNALL: I think it is important to underscore one of the things Gary Porter has noted. With reference to the issues that need to be developed, the MIAs and the reparations for rebuilding North Vietnam, the point I want to make is that the U.S. did change its policy as a result of that war. We are still operating on the same strategic doctrine, we still have essentially the same foreign policy, although other governments may have begun to change their policy toward us. We are still living in the legacy of Richard Nixon. I do not think we want to make too much out of the secret agreement to provide $3.5 billion to North Vietnam. After all, Nixon also had a secret agreement with Thieu to provide American troops and support if the North overran the South. The point is that the U.S. is still operating with the same power base. Issues were created that were clearly false issues. The issue of the MIAs is a false issue. The issue of POWs is a false issue. If we continue to operate with that agenda, particularly in the Congress and Executive Branch, there will be no change in the relationship with Southeast Asia. Ten years after, we have only a vague national policy, a strategic doctrine, and really an emerging foreign policy.

GURTOV: I would like to address myself primarily to Scott McNall's paper, not only because I find it most provocative but also because I think it asks some of the fundamental questions that have to be answered. At least an attempt has to be made to answer them before one can begin to develop a coherent response to some of the issues posed in the other papers. The part of McNall's paper that I find most stimulating and at the same time most in need of an alternative view, which I will try to give, is his suggestion, in answer to the question, "Why did we get into Vietnam?" that one can find the answer in the attempt of American policy-makers to use Vietnam as a testing ground for certain strategic theories. I certainly agree that one of the persistent aspects of American policy in Vietnam, and for that matter in American foreign policy as a whole, has to do with the image problem that McNall talks about, and with the attempt to maintain that image whether in Southeast Asia or worldwide. But to speak about Vietnam as an attempt to apply and prove theory is certainly not, at the fundamental level, a satisfactory explanation of Vietnam. The question that is posed by his assertion, or his conclusion, or his hypothesis that the limited war theory has a lot to do with an understanding of Vietnam is, "Where does the theory come from?" Behind the theories, whether they happen to be theories of limited war, theories of containment, theories that talk about graduated escalation, massive retaliation, or the balance of power, is a fairly common set of values—political values—that sometimes assume the guise of moral values, or personal values. This set of values, which I would say constitute an American political culture, tend to have a particular inclination towards interventionism in the rest of the world. There is an ideology of American foreign policy and that ideology comes from particular roots in American life. If we want to understand why Vietnam, or for that matter why the Dominican Republic, or why Lebanon, or why the Congo, or why Angola, we need to understand ourselves. One has to look at the qualities of American culture, which is to say, such qualities of American politics and foreign policy as our aggressiveness, our competitiveness, our faith in technology to give an answer, our extraordinary sense of corporate loyalty and identity, our super-patriotism. McNall was right to identify questions of will, determination, and resolve—the kinds of words we read in the Pentagon Papers. All of those things are important, but one must think about them in the context in which they were written. In a negative way, one of my favorite documents in that collection is by Walt Rostow. It is a memorandum in which he reminds President Johnson about the American will and resolve that had previously been shown over Berlin and the Missile Crisis in Cuba. Rostow says that all we really need to do in Vietnam is to show that same resolve and steadfastness of purpose, and to act like the number one power that we really are. That is what I submit Vietnam really is about. The theories come from that set of attitudes and values. But it is not only a matter of saving the theory; it is a matter of saving the values, saving what in a larger sense came to be known as the American way of life. This is where one gets the translation into foreign policy ideology and then specific foreign policy tactics. Theories of limited war do not explain why Vietnam happened. They explain the different modes of American participation and of American tactics in Vietnam. I think that is a distinction of real substance and not merely one of semantics.

PIKE: I have four points that seem to be worth making, although in no particular order and perhaps with no equality of significance. From the people I have heard speak, there seems to be a fairly general desire for an improvement of U.S.-Vietnamese relations. I think this is also true of the world in which I live in Washington, D.C. I have not personally encountered anybody who is flatly and hawkishly opposed to a normalization of relations. I am sure there are such people. But these are not among the professional foreign policy community people with whom I deal. Further, there is a general sense of parity on both sides—Vietnamese and American—and a feeling that there will be a gradual movement toward normalization. This is a measured effort on both sides; that is, there have been gestures made on both sides. The gestures have been limited and modest, but a trend is in this direction.

It is simply a question of when and at what pace the normalization is going to proceed. (The same is true, of course, with regards to Chinese-American relations. No one can really anticipate the pace here either, especially not in 1976. Probably after the elections in this country there will be some clarification.) One thing we must all keep in mind is that public statements by North Vietnamese officials, like public statements by American officials and public statements by all officials, contain a certain "necessary" verbiage. I have come to the conclusion that in politics and religion, because of this "necessary" verbiage, it is dangerous to try to build a case from, or to cite as evidence a single sentence extracted from an official communiqué. The thrust of North Vietnamese policy, both in what is said and in behavior, is relatively clear and unambiguous now. First, the North Vietnamese want to secure economic assistance from whatever source they can. Second, they want to pursue what they call independent foreign policy with respect to the Soviet Union and China. And finally, they want to normalize relations with the United States. All of their behavior and all of their statements, it seems to me, are quite consistent with this.

I had a little trouble understanding Scott McNall's paper, which I felt was very good and provocative. Mr. McNall appears to believe that the basic reason the U.S. went into Vietnam was to prove that we would fight a nuclear war. I think that this was a factor—and I am not meaning to characterize his presentation as a suggestion that this is the only reason—but my experience as an observer on the spot in Vietnam over the years was that the reasons the U.S. was there, the rationale, the objectives, the goals, and so on, were developmental. The reasons were changing, they were fads. The original impetus was not the middle impetus, the late impetus or the final impetus. There are probably a dozen or so of these shifts of impetus that future historians will eventually isolate. Also, both the Munich syndrome and the Korean experience contributed to the reasons why the U.S. went in. There was also the notion that if you do not stop aggression now, you have to stop it later at a higher cost. That was the force at the beginning. For a period the impetus was to contain China, or at least the perceived expansionism of China. That also evaporated. China was considered benign, or inward-turning after the Cultural Revolution, certainly not a threat or justification of American involvement. The ideological balance of power was also a fairly strong notion for a period, among many policy thinkers in the government—in and out of Vietnam. After 1968, I would say the chief objective of America in Vietnam was to get out; we were in effect fighting to get out of the situation. So the objectives, the goals, the rationale, changed over the years; one reason simply cannot be specified. I am not suggesting that Mr. McNall is saying this; I am simply trying to demonstrate that this thesis is relevant at the point where it runs through earlier policy. Although in the final line of his paper, I am not sure how Mr. McNall views credibility. Credibility is not machismo. I think it becomes that sometimes, because there is ego involvement by leaders of policy. What is important in international relations is constancy of intent and reliability of purpose. Nations dealing with other nations want to see this consistency in pursuit of national interest. They want to know what they can expect and what they can anticipate from other countries. That is why traditionally there was such a premium placed on the detailed language of official documents such as treaties. Nations and individuals, I think, are very much like children in their relationships with their parents. Children above all want to know what they can and cannot expect from their parents, how their parents are going to behave. They want the parent to be consistent and not forever changing and reversing. That is what the sense of credibility is, and that is why one cannot operate in the international arena without it. One country has to know what to expect from other countries, how other countries are going to behave, what the other countries can be depended on to do. Credibility is a necessary ingredient.

One final point to underscore what Don Weatherbee said earlier, which is a hot subject in Washington in both academic and government circles right now. That is this notion of (this is not his language, it is mine) the "polarization of Southeast Asia." Over the next ten years what we are going to see are two poles, Jakarta and Hanoi, and a polarization of all the countries in between. This is now being considered as a thesis. I do not know of anyone who is saying that this absolutely will come about, but it is one thing being discussed in and out of government circles, and it is probably something you will hear a great deal about in the future.

MEISNER: Jayne Werner amazed me by talking about the Portuguese back in the old days not getting kicked out of Africa (which is not what people are talking about today) but when it all started. She also referred to the kind of historical context of anti-colonialism in which the Vietnam and other Indochina situations have been set. The paper by Phan Thieu Chau I consider to be a very cautious but positive re-evaluation of a historical stance toward the events in Vietnam by a Vietnamese person who was a significant participant for a period of time. It is a very welcomed kind of thing to see happening, and I think it indicates a shift that a number of Vietnamese people must be going through. I was going to talk about some of the same issues but will now leave it aside. All of them involve historical learning, and I think people know that history, or the interpretation of history itself is a political event. In a country like the U.S., even in the field of Asian politics, it has been very significant. The interpretation of events in China during the 1940s, which came to be known as the "loss of China," became the

American politics of the 1950s, and these in turn were somewhat transformed and ended up in the liberal policies of the 1960s. Now, do we have any historical learning going on today, or do we have the same kind of interpretation of history, which is to say, do we think that there has been a "loss of Vietnam"?

You recall President Ford saying shortly after the war in South Vietnam ended that we should not talk about what had happened because we understand that and we should now go on. Let's not talk about the history of it. It is not limited to Republicans, by the way. I remember one of my first political experiences being that of attending a banquet for the Americans for Democratic Action. It was right after the Bay of Pigs and a historian there, his name was Arthur Schlesinger, Jr., was giving a banquet speech in which he said, "You know, we really should not worry about this Bay of Pigs invasion and what it means because in the long course of the writing of history they will not treat it as more than a mere ripple. Let's not worry about it." I remember hearing him say that. Then there was Mildred Colby's recent statement in *Time* magazine when she was asked if war ended in defeat for the U.S. and Europe, and was there any sense in which the U.S. succeeded in Vietnam. Colby said, "Well, the military equation did not work, but we won the people's war. By 1972 and 1975, there were not any true guerrillas in Vietnam. The people were all on the government's side. The communist victory in Vietnam was no more a result of a guerrilla war than was the Nazi victory in France or Norway." There is this desperate attempt to interpret—a climactic and desperate false interpretation. Then there also is a one-sided or unbalanced interpretation of the present; a good example is the question of relations between Thailand and its neighboring states. Here one can see the current idea that neighboring states are centers for promoting insurgency inside Thailand, an idea that ignores the constant use of Thai forces in various secret guises within the other Indochinese states during the war that was just concluded.

The possibility of normalization of relations between ourselves and the Indochinese people and the possibility of aid for reconstruction in Vietnam—there are tendencies among some people to blame American public opinion as a kind of villain in this situation. This is a difficult and very peculiar charge to make for a number of reasons. First, there was no great celebration in government circles of the climactic, momentous acts of public opinion during the complex anti-war movement. It is an amazingly powerful force. As we were reminded before, public opinion was seen in part as a weapon of war, of something that would have to be controlled in order to keep fighting a war like the Vietnam War. Second, it is quite true that a number of dominant ideologies that have served to justify and underline American involvement abroad—such as the benevolent internationalism coming out of World War II, which we now know as interventionism or perhaps imperialism or other such things—are now somewhat discredited. The concept of monolithic anti-communism that has existed in the past is certainly on shaky ground today. That brand of patriotic valor that is associated with war movies, the World War II John Wayne image, was transmuted by the disillusionment of the American army in Vietnam into a kind of patriotic gore, if I may paraphrase from Edmund Wilson and the Maryland State anthem. Then finally, the bloodless, bureaucratic ideology of national security also has its troubles, although judging from today it is still a current form of thought. But people have their own reasons for being reluctant to aid Vietnam. One of those mentioned is the economic problem in the U.S. People should remember in discussing this that one of the reasons, perhaps a very large reason, for the economic problems of the U.S. was the distortion of the U.S. economy based on carrying out American military and other policies in Indochina over a substantial period of time. There is also a connection between people's economic difficulties here and what has just concluded overseas. It is also quite relevant for us, as scholars, to recognize the fact that a generation of experts in various disciplines has systematically misled the American people about the meanings and facts and tendencies of the long-desirable development of that region, and the underlying kinds of forces that were at work there. Many people are still reluctant today to identify with the substance of change in Southeast Asia, although I think this conference and a number of the papers have been the beginning of the correction of that kind of thing. But if you insist that people are at fault in not understanding, you have to examine the roots of popular misunderstanding. Finally, if I could borrow a quote from Brecht paraphrasing his short poem that, "if the government is not satisfied with what the people are doing, then it should elect itself a new people"—this is, I think, a reasonable comment, and so let me end there.

WEATHERBEE: We should not simply think in terms of military/political categories. Perhaps one of the greatest impacts on the internal evolution of the non-communist states in Southeast Asia will come if the communist states of Southeast Asia are able to demonstrate dynamic progress in economic modernization and development in environment analogous to that in non-communist Southeast Asia. It is precisely these areas that are still plagued by the problems of stagnation, lack of progress, corruption, and so on. In a sense, this demonstration and the possible effect of future demonstrations in terms of the reordering of a modern society, may have a greater impact than any possible political or military threat.

WINN: I would like to direct my statements primarily to the very interesting presentation from our representative from Washington,

Douglas Pike. He mentioned that when one returns to Washington, one realizes that one's perspective isn't important, that it has to be played down. My counter is that one's perspective is on a continuum of specialty versus general analysis. I liked Mr. McNall's strategic perspective, not that I think the U.S. was fighting, or that there was a connection with, a nuclear confrontation in Vietnam, but that there was a distance in terms of the analysis of the expertise. Instead of taking the perspective of the people, land tenure, or other specific data that have been given, there was instead a general tendency towards "backroom" analysis, toward the "darkroom" approach, toward the "Let's divide Korea according to the 38th parallel because it looks good on the map" approach. This is a danger that can arise from people arguing that one should not worry so much about the specific detail of a country in which one is involved—one should see things in more of a global perspective. I think that is a game of theoretical approach, which has been used disastrously in Vietnam. The two should be balanced.

Secondly, with regard to Mr. Porter's comments and regarding tomorrow's discussion on Korea, I think that the State Department, in its new relationships or potential relationships with Vietnam and North Korea, should make overtures; it should not be bound by such statements as I heard in discussion at the State Department last week wherein someone said that unless Russia and China talk to South Korea, the U.S. will not talk to North Korea. This is like sitting and waiting for Godot; this is an opaque perspective. I think the U.S. can talk in secret, and certainly we can talk openly. The Paris Peace Agreement went down in flames through mutual duplicity, which brings in the question of the values of treaties, for that matter. But this is not the basis for a new relationship with Vietnam. We have to say that this is a new country and we must have some type of economic relationship, not 3.2 billion dollars; but to have the kind of non-communicative relationship we have had with North Korea would be a major error. My field is international relations and there are many theories, but one is that if you do not communicate, you can only end up with a conflict situation. The reverse side of this is that communication brings both cooperation and conflict, but at least that is an advance.

Finally, and I think most significantly, Mr. Pike made four points regarding United States policy in terms of its perspective toward Asia. He said, in short, that we are first interested in détente and peaceful coexistence; second, flash points; third, resource allocation; and, fourth, non-proliferation. I think there is a fifth point that should be brought up, and that is the question of human welfare, freedom, and the rights of people throughout the world. We have made some reference to the fact that there is a link between domestic and international affairs; I think that this could be very strongly put forward. Our policy regarding Korea is going to be linked to American reaction to oppression in that country. Our foreign policy is linked to domestic affairs. This is a fifth area of State Department emphasis that should be further amplified.

PIKE: When I listed Salt flash points, the economic resources and nuclear proliferation, I was not trying to put a value judgment on them and exclude human rights, and there is an office for this at the State Department. Every policy paper has a consideration of the human rights of people, and so on. I simply listed these as being the points with which the principles of the government are overwhelmingly concerned in their day-to-day work. If one attends to those four points, one is very busy, and one really cannot devote oneself in much detail to anything beyond this. I am not saying that it ought to be that way. In that sense, I was just being rhetorical. That's the way it is. Human rights themselves have become an "in" subject, almost fashionable; unfortunately, in government now ecology is "out" and human rights are "in." It is unfortunate that serious subjects like these have acquired a kind of "chicness." It hurts them in the long run. For the moment, the fact is that human rights is a very central issue, that it permeates all of these. It is certainly true for the Salt and détente issue.

CARRIER: The question I have is addressed to Professor Oliver. Gareth Porter mentioned that the issues in Vietnam included such things as who owned land, who was landless, questions of the agrarian relationship with landlords; the other question was of national independence. Now, Syngman Rhee was widely acclaimed in 1945, and this was obviously a staged kind of acclaim, or it may have been that he misrepresented himself or others misrepresented him as an indication that this was a person who stood for Korean independence, social revolution and the adjustment of all colonial issues that had been raised over many years of Japanese occupation. Furthermore, this was not a defeated power, but a liberated Korea. I would, therefore, like to ask this question: these political parties in South Korea—who did they represent? Certainly not the nation, certainly not the masses of people. How could they, without any prior political existence, or any activities in the political arena, claim that they represented the people? And certainly Syngman Rhee could not make such a claim, then or afterwards. In other words, if we are going to reassess the American role in Asian politics, we are going to have to start dealing with the fundamental questions that Professor Meisner and others have raised —issues that require some kind of class analysis.

OLIVER: I would like to respond in length, but I will try to be abbreviated. How do we know whether President Rhee represented the Korean people then or afterwards, Professor Carrier asks. We have one measure of the afterwards, because there were four presidential elections. He carried them overwhelmingly, or with what we would call a "landslide," and in every one of these elections the United Nations' observation team supervised and organized. It was the only nation in the world that had such supervision and observation. After every election the United Nations' Commission reported to the U.N. that the elections were fairly conducted. Several members of the U.N. Commission told me personally that the elections were much more fairly conducted in Korea than elections that were conducted in their own countries. Syngman Rhee did get overwhelming support. As to the situation in 1945, actually Syngman Rhee had been elected the President of the Republic in exile in 1919, after the 1919 Mansei Revolution. His name was widely known in Korea and very few others were. I would like to agree with Professor Carrier. I think there was a great deal of pro-communist sentiment in South Korea in the fall of 1945. And in the winter of 1945–46. If it had not been for the activities of Syngman Rhee, his radio speeches, and his travels down through the peninsula, Koreans in the South might well have shifted towards a strong pro-communist sentiment. The reasons are rather obvious. After Korea was taken over by Japan in 1910, England had no interest in maintaining Korean independence. The treaty with Japan in 1903 precluded any notion such as that. The United States was indifferent to helping the Koreans, despite the friendship Rhee had with Woodrow Wilson and despite Wilson's declaration of the right of the people to self-government. The Koreans could not get Wilson or the State Department interested in Korean independence in 1919 or 1920. China was too beset with its own problems to have much interest in helping Korea at that stage. But following the 1917 revolution in Russia, there was a good bit of assistance from the Soviet communist regime for the Korean population in its efforts to resist the Japanese. So the Koreans, who moved into Manchuria and then into Siberia, were treated very well and allowed to retain their own language schools and were given assistance in organizing their own communities. When the Korean guerrillas wished to attack the Japanese, they received inspiration, guidance, assistance, and training from the Soviet Union. There was every reason why the people of Korea, both North and South, would have an actual tendency to be sympathetic toward Russian communism. There was a large amount of such sympathy and I think R. Scalapino's and C. Lee's book on *Communism in Korea* offers abundant evidence to the fact that there was a lot of pro-communist sentiment there.

Now, in regards to Syngman Rhee, we have had a reference to the fact that it depends on one's perspective, where one stands on an issue. When a person goes back to Washington, he finds a different perspective than the one he had out in the field. I found this illustrated over and over again in my experiences with the Koreans working in Washington, D.C.; it was easy to absorb the kind of attitude that was prevalent there. I would go to Seoul and find an entirely different attitude prevalent there, among Americans as well as among Koreans. Where one stands in the world depends on and very considerably affects one's judgment of events. Syngman Rhee was not in Korea during this period when a lot of pro-Russian, pro-communist sentiment was developing. He was in Washington, and before that in Hawaii. He was outside where he could observe what was happening in the world. He was able to bring back an anti-communist foundation, based on his own principled observation of what was going on. During that winter of 1945–46, by educating the Korean people Rhee very skillfully put forth the proposition that their future independence did not lie in their acceptance of a communist form of government.

RHEE: I'd like to reply to Mr. Carrier's questions about Syngman Rhee. In the beginning—that would be from 1945 at least up to 1950 —there was no question that Syngman Rhee was still a popular person in South Korea. When one talks about the decline of his legitimacy in South Korea, that would be after 1950. But even that would be too early. I think the major decline of his political legitimacy started somewhere around the late 1950s. So I would disagree with the view that when Rhee returned from Korea after liberation that he was not representing anybody.

OLIVER: Thank you for that observation. I'll add one little bit. Two or three reasons are involved with the decline of the popularity of Syngman Rhee in the late 1950s, say from 1950 on. He stayed in office too long; he was too old—he had an opposition. Another major factor was that the economic conditions in South Korea were absolutely dreadful during the 1950s. True, we sent millions of dollars worth of American aid, but there were three billion dollars worth of damages resulting from the war. Things were terribly distraught and disrupted. At the same time, President Rhee and his administration were building up the educational facilities remarkably quickly. Well, I think it is practically a truism that you can't take youngsters out of rice-paddy ignorance and limitation, give them a high school or college education, and then not have any jobs for them, without creating a vast amount of frustration and disruption, disappointment and rebellion. And that's what happened in Korea, in my judgment.

PORTER: The fact that Syngman Rhee was not the man in 1945 who represented the landlords, for example, and who was not the man who represented collaboration with foreign enemies, does not necessarily mean that there was not entente between certain social forces. In the case of Vietnam, from 1946 to 1954, it was Bao Dai who represented the collaborationist element in Vietnamese society, who represented the large landlord elements of Cochin China, who gathered around the French presence in Cochin China. In the history of both of these countries, you have a colonial period, in which many of the landed and wealthy elements in society had to make a choice—whether they would come together with people who had formerly been anti-communists or not. The anti-communists also may not have been pro-colonialists in the past, but may have had anti-colonialist sentiments; they also had to make a choice. In the case of Diem, he made a choice to join forces with the U.S. and with the most repressive elements of society against the communists. And this was sort of the basic political line of development from 1954 on.

PIKE: I see the role of human rights, civil rights, and foreign policy as pretty much a straightforward continuation in a somewhat different language of an almost traditional foreign policy debate in the U.S., which is traceable back to the Spanish-American War and the Monroe Doctrine, the so-called realist school versus the idealist school. I don't think you can dogmatically say the realist school is right, or that the idealistic school is right. It is like determinism, and a lot of other philosophic questions. You can have strong opinions, as people indeed do, but you can't in all honesty simply objectively state that you are right and the other school is wrong.

RHEE: I never mentioned this dichotomous school of realism and idealism. In fact, on these two things you cannot make distinctions of black and white. They spill onto each other. We've been blasting away at the Soviet Union and the communist bloc states with "Voice of America" propaganda and many other broadcasts and so on. Are we, in doing this, just aiming at an idealistic policy? Or are we, by attacking the Soviets' lack of human rights and civil liberties, somehow attempting to create a political situation in the Soviet Union?

   That idealistic policy had rather idealistic edges in it. What was the value of American propagandistic policies against the Soviet Union's lack of human rights and civil liberties and the totalitarian nature of the state? Was it idealism or realism? It seems to me that was the height of realistic foreign policy, by attacking the most vulnerable part of the Soviet Union. Isn't this why Solzhenitsyn has become a major issue—not because we are in favor of his position so much, but because he is political dynamite we could exploit?

AUDIENCE: I would like to see something concrete, to have you show another side of the nations' relations in the postwar relationship between Vietnam and America.

PIKE: I see on both sides a desire to divide the future of our relationship into two stages. One is a "let the dust settle" stage. During this interim period, neither side does anything to freeze relations as American-Chinese relations were frozen after the Korean War. After a period, an indeterminable period, both sides will begin to move towards so-called normalization of relations. I think this is moving faster than I expected, than most people would have expected, a year ago. There have been measured gestures on both sides; quite limited, quite guarded, quite cautious. There is no sense of urgency, I would argue, on either side. This is my perception. The North Vietnamese make certain gestures, but they are quite measured. On the American side, the overriding syndrome is the "gone with the wind" syndrome. It is a kind of general unwillingness on the part of Americans—including official Americans—to address themselves to Vietnam. This is a nation-wide phenomenon. It is, perhaps, understandable. It is temporary in any case, as it is going to burn itself out.

For example, at the fall of South Vietnam, I expected that we would go through a terrible period in the United States of recrimination and accusations. I was afraid of this and I did not want it to happen, but I was reasonably sure it would happen. The way the war was closed foreclosed that possibility. Actually, the American-Vietnamese relationship is in much better shape than we had any reason to expect it to be a year ago.

WEATHERBEE: I think it depends on the vantage point from which one is viewing the question of American-North Vietnamese relations. People on the panel have been involved in Southeast Asian studies and Vietnamese studies. But one of the arguments against the kind of allocation of resources the United States made in Vietnam over the years was that really the United States did not have the vital interests on the mainland of Southeast Asia. That was a malappropriation of our resources. In a sense now, we are saying that's true, that Vietnam is no longer that important. It has been, in a sense, relegated to a kind of back burner. It is more than just the "gone with the wind" syndrome. We have turned to other things. We have turned to Angola. We have turned to détente. For the great majority of Americans, Vietnam is no longer an important issue. For the people who have been involved and committed, it is in the aftermath. But, for most people, Vietnam is not the kind of issue any more to generate a public demand for quick normalization of relations.

WERNER: I think it is pretty clear that the Vietnamese want to normalize relations with us much more than we want to normalize relations with them. I think the record on that over the past nine months or so is very clear. The Vietnamese have stated that they want to normalize relations with us.

PIKE: So have we.

WERNER: In what context? The North Vietnamese have taken very concrete steps in opening up the door to American investment and making contacts with American banking interests, showing that they would certainly like to pursue this question as soon as possible. Further, I think we need to recognize that the North Vietnamese have made substantial gestures on the MIA question, that they have indicated recently their willingness to provide more information.

PORTER: There is a lot of obscuration going on here. I would like to comment on the point of who is obstructing a new relationship—Vietnam or the United States. Even the most hawkish Congressman in the House of Representatives, G. V. "Sonny" Montgomery, who is the chairman of the Select Committee, is now saying privately—I don't think it is unfair to reflect his private attitude on this point—that the State Department is still pretending there's a war going on. They are still carrying on the war by other means. This committee has to play a part in dragging the U.S., kicking and screaming, into a new era in Southeast Asia. The fact is that Kissinger does seem to feel that he has a personal political interest in holding off the Vietnamese at arm's length, trying to prevent trade from taking place between the two countries. The Vietnamese are perfectly capable of getting along with the United States. In fact, Montgomery was in Hanoi and talked to the Vietnamese, and found out that they are really not such ogres after all —he wonders why it was necessary to have a war with them.

The Vietnamese made it very clear that they do want trade. It is one of the main points they emphasized in Paris when they met with the MIA Committee there. They feel strongly that the U.S. policy of forbidding any trade with Vietnam is an act of hostility that has no rhyme or reason either in American or Vietnamese interests. American companies have talked to the Vietnamese and they are ready to go to the stage of making agreements on trade. The only thing that stands in the way of this is the trade embargo imposed by the United States government. The United States government is telling U.S. businessmen that their assets in South Vietnam have been nationalized. This is not, in fact, true. The South Vietnamese authorities have not taken steps to confiscate American businesses with assets in Saigon. So, there is a continuing policy here of trying to do everything possible to discourage normal relations between the two countries.

Also, the Vietnamese have offered to negotiate without conditions on the two outstanding problems of MIAs and reconstruction aid. They have made it clear that they are flexible on these negotiations. They are not tied to the figure of $3.25 billion. Deputy Premier Prime Minister Phom Yin told the committee that we always retain our principles, but we are always realists. He understands that there is no way they will get that much money. The Vietnamese also point out that it is more important to have the principles of the United States' willingness to do something to help heal the wounds of our war in Vietnam than how much money they get. And we should realize that the Executive has the power to begin trade with Vietnam immediately, whenever they want.

PIKE: No, there are statutory regulations. There definitely are.

PORTER: No, there are not.

SIMON: I think it is noteworthy that this panel represents virtually all shades of the political spectrum on U.S. policy towards Southeast Asia. Two or three years ago it would have been highly unlikely that this panel could have convened.

PORTER: Do you think we are moving to the left or the right, though?

SIMON: Well, actually, that's the end of my complimentary statement; now comes the thrust. There are those who believe that the United States should be engaged in expurgating its past sins in terms of its future foreign policy. Others are less concerned about our past sins than in trying to determine what America's new strategic and foreign political relationships should be in Asia. Unfortunately, these two viewpoints have yet to meet in any meaningful dialogue.

Part II

U.S. POLICY: WHITHER KOREA?

United States Policy toward Korea in the Shadow of Vietnam: A Reassessment

Gregory Henderson

During four hundred years of expanded world contact, world politics has been dominated by Europe, by Europe's ideas of arms and power politics and confrontation, by its entrancement with the individual, and by its theories of wealth and materialism as prime movers of men.

Now this domination is receding, probably permanently. Great Britain, Europe's leader in world expansion and domination, has become quietly but with startling suddenness and permanence, a backwater. Europe's colonies have been finally, and historically with fair rapidity, divested. New independent governments, all outside Europe, have proliferated and come to dominate the United Nations.

Through world trade, investment, and diplomatic relations, through Christianity, democracy, and Marxism, ideas and values associated with Europe continue some hold even after colonialism's formal end. Yet one notices that this hold also is ebbing. Much of Asia practices a defiant self-sufficiency with confined roles for international investment and modest roles for trade. Marxism has given way to Maoism and its stepson, Kimism. Democracy has given way to Indiraism, Marcosism, and Parkism. Christianity almost has been extinguished on the East Asian continent, flourishing only on its periphery. In its place rises strongly centralized, overwhelmingly ideological, mass concensual politics. From its Asian capitals, this then spreads to the Third World; the U.N. reflects these trends.

What we see is the drift of the world's political and perhaps ideological center away from Europe towards Asia. The pace is unrushed: China is, as usual, unhurried. But the trend and the direction seem unmistakable, while not often articulately recognized.

The Maoist portions of these trends we once feared and warred to halt their fancied expansion. Now an in-between stage has been reached. They are more accepted by us and most Asians; but whereas some states we created or supported remain hostile, we still cling to

165

a politics of confrontation otherwise outworn and persevere in our archaic vision of a world of security and military terms. In the wake of America's last two wars, both in East Asia, these terms exercise a fatal fascination and enchainment for American policy, especially in Korea. This enchainment contributes to delaying the communication, mutual recognition, and trade that would presage a much increased prosperity —perhaps especially in Northeast and Southeast Asia. It also distorts and largely determines the new forms of political and social expression which have arisen outside the socialist world in Asia, erecting governments of sham populism behind which stand rigid militarist elites and dangerous power and wealth discrepancies. The tensions then arising threaten Asian and world peace, impeding the emergence of a safer, better-communicating world.

Nowhere is the enchainment of militarist policies now so great as in Korea. The effect of Vietnam's fall has been, catastrophically, to escalate policy *machismo* in armament, in non-compromise, in dialogue breakdown, in hostility, in repression. South Korea leads in these but Washington seems unreluctant to follow. Nowhere does the militarization of foreign policy contribute more to a slowing of necessary adjustments and greater four-power communication. The origin and victim of these trends continues to be the division of Korea; it is the chief knot to be cut in moving toward a better post-Vietnam Asia. Korea is thus a policy keystone in the part of the world toward which world politics now shifts: it has been important; it now becomes more so. Change in our policies there is particularly long overdue.

The United States stands before history as the principal co-author of the division of Korea—a responsibility we Americans have for no other of the world's dozen divided nations.[1] We drew the line of demarcation not merely for the surrender of Japanese forces but between the occupation zones, however temporarily that division was expected to last. We drew it without the Koreans' knowledge, support, pressure, or advice. We drew it in the face of expert warnings that predictably the Soviet Union might exploit such a "temporary" line for permanent purposes.[2]

The consequences have been even more horrendous than anyone could then have foreseen, not only for the Koreans but also for the security and development of Northeast Asia and for world peace. The Korean War has not exorcised these dangers. Nor have the short-lived North-South talks; both sides share responsibility for their breakdown. The hostilities that have been implanted fester and eat into the political fabric of the entire region, corroding the possibility of compromise; confrontatory alliances acidulate the surrounding area. The arms race inexorably increases the explosive charge behind these hatreds. Relations between the allies of the two antagonists are threatened. In trying to get along better, the major powers are being constantly pulled at by their Korean clients, North and South, each time with the message: "Don't compromise, stand with us, be more hostile." Mounting trade, expanding diplomatic relations with both Koreas, and swelling propaganda edge Korea's hostilities outward from Northeast Asia into the world arena.

Gradual change in our Korean policies offers the key. Changed policies can stop the current slide toward heightened tension and possible hostilities and can open a path toward the relaxation of tension in the direction of eventual unification. The key lies in a correct reordering of our regional priorities. Our first objectives should be the security, the peace, and the expanding interstate communications and economic development of the Northeast Asian area—and hopefully later the whole East Asian area. It is an area of great promise, to which we belong historically as well as through our role in World War II, and also through our large trading and Alaskan stakes. We also still seek our classic objective of an East Asia not dominated by a single power.

Our Korean policies must contribute to, not detract from, these objectives. Faced with outright communist aggression in 1950, policies to defeat that aggression in alliance with the Republic of Korea (ROK) were essential to basic U.S. regional aims. Twenty-five years later we faced a changed situation. Our Korean alliance, instead of contributing to, is beginning to detract from peace and more open communications in East Asia. Also, in long-range terms, a united, independent Korea would counterpose some fifty million energetic Koreans and a considerable industrial plant against Asian domination by a single power, would remove a major source of tension, and would improve interchange and communications. A divided, hostile Korea is not only an irritant that aggravates regional instability; it is also a less effective block to great-power domination to which the peninsula might even fall eventual prey.

A unified, independent Korea should not, as it is currently, be abandoned by our policies; Korea is very deeply in the interests of the United States and its overall Asian policy, and should be an important American long-term commitment. Any communist aggression should reinvoke our defense treaty and our determination to defend South Korea. In all other respects, however, our interest in regional security and the prevention of great-power domination should have priority over our alliance with South Korea.

This is not how we have been acting; it does tell us much about how we could act. Our present concentration on military aid increases tension, encourages repression and intolerance in the South—and by reaction in the North—and discourages communication between the Koreas. This emphasis on military aid should be phased out and replaced by increasing communication among the four powers to limit arms to each Korea through reinvoking Paragraph II.A.d. of the Armistice Agreement, which bars the introduction of new armaments. We should also emphasize common objectives of tension-reduction and neutralization in the peninsula by, among other things, the application to Korea of the "two-Germanies" policies. Communication among the four powers about Korea is the one force capable of propelling the two Koreas somewhat toward each other. Such policies are likely to induce compromise into Korean positions, much as our present policies induce intolerance and alienation. The ultimate objective of our Korean policies is clear and we should begin forthrightly to state it: a four-power guarantee of the neutrality, unity, and independence of the Korean peninsula.

II.

The period since the breakdown of the North-South talks (at least since early in 1974) has seen growing doubts regarding the importance and the feasibility of unification. These doubts are probably of South Korean origin, but they have proved insidiously infectious abroad: bureaucracies are easily convinced to support the status quo and to pursue the paths of least trouble and resistance. Continued division would seem in the short run to be that path, both Koreas now being viable states, stronger than three-quarters of the present U.N. membership, and far more hostile toward each other than are the four major powers. Unification soon—within the context of current regimes, current propaganda and the current lack of popular communication—seems most unlikely.[3]

Yet policies in favor of unification have, for the long run, far more persuasive grounds. For Koreans, the case for unification is well known. The peninsula has the greatest ethnic, linguistic, and historical homogeneity and unity of all the divided nations, and there is a popular desire, which is revealed by polls and in the politics of both states, to have unification. This popular desire appears to be much more widespread on both sides in Korea than is manifest in their present governments, or than it has been in almost any other sundered country, such as Germany, India-Pakistan, Pakistan-Bangladesh, Palestine, Ireland, Cyprus, or even China-Taiwan, Vietnam, and Mongolia, in whose riven parts the past experience of unity is briefer than in Korea. Such grounds cannot be dismissed as "sentimental"; they are a people's birthright, an important political fact. They are given more cogency by Korea's unique emplacement within the cross-fire of the four great powers. Korea's independent unification, unlike Germany's or Vietnam's, would threaten none of its neighbors, particularly under a unification of the Austrian type with the declaration of permanent neutrality.

Equally cogent is that a divided Korea has been, is, and for years will continue to be a threat to world peace. If Korea is *not* united, one or another of the far stronger surrounding states, under circumstances not visible today, may reduce or destroy Korean independence or its economic or political actuality. Koreans worry far more about such long-range threats than we do, and with reason, because present-day power balances will change, as all such balances have changed. We cannot be sure what new balance or imbalance of powers will appear. A perfectly conceivable scenario is one in which Japan, facing a far stronger China or a militant U.S.S.R. in the Far East in the next generation, and possibly with weakened economic and American support, might feel that greater control of South Korea would be one of the few steps between itself and destruction. Japan felt this way about Korea between 1884 and 1910 and acted accordingly. Both Koreas would be likely to read in any such threat the necessity for unification. This scenario is not, of course, in any way a prediction, nor an ascription to Japan of any such present intention; it is merely a conceivability in a world in which much that has occurred, including events in Korea and Japan, has been beyond prediction over a twenty year period.

It is less often observed that different but equally strong arguments commend Korea unification to the longer-term interests of the four great powers and also separately to the United States. It is strongly in the interests of all the major powers to have a stable Northeast Asia of Eastern Siberia, Manchuria, Korea, Japan and Alaska, open to inter-communications of all sorts, for the region has elements of a rapidly developing, exceedingly productive economic (but not political) unit or area.

The end of the Korean division would likewise remove a major threat to regional and world peace. All the great powers want to lower their risks and their military expenses in this area, especially in Korea, where expense and risk have alike been great.

To be sure, there are difficulties to a four-power concert on Korean unification. The fall of Vietnam has contributed to one difficulty by strengthening Peking's support for Kim Il-sung and the North as the only legitimate heir to a unification that Peking apparently now perceives as feasible under the Democratic People's Republic of Korea (DPRK). It is vital that the United States help mitigate these fears less through the provision of arms than by the encouragement of a viable political system that will give Koreans something to fight *for* rather than *against*; for only thus can the ghost of the Korea-Vietnam parallel be laid. Another difficulty may be Japan, which has been rather evasive on the subject of unification. Current Japanese policy strongly supports the defense of South Korea. Many Japanese appear grateful for a South Korean buffer, which they can more easily manipulate than they could a united Korean state. Some Japanese, on the other hand, would like to be midwife to a more neutralist Korean unity. Japanese policy thus seems unconcerted; it would be unlikely to oppose strongly the unification efforts made by any of the other three great powers, and could well cooperate with them. American understanding or encouragement of Japanese movements toward the recognition of the two Koreas, which thereby encourages a neutralist approach on the part of Japan, would be helpful. Through their recognition of the South, and persuasive diplomacy, the U.S.S.R. and even Peking could gradually be edged toward similar more neutralist and pro-unification positions.

On balance, longer-range policy support for greater four-power neutrality and support for unification would be wise—and far from impossible or impractical—in the next generation. Such a policy can be worked on and toward, just as we work on many other policies which ultimately may or may not succeed. Compared to the solutions to other current problems such as the population-food equation of South Asia, the harmonious and rapid economic development of the African continent, and, perhaps, even the peaceful solution of the Middle Eastern crisis, the attainment of more open interstate communications and development in Northeast Asia may well be easier, less obdurate, than these other problems. It may also be of the same general order of importance. A vital component of any such process would be the reduction of tension and the increase of communications in the Korean peninsula. Unity of the peninsula is not, to be sure, an absolute requirement; but a peaceful unification with lowered levels of armaments, four-power guarantees of unification and independence, and no exclusive alignments would complete the arch of such policy. In the long run, four-power interests and those of the Korean people roughly but powerfully coincide in Korean unification. Such interests exceed by far those that any great power has in its alliance with either North or South Korea; and, while treaties must be respected, the relegating of alliances with either Korea to second-tier importance would conduce to the stability and development of Northeast Asia.

III.

We are left, then, with the concept of a unification desirable for both Korea and the United States and for which both have responsibility, but which has no immediate prospect of being attained. But we do have the intermediate goals of more extensive communications and the relaxation of tension—closely related goals—which are desirable in themselves and necessary waystations on the road to unification. These goals also are not being reached. Indeed, heightened levels of propaganda and tension have brought retrogression. The unification formulae proposed by each Korea, or the history of contact between the two states, may or may not be of enduring importance. It is rather more necessary for us to ask what are, in general, the constraining factors. What is taking them backward?

Strong stress is usually placed upon the differences and incompatibilities in approach toward unification on the part of the two Koreas, with the implication that rejection by the North of any step-by-step formula, its "commitment to mass mobilization and revolution," and its armed aggressiveness in incidents, are the major obstacles to unification. The North is excoriated for trying to seek equality in power and representation despite the fact that its population is only one-half that of the South. Foreign influence for good or ill is discounted; without evidence, it has been chic to say that the influence which external sources can now exert upon the two Koreas is questionable.

I would like to advance the following alternate appraisal of the immediate causes and blame for the breakdown in the contact between the two Koreas:

1.   The record shows that the Democratic People's Republic of Korea has consistently paid far more attention to unification than has South Korea; it continues to do so today.

2.   This attention is consistent with the North's ideology of *chuch'e,* or self-reliance: the larger and more powerful a Korea is, the more its potential for independence and self-sufficiency. The South, in contrast, lacks any viable or consistent ideology and advances no concept of which unification is a deeply structured part.

3.   The North has made what is almost certainly the most original and far-ranging of the unification suggestions advanced until now—that of confederation. The confederation notion, as first detailed in Kim's speech of August 14, 1960, is not a one-step concept and does not necessarily contrast with South Korea's "step-by-step" concept.[4] It is potentially broad enough to serve more than narrowly North Korean ends. It could proceed from a small-scale overlapping of lower-level governmental enterprises (conceivably even joint archeological expeditions) moving gradually upward over time to increasingly complex governmental and administrative overlapping, all the time under separate political and social systems, until joint operation of upper governmental functions is finally invoked. The fundamentally gradualist notion behind confederation is not being given nearly enough due.

4.   The ROK version of a step-by-step increase in communications and interchange also has merit; it is most desirable. Somewhat less governmental along the lines of the German experience, it might or (as with Germany) might not lead to unification. Much of what South Korea says on this question rings with doubt. Of course, one is entitled and even obligated to view the North Korean proposal with suspicion; it must be taken for granted that the DPRK wants unification

on substantially its own terms just as the ROK does. But the greater seriousness of confederation as a logical proposal with a logical but definite unification result is not a proposal to be condemned out of hand, granted Korea's "shrimp-among-whales" position.

5.   There is a great deal that Kim Il-sung says under various pressures and for various audiences, which is in the highest degree hostile, paranoiac, dogmatic, and seemingly quite unpromising for negotiation. Professor Scalapino cites such instances, and ROK propaganda makes hay, perfectly legitimately, with many of Kim's remarks. History contains many parallel situations. If we believe everything Soviet propaganda mouthed and never bothered to probe beneath it, no agreements whatsoever would have been possible. Yet we find common ground with the U.S.S.R. because we have diplomatic relations with the U.S.S.R. and we probe. We have no diplomats in the DPRK and we do not probe. There may be more secret probing than we know about, but I think there would be indications of probing if it were being done seriously. Of course, it is inconvenient (it might also be crucial, we don't know) that the DPRK seems to have no Chou En-lai who is sufficiently secure and at ease to meet privately with secret emissaries. That we do not seem to probe, however, is still hard to understand; not probing is the cardinal diplomatic sin in anyone's book. Korean affairs deserve far more attention, imagination, and plain old-fashioned diplomacy than they appear to be getting.

6.   When one asks whether there is any indication that there is something to probe, any conceivability of "give," the answer seems to me to be cautiously "yes." For example, in regard to the prior conditions of the U.S. troop withdrawal, ROK troop reductions, etc., there is Kim Il-sung's *Yomiuri* interview of January 1972, in which he said that steps to bring the two Koreas closer, including a peace pact and a nonaggression treaty, could be undertaken even before U.S. troops withdrew.[5] Regarding his apparently adamant stand against Park's proposal to admit both Koreas simultaneously to the United Nations, a proposal which I personally regard as realistic and in the long run (though perhaps not short run) helpful, there is initial reaction from communists like Kim Byong-sik that such a proposal should be carefully considered. There since has been a freeze in position, but North Korea here runs against the trends started with Germany. Because the North is anxious to be less isolated, pressures on North Korea to come closer into the stream of international action can be exerted. Many more examples could be given indicative of the possibility of "give." Of course, we do not know what we would find if we did probe. Kim is not a flexible liberal—not even such communist friends as he has would say that. But there is ample ground for probing and it should begin soon; the situation is not getting any better without it, nor is Kim getting any weaker.

7.   The North's creation and direction of a revolutionary force within the South is often overdrawn along the lines of ROK propaganda. Kim expects such revolutionary forces to appear, but expects they will be Southern. He expects to help them at some point. But there also have been messages from him that "Southerners" must do most of the job and cannot ask the North to do it all. It is, in the final analysis, a serious and open question whether history will show Kim Il-sung or Park Chung-hee to have been the more effective inspirer of subversive activity within the Republic of Korea. The Center for Defense Information in Washington, D.C. evidently inclines toward the latter interpretation: "The danger to South Korea posed by the Park regime's repressive policies is in many ways more serious than the danger of invasion from the North"[6]; or the danger of South Korea's subversion. The myth of North Korean subversion is more a propaganda tool of Park than its actuality is an effective tool of Kim.

8.   A too unilateral blame is often laid on the North for the breakdown of the agreement of July 4, 1972, following, in this respect, the especially high-decibel ROK propaganda. The blame distinctly is shared. The purposeful mistranslation into English by the ROK of the July 4th text by saying "unification shall be achieved through independent Korean efforts without being subject to external imposition or interference" when the original contained the phrase "without reliance upon outside force or its interference" revealed ROK ambiguity and ambivalence about abiding by the terms actually arrived at. In the ten days following the signing of the communiqué, the ROK government made it clear in the National Assembly and in announcements that it did not consider the U.N. Command (i.e., the U.S. troops) to be "outside forces," which is a strained and unconvincing, if not utterly deceptive, interpretation of the terms of the agreement.[7] On July 11, 1972, the ROK Prime Minister stated that the DPRK, with whose representatives the ROK had one week before signed an agreement, was "not a legitimate political entity."[8] Numerous were the explicit and acerbic statements that the ROK would not alter its anti-communist posture. This is, under the circumstances, hardly the language of determined sincerity. One can, of course, point to DPRK propaganda statements claiming that the ROK has completely accepted the line of the "respected and beloved" national leader Kim Il-sung and other aggressive or gloating statements (even in 1972, let alone 1974–75) not calculated to create the appropriate atmosphere for a peace conference. Blame does not fall solely on either side; it takes two to tangle. But we should be aware that there are serious, committed anti-communist analysts of ROK-DPRK relations who believe on balance that South Korea has been more disruptive of negotiations since 1972 than the North; that, at the very least the responsibility is deeply shared.

9. The one-man-one-vote principle in international affairs, commonly invoked to give the more populous South Korea a greater weight in unification schemes, rests on the assumption of a single political unit. One should recognize that this cannot apply to today's Korea. The ROK takes the position that each Korea be recognized as an independent nation in the United Nations with no vote differentiation based on a population difference. Yet one argument insists on one-man-one-vote in the preliminary arrangements long before Korea becomes one unit. At some point, of course, population must be taken into account in any unification formula. If Korea ultimately becomes united, such a principle should be recognized. The initial meetings and bodies that perform preliminary roles, however, can no more be stuffed into a population/representation mold than could the Congress of Vienna, or the Paris Peace Conference, or the United Nations.

10. Finally, there is the question of interpreting the military situation. ROK propaganda frequently leaves the impression that the DPRK is again resorting to armed disruption which, by implication, we are led to believe is on much the same scale as in prior years. No statistics are given.

The statistics of the U.N. Command, obtained from the Pentagon, regarding North Korean armed violations in the DMZ area are as follows: 1967–829; 1968–761; 1969–134; 1970–106; 1971–58; 1972–1 (sic); 1973–7; 1974–9; 1975–17 (through August).[9] Those questioning or seeking solace from these figures murmur that the U.N. Command no longer counts as violations what was counted in prior years. The U.N. Command seems never publicly to have admitted or explained any such change in its recording. My understanding is that even if this is true, the recent figures would not rise above the general range of fifty to sixty armed violations—still vastly below the numbers of the past. Even U.S. sources cast substantial doubt on how reliable some of the allegations of North Korean naval incidents are; the former ROK Naval Chief of Staff recently stated that at least two main naval incidents, allegedly perpetrated by the DPRK, were actually provoked by the South for propaganda exploitation. As another example, some reliable sources have denied that "on November 15, 1974, a DMZ police squad . . . discovered a tunnel . . ." and have reported that this tunnel was "discovered" in June 1974, the ROK announcement of its "uncovering" having been manipulated to impress President Ford on his visit to Seoul. The possibility that whole divisions could rush through the tunnel has been somewhat scotched by reports that individual ROK soldiers have asphyxiated for lack of air while exploring part of it. These are propaganda-laden days, and no doubt there are other past and future "discoveries" on the ROK agenda. If we report versions coinciding with ROK propaganda, we should also cite non-communist sources that qualify these versions.

In essence, the DPRK abandoned its large-scale, trained-guerrilla tactics during 1970; solid evidence of any resumption does not exist; the statistics of the U.N. Command dramatically evidence this change.

Returning to our original question of the constraints on the reduction of tension, let us summarize before going further:

1.   There are the feelings, the intransigence, and the differences in concepts of unification and in the actual unification proposals by the two Korean governments. These are great obstacles that can become insurmountable. But this bleak prospect must also be seen in light of the following qualifications:

(a)   Responsibility for the hostility and for the breakdown in communication efforts is shared.

(b)   North Korean intransigence remains only a little tested by South Korea and under circumstances that the ROK itself prejudiced during its July 6–14, 1972, statements; it remains scarcely tested by the Japanese and not at all by the United States or other Western powers. North Korea has greatly enlarged its relations with non-communist powers in the last two to three years (as of September 1, 1975, it was recognized by eighty-eight nations) and hence non-communist information into its system has increased.[10]

(c)   Both Korean positions contain some gradualism and some possibility of movement and compromise—how much is uncertain until they are tested. Both positions have hopeful elements.

(d)   Though much of the hostility is quite deeply rooted, the people living under the two regimes can be presumed in general to be less hostile toward one another than the governments that represent them.

(e)   Any conclusion that the DPRK and ROK unification plans are too far apart for compromise or that compromise is not worth achieving is in itself unwarranted, although one certainly can doubt that either leader honestly desires unification on any but his own terms.

2.   The foreign and other policies of the four great powers no longer constitute the constraint they were before the current era of détente, and would allow for considerably more compromise and movement than is being achieved. This is a distinct change from the 1946–55 period and is worth stressing. Indeed, the four powers have much to gain from a compromise regarding Korea, and even from neutralized unification.

More armaments per square mile are deployed in the Korean peninsula than in any other similar arena in the world—more, even, than in Vietnam before the debacle. This perilous condition has endured for an even longer period than it did in Vietnam. The two Koreas cover about 85,000 square miles, roughly the size of Minnesota, but they boast more men in their standing and para-military forces (circa 4,850,000) than Minnesota's total population (3,947,000 estimated in 1974).

For both Koreas, the armed forces have become the largest cohesive vested interest in their states; they probably have hegemony over and certainly enormous influence on, the politics and political postures of both countries. The leaders of both Koreas, their Prime Ministers and chief associates, are all military men. Scalapino and Lee's *Communism in Korea* has well expressed the puissant influence on DPRK decision-making of its military and former military leaders.[11]

That these vested interests constitute an enormous constraint on any movement toward the reduction of tensions, let alone toward unification, seems both logical and obvious. Once established and entrenched, its own organizational dynamic seeks to enhance the military, both as function and as group to which loyalty is felt, to enlarge it, to equip it better, to expand its scope and influence. The rationale for such enlargement is couched in terms of hostility to the other Korea: each military guards a separate Korea from its twin, not a united Korea from external enemies. The chief threat to each military's existence is the lowering of the perception of threat and hostility, the relaxation of tension or any trend toward its neutralization that might be a threshold to unification. Official statements have specified that it was the mounting desire for contacts between the two Koreas and for the discussion of unification, especially in student circles in 1960–61, which roused the special apprehension of the military establishment in the ROK and led to the 1961 coup and Park's rule. Even within this regime, the contacts with the North initiated by Lee Hu-rak and the CIA of the ROK caused military dissension, leading to a serious internal struggle within the top echelons of the ROK power structure.[12] The ROK military is the South's strongest anti-accommodation force.

Such attitudes feed on their own training and propaganda. A recent paper describes in detail the sharp rise in the political propaganda component in the education programs of the ROK army and especially the expanded attention now given to the "infiltration" and "subversive" threats.[13] With compulsory military training, such education affects almost all males in South Korea.

Our knowledge of the decision process in North Korea is far more slender, but Dr. Scalapino has observed: "It is assumed that the Military Affairs Committee [of the DPRK] discusses and determines policies relating to the campaign for southern liberation. . . . the Party and the military are intimately bound together. . . . The militarization of North Korea, resulting from the elevation of southern liberation to a top priority, inevitably has cast the military into a role of cardinal importance."[14] As thus described, the entire context of the function of the military, in the North as in the South, suggests that the military is essentially the chief enemy of accommodation and a relaxation of tension. Here, more than in the hostile ideologies themselves, specifically is the main seat of that extremism and intransigence that we all see on both Korean sides, and that almost forecloses the possibility of any progress toward more open communication and unification.

In neither the North nor the South, of course, are civilians a cohesive group opposing the views of the military; far from it. Moreover, our ability to penetrate the caliginous thickets of North Korean policy councils is almost nil. But it probably can be hypothesized that the groups advocating greater liberality in counsel, more communication, and more trade are civilian intellectual, student, and economic groups. As in the South, it is quite likely that those voices contributing to such glimmers of accommodation as the DPRK position are voices within its civilian circles trying to establish ground within an overwhelming military-party establishment. It is precisely these civilian voices in counsel which we should seek to strengthen. Unfortunately, it is these voices which our present policies weaken.

The task, then, of moving toward some sort of accommodation, some sort of relaxation of tension, becomes intertwined with the task of lessening the grip on the policy and politics of both Koreas, which is exercised by bloated and enduring military establishments with vested interests in hostility and in the division which produces it. At least in the South, and conceivably even in the North, that task is linked with the restoration of more liberal internal political processes. The formula oversimplifies, of course; no large militaries are homogeneous under the surface. But years of observation have shown most readers of the political fate of developing countries that the grip of the military is far stronger than is wise for stability or for the peaceful resolution of outstanding issues.

The military of each Korea is the special domain of foreign influence. It is the irony of the present plight of the two Koreas that the particular vested interests most powerfully inhibiting movement toward accommodation are cast most closely in the image of, and are most extensively supported by, two powers whose real interests would be served by a relaxation of tension and by accommodation.

The reasons have nothing to do with "a plot" or even with planned military intentions. I hold no such theory. For half a millennium Korea was one of the most pacifist of states in the world. When mustered out in 1907, its army numbered only some 6,000 men, inadequately armed and poorly trained; its once-vaunted navy was long dead. From then until 1945 there was, within Korea, only the Japanese army which, with a few unimportant exceptions, allowed no Korean enlistment until the late 1930s, and did not have any significant number of Koreans until the last eighteen months of World War II. Liberation, division, tension, independence and hostility thus found a Korea without a native Korean military tradition.[15]

This vacuum was filled by the Soviet and American military occupations, each rapidly creating armed forces in its own image, training them in its own system, arming them with its own weapons; each the bastion of its own viewpoint and doctrine, methods of organization, and language. Training manuals were either in Russian or in English or awkwardly translated versions; the first officers' class in the South opened in an English language school. American and Soviet advisers had much to say about personnel selection, procedures, promotions, and training. Promotion and preferment was influenced by a Korean's adaptation to the foreign system, its language, and its advisers. In no other area of national life was training abroad so common.

With war, this system was multiplied a hundredfold. More permanent schools were set up, then armed service colleges, each modelled after those in the United States or the U.S.S.R. Training abroad increased enormously, but 95 percent of it involved no contact with foreign civilian elements. It was vastly greater than all civilian foreign training programs combined. Though known under such titles as "military aid," it was an extensive system for transmitting foreign procedures, institutions and values—chiefly military values—from the patron culture to the client culture. Rewards for achieving and punishments for not achieving are patent throughout any military system, far more so than in the civilian world. As virtually all young men were processed through such a system, year after year, the effect was to create a rising *imperium* of somewhat Japanized American or Soviet military values within a declining *imperio* of less revolutionized, less foreign-supported, more native but more discarded civilian values. The two military-dominated Koreas of the last ten to fifteen years are the creation of this kind of foreign-initiated, foreign-supported process.[16]

However unintended the scope of these foreign inputs may sometimes have been, and however much a response to the local situation, to speak under these conditions of American or Soviet "noninterference in the internal affairs of Korea" is nonsensical. In addition, how can one speak of U.S. noninterference in Korean political affairs when an American four-star general, together with other U.S. generals and flag officers, exercise operational control over a 625,000-man Korean military establishment? Chinese influence on classic Korea was longer lasting and more touted than American influence, but it lacked the persuasiveness of the absolute systematization and discipline of armies and the minute personal supervision exercised since 1945, particularly by Americans, over South Korean military educational institutions. It will be exceedingly difficult to liberate traditional Korean civilian values from this new militarized and essentially foreign influence with its systemic repressiveness and intolerance.

Of the Soviet and U.S. military influences, that of the United States is certainly the greater in measurable ways, probably far greater in all respects. There have been no Soviet troops and comparatively few Soviet military advisers in North Korea since the end of 1948. American combat troops were absent only for the fateful twelve months from June 1949 to June 1950 and very many KMAG (Korean Military Advisers Group) advisers remained. The American presence has been pervasive for thirty years. Americans fought by the hundreds of thousands alongside Koreans either in neighboring or in actually integrated units. The training of Korean military in the United States has been greater than the training of North Koreans in the U.S.S.R. It has now been shown in U.S. statistics that the United States, since 1963, has provided arms and military training to South Korea costing three times that which the U.S.S.R. and China combined have given to North Korea: our $2,624,000,000 for the South as against their $805,000,000 for the North.[17] In 1969, the gap was monstrous: $489 million for the South, $9 million for the North.[18] Figures for the preceeding decade are not available from the same source, but it appears that the discrepancy may be even larger. I do not know of any responsible statistics positing total communist military aid to North Korea as high as $2 billion; indeed, it is hard to find any figures at all. Total help must have been great, although more cheaply costed than ours: statistics and costing are problems and the comparability of totals controversial. Total U.S. military aid to South Korea from 1945 to 1975 is some $6.5 billion to $7 billion, far more than the United States has given to any other country except Vietnam.[19] It is still growing by some $160 million or more per year, with requests over, or in November 1975, exactly at $200 million. Political scientists recognize that giant inputs in one sector cannot be confined to that sector alone but spread throughout the polity. Military inputs, both as incentives and as training and socialization, are inevitably political inputs as well. The overwhelming effects of such inputs on the institutional, social, and political developments of South Korea, thus inexorably smothered in our military embrace, have been starkly, if not ludicrously, clear in the political systems and the governmental and legal values of the Thieu and Park regimes. It is a supreme irony that these regimes ruled or rule over two of the most pacifist ancient polities one could have found (until World War II) anywhere among the earth's political kingdoms. It is worth observing that such a contrast with deeper native values by itself probably adumbrates future instability in both areas: deep struggles between civilian and military values within the political-social domain.

The argument that constant inputs of military aid are necessary for South Korea's defense seems to me to have been laid convincingly by the figures of the State Department's own Disarmament Agency. If more evidence is needed, the following tabulation might provide it:

TABLE 1: THE MILITARY ESTABLISHMENTS COMPARED

	ROK	DPRK
Troop numbers:	625,000+	450,000+
Foreign troops:	40,000–42,000 (U.S.)	None since 1958
Atomic Weapons:	152 shells for 155-mm guns[a]	None ever indicated
	56 shells for M8-inch guns	None ever indicated
	12 load and reload for Sergeant missiles	None ever indicated
	12 Lance warheads[b]	None ever indicated
	198 bombs for 54 F–4 fighter-bombers	None ever indicated
	50 nuclear land mines to destroy whole forests and passes	None ever indicated
	80 loadings for Honest Johns	None ever indicated
	144 Nike Hercules missiles	None ever indicated
Total number of nuclear weapons:	704	
Foreign arms and training	$6,500,000,000	About $2,000,000,000[c]
Annual cost of U.S. troops:	$ 300,000,000[d]	No foreign troops in DPRK
U.S. nuclear arms:	Indeterminant but hundreds of millions of dollars, including upkeep and renewal costs	No known nuclear weapons
Population:	34,000,000	16,500,000
Militia and paramilitary:	2,400,000	1,400,000
Air Force:	About 333 combat aircraft when announced sale intentions have been completed	573 combat aircraft[e] (of which 420, however, are largely obsolete)
Modern, high-performance aircraft:	203	153
Foreign Air Force:[f]	U.S. Wing of F–4 fighter-bombers	None within DPRK (though present in neighboring PRC and U.S.S.R.)
Diplomatic Recognition:	93	88

NOTES TO TABLE 1

[a] Center for Defense Information estimate, Washington, D.C., 1975. See also Congressional Testimony of Dr. Leader, Defense Information Center, and Admiral LaRocque, its head. *Jiji* has comparable but somewhat smaller estimates. In 1973, the Defense Department (Senate Document 33–439, p. 209) said that the cost of the 155-mm nuclear shells was $452,000 each, compared to a cost of $191 for conventional shells for the same gun. (*Korea Week,* February 28, 1975.) For most recent ROK armed forces figures, see *Korea Week,* September 17, 1975, and October 31, 1975, based on official South Korean news agency (NNS) figures; ibid. for recognitions.

[b] *Jiji.* Lances have a 15-kiloton load and a 70-mile target capability.

[c] Since the Armistice Agreement forbids the introduction of more weapons into the peninsula by either side, these figures imply that, since 1953, the United States has been violating the Armistice Agreement it signed in Korea at a rate considerably greater than that of the communists, most of whose arms (about 85 percent) come from the U.S.S.R. which was not signatory to the agreement. Caution must be employed relative to arms costing, however, since U.S. arms and training are considerably higher costed than roughly comparable Russian and Chinese products.

[d] Hearing before the Committee on Armed Services, U.S. Senate, Part 8, Manpower, FY 1974, p. 5351 gives annual recurring costs of $260,000,000 for a somewhat similar infantry division and, on p. 5362, some $30,000,000 for the recurring costs of 2 squadrons of F–4s. Support for the Taegu Support Squadron was $3,100,000.

[e] See ISS, *The Military Balance,* and Young-hoon Kang, "The Military-Security Implications of the North-South Korean Dialogue," *Korean Affairs,* Vol. IV, No. 2, July 1974, pp. 1–7, presenting a ROK military view.

[f] Leader testimony, op. cit., p. 3.

It is the opinion of the Center for Defense Information in Washington, D.C., that "insofar as military capabilities are concerned the South Koreans have a significant edge. . . . Large numbers of South Korean troops are tough combat veterans of the Vietnam war. The North Korean Army has not had any combat experience since the Korean War."[20] In addition, Clausewitzean doctrine advocates at least a 50 percent edge as normally needed for attack. It would appear that the ROK is closer to such an edge than the DPRK. ROK propaganda avers—and it was until recently widely accepted—that the North has a significant edge in one field, that of fighter aircraft. In numbers, the North apparently does lead two to one. In the fall (September 2-October 23) of 1975, however, the United States announced that it intended to sell South Korea sixty F-5Es and F-5F fighters with ground equipment and ten spare engines, eighteen F-4D Phantoms, eighteen F-4E Phantoms, and twelve Harpoon ship-to-ship missiles for a total of $510,300,000 (over one-third of the entire ROK 1976 defense budget).[21]

With these aircraft, particularly the F-4s, ROK air power becomes more than a match for anything the DPRK has, most particularly in its offensive capability. From present fields, the North's MIGs can get little past Seoul and back on their fuel capacity and if their fields are moved southward they become more vulnerable. The ROK's new Phantoms, however, can fly anywhere in North Korea and indeed over most of Manchuria and the Maritime Provinces, all of industrialized Japan, and much of northeast China including Peking, and back from present fields on their fuel supply. The North's numerical superiority now becomes largely meaningless. In addition, discussions are now in progress that may lead to the local manufacture of a Korean fighter plane. And, or course, two U.S. F-4 fighter-bomber squadrons are now in Korea. "Defensive" and "offensive" are not easy to define satisfactorily with regard to air forces. Perhaps the capabilities of North Korea's air force have not been fully appraised in publicly available literature. However, Air Force General George Brown told the House Defense Appropriations Subcommittee in 1974 "that the North Korean Air Force is essentially defense oriented and not offensively oriented."[22] This appears true; it also appears that the ROK Air Force is moving with U.S. help toward a more offensive capability than that possessed by North Korea.

The dangers involved were further increased in late October 1975 when France announced its intention to sell South Korea equipment and technology that will produce the explosive material for atomic bombs by means of reprocessing nuclear waste into weapons-grade plutonium. This equipment would be in addition to two nuclear research reactors now in operation in South Korea, a nuclear power plant to be complete this year within half an hour's drive northeast of

Pussnat Kori, and advanced plans to build four 600,000 kilowatt French and Canadian Candu nuclear power stations in the next three to four years. India already has detonated a nuclear device whose plutonium was obtained from the waste product of a nuclear reactor supplied by Canada for peaceful purposes. The 310-page Directory of *Korean Scientists and Engineers in America* alone lists 1,000 engineers qualified to work in nuclear-related installations and eighteen specialists in nuclear physics and nuclear engineering. In addition, Seoul has purchased Lockheed Aircraft's complete facilities for manufacturing solid-fuel rocket motors, a sale reportedly once opposed even within the State Department.

International Atomic Energy Agency (IAEA) and other restrictions provide safeguards against the use of plutonium produced by nuclear power plants. Beginning in 1977, the Kori plant alone will be capable of producing some ninety-two kilograms of plutonium per year, enough for nine explosive devices of the Indian type. One must assume, however, that a government that breaks every international and humane law to kidnap its citizens from foreign countries will break every supervisory limitation and abscond with the technology it is determined to acquire. Foreseeable, therefore, in a period of some years, is a South Korea capable of carrying atomic weapons either in or protected by sophisticated aircraft on bombing missions within combat radius of at least 400 miles (depending on heights, speed, and payloads) of South Korean airfields. This will mean that every point in North Korea, Shen-yang, Kirin, Mukden, Vladivostok, Japan up to northern Hokkaido, Peking, Shanghai, and much of the northeast China Plain can be bombed by the unchecked decisions of a single man, Park Chung-hee, whose ruthlessness, intolerance, determination, and cruelty are well known. South Korean signature on the nuclear anti-proliferation treaty may mean little, if anything.

It is understandable—although I do not agree—that many Americans find it necessary to extricate U.S. troops and planes from these dangers. Such judgment is backed with stern political realities according to the Chicago Council on Foreign Relations poll, which showed that only 19 percent of U.S. leaders and 14 percent of the general American public favor U.S. military involvement if North Korea attacks South Korea. If this fairly represents U.S. opinion, we hardly have a mutual defense treaty with the ROK. In view of this, it is also understandable to support a strengthening of the ROK air force. Provision of F-5 fighter planes and Harpoon missiles could rationally follow from this. Provision, however, of the offensive deep-penetration advanced F-4E and F Phantoms, when combined with the prospect of atomic weaponry under ROK control, appears as an error in judgment unwarranted by any military necessity.

The information about the sale of nuclear technology and Phantoms is new and its technical nature will require some further analysis. If, however, these sales go forward as planned, and unless controls far more extreme can be imposed, it appears that the United States, Canada, and France are enabling South Korea to release unparalleled and inadequately checked military danger in the Korean peninsula and in Northeast Asia of a dimension unjustified by any of the known threats with which South Korea is confronted. This questionable judgment carries the capability of upsetting the power balance in Northeast Asia, threatening the area with nuclear war within the next ten to fifteen years, raising Soviet and PRC arms levels to North Korea and in Manchuria and the Maritime Provinces, tempting the nuclearization of North Korea, strengthening the military in both North and South Korean councils, destroying the last chances for a democratic comeback in South Korea or of accommodation between North and South Korea, increasing communist and Third World support for North Korea in and out of the United Nations, and, by the mid-1980s, thrusting the Korean peninsula forward again as the seat of worse threat, tension, and danger of war than those now tragically engulfing the far smaller populations in the Middle East.

The potential effects on Japan alone are most disquieting. Political divisions are almost certain to be exacerbated and consensus decision-making gravely undermined if not destroyed, which is a powerful impetus given the conservatives toward arming Japan with nuclear weapons and moving the socialist opposition further leftward while increasing its strength. Japan might well then teeter between a far greater militarism and a leftist neutralism with an enhanced possibility that her constitutional government might be overthrown and her liberties suppressed. Whether in Japan or in Korea and among her other neighbors, does any cause we might have in Korea justify even the possibility of invoking these results?

It is often asserted that China and the U.S.S.R. maintain near Korea's borders substantial armaments and nuclear weapons, which, it is implied, in some way must be balanced within the Korean peninsula. Military planners are well aware of the obvious unfeasibility of placing sufficient armaments within the Korean peninsula—let alone in less than half of it—to balance or even deter the world's two largest armed forces. To try this or even suggest that it could be tried would write a blank cheque on the largest bank account on earth, made out to the Pentagon and the ROK armed forces. I doubt that the record of the last decade suggests the efficacy, let alone wisdom, of such a course. What the United States says it is doing is stationing forces in Korea sufficient to deter a North Korean attack. The U.S.-South Korean Mutual Defense Treaty is specifically designed as protection against any armed threat from China or the U.S.S.R. Former Secretary of Defense Schlesinger does not think that such a threat exists, recently testifying that "in the present political climate we believe these nations would see aggression as contrary to their interests." Sino-Soviet experts have recently gone somewhat further than the Secretary: "For both Russia and China, their stakes in improving relations with Tokyo and Washington are now, and for the foreseeable future, much greater than their stakes in helping Pyongyang reunify Korea."[23] The crushing weight already imposed on the Korean political system by existing military machines is patent. Were Korea to become still more the military parking lot of four-power armament, that weight would deform Korea's political structure and values past recognition, redemption or hope of defense.

In conclusion, then, not only is each military establishment the major deterrent to accommodation between the two Koreas, but also each in its particular client relationship to the three largest powers reflects its patron's influence. In the South there is not only the exceptional military influence of the United States but even operational control exercised by U.S. generals. External powers have influence on the two Koreas; it is their will to use it which fails.

IV.

What is the U.S. interest? Surprisingly—or after Vietnam is it surprising?—the definition of this interest remains somewhat opaque, in part because American policy-makers have never been able to make up their minds regarding how vital the Korean peninsula or its southern half is to the U.S. or to the security and the orientation of Japan. Actually, from a military threat viewpoint, I think there is a growing concensus—with which I would agree—that the Korean peninsula is not vital to Japan, let alone to the U.S., under present strategic-arms conditions. Perhaps it never really was. But U.S. commitments and treaties, in a world dependent on security commitments, create important interests that tend to be fungible, which is the reason we went to war in Korea in 1950. History does charge us with a commitment to a free South Korea and to preventing a takeover of the ROK by forceful and illegitimate means directed by an outside power. That is very much a part of our credibility in Asia and elsewhere. I would also add to the formulation the U.S. interest in the United Korea sketched above; this addition to the definition of our interest is less explicit in our present policy and less widely agreed.

But the situation recently confronting us in Cambodia and Vietnam sheds stark light on what our *long-range* options in Korea are likely to be. Both in Cambodia and Vietnam there were far more expensively armed and maintained troops on "our" side than on the communist side. The same was strikingly true in China from 1946 to 1949. The same is true, as official figures now confirm, in Korea today. What confronts us is not in basic terms a war of arms but a war of ideas and politics, which we (as also Kim Il-sung and Stalin in 1950) have allowed arms to obscure. We constantly seem to learn too late that our problem is not arms; it is political viability.

Political viability in Korea is likely, in the middle to long range, to lie in the opposite direction from support of the military establishment. It is likely to lie in the direction of being certain that Koreans have something of those rights and freedoms which the textbooks we gave them thirty years ago and on which they have been raised tell them they should have: namely, the rights and freedom which their patrons and closest associates have. In highly literate states, when education, association, and international media reception all go in one direction and political reality goes in another, viability in the long run is doomed under whatever political system may be obtained.

The State Department has unhappily selected or acquiesced in a policy option for Korea that is contrary to longer-range American interests in the Korean peninsula and Northeast Asia. It is an option most likely to increase tensions, least likely to encourage the trend toward accommodation and eventual conceivable Korean unification. It supports the present South Korean regime with one of the largest U.S. military aid programs, it has no other kind of significant program, and it puts exceedingly little apparent pressure or influence on the Park regime.

1.   The option that is being followed not only concentrates U.S. policy on military aid but it does so exclusively; no civilian interests or enterprises in Korea get any significant U.S. official aid. We are, for example, quite unwilling to symbolize our interest in Korean students and their interest in democracy by donating a student center to the New SNU campus at Kwanak-san. Our aid items thus constitute powerful political signals to the internal Korean polity. Little is done by the State Department or any other U.S. agency to counteract the anti-democratic implications of these signals.

2.   We not only give nothing to groups interested in democracy but the State Department also has announced that during the last decade the United States has been giving military aid to the South at three times the cost that communists have given such aid to the North. Nonetheless, no explanation of such a large discrepancy or the need for it has been forthcoming.

3.   Aid of this sort is given at precisely the time when the ROK military establishment, its arms, and its counsels, constitute the chief support and pressure for the repression of the rights and freedoms of the Korean people. The U.S. government gives no aid to universities and churches or to intellectuals in this struggle. It supports only the military side. Thus, it not only intervenes in an internal Korean political controversy but also intervenes clearly on the side opposing ex-

plicit U.S. political policy interests as expressed in our highest circles
for thirty years.

4.   In its intervention, U.S. policy supports two trends in the
South. With U.S. support and benediction, it tends further to clamp
the hold of the military on South Korean decision-making, a hold
consistently opposed to the accommodation or reduction of tension in
the Korean peninsula. It also tends to prolong the life of a regime most
likely to bring the cause of anticommunism into ill repute in Korea by
connecting it with flagrant injustice, repression, torture, wealth inequalities, and social injustice. (This is a repetition of the Chen Li-fu
epoch and methods which softened up Chinese opinion in the 1930s
and 1940s for the communist takeover in China, and of recent Vietnamese repressions, inequalities, and injustice which sank—or
speeded the debacle of—the Thieu government.) By so doing, present
U.S. policies foreclose the chances for moderation or neutralization in
Korea and, in the longer run, make an extremist and leftist reaction
more likely, thus playing into the hands of the communists and risking
an eventual reaction of hatred by moderate Koreans against Americans.

5.   The effects of our policies in the North are equally bad. Knowing that its forces are already fewer and its receipt of foreign arms aid
vastly less, yet determined despite this to maintain as much *chuch'e*
independence as possible, the North feels pressured to turn more and
more of its resources toward military purposes, and away from any
trend of reducing the level of the military in its councils. Thus civilians
are undercut, the military voice loudened and any conceivable spirit of
accommodation undermined before it has a chance of being heard.

6.   Finally, such policies run counter to the interests of détente
among the four powers by signalling to Russia and China a U.S. unwillingness to recognize a reduction in their military aid to Pyongyang by
a reduction in our military aid to the South. We thus are cast in the
role of increasing tensions rather than decreasing them while we are
soliciting, in effect, comparable external and internal increases from
the communist side. Instead, mutual *reductions* of troops and armaments should be the aim of our policy in Korea; our signals should
concentrate on encouraging such trends.

7.   In short, I would conclude that the Korean military establishments with their military outside support are the major constraints on
any movement by the two Koreas toward accommodation, and that the
U.S. policy's military orientation disruptively abets this constraint.

8.   State Department decision-making of this sort is seen by more
and more members of Congress as running counter to long-range U.S.
interests in Northeast Asia. Thus it contributes to the recent—and
inauspicious—trend for Congress, restive at State's policy-making, to

substitute its own policy-making. Such trends deserve (and appear to be getting) increased public discussion.

There has been a two-pronged tendency for a retreat of U.S. influence from Korea. Outside the government, disenchantment with our failures in Asia has abetted isolationism. Inside the government, there has been disillusion with the leverage we can exercise and the limits of our influence, a tendency which, while decrying isolationism, is in fact its sibling. It appears from the tenor of discussions with experts from the U.S.S.R. that a somewhat parallel retreat and disillusion characterize Soviet policy toward North Korea, including the provision of Soviet arms. China has played a very small role in providing arms but its reported—and quite probable—emphasis on "non-interference" in Korea in the Peking talks of October 22, 1975, with Secretary Kissinger argues somewhat similar policy experiences and conclusions.

We can of course tell the two Koreas, specifically Park and Kim: "This is your peninsula, you've got to work out its peace, independence and accommodation; we're going to wash our hands of it and walk away." The recent State Department line has come close to doing this. This is exactly what we did so disastrously from 1947 until the Korean War erupted in June 1950: we espoused a pull-out policy which led directly to that conflict. It is certainly the opposite of the policy we have been pursuing with occasional success in the Near East, where we have never exercised sovereign powers nor had the direct responsibilities which flow therefrom.

To walk away from Korean unification would invoke the following parable: The owners of two big estates come into their smaller neighbor's garden. They take over his place for a while; they train two bulldogs to the greatest pitch of ferocity—specifically to sic each other—and provide them with the best meat, spiked collars, and little knives strapped to most parts of their anatomies. After years of training, they then let the dogs off their leashes and walk back to their estates to watch what happens. In the parable, it's only the bulldogs who get slashed to death; in real life, it's the entire Korean people. Americans and Russians both must remember that the Koreans did not ask us to divide their country, did not request that we occupy and rule them, did not solicit the governments or the armies we unleashed over their heads. Nor, unlike the Germans, had they given us the pretext for doing any of this. Both the United States and the U.S.S.R. have in Korea a responsibility that is unique among the dozen or so divided nations of the world. They must act accordingly.

Practical grounds argue for continued interest quite as strongly as does moral responsibility. Korea cannot be united without some sort of informal or formal agreement among the four great powers. Nor, in my view, can tensions be reduced as fully as they should be without some kind of great-power agreement on the supply of arms, and in the event of increased tension, on the supply of oil, spare parts, and ammunition currently provided by the outside powers. There is the almost-forgotten Armistice Agreement of 1953 to which the signatories should return. There is the present impasse in contacts between the two Koreas: leaving Korea to the Koreans would result in the resurgence of hostile feelings and armed incidents which could threaten world peace and détente. The consequences would be much the same as leaving Israel and its neighbors to settle their differences alone. Finally, there is the demonstration in Nixon's Peking visit that only contacts among the four powers could drive the two Koreas into initiating contacts. The implication is clear that more prodding by the powers is going to be needed to drive them back again to the negotiating table.

The last factor is crucial and is likely to become more so. The two Koreas are becoming more hostile; the four powers are on the whole slowly becoming less so. Unless the two Koreas can resume peaceful contacts stimulated by the great powers, the trends toward hostility are in both cases likely to increase. There is a distinct possibility of some amelioration in Sino-Soviet relations after Mao's death. It is conceivable that in the fairly near future the Japanese socialists will come to power, probably in some kind of coalition government. While this is unlikely to have revolutionary effects on Japanese policies or to shake the U.S.-Japan relationship fundamentally, it is sure to bring close Japanese ties to Peking, Moscow, and Pyongyang. The future of U.S.-U.S.S.R. relations seems more opaque, but it appears improbable that the two nations will discontinue their dialogue and be unable to discuss, and even agree on, certain common problems. Nor must we await Mao's demise or the enthronement of the Japanese Socialist Party, if it comes. China's support for Kim Il-sung seems to have been strengthened somewhat in the wake of Vietnam, and its willingness to negotiate on Korea may temporarily have receded. Nevertheless, four-power communication in general is slowly gathering momentum, and it is far better than anything the two Koreas are displaying or are likely to display soon, unless we influence them.

The foregoing considerations indicate that from now on the four powers should have Korea on their agenda: on a back-burner for the most part, but still under enough flame to prevent congelation. For the time being, this need not involve the problem of four-power conferences. Occasional contacts and/or discussions among the four powers and, hopefully, some understanding on mutual reductions in arms supply to both Koreas will probably be enough to arouse intense apprehension in Pyongyang and Seoul and propel the two back into communication; it sufficed in 1971–72.[24]

For the future, there can be progress in the relaxation of tension in Korea if the four powers come to perceive that the Korean peninsula —an inter-communicating Korea and ultimately a united Korea—is a long-range *opportunity,* not just a liability, for the achievement of improved relations among themselves much as Austria was twenty and more years ago. The *opportunity* for a Northeast Asia of improved intercommunication and trade is deeply in the interests of everyone, especially the non-communist powers. In perhaps no other area are vast underdeveloped resources, like those in eastern Siberia, Alaska, and Manchuria, so closely juxtaposed with the thickest-settled, rather resourceless, and highly industrialized areas of Japan, both Koreas, and southeastern Manchuria. As long as they have to provide much of the armament, any reductions in supplying them remain more in American and Soviet interests than in the two Koreas themselves.

Such a perception necessarily must be linked to another one: namely, that the achievement of a more stable, more peaceful, more intercommunicating Northeast Asia must have priority over the relations and alliances between the patron states and their client states. This does not mean abandonment, nor yet forgetfullness; it does mean priority. The two are not at all mutually exclusive. Granted the annoyance and embarrassment which Pyongyang causes in Moscow, and to a lesser extent in Peking, and which Seoul causes in Washington and Tokyo, I regard acceptance of such a principle as relatively easy if one presupposes a slightly broader view of the long-term interest in peace than is now prevalent. The more each great power clasps "its Korea" to its bosom, the more the interests of everyone—including the Korean people—will recede.

The ultimate aim of such a four-power entente on Korea would be agreement on a united, independent Korea, hopefully neutralized with a position and an accommodation somewhere between the Austrian and the Finnish neutralization. No alliances would be permitted, no atomic or strategic arms could be located there, armies would be sharply reduced, and general freedoms and democratic process would prevail although there might be limited curbs on outspoken sentiment, movements, or action considered threatening to the four powers. While Finland's accommodation is not perfect, it is far more desirable for everyone—including the Finnish people—than is the irascible instability and intense repression of today's Koreas, or of any divided and highly militarized Korea that is foreseeable.[25] Such a solution is perfectly conceivable, probably not within fifteen years, but quite possibly within thirty or forty. One cannot predict it, of course, but it is eminently worth working toward, not only by us and the other three great powers, but also by the two Koreas through some combination of the ROK's private gradualism and the DPRK's confederation gradualism.

V.

The effect of South Vietnam's debacle on South Korea—and even the U.S.—has been traumatic, producing a specious and temporary facade of political concensus for escalating Korea's armament and tightening its armed camp atmosphere of fear and repression. Such trends are deleterious to the ends to be sought and to American objectives in Korea and Northeast Asia: relaxation of tensions, increased communication and trade throughout the area, détente, and unification. The real lessons of Vietnam have been more unlearned and indeed more openly flaunted in Korea than in any other place.

In my view then, constraints on Korean unification, although heavy, are not irremovable. I think there are fundamental reasons of Northeast Asian security why we should work toward unification, however slowly. Historically, we and the U.S.S.R. must regard ourselves as responsible to the Korean people for helping them (and ourselves) attain this end. Some rigidity on both sides especially in Pyongyang must be removed; but I join a small number of other observers in the feeling the Pyongyang may not necessarily be as rigid as it tends to be described, and that its position must be far better probed. I would on the whole share a wider feeling that the German-type communicating coexistence solution is probably the right way—though not necessarily the only one—to achieve longer-run tension relaxation while believing that, unlike Germany, Korea could eventually go beyond division toward unity. In this respect, I find myself nearer Seoul than Pyongyang on the question of intermediate measures. Ultimately, neither system in the divided house can triumph altogether and we must be willing to accept some sort of intermediate ground—probably nearer Finland's accommodation than Austria's, much as I personally would prefer the latter. It would be far kinder than the present to Korea's long-suffering people.

For the moment, we must recognize that supplying or selling arms at a good deal more than the communist rate is destabilizing, provocative, a violation of agreements we signed, unwise interference in the internal political affairs of South Korea—and on the wrong side of a domestic dispute. Such grounds are quite different from, and far more basic than, "punishing Park." The U.S. military presence in the South, minus U.N. status and operational control over ROK forces, is less of a domestic interference than is our military aid program. A circumscribed U.S. military presence is far more removed from internal matters. Once the post-Vietnam era is bridged, we can reduce our forces, which are chiefly of symbolic importance, to some 20,000; but we should, for the present, be cautious about removing such a symbol entirely. The assessment flies in the face of present trends towards upping South Korean armies and pulling "our boys" out of harm's way: a prelude to a long-term Vietnam-type debacle.

All steps, including any reductions in supplying arms, should be linked to informal four-power entente and we should try to obtain understandings on similar measures—certainly for restraint—on the communist side. Such steps will render the security of South Korea more dependent on our mutual defense treaty. We should keep reminding Park that any invocation of this treaty's terms depends on U.S. Congressional agreement and that he seriously, perhaps disastrously, undermined Congressional will to support Korea by policies violating basic human rights and throttling opposition. Finally, we should use four-power intercommunication and public diplomacy to keep the two Koreas glued to the task of extending their own intercommunication and the relaxation of tension.

Further down this path could lie both a better Korea and an exceedingly prosperous Northeast Asia. If, however, the present situation drags on without substantial improvement, it is possible that in a number of years Korea may take the path followed by mainland China, Vietnam, Cambodia, and Laos—the path in which, with forces of superior numbers and arms and far more munificently financed, we nonetheless lose because of the ultimate lack of political viability of the hollow shells of arms, inequality, and injustice that we persistently support.

NOTES

1. G. Henderson, R. N. Lebow, John G. Stoessinger, *Divided Nations in a Divided World* (New York: David McKay & Co., 1974).

2. *Foreign Relations of the United States: Conferences at Malta and Yalta* (Washington, D.C.: Department of State, 1955), pp. 358–61. The briefing paper was prepared by Dr. Hugh Borton. George M. McCune, then a chief Korea specialist for the State Department, is known also to have voiced his alarm to policy-makers over the consequences of any "temporary" division.

3. Dr. Nathan White has recently stated the status quo case in "Search for Peace: The Four Powers and Korea," *The Korean Journal of International Studies*, vol. VI, no. 1, Seoul, 1974/75.

4. See Rinn-Sup Shinn, "North Korea Policy toward South Korea," in Young C. Kim, ed., *The Major Powers and Korea* (Silver Spring, Md.: Research Institute on Korean Affairs, 1973), p. 89.

5. Ibid., p. 102.

6. Dr. Stefan H. Leader, Center for Defense Information, testimony before the Subcommittee on Asian and Pacific Affairs, the House Committee on International Relations, House of Representatives, *Our Commitment in Asia*, 2 October 1974, p. 160.

7. Rinn-Sup Shinn, "Korea: Foreign and Unification Policies," *Problems of Communism*, January-February, 1973.

8. *Dong-A Ilbo*, 12 July 1972.

9. *Annual Reports of the United Nations Command*, Seoul, Korea, 1968–72. Thereafter, statistics have been obtained personally from the Department of Defense, Washington, D.C.

10. *Korea News*, Washington, D.C., 17 September 1975, p. 7. Seoul at the time was recognized by ninety-three, apparently before the shift of Laotian recognition from Seoul to Pyongyang. See also *Far Eastern Economic Review*, 24 October 1975, p. 28, which notes that at the end of 1970, Pyongyang was recognized by only thirty-six governments.

11. Robert A. Scalapino and Chong-Sik Lee, *Communism in Korea* (Berkeley: University of California Press, 1973), vol. II, pp. 919–1010, and Chapters VI-VIII.

12. On or around 10 March 1973, Major General Yoon Pil Yong, commander of the crack Capital Defense Command was dismissed and arrested. On April 28, the ROK government confirmed that Yoon, two Army Brigadier Generals, five field grade and two company grade officers had been arrested and tried by a military court, receiving one to fifteen years in jail for corruption, influence-peddling and "organizing a private organization with his followers to undermine the chain of command." On 6 October 1973, the *Christian Science Monitor* reported that General Yoon had been "quietly let out of jail in September." The Capital Defense Command is responsible for the personal safety of the president from uprising and can call on any military units to carry out its duties. It is thus the key, inner ROK praetorian organization. The affair was held highly secret, but it is apparent that General Yoon had forced a show-down with ROK CIA chief Lee Hu-rak, reportedly on the grounds that the negotiations with North Korea which Lee Hu-rak had started and led were dangerous both to the ROK and its relations with its friends. Yoon reportedly represented considerably more military opinion than that within his command alone in bringing this matter to a head. (The fullest English-language description is probably that in *Korea Week*, issue 122, 30 April 1973; issues 120, 31 March 1973, and 133, 18 October 1973, as well as the *Christian Science Monitor* and the *Far Eastern Economic Review* numbers during April 1973, contain added references.)

13. Kim Jai-hyup, "Political Dimensions of Total War Programs: Some Observations from the Curricula Changes of the Three Military Schools in Korea during 1963–1971." (Washington, D.C.: *International Studies Association,* 19–20 February 1975).

14. Scalapino and Lee, op. cit., vol. II, pp. 935, 936.

15. G. Henderson, Korea: *The Politics of the Vortex* (Cambridge, Mass.: Harvard University Press, 1968), pp. 334–38.

16. Ibid., pp. 338–42.

17. *World Military Expenditures and Arms Trade 1963–73* (Washington, D.C.: U.S. Arms Control and Disarmament Agency, 1975), p. 89.

18. Ibid., p. 99.

19. *U.S. News and World Report,* 20 January 1975, published total aid figures—economic and military—for all countries, which the United States have given since 1945. The largest was for Vietnam with $22.49 billion; the second, Korea with $12.24 billion. No other country received as much as $10 billion in aid, including the U.K., France, and India. Even Israel, through mid-1974, received $5.63 billion, less than half what we have given Korea.

20. Leader testimony, op. cit., p. 3.

21. *Congressional Record,* 9 October 1975, p. 18152; and *Congressional Record,* Senate, 21 October 1975, pp. S 18377–18378. Also *Korea Week,* 31 October 1975.

22. Leader, p. 4, gives this quotation.

23. Donald S. Zagoria and Yong Kun Kim, Chapter 2, p. 14, in William J. Barnds (ed.) *The Two Koreas in East Asian Affairs* (New York University Press, 1976).

24. Dr. Nathan White of the Institute for Defense Analysis, "Search for Peace: The Four Powers and Korea," op. cit., comes to a similar conclusion. Communication is, however, far from unification.

25. I agree that two Koreas accepting each other's existence, communicating with each other, and allowing their citizens to communicate would probably be less at dagger's points than they are now, but I believe there would always be a frustration and tension which Germans, with the greater size and independence of the two Germanies, do not have to feel. I also agree that the transition to a united neutral state and the problems of keeping it that way are going to be severe and will involve instabilities and dangers of their own. But I find such instabilities less lethal than the over-militarized variety. The Finlandization of Korea would in fact activate a condition planned for states bordering the Soviet Union after World War II, when it was felt that the U.S.S.R. merited a non-threatening border belt.

American Policy to Korea in a Tokyo-Peking-Pyongyang-Moscow Quadrangle

T. C. Rhee

The problem of American commitment to South Korea has re-emerged as the focal point of major controversy in the wake of the debacle in Indochina and in the face of deterioration of democracy in South Korea. This paper intends to analyze the important economic and political changes in Korea—both the South and the North—and to relate it to the pressing need for re-evaluation of American policy to that region. The first portion addresses the loss of national and "popular" legitimacy[1] in South Korea.

President Park's South Korea bills herself as a "land of Western-style democracy"—immeasurably freer than totalitarian North Korea. But the reality of "democratic rule" in South Korea is not even re-motely comparable to that practiced in the United States and others in Western Europe. The Seoul government has been explaining away this important difference by the convenient rationale that "Western democracy" to be functionable in Korea would have to be "tailored to suit the situation." The so-called "tailoring" has been so fundamental that the very notion that South Korea is "democratic" or "free" is impossible to sustain.

For this major distortion of the basic definition, South Korea has offered two main reasons: one, the need for "national security" against the imminent military invasion of the North; and two, the economic stability and progress for achieving modernization and econo-politico-military self-sufficiency. Because of the former the latter was essential, so goes the reasoning, and to achieve the former the progress in the economic area so spectacularly forged under Park's leadership has to be protected by all means—including the sacrifice of "Western-style democracy" regardless of the political price it exacts in the process.

However, what in essence is the source of the Park regime's un-shakable paranoia of North Korea's military attack, and its frenzied, tragi-comic attempts to overcome the indescribable fear of its own population?

It is indeed a strange paranoia for a nation whose population is almost three times the size of North Korea's, and whose armed establishment ranked fourth in size in the world—along with the self-proclaimed "Economic Miracle on the Han," a vaunted performance matched only by the West Germans. The nagging fear of the regime is all the more incredible as President Park had grandiloquently "decreed" that the economic goals for 1980 were to be the achievement of a $10 billion export per annum and an annual per capita income of $1,000.[2] To accomplish this miracle, which he had not abandoned even after the massive dislocation of world economy after 1973, Park had calculated that his ever expanding export should be able to show an annual increase of no less than 25 percent from 1972 to 1980 together with the G.N.P. growth rate of an astounding 16 percent per annum in the same period.

Why, despite all these magnificent achievements and more, is Park so petrified by the specter of North Korean attack, a nation he offhandedly dismisses as a total failure—economically bankrupt with totally enslaved people without soul, certainly no match for his well-managed South Korea?

There are three main reasons for this. Firstly, there is the growing problem which former President Ford referred to as "popular legitimacy and social justice" without which "subversion or aggression" could not be resisted. Park's loss of legitimacy had been gradual up to 1972, but since then it has become *complete,* through economic failure as far as the great majority of the masses is concerned, through political repression at a level and intensity unmatched anywhere on this side of the communist states, and through humiliating and slavish reliance on Japan in total defiance of the nation's inner agony.

Secondly, his touted economic progress so frequently praised has absolutely no beneficent meaning for the overwhelming majority of the people. The fruits of suffering by the people have been ruthlessly cornered by the few corrupt government officials at the very top. The economic conditions of South Korea for the masses have neared the brink of desperation of the kind only to be envisioned in futuristic fiction.

Thirdly, as North Korea transformed herself in her basic character from the image of a slavish puppet state paying homage to foreign masters and ruled by a foreign trained marionette, to a state placing heavy emphasis on her own nationalistic roots, self-respect and self-reliance, South Korea under Park has voluntarily handed the nation back to Japanese control as a quasi-colony, a unique phenomenon of self-demolition unheard of in modern annals of man and nations.

In assessing the fearsome wave of political terror and repression that has swept South Korea since 1972, it is important to remember the close relationship between the regime's early promise of efficient and clean government and its totally disappointing performance.

The wave of extremely damaging scandals involving the conditions of the rich few—both official and private, closely connected to those who are in power—in the cities had so alienated the people that it now definitely touches on the very legitimacy of the regime. Long threatened in its "revolutionary public image" born of earlier pledges and solemn oaths (which the present regime somehow desperately wanted to maintain prior to October 1972), albeit physically "secure" for the time being behind the omnipotent and omnipresent internal security measures for survival, the Park regime felt compelled to take increasingly repressive measures against any kind of public and private criticism. In this context, the so-called *Yushin* ("Revitalization") structure of October 1972 and the massive and wholesale political changes effected in South Korea since then had to be viewed as legitimation of political terror and repression for the purpose of prolonging the unpopular regime.

The present regime once perhaps entertained the idea of peaceful and democratic transference of political power. However, under the highly charged atmosphere of intense political opposition then on the rise—certainly not confined to a small group of ambitious opposition politicians—it suddenly occurred to Park with paralyzing impact that the advent of a new regime under the control of the emotionally aroused opposition—no matter what its composition—and under tremendous public pressure for cleansing the nation of corruption and those who were responsible for it, was totally unacceptable and fearsome. Unacceptable because, obviously, it could immediately threaten the well-being of those who had perpetuated, abetted the irregularities. Thus fearful to the point of panic over the changes they felt they would neither be able to control nor contain, Park reneged on his early promise of establishing genuine democratic institutions and processes in Korea.

Quietly preparing his plans for the constitutional coup since his controversial election victory for the third consecutive presidential term in 1971,[3] Park had taken a series of major steps. Most significant was the early morning passage on December 27, 1971, without the presence of the opposition, of the "Special Law for National Protection," which included the following provisions: 1) national mobilization of men and material in case of national emergency; 2) severe limitations on residence and citizens' mobility; 3) prohibition of assembly and demonstration; 4) severe curtailment of freedoms of speech and press; and 5) prohibition of collective bargaining. Also, he had eliminated all open opposition within his own party through a carefully orchestrated round of purges; removed potential dissenters from the military leadership (especially the army's) through court-martial on trumped up charges of corruption, counter-revolutionary conspiracy, etc., vastly reduced the cabinet authority to mere "administrative functions"; imposed strict control over the nation's mass media through the extensive use of the KCIA under Lee Hu-rak; and totally stifled student dissent and all other activities.

Then, during the night of October 17, 1972, Park declared martial law, abolished the Constitution, dissolved the National Assembly, outlawed all political activity, imposed censorship on the press, and closed all the universities. With dizzying speed, under the protection of the martial law, he made a series of major revisions in the Constitution that made him the first permanent dictator of the country in history. Without political debate, and with the opposition and the people terrified, Park submitted the revision to the national referendum, which managed to register 92.6 percent support.

Park explained that the sweeping changes were necessary because, "We have always attempted awkwardly to imitate closely the democratic institutions of others," and because, "We can no longer sit idle while wasting our precious national power in futile endeavors." He promised that the new constitution would "guarantee maximum efficiency in regimenting national strength."

The amended Constitution in fact provided all the power that any dictator could desire for permanent rule. Under the new system, the President is selected by a newly created National Conference for Unification, a body consisting of more than 2,000 members all handpicked by Park, and of which Park himself is the President. No limitation is imposed on the President's term of office (now extended to six years from the earlier provision of four), guaranteeing Park perpetual rule. One-third of the National Assembly is appointed by the President, while the rest are elected through the complicated election law—revised to give the government party an undisputed edge. This assures Park total control of the legislature, which itself was stripped of all powers to check the executive branch, such as the right of oversight, right to vote "no confidence" (in fact, an impeachment) in the President and the cabinet. Moreover, the session of the National Assembly is now limited to two weeks in a year.

As if all these powers were not enough, Park had gained the additional power to: 1) dissolve the National Assembly whenever he wanted—a power denied him under the old Constitution; 2) declare presidential emergency decrees "to temporarily restrict civil liberties" whenever he deemed such action necessary to face "national emergency"; and 3) indefinitely eliminate local autonomy to preserve "national unification."

Having systematically eliminated all democratic elements and guarantees against arbitrary rule, Park had created a dictatorship with all the trappings of a vicious police state with its prevalent atmosphere of terror. South Korea under this system of the "October Revitalization" since 1972 has become a state of summary arrests, disappearance of critics, kidnappings, "accidental deaths" (assassinations through underhanded methods all carried out by the KCIA), liberal use of torture, secret trials, secret executions, brutal and total censorship, omnipresent agents and agents-provocateurs, "house arrests," intimidation of citizens against contact with foreigners including the members of the U.S. Embassy, total and unabashed use of state, local, private, and public institutions of all kinds for partisan purposes, total penetration of business, educational, religious, charitable organizations, unparalleled corruption, massive accumulation of private fortunes through bribery, extortion, and simple theft of state properties, etc. The list indeed is too long to catalogue.

Among the major milestones of Park's dictatorial rampage, however, one could list the following:

1.   Nine major "presidential emergency decrees" since 1972, all designed to escalate the campaign of terror and suppression of free and responsible criticism. By some accounts, there have been no less than 2,000 decrees of all kinds, including various legislations rubber-stamped by the National Assembly such as the "National Security Act," "the Special National Defense Law," the amendment of the Criminal Code,[4] and various other laws sanctioning protective summary detention, surveillance, and limitation of travel and domicile, etc.[5]

2.   The famous (or notorious) case of the Kim Tae-jung kidnapping in Tokyo by the KCIA on August 9, 1973, a year after the so-called "October Revitalization." Under constant house arrest and harassment since his forced return to Seoul in 1973 after abduction in Tokyo, his movement and speech have been completely controlled by police and the KCIA—so much so that he cannot even go to the hospital for treatment for fear of "accidental death."[6]

3.   Mass arrests of students, professors, journalists, novelists and poets, artists, priests, and ministers, both nationals and foreigners, and military officers; and the torture, imprisonment, expulsion, etc., of the same.

Especially noted is the persecution of the students. Student activities are under heavy surveillance. No meeting of any kind is allowed for students for fear of demonstrations. Since 1974, any meeting of more than ten university students is forbidden. As of November 1975, an additional 859 students have been arrested for violation of this decree. They are held incommunicado without visits from their families—no formal charges have been made and no trials were held. No information of their whereabouts, their health, etc., was ever released. Moreover, there have been a series of further arrests of students who have been found organizing and planning demonstrations.

Simultaneously, Park began to attack systematically two chief centers of opposition: the churches and the universities. The result has been the mass arrest of ministers for the alleged misappropriation of funds, the closing of universities around Seoul, and the mass arrests of the students, one of whom "committed suicide by disemboweling himself on the campus of Seoul National University," leaving behind a note to Park: "Do not mistake the silence of the masses as support for your regime."[7]

4. Murders of professors, opposition politicians (the latest case involves the mysterious death of Mr. Chang Jun-ha, former member of the National Assembly, the editor of the prestigious *Sasange* monthly, and a recipient of the Magsaysay Award).

Chang's death on August 17, 1975, is merely a small example of Park's unending campaign of terror and intimidation—carried out both in Korea and abroad[8]—designed to totally eliminate any opposition to his policies. Despite the government report that Chang fell more than forty feet to his death during a mountaineering adventure near Seoul, his body showed no sign of damage from the steep fall from the rough rock surface he was allegedly climbing, except a small wound on his elbow. Witnesses testified they had seen two young men in military fatigues talking to Chang in the woods just before his death.[9]

Of a more serious and fundamental assault on democratic values and institutions are the mass arrests, forced retirement, and firing of university professors who are critical of Park's policies of repression. The suppression of the professors is the most severe in the nation's major universities, involving the prestigious Seoul National University, Yonsei University (established by American missionaries), and Korea University, etc. The Korean Theological Seminary (Christian) was forced to choose between the permanent closing of the school and the firing of two dissident professors. The Seminary, under the tremendous pressure, fired the two professors.

5. The repeated arrest, imprisonment, and torture without trial of the noted poet Kim Chi-ha. As a poet critic of the Park regime, the Solzhenitsyn of Korea, Kim is languishing slowly to his death in prison, denied even the barest needs, including visits from his family members.[10]

6. Suppression of the press, which has been completely silenced by the persistent brutality of the KCIA and police through arrests, torture, imprisonment, and periodic "indoctrination sessions" in KCIA torture houses set up in various places and hotels. The KCIA control of the press has gone so far as to place its own agents in newspapers, etc., as managers, editors, and reporters. One editor-in-chief of a major paper was threatened not to meet with or accept visits from members of the American Embassy. As a result, after long harass-

ment and intimidation, neither side ventures for a conversation. Telephone bugging is so rampant, nobody dares to use the phone for any serious conversation.

Under the circumstances, the freedom of press in Korea is now much worse than what it was under the Japanese colonial rule.[11] I know from a well-placed and reliable source that the KCIA would not hesitate to "eliminate" individual Americans who stand in their way.

7.   Complete governmental control of the Christian movement as a major menace to his regime—through dissolution of churches; intimidation of church members and various hindrances in order to block holding of church services; arrest and imprisonment of ministers and church officials either through trumped up charges or without charges whatsoever. The Park regime has recently organized a pro-government church organization called the "Dae-Han Ku-Kuk Sun-Kyo Dan" (Korean National Salvation Evangelical Corps) of 503 "registered" ecclesiastics under the nominal leadership of Park's own daughter who is in her early twenties. With this government-sponsored, pseudo-Christian movement, Park's daughter travels to various evangelical meetings, organized by "ministers" whose identities are unknown and oftentimes in military uniforms, persuading people to volunteer for military training, propagandizing that there is no Christian persecution in South Korea, and spreading bribes for silence.

In recent years, particularly since 1972, there have been: a) concentrated efforts to effect a political penetration of the Christian church for eventual politicization for Park; b) pressures on ministers through various means to wear military uniforms and to issue statements of support for Park, and to deny allegations of Christian persecution;[12] and c) persecution of the "Church of Galilee," a church organized by professors driven out of their universities for their criticism of Park—under constant harassment and threat, this church cannot even meet for prayer.

8.   Surveillance of the military. Despite the series of purges, forced retirements, internal surveillance by various military agencies and by the KCIA agents planted in all units down to the platoon level, Park's fear of the military has not been allayed. Recent measures taken to both cajole and to intimidate the top generals have been: a) December 1975 decision to upgrade the military pay, with enormous increase; b) an extreme degree of limitation on foreign travel; and c) promise of lucrative positions after retirement.

Since Park's own military coup in May 1961, the role of the Korean military has been subject of a high sensitivity in South Korea. The undeniable political fact is that the military coup of 1961, which created the present regime, has set the dangerous precedent of releasing the military from its political neutrality. The heavy involvement of the retired officers in every possible profession—government, business, banking, diplomatic service, etc.—had severely loosened the military discipline, highly politicized the officer corps, and dangerously relaxed important civilian control. This political tendency is assessed as strong even among the younger junior officer corps of the service academies. Since the present regime is in "solid control" at least for the moment, and the opposition is totally crippled, the only way to replace it would be through another military coup.

The high rate of turnover and the retirement among top echelon officers, and their eventual employment in key posts over the last thirteen some years, conceivably has created a solid phalanx of military support for the Park regime. However, the political loyalty and dependability of the middle and lower echelon officers—of junior and middle grade field ranks with better education and motivation for their profession—could very well be shaky.

If urban "prosperity" at the expense of the rural stagnation is not reversed and compensatory development in the farming regions soon achieved, there could be serious political challenge among the officers whose social and economic backgrounds are rooted in the countryside. Their background and keenly felt affinity for the neglected farm population, plus the difficulty of city living with their meager pay even after the recent pay raise, the urban demoralization felt within the context of the widening gap between the rich few and the poor masses, and the uncontrolled high living could easily propel these military elements into the political arena with ferocity unheard of before. Indeed, when one takes into account the fact—despite Park's paranoiac screening of politically undesirable elements—that an increasing number of entrants into the service academies come from rural rather than urban areas, the political commitment of the future officer corps could not be easily discounted.

Reporting from Seoul in February 1975, Richard Halloran of the *New York Times* indicated that there were signs of cracks in the army's loyalty to Park. Although the voice of dissidence in the army was muted and sporadic, as Halloran reported, and although the possibility of a successful coup was highly uncertain due to "elaborate apparatus" of surveillance and detection within the army, the unspoken military pressure will never disappear in the fear-ridden minds of the Park regime. In the process of total dissipation of legitimacy and even its semblance, military disloyalty to an unpopular and repressive government may provoke a truly bloody action by the officers and men. As was indicated in Halloran's report, there already have been telltale signs of military unrest. Retired general officers and the flag officers of the navy had urged Park's "retirement," while discontent spread through the colonels ranks, who most importantly did not take part in Park's coup, and through all graduates of the regular academy in the mid-1950s whose education and outlook have been totally different from the ragtag corps of generals with varied and indifferent backgrounds. In the fall of 1974, some twenty-eight young officers wrote a critical letter to a *Newsweek* correspondent in Seoul asking for its publication with their names. Other incidents involved reported cases of military riots against the military police who were sent to disperse and arrest officers in political meetings; surveillance of Christian chaplains in the military; the installation of numerous antiaircraft batteries in Seoul largely to protect Park himself from his own air force pilots; and paranoiac control of the air force units to the point of jeopardizing their combat readiness.[13]

Judging apparently that the above measures were not enough to keep him in power, Park had begun to take further steps to institutionalize his national surveillance by the following:

1. Establishment of *Student Corps for National Protection*—Organized nationally in the fall of 1975 for the alleged purpose of national mobilization against North Korean attack.

The organization was undertaken immediately after the dissolution and prohibition of all extracurricular activities in educational institutions from the elementary level to university (such as various legitimate research clubs, Christian and other religious organizations, and even Boy Scouts) as an added measure of total control of academia.

With the Corps, the schools instantly have transformed themselves into massive military camps, the cadres of which were appointed by the government with the power of surveillance, and summary punishment, of fellow students suspected of anti-Park activities. The head of the Student Corps is Park himself, who has direct control down to the company level commanders.

2. *People's Defense Corps*—It was organized in 1975 to mobilize all of the male population between the ages of seventeen to fifty for the ultimate purpose of controlling the entire population, whose first oath was not to engage in any political activities, thus completely eliminating the very foundation of political opposition. Even with this measure, the Park regime proclaimed Emergency Presidential Decree No. 9 in May, which declared that any discussion of the *Yushin* Constitution or Park's rule was an act of national treason.

3. *National Security Act*—It was passed in the early morning hours of July 9, 1975. The act forces an additional levy in the form of a "Defense Tax" even on foreign firms; limits residence for citizens; and provides an extraordinary state power of preventive arrest of all "ideological criminals"—a new category of offense against state security. As the Japanese have commented sardonically, the Act resembles closely the detested Japanese "Peace Preservation Regulations" of the Meiji period.

4. *The Defense Tax*[14]—The ultimate use of this newly imposed tax,

paid both by the citizens as well as foreign and domestic corporations, is unknown and unexplained. Reliable sources indicate that it is being used by the Blue House (Park's official residence) for political and other secret purposes. The same sources charged that the fund for the most part is used to bribe senior military commanders and journalists to control and muzzle them, as Park is still unsure of their loyalty.

The result of the unlimited political repression and the atmosphere of constant terror had created a surrealistic social climate eerily similar to Francois Truffaut's 1960 movie, *Fahrenheit 451,* with its description of Superstate and the terrorization of the population. People in South Korea have become increasingly wary of reading any book for the fear of official suspicion of intellectual dissent, giving rise to wry jokes in South Korea that the "Age of Comic Strips" has finally arrived for the adult population. With freedom of speech and press in total jeopardy, South Korean opposition spreads in sullen defiance of silence.

Warnings and advice of all kinds notwithstanding, Park's Korea is heedless of the painful lessons of the collapse of Indochina—of Thieu and Lon Nol. The idea that South Vietnam had fallen due to "internal collapse" and as a result of the loss of "popular legitimacy," either has not dawned on Park or he is afraid of change, having gone too far in the wrong direction for too long.[15]

It is truly pertinent to quote for the regime the following statement by an anonymous person: "Dictatorships don't realize when the game is over." For it is true that dictatorship of any criminal regime, solely based on the exercise of brute force and repression in callous disregard of popular will and welfare, carries in itself the seed of its own violent demise. Free political expression and the consent of the governed cannot long be suppressed especially when there is no chance of peaceful transference of political power. To rectify such conditions, violence is not only tolerable but strongly recommendable.

II.

This section focuses on South Korean economy: Park's embrace of Japan and his sense of national value.[16]

For all his vaunted "economic progress" since 1961, the lethal defect in Park's economic "growth" has been his insensitive, blind, and total dependence on Japan, despite the deeper political meaning in the context of Korea's sad past history of Japanese domination.

The perennial problems of trade deficit,[17] foreign loans and other forms of economic and financial aid from Japan, on which the very survival of the South Korean economy so precariously rests, will not remain purely economic, but inevitably will have serious political complications.

The status of Japanese economy in Park's Korea has been an exclusive factor since the early years of his rule. But, besides the possibly sinister political motives behind Japan's policy of "economic cooperation,"[18] there are several serious problems for Japan's economic future. The problem of rising wages at home threatens to significantly diminish Japan's profit margin. The growing manpower shortage, either from excessive economic development or from the exceptionally successful postwar birth control program, limits the possibilities of continuous economic expansion and further raises the question of high wages. The cutthroat economic competition among the firms in Japan and the general trend of cartelization have largely destroyed small and medium enterprises, and their salvation can only be found overseas in low-wage and unemployment-ridden countries such as South Korea. Moreover, the growing global resentment against the rising invasion of "Made in Japan" goods inevitably forced Japan to devise devious means to skirt that problem—by setting up "transformation" industries and phony "joint ventures" in underdeveloped countries—with the collusion of the ruling elite.[19] Lastly, and increasingly most important, the existence of huge surplus capital and foreign exchange (accumulated prior to 1973) forces Japan to seek an overseas outlet for economic and ultimately political penetration.

All of the above factors had converged with Park's obsession with "economic growth" *at all costs* (including the possible subjection of his nation to a new form of colonization) to allow the present level of dependence on Japan. For some years now, more than several hundred Japanese firms of different types have been hyperactive in South Korea —showing a keen interest in *all* kinds of vital industrial projects. As a result, numerous "transformation industries" have been set up in Korea to enable Japanese capital investment and to take advantage of the local availability of a cheap and abundant labor force—a labor force deliberately driven to poverty by an official South Korean policy for the dual purpose of political control and inequitable economic growth at the expense of the masses. Besides the overt massive capital investment, Japan has introduced into Korea an undetermined sum of funds through covert financing in cooperation with the numerous "phantom partners" in supposed "joint ventures." In this way, Japan has succeeded spectacularly in collecting profits from the so-called South Korean exports, which in fact are nothing but assembled products from imported Japanese components.

Between 1965 and 1969 alone, Japan's investment in Korea—through both channels described above—had increased more than twenty-three times. Since then, despite the paucity of data released by South Korean authorities, especially after the total clampdown since 1972, the cumulative increase could well have reached forty-five to fifty times the figure of 1965.[20] The 1970 data of the Bank of Korea showed that Japan had become the second largest investor in Korean economy, following only the United States, with 34.7 percent of the total foreign capital in South Korea. By 1973–74, Japan had a cumulative total of $436.9 million in "formal equity investment" as compared to the second investor, the United States, which had the figure of $174.3 million.[21] Of the new authorizations alone given in the same period, 94 percent went to Japanese firms.[22] The cumulative total for Japan by 1975 (first quarter) was $498.2 million (61 percent of the total foreign investment), as against the United States figure of $202.2 million (24 percent).[23]

In addition to all this, Japan has been advancing to South Korea millions in commercial loans, which in fact will increase South Korea's dependence on Japan to a still higher le⁻⁻¹ because of the termination of the reparations payment agreement signed at the time of the normalization in 1965.[24] As the Third Five Year Plan (1972–1976)[25] has largely been a failure due to many causes, South Korea has been begging Japan since last year to float some $2,000 million annually in terms of governmental, private, and commercial loans, and other aids.[26] Certainly, this will have an added impact on South Korea's dependence on Japan.[27]

The economic and political implications of the rapid growth of Japanese influence on the South can hardly be underestimated. In economic terms, the growing Japanese involvement could mean that it would be almost impossible for South Korea to adopt economic policies in close conformity with indigenous national interest and needs. Already in the present form, Japan's economic domination of the South had amounted to a subtle yet stronger form of "colonialism" —an experience in the long run not much dissimilar to the years of Japan's domination of Korea until 1945. Additionally, Japan's heavy economic stake has already shown that Japan wished to increase her political influence in domestic political affairs in Korea to the point of pre-emption.[28] Moreover, Japan's economic dominance augurs a deleterious effect on the chances of Korean unification. Selig S. Harrison, in his impressive discussion in *Foreign Policy,* puts it this way:

> Many politically-conscious South Koreans respond that the Park approach to development actually prolongs and reinforces [the national division] by its very nature, leaning excessively on foreign help [especially Japanese] in a preoccupation with rapid growth per se and thus multiplying the vested interests with a stake in perpetuating the status quo.[29]

There have indeed been numerous cases of suspected, although skillfully camouflaged, political collusion between the Park regime and the LDP government in Japan—especially with its right-wing elements such as Kishi, Sato, Tanaka, Fukuda, et al., and the *Seirankai,* in terms of political conspiracies and mutual support in political funds.[30]

The same fear of major complications because of Japan's heavy involvement in South Korea has often been voiced by the Japanese themselves. Among the most notable ones are Tokuma Utsunomiya (a liberal member of the LDP) and Professor Eto Shinkichi of Tokyo University. If the present trend continues much longer without abatement, mainly through major changes in Park's thinking, it would undoubtedly constitute the disruptive renewal of the aggressive Japanese stance on the peninsula and even in the continental affairs,[31] and will most assuredly complicate the Korean problem beyond reprieve. The main fallout of this dangerous turn of events would not only be borne by the South Koreans but unmistakably by the Americans themselves with their continued commitment to South Korea and Japan.

Such Japanese economic penetration with the ultimate objective of political control will create a political atmosphere of increasing corruption and irregularities in the management of the South Korean economy, and would eventually lead to a political crisis of truly major proportions—a crisis justifiably compounded by the aroused anti-Japanism.[32] Japan's deliberate silence and reluctance to reorient her economic relations with South Korea on the basis of sound economic principles and with due regard to Korean national sensitivity show to a great extent her extra-economic ambitions—a factor not only economically devastating to South Korea's rivalry with the North but more critically heating up Peking's apprehensions on the Korean question.[33] The ultimate outcome of such a development would be enormously detrimental to the United States as well, for instance in the possibility of collapse of détente with Peking. Lastly, but equally important, it is well to point out that the present regime, solely responsible for the reintroduction of Japan on a massive scale contradictory to Korea's true interest, will have to answer for its conduct to the people in a Draconian manner—far more severe than any which has been meted out to unpopular regimes in the past. In many respects, despite his lapses and crudities, Syngman Rhee was an angelic personification of true nationalism nowhere comparable to the traitorous behavior of Park and his officials.

Park's oft-repeated phrase has been the "establishment of a correct sense of values"—a rhetoric he has consistently used to justify the present dictatorship. What does he mean by this lofty slogan? How faithful has he been to his own statement of high values?

A revealing glimpse can be had in the following episode. One Min Kwan-sik, who once held the position of Minister of Education, visited a South Korean high school in Tokyo *(Hankuk Hakkwan)* on April 12, 1973, while he was still holding the cabinet post. In a speech given on the occasion, "as Minister," he "expressed his satisfaction" that the numerous South Korean young women were "making 'devoted' efforts at home and overseas to acquire much-needed foreign exchange" for the Republic's national task of economic development and modernization. The Minister was reported to have paid special praise to "The laudable patriotic sentiments of the large number of South Korean *kisaeng* and nightclub hostesses [carrying the passports stamped with "Artistic Delegation"] who have come to Japan and are working day and night selling their _____ for the nation."[34] As Mr. Chung Kyungmo, a well-known journalist and critic, had written in *The Japan Interpreter,* such an obscene description is rarely used even in private company but was obviously considered appropriate by a Cabinet officer on Japanese soil to an audience of Korean high school children.[35]

Indeed, prostitution in South Korea is not only a state sponsored institution, abetted by the highest "political authority," but it is also treated as an indispensable source of national revenue. *Time* Magazine in its June 4, 1973, issue described South Korea as "Japan's bordello" —a term both humiliating and repugnant to the nation in light of its acute past experiences with Japan.

On another occasion, during a South Korean-Japanese Parliamentarians' Conference in Tokyo in September 1971, General Min-Ki-sik (retired), chairman of the Military Affairs Committee of the National Assembly, and former chief of staff of the South Korean Army, approached the then Prime Minister, Sato, with the statement that: "If Japan does not help us, South Korea will be destroyed. *We want you to think of the ROK as part of Japan and give us some real military assistance.*"[36] (Emphasis added.)

Basically, the serious economic problem for South Korea emanates from its policy of exclusive emphasis on industrial growth and export-orientation at the expense of its agricultural policy in a nation of 50 percent peasant population.[37] What South Korea has not realized is the fact that the Japanese model for economic growth that she tries to imitate so closely, was preceded by a successful agricultural revolution that had provided Japan with a solid base for modern industrialization.[38]

Through the failures of the three successive Five Year Plans (1962–66, 1967–71, 1972–76), South Korean agriculture is in a state of serious stagnation. First, agriculture's annual growth rate in general has been significantly below the level of industrial growth. Prior to 1972, agriculture's 4 percent rate contrasted poorly with the industrial growth rate of 20 percent to 25 percent. Even after the Third Five Year Plan, which had promised the rectification, no significant change was made. On the contrary, the agricultural production rate had declined to the level of 1.3 percent or less according to the government figures.[39] However, the real picture is gloomier with the growth rate registering less than zero percent.[40] Second, without the compensating improvement in scientific methods and other forms of mechanization to improve the productivity, the size of the arable land has consistently shrunken as a result of ill-conceived industrial projects. For instance, in the period of 1967–1970 alone, there was a reduction of some 9 percent. In a land of peasants, who still comprise some one-half of the total population, with the constant need for grain imports and the increasing difficulties for export of industrial products, such a policy for haphazard industrial expansion seems extremely unsound. Third, largely due to agricultural retardation, an increasing number of migrant farmers have inundated the urban labor market, pushing up the unemployment in the cities and reducing the farm labor force by more than 10 percent in the past several years. This latter point is significant as mechanization and other improved methods of cultivation, which were the key projects in the Third Plan, were not implemented. As a result, the national unemployment rate was pushed up alarmingly even before the economic debacle since 1973. The unemployment rate in Seoul had reached 14.7 percent to 23 percent by 1971–1972. As the trend continued, somewhere between a quarter to a half million people had migrated into the cities every year, creating a new cycle of unemployment.[41]

The real truth behind South Korea's agricultural policy is that the regime has no intention of improving the farm income nor in general the welfare of the farming population. In fact, South Korea's anti-inflation policy "requires" low prices for farm products. According to Chung Kyungmo, the Seoul government's rice purchase price, which was deliberately kept low, had never exceeded the farmer's production costs. Consequently, the impoverished farmers were forced to abandon their fields and begin to migrate into urban areas, resulting in the sudden urban population explosion and unemployment. A Seoul National University survey in 1967 had found that 32 percent of the heads of the households in Seoul had no gainful employment.[42]

Although it might have been a genuine headache and even a political dynamite, Park has found in the untoward phenomenon a certain valuable advantage. As his policy has always been one of industrial growth, of expanding exports, and of attracting foreign capital, he found the idle and unemployed labor force in the cities a major asset because lower wages attracted foreign capital and facilitated export trade. Moreover, Park has considered the increasing foreign investment as the ultimate guarantee of his political longevity. As Chung and Professor Gerhard Breidenstein stated:

> The government finds it very useful to have an industrial reserve army, which will make no complaint no matter how low the wages are, "encamped" in large numbers in the cities. . . . [In fact,] the Park government's apparent lack of policy toward rural migration to the cities is actually the regime's policy![43]

In fact, it seems beyond doubt that Park's policy is to keep "stability through poverty," as Chung aptly described:

It is in the Park regime's interest that the populace be so hard pressed in making a living, just trying to stay alive, that it will lose all interest in politics. People know that to get in trouble once means loss of job and harassment by the [KCIA], ending in extreme poverty or starvation. The poverty of the people has become a unique "mass base" of the Park government.[44]

Apparently, Park has found in "poverty" the reverse of the political truth so beautifully expounded by Saint-Just, who said: "Les malheureux sont la puissance de la terre"—that all the deeply engraved social ills led inevitably to revolutionary conditions.[45]

A classified internal document of Japan's Foreign Ministry, "The Reality of the Fake Enterprises in the ROK,"[46] was compiled by the Northeast Asia Division of the Asian Affairs Bureau on the basis of information collected by various unnamed "organizations in South Korea at the request of the Ministry" in 1972. The existence of the top secret report on South Korea was made known on February 3, 1975, during a Diet interpellation session of the Lower House Budget Committee. Ataka Tsunehiko, a member of the Japan Socialist Party (JSP), in a debate on Japanese economic aid to Seoul, requested the revelation of the document. Foreign Minister Miyazawa admitted that the Ministry in fact was in possession of the report, but refused to publicize it because of the possible diplomatic complications with Seoul and because of the possibility of "untoward incidents" toward those who were directly involved in the collection of the data in South Korea.

However, an abridged version of the document was partially released by Aoji Shin, the representative of the Japan-ROK Solidarity Liaison Council, in a press conference on May 8, 1975. Aoji stated that the original document existed in mimeographed form (276 pages), and that the fifth chapter of the report dealt with the "fake enterprises and their relations with political and business circles," and cited numerous names of the high officials of the Park government and top business leaders who were implicated in the massive distribution of "political funds."

Divided in seven chapters, the secret document dealt with: 1) the origins of the "fake" enterprises; 2) the process of their appearance; 3) the reality of the same; and 4) their relations with political, official, and business circles.

The report concluded that there was a direct link between the foreign aid, regarded as the "most important concessions" in Park's Korea, and the origins of the "fake" corporations. The secret document revealed that "Any person, who was able to make money (to be used for social entertainment) and find a political channel, could gain access to concessions in some way or other," and that many who play the role of intermediaries for "concession hunters" were in general "American and Japanese" who were mostly "ex-bureaucrats and Government-patronized businessmen"—well acquainted with official and business circles in their respective countries.

Aoji stated that the Japanese government continued to offer loans to South Korea despite the major findings of irregularities in the use of those funds, and the massive corruption that now swept through Park's regime. According to Aoji, one very important "fake," which was connected with a Japanese corporation, had a direct link with Kim Jong-pil, Prime Minister until December 1975.

In a further comment on the report, Ataka charged that "most of the loans given the ROK by Japan in the past were used by political and business circles" of the two countries "for their own personal interests"; that Japan invariably increased the loans simply to secure the repayment of the previous ones; and that the "fakes" were the direct result of such bankrupt policies. Ataka was particularly emphatic in pointing out the possibility of strong anti-Japanese feelings amongst Koreans as a result of their ultimate sufferings under such practice.[47]

Among the corporations branded as the "fakes" were more than ten of the most prominent and "model" business concerns of South Korea, which the Park regime had repeatedly cited as successful examples of its economic progress. They were: Daehan Shipbuilding Corporation; Hankuk Fertilizer; Shinjin Motors; Donam Wool Spinning; Taerim Fisheries; Taewon Paper; Taeson Shipbuilding; Punghan Industry; Daehan Plastics; Kongyong Chemicals; Hankuk Chemicals; Daewoo Industry; Hanil Synthetic Fibre; Ssangyong Trading; Samsung Moolsan, etc. Every one of these corporations is in various stages of bankruptcy.[48]

As the Japanese Foreign Office report attests, the root cause of this prevalent evil that has placed the nation on the brink of paralysis is the uncontrolled influx of foreign loans. As of March 1975, the government acknowledged a total of $7.5 billion in foreign loans (debts)—a sum clearly beyond South Korea's ability to repay and a sum that is more than half the total G.N.P. of South Korea.

Liberally imported on the grandiose pretext of "modernization of the fatherland," the foreign loans have in fact been squandered by bankrupt corporations through officially sanctioned irregularities, which in turn had financed all of Park's anti-democratic escapades. For example, the operational mode of the South Korean haute fraudulence runs something like the following. An "entrepreneur" (a term commonly used in South Korea to denote a person without a penny of capital to his name) concludes an $8 million purchase contract with a foreign firm, and proceeds to get a foreign loan to cover the contract. He then "persuades" the foreign firm to mark up the total sum of the contract to a fake amount of $10 million. A cash delivery of the difference—$2 million—is "diplomatically" arranged; a part of the difference is promptly "donated" to Park, while the rest is "invested" in foreign currency neatly tucked away in secret accounts, a luxury residence, and other choice real estate properties. While the foreign contractor now fulfills the $8 million purchase order with plant facilities and machinery, either too antiquated to be operable or simply "incomplete," he feels no longer obligated but in fact sees an opportunity in the deal for easy profit. After all he had already done a great favor by jacking up the contract and handing over a sizable sum of cash. The South Korean "entrepreneur" feels no responsibility for the loan, since it was guaranteed by the state. The ultimate responsibility for the delinquency is not his but "South Korea's." All he has to do now is to declare bankruptcy at the proper time after due "preparation," which would be "understood" by the "state" already well oiled with a handsome kickback. The result of this connivance is obvious: the enterprise normally goes bankrupt *even before* the "factory" materializes. This kind of shenanigan has created a brave motto in Seoul: "the enterprises may die but the entrepreneurs never die."

Although President Park's dictatorship has been omnipresent and extensive, it most certainly was not confined to "arranged kidnappings," intimidations, the KCIA activities against critics at home and overseas (particularly in the United States), and massive public relations lobbies and bribery aimed at foreign government's high officials, and members of their legislatures. It again did not limit itself to the suppression of freedoms of speech, assembly, press, academia, religious activities, foreign nationals including members of the American Embassy, etc. The most substantial part of his dictatorship applied to "cornering" the whole nation's finances.

According to well-established sources in South Korea, it is strongly suggested that the infamous *May 16th Foundation*[49] (established to commemorate his "military revolution" of 1961) belongs to him in its immense financial entirety. The Foundation encompasses numerous satellite "enterprises" under its ever widening control: Cultural Broadcasting Corporation (Mun-hwa Bangsong); *Kyunghyang Shinmun* (formerly a Catholic daily of great prestige and integrity which had fought a brave battle for democracy against Syngman Rhee); *Pusan Ilbo* (daily in Pusan); and a series of textile firms, etc., valued at some $160 million. Moreover, it has been charged that the omnipresent Foundation had taken over the Walker Hill[50] complex in Seoul—the renowned "Las Vegas" of Korea—which had previously gone bankrupt under private management.

To top it all, according to *Minjok Shinbo* (a newspaper published in Japan by Koreans), Park has reportedly purchased land of some 400,000 *pyung* (valued at $18 million) in Nasu, Japan, where Emperor Hirohito owns a villa. The same story was taken up during the Japanese Diet debate in the Lower House Budget Committee on November 13, 1973.[51]

Indeed, the picture of high level corruption becomes clearer, when one adds the general profile of "several dozen" who control the nation's economy through underhanded and covert channels. For instance, 1972 statistics, released by the South Korean Tax Agency, showed that 2,965 persons paid especially high taxes—under the so-called "composite income tax"—of $12,500 on the average. Judging from this, it can easily be concluded that of 2,965 only "several dozen" at the most are enjoying the monumental wealth reaped through the handling of foreign loans and illicit "private loans" described above which totalled some 500 billion *won*—almost twice the amount of total money in circulation issued by the Bank of Korea. Chung Kyungmo writes, along with the other sources already cited:

> It is widely rumored that the combined private property of the four highest government officials (not private businessmen, but present or former senior bureaucrats linked to the Park administration) is more than 50% of the total currency issued by the Central Bank of Korea. South Korea's Central Intelligence Agency (SKCIA) chief Yi Hu-rak [who was relieved of his post as a result of Kim Dae-jung case] was severely criticized in the National Assembly in 1970 for having acquired private property worth 30 billion won [some $6-7 million at the current exchange rate]. At that time, the Bank of Korea's total currency issue was 190 billion won.[52]

It is no wonder that the South Korean economy hovers danger-ously near the brink of total disaster. Its so-called success has been entirely based on monumental foreign debt, some $7.8 billion by 1975 —a sum clearly out of proportion for the Korean G.N.P. The salvation of Park's economy lies in still more loans, and more loans will further intensify the rate of corruption. It has become an irreversible cycle, which cannot and will not be arrested without basic reforms in psy-chology, politics and business mentality. No amount of foreign arms, defense commitments and extraordinary measures of national "mobi-lization" can save the regime.

The problem of Park's system (which he calls "capitalism") has been the total absence of what Max Weber defined to be the "puritan" morality of "penny-pinching asceticism" which accumulated the re-quired capital for others.[53] So was the case in Japan, which was Park's model for development, where the samurai class applied their ethic to modern capitalism, wherein honesty, frugality, and hard work played their major role. Nothing of the kind exists in Park's Korea, where everything and anything is totally dependent on the fruits of others' labor. As indeed Chung cites most aptly, John M. Keynes suggested in *The General Theory of Employment, Interest and Money* (1936), that the survival of capitalism depended on the "expansion of effective demand by the redistribution of wealth, not because economic inequality was immoral or unethical, but because . . . a more equitable distribution" was indispensable.[54] Surely, neither by Weber nor by Keynes does South Korean capitalism qualify itself for the description, nor can it survive with its massive inequity and lack of "profit motive," wherein no capital is formed and the only *modus operandi* is fraud. So, without democracy and capitalism, where can one find a convincing rationale for the defense of Park?

III.

The thorny question of American politico-military commitment to South Korea has re-emerged as a pivotal issue since Indochina and demands a comprehensive examination against two fundamental points. Firstly, does American support for Park's regime in Seoul still hold the same intrinsic value as the American support for the Rhee regime of the 1950s? And very importantly, will that commitment for Park benefit American national interest? Or can the American policy at present continue indefinitely despite the wholly changed conditions within South Korea? Will that make sense for the United States in Asia for the long run? Will that commitment be possible in light of the deterioration of the Park regime, which cannot be distinguished at all from Kim's in the North?

Secondly, as Selig S. Harrison so aptly posed in his major article in *Foreign Policy,* is there a need for a "detached American approach to Korea . . . one that rests not only on distaste for [Park] but on a more comprehensive appraisal of North Korea"?[55] What was the character of the Kim regime in the North in 1950, which compelled American intervention on behalf of Seoul; what is the change that has taken place, if any, in North Korea since then that needs scrutiny; what does that change imply for American policy to Korea; and, lastly, could there not be reason to fundamentally rethink and retool American response to the Korean problem for the 1970s and beyond.

I have already described in some detail the process of disintegration (under Park) of South Korea's vital "popular" and national legitimacy. What impact could that crucial transformation have on the viability of South Korea for which America has paid in blood and treasure? There are several important assessments which need re-emphasis in evaluating the Park regime and its implied influence on American position not only in Korea but in Asia as a whole for a period to come.

Professor Edwin Reischauer had persistently and persuasively argued with wide concurrence:

> What South Korea has to fear from the North is not open aggression so much as subversion. So long as the people of the South continue to fear and hate the Communists. . . ., there is no chance of successful subversion, but disaffection with the Park regime is beginning to erode these attitudes. Park is embarked on a policy that seems almost designed to destroy popular support for his regime and make the distinction between the [two Koreas] seem no longer very important. He is running the danger of turning many of his own people into Communist supporters, willing to risk the rule of the North in order to get rid of his oppression.[56]

Too far-fetched a conclusion? Park's policy of unlimited and unabated repression will shortly "neutralize" most of the population—if not all. In the process, a drastic political and military change on the peninsula might not be a matter of great alarm to the "ideologically" neutralized majority. In fact, should Park's dictatorship continue without chances for restoring a democratic rule, the people in South Korea might very well be tempted to make the distinction between the North and the South not in terms of anti-communism but in terms of corruption, livelihood, and stance on nationalistic zeal.

Professor Paul K. Ryu, a respected judicial scholar, a former president of Seoul National University, and most importantly an ardent anti-communist, had argued:

> The operative portions of Mr. Park's "Korean democracy" are replicas of the North Korean pattern, which styles itself as "democratic centralism." The only difference lies in the fact that Kim Il Sung avows such centralism, derived from the Soviet Union, whereas Park Chung Hee merely practices it. Park's centralism is ominous. It plays into the hands of [Kim], just as Hitlerism unwittingly served Stalin.[57]

The important question here concerning Park's rule is not merely the "denial of civil liberties and human rights" as it so often seems to be treated by the United States Congress and the Administration.[58] The real crux of the issue is what ultimate political effect it will have on the domestic political atmosphere bearing on the degree of popular support for the regime and its viability, as the collapse of Park could easily presage the collapse of the state itself. The dilemma, then, is that the collapse is *inevitable with Park* and could be inevitable "without Park" depending on how swiftly and determinedly America moves to review the whole policy.

The political truism in all this is the eternal historical verity that the successful defense of a state does not depend on arms alone, but more fundamentally on the status of national will, popular loyalty freely given, societal cohesion, and national morale. History is strewn with the carcasses of the regimes that committed the acts of self-immolation: Chiang Kai-shek's KMT government, Thieu's Vietnam, and Lon Nol's Cambodia readily come to mind in our life time. There are numerous others in the annals of man.

Even the Ford Administration acknowledged as much. After months of pondering the bitter lessons of debacle in Indochina, President Ford finally stated in Honolulu on December 7, 1975, that "Popular legitimacy and social justice are vital" for "resistance against subversion or aggression."[59] Former Secretary Kissinger at least on two occasions commented on the theme. On August 14, 1975, in a speech before the Southern Commodity Producers Conference in Birmingham, Alabama, he said:

> Our smaller allies and friends around the world are important factors in global stability. *We have learned the lesson of Viet-Nam: American military involvement cannot substitute for a nation's efforts to mobilize its people to defend itself. Nor will we permit allies to blackmail us by pretending that their security means more to us than to them. . . .*[60] (Emphasis added.)

Kissinger again on November 6, 1975, stated before the House Committee on International Relations on the question of America's "security assistance program" that "[there] are many factors which must be considered in any foreign transfer of American defense services and equipment"; and that the United States would have to ask serious questions on "*the nature and extent of the threat to the security of the recipient nation*" and on the "*capacity* [of the nations involved] *to maintain stability,* its will to defend its own interests."[61] (Emphasis added.)

Professor Gregory Henderson, a former specialist on Korea in the State Department, has written:

> In the next years, the testing ground shifts to Korea. Again, the question will not concern arms—we have been giving these to the South at three times the rate anyone has given them to the North. South Korea's defense depends on whether Park so rules that loyalty is felt and given freely in a system where men are not cowed but have and feel some stake. . . . [Unless] the South can create a politically viable system, it will, probably within the next several years, be doomed as Vietnam and Cambodia were doomed.
>
> Park's political methods are forged for subjects, not citizens; for privates and corporals, not South Korea's educated and politically sophisticated civilians. . . .[62]

Should the political terror continue under Park, who refuses "to pay even lip service to democracy" with the ever convenient excuses of "national security" against the Northern invasion, which is discounted even by the American military, the "once firm political terrain of loyalty" will be softened and turn "South Korea into the sort of political quagmire that we know only too well from Vietnam."[63]

What should the United States do with "an ally"—seemingly so determined to dig its own grave? By most accounts, it seems that South Korea's Park has been totally impervious to American advice cautioning him on the damage of his policies, although it is difficult to tell what the conditions of American representation have been since the early 1970s.

Judging by the past record, and the vital importance of American commitment to Park for his survival, it seems eminently reasonable to assume that *given the proper pressure—unqualified and resolute—*the United States should be able to achieve a mutually desired result in restoring the democratic rule in South Korea. Although State Department officials have implied through their statements (private and public) that the basic political, economic, and military conditions of the world had so changed of late that the American pressure on South Korea would not only be ineffective but might even have undesired results,[64] one is not certain whether that indeed is the best judgment. Besides the reported plans for a "Korean coup" during the Eisenhower administration to deal with intractable Syngman Rhee, Kennedy's heavy pressures on Park's *junta* in the early 1960s had successfully effected a change in Park's plan—resulting in the transfer of power to a duly "elected" government in 1963. And what about the American pressure —exerted by Ambassador Walter P. McConaughy—during the crisis of March and April, 1960, which eventually topped the Rhee government?

Understandably, in the aftermath of the wrenching experiences of Watergate, Indochina, the CIA-FBI investigations, and the heightened assertiveness of the Congress on foreign policy issues, such a notion might not be so easily entertainable. However, one should not lose sight of two very important differences in the case of South Korea. One, it is the Congress itself that is now demanding action in South Korea, and it is the Ford administration that seems to dig in against any change.[65] Second, the reaction of the South Korean people to American "pressure" against Park would most emphatically be positive, even laudatory as the true restoration of the great "America" that once was an important symbol and idol. The image of great respect once held by the Koreans for the United States, so badly tarnished in recent years through the support of moribund regimes on the simple basis of blind and self-destructive "anti-communism," would be restored. One must never forget what happened to Ambassador McConaughy after "his" interventions against Rhee in 1960. After all, is it not important that *Park is not* Ho Chi Minh, nor Mao Tse-tung, nor even Castro?

The *New York Times* editorial on August 4, 1974, put the problem in the right perspective, and despite the collapse of Indochina and the revived concern for South Korean security, it still is no less valid:

> ... [The] South Korean regime is consistently turning deaf ears to all outside advice and warnings. Under such circumstances, *the Administration would do well to reconsider whether it has expressed its concerns to Seoul in strong enough terms....*
> The United States should not be in the business of molding other societies to suit its own convenience. But neither should it continue the flow of military support to regimes which are, by their own ill-considered actions, undermining the security which that support is designed to provide. (Emphasis added.)

But whatever the short-term considerations, the most urgent and pressing task with which the United States will sooner or later have to grapple is to identify the options for American policy for the long-term posture: 1) What should be the basic stance of the United States to the problem of both Koreas; 2) what is North Korea today, and what should be America's relations with her; and 3) given the above, what would be the outcome of Korean unification, if achieved by the North, to the United States interests?

To date, the most convincing case made for the necessity of an overall reassessment of North Korea is by Mr. Selig Harrison. As he so perceptively argued, almost twenty years of major changes later, there has been "[no] substantial attempt [made] to confront the implications of a Northern-dominated unification" of Korea through "military or political means, or a combination of both."[66]

Indeed, as would most observers agree, significant changes on both halves of the peninsula over the past decades have largely nullified the basic assumptions of the American policy toward Korea and its basic goal as well. Undisputably, the initial American commitment to South Korea's defense was both convincingly rational and relevant. Not only was South Korea's legitimacy widely accepted as the true "representative of Korean aspirations," as against the image of the North as the "pristine" state of "illegitimate dictatorship" without popular support, but in the heat of the Cold War Kim Il-sung's invasion was generally viewed as the opening shot of the international communist conspiracy for world domination.[67]

A quarter century later, none of these facile assumptions has survived the test of history. The theory of international communist conspiracy and the communist monolith has exploded in the face of intense Sino-Soviet conflict and the "normalization" of relations between Washington and Peking. On the other hand, if South Korea ran the slippery road to a total dissipation of legitimacy especially under the dictatorial rule of Park, ex-Lieutenant of the Japanese Imperial Army, then Kim of the North "has earned his nationalist credentials."[68]

Non-communist Western visitors to the North, including a few Americans, have brought back a portrayal of North Korea, if dictatorial, far removed from the stereotype still operative in the formation of American policy. Harrison, as one of the two American visitors to North Korea in 1972, argues that "Pyongyang's priorities today are incontestably Korean. It has left behind even a 'national Communist' identity and is best described as a 'Communist nationalist' regime."[69] Harrison continues:

> The most striking surprise greeting a visitor to the North is an atmosphere of enthusiasm and elan contrasting sharply with the mood of disenchantment that has progressively overtaken the South. Kim has effectively used his monolithic control to make himself the personification of nationalism, and nationalism is the psychological cushion that softens the impact of an unusually rigid brand of totalitarianism. [Kim's persistent emphasis on unification made the Northerners think of themselves] as the historically-destined liberators of a South that has lost its authentically Korean character.
> [More importantly, they are confident] that Seoul, dependent on anti-Communism for its unity, would fall apart if a meaningful relaxation in the North-South climate were to develop.[70]

Expressing much the same view, an Australian Sinologist, D. Gordon White, after his visit to North Korea in 1974, has written that despite his exposure to Chinese national pride, "nationalism in its present form in [North Korea] is the most intense I have yet to come across," and that Kim's idea of *Chuch'e* (self-reliance) involves an "independent line in politics, self-reliance in economics and self-defense in military affairs."[71] Among some of the signs of intense nationalism, White cites: 1) complete elimination of all Chinese characters from the writing system; 2) the availability of Kim's writings to the virtual exclusion of others—such as the Soviet and the Chinese; 3) the view that the "Korean Revolution" was a "war of national liberation" and nothing else; 4) the recurring theme of Korean cultural identity; 5) the view that the Korean revolutionary experience is a model for the Third World much more than the Soviet or the Chinese "competitors."[72] However, more significant from a political viewpoint, the North Korean regime is extremely reluctant to acknowledge the debt of blood and material it owes to the Chinese and the Soviets for its revolutionary success and during the Korean War.

It is this kind of emphasis on emotional nationalism and her cultural identity that gives today's North Korea her intrinsic strength against the South. Not only is Park's service in the Japanese Imperial Army under the Japanese name of Lieutenant Masao Takagi damaging, but South Korea's ruling clique is tainted with the same record of disservice to the nation. If the past was to be deemed irrelevant for the present, nothing in the record of South Korea's economic and political development so far under Park's rule nullifies the past, nor sets a resurrection of his national credentials. Although it may be very difficult for policy-makers of the State Department to realize the central importance of this, despite their own variegated ethnic and national backgrounds, nationalism in Asia in modern times has been the sole motive force and the overriding rationale for every movement, every revolution, and every human sacrifice; and it will most assuredly continue to play a central role for ages to come. Anyone who cares to examine the turbulent history of Asian communism ought to be able to discover, especially through the experiences of the Vietnam conflict, that the neglect of Asian national aspirations in whatever manner, shape or form will ruin everything in their path—individuals, policies, governments and states.

What has generally marred Park's "economic miracle" is not so much the inequities, which are not found in the North, as Park's "lack of nationalist ethos"—his "unrestrained embrace" of Japan in total "insensitivity" to the "political meaning" of Japan's benighted colonial rule as well as his inglorious part in it.

South Korea as such presents a serious dilemma for the long-term commitment of the United States. Without a major reassessment of the American role vis-à-vis South Korea and the North, it is clear that the United States will continue to experience extreme difficulties unnecessary and detrimental to America's overall posture in Asia.

It has been true that the American commitment in Korea has had the beneficial effect of stabilizing the region for the past quarter century. It is also true that the area had and still possesses far greater strategic and political significance for the United States than Indochina. It is an area where the "security interests of all the great powers intersect," in which clearly American anchorage will have to be maintained in some form to enable American presence in Asia as a force of peace and order. But is there a compelling and irresistible reason to accomplish this with a policy whose foundation for existence has long disappeared?

It seems reasonable and logical, under the circumstances, that there should be a termination of that commitment confined merely to South Korea. It seems equally clear that a new commitment based on the reality of the present will have to be made not only to ensure America's continuing role in Asia, but also for the general welfare of the states in the region. As Harrison argues bluntly but realistically, the American "disengagement" from South Korea might not inevitably lead to a Northern domination of Korea, and even if that should come to pass, it would not necessarily "lead to adverse consequences for the United States and might even have its advantages."[73]

The alternative to "disengagement" would be immeasurably more disastrous. In fact, an American failure or postponement of "disengagement" would have to be measured against a much worse scenario: the ever continuing and intensifying exposure of the United States to a dangerous quicksand in an "increasingly supercharged Korean environment." In an atmosphere so disfigured by Park's insane repression and economic inequities, anything is possible in South Korea in the way of domestic political upheavals or military coup. Committed to defend the regime within these possibilities and conditions would be a sheer folly. Indeed, in a very complex political situation of the region, it would be extremely difficult to reconcile American interests with the present policy of military commitment.

Under the circumstances, what is important for the United States is to realize the fact that Kim Il-sung's regime in North Korea has "emerged" as a credible "contender" for the governance of all Korea, and as such "the North may well have greater political dynamism rooted in a firmer nationalist ethos."[74] Moreover, buttressed by a strong sense of national identity and determination for independence, the Korean unification under the Northern leadership could very well enhance Korea's ability to offset the influences of the intersecting great powers and help maintain the regional stability sought by the United States.[75]

Whatever the case, any long-term American misjudgment of Korean national aspirations would be as catastrophic as the misjudgment of Mao Tse-tung's Chinese Communist Party and Ho Chi Minh's Vietminh forces in the past. In this connection, too, a persistent American pressure on Japan for a greater Asian role—especially on the peninsula —would not only be myopic but also suicidal for the American interests in Asia for a long time to come.

Additionally, it is well to realize that, in dealing with the Korean problem, the United States will have to contend with and adjust to the new global forces, philosophies, and trends—as new parameters of American latitude. Indeed, there has arisen an ill-definable combination of regional international systems, competing political philosophies and forces of an awesome nature yet in the process of infinite transformation. One cannot readily tell where and how all these new elements would ultimately lead. However, of the major evolutions of the past decade or so, some of the more significant ones with revolutionary policy implications are:

1.   The sharp historic shift in global economic equilibrium, largely brought about by the decline of American economic colossus and the simultaneous rise of competing industrial powers. The gradual but truly revolutionary reallocation of vital natural resources, of which the OPEC cartel is only the proverbial tip of a gigantic iceberg. The wide dissemination of sophisticated technology equally suited for economic growth as well as for military application. And the breakdown and dissipation of capital accumulation in the traditional powers of the West.

2.   The emergence and congelation of the third force (or the Third World) in the global politics in direct challenge to the traditional powers' dominance. Despite the fragility and disunity of this force, the "permanence" of its politico-economic influence would be well assured as long as the conflict among the superpowers continues—thus effectively preventing their collective countermeasures against such an existence.

3.   The decline of the American military power relative to the Soviet ascendency due to escalating economic strains, waning national will and purpose, disintegration of forebearance, obsession with racial issues, psychological debility to face foreign policy issues, exaggerated national complacency and bloated pride, lingering "pactomania" without careful criteria, and in neglect of historical lessons.

4.   The revival and rise of impassioned nationalism, which, given the nature of the existing power politics, thrives on manipulation of the superpower contention. Given the nature and durability of the major conflicts in the world, this new force will remain impervious to external attempts for control, and will by itself become the single most important determinant for great powers' policies.[76]

As long as these presently perceivable forces remain, the foreign policy options of the United States will suffer progressive contraction; and unless and until the United States makes major adjustments in areas of explosive tension, such as Korea, she will experience an inevitable decline of her influence in the global arena.

With the mounting difficulties to be expected from the United States commitment to South Korea, what should be the ultimate American policy objectives in Korea—objectives that will not unduly upset the present balance, nor provoke other interested parties, and might even be acceptable to others in the region?

To arrive at a reasonably convincing scenario for American policy, let us make a few basically acceptable assumptions for the sake of argument:

Firstly, it is highly desirable to devise some form of methodology to achieve the Korean unification. Based on the strength of the argument to date, it is reasonable to conclude that the Korean problem in present form would be extremely perilous to the United States and others. It is therefore eminently advisable that the United States devise new approaches to change the basic dimension of the problem—*such as probing the conditions under which the natural outcome of "evolutionary changes" on the peninsula (without the continued American presence) including the Northern-dominated control of Korea would be acceptable.*

It would be true, however, that under the prevailing circumstances, a unified Korea might be a source of serious apprehension to some of the interested parties. For instance, a unified and highly nationalistic Korea would be a source of particular concern, of constant irritation, and even a threat to Japan—especially, if it were to be achieved by a regime closely affiliated with either China or the Soviet Union, or with both, reinforced by hostile stance or ideology. *Provided that* the regime in this case is clearly aligned with either China or the Soviet Union (or both) *against the United States,* such a proposition would be unacceptable and would not be treated seriously by Washington.

On the other hand, one could easily envision vigorous Chinese opposition if the unification were to be achieved through a formula that would allow Japan a clear edge on the peninsula. Under certain conditions, the Soviet Union herself might side with China to frustrate such a development—namely, a more aggressive Japanese-American cooperation further conditioned by a Sino-Soviet détente. Given these possible scenarios, a unification formula in exclusion to the above would be both possible and acceptable to all parties.

Secondly, one could assume that the present conditions of power relations would remain relevant for an indefinite period, and that the presently operative assumptions would still be valid. Included in these are:

1. The continued state of tension and friction between the Soviet Union and China—regardless of possible reconciliation. It can

be assumed that the process of détente, if it is possible, would be slow and difficult, negatively affecting their concerted action.

2. The continued evolution of Sino-American détente, provided there is no sudden shift in Peking's policies to Moscow in favor of reconciliation.

3. Even with some inevitable changes, the basic Japanese-American relations will largely remain the same as present, except in some unforeseen circumstances.

4. Delicate yet basically "harmonizable" relations between the dual sets of ties in East Asia—namely, Sino-American, and Japanese-American relations, provided the Soviet-American frictions and the Sino-Soviet conflict in their various forms continue. In addition, one should also point out the unlikely chances for a Sino-Japanese entente.

Assuming that the present equilibrium among the four major interested powers remains, it would be safe to presume that none of them would be able to enjoy a clear edge against the others in Korea. Within this hypothesis, we can expect an effective restraint between the Soviet Union and the United States, and China and Japan.

Having examined the assumptions, let us turn to the following scenarios and their respective consequences:

1. *A Soviet Attempt to Dominate Korea—*

Although this would be the least likely scenario, under present conditions, any Soviet effort to pre-empt in Korea at the expense of the other interested powers (despite the geographic difficulties of maintaining an effective dominance in Korea without the Manchurian link) would so alarm the Chinese that the PRC would be compelled to make major concessions to Japan to effect joint efforts to contain the Soviet Union. Such an effort by China would not only be acceptable but essentially indispensable for Japan to safeguard her national security.

The presence of such a hostile power on the peninsula would have a catalyzing effect on Sino-Japanese cohesion that otherwise would be well-nigh impossible. Moreover, the Soviet actions for domination of the peninsula would be an act of unintended self-negation of the long sought Soviet objective of preventing Sino-Japanese entente.

Any clearcut Soviet pressure, either in the form of massive and overt support for the North against the South, or in the form of covert but open-ended ties with the South,[77] would clearly constitute a major cause for the United States to align herself with the Sino-Japanese coalition.

In view of these possibilities, Soviet action for predominance in Korea would be impossible and undesirable. Moreover, if the Soviet desire for an Asian collective security arrangement is genuine, it would be inconceivable for the Soviet Union to provoke the others in the region with major changes of policy in areas such as Korea. The various difficulties involved would be keenly appreciated by Moscow, and in this regard, the neutralization of Korea would be considered an acceptable option.

2.   *A Chinese Attempt to Establish Predominance in Korea—*

Peking's hegemonic efforts in Korea—whatever form they might take under conceivable circumstances—would unquestionably provoke Japan to the point of either a massive rearmament with nuclear weapons, and/or an across-the-board settlement of all pending differences with the Soviet Union to contain and eventually "remove" the Chinese from the peninsula. This would hold true, especially *if* the Sino-American détente improves out of *increased need* to contain the Soviets, or to prevent a sudden turn of adventurism in Japan's Asian policy.

In these given circumstances, and provided the existing conditions of power relations basically remain the same, the Soviet Union would not only welcome the Japanese overtures but also would consider them as a major opportunity to improve her position in the area. In essence, the PRC's peninsular policies would have inadvertently created a situation dreaded by herself and the United States. The global balance would have been altered fundamentally to the detriment of the PRC, the United States, and others.

On the other hand, it is conceivable that the same Chinese actions in Korea might not be unduly alarming to the United States—unless there is a major change in the PRC's overall policies, especially in those that affect the American position adversely, or unless the Chinese policies critically inconvenience Japanese-American relations that the United States still considers vital for her role in the region.

Indeed, as long as the present security arrangement between the United States and Japan continues *basically unchanged,* this Chinese attempt in Korea could seriously complicate American relations with Japan, and may have to be resisted by Washington. However, even in such an eventuality, American resistance to the PRC would have to be measured ultimately against Washington's existing relations with Moscow. If the latter is in a state of serious tension, and also, if the American perception of balance against the Soviets is unfavorable to the American interest, then Washington's countermoves to Peking would have to be taken in moderation.

As long as the United States considers Japan central to her objectives in Asia, the PRC's hegemonic moves in Korea would pose a virtually insoluble dilemma and crisis for American policy.

Whatever the case, as long as the United States persists in the present course of commitment to South Korea, her position in East Asia will remain totally untenable. For instance, if the PRC should want to exert pressure—albeit limited—on the United States for a variety of plausible and predictable reasons, her policy options in Korea would be both logical and readily available. However, considering the range of possible consequences all potentially damaging to Peking's basic objectives, the PRC's basic posture toward Korea could well be served by a genuine neutralization of Korea.[78]

3. *The United States in Korea—*

There is not and will not conceivably be any compelling reason for the United States to attempt domination of Korea. This would be unthinkable except in cases of extremely serious crisis or other totally unforeseen events.

If it should occur, however, for whatever reason, the American relations with China would unquestionably suffer a grievous blow, and could easily force a reconciliation or even a military alliance between Peking and Moscow. An alliance would then so thoroughly alarm Japan that Tokyo's policies might also be fundamentally altered against the vital interests of the United States. Put another way, the continued American commitment or outgoing policies in Korea could easily alienate the United States among all the major powers of the region.

Given the myriad of possibilities of monumental complications the United States could be forced to face in Korea, it is entirely conceivable to expect a major American reappraisal of Korean policy at the latest after 1976 elections. Although presently unconvinced, once the United States realizes the basic disconnection between Korea and the Japanese "national security," the Korean neutralization would be entirely acceptable to the United States as the best possible course of action.

4. *Japan's Dominance in Korea—*

Japan's determined efforts to penetrate and dominate South Korean economy and eventually its politics would be so fraught with perils that it would be impossible to adequately catalogue all the possible adverse consequences to peace in East Asia. Not only would it destroy all the chances for harmony with China, but also it would have other unmistakable effects:

(a) Inevitable jeopardy of Sino-American relations, exclusively due to persistent American policy of strong encouragement for Japan's major role in Korea to the point of complete substitution of the United States.

(b) Inevitable reconciliation and even an alliance between China and the Soviet Union, effected largely through Chinese concessions.

(c)   Almost complete isolation of Japan in Asia and the certain rise of vehement anti-Japanism.

(d)   Eventual ruination of the Japanese-American ties.

The tragic mistake of the present American policy in East Asia has been caused by the inexplicable and undefinable American obsession for the "Japanese connection"—blindly expecting that Japan's interest will indefinitely remain coterminous with that of the United States. Or failing in that expectation, the United States will always be able to contain and direct Japan's policies to her advantage, regardless of important internal changes in Japan.

On the other hand, with superb cynicism and skillful manipulation, Japan has been spectacularly successful thus far in misleading the United States with the *diligently cultivated notion that the preservation of South Korea* (*always* in the context of her conflict with the North and most preferably ruled by Park) is absolutely essential for her own existence; and tried to intimate with the thinly veiled threat that without "Korea" she might have to go nuclear. Embedded in this is the important implication that the "nuclear" Japan might not accord a friendly treatment to the United States.

Unless and until American policy changes basically in this important myth, Japan's dangerous domination of Korea will have been achieved unwittingly by American blessing and succor. As such, the present American policy would be an ironic and unintended repetition of the Taft-Katsura Agreement of 1905, and the Root-Takahira, Lansing-Ishii formulae of 1908 and 1918, which inadvertently acknowledged Japan's "special interest in Asia due to geographic propinquity." Consequently, the American policy is not only morally reprehensible but destructive to its own long-term national interest.

As regional conditions now stand, and within the context of the global power equation, South Korea could not be, nor would be threatened by China, the Soviet Union, and certainly not the United States. The only interest this "South Korea-Japan" linkage concept defends is Japan's own economic and financial dominance of Korea. As it is, in defending this faulty principle, the United States would be supporting Japan's aggressive continental policy, as once the Anglo-Japanese Alliance had done from 1902–1922 with catastrophic result.

In the final analysis, the ultimate and inevitable outcome of this mistaken concept will be: 1) Japan's rise to prominence in Asia as the major source of instability; 2) the rise of chauvinistic nationalism and its lunatic fringe elements in Japan; and 3) a gradual revival of destructive "Pan-Asian" concept of the 1930s and 1940s.

Under the circumstances, then, the only sensible policy of the United States should be to encourage the course of events that would enable a gradual unification of Korea—even under North Korean control—and to effect a genuine neutralization. For, in the Korean context, the two will have to proceed side by side. *Neutralization of Korea with the great powers equilibrium (to be distinguished from the maligned concept of "great powers guarantee"),* along with viable nationalistic ethos and defense capacity, would be the only sensible and lasting solution of the peninsular problem.

IV.

Here are recommendations for American policy change on South Korea:

1.   Unequivocal "advice" to Park's regime for the restoration of a genuinely democratic government—with full restoration of the old constitution; new election for a popularly elected government; major purge (judicial punishment through laws which existed prior to 1961) of those who are responsible for corruption, terror and propaganda, including diplomats; restoration of the military dicipline.

2.   Equi-distance policy toward North Korea, either through immediate recognition (even without reciprocity)[79] or through the establishment of diplomatic contact for political negotiation of the Korean problem.

3.   Phased military withdrawal of Korea, to be effected simultaneously with #2 and especially with the implementation of #1.

4.   Six power conference for unification and neutralization, among South Korea, North Korea, the United States, the Soviet Union, China, and Japan.

5.   Demobilization of military and paramilitary forces on both sides to the level of 50,000 men each until the achievement of national unification and neutralization, by which time the unified Korea can rebuild her armed forces—as the military for all Korea.

1. Describing his "Six Principles" of Pacific Doctrine in Honolulu on 7 December 1975 President Ford stated: *"We must reach beyond our concern for security; . . . We recognize that force alone is insufficient* to assure security. *Popular legitimacy and social justice are vital prerequisites of resistance against subversion or aggression."* (Emphasis added.) "President Ford's Pacific Doctrine," *Department of State News Release* (hereafter cited as *DSNR*), 7 December 1975, p. 2.

2. For a similar fantasy, see, "Building Profits in South Korea," *Far Eastern Economic Review* (hereafter cited as *FEER*), 5 September 1975, p. 57.

3. Park had promised to the nation that he would retire after his third term in 1975. During the campaign in 1971, he also promised that he would build up "democratic strength" and "national harmony."

4. On 19 March 1975 Park's ruling Democratic-Republican Party and its affiliated group, *Yu Jong Hoi,* railroaded through the National Assembly twenty-four legislative bills in less than thirty seconds without any debate and with minimal adherence to parliamentary procedures—and in the absence of the opposition members. Included in the twenty-four laws passed was the amendment of the Criminal Code (Paragraph 2, Article 104), which provided the severe penalty for those Korean nationals, making insulting remarks or criticism of national organs constitutionally established, or disseminating distorted facts or falsehood, or otherwise endangering national security, interest or dignity of the state—they shall be punished by seven years of imprisonment; and to make comments concerning the above through foreign nationals or foreign organizations shall be treated the same with the additional suspension of legal rights for ten years.

5. The Emergency Decree No. 9, proclaimed on 13 May 1975 prohibits at the pain of harsh imprisonment and the loss of civil rights: 1) rumor-mongering, through distortion of truth and the dissemination of untruth; 2) any activity in denial of and opposition to the *Yushin* Constitution (of 1972) through any advocacy, petition, instigation, propaganda for the repeal thereof; through the medium of newspaper, broadcast, press, public handbills, documents, books, records and other material; 3) any student assembly, demonstration and the press reports thereof, and any student political activity; and 4) any criticism of the decree itself. Violation of the decree will be punished by imprisonment of at least one year and the loss of civil rights for at least ten years. Public officials who neglect their duties in implementing this decree will be summarily fired from their positions and punished. The military units can be mobilized at any time in order to carry out the decree, etc. For the United States reaction, see, Assistant Secretary of State, Philip C. Habib's statement before the Subcommittee on International Organizations of the House Committee on International Relations, 24 June 1975. *DSNR*, 24 June 1975, pp. 3–4. *Han-Kook Ilbo* (hereafter cited as *HK*) reported on 15 April 1975 that "preventive detention of 'ideological criminals' was being planned" in South Korea through another legislation. For the full text of the proposed bill—"Societal Security Act"—see *HK*, 29 June 1975.

6. For the Kim Tae-jung kidnapping, see among others, "Abduction in Broad Daylight—Showa: Turbulent 50 Years (48)," *Mainichi Daily News* (hereafter cited as *MDN*) 15 July 1975.

7. 28 April 1975.

8. For the terror campaign of the KCIA in the United States itself to "harass foes," see, David Binder, "Threat to Koreans in U.S. By Seoul Stirs Concern," *New York Times*

(hereafter cited as *NYT*) 17 August 1973; "Seoul's Man in the U.S. Is Mr. Lee and Mr. Yang," ibid. Mr. Lee was Seoul's minister to Washington.

9. For earlier threats and imprisonment of Chang, see, Norman Thorpe, "South Korea: Democracy Rolls On," *FEER*, 25 June 1973, pp. 23–4.

10. For the ridiculous nature of Park's charge against Kim Chi-ha, see, Bruce Cumings, "The Kim Chi Ha Case," *The New York Review*, 16 October 1975, p. 42.

11. For the total destruction of the nation's leading daily, *Dong-A Ilbo*, see, Jerome Alan Cohen, "Lawyers and Politics in Korea," *MDN*, 13 April 1975.

12. On Christian opposition to Park and religious persecution, see, Fox Butterfield, "Something New in Korea: An Opposition," *NYT*, 4 August 1974.

13. See, "South Korean Army's Loyalty to Park Shows Signs of Cracking," *NYT*, 3 February 1975. See also my "South Korea's Economic Development and Its Socio-Political Impact," *Asian Survey*, July 1973, pp. 677–690.

14. A report said that "Seoul did not specify the exact purposes for raising the money [through the new defense tax]." See, for the background story, Kim Sam-o, "Taxes: A defence burden in South Korea," *FEER*, 1 August 1975, p. 59.

15. See, for instance, Fox Butterfield, "How South Vietnam died—by the stab in the front," *The New York Times Magazine* (hereafter cited as *NYTM*), 25 May 1975, pp. 30ff. Such descriptions as "We beat ourselves," or "We are a country that destroyed itself" have apparently meant nothing for the Park government.

16. Unless otherwise indicated in the text and in footnotes, the content of this section is an updated version of my 1971 writing and its improvement in 1972 as cited in Note #13 above. See also, "Japan: How Seoul Was Won," *FEER*, 1 August 1975, pp. 52–53; "A sweet and sour affair," ibid., pp. 52–55; "Tension at Masan," ibid., pp. 55–56.

17.

1970 deficit (against Japan)—	$ 573.4 million
1971 deficit	—$ 693.1 million
1972 deficit	—$ 627.8 million
1973 deficit	—$ 456.4 million
1974 deficit	—$1207.5 million
1975 deficit (Jan.–Apr.)	—$ 570.2 million

Cited from *FEER*, ibid., p. 54. For other figures, see, "ROK's Trade Deficit With Japan Increasing," *MDN*, 9 August 1975.

18. See, among others, "Japan '75 Focus: Hidden Forces Against Change," *FEER*, 23 May 1975, pp. 17–18, 20; also, Koji Nakamura, "Japan: The Premier's [Miki's] new political spots," ibid., 19 September 1975, p. 20.

19. For the historical discussion of the impact of the foreign resistance to Japan's expansion overseas in the direction of the Western Hemisphere and elsewhere on Japan's foreign policy change, see, Akira Iriye, *Pacific Estrangement: Japanese and American Expansion, 1897–1911* (Cambridge, Massachusetts: Harvard University Press, 1972), passim.

20. See, Note #16.

21. Selig Harrison, "One Korea?" *Foreign Policy*, No. 17, Winter, 1974–1975, p. 46.

22. Ibid.

23. These figures do not include Japanese and U.S. capital invested in South Korea through multinationals incorporated in third countries. See, "A sweet and sour affair," *FEER*, 1 August 1975, p. 54.

24. See, Susuma Awanohara, "Japan: Quietly Keeping up the Flow," *FEER*, 19 September 1975, pp. 53–54.

25. For further discussion of the Third Five Year Plan, see below in the text.

26. A World Bank group concerned with South Korean economy recently suggested that Korea's "debt-financed" economy will need $2,000 million in foreign loans annually for some time to come. See, Susuma Awanohara, op. cit., (Note #24).

27. For some of the additional pictures of South Korean desperation, see, *HK,* 14 January, 7 June, 10 June, 16 September, 1975 and *Yomiuri Shimbun,* 23 September 1975.

28. Numerous articles by Kohi Nakamura of *FEER* in recent years had specifically catalogued the accusations.

29. Harrison, op. cit., p. 47.

30. See Note #28, and Jon Halliday and Gavan McCormack, *Japanese Imperialism Today* (New York: Monthly Review Press, 1973), pp. 135–64.

31. See, for instance, "Japan To Play Bigger Non-Military Role in Asia: Miki," *MDN,* 9 August 1975; for the possibly implied warning from Peking, see, Note #29; and Halliday and McCormack, op. cit.

32. See, Takehiko Takahashi, "Anti-Japanese Mood in South Korea," *MDN,* 19 June 1974.

33. See my "Peking and Washington in a New Balance of Power," *ORBIS,* XVIII, 1, Spring 1974. The recent return of the Soviet helicopter crew by Peking may portend a new trend in Chinese thinking on this issue.

34. Chung Kyungmo, "The Second Liberation of South Korea and Democratization of Japan," *The Japan Interpreter,* 9, 2, Summer-Autumn, 1974, p. 179.

35. Ibid.

36. Chung, op. cit., p. 181.

37. See, Willard D. Keim, "The South Korean Peasantry in the 1970's," *Asian Survey,* September, 1974, pp. 854–68.

38. See, Thomas C. Smith, *The Agrarian Origins of Modern Japan* (Stanford, California: Stanford University Press, 1959).

39. See, the World Bank report to IECOK as cited in *HK,* 3 May 1974.

40. By the first quarter of 1ᶜ/3, according to the Bank of Korea statistics, the agricultural growth rate was –0   ꝑercent.

41. See, among others, "Seoul Population Snowballing," *MDN,* 1 March 1973.

42. Chung, op. cit., p. 183.

43. Ibid., p. 184. Chung cites from Breidenstein, "Capitalism in South Korea," in Frank Baldwin, ed., *Without Parallel: The American-Korean Relationship Since 1945* (New York: Pantheon, 1974), p. 350.

44. Chung, op. cit., p. 184.

45. See, Hannah Arendt, *On Revolution* (New York: Viking Press, 1963), pp. 56, 106.

46. A "fake" enterprise means a corporation in a state of financial bankruptcy. Many South Korean enterprises, financed by funds from the United States and Japan, have already gone bankrupt. Some "fakes" at the time of the secret report in 1972, have since been "placed" under banks' control, or have undergone superficial cosmetic reconstruction through personnel changes.

47. The data on this report are from *Mainichi Shimbun,* 9 May 1975.

48. Ibid.

49. The Foundation was originally registered under the name of Park's wife, before the assassination.

50. Originally named after Gen. Walton Walker, the commander of the U.S. Eighth Army in Korea in 1950, to commemorate the American military assistance against the North Korean invasion for the defense of South Korea's democracy.

51. See, *Han-Min-Shin-Bo,* 15 June, 15 August, 1975.

52. Chung, op. cit., p. 183.

53. Weber, *The Protestant Ethic and the Spirit of Capitalism.* Cited from Chung, op. cit., p. 184.

54. Ibid., p. 185.

55. His "One Korea?", *Foreign Policy,* No. 17, Winter, 1974–75, pp. 35–62.

56. "Is it time to disengage?—The Korean Connection," *NYTM,* 22 September, 1974. Full text, pp. 15 ff. Quote from p. 64.

57. Letter to Editor, "Korea: Park's 'Ominous Centralism,'" *NYT*, 7 June 1975.

58. The very same problem existed vis-à-vis Greece under the Colonels. On Korea, see, among others, *Special Report—Human Rights in the Republic of Korea*, no. 5, *Department of State Publication 8778*, East Asia and Pacific Series 212, September 1974. Also, *Human Rights in South Korea: Implications For U.S. Policy* (Hearings Before the Subcommittee on Asian and Pacific Affairs, and on International Organizations and Movements of the Committee on Foreign Affairs, House of Representatives) 2nd Session, 93rd Congress, 30 July, 5 August, and 20 December, 1974 (Washington, D.C.: U.S. Government Printing Office, 1974).

59. See Note #1.

60. "American United and the National Interest," *DSNR*, 14 August 1975, p. 3.

61. *DSNR*, 6 November 1975, pp. 2–3. See also, the statement by Philip C. Habib, then Assistant Secretary of State for East Asian and Pacific Affairs, before the Subcommittee on International Organizations of the House Committee on International Relations on 24 June 1975. *DSNR*, same date, pp. 3–4.

62. Letter to the Editor, "The Korean Task," *NYT*, 20 April 1975.

63. Reischauer, op. cit., p. 65. On American military comments on South Korean warnings on the Northern invasion, see, Richard Halloran, "U.S. Warns Seoul on Tainted Image—Americans Say South Korea Impairs Its Credibility by Exaggerating Red Threat," *NYT*, 30 March 1975.

64. For the implied American position, see Habib's statement. See Note #61. The State Department seems to feel that an aid cut off, proposed by many, will simply re-direct South Korea to other sources of supplies, in fact, far more sophisticated weaponry than the American government has so far allowed Seoul, thus far more dangerous for East Asian stability and peace. For South Korea's nuclear goal, see, *NYT*, 2 November 1975. On plans for "Korean coup," see, *NYT*, 4 August 1975.

65. See, Leslie H. Gelb, "Realism Vs. Idealism in American Foreign Policy," *NYT*, 30 November 1975. For Senator George McGovern's proposal on Korea—"A phased withdrawal of American troops from Korea within the next year," see, *NYT*, 26 October 1975.

66. See his "One Korea?", loc. cit.

67. For the refutation of these assumptions, see *inter alia*, Charles E. Bohlen, *Witness to History* (New York: Norton, 1973); Ernest May, *"Lessons" of the Past* (New York: Oxford University Press, 1973); Allen S. Whiting, *China Crosses the Yalu* (New York: Macmillan, 1960); Nikita Khrushchev, *Khrushchev Remembers* (Boston: Little, Brown, 1970); Wang Ming (Ch'en Shao-yu), *Half Century of the Chinese Communist Party and Mao Tse-tung's Betrayal* (Moscow, 1975).

68. See, D. Gordon White, "Report from Korea: The Democratic People's Republic of Korea Through the Eyes of a Visiting Sinologist," *The China Quarterly*, 63, September 1975, pp. 515–522.

69. Harrison, op. cit., p. 38.

70. Ibid., pp. 38–9.

71. White, op. cit., p. 515. For a similar report, see, Stanley Moore, "North Korea: Identifying the Peninsula Threat," *FEER*, 22 January 1972, pp. 16–18.

72. White, op. cit., pp. 515–17.

73. Harrison, op. cit., p. 51.

74. Ibid.

75. For a similar view, see, Gregory Henderson's article in the *Los Angeles Times*, 1 June 1975. See also, Harrison, p. 57. In this connection, I. F. Stone's views are to be noted, "Korea: An Old-New Tunnel for Old-New 'Light'?", *NYT*, 2 June 1975.

76. Kissinger, for all his brilliant account of Metternich and his policy, has failed to understand the forces of nationalism as the main pillar of modern politics amongst nations. As Metternich was once so obsessed with "cabinet diplomacy" of manipulation ignoring the new age of nationalism, Kissinger seems unable to shake himself loose from

the temptations of momentary "juggling acts" rather than acknowledging the historical forces and adjusting to them.

77.   Possible in case of an irreparable deterioration of the South Korean-American ties or a severance of South Korean-Japanese relations due to a major change in Japan's policies vis-à-vis the North and/or the complete domination of the North by the PRC solely against the Soviet Union. It is also possible that a change of Japanese policy could be effected through the fall of the LDP government in Japan and its replacement by a coalition cabinet.

78.   See, for instance, "China Backs Asia Peace Zone," *MDN,* 10 August 1975. It was reported that the PRC would support a "zone of peace, freedom, and neutrality."

79.   See Kazushige Hirasawa, "Japan's Emerging Foreign Policy," *Foreign Affairs,* October 1975, pp. 155–172.

Will South Korea Be Another Vietnam?

Anthony Kahng

After the collapse of the American-supported regimes in Indochina, many observers focused renewed attention on Korea and are asking: Will South Korea Be Next? If so, to what extent do the lessons of Vietnam apply to Korea? Were American actions in Vietnam and Korea based on sound understanding, or on delusion? And what are the implications of all of this for peace and reunification of Korea? Since the Korean situation is often compared with Vietnam because of the common fate of division into North and South by foreign powers and their similar war experience, the objective of this paper is to reassess the intertwining of the Vietnam and Korean questions in the context of American foreign policy in Asia.

In order to understand the problem one must examine the South Korean reaction to the Vietnam debacle. To counter fears expressed in Washington that the impact of the fall of Vietnam and Cambodia would be felt more in South Korea than anywhere else in Asia, South Korean Foreign Minister Kim Dong-jo said on April 30, 1975, that his government was "unconcerned by the fall of Vietnam to the Communists" and "was confident that the United States would honor its commitment to defend South Korea." He pointed out that the defeat of South Vietnam and Cambodia was a good lesson and said:

> We have to stand on our own feet—self-reliant in defense, self-sustaining in economy. These have been our principal national policies in these several years.[1]

While it is a well known fact that the South Korean Foreign Minister is not a loyal follower of North Korean President Kim Il-sung, listening to his admonition about "self-reliance" one would have to conclude that he studied "Juche" very well.

At the end of a week of tension generated by the dramatic events in Indochina, the second Korean response took the form of a well organized defense alert in Seoul. In a dispatch from Seoul on May 11,

235

1975, to the *New York Times,* Richard Halloran said that hundreds of thousands of South Koreans were mobilized to attend a rally in Seoul in support of President Park's call for increased preparedness against possible aggression from North Korea. A large effigy of North Korea's President Kim Il-sung was burned at the rally, and a number of youths wrote slogans in blood denouncing the North Korean government for its "aggressive ambitions." One and a half million people were mobilized and the resolution adopted at the rally said: "The United States Government and Congress should not forget the lessons of Vietnam." It also asked the United States to "strengthen" the present defense treaty between the two countries. Since the United States is committed to respond to any aggression against South Korea in accordance with due congressional processes, some members of the National Assembly have urged that the treaty be revised to provide for automatic involvement of the United States in the event of another war in Korea.[2]

President Park seems to have cried "wolf" when he overemphasized that the communists in North Korea set 1975 as the year of aggression against the South. In response, President Ford and his senior officials issued regular assurances that the United States intends to stand by its security commitments. For example, Secretary of Defense James R. Schlesinger warned:

First, if North Korea starts trouble, the United States "will go for the heart of the opponent's power . . . and take more vigorous action than . . . during much of the Vietnam war."

Second, he went so far as to suggest that the United States would not hesitate to use tactical nuclear weapons in Korea if the administration considered that necessary.

Third, he indicated that the administration was not contemplating a withdrawal of United States forces in the immediate future. Instead, he agreed with President Park of South Korea that in about five years, reduction could begin, but he added: "I think it is at least arguable that a U.S. presence will need to remain for the indefinite future."[3] [The Carter administration has since decided to withdraw U.S. ground forces in four to five years. Editor's note.]

In a similar vein, President Park has emphatically insisted that American forces must remain at their current levels for the foreseeable future. Nevertheless, he recently said that in five years his nation would no longer need American ground, air, or naval forces or even logistic support to help defend itself if North Korea attacks without Chinese or Soviet aid. "If the North Korean Communists launch an attack against us without any external help," said the President, "then we would be able to repel it successfully if proper air and naval support is given by the United States, with appropriate logistic support."[4] In the United States, meanwhile, a different evaluation was being advanced. Richard Holbrooke, new Assistant Secretary of State for East

Asia and the Pacific, cautioned us when he said: "We run a risk in
Korea as great as we did in Vietnam that we may get trapped in a small
and secondary country to which we must remain committed."[5]

Now, just how great is the danger of another Korean war? Will
South Korea be tempted to distract attention from domestic affairs by
creating an incident to involve the nation in a military strife? It is
extremely important to assess correctly both the danger of war and the
prospects for peaceful change in Korea. In a recent Seoul-datelined
report by Jack Anderson, long a conduit for "intelligence" handouts,
we learn that "the fears that North Korea might resume the Korean
war are subsiding. An intelligence estimate from the U.S. Embassy
discounts the likelihood that North Korea's Kim Il-sung will attack."
This view is shared, incidentally, by the Joint Chiefs at the Pentagon.
First of all, U.S. Army Chief of Staff, General Weyand, declared on
June 20, 1975: "There is very little chance of a major attack from the
North."[6]

The following quotes from the *Wall Street Journal* and *Time* Magazine are contrary to President Park's war propaganda:

> New Korea war? Scare stories are overdone, U.S. analysts say. They find
> outlook calm, dismiss war talk. . . . More rhetoric than reality. When you read the
> intelligence reports, you don't get scared. The intelligence community is chuck-
> ling over the worry (war scare) aired in the Press, so say U.S. officials.

The *Wall Street Journal* continues:

> South Korean President Park Chung-Hee whips up concern to ensure contin-
> ued U.S. military support . . . Park exploits war fear to tighter-than-ever control
> over his political foes.[7]

And *Time* Magazine stated:

> In the opinion of senior U.S. officials in the Pentagon, the State Department
> and the U.S. intelligence community, South Korea does not face an imminent
> attack from the North.[8]

On May 2, 1975, Richard Halloran, who has been covering South
Korea for the past few years for the *New York Times,* wrote from Seoul:

> South Korean and Western analysts of North Korea point to three tempta-
> tions for Marshall Kim. One is obviously the Communists successes in Cambodia
> and Vietnam that must fan his own desire to achieve a similar victory. A second
> is the deepening trend toward isolationism in the United States. A recent poll
> indicated that 65 per cent of Americans would oppose United States intervention
> in a new Korean war and only 14 per cent would approve. Moreover, the United
> States is preoccupied with the aftermath of the Vietnam war, the crisis in the
> Middle East, international economic disruptions and a variety of domestic prob-
> lems. President Kim has a record of provocation when American attention is
> elsewhere.
>
> The third, and most important, temptation is the continuing and spreading
> unrest in South Korea caused by President Park's repressive politics. There has

been a steady erosion of popular support for Mr. Park's Government similar to
that leading, in the eyes of many observers in Asia, to the downfall of the South
Vietnamese regime.[9]

In other words, it is the "third temptation" of Halloran's analysis
which explicitly implies that South Korea's problem is not the North,
necessarily, but her internal situation that is highly explosive.

Since October 1972, when martial law was instituted, President
Park has placed severe restrictions on the exercise of fundamental
human rights and civil liberties. As a result of these repressive measures, the South Korean government has been charged with extremely
serious violations of human rights, including extensive torture of political prisoners—all strikingly similar to the days of Thieu in South
Vietnam.[10] Is this the way to win the "hearts and minds" of the Korean
people? Why is South Korea unable to maintain the law and order
without martial law?

William J. Butler, upon his return from an investigatory mission
to South Korea on behalf of Amnesty International in 1974, testified
before the Subcommittee on International Organizations and Movements of the House Committee on Foreign Affairs concerning violations of human rights in South Korea:

> Political liberties have been severely restricted in South Korea ever since a
> military coup, led by Park Chung-Hee. In 1972, he declared martial law and
> dissolved the National Assembly. And in January 1973, he decreed the imposition
> of a new constitution under which the President was to have the dictatorial power,
> be eligible for re-election to any number of terms, and appoint one-third of the
> members of the National Assembly.
>
> The increased concentration of power in President Park's hands led to grow-
> ing opposition in all sections of the population. Large-scale student demonstra-
> tions and strikes began in October 1973. Some 100 students were arrested.
> Statements by groups of intellectual and political leaders supported the demands
> of the students; five of those who signed the statements were arrested. At first,
> they were charged with espionage for North Korea, but later this charge was
> dropped, and they were accused of "communism."[11]

In discussing the human rights situation in South Korea and its
implications for U.S. Policy, Congressman Donald M. Fraser, Chairman of the Subcommittee on International Organizations and Movements, pointed out:

> U.S. military assistance to countries with oppressive regimes is not only
> morally wrong but practically unsound. In deciding upon the level of military
> assistance to South Korea, we should have not only taken into account the threat
> of aggression by the North Koreans, but the fact that our assistance strengthens
> the South Korean Government's ability to oppress its own people.
>
> Because the South Korean Government is increasingly oppressive and pays
> little heed to internationally recognized human rights for the Korean people, the
> military assistance to South Korea should be reduced or eliminated.[12]

In these grim circumstances, the South Korean opposition leader,
Kim Tae-jung also pointed out in a memorandum on the security
situation in East Asia that he gave to Congressman Stephen J. Solartz:

> I don't believe that our present situation is the same as the Vietnamese situation. But if we don't change the suppressive and corrupt rule early, we can't avoid the fate of another Vietnam.[13]

Outlining his Vietnam-Korea analogy, Mr. Kim wrote:

> I believe most people in this country are becoming skeptical about fighting against Communism under the present dictatorial rule, disappointed with the big gap between the haves and the have-nots and angry with the extent of corruption and the luxurious life of the privileged class. Their loyalties to the nation are eroding day by day.[14]

As for the perspective of the "threat from North Korea," he said:

> I don't see that there is an imminent threat of an all-out attack from the North at present. Kim Il Sung, the North Korean leader, will take a lesson from Indochina and not repeat his failure in the Korean war, that of all-out attack. He will try to organize guerrillas to infiltrate among a people dissatisfied with suppression, poverty and corruption in the South. He will urge that guerrilla activities in the South are staged within the South with no obvious connection with the North. This is the precedent of North Vietnam when it communized South Vietnam.[15]

In the aftermath of Vietnam, President Park has become increasingly jittery and is overreacting to the slightest provocation. Therefore, it comes as no surprise to South Koreans when President Park proclaimed the ninth Presidential Emergency Decree on May 13, 1975, under which the final semblance of democracy was completely suffocated. Since the inability to govern the nation without martial law is so deeply rooted in the very nature of the South Korean political system, it is rather naive to believe that a better possibility would be the replacement of President Park by a moderate political alternative. Richard Holbrooke recently suggested that "there is nothing wrong with this suggestion. Indeed, if it had a good chance of happening, it would be worth pursuing. But it seems highly unlikely."[16] In essence, what we are witnessing in South Korea today is the final stage of the so-called "Korean style of democracy."[17] The agony is compounded by the fact that the great threat to the stability and security of South Korea arises not from external aggression but from the oppressive nature of the South Korean right-wing dictatorship itself. It is already the 25th hour in Korea!

II.

To begin with the Vietnam-Korea analogy, one may wonder whether there is a parallel between them. Are Vietnam and Korea the "twin of the Cold War" legacy? After the debacle in Vietnam, the analogy of the Cold War twin has been the subject of extensive critical commentary and continues to be fascinating. A classical Vietnam-Korea analogy appeared in 1950. Jacques Soustelle, former Minister of Colony and Governor General of Algeria, expressed a French version of the Cold War analysis in his article, "Indo-China and Korea: One Front":

> The glow from the Korean battlefields lights up the whole Asiatic front from Manchuria to Malaya. On certain sections of this front calm reigns—in appearance at least. On others, for examples in the Philippines and in Burma, guerrilla warfare is endemic between the native governments and rebel forces. . . . along two portions of this immense area the cold or tepid war has given place to, simply, war. There two Western Powers have engaged their armies. The United States has been fighting in Korea since June 26, 1950, and France has been fighting in Indo-China since December 19, 1946.
>
> The two conflicts differ from each other in many ways. However, each clearly has a place in the same strategic and political complex. They share a basic common factor. Each results from the expansion of Soviet power toward the sea, pushing its satellites ahead, and exploiting against the West the nationalism, even xenophobia of the Asiatic masses. There is another common factor also. The Government of President Syngman Rhee can no more withstand the assault without external aid than can the Government of Emperor Bao Dai.[18]

In an arrogant expression of dealing with a colonized people, Soustelle asserted that "no one, even the Indo-Chinese themselves, could have done for Indo-China what France has done. France did all that was in her power for the people of Indo-China, often more than she did for her own people."[19] To that school of political thinkers who believe in their "civilizing mission" it is irrelevant sentimentalism to question what the people of Indochina could have done for themselves if they were left alone to determine their own destiny. Of course, this type of politics is practiced under different names. The British called it the "white man's burden"; nineteenth century Americans called it "manifest destiny." It is now being called the "responsibilities of power." Is there any qualitative difference between these terms? In Soustelle's conclusion these terms are based on a common assumption that "the entire strategy of the West in Asia must be conceived as a whole and that it would be foolish to consider Korea and Indo-China separately. President Truman understood this, and increased the aid promised to the French and Viet-Nam forces."[20]

On the basis of a parallel vision, Washington was so certain that Ho Chi Minh and Kim Il-sung were ordered by Moscow as part of a plan to destroy the free world because all evil flowed from the Soviet Union.[21] A recent study by Professor Robert R. Simmons casts a serious doubt on the credibility of this assumption. Based upon a fresh reconstruction of the available evidence, he suggested a different hypothesis:

> Although the Russians certainly armed the North Koreans, and did expect a war, the timing of the war—which was primarily a civil conflict—can best be understood in terms of the indigenous conditions on the Korean peninsula.
>
> All Koreans were united in their urgent desire for an early reunification. However, the specific timing of the June 24 invasion was caused by intense

intra-Korean Worker's Party rivalry in the north, combined with appeals from South Korean-based guerrillas who had powerful supporters in the north. These pressures forced Kim Il-sung into a war date earlier than one which his Soviet mentors and he probably agreed upon.[22]

Was it a mistake then to go into Korea? Was the entire Korean action and the United Nations official policy with respect to it a mistake? Or if the policy was correct, is the refusal to compromise that policy an error? These questions were posed by Professor F. S. C. Northrop, one of the most spiritual and moral advocates of the American intervention in Korea. He was particularly outspoken when he explained:

> To these questions the answer is unequivocally "No." Communistic doctrine and deeds, being what they are, the North Korean Communist invasion of South Korea if unstopped would truly have become an Asian Munich. Furthermore Communist ideology which affirms that ideals are not merely neutral and impotent, but morally evil unless they are backed with all the materialistic might they can muster, could hardly be stopped with words uttered by Prime Minister Nehru or the President of the United States or by a mere overwhelming majority positive legal vote of the United Nations. Police action, as well as official words, was necessary.[23]
>
> If the United Nations policy in Korea was correct, and if the principles defining that policy should not be compromised, is there anything else that could have been done or can now be done to win rather than to alienate the moral and living law values, as well as those of the West and the lessons of Munich.[24]

Professor Northrop underwent a severe shock when the Indian newspaper editorials described "the police action of the United Nations as a greedy struggle between the two major powers of the world, in which the interests of Asians were largely overlooked, and with respect to which the United States was, if anything, slightly the worse of the two disturbers of the peace."[25] Although he was carried away with his self-righteous moral judgment, his positive attitude towards American intervention in Korea was an eloquent defense of the basic assumptions of the American value system. The United States acted exactly on the same assumption in Indochina as W. W. Rostow explained: "It is on this spot that we have to break the liberation war— Chinese type. If we don't break it here we shall have to face it again in Thailand, Venezuela, elsewhere. Vietnam is a clear testing ground for our policy in the world."[26] With this anticommunist paranoia, the United States backed the French in their utterly anacronistic effort to reconquer Indochina. Certainly the United States did not support France for the purpose of maintaining French power in Indochina. The United States looked at the Indochina war as part and parcel of its overall strategy of containing communism throughout the world.

Vietnam, as we have learned from the Pentagon Papers, was no aberration. It resulted logically from the decisions made and the attitudes assumed throughout the Cold War. Therefore, Vietnam and

Korea are part of the same pattern. The American intervention was based on the belief that the failure to contain the war of national liberation in Southeast Asia would threaten the entire imperial systems on which American economic and political hegemony rests. By the same token, the Vietnamese war was indeed a people's war, a war of the American people against the Vietnamese people, a war which, until they became tired and frustrated, was fully if not enthusiastically embraced by the great majority of Americans. This is an important lesson, if it shows us how deeply embedded in our culture are the roots of racism and anti-communism. James C. Thomson, former East Asia specialist at the State Department and the White House, makes an issue of this point when he said:

> There is an unprovable factor that relates to bureaucratic detachment: the ingredient of cryptoracism. I do not mean to imply any conscious contempt for Asian loss of life on the part of Washington officials. But I do mean to imply that bureaucratic detachment may well be compounded by a traditional Western sense that there are so many Asians, after all; that Asians have a fatalism about life and a disregard for its loss; that they are cruel and barbaric to their own people; and that they are very different from us (and all look alike?). And I do mean to imply that the upshot of such subliminal views is a subliminal question whether Asians, and particularly Asian peasants, and most particularly Asian Communists, are really people—like you and me.[27]

By putting it another way, Thomson asks: "Would we have pursued quite such policies—and quite such military tactics—if the Vietnamese were white?"[28] Prime Minister Indira Gandhi asked a similar question in a rising voice in a speech to Asian delegates at a conference: "Would this sort of war or the savage bombing which has taken place in Vietnam have been tolerated for so long had the people been European?"[29] The seizure of an American cargo ship, the Mayaguez, by the Cambodians in mid-May 1975, gave the United States an unexpected opportunity to reinforce those words with action. Professor Chomsky sums up this incident in his recent article:

> The essential features of U.S. policy were clearly illustrated in what, let us hope, was the final incident of the American war in Indochina, the Mayaguez incident.[30]

Anthony Lewis, a serious and effective critic of the war, expressed his dismay when he said:

> For all the bluster and righteous talk of principle, it is impossible to imagine the United States behaving that way toward anyone other than a weak, ruined country of little yellow people who have frustrated us.[31]

In conjunction with Thomson's question, what Tom Englehardt has to say is very much worth hearing. In his view, it's hardly a wonder that Vietnam did not sear the American consciousness. Why should it have?

For years, Americans had been watching the whole scene on their screens: REV, DEV, WHAM, endless My Lai's, body counts, killing of wounded enemy soldiers, aerial obliteration, etc. We have grown used to seeing it, and thrilling with pleasure while reaching for another handful of popcorn.

American moviemakers have successfully tied extermination of non-white peoples to laughable relief, and white racial superiority to the natural order of things.

It is a "united front" among whites. . . . Yet no matter how low, no matter what their internal squabbles, no matter what their hostilities towards each other, in relation to the third world the whites stand as one.[32]

Among the many factors, ideology, idealism, and even domestic politics played a very significant part in the decision to go into Vietnam and Korea. As Soustelle believed that what the French "civilizing mission" in Indochina has done for the people more than the Indochinese could have done for themselves, there were many Americans who believed, or convinced themselves, that what we were doing in Southeast Asia was not only necessary for our own security, but good for the people who lived there. The imperialistic drive also rests on a missionary impulse to mold other societies in our own image. Moreover, no president has even been willing to be responsible for the loss of any country anywhere to communism.

In 1965, when President Johnson was stepping up the war in Vietnam to the accompaniment of growing restlessness at home, he needed a device to persuade the American people that the war was indeed a "collective response against the Communist aggression." The key at this critical juncture was domestic politics: the need to sell the American people, press, and Congress on support for an unpopular and costly war. It was against this background, in May 1965, that President Johnson sent his presidential jet—Air Force No. 1—to Seoul to bring President Park to Washington for a conference. As a result of that conference, South Korea has become a reservoir for recruitment of innocent Koreans to support foreign intervention and a war of aggression in Indochina.

Korea by herself has never been an aggressor and it is the first time in history that Korean troops have been used as mercenaries in a foreign war. Since 1965, a total of 360,000 troops of the South Korean army and more than 16,000 civilian contract workers have served in rotation in Vietnam, and leaving behind them a record of beastiality that will have earned for them for years to come the hatred of all Vietnamese.[33] In every respect, the South Korean mercenary activities in Vietnam on the side of aggression against Asian people marked the darkest and the most shameful chapter in her history. A recent, well-documented study by Frank Baldwin, "America's Rented Troops: South Koreans in Vietnam," calls our attention to the benighted American attempt to internationalize the war as a cover for the American intervention as it did in Korea.[34]

The internationalization or "more flags" strategy, of course, had a precedent in Korea itself in 1950, when the United States maneuvered to cover its intervention in South Korea with the multi-nation flag of the United Nations. In the 1950s, the member states of the United Nations numbered over fifty and, needless to say, there was what at that time the late Vyshinsky called "the mechanical majority" under the American control. This is the reason why the United States succeeded in its attempt to internationalize the Korean intervention under the guise of the United Nations Police Action. By contrast, it is ironic today that the United States is in a minority position and condemning "the tyranny of majority" achieved recently by so-called nonaligned or Third World countries. It is the United States that invented and organized the first "massive" voting block in the forties and fifties to support an imperial foreign policy. Therefore, block voting in the United Nations is not a new idea, and not an invention of the Third World countries. They just happen now to be the majority in the United Nations, and like the OPEC nations, who have learned the laws of supply and demand, they are using the old political tactics of the West against the nations that used them in the first place.

In response to the call for the United Nations Police Action, fifteen members other than the United States and South Korea offered to contribute troops.[35] Almost 90 percent of the non-Korean forces fighting under the United Nations flag were United States forces and, for all practical purposes, the United Nations Police Force became identical with the Far East Command of the United States. It is time to call a spade a spade and to designate things by their proper names: the so-called United Nations presence is nothing but a United States intervention in the Korean civil war.[36] According to Baldwin, the United States made a similar attempt in Vietnam:

> U.S. Secretary of State John Foster Dulles tried to internationalize the war in April, 1954, by forming a coalition of the United States, England, France, the Associated States (Laos, Cambodia, and Vietnam), Australia, New Zealand, Thailand and the Philippines to intervene in Vietnam. This effort failed but after the Vietnamese victory at Dien Bien Phu, Dulles succeeded in establishing the Southeast Asia Treaty Organization (SEATO) as an arrangement for internationalizing the war and sanctioning U.S. military intervention if necessary.
>
> In 1964 massive, direct intervention became necessary. SEATO was ineffective, however, and could provide only a weak legal rationalization for U.S. actions; the organization never took important military or political collective action. Therefore, in November 1964 the Johnson administration developed a hasty strategy with military/diplomatic elements: a "More Flags" campaign to involve additional countries in South Vietnam on an ad hoc basis. "More Flags" was intended to establish a pragmatic justification for U.S. intervention—the visible, committed presence of allies who would associate themselves with U.S. actions in Vietnam, militarily, if only in a token way, and diplomatically. Allies would be the functional equivalent of collective action by SEATO or the United Nations.[37]

Baldwin's analysis is accurate when he said that "their major political value to the Johnson administration was to make it appear that U.S. intervention had broad international support."[38] It comes as no surprise, then, to discover that the United States secretly paid a high price in dollars and military and economic aid to obtain the 1965 deployment of South Korean mercenaries to Vietnam. Although the United States and the South Korean governments claimed that the South Korean troops dispatched to Vietnam were highly motivated volunteers who desired to serve their country and defend the free world, the deception was exposed by the Pentagon Papers and in testimony before a Subcommittee of the Senate Foreign Relations Committee in 1970. In fact, Saigon at first opposed the idea of South Korean mercenaries and yielded only after pressure from Washington. A revealing description of Washington's efforts is given in Baldwin's article:

> The U.S. effort to introduce South Korean and other foreign troops into Vietnam in April 1965 met unexpected resistance, not from the "allies" but from the Vietnamese themselves. Chester Cooper has written that "one of the most exasperating aspects" of the U.S. attempt to involve other countries in Vietnam was "the lassitude, even disinterest of the Saigon government." Saigon saw the program as "a public relations campaign directed at the American people." For once Saigon was correct.
>
> On April 15, 1965, Washington instructed Ambassador Taylor in Saigon to "discuss with GVN introduction of R.O.K. regimental combat teams and suggest GVN request such a force ASAP." Taylor, somewhat startled by the rapidity of Washington's build-up and introduction of foreign troops, reported that South Vietnam would not welcome R.O.K. troops. Taylor cabled the State Department on April 17 that "it is not going to be easy to get ready concurrence for the large-scale introduction of foreign troops unless the need is clear and explicit." Taylor requested new instructions to persuade the South Vietnamese to accept the Korean troops.
>
> The Taylor-Washington colloquy illustrates that the central U.S. purpose in putting South Korean and other foreign troops in Vietnam was not military necessity but to assuage domestic opinion. The administration needed the semblance of "allied" cooperation to mask the American takeover of the war. With American support contingent upon acceptance of Korean and other foreign troops, South Vietnam had no choice but to acquiesce and request aid from its new-found "allies."[39]

President Nixon's statement of July 1969 that the defense of Asia is primarily a responsibility to be borne by Asians has been termed the "Nixon Doctrine." The South Korean collaboration with the United States under this scenario "Let Asians Kill Asians," has turned its economy into a "bonanza." The economy of South Korea has profited enormously from the Vietnam-related procurement, but that is a costly and highly dubious form of foreign aid. How much did South Korea receive in any form of military or economic assistance in return for the mercenary activities? "From 1966 the United States has provided South Korea with approximately $3,158,000,000 in military assistance." Baldwin suggested correctly that "it is also possible that the R.O.K. need for armaments would have been much less if the U.S. and South Korea had not exacerbated tensions in Northeast Asia by using South Korean forces in Vietnam."[40]

According to former Defense Secretary Melvin Laird, there is no doubt that the substitution of mercenaries for American troops in counter-insurgency warfare has many advantages for the United States military establishment. For example, James Otis (pseudonym) explained in his article in *Ramparts* magazine:

> To be specific, the normal salary of a ROK army private is $1.60 a month. But if that private elects to serve in Vietnam, he can earn 23 times that amount, or $37.50 a month. In one day, he earns almost as much as he would have made in a whole month had he remained in his homeland—courtesy, to be sure, of the American taxpayer. The middleman of this operation is the government of South Korea, which receives a kickback of well over $300 million per year for the service.[41]

Laird also pointed out in his Fiscal Year 1971 Defense Program and Budget that Vietnamization or Koreanization is the essential ingredient of the Military Assistance Program:

> . . . we are to honor our obligations, . . . and reduce the likelihood of having to commit American ground combat units. When looked at in these terms, a Military Assistance Program dollar is of far greater value than a dollar spent directly on U.S. forces.[42]

The Military Assistance Program is expected to accomplish the following goals:

1. Domestic opposition to foreign operations is reduced because our involvement is less visible and less costly.

2. Opposition abroad is reduced because people are not confronted with the overt presence of our expeditionary forces.

3. Finally, troops cost the U.S. much less to maintain.

These benefits were summed up by former Defense Secretary Clark Clifford in an unusually candid statement to the Congress of January 15, 1969: "Clearly, the overriding goal of our collective defense efforts in Asia must be to assist our allies in building a capability to defend themselves. Besides costing substantially less (an Asian soldier costs about 1/15th as much as his American counterpart) there are compelling political and psychological advantages on both sides of the Pacific for such a policy."[43]

Accounts of the conduct of American troops, especially at Song My and My Lai in March 1968, have stung the national conscience and raised question of the Nuremberg legal principles as applied to American involvement in Vietnam.[44] "From the outset, it was understood, and, explicitly affirmed, at the highest level of policy-making, that the

U.S. intervention in South Vietnam and elsewhere was to be pursued in defiance of any legal barrier to the use of force in international affairs."[45] Therefore, Professor Chomsky concluded that "the American record in Indochina can be captured in three words: lawlessness, savagery, and stupidity—in that order."[46] In this context, it is equally disturbing that there was a devastating description of South Korean troops' behavior by Jesse Frank Frosch, an army intelligence lieutenant assigned to the advisory team at Quant-ngai province at the time of the Song My incident in March 1968. He said that the Song My area was the scene of a "staggering slaughter of civilians" by troops of the South Korean Marine Brigade in late 1967.[47] Such a shameful chapter can never be concluded so long as conscience and memory remain.

While South Koreans were serving as mercenaries in Vietnam, what position did North Korea take? Wilfred G. Burchett, one of the most authoritative Western reporters in East Asia, gave us North Korea's perception on the Vietnam-Korea analogy:

> In North Korea, the Vietnamese war is seen as a second edition of their own war, except the United States has no UN flag to hide behind this time. For a Korean, the problem seems so completely identical that it is accepted not as demagogy but as simple truth when the leadership says: "The Vietnamese war is also our war." Vietnam is also a country divided against its will. It has a 17th parallel instead of a 38th. And if the U.S. government was not responsible for a line being drawn along the 17th parallel, at least it was clearly responsible for its becoming a permanent barrier dividing country and people. In both cases, the lines were drawn temporarily at international conferences for quite plausible reasons and perpetuated by U.S. trickery: for Korea's 38th parallel, to facilitate the disarming and dismantling of the Japanese occupation regime; for Vietnam's 17th parallel, to facilitate a separation of combatant forces to make a ceasefire effective. In both cases, once the lines were made quasipermanent, the United States built up armed forces in the southern areas with an avowed aim of annexing the northern areas by force. In both cases the United States rejected the most elementary, democratic procedure by which the whole people of these countries could have expressed their will and had a regime of their own choosing. Both countries have been subjected by the same enemy to merciless bombings and other atrocities that amount to attempted genocide against their peoples.[48]

There is no doubt that next to reunification and construction of a socialist state, solidarity with the struggle of the Vietnamese people is the most important theme in North Korea. At this point, many third world countries regarded the Vietnamese struggle as their own struggle and also expressed their solidarity with North Korea. Burchett gives a vivid description of his observation on the expression of North Korean solidarity with Vietnam:

> It is expressed by posters and slogans everywhere; in art forms, in theater, and mass calisthenic displays, but also in practical forms of very considerable aid for the Vietnamese people. In almost every factory I visited, part of the production was set aside for Vietnam. Sometimes a whole department, in some cases individual machines, were working for Vietnam. Big posters over departments,

sections or machines announce the fact. Tens of thousands of tons of chemical fertilizers, tractors, rolled steel, small turbines for generating rural electricity, diesel engines, have all been sent as gifts to the Vietnamese people. "They are fighting for us," is the simple and universal expression one hears in explanation.[49]

In the final analysis, what are the major implications of the Vietnam-Korea analogy for the post-Vietnam-Korean situation? Immediately following the Vietnam defeat, McGeorge Bundy, once President Johnson's national security adviser and now the president of the Ford Foundation, suggests that:

> There is at least one lesson about Vietnam which deserves to be learned and understood by all of us just as soon as possible: it is that the case of Vietnam is unique. It does not make sense to set as a central objective the redesign of our foreign and defense policy so as to avoid "another Vietnam." The world is so shaped, geographically, politically and historically, that the particular set of circumstances which led to the American role in Vietnam is most unlikely to be repeated.
>
> There may be a real crisis of confidence, for example, in Korea, where our historic obligation is open, explicit, and underlined by the presence of troops, and where the energy and determination of the people on the spot are so different from what we ever found in South Vietnam.[50]

Not only is Mr. Bundy refusing to re-examine his distorted perception of history, but he is smoking the wrong weed in his pipe. If Vietnam has turned into a defeat of an imperial foreign policy, a repeat performance of Vietnam in South Korea now may shatter the very backbone of American foreign policy in Asia.

Even before the collapse of Indochina, the Korean situation was often compared with Vietnam. For example, General Westmoreland, the commander of the United States forces in Vietnam at the time of My Lai massacre, gave his version of the Vietnam-Korea analogy:

> There is a strong parallel between the situations in South Vietnam and in Korea. But the Vietnam situation has been far more complex because of a well-established guerrilla movement and political subversives in the South, in addition to invading armies from the North. Further, it is much simpler to defend a peninsula than to defend a country whose borders extend along its entire length, enabling an enemy to take sanctuary in nearby countries.
>
> The Korean war was not brought to a conclusion until President Eisenhower threatened to use atomic weapons, and the Vietnam war was not concluded until Haiphong Harbor was mined and the United States used air power against North Vietnam where it hurt.
>
> Both the Communists in Korea and Vietnam finally agreed to an armistice and a cease-fire respectively only after they had concluded that they could not win militarily, and after face had been saved by a local battlefield success.
>
> Now, twenty years later, South Korea is independent, has a growing economy and is beginning to open communications with North Korea.
>
> I believe Vietnam will follow a similar pattern. In due time, North Vietnam will probably accept the prevailing situation—two independent countries—and conclude that it is to its interest to stop fighting and to coexist in peace. This could

take years. But I would not rule out a peacefully unified Vietnam in the far distant future.[51]

General Westmoreland led us to believe that we were winning hearts and minds, building a nation in South Vietnam with his strategy of "search and destroy." A more disturbing question is that if we apply exactly the same legal principles of Nuremberg and Tokyo trials to Westmoreland that were brought to bear in the case of General Yamashita, hanged for crimes committed by troops over which he had no control in the Philippines, what would be his defense?

Recently, Professor Edwin O. Reischauer, former Ambassador to Japan, cited the lessons of Vietnam in warning the United States that "the defense of South Korea, regardless of the nature of its systems, is not vital to American interests." In his Vietnam-Korea analogy, he explained:

> False analogies between Korea and Vietnam originally helped get us into a fundamentally worse situation in Vietnam. Let us not now reverse the process and panic over Korea because of analogies mistakenly drawn with Vietnam.
>
> South Korea simply is not vulnerable at present to the two basic ills that destroyed South Vietnam—the uncertain loyalty of its people, and the resultant possibility for easy penetration and subversion by the North. At present it would require a massive external flow to overthrow the South, and there seems no sign of this happening.
>
> This may sound reassuring, but it concerns only the false crisis derived from mistaken analogies with Vietnam. Back of this, however, is a real danger that is escaping adequate attention, in part because of the red herring of Vietnam.
>
> It is not an immediate crisis, but rather a situation that over a longer time span may produce conditions like those that proved fatal to South Vietnam. In other words, an ultimate, Vietnam-like debacle may be in the cards for us in Korea unless we start to do something about it soon.[52]

Contrary to Professor Reischauer's call for a realistic reassessment of our assumptions on which American foreign policy rests, the most popular American mythology about South Korea is expounded by one of its official spokesmen. Raymond M. Kell, Honorary Consul General for Korea in Portland, Oregon, made it more explicit when he said:

> Korea and Vietnam are similar in that each is an Oriental country that an impulsive, well-intentioned, erratic and impatient United States set about to save from Communism. Each has watched with dismay and disbelief as the U.S. gyrated from hard-line anti-Communism to detente, to isolationism from total support to humanitarian crumbs.
>
> But the comparison stops there. Korea is disciplined, dedicated and militantly anti-Communist.[53]

To put it another way, Mr. Kell assumes that the Koreans have something to defend against communism and are very much capable of defending it. Now the most crucial questions are: Is there a sort of political value system that is capable of holding people together and worth defending? Are they going to defend the "Korean style of democracy"? If so, how viable is it? Will South Koreans fight to defend the repressive dictatorial government in Seoul? What is the central problem to all Koreans in South and North? This is the heart of the question.

III.

The Vietnam experience cries out for us to re-examine our basic assumptions on which our Korea policy rests. It means reviewing a set of attitudes, the decisions that flowed from them, and the perceptions on which they were based. Inevitably, the process of re-examination of American foreign policy must bring into question the men who have dominated the policy-making process and their perception of the American values. On this premise, let us turn to the basic question: Will South Korea Be Another Vietnam? The answer is unequivocally "yes." Why?

One finds very little honest self-appraisal in the wealth of current literature on Vietnam. Where did we go wrong? In essence, the deep roots of American self-defeat in Indochina lie in the basic assumptions of the American value system rather than with the fault of individuals like Richard Nixon, Dean Rusk, Walt Rostow, Maxwell Taylor, William Bundy, Robert McNamara, Lyndon B. Johnson, General Westmoreland, and Henry Kissinger. They shared a missionary impulse to mold other societies in our own image and common cultural arrogance. President Ho Chi Minh was correct when he said in a letter to President Johnson:

> Vietnam is thousands of miles away from the United States. The Vietnamese people have never done any harm to the United States. But, contrary to the pledges made by its representative at the 1954 Geneva Conference, the U.S. Government has ceaselessly intervened in Vietnam. It has unleashed and intensified the war of aggression in South Vietnam with a view to prolonging the partition of Vietnam and turning South Vietnam into a neocolony and a military base of the United States.[54]

The only way to understand the meaning of this letter is to put ourselves in Vietnamese or even Korean shoes by imagining how we would react if the positions were reversed. In the vocabulary of imperial power politics, it is irrelevant sentimentalism to express a humane response to such a letter. Watching the stubborn refusal of successive American administrations to re-examine the basic assumptions of their foreign policies in Asia, one is reminded of the ancient Greek saying: "There is nothing more terrible than power combined with ignorance."

What we are confronted with in Korea, in essence, is a value conflict. Perhaps it will serve a very useful purpose to look into the question of compatibility of the two different value systems. To begin with the American value system, it is based on a triangular relationship with Adam Smith's economics, social Darwinism, and Protestant Ethic at the vertices of the triangle. These three social forces operate the American value system and in their definitions lie the underlying philosophy of it. Of course, the basic assumptions of the Korean value system are profoundly influenced by Buddhist-Taoist-Confucian mentality. The Koreans are not American in outlook and never would be. To what extent is the American value of democracy valid or viable in Korea? A study of the "Korean Development" by Cole and Lyman explains it in the following terms:

> In Korean political culture, democracy has largely been an import from the West. Its early acceptance as the norm for an independent Korea originated in part during Japanese rule, in the close association between nationalist efforts within Korea and the sympathetic operation of Western missionary school and churches.
>
> The conflict between acquired values and traditional habits of thought continued after independence. Under American influence, the non-Communist nationalists in the South set up democratic forms of government.
>
> But the practice of democracy in the South was hampered from the beginning by a lack of suitable institutions or experience, by the first president's determined quest for autocratic power, and by the international circumstances surrounding South Korean independence.[55]

During the hearings before the House Committee on International Relations, Professor Gari Ledyard of Columbia University expounded on the same aspect of Korean democracy:

> Korean progress in building democratic institutions is an extremely complicated question of which few statements can be made without extensive qualification. South Korean political figures have claimed that Korea's traditional Confucian political order is not congenial to democracy and in fact encouraged political authoritarianism and makes little provision for the expression of popular will.
>
> Such claims are ridiculous and self-serving. The parroting of these statements by American officials and apologists, most of whom are totally ignorant of Confucianism and the Korean historical experience, is more disturbing.[56]

Another comment on the fragile nature of Korean democracy came from Professor Reischauer. In his view:

> Except for a brief period in 1960–61 of ineffective Democratic government, Korea's democracy has always been imperfect and incomplete. Individual rights and freedoms were often curtailed.
>
> But at the same time, there was enough individual liberty and democratic participation in government to make people feel that there was sufficient difference from the completely repressive regime of the North to make the South worth fighting to preserve. This situation, however, has been changing of late. . . . Step 1 has been taken toward the making of a Vietnamese situation.[57]

The quesion as to what political value system Koreans should choose must be examined in the widest historical perspective. The fundamental differences between the United States and Korea, including many Third World countries, are:

1.   Korea and many Third World countries are confronted with two formidable tasks. On the one hand, they inherited the legacy of feudalism and old social law and orders; and on the other, they have to modernize their society that has been severely retarded under the colonial exploitation. The tragic combination of feudalism and colonialism deformed the social, economic and political structures. In these grim circumstances, the difficulties are compounded by the burden of two simultaneous historical tasks.

2.   Unlike most of the other countries, America never has had a feudal period in its history. The result has been that American people have been far less class conscious. On the one hand, the absence of feudalism in American history shortened the course of modernization; and on the other, it became a severe psychological obstacle that hampered their understanding of the Third World countries including Korea.

Historically, almost every nation state evolved out of a three-stage process. The first, of course, is the primitive society. As a result, some nations are rich in their cultural and archeological treasures from this primitive stage. The second stage is the feudal society. Many Asian, African, and South American countries are still at this stage of their historical development. At this time in history, all these colonizing powers shared one ideological assumption—the supremacy of the values of Western civilization and the moral duty of the West to impose at least some of these values on colonized people. The third stage is the contemporary world of modernization. (See Table 1.)

With this historical background of feudalism and colonial experience, Korea is a Third World country. At the same time, Korea represents a beautiful example of two competing forms of political value systems. After the artificial division of Korea into North and South in 1945, South Korea has over the last thirty years emerged ponderously from a colonial world into a neo-colonial one under the tutelage of so-called American democracy. It is ironic that the "August Liberation" in 1945 did not bring a true national liberation contrary to South Korean expectation. In view of her history, if the South Koreans were given an opportunity to manifest their collective nationalism, there is no doubt that it would take a form of anti-imperialism.

By contrast, North Korea moved from the same historical legacy of feudalism and colonialism to socialism with cosmic speed. A careful examination of North Korean experience suggests that communism has become a means by which an underdeveloped society attempts to undergo, very rapidly, the process of modernization, to transform itself politically, economically, socially, and intellectually. The North Korean experience also defines communism as a process of change, of

TABLE 1: HISTORICAL CONDITIONS AND POLITICAL CHOICE

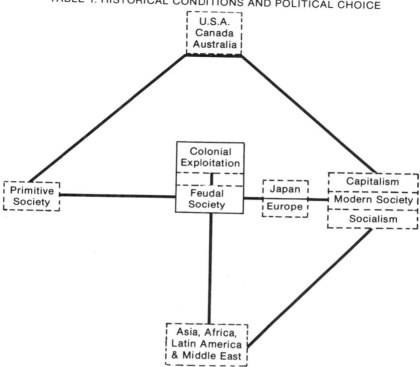

transformation, as a form of nationalism, a stage in the internal re-structuring of what we consider backward societies.

As compared with North Korean President Kim Il-sung, South Korean President Park has no philosophically, politically, or economically clear conception of what his aims were. More particularly, "President Park is hardly an ideal nationalistic leader. During Japan's colonial rule, he collaborated as an officer in the Japanese Army in Manchuria, where Korean guerrilla fighters, including President Kim Il-sung struggled against the Japanese. President Park thus suffers a handicap similar to that of former President Thieu in Vietnam, who had served the French colonialists against his own people."[58]

Finally, what should the United States do? First of all, the United States must recognize that the struggle of the Korean people towards reunification is part and parcel of the struggle of the people of the Third World against colonialism, racism, and foreign intervention. There is no force on earth that can stand in the way of its unity. Therefore, we suggest the following:

Pitted against the Korean determination to unify the country, the American determination to prop up the status quo of "two Koreas" is destined to fail as it did in Indochina. Who do you count on? Without historical roots, the Americans will not be able to find a foothold for their actions in Korean culture. Our views at this moment are in full agreement with the American Ambassador to Yugoslavia, George Allen, when he said:

> If the United States had tried with all its might, using money and perhaps bayonets, we might have installed a Jeffersonian democracy in Yugoslavia, but it would have stood only as long as our money and our bayonets held it up. As soon as they are withdrawn, it would have fallen like a house of cards. No system will last unless it evolves out of the soil of the country itself. Those which stand the test of time must grow out of the soil of countries concerned, and not be imposed from the outside.[59]

The divided Korea has been an international political liability. How can we turn that liability into an asset for peace and political stability in Asia? The only practical answer to that question is the reunification of Korea. The reunification problem is absolutely central to all Koreans in South and North. Even according to the South Korea sponsored opinion surveys, over 90 percent of South Korean people feel that national reunification is a supreme national goal.[60] North Korean President Kim Il-sung, in his speech at Pyongyang Mass Rally in welcome of Algerian President Houari Boumedienne, said on March 4, 1974:

> Today the Korean question, after all, boils down to the question of whether reunification or division; whether one Korea or two Koreas. The entire Korean people are unanimous in desiring the reunification of their country.
> But the great powers want the division of our country. To divide and rule is an old method of imperialism.
> What is the use of holding the north-south dialogue, if our nation is to live divided? The north-south dialogue must be conducted, under any circumstances, for the purpose of achieving the reunification.
> If the South Korean authorities really want the reunification, they should retract the "special statement" of June, 1973 advocating the membership of two Koreas for the United Nations and approach the talks for reunification in conformity with the interests of the whole nation.[61]

At this critical juncture, the United States must recognize the legitimacy of the Korean aspiration for reunification instead of cynically continuing to follow a "Two Koreas" policy. In every respect, the "Two Koreas" policy lacks logic, realism, and principle.

The continued presence of the United States military forces in the Korean peninsula is the major obstacle for reunification. On July 4, 1972, a Joint Statement of North and South Korea on the independent and peaceful reunification of the country was issued. They agreed that "reunification should be achieved independently, without reliance upon outside force or its interference." How can foreign forces, whose very presence is seen as a threat to one of the parties, possibly contribute to a reconciliation between the two parties? The only way to repudiate the allegation that the South Korean government is a "puppet" of the United States is to make South Korea itself independent of the United States military presence. That is the real meaning of the withdrawal of all military troops from South Korea. If all the past economic and military aids have not produced a viable democratic state in South Korea, how is it possible to believe that ten or twenty more years of military presence and aid will make the difference? The excessive dependence on military forces is the surest sign of moral weakness of American foreign policy in Asia.

The fundamental cause of conflict between the United States and Asia is the basic assumption of American security that the United States claims the entire Pacific Ocean stretching right up to the shores of China as its security zone. In this context, the Vietnam and Korean conflicts are only a partial manifestation of that imperial assumption. If we persist with such a pompous assumption, China has equal right to contend that the entire Pacific Ocean stretching right up to the shores of California is the security zone of China. After the debacle in Indochina, should we still persist with the same assumption? What Professor Paul T. K. Lin has to say is very much worth hearing:

> It should not be forgotten that the only truly international aspect of the tension that has existed in the Taiwan area for 25 years has been caused by the presence of U.S. armed forces. To eliminate this tension requires more than the recent token withdrawal. *Fu di chou xin,* the Chinese saying goes—to stop the pot from boiling, one must pull the firewood out from under.
>
> There are in addition those who believe that China might not be so eager to see the United States pull out of the area, since this would leave a "power vacuum" which the Soviet Union might be tempted to fill. But how can such geopolitical analyses have any relevance to the case except, indeed, to underscore the urgency of Taiwan Province rejoining its powerful motherland? Besides, the recent victories of peoples fighting for their independence have shown that "power vacuums" resulting from the retreat of imperialist power are likely to be filled quickly and effectively by people's power. In this way, the countries and areas concerned cease being pawns in the superpower game and achieve a genuine stability allowing for progressive change.[62]

The fundamental error in American foreign policy in Asia since 1945 was a failure to recognize that socialism is a vehicle for nationalism. The Vietnam War was from the first shot to the capture of Saigon a war of national liberation. The liberation forces fought against French colonialism and the American intervention. The United States assumed that communism is not a legitimate response to the problems of the Vietnamese society, that communists cynically exploit the problems of the Vietnamese people in order to promote their own interests, which are the interests of an international ideological movement concerned with the destruction of the free world, and the spread of a noxious, totalitarian system. In other words, the great weakness of the American view of communism in Vietnam is that it tends to substitute moral fervor for understanding. The United States has developed a very righteous pose of moral indignation toward communism, but it has made little effort to see its nature clearly, in relation to objective historical conditions in Vietnam.

To a large extent, the American policy devoted itself to persuade the Vietnamese to adopt the presumably democratic alternative to communism. But what we call the democratic alternative, which is the route that the West presumably traveled to its present wealth, power, and freedom, appears to be an alternative no longer valid in the Vietnamese society, which faces a configuration of circumstances much more closely resembling those faced by the Soviet Union in the 1920s and by China in the 1940s than those faced by the United States in the nineteenth century. Against this background the Vietnamese people have chosen communism as their political answer to the unique problems of their society. Why? Professor Bernard P. Kiernan properly sums it up:

> Modernization in the emergent world will produce left-wing authoritarianism not only because the sum total of the conditions of the emergent world dictates an authoritarian transformation, but because such a transformation is defined as a left-wing process. The difference between left-wing and right-wing dictatorship is, by definition, a difference in attitude toward change.
>
> Left-wing authoritarianism mobilizes the society to carry out a revolutionary change, involving the political awakening of the masses and the modernization of the society. By definition, left-wing authoritarianism is authoritarianism dedicated to modernization. Right-wing authoritarianism, on the other hand, is committed to preserving the status quo, its purpose is to prevent change.
>
> The choice, in the emergent world, is not between democracy and dictatorship; such a choice is probably irrelevant. It is between right-wing and left-wing authoritarianism. As between the two, only the dynamic force of left-wing authoritarianism can hope to solve, in the long run, the modernizing problems of the emergent world.[63]

If this perception is right, then we can expect South Korea to be another Vietnam.

1. *New York Times*, 1 May 1975.
2. *New York Times*, 11 May 1975.
3. *New York Times*, 14 September 1975.
4. Ibid.
5. Richard Holbrooke, "Escaping the Domino Trap," *The New York Times Magazine*, 7 September 1975.
6. *Wall Street Journal*, 27 June 1975.
7. Loc. cit.
8. 28 April 1975.
9. *New York Times*, 3 May 1975.
10. *Background Material*, Amnesty International of the USA, 19 July 1974.
11. Ibid.
12. *Human Rights in Korea: Implications for U.S. Policy*, Joint Hearings with the Subcommittee on Asian and Pacific Affairs (Washington: Government Printing Office, 30 July 1974).
13. *New York Times*, 25 September 1975.
14. Loc. cit.
15. Loc cit.
16. Richard Holbrooke, op. cit.
17. Sugwon Kang, "Thoughts on the 'Korean Style of Democracy': A Response to Pyong-Choon Hahm," *Journal of Korean Affairs*, vol. IV, no. 1, April 1974, pp. 26–35.
18. Jacques Soustelle, "Indo-China and Korea: One Front," *Foreign Affairs*, October 1950, p. 56.
19. Ibid., p. 61.
20. Ibid., p. 65.
21. Gaddis Smith, "After 25 Years—the Parallel," *The New York Times Magazine*, 22 June 1975.
22. Robert R. Simmons, *The Strained Alliance: Peking, Pyongyang, Moscow and the Politics* (New York: The Free Press, 1975), p. 103.
23. F. S. C. Northrop, *Philosophical Anthropology and Practical Politics* (New York: Macmillan, 1960), p. 161.
24. Ibid., p. 162.
25. Ibid., p. 155.
26. Ronald Steel, "Is America Imperialistic?", *At Issue: Politics in the World Arena*, Steven L. Spiegel (ed.), (New York: St. Martin's Press, 1973), p. 74.
27. James C. Thomson, "How Could Vietnam Happen?: An Autopsy," *At Issue: Politics in the World Arena*, ibid. pp. 274–275.
28. Ibid., p. 275.
29. *New York Times*, 6 February 1971.
30. Noam Chomsky, "The Remaking of History," *Ramparts*, September 1975, p. 52.
31. *New York Times*, 19 May 1975.
32. Tom Engelhardt, "Ambush at Kamikaze Pass," *At Issue: Politics in the World Arena*, op. cit., pp. 41–42, and p. 33.
33. James Aronson, "South Korean Mercenaries in Vietnam: An Expose of the Nixon Doctrine Ingredients—Murder, Rape, Arson," *Korea Focus*, vol. II, no. 1 (January-February 1973), pp. 21–30.

34. Frank Baldwin, "America's Rented Troops: South Koreans in Vietnam," *Bulletin of Concerned Asian Scholars,* vol. 7, no. 4 (October-December 1975), pp. 33–40.

35. Australia, Belgium, Canada, Ethiopia, France, Greece, Luxembourg, the Netherlands, New Zealand, United Kingdom, the Philippines, Thailand, Turkey, and the Union of South Africa.

36. Simmons, op. cit.

37. Baldwin, op. cit., p. 33.

38. Loc. cit.

39. Ibid., p. 34.

40. Ibid., p. 40.

41. James Otis, "Seoul's Hired Guns," *Ramparts,* September 1972, p. 18.

42. U.S. Department of Defense, *Fiscal Year 1971 Defense Program and Budget* (Washington, D.C.: Government Printing Office, 1970).

43. U.S. Department of Defense, *The 1970 Defense Budget and Defense Program for Fiscal Years 1970–74* (Washington, D.C.: Government Printing Office, 1969).

44. Telford Taylor, *Nuremberg and Vietnam: An American Tragedy* (New York: New York Times Co., 1971).

45. Chomsky, op. cit., p. 54.

46. Ibid.

47. Aronson, op. cit., p. 25.

48. Wilfred G. Burchett, *Again Korea* (New York: International Publishers, 1968), p. 166.

49. Ibid., p. 169.

50. McGeorge Bundy, "Vietnam," *New York Times,* 29 June 1975.

51. W. W. Westmoreland, "Vietnam: No Peace Within Striking Distance," *New York Times,* 18 April 1974.

52. Edwin O. Reischauer, "Korea and Vietnam: The Nonparallels," *The Washington Post,* 28 June 1975.

53. Raymod M. Kell, "Korea: In Pursuit of a Delicate Balance," *New York Times,* 2 May 1975.

54. *New York Times,* 21 March 1967.

55. David C. Cole and Princeton N. Lyman, *Korean Development: The Interplay of Politics and Economics* (Cambridge, Massachusetts: Harvard University Press, 1971), pp. 57–58.

56. *Human Rights in South Korea and the Philippines: Implications for U.S. Policy, Hearings before the Subcommittee on International Organizations of the Committee on International Relations, House of Representatives, 94th Congress, First Session* (Washington, D.C.: Government Printing Office, 1970), p. 14.

57. Reischauer, op. cit.

58. *Human Rights in South Korea and the Philippines: Implications for U.S. Policy,* op. cit., p. 8.

59. Quoted in *Annals of the American Academy of Political and Social Science,* vol. 393, (January 1971), p. 65.

60. *Human Rights in South Korea and the Philippines,* op. cit., p. 36.

61. Kim Il-sung, *For the Independent, Peaceful Reunification of Korea* (New York: International Publishers Co., 1975), p. 217.

62. Paul T. K. Lin, "The Road Ahead: A Call for a Farsighted U.S. Policy toward China," *New China,* vol. 1, no. 3 (Fall 1975), p. 35.

63. Bernard P. Kiernan, *The United States, Communism, and the Emergent World* (Bloomington, Indiana: Indiana University Press, 1972), pp. 155–156.

United States' Imperialism and Asia: The View from North Korea

Fred J. Carrier

Since its founding in 1971, I have been a member of the American-Korean Friendship and Information Center, and currently I serve as co-chairman. It was as a representative of the Center that I made my journey in 1973 to the Democratic People's Republic of Korea where I learned firsthand some of the views expressed below. Our Center is not affiliated with the DPRK, and certainly I cannot speak in any official capacity for that country. An official representative of the DPRK should be here today. I strongly protest such an absence, pointing out that it is the government of the United States that makes this presence impossible, thus thwarting a free exchange of views.

With this explanation and protest recorded, I will try to accurately express the political views communicated to me by spokesmen of the DPRK. To speak the truth on such matters seems to be both an act of friendship to the Korean people and an act of good citizenship on behalf of the American people. Such exchanges are essential to understanding. Therefore, our Center takes a friendly attitude toward North Korea, which also stems from political commitments: we view a certain force in the world as regressive, namely imperialism, and a certain force in the world as progressive, namely socialism. The world is in the throes of changing from an imperialist era, which for more than a century past was marked by Western domination of colonies and economic control over semi-independent areas such as Latin America. The change is toward national liberation, a political process that ultimately entails national control of resources (generally through nationalization of land and capital property) and development through collective planning or socialism.

We strongly feel that Americans need to be reminded of this view of the world, so that they will not mistake U.S. foreign policy goals (to preserve as much of the imperialist framework as possible) for world realities (the collapse of imperialism and the growth of socialism).

Historical change that is impelled by the needs of masses of people cannot be thwarted or re-directed against the interests of these same people, no matter how powerful may seem the imperialist forces. Hence, the failure of U.S. policy in Asia cannot be a surprise, for from its inception it stood opposed to one billion Chinese, Koreans, Vietnamese and other Asian peoples. History is on the side of revolutionary change.

I would like to make another disclaimer at this point. Many people who have addressed this symposium began by saying that their views are not to be considered as representative of the institutions that they serve, whether the State Department, the U.S. Army War College, Arizona State University, and so on. I have to say that, on the contrary, the views I express here are not necessarily my own. These are views, as I understand them, of Kim Il-sung, President of the DPRK, and of the state that he leads. But in saying this I do not want to make it impossible for the discussants to take critical issue with me. I am not going to hide behind the mantle of Kim Il-sung. I agree with at least some, perhaps much, of what I am about to present, and in any case I am prepared to give the best explanation of Korean political thinking.

In the first place, I would say that one cannot understand the views of the DPRK unless one takes a Marxist-Leninist look at the world. Unlike Professor Henderson I do not feel that Marxism is somehow passé. I think on the contrary it is very much alive, that Maoism and *juche* are Asian adaptations, improvisations that are essential to any living philosophy, theoretical reflections of historical necessities. Marxism, as it has guided revolutions in China and Vietnam, was hardly a set of dogmas pronounced by Marx in the nineteenth century. What Professor Henderson and others who underestimate Marxism do is create a straw man—a set of final dogmas that they call orthodox Marxism—in order to dismiss that philosophy as a set of dated doctrines that cannot possibly answer all the questions of the moment. That kind of academic Marxism, however, is far from the living thoughts of Kim Il-sung or Fidel Castro and, of course, a parody of Marx's views, which aimed at a scientific analysis of social evolution as it continues.

To begin to understand the political thought that guides the DPRK, it is necessary to consider seriously the view that the world is involved in a revolutionary struggle that in its most encompassing scope constitutes the struggle between socialism and capitalism or capitalism-imperialism (capitalism in its late stage became characterized by the quest for monopoly of the world's resources or imperialism). It is a world struggle, it is a world revolution against a counter-revolutionary force that opposes socialism and liberation of nations that will seek to control their own resources. This great struggle began with the Bolshevik Revolution, which introduced and stubbornly defended a rudimentary socialism, and later the Second World War played a critical role in extending socialism into the heart of Europe as well as eastward. The Chinese Revolution was nurtured by the struggle against Japanese fascism, as was the great revolution in Vietnam—and these socialist movements marked a very decisive change in the world revolution. Angola is now continuing the process, so that a new era is rapidly evolving.

There is a sense of optimism in the DPRK, as there is throughout the socialist world, for the simple reason that the forces for revolutionary change are becoming dominant. In only a little more than half a century, more than one-third of the world's people have adopted socialism, pointing out the direction history is moving. Such change is inexorable, not because Marxist theory argues thus, but because the colonial peoples who constitute a large majority of the world have found ways to liberate themselves from imperialism.

Perhaps the anti-capitalist character of this perspective needs some elaboration. From the founding of the Third International in 1919, the revolution announced its worldwide anti-colonial character, identifying the proletarian struggle with the struggle of colonial peoples. Both the proletariat in Western countries and the natives in the colonies were victims of the same system of international capitalism by which a miniscule minority of bourgeoisie pillaged the resources of the planet. Imperialism was implemented by national states whose armies not only occupied territories but also enforced, in the guise of law and order, the instruments of capitalist monopoly of colonial wealth. To cite one instance, to whom did the land belong? To the natives whose ancestry had for centuries been identified with "national" soil or to the white intruders? Occupying armies made possible law by decree, which gave the lands to the already rich from the West.

Thus, a second aspect of the DPRK view concerns the former colonies or the Third World, which is a vital part of the anti-imperialist struggle, aided by the socialist countries and at the same time through its own liberation accelerating the movement toward a socialist world. This Third World Revolution in its most dramatic form involves People's Wars, such as Vietnam, aiming at the liberation of a national soil from foreign exploitation. It can be seen as separate national liberation wars or it can be understood, as the DPRK does, in relation to the shared task of destroying imperialism. The revolution in Angola is not irrelevant to Korea, to the larger framework. Far from it. Every blow against imperialism weakens its tenacity, and every revolutionary success engenders new strikes.

The struggle of the Third World encompasses the great majority of the people of the world, more than eighty nations, and the bulk of the world's resources. Guerrilla warfare is only one of the tactics, but each national liberation effort, with varying degrees of political consciousness, is creating a new era. The countries of the Third World, the so-called non-aligned countries, are heading for socialism. At least that is the DPRK's view, and I think it is correct. The reason the Third World must take a socialist course is because to accomplish a liberation that touches the economy and redistributes wealth, they must destroy the old international economic order. Capitalism through colonialism had appropriated the world's wealth for the benefit of the few. Now, national liberation of *juche* demands a redistribution, both logical and just, by which each nation will collectively control all of its own resources. The Third World can do this by nationalizing the land, as in Cuba, or the most valued part of the land, as in Venezuela; or it can unify to control the production and prices of a raw material, as OPEC does; or it can seek an ever enlarging share of national ownership of its mines, plantations or other capital-producing resources. This process is what Kim Il-sung has stressed repeatedly:

> If non-aligned countries are to gain and keep independence, they must achieve economic self-support by building independent national economies. This will require solidarity. If non-aligned countries fight in firm unity, they can defeat imperialism. They should unite to destroy the old international order set up by the imperialists and establish a new international order that will meet the interests of the world's people.[1]

Now we can turn to a third point, what we ordinarily conceive of as nationalism, how that affects the DPRK's view. In the DPRK they shun the term nationalism, preferring the concept of proletarian internationalism. This is because the revolution, although it proceeds within nations and therefore has a nationalist dimension, is also part of a world revolution. Each anti-imperialist step leads the world closer to socialism. For this reason all the world's people have a stake in each particular battle.

Regarding Korea as a nationalist revolution, from the eyes of the DPRK, how does their recent experience look? The revolution has proceeded rapidly in the northern part of the country and it would, of course, have made a socialist Korea except for the fact that the U.S. intervened to abort the democratic revolution in 1945 and the socialist revolution in 1953. American intervention, with consequent division of the country, did not create the kind of democratic society that words proclaimed. In the South, therefore, there is unfulfilled revolutionary potential that must one day liquidate the artificialities of South Korean society imposed by U.S. military power. That is simply because at least 75 percent of the population of the South are among the dispossessed classes. For details, I will refer to Professor Rhee's paper where he more fully analyzes the nature of South Korean society and, in that context, I reiterate Professor Kahng's apt phrase, "Whatever does not spring from the roots of native soil will not flourish."

A fourth point to consider, one which would certainly surprise any economists within our midst, is that the DPRK believes—and again I will put myself in agreement—that capitalism as a world system is facing its most serious crisis since World War II. Moreover, this crisis is a permanent one that will be deepened to the extent that national liberation accomplishes its ends.

The capitalist world is riddled by what Kim Il-sung would call "internal contradictions." Let's translate that as simply class struggles that will not go away but instead are bound to be aggravated as the redistribution of world wealth occurs. Even though the U.S. might in some ways come out of its current "recession," keeping its society intact and its unemployed quiescent, there are many contradictions within the so-called "free world" that must be resolved: specifically in the context of this conference, between Japanese and Korean interests, between Japanese and American interests, and between Korean and American interests. These conflicts plus internal class differences are bound to come to the fore.

Now if that is a complicated matter or if it seems too theoretical, I would turn to Korea itself and say that the DPRK feels the contradictions are evidenced in Korea. For example, we can contrast the economies of the North and South. The North's economy is, of course, a socialist one for which they use the term *juche. Juche* means that the economy is fundamentally a developing economy that is moving in the direction of greater independence. We can see this very strikingly by noting the way in which the DPRK has developed its own resources. It has resources such as coal and minerals in its own soil and it is building an industrial plant based upon these resources. It manufactures from its raw materials, with its labor, and not only satisfies its own needs but exports manufactures to more than seventy countries. Its manufacturing includes heavy machinery, which supports its own industrial growth. Such an economy is a viable one. It does not collapse when there is a depression in the United States. While the DPRK does trade extensively with the U.S.S.R., the Soviet Union does not have depressions. That is an important point.

On the contrary, if we look at South Korea, which is currently gripped by depression, we can trace all the attendant sufferings to neo-colonialism. Although some of our panelists dismissed neo-colonialism as inapplicable to South Korea, and one even repeated the Cold War myth that South Korea is a showplace for capitalist development, I would not belabor the point except to cite from the *International Policy Report* of December 1975. Summing up the neo-colonial quality or character of the South Korean economy, the report points out that the South is no longer able to balance its imports and exports. To the tune of $3 billion annual excess in imports, South Korea will have to be financed by either the U.S., the World Bank, or some other country.

In brief, South Korea's pattern of export-oriented growth controlled by foreign capital, the source of her past prosperity, is also the source of her present malaise. South Korean economists, the products of the finest U.S. business schools and training programs, have faithfully followed the favored models of export-led development. In so doing, they have staked the future on the continuing expansion of a few markets in highly developed countries like Japan and the U.S., and they have counted upon the steady flow of Western capital investment. As long as international markets remained buoyant, the export-geared South Korean economy surged ahead.

> The basic structural features of South Korea's export-oriented industry concentrated in the light manufacturing sector—high dependence on imported raw materials, energy and intermediate products and low value-added component—leave it relatively little room to maneuver when terms of trade deteriorate. Some economies can ease an external payments crisis through import substitution. South Korea can do little here. Her textile industry spins and weaves imported cotton; her steel mills and shipyards work on imported ore and scrap iron; her sawmills process imported lumber; her electronics industry assembles imported components. All her industries run on imported energy.[2]

The point is that the South Korean economy, apart from between $3 to $4 billion of foreign ownership, must import its resources and must export its low value-added commodities to the U.S. and Japan, countries that are facing their own need to reduce imports.

So the difference between North and South is a crucial one. A fuller analysis would go far beyond the limits of this paper. As far as the South Korean miracle, I would suggest that what further needs to be stated is that there is a vast difference between a society that is a popular society, a society built on the people contributing collectively to development and sharing equitably in the wealth they are creating, and a society called "middle class," which in fact serves the affluence of a small minority. This difference is accentuated when the capital of the bourgeois society is substantially under foreign control.

To turn to a fifth question, the role of the U.S.—how does the DPRK see it? All I can do is quickly outline a few things that would require a whole session for fuller consideration. The U.S. is, of course, an imperialist country. It wishes to control the former colonial areas of the world through capital investment. To do so it must repress national liberation movements. The U.S. is the source of counter-revolutionary force in the world. The proof of this, aside from Vietnam, and from a lot of other places in the world, is Korea. The U.S. occupied South Korea in 1945, even though Korea was not an enemy but a victim of Japanese imperialism. The U.S. established a protectorate, or first military rule and then a protectorate in 1948. When the protectorate was about to be destroyed because of a national revolution in 1950, the U.S. used war to prevent Korean liberation.

The Korean War was not a war of aggression on the part of the DPRK, if for no other reason than because Koreans are not acting as aggressors when they seek social change and the end of foreign domination of their own country. We used to hear during Vietnam War days of the invasion from the north, but when we understood better the class character of the Vietnamese revolution, we realized that it was actually liberation of Vietnam that was involved. Likewise, for the U.S. to preserve a South Korea, it was necessary to develop it as a neo-colonial state under the rule of a comprador bourgeoisie, which meant thwarting the social aspirations of the majority of Koreans. Even now, twenty-three years after the war, the U.S. keeps its army there to preserve South Korea's military state against the dangers posed by its subjects and not merely from the North.

In a conference on reassessing the role of the U.S. in Asia, I would like to point out that when U.S. policy speaks of maintaining peace in the world or halting aggression, it might well appear suspect to Asian eyes. We should not quickly forget the three major interventions in Asia. First, the support to the Chiang Kai-shek regime as the "legitimate" expression of the Chinese people, as the movement that represented "freedom" according to the U.S. conception. This intervention was a total failure, culminating in the stubborn refusal over a quarter of a century to recognize the People's Republic of China. Second, the U.S. backing of a colonial war in Indochina, which sought to preserve a colony for its French masters; and when that attempt failed after 1954, to replace French rule by an American protectorate. This Vietnamese intervention was of course also a failure from the U.S. point of view, but a very liberating Vietnamese success in the eyes of the rest of the world. Third, we get to the case of South Korea, and this is really the concern of my presentation. What about that attempt—how successful is it apt to be finally?

I would like to have had time to talk about the Korean War in some detail because I think the American view is at last being subjected to realistic analysis. The Cold War and the hysteria over communism really stunted political awareness so that the scholarly community in the U.S. virtually abandoned its intellectual responsibility. Then, after 1964, scholars were rightly preoccupied with Vietnam. Only now are American scholars taking some of the lessons of Vietnam and applying them to Korea—for example, the U.S. contention that it was halting aggression from the North when, in fact, it was suppressing a national liberation movement. Applying some of our late perceptivity to Korea in 1953, the ridiculous question of whether or not North Korea made the first move is irrelevant, in addition to being uncertain. The reassessment that has begun, and this conference is a part of it, must continue if we are ever to reach political maturity.

Whatever the origins and earlier conduct of U.S. intervention, the critical point that must be examined, one which is of vital concern to the DPRK, is the effects of the Vietnam War on future U.S. policy in Asia. To gain an accurate perspective on the post-Vietnam era, that is why we are here today. Only now can the academic community formally recognize that the U.S. suffered a very grievous loss, but that it was only a loss, comparable to the "loss" of China, in narrow, chauvinistic, counter-revolutionary terms. For much of the world, and certainly for the Vietnamese people, it was a great victory. The U.S. goal was to stop the socialist revolution, to prevent the liberation of Vietnam. National independence for Vietnam meant the reclaiming of its soil from the French and from all Western imperialism. The U.S. used massive military power to preserve Western domination in Asia, but despite that it could not succeed because the only thing it could do, and this is all it can do in Korea, is preserve for a time a regime without popular support. It cannot substitute a viable society of national independence for the selfish cliques it has fostered. National unity and independence have to grow from the soil of the country, not as transplants. That is what the U.S. tried—to provide blood to a lifeless bourgeoisie without arterial ties in Vietnamese society.

The DPRK is very much aware, and I think many of us are, that the U.S. defeat cannot be reduced to a simplistic military analysis. The U.S. has the power to destroy anything it chooses. On the other hand, this does not mean U.S. military power is invincible. During the Korea War, the U.S. was held to a standstill despite superior weaponry including the most devastating air power used until that time. What was lacking was the ability of the U.S. infantry to sustain a long, tough war in Asia when the political terms were not impelling. In Vietnam the loss was due to many forces and it may profit us to quickly list them. Basic to the revolution was a people determined to accomplish their liberation. Already armed with a base in the liberated north of their country, this liberation movement was able to draw support in weapons from a strong socialist community of nations. Beyond that, the U.S.S.R. and People's China provided a shield against the nuclear annihilation of Vietnam. Also, in the U.S. an antiwar movement grew in proportion to the revelation of U.S. motives and practices in Vietnam.

North Koreans ask why we who led the anti-Vietnam War movement are not more active in regard to Korea. It is a bit hard to explain. The basic reason, however, lies right in Korea. The antiwar movement was always a reflection of the Vietnamese determination to continue their revolution until victory. That determination, in turn, grew along with the number of people actually involved in combat. Vietnam's revolution, as a People's War, lasted from 1946 to 1974. During that twenty-eight year conflict, the National Liberation Movement developed a network of support that literally reached every single village of the country. To compare Vietnam and Korea, one immediately notes that Korean liberation was from the start largely due to Soviet occupation. While help from the Soviet Union brought benefits, it also diminished the urgency of the revolutionary struggle as a guerrilla struggle. Korean revolutionaries concentrated on building a socialist North as a weapon against imperialism, but at the same time they could not, because of circumstances beyond their control, create the politically conscious movement at the village level in the South.

That leads directly to what might be the summation of this paper in the sense that ultimately we are talking about what could be done to change U.S. policy in Korea. One thing we can do is give serious attention to the DPRK's proposals, which are very practical and, I think, just. Behind their proposals are certain attitudes which prevail among the people of the North. First of all, they are going to build and are building a strong socialist North that will be capable and willing to help the South build socialism when the time comes. The Koreans in the North are heavily indoctrinated to believe in their brotherhood with the people of the South, and in their responsibility to be ready to provide them with the industrial base from which a strong, unified, independent Korea can come. Meantime they give support, most of it I suspect verbally, to the revolutionary forces in the South. They are justly concerned with pressuring the U.S. to end its intervention in Korea. They depend heavily for support in this matter on the socialist countries, especially China and the U.S.S.R., on the Third World countries, and on the United Nations, which is increasingly becoming a world forum. And, of course, the U.S. is getting worried about what it calls the "tyranny of the majority" in the United Nations. The U.S. did not oppose the tyranny of the minority that operated for nearly twenty-five years, but with China's entrance and the addition of a number of Third World countries, now that the majority is exercising what might be called democratic conduct, this suddenly becomes tyranny.

The DPRK believes—not only regarding Korea but also in Angola and elsewhere—in supporting all national liberation struggles because they in turn will weaken the U.S. ability to dominate Korea.

Finally, the last point I will deal with concerns the steps the DPRK envisages toward a unified Korea. Naturally these things are subject to rapid change, but I would say there are four steps that they expect to happen. First, they would like a peace treaty with the U.S. to supersede the armistice of 1953. They have proposed this treaty to the U.S. Congress but, of course, with a deaf ear from our own government. Secondly, détente should apply to both North and South Korea. The DPRK would like to pursue that policy and has advocated a number of practical steps. Third, when détente is implemented, it would lead to South Korea supporting the idea of withdrawal of all U.S. forces.

Until foreign soldiers leave Korea, independence cannot be accomplished. Fourth, then, there is the possibility of a Korean confederation.

The question might be raised, why Korean unity and not a unified Germany? The Korean situation appears to be different than that of Germany. Korea has a different economy than the two German states. The North is developed, the South is not. In fact the South is neo-colonial. The North has resources and technology that could fashion a strong, unified Korea. In Germany both East and West are developed countries. Secondly, different from Germany, the South Korean government is totally dependent on the U.S. and lacks the popular support that both German states enjoy. South Korea's military is under the command of the U.S. with 42,000 American troops present, a sign of its neo-colonial status. So the economic situation—added to the larger geopolitical situation that was mentioned earlier by both Professors Henderson and Rhee, namely that a strong United Korea is not antithetical to the interests of the U.S.—suggests possibilities for one Korea. It would be independent even though it would become a socialist state; such a Korea would not be as much of a liability to the U.S. as the current unstable South. So all of these things are of bearing.

To sum up, from the DPRK's view, what history has fashioned as one people—and by history it is meant the long evolution of a race, culture, language, with all of these identified with a national soil—imperialism cannot sunder. Time is on the side of people. The Korean people will ultimately decide the fate of their nation.

1. Cited in *Pyongyang Times,* 14 November 1975.
2. *The International Policy Report,* vol. 1, no. 1 (Washington, D.C.: The Institute for International Policy), December 1975, pp. 7–8.

Discussion

TOTTEN: I would like to ask Professor Henderson to give us a clearer picture of what he sees as a possible confederation between North and South Korea. I would like to ask Professor Rhee to comment on the viability of the economy in Korea. He spent a great deal of time dealing with the question of civil liberties there, and I was wondering if he felt the economy is doing well. To Professor Kahng I would like to direct the question of whether he was saying that right-wing authoritarianism will have to be replaced by left-wing authoritarianism, and whether he sees any possible democratic path to modernization in Korea or elsewhere. To Professor Carrier I would like to inquire whether he thinks that North Korea will be threatened by a meeting with the South, since the people in the South have quite a different background and have had much greater contact with the rest of the world than the people in the North.

OLIVER: I am rather surprised that Mr. Carrier expected me to be critical. I feel a little bit like the Korean husband. He and his wife quarreled about one another's relatives even as Americans sometimes do. One evening they sat cross-legged on their floor, she embroidering, he with his long-stemmed pipe in his mouth. He took his pipe out of his mouth and said, "Wife, now tonight I will say something good about your relatives." "Yes?" she said. "Yes," he said, "I have decided that I like your mother-in-law better than I like my mother-in-law." I must confess that I find communist rhetoric rather amusing, like *Alice in Wonderland,* as long as you do not get too much of it. I got rather too much of it this morning. It is pleasant to get out of the rabbit hole and into the real world for a moment or two. I listened to Mr. Carrier tell us that the world is engaged in a struggle for survival between communist and non-communist nations. I heard him declare that he thinks victory for the communists is inevitable and that he prefers that victory. All I have to say is—okay, Mr. Carrier, I do not; you and I differ very fundamentally and there is not much point in discussing it.

   I listened to Anthony Kahng, who insisted that South Korea must be communized, and who, with lots of eloquence and wit and a kind of charm that makes him interesting even when he is devastating, argued in his conclusion that left-wing authoritarianism, communist dictatorship, is the only hope of the world. Well, Mr. Kahng, have your own preferences, they are very different from mine.

   I listened to Dr. Rhee's paper and I hear him bewailing the abridgement of civil liberties and regretting that leadership gets entrenched in power in Korea. I thought surely he was talking about North Korea and then discovered that he was talking about *South Korea!* We do not have one civil liberty in South Korea; we have a leadership entrenched in South Korea—that is far from an ideal situation in South Korea and whatever can be done to improve it ought to be done.

In terms of Dr. Henderson's paper, I am going to take a different approach. I admire and respect Dr. Henderson very much. I have known him for quite a number of years and I know that his attachment to and concern for the welfare of the Korean people is both sincere and intelligent and deep-seated. I agree with him that American troops should be kept in South Korea. I agree with him that we should reduce their number somewhat as opportunity provides. I agree with him that Korea for its own sake could be reunified. I agree with him that we should exercise a discreet influence to get more civil rights and civil liberties instituted in Korea. I agree with him that we have interfered aggressively in Korean affairs in the past. I am not sure, however, that I can agree with him that we ought to continue to interfere aggressively in Korean affairs in the future. The biggest interference, the most devastating interference, the vital fundamental interference in Korean affairs was when Franklin Roosevelt, in the winter of 1941–1942 and certainly by the spring of 1943, decided to use Korea as a pawn with which to entice Russian entry into the Pacific War. Following that in December 1945, the power trusteeship in Moscow announced that the future of Korea was to be decided by four outside powers, without Korean concurrence and without Korean consideration. It did not work. I am *not* prepared to have the future of Korea again determined by a four-power interference—Russia, Red China, Japan, and the United States. Of these four powers, can anyone really say that Russia is a friend of the Korean people? That Japan is a friend of the Korean people? And I think we have to add that the United States is only reluctantly a friend of the Korean people. We do not have deep-seated interest in what happens in North Asia. How can the Korean people trust their future to a four-power conference composed of powers such as these, powers which will decide for their own good, in their own way, what is going to happen in Korea? By what means are these four powers to exercise their full influence in Korea? Are they to reach a determination among themselves and then announce to the Korean people what it is? Is Finland really a good model for Korea? I doubt it. Can we really expect a non-communist Korea to emerge from the Henderson formula? I doubt it. Is there really anything unique or special in the military influence exercised in both North and South Korea? I doubt it, because wherever I look around the world I find militarism dominant in governments—everywhere perhaps but in Japan. Is it conceivable that the Koreans will welcome either Russian or

Japanese influence? Is this not merely another term for foreign domination?

KENNEDY: I will go directly to the issue that is at stake. At some point, this marvelous world of theory has to stop and someone has to sit down and devise a course of action. The person who does that is the planner. For the Army's part in that, only one part in the varied kaleidoscope of parts in the government, the Army War College has a model that it offers to its prospective Army planners. The model proceeds from the identification of the national purpose and goals to an examination of the world environment. It then goes on to identify U.S. interest in that environment, specific objectives that need to be obtained to support those interests, the evolution of a national policy that will enable us to attain those objectives, and finally in the Army's business, the military strategy that will support that national strategy within the political and fiscal constraints established by our civilian superiors. For a moment let us by-pass the question of national purpose and goals and go directly to the question of interest.

Is there a single overriding interest for the U.S. in the Pacific area? I feel that there is such an overriding interest and it lies in Japan being able to continue as an independent, relatively unarmed, non-nuclear power, free of domination by either of the inherently unstable great powers that presently dominate the East Asian mainland. How do we go about assuring that Japan is able to do that? Certainly not by lecturing here. We have to look at the world from Japanese eyes if we are going to get an appreciation of how to go about that. There are three ways to exert pressure on Japan. First there is the area to the north, toward Kurile and Sakhalin. Japan has already launched a very effective diplomatic offensive of her own in that region in its efforts to get back from Russia the four islands that were stolen, or conquered if you will, in World War II. A second essential avenue is Korea. A final southern avenue is Taiwan and the Rykukyus.

I had an opportunity a few weeks ago to discuss very extensively this issue of what Korea means with Japanese officials, and as a sort of counterweight to them, Japanese newsmen. I find their appraisal entirely different from anything I have heard or read in the papers. I did not raise this particular historical cliché, but it was finally raised not by Japanese military, not by the Japanese government, but by a man you would recognize immediately as the representative of one of the most liberal Japanese newspapers. He said, "You must realize that Korea is a knife aimed at Japan's throat, geographically speaking." Regardless of whether they are right or wrong, this is the Japanese appreciation of the situation. If we want to see an independent, unarmed or at least a relatively unarmed, and non-nuclear Japan, then I think it is clear that we must secure the Korean peninsula from domination by a hostile power that is able to intimidate Japan. That is the primary interest that we must deal with in the Pacific Ocean.

That function is being carried out at present, and has been carried out very well for a number of years, by the U.S. 2nd Infantry Division, which is in a reserve position several miles behind the demilitarized zone along the 38th parallel. The Japanese make no bones about it; they paint the picture and they spell it out in no uncertain terms that this infantry division is their security against an invasion from the North of Seoul.

It might come as a surprise that China has indicated in various ways that she has a certain degree of concurrence with this assessment. China feels that we must retain our present commitment in Korea with the present degree of forces, which is essentially a token force with the capability to reinforce that force very rapidly if there is an attack by the North. The North, however, has assumed a very important role that the South cannot. It has the initiative because it has the same claim on Russia and China that the North Vietnamese have. It can attack tonight and it can then turn to the Russians and Chinese and say, "If you do not support us, then we will expose you to the rest of the communist world and the Third World as an imperialist, socialist imperialist, or whatever you want, as having abandoned the communist effort." There is a very good chance that both Russia and China would have to answer to that ticket.

Primarily because North Korea has the advantage of the initiative, it can concentrate its forces and it can attempt to punch through. It lies about twenty-five miles (a very easy morning's motor-march if it were unopposed) to the capital city of Seoul. That is the strategic relationship.

Yesterday, Dr. Rhee raised the question of where idealism fits into this. I think it is an extremely important question because it goes back to the national purpose and goal that I mentioned earlier. There is a fundamental difference between a view of the world and of mankind as an individual person who has an intrinsic worth, and a view of mankind as a mass of protoplasm to be shaped by whatever self-appointed elite who happens to have gained control of the levers of power. We can pull back to the Potomac if we want, but as long as we espouse that principle we are going to be in trouble with the Russians. And when the Chinese are able to settle their accounts with the Russians, we will be in continual trouble with them by their own announcement.

What should we do with the problem, the fact that we have policies facing us in South Korea that are certainly not desirable to us and that are opposed to some of the very concepts about which I am talking? Most certainly we should not use the U.S. Army to influence in any way, by manipulation of aid or whatever, the make-up of the Korean government. That was done in Vietnam and it resulted in the murder of President Diem. The U.S. has no business going in and reshaping the Korean government to its own image. The U.S. can express its ideals—and I think this has been done quite effectively—by stating that we do not agree with many policies that are present in South Korea. This is a long way short of saying that the U.S. is going into Korea and reshape it. The U.S. has precedents for this restraint in policy. We did not support human rights in East Berlin in 1953 when men were throwing rocks at Russian tanks. We did not support human rights in Budapest in 1956 when Russian armored columns were grinding down Hungarian freedom fighters. Again in East Berlin, we did not choose to intervene when East Berlin was turned into a big jail with the erection of the Berlin Wall against the spirit of the Four Power Agreement. We did not intervene in 1968 in Czechoslovakia when they made a rather futile grasp at freedom. With these precedents of policy, it is in no way inconsistent to say that we have no business in trying to reshape the government of South Korea. We are not the world's policeman and we should not be going out on misdirected crusades.

CHO: Among the commentators, I am the only Korean. Furthermore, I am a South Korean and I fought during the Korean War as an officer. I feel that I have to mention these facts as they undoubtedly influence my opinions. Dealing first of all with Mr. Carrier's point of view, I was very interested in hearing about North Korea's situation. He was depicting North Korea as a paradise; my major study is North Korean politics and I do not agree with this assessment. First of all, I do not think that any nation is a paradise. We are living in an imperfect society in a perfect world. There is no question that South Korea is not a perfect society. We must strive to attain larger amounts of civil liberties there and more intellectual freedom. But on the other hand, ask people and you will find that South Korea is not that bad a nation. There is room for reform, and in this sense my philosophical foundation is gradual reformism. I will strive for this goal in South Korea, and I would like to change certain South Korean wrongdoings if possible. As an intellectual, maybe I can achieve this through writing or some kind of public movement. Perhaps these are the ways I would be most effective.

On the other hand, what I am afraid of is a remedy consisting of drastic social change in South Korea. If there is drastic change, then naturally we are going to create tension within society, and most likely we are going to have a war. The one thing I am afraid of is war in Korea. We have to avoid war. I now live with the knowledge that I myself killed many Koreans during the Korean War. As an officer I was involved in the bombing. But the tragedy I witnessed during the Korean War makes me urgently want to work toward averting another war. If possible, I would dedicate my whole life to stop this kind of war.

The papers presented here have not offered solutions that would be a guarantee against war. The only important solution, in my judgment, was presented in Professor Henderson's paper. I think it deserves more attention. There should be some kind of Big Power, or at least a "Big Four" conference to stop a potential Korean war. This sort of conference could aim at guaranteeing some kind of reunification of Korea, and perhaps pave the way for eliminating conflict later by a gradual process. On the other hand, Professor Henderson's paper did not elaborate on how he proposed to proceed with the so-called "Big Four" conference. I know that the other countries refused when the U.S. proposed such a conference. We have to strive, but we need some kind of international guarantee for security and also peace in Korea.

I also felt that Dr. Rhee's paper was very good. While I take a position of "gradual reformism," he accuses the South Korean government of borrowing so much money from Japan that it is taking the risk of completely destroying the country and creating a situation of dependence that would relegate South Korea to a position of a Japanese colony. We must be more realistic than this and accept the fact that South Korea has few resources other than its manpower. Without having the benefit of capital from the outside, either from the multicorporations or from Japan or Europe or wherever, there is little chance for South Korea to modernize. As far as we want to maintain the South Korean government or systems in the framework of capitalism, then the problem becomes one of how we are going to control the inflow of capital so that this kind of large capital does not control or destroy South Korea completely.

These are my solutions. If I were a politician, I would first of all borrow as much capital as quickly as possible. I would invest this in industry, and the profit gained from the sale of these manufactured goods would be used to support the people. The only problem is that South Korean politicians often become corrupted by their positions. This in turn influences their judgment in internal policies, but until that policy sets in we would be okay. The success or failure of the South Korean government is dependent upon the consciousness of its political leaders. In this sense I would urge South Korean politicians to be more honest and effective. But I do not necessarily think that the borrowing of money from the outside will eventually lead to total destruction; rather, that is probably the only way to survive in the given framework of South Korea's political situation.

AUDIENCE: Dr. Carrier, you noted the North Korean *juche* policy, its independent economy, and strong industrial base. If this is to be a system that should press the people in the South to perhaps adopt a revolutionary struggle, I would like you to justify something that has appeared in various journals, including the *Far Eastern Economic Review*. The June 6, 1975, edition states, "It is increasingly evident, however, that Western traders are expressing alarm at North Korea's inability to fulfill financial obligations. One Japanese source estimates North Korea's outstanding debt at $1.3 billion. This figure includes $550 million which she owes to the West and $750 million within the communist bloc. South Korea's exchange bank gives higher estimates of North Korea's debt, placing it at $1 billion owed to the West, $700 million owed to the communist bloc, for a total of $1.7 billion." In April, the London *Economist* also reported that North Korea owed about 300 million pounds to Western creditors. Can you please rationalize this in light of your lauding the North Korean *juche* policy?

CARRIER: Well, first of all, the estimates are questionable. I do not have any inside information on the subject, but I would like to note one difference. It is a very critical one between whether the DPRK has certain outstanding debts and whether South Korea has outstanding debts. The DPRK may have debts and she may not be able to immediately repay them without obviously interfering with trade. But the DPRK does not depend on any capitalist country for markets. It is not dependent for food or raw materials or imports. Therefore, its industry and its population can continue to work and to eat. As far as its debts to the socialist world, I would say those sources are totally inaccurate. I happen to have certain information with regard to debts to the Soviet Union and those debts are not immediately pending. They can be programmed for over twenty-five or fifty years at low interest rates. It is not a critical problem. The South Korean debts are due to the fact that they can no longer import essentials. Very little of the DPRK's imports are essentials. It could present a problem to the standard of living, but it is not going to destroy the substance of what I said.

AUDIENCE: Thank you. In addition to that, you may be aware that North Korea has recently imported a substantial amount of arms that were built, I believe, in Austria, because of the Soviet Union's unwillingness to credit North Korea by supplying arms. Do you know anything about this, Professor Carrier?

CARRIER: I do not; however, I do doubt it. It can be a very critical matter. When I was there I saw a lot of the arms, and I do not think that they were from Austria; but that is not something that I care to go into right now. It is certainly not a critical factor in their defense.

WEATHERBEE: I have listened to the speakers, and I think, particularly, Professor Carrier used the word "détente" in the sense of whether we could or should be applying détente to the two Koreas. I do not think détente is a kind of structure that can be imposed upon the two Koreas or on anybody. Détente, according to my understanding, is a condition that is derived from a mutuality of perception on both sides and a degree of reciprocity in terms of the arrangement, which both sides are willing to make in order that they can live with some degree of relaxed tension. *I* am not sure of this majestic notion, and I really do not think that it is that way. That concludes my comment.

My question relates to Professor Henderson's model and Professor Carrier's exposition of what he saw. I must say that I noted a slight hint of advocacy of the DPRK's position. My question is, what would be the DPRK's perception of a process that involved "Four Power" guarantees of any kind of reunification program for the two Koreas, particularly guarantees that would involve a continued commitment to the integrity of a South Korea?

CARRIER: The DPRK would not accept such a situation if it has the power not to accept it; and I do not think the Soviet Union or the People's Republic of China are ready to enter into such arrangements. For these reasons it is not important to pursue it further.

HENDERSON: Oh, I think it would drive Kim Il-sung wild. There is no question at all that the thing that both Koreas fear more than anything else and hate more than anything else is "Four Power" discussion or planning with regard to the Korean peninsula. This is one of the reasons, in a way, why I advocate it. The reason why the talks between North and South Korea were begun did not arise at all from the Korean people themselves, it arose from Nixon's visit to Peking. The minute we take our hand out of the Korean peninsula—which after all we divided, not the Koreans—it is our responsibility. The minute we take our hand away, they fight harder and faster and more strongly than at any other time, because they are the two most hostile powers in the world, even more hostile than the Arabs and the Jews. They are much more hostile than any of the "Four Powers" are to each other. The only mechanism we have to drive these two bad children back, so that they get a little bit closer to each other and at least talk to each other, is whispering a little bit among ourselves. There is a great limit to what we can do, but it has been proved to be an effective mechanism in the past, and it can be an effective mechanism again. If we do not do that, we will get a drift toward more and more danger in the peninsula, toward more and more open conflict and an open breach of world peace. That would be our reward. It is not a perfect world. This is not the kind of world I would like. I would like a world where we see a beautiful united Korea, where the Korean people have the right to say everything about themselves, and so on. I would like to see a situation where we stay strictly out, which is the best thing, and it is what they deserve. But that is not what we are doing at the present time, and that is not the situation we face. I believe that some "Four Power" influence, however unattractive, and perhaps because it is unattractive, may be one of the few mechanisms we have for containing the enormous potential ferocity that could break out at any moment in that corner of the world.

WINN: I want to make a brief statement about each of the four papers given, and then something of a summary. I believe the topic of this session is "United States Policy: Now What?"—and I would like to examine this in reference to South Korea. First, Professor Henderson's paper is cogent with respect to an American withdrawal, but that is not his argument; that is not his desire. With respect to Professor Rhee, I do not believe that the Japanese, beyond economic involvement, are interested in political domination in Korea. If anything, they have a general distaste for interaction with Korea. As for Professor Kahng, I would hope that he is incorrect regarding the individualistic orientation within Korea. I think there is an individualistic orientation and that is the major factor that differentiates it from a totalitarian regime. Finally, Mr. Carrier's views are generally known, but I think one should take note particularly of his statement regarding the DPRK's position on active world revolution.

In terms of United States foreign policy, I think that we are talking about military involvement; we are talking about nuclear weapons; we are talking about troops; these are specific policy-relevant questions. I think the first thing we have to ascertain regarding nuclear weapons and those troops is a straight statement from the Defense Department as to what the military strength of North Korea is. Is there a reason for having nuclear weapons as a deterrent to, for instance, a "nuclear" force in North Korea? Otherwise, we will be well-advised to revamp and begin to withdraw.

I would also like to make a few comments on human relations. Human relations are not an idealistic factor. Vietnam has told us that realism includes idealistic or thoughtful considerations. The abrogation of those relations affect American support, Congressional support, the continuation of American arms, and the continuation of Japanese support for American base support of the Koreans. The continuation of President Park's government is conditional because his generals may not want to support him if they feel that the government's position is reducing South Korean security. In other words, individual freedom is national security on the one hand, and individual freedom on the other. They do not have to be divorced, it is not a continuum of opposites. It is the ability to have security militarily and individual freedom. There are many historical analogies where there is not any need to have one off-setting the other—the same way that there is no opposite between idealism and realism, they are one in the same. If South Korea maintains a commitment to liberal democracy, I would say that the first indication of that for the world is the government's allowing for change in the direction of a peaceful transfer of executive power.

CARRIER: In closing I want to say something that is not self-serving, it is about the DPRK. I did not depict it as a paradise; if it seems like a paradise it is because the United States government and the Republic of Korea have tried to portray it as a prison, as a hell. When the truth is told, it sounds like an ideal is being made up. Full employment may sound like a dream, but it is real. I would like to close by saying that I am not as limited as it may seem here today. I would like to cite Gandhi on one point. "To the hungry, God comes in the form of bread." I would like to add to that point, to the unemployed, God may come in the form of the security of their job; to the uneducated, in the form of schools; to those without care, hospitals. That may be to them the equivalent of paradise.

RHEE: I will mention one other thing. In South Korea there is no Christian church movement at all. The Christian church has been totally penetrated, totally demolished. Why? I would like to see South Korea remain non-communist; I would like to see South Korea retain the element that would give it the character of a non-communist state —that can be defended. But if South Korea deteriorates, it is impossible to defend. In other words, the problem of South Korea is not the problem of Korea alone. It is also the problem of the United States. Now think about the implications of those two astounding facts and see in your mind whether that type of regime is defendable.

HENDERSON: I wish I could respond fully to all the things that have been asked and said. I was asked the question of how a confederation could come into being. Again I have no chance to fully answer that, but I do feel that confederation as a process can, and even has to be, gradualist. It is true that Kim Il-sung does not always present it that way, but I think it can be made to go in that direction. A gradual overlapping of certain minor governmental functions—even archeological expeditions, things that do not relate to the security of the country first—should be expanded through the years. This is the only way that I can see that the problem can be solved; it is a long, intense, difficult problem, but I think that this is the way to go about it. Essentially, this is not too dissimilar from the South Korean view, which is also one advocating a gradualist approach—not starting at the top with national assemblies and conferences, but through minor things and expanding. In this sense, I think the two points of view are possible to combine.

I do want to say a word about Dr. Oliver's and Mr. Kennedy's thesis of noninterference—that we should not interfere as foreign powers, we should not interfere as the United States. I would almost like to say "nonsense" to this, because it is not a statement of the reality that we have created in the last thirty years. It is completely on cloud nine. We, the United States, created the South Korean army, unilaterally, without asking the Korean people. We fueled it, we educated it, we established its schools, we had hundreds of thousands of American soldiers fighting alongside it and in combined units in it. We have given it virtually all the muscle and arms and everything else it possesses, and we still control it through the tactical command of a four-star American general. Under such circumstances, to talk about the non-interference of the United States in South Korea is arrant nonsense, approached arrant dishonesty. It is simply not a statement of where we are.

Now the same is true, to a somewhat lesser degree, in North Korea. The communists created the North Korean armed forces, the communists have shaped the North Korean state also in their image, of course. But it is also true that there have been no foreign soldiers in North Korea since 1958, and that their military aid has been greatly less than ours to South Korea. Therefore, in statistics we stand accused of being the people interfering more, and by that interference creating tension and danger in the Korean peninsula rather than the opposite.

We do have two alternatives. One is to say that this is your country, we have nothing to do with it, we are going to give no aid, we are going to give no soldiers, we are going to pull everything out and say, "bye-bye." I regard that as completely irresponsible. If that happens we are going to have a tragic war that can only decimate the Korean people. I think we have enough responsibility to our acts in dividing Korea on August 10–11, 1945, not to do that. The other alternative is to use our influence, but to use it in a way to create stability, to create communication, and to create a peacefully operating Northeast Asia and united Korea rather than the dangerous, explosive, ferocious situation we are helping to create today.

SEOUL'S VIEW AND AMERICAN REACTION

Korea: In Search of Peace and Prosperity

Pyong-choon Hahm

In discussing America's role in Asia, it is important to remember that the United States is a Pacific power as much as it is an Atlantic power. In fact, it may be wrong to compartmentalize the role of the United States by confining it to any particular region of the earth, because the United States is a global, not a regional, power. It is only in this global context that we are to discuss America's role in Asia as a Pacific power, keeping in mind that what it does or does not do in Asia is inextricably linked with its role in the other parts of the world.

As a Pacific power the United States has a serious and immediate interest in the events that transpire along the entire rim of the Pacific basin. This means that the western Pacific region is of great importance. There is a segment of this rim that we call Northeast Asia, which has a greater importance to the United States than the rest of Asia. The reason why Northeast Asia has a greater strategic significance is that there the three greatest powers of the world—Russia, China and Japan —converge around the Korean peninsula. If we include the United States, it is there that the interests of the four greatest powers of the world today come together.

The convergence of four world powers signifies that there is a potential for tension, competition, even conflict in this area. In recent years the United States has been trying to create a certain balance or equilibrium of power as a means to stabilize the situation in this important part of the world. It is true that there have been criticisms of the current détente policy on the grounds that, unlike the days of Metternich, ideological entente is impossible today, and therefore the U.S. would become a party to the ideological conflict rather than a "balancer" as Britain was in the nineteenth century. The critics further argue that the U.S. no longer possesses the independent leverage and preponderance Britain enjoyed with her *Pax Britannica* to play the balance of power game effectively. Be that as it may, one thing is clear;

285

it is in the interest of the U.S. to secure stability in the region, and U.S. involvement is necessary for such stability.

Southeast Asia is rich in resources, has a very large population, and encompasses an area perhaps even larger than the Northeast Asia region. But in terms of strategic interest of the United States, Northeast Asia has greater importance. Geopolitics and history have made Korea a focus of big-power convergence in Northeast Asia. Given these geopolitical features, it was not difficult for the United States policy-makers to recognize important strategic interests in the Korean peninsula. Since 1950, the United States has maintained a political, military, and economic presence there. Since the fall of Indochina to the communists, however, there has been some debate in the United States as to the continued wisdom and advisability of U.S. involvement in Asian land war. But the question has to be faced in a more fundamental way.

It has often been asked why the United States must be involved in a distant part of the world such as the other side of the Pacific basin. Since 1945, the American policy-makers have looked upon such distant involvements as a way to keep potential conflict away from the American shores. They have also sought to contain the conflicts within a local, and a non-nuclear, conventional scale. They believed that this was the way to prevent possible cold war conflict from escalating into a global nuclear holocaust. Did this mean that the United States was promoting, instigating, and creating these conflicts for its own territorial gain and to satisfy its "arrogance of power" as a twentieth century superpower? I, as a friend of the United States, do not think so. It is the communists who, out of their revolutionary evangelical zeal to change the world into their own image, have been undertaking an expansionist and aggressive course of action against the non-communist world. The United States policy-makers were merely reacting to these communist moves.

In this day of détente and Sino-Soviet conflict, there is almost a wishful thinking that communism has had a change of heart that fundamentally altered its nature. I, for one, do not believe this. To the communists, the non-communist world still remains a place where evil dominates and oppression and exploitation continue. They still believe that the communist system is the only moral, ethical, humane, and good system. From this ideological perspective, the communist revolutionary imperative is derived. We need only to read the official pronouncements of the Soviet government and party to learn that the so-called peaceful coexistence does not preclude "revolutionary struggle." On the contrary, peaceful coexistence is a tactical means by which the cause of revolution is to be advanced. The practical application of this ideological perspective is well illustrated in the cases of Indochina, such Portuguese colonies as Mozambique and Angola, or even Portugal itself. The Soviet Union is proudly proclaiming its commitment to aid and assist national liberation anywhere in the world.

Nowadays we also hear that some of the big communist parties in capitalist countries, such as Italy, France, or Japan, have declared their so-called independence from Moscow and Peking. This is only a matter of semantic quibble. There may be a different evaluation of the most effective tactical means to acquire power in each capitalist country. But no matter how political power may have been gained initially, we have yet to see a communist country become non-communist. The ideological solidarity and the common ideological imperatives will remain. Given the global perspective of communism, the U.S. response must be global also. A diminution of U.S. influence anywhere in the world necessarily means a communist gain made that much easier in the rest of the world.

Let me come back more specifically to the Korean peninsula. North Korea still has its "revolutionary commitment for national liberation" against the Republic of Korea. North Korean communists are still committed—perhaps more fanatically than ever—to the "revolutionary liberation" of their compatriots in the South. As economic development and industrial progress proceed at a rapid pace in the South, this only increases the North's fear that "people's revolution" would become impossible by virtue of capitalism's success. The North had already intensified their propaganda even before the tragedy of Indochina. They were digging tunnels, not just one or two, but over a dozen of them under the demilitarized zone even while they were agreeing to dialogue with the Republic of Korea. They have stepped up guerrilla infiltrations, the propaganda and diplomatic offensive to isolate the Republic of Korea in the international community, and infiltration of espionage agents through third countries.

Against this kind of serious threat, the Republic Korea has set the prevention of another war as the highest priority objective. This decision was based on the premise that war is the most savage and cruel destruction of humanity, and therefore, must be avoided. In order to prevent another revolutionary violence waged by the communists in the name of national liberation, the Republic of Korea has been compelled to strengthen its military defense capabilities. Every citizen appreciates the necessity of "eternal vigilence" in view of the ferocity of continuing communist political warfare. The maintenance of full-time alertness and ever-ready preparedness has proved to be the best defense. It was almost total lack of military defense that invited the North Korean invasion in 1950. The Republic of Korea may not repeat the same mistake in the future.

This does not mean that the government and the people of the Republic of Korea would not prefer a more relaxed and freewheeling lifestyle. They know that continuing wartime controls and regulations mean restraints on their personal freedoms. For the past twenty-five years—and no one knows for sure how many more years in the future —the balance has been struck more in favor of national security than of individual freedom. And yet, non-violent and loyal dissent has been fully permitted. What has not been permitted, however, are those varieties of dissent that are illegal and disorderly.

Ultimately, the best national defense is economic strength and continuing economic development. The capital city, Seoul, is located only twenty-five miles from the cease-fire line. This vulnerability has made public optimism, which is vital for continuing economic development, very difficult. But the citizens of the Republic of Korea have made possible the impossible. The Republic of Korea lacks natural resources. It has been totally dependent on the Persian Gulf area for its oil. It started its economic development with little investment capital. It had to borrow technology from abroad. But it did have a highly motivated, disciplined and literate population that was intelligent enough to master new technological skills very rapidly.

During the past dozen years, the G.N.P. grew on an average of 10 percent annually in real terms. Export grew 40 percent annually from $30 million in 1961, to $5.4 billion in 1975. Per capita G.N.P. was $80 and about $550 respectively. Moreover, the Republic of Korea committed itself from the beginning to private-enterprise and private-property-oriented capitalism as a means for rapid industrial development. This meant that its economic system was an open system and thus able to give and take with the rest of the world. This openness in economy has meant openness in politics also, greatly moderating the rigid preoccupation with national security.

This resolve on the part of the Republic of Korea to deter another war and defend itself has not meant that it wishes to continue the course of confrontation and tension with North Korea. It opened dialogue with North Korea and tried to persuade North Korea to engage in negotiation and relaxation of tension. The Republic of Korea wished to have some kind of agreement with North Korea that all violent means, including revolutionary violence, should be ruled out as a means to achieve unification. The Republic of Korea policymakers have decided that, although unification may be a supreme goal for the nation, even such a goal should not justify another fratricidal holocaust. They have made it clear to the North Korean communists that the only acceptable means for unification is a non-violent one. Inasmuch as peaceful reunification is possible only as the basis of reduced hostility and negotiation, they have urged the communists in the North to accept the Republic of Korea as an entity to negotiate with rather than an object to be destroyed in the name of revolution.

This was the reason why the Republic of Korea called upon North Korea to join it in seeking membership in the United Nations, pending national unification. Of course, the North Koreans have refused the proposal, denouncing it as "an insidious conspiracy" to perpetuate the national division. But without the willingness on the part of North Korea to accept the Republic of Korea as a party with whom to talk and carry on negotiation and dialogue, there cannot be a meaningful interaction that might lead to a peaceful reunification of the nation. In this, the citizens of the Republic have a strong conviction that time is on their side. The reason is that the rapid economic and industrial development will continue and the standard of living will continue to rise in the Republic of Korea. As time goes by, the Republic will become stronger and more prosperous. The communists in the North will have no choice but to accept the undeniable reality. Peace and prosperity, thus, are essential not only for the continuing survival and well-being of the Korean nation but also for their reunification.

Finally, I should like to touch upon the American role to be played in Korea in the years to come. The U.S. troops are currently in Korea to render effective the policy of the Republic of Korea to deter war. The U.S. troops are not there merely for military gain or superiority. But they are there to prevent another bloodshed and tragedy on the Korean peninsula. Our two countries proudly share this common objective.

Also, the U.S. military presence on the Korean peninsula has been essential for the continuing security of Japan. In this sense, both the Republic of Korea and the United States have contributed significantly to the continuing viability of democracy and economic prosperity of Japan. Once this sense of security is denied to Japan, Japan will have to face a very stormy and disruptive national debate as to her own security in terms of remilitarization and even nuclearization.

The United States will have to continue to play an important role in promoting economic development in all the nations in and around the Pacific basin. The bilateral trade and economic cooperation between the United States and the Republic of Korea is, of course, important in and of itself. But it has a further significance in terms of greater economic cooperation among all the nations in and around the Pacific basin. There is growing technological cooperation among these countries. In this the United States has to play a leadership role also. As Korea's economic growth continues, Korea is becoming an important trading partner of the United States. Already it is the twelfth largest partner of the United States having over four billion dollars of two-way trade. Korea has become one of the largest purchasers of American goods and agricultural products. This kind of economic and trade cooperation will continue to figure as the most important aspect of the U.S.-Korea relationship. We hope that in building peace and prosperity in Korea, the Korean people and the American people will cooperate in building peace and prosperity throughout the Pacific basin and throughout the world.

Discussion

HENDERSON: I stand here today in the expectation of giving a scholarly paper on the "Reassessment of America's Role in Korea" with all these estimable gentlemen around to criticize. I have a paper with me, a rather too long one and no one really wants to hear somebody just read a paper. I also stand here as perhaps the American critic who has written and spoken longest against the Park regime, and I could give a diatribe against today's Korea and yet that too would be dull, for what could I say that would be new? What fresh resolution could we obtain from a rehearsal of these now almost ancient woes?

I thought that I would do something else, because I have the uncomfortable sense that we may be standing on the edge of a volcano and that those of us who know or can sense this seem to be rather few. We seem to be dancing on this volcano, pursuing our daily labors and dreams without really telling ourselves or others where we have been, why the earth is hot underneath us, when or where the eruption may come, and above all, where we are going.

Once there was a nation state called Korea. One of the oldest nation states human beings had ever formed. Before the 14th century, when the nation states of Europe began to be formed, it already stood. That nation state exists no more. An echo of it sings to us in the determination of certain Koreans that it exist again. It was the home of one of the world's most ancient and continuous civilian governments. China held up behind it a military umbrella. In its shadow there flourished a culture looking down on arms, denegrating the military and preventing their coming to power in the Korean state. In counsel, when questions of security arose, which they did on the whole rather rarely, the counselors would stand up and prevent military decisions. They pointed, time and again, to the immorality of a resort to arms and to the dangers to the internal state and to the being of Korean men and the tone they wished to make in the world of military enterprise and its effects on people. When the Korean state ended, the army was about 6,000 strong—this in a country of very strategic location. The navy, once renowned, had turned into a few mud scows incapable of doing anything. And morality and ethics were so much to the fore that the nation had, in this sense, been unable truly to defend itself.

One can exaggerate and idealize of course, but the impression that this state gave others was of courtesy and gentility. Its arts were soft and flowing, its expressions reticent, its language decorous, and respectful of others. It knew no democracy, of course, but it also, for

291

centuries, abhorred dictatorship. For centuries its political history concerned the control of the monarch by the Censorate, the Secretariat, the Pebeonsa, and the other state organs of the Confucian Yi Dynasty. When the monarch tried to extend his palace, as he sometimes did, or spend his time hunting, Korean officials stepped forward in numbers and at the risk of their lives, to chide him. Koreans were no democrats but to say that they were authoritarian in the tradition of Stalin, or Kim Il-sung, or Park Chung-hee would be a lie outraging heaven itself—the annals of the Yi Dynasty be my witness and bond.

Where is this land? Where, as the Czech National Anthem puts it, "is your home"? One can see the print of 17th century Puritans in today's Americans. One can see Luther in today's Germans. And even Descartes in today's Frenchmen. But where is Korea in today's Koreans? Where once gentility and politeness stood, the world knows Korea, both Koreas, as the roughest and most intemperate of modern states. The land bristles from one end to the other with arms. Nor are these kept to themselves. Kim Il-sung trains agents in Mexico to overthrow its government and others. He rushes to Ceylon to subvert them. North Koreans man planes and missiles in the Arab Near East. South Koreans sally forth to terrorize the villages of Kuang Tri where even now the memory of Korean soldiers make Vietnamese pale. Park dashes into the Federal Republic of Germany to make off with Korean citizens, into England to extract a physicist, into Japan to manhandle and kidnap Kim Tae-jung. There are said to be Koreans once known for their ethics and moderation. Now Americans and Japanese and Germans, never known for their moderation and only occasionally for their ethics, have to pressure Koreans to observe minimum humanity to other Koreans. On the thrones of Pyongyang and Seoul sit no men who any Yi Dynasty official would have recognized as Koreans. They are some sort of strange monsters whose names once civilized men would not have sullied their tongues to utter. Korea has become the home of ferocity and intemperance. Around it a wave of corruption widens, toppling the Board Chairman of America's ninth largest company; driving to suicide a close confidant of the White House; connecting even the community abroad with the seductive smiles and oozy corruption of Park Tong-sung. Where once was a people who had words for a clean poverty and men to go with these words, now stand men of a brasher and flashier materialism than the most unblushing Texan, men who talk no more of morals and ethics and behavior but of Mercedes, Cadillacs, "Thieves Villages," and Beverly Hills.

Men go to Kyung Ju and excavate the great tombs of Silla and take exquisite movies of them and think they have found Korea's past, but the corpse of Korea is not to be exhumed. It is not to be found in its sons and if it lives not there, then in whom can it be found? Far from being excavated it is only being buried deeper and deeper. The men of the past, the real Korean spirit, is not even honored. The words of Shakespeare seem to come to us, "but yesterday the word of Caesar would have stood against the world, now lies he there and none so poor to do him reverence." What has brought us to this new world, to this new intemperate, intolerant, materialistic Korea? To this new frontier of a land no man described or foresaw, nor in his worst nightmares dreamed? And what does it do to the policy of accommodation and détente that we so need in a peninsula so desperately threatening both itself and the rest of the world?

We know the answer to this question. And it arises unfortunately in the topic of today, in the so-called foreign policy of the Great Powers. It arises in the fact that Korea was divided without the knowledge, consent, input or advice of the Koreans; divided essentially by the Americans and with the subsequent consent and considerable enthusiasm of the Soviets. This has become one of the worst crimes of the century and it is fabulous to see how deeply it has riven not only the peninsula, not only threatened world peace, but also revolutionized and transformed the Korean man.

Once sundered, the two sundered parts developed hostilities worse than any of those of the patron states. Group hostility acted to drive men apart so that within weeks of the so-called liberation, Korea in many ways had not yet been liberated. There stood hostility, including Professor Oliver's Syngman Rhee who was making speeches when he first landed that were harsh, and which the American government objected to partly because of the extreme extent of their hostility and their completely unaccommodating spirit. Mr. Oliver will give you an opposite side to that coin. Having developed these hostilities, they then erupted in war. This war then increased the hostilities and the perception of them.

But it did another thing in foreign policy. It increased the perception of outside powers that Korea was not a place for the Koreans, was not a place of a people of a certain character, was not a place with social problems and a society, but was principally and foremost only a "hostility problem." This went far beyond Korea and as Allistair Bucken has said, "U.S. foreign policy not only to Korea but to the rest of the world became, from the point of the Korean War, increasingly militarized." It continues in many ways despite the growing concern over this in the American Congress.

For some years of course, economic policy and economic aid were considerably important. They have, however, now greatly declined. And it is almost exclusively on the military, on aid and support to it, that present American foreign policy and its results appear to be based. In many ways we have no foreign policy to Korea in the normal sense of that word. We have a military policy to Korea, and whenever an American department or American official speaks of Korea, it is almost automatically linked only with arms, with military, with security and with security dangers. No other thought appears to pass through the American mind.

One wonders whether anyone has been giving serious thought in all this time to what effect these foreign policies are having in terms of their political and even sociological outcomes. One wonders what kinds of studies the future will tell us have been produced. One cannot separate military aid from politics, all inputs of the size and extent of those we have been making in Korea are necessarily political inputs as well. And when you give, for example, a few destroyers as we did to Great Britain, you can expect that the results are very containable in political terms because you have a polity of firmly established institutions, and the size of the military aid that you give is infinitesimal. But you continue military aid in an era of developing nations and give to nations who, by their own definition, have institutions less formed and less able to withstand the effects of the outside, the seductions of outside aid. When you then escalate the aid so inexorably that it surpasses everything else entering the economy, and when you add to that as we have added, schools and training institutions and the presence of hundreds and thousands of Americans cheek-by-jowl with Koreans, when you make the umbilical cords connecting Korea and the U.S. 90 percent military umbilical cords, you cannot then turn around and say that you are having no political effects. You cannot turn around and say we are not interfering in the internal affairs of foreign nations. This is an absolute impossibility. We are not only interfering in the internal affairs of foreign nations we have revolutionized, but in the case of the Korean state we have produced a state that never existed before in history, and pray God may never exist again.

We have also revolutionized the values and fabric of Koreans' lives. We seem not to realize that when we set up schools all over the peninsula in a military world, we are sharpening the perception of hostility on the part of the entire population. That the military as an institution wants to aggrandize itself, as all institutions do, and that it can do so only by perceiving more and more danger and more and more hostility on the other side. By this process we are infecting the entire community with precisely the type of spirit we do not need in order to face the future in the Korean peninsula—a spirit in which both sides become more and more hostile to each other all the time; a spirit in which we constantly abet this process by giving or selling military aid in spite of the fact that our own figures show that our military aid in stated dollar value is three times that of the communists, and that we are now mixing it with the dread potencies of possible nuclear weapons. I am of course delighted to see that at last the State Department has gotten up on its legs enough to cancel the deal between

France and Seoul on the conversion of plutonium. But it appears that the danger is not by any means entirely over.

What is the way we must go? It is clear that we must cease the present policies of emphasizing only the military and aid to the military. I personally feel that the retention of American troops in Korea is far less a political interference in the internal affairs of South Korea than the aid we are constantly giving in that area. I would advise some retention of American troops, although I think they can be reduced. We must adopt a long-range policy to try to solve the essential problem of Korea: its division. If this problem is not overcome in the long-run, it will continue to be a festering sore, not only dividing and unattractively revolutionizing Koreans themselves, but also feeding world war fevers and the dangers of conflict, which I think are very great.

We must adopt a positive policy toward Korean unification, and this means placing increasing emphasis on "Four Power" discussion; on some kind of accommodation between the "Four Powers" looking in the long-range future. This obviously cannot come about tomorrow. The long-range future may be twenty or twenty-five years after a "Four Power" agreement for the unification, the neutralization, and the partial demilitarization of the Korean peninsula. Some solution—hopefully as similar as possible to the Austrian one, but if not, then even the Finnish one—would be infinitely preferable for the Koreans themselves, as well as for everyone else concerned, than the kind of mindless inflammation we now are producing through what I consider to be especially ill-conceived and especially thoughtless and disastrous foreign policies.

BAERWALD: Dr. Henderson's very carefully thought through opinions are quite different in tone from those of Ambassador Hahm. I think we should return to Dr. Henderson's impassioned plea to go beyond cold war rhetoric and should try to look at the situation within a broader historical perspective. From that perspective I would like to pick up at least a couple of points from Ambassador Hahm's paper.

Ambassador Hahm says that once the sense of security is denied to Japan, Japan will have to face a very stormy and disruptive national debate as to her own security in terms of demilitarization and even nuclearization. There are several things in that sentence that strike me as being false. First of all, Japan has been involved in a very serious debate about its policies toward Korea for a long time. This would not just be a new dimension if Korea were to be unified one way or the other, but would be a continuation of that debate.

Secondly, Ambassador Hahm's remarks strike me as being very much in the tradition of the old argument that Korea is the dagger that points at the heart of Japan—an argument that Japanese militarists used in an entirely different context for their purposes some years ago, much to the disadvantage of Korea itself. The heritage of that relationship lasted between 1910–1945, and I think still very badly mars the kinds of relations that could be possible between the two countries.

Let me try to be very specific. The debate in Japan has revolved around the whole question of with which Korea should Japan associate itself. It is also well known that the governing liberal democratic party has identified itself with American policy, has identified itself with the government of President Park Chung-hee. On the other hand, even within the governing party there are voices of dissent, and certainly the voices of dissent become very shrill and harsh when one deals with the opposition parties.

I am not certain what kind of solution Ambassador Hahm envisages, if it be a solution indeed, should Korea be unified—presumably under the North in terms of the sentence I mentioned earlier. The effect of the tremendous overemphasis in that region in American policy, which of course has been largely militaristic, would be along the lines of thinking in military security terms rather than trying to build a very different kind of setting for the debate that is supposedly taking place. I am not sure, in conclusion, what kind of volcano Dr. Henderson had in mind.

PAUKER: I am not a specialist on Korea, although I have been in Southeast Asia every year for the last twenty years. I am not knowledgeable about internal Korean affairs, and therefore I can only look at it from the point of view of someone who reads the American press and is concerned with American policy towards Asia and the Pacific. In that context I use the kind of "feel" for the problem that familiarity with other parts of Asia has given me. I will not try to emulate the eloquence of Professor Henderson, which is quite formidable, in part because I lack his talent and in part because I am suspicious of eloquence that sometimes may distract the minds of the audience from the logic of the argument. I would like to ask a number of questions that are of considerable importance to someone concerned with American security problems.

The problem of Korea, it seems to me, is an extremely difficult one for American policy-makers to handle, and that is why I would have preferred Professor Henderson giving us more precise and operational suggestions of how to go about coping with these problems. I find it very difficult to reconcile American policy with the necessity to maintain intimate political-military relations with a regime whose internal policy is unanimously condemned by the American press, and therefore is seen through the eyes of the American press and the American media by American public opinion. How far the policy of the regime in South Korea differs from that of other Third World countries is, to my judgment, not highly relevant, because our relations with other Third World countries are almost without exception less intimate than our relations with the government of South Korea today. Therefore, the situations that may compare unfavorably with the internal situation in South Korea are not to that same extent our concern.

But I cannot look at the situation of South Korean-American relations only in this context. I also have to look at the point of view of broader American interests especially as the title of this symposium urges us to do, in the context of the events since the fall of Indochina in the last nine months or so. The U.S. is present today on the mainland of Asia only in South Korea plus a small residual presence in Thailand, which is about to be phased out. Within the next year or so our presence in Thailand will drop below the level where it is of any operational significance—both to us and to those who observe these situations in order to reach conclusions about future American intentions and capabilities with regard to Asia and the Pacific. Therefore, our presence on the mainland of Asia for the foreseeable future consists of the 2nd Infantry Division in Korea, of certain elements of the U.S. Air Force in Korea, and of other related military elements.

The question is what is the function of these American military forces in Korea? It is often said, and I am sure this is a well-known argument, that the 2nd Infantry Division is not necessary in South Korea because the South Korean ground forces are superior in number and perhaps in quality as well to the military ground forces of the potentially aggressive regime in North Korea. It is also said that American air power may be unimportant from a purely military point of view because North Korea outnumbers and possibly outclasses South Korea in its air power capability. But it is also answered by others that air power is very rapidly deployable and therefore we do not have to have military presence in South Korea if the objective is only to establish and maintain a balance in the field of air power between the North and South.

This argument of course fuels those in the policy-making community, which includes the executive branch of the U.S. government, the Congress, the academic media, and other observers and commentators. But the problem has to be seen in a broader perspective than that. It is not just a matter of contributing to or helping shape the military balance between the two enemy border countries, but it has to be seen from an American point of view in terms of broader American interests in Asia and the Pacific. And from that point of view, the events of last April in Indochina are extremely important.

Naturally the communist victory in Indochina gave, quite legitimately, cause for all the other countries in Asia, and the rest of the world for that matter, to re-evaluate, to reassess their attitude and their

views toward the government of the U.S. The question asked in countries that are old established allies of the U.S., and in countries that are
neutral but count on the U.S. as an important factor in the political-
military equilibrium in Asia, is "What are future American intentions?" Obviously the U.S. would not have been forced or compelled
to accept a communist victory in Indochina if it would have been
willing and able to go all out with its immense resources. What really
matters in this was that the U.S. was not prepared to do so, for reasons
that are very complex but easily understandable to an audience like
this who lives in the U.S. and is part of the American community. The
issue is, if the U.S. was not willing to use its resources to prevent a
communist victory in Indochina, what are American intentions toward
other parts of Asia in the future?

In this context, the presence in Korea becomes, and I would say
unfortunately because of the other elements in this complicated equation, a very important one. If at this time the U.S. would withdraw from
South Korea, this action would be interpreted in Southeast Asia, and
would probably be interpreted in other parts of Asia and the world as
well, as an additional and perhaps even more important sign that the
U.S. has lost interest in Asia or has lost the will to play an important
role in the political-military equilibrium of Asia.

That brings me to my last few remarks. Although this is the case
as seen from the view of a strategic analyst, that does not mean that
the future presence of the U.S. in South Korea should be taken for
granted. We are in an election year and we know that the currents that
go through Congress and through American public opinion are, and
I think for very legitimate reasons, increasingly hostile to American
involvement in overseas adventures. It is not an appealing notion to
the American public to either be held hostage by a foreign country or
to risk getting involved in a conflict between foreign countries.

In the light of this, it is surprising to me that the balance in the
equation that the government of South Korea has established between
the amount of threat from communist subversion, on the one hand,
and the danger of alienating the American public opinion to the point
where our continued presence in Korea will become impossible regardless of the broader strategic considerations on the other hand, has
been solved by the government of South Korea the way it has. In other
words, I wonder whether the threat posed to the government of South
Korea by various kinds of subversion, political disloyalty, or whatever
it may be, is so great that this warrants creating a situation where
American public opinion of the American Congress is very likely in the
foreseeable future to consider our continued military presence in the
peninsula impossible.

LEE: I have always frowned upon someone who makes instant analyses after someone makes a speech. And here I am, now compelled to make some kind of comment on the papers and ideas presented.

Regarding Professor Henderson, first I would like to say that he is very critical of the South Korean regime, referring to it as dictatorial, authoritarian, and comparing President Park with Stalin and Kim Il-sung. What kind of a democracy does he have in mind with which he is trying to compare Korea? If you perhaps asked Chairman Mao to discuss the democracy practiced by the U.S., his answer would be far different from what you claim to be a democracy that is in fact practiced today.

The fundamental question that Professor Henderson should be answering is, "Is it possible to transplant a Western form of democracy into a soil that is culturally different from the U.S.?" Perhaps he is referring to the Western type of democracy when he describes the situation prevailing in Korea today. It has taken 200 years to develop the political system that exists in the U.S. today. It took 100 years to emancipate the Blacks. It has taken another 100 years to legislate the Civil Rights Act of 1965. I would like to remind you, ladies and gentlemen, it was only fifty years ago that the U.S. for the first time provided universal suffrage for its citizens through the 19th Amendment.

Do you think you find corruption only in Korea today? I could ennumerate hundreds of examples of corruption in the U.S. today. South Korea never had an Allende affair. It never dispatched any troops to a distant country to overthrow somebody else's government. There was no Cuban fiasco, which is comparable to what was done here in the U.S. some years ago.

You talked about the military aid, or perhaps the economic aid that in certain forms might interfere with domestic affairs of other countries. The U.S. has provided billions of dollars since 1945 for the national security of the U.S. The U.S. has never provided anything in purely humanitarian grounds. If the U.S. provided military-economic aid to South Korea, it was in the name of the national interest of the U.S. After all, the U.S. has provided military-economic aid even to Tito of Yugoslavia, which is a communist country, to Trujillo of the Dominican Republic, and to Batiste before Castro came to power in Cuba.

Jo: You have raised some fundamental questions. The very question of American foreign policy posture cannot be based upon only a narrowly defined, so-called "national interest" in terms of material and security benefits. It is precisely for those reasons that we talk about the necessity to shift American policy in a different direction. Even Kissinger, while he may not be such a superb moralist, did say that America cannot be true to itself without moral purpose. I would also add that one cannot separate realism completely from idealism. The breach of the two is something for which we strive, and it is for that reason that there is some *reason* to reassess American policy for the benefit of not only the U.S. but also those countries that are related to the U.S.

RAY: I was described in today's program by my non-conventionality of ideas. That was a polite way of describing an "original thinker." Actually that means that when I make presentations to groups like this I usually end up disappointing those that are very much to the left or those who are strong supporters of traditional American policy. I make everyone mad.

How are we to come to grips and reassess American policy in Asia, and perhaps American policy around the world? We have had in the presentations that preceded me, four or five basic approaches to American policy. In many respects I have things to say critically of each of them. I share much of the humanism and the moral concerns that Professor Henderson expresses for Korea. I likewise share with Professor Pauker the uncertainty as to the real meaning of the statements of American political decisions. I was also somewhat disturbed about the lack of exploration of American policy. If indeed this is the impact of American policy, then what is the basis of that policy? How is it that American policy came to that position?

I am also fairly sympathetic with the comments made by Professor Lee in criticizing something that I think runs through many American perceptions of the outside world, and is held by those who defend or those who criticize policy—and that is a certain degree of pretentiousness in the liberal critic. Some of the political corruption in America has indeed been exported to Korea through the institutions of American corporations.

Ambassador Hahm illustrated a second school of thought, one which, perhaps has more advocates in this country than any other. That is perceiving American policy as always responding, never initiating, reacting to aggressive threats from the other side. I think that is rather myopic, and I am not sure whether it is accurate in many cases historically. I will not go any further with that. Ambassador Hahm also brought up the "ideological crusade" approach to American foreign policy—that we are really motivated by extreme fears of communism and other evil things that go about in the night. To a certain extent I am struck by those passages, they strike me as something of a mirror of the more hard-line, ideological statements that one finds coming out of the communist bloc, and to a certain extent they feed upon one another and they are mutually reinforcing. But to a very great extent I think one can explain our intervention in Vietnam as a product of this sort of ideological crusade.

A fourth view, and it is one that I have some difficulty sorting out from the third one, is the "balance of power," or the "strategic interest" approach. There was something that Professor Pauker said that got to the crux of why I have trouble sorting them out. That is his comment that we were not willing to use all of our resources to prevent a communist victory or take-over in South Vietnam. As I observed, with a great deal of frustration from 1965–1973, our activities in that unhappy country, it was not a lack of will that was really frustrating our efforts, but it was the irrelevance, culturally and politically, of the resources that we committed to that country. What often characterizes and has propelled American policy, and one of the things with which we have to come to grips, is this compulsion we have—and I think its roots are more idealistic and ideological than they are strategic—to intervene. We seem to feel the need to demonstrate that we have a will to stand up to aggression. This is a perception that is at the crux of many of our problems. I think that there are more important strategic issues that Dr. Pauker raised.

The fifth view is economic imperialism. That really is the underlying basis of American policy, economic imperialism. I think it is a key element in American policy and therefore should not, and cannot, be ignored. Professor Lee in his comments also understood that American aid is not given out of altruism but does indeed express a strongly perceived notion of national interest. Those statements, I think, can indeed be tied in to a larger pattern of explaining American policy; as long as we can do that, our ability to reassess in the light of the tremendous changes that are occurring will be greatly enhanced.

SIMON: One of the advantages of being a late discussant is that I can be very brief indeed by saying that everything I have been thinking about has already been said by the previous discussants, with one or two exceptions. I will look at those exceptions.

I would like to briefly address the relationship between the international environment of the Korean peninsula and some of the questions of domestic ROK politics that were so vigorously presented by Professor Henderson in the case against the continued American military and political support of the Park government. This contribution and this support allow for the creation of an internal regime, one that presumably contributes to the high tension and hostility on the Korean peninsula. What I would like to do is briefly look at the question of the ROK's need to maintain a garrison state because of the North's alleged unification efforts on the peninsula. It appears that Japan, the United States, the People's Republic of China, and the Soviet Union do not want to see a change in the political boundaries currently existing on the peninsula, because of the unpredictability of a unified Korea's role in Northeast Asia, and perhaps more importantly because short-range unification could only come about through revolution or war.

If such an event was to occur, there would be intense pressure on both the Soviet Union and China to pre-empt the other, hence the possibility of a Korean war turning into a Sino-Soviet war. That is a consummation, of course, that all four major powers devoutly wish to avoid. If this strategic analysis is accurate, then the next question is, "How then can the communication of this lack of desire on the part of the major powers for any change in the status quo, at least in the short-range and medium-range, be communicated to both Pyongyang and Seoul?" Another way of phrasing this question is, "How can hostility and tension be reduced between the two Korean antagonists?" First of all, each side must be assured that the other one is not bent upon military invasion; secondly, that even if one side was bent on military invasion, its major members would not permit it. If that can be communicated, then it comes down to the internal politics of the two countries—that is, in effect, the garrison state that exists in both the North and South are rationalized rather than caused by the so-called external situation. In reality the garrison states are a function of internal politics and the incumbent elite. If this is the case, then a reduction in U.S. military aid would probably have very little effect on the regime in North Korea. I would be very interested in asking Professor Henderson to address himself to this particular question.

OLIVER: I would like to suggest a different emphasis than I think Dr. Henderson was giving us. He is indeed a friend of the Korean people, as he reminded us, and has been for a long time. We admire and respect that. Some of the rest of us have been friends of the Korean people, too, and are proud of that fact. I do not quite go along with Dr. Henderson in idealizing the Korean past quite as much as he did. It's an important question, because he posed an idealized past against a monstrous present. I think most of us who know something about Korea realize that for 4,000 years or so Korea was under an absolutist monarchy without civil liberties, with a lot of barbarism. Korea was divided many times in its past, not just in the last fifteen years or so. Koreans are like other human beings. They have had their problems and their failures and their short-comings as well as their glories and wonderous achievements. I do not think the Korean past belongs in the "garden of Eden" category, nor do I think that today either North or South Korea is inhabited by monsters. It is true that the Korean soldiers were a little bit severe in Vietnam, but I seem to remember Lt. Calley, an American, who was not altogether kind in his dealings with the Vietnamese population. I seem to recall there were bombs dropped on civilian centers, and I do not believe those bombs came from Korean planes. I think the communists in Vietnam also engaged occasionally in unkind behavior toward their enemies. It was a messy war, as wars tend to be.

I would like to turn my attention primarily to Dr. Henderson's suggestion that the four major powers concerned in Northeast Asia should devote attention to a solution of the Korean question. Dr. Rhee, in 1945–1946–1947 when he went into Korea, was opposed to the American policy at that stage. I am proud that he was because the policy was a four-power decision, which had been reached at Moscow and announced on December 17, 1945, to impose a trusteeship upon Korea—a trusteeship that would have inevitably led to communist domination of Korea. It is true that Dr. Rhee led the opposition to that trusteeship, and I think he is primarily responsible for its not having been put into effect. If the four-powers were to take up the Korean question again, and to agree among themselves to a solution without Korean participation, I would be shocked and worried and fearful. How would they set about imposing their solution upon the two halves of Korea? It seems to me the whole idea is exceedingly impractical in operation. What kind of solution should we seek? I do not think the solution of Finland—a neutralized Korea under communist influence, as Finland is—would be the answer, because I do not think the Koreas would accept it and I do not see any practical way of imposing it upon them. I do not think the solution is the solution recently found in Germany of taking the two divided parts and making two separate nations of them. I do not think the solution is the solution of Vietnam, which of course is communization of the entire area. I think a solution that is more feasible, more practical, and in the long run better not only for the Korean people but also for the world, is the solution that South Korea is attempting to achieve. I think there will be, and we should certainly put all of the emphasis we can in assisting, a meeting again between representatives of North and South Korea. Gradually and by small increments there will come a certain kind of cooperation, so that the two may come to live in a little more harmony than they do now. Although history is long and very indeterminate, the Korean people are a sturdy people and they have been there for a long time —and they are Koreans, after all, North and South. If we do not get too impatient, if we do not try to impose a solution from outside, we will see Northern and Southern Koreans becoming a little more agreeable toward one another.

BERTON: I would like to focus on the criteria for American involvement abroad. As I was preparing to talk about the impact of the Soviet Union on U.S. policy options in Korea, I received a thick envelope from Harvard's Center of International Studies. It turned out to contain a pamphlet entitled "Foreign Policy Leadership Questionnaire." When I began to fill out this questionnaire (which apparently was sent out to a random sample of academics, businessmen, industrialists, military officers, etc.), I saw that one part of it was very relevant to our discussion of American policy in Korea. It is a topic where passions run high, where people are concerned about political oppression in South Korea, the importance attached to American bases on the peninsula, and what not. So, what I decided to do was to expand that portion of the questionnaire on American options in dealing with under-developed countries. I added four to the seven original questions, and I think that presenting and discussing them would serve to interject a cool, detached, theoretical note into the proceedings. It would also be useful to look at Korea from the perspective of American foreign policy.

If you look at the questionnaire (which I have circulated) you will see rather quickly that making a choice among the questions is quite difficult. I would like you to rank-order all the choices for one to eleven (please do not say that numbers two and three are equally important). Here are the questions:

1. Is a stable government, capable of preserving internal order, the most important criterion in determining American involvement?

2. Is the fact that a government is neutral or pro-American in its foreign policy the overriding criterion, or the second or third or eleventh item on your list?

3. Of what importance is rapid economic development? Here, of course, we all are keenly aware of the tremendous economic development (another economic miracle similar to that of Japan or West Germany) that has been taking place in the southern part of the Korean peninsula.

4. How important is the ability of a government to maintain civil liberties? And here again this rings a bell in terms of the Korean peninsula.

5. What weight do you attach to the fact that a government maintains the free enterprise system? Is this an important element in determining U.S. support?

6. The commitment of a government not to engage in un-provoked aggression against other nations—how important is this?

7. To what extent should the availability of broad opportunities for American business investment determine our policy? And I am quite sure that for many people this is indeed an important criterion.

8. How much value would you place on the decision of a government to provide military bases for U.S. armed forces?

9. How important is an agreement to make bases available for vital communication facilities?

10. Of what consequence to U.S. security is the strategic location of a country?

11. Similarly, how important is the strategic location of a country to the security of one of our important allies?

Now I know you cannot complete the questionnaire in a few

minutes, but I think that attempting to answer it and trying to rank-order the choices will give you a clearer perception of the complexity that confronts real decision-makers. It is easy for us academics to pontificate and talk about this or that factor or to point to this or that reason why we should support or not support a given country. Even this brief list of eleven criteria, I think, will show how tremendously difficult things are, and how it is never a question of right or wrong —white or black—but rather of groping in an immense area of gray.

TOTTEN: I will try to delineate the problem in its clearest, starkest form, and get to the essence. There are two garrison states and two authoritarian regimes facing each other on the Korean peninsula. The danger of war breaking out is great despite the fact that the surrounding nations, including the Soviet Union, the United States, Japan and China, for their own reasons, would not like to see it. In general, neither the regime in North Korea nor the regime in South Korea want war, nor do the people. But we know that wars have broken out in the past despite universal lack of wanting it to happen. It seems to me that all of us here do want to see the North and the South negotiate. It is the most horrible border in the whole world at the present time. You cannot have mail, you cannot cross and visit your relatives. You cannot find out whether relatives are alive or dead. People must be able to communicate. People must be able to trade. But the important thing is that people must be able to feel safe in their beds at night—and that means the dismantling of the military forces in both the North and the South.

If you compare Japan and Korea at the present time, people in Japan can sleep. A communist may live next door to a non-communist, but when they meet in the morning they will bow to each other. They will get on the subways together and there is no fear that one is going to kill the other. One will vote one way in the political election, another will vote another way. The question is how to achieve this harmony given the situation as it is in Korea. I think in the negotiations. There are of course the military problems, and many other problems. The North, which wants foreign troops out including the United States military forces, has been giving signals that it would negotiate even before those are out. The North also talked about allowing the discussion of communism in the South, and as far as I know the North previously has opposed this violently. But I think it should be the other way around. This seems to be a great opportunity, because it can make a point for negotiations. If the South allows people to openly advocate communism, then it means that reciprocally in the North opposition ideas should also be advocated. The Swedes, for instance, are known as people who take an impartial view. The South could go to the North and then interview people who could come to see them. Of course their names would be taken down by the North and so on, but then this group could come back in six months and ask where these people are and see if they have been tortured or mistreated. The same could be done for groups from the North coming down to the South. The object, of course, is to try to build up some trust between the North and the South, even though systems of different types may be continued in the North and South. I see that it is possible that this kind of a thing could get started soon. I agree with Mr. Oliver that this negotiation should take place and should be done mainly by the Korean people. The big nations can make conditions for this kind of negotiation, but it must be done by the Koreans. But I disagree with Mr. Oliver on the timing. I think that a waiting will allow nuclear weapons to develop in Korea. At the moment, the more rapid nuclearization of the South has been stunted by the present American insistence that the South Korean government stop its purchase of the French nuclear materials. But on the other hand, it could happen soon. I think that the world and Koreans should push for faster negotiations between North and South Korea with the objective of eventual disarmament in Korea and full civil liberties for people in both the North and the South.

JO: On the solution question of a four-power guarantee of Korean neutrality and independence, Professor Henderson is on the one hand aware of the fact that neither North or South Koreans are interested in four-power solutions. On the other hand, neither the United States, the Soviet Union, China, or Japan are interested in change of the status quo. That being the case, what happened to the feasibility of his plan of four-power guarantee? Is it such a long-range thing that we cannot talk about it in a feasible manner or in the foreseeable future? On the one had, Ambassador Hahm said the ideology of détente is difficult— yes, we all realize that—but that does not mean the conflicting sides should refrain from having a dialogue and even détente, even if they cannot go so far as to Koreanize the peninsula's problems.

HENDERSON: In all the history of my attending these conferences, I think I have never attended one where so many surgeons dissected a single corpse. As all the commentators by their silence in essence told us the paper of Ambassador Hahm really did not say anything new whatsoever and so they turned their attention almost entirely to mine. The first point I would like to respond to, that is very welcome and certainly extremely called for in criticism, is that I did not give a proper organizational, specific conclusion for what my policy recommendations would be. I would advocate cutting American military aid, and phasing it out in the very, very near future. I would advocate, too, the retention of American troops for a short time but their reduction probably within a year and a half or so to around the 20,000 troop level. I would make American presence and any kind of future aid dependent on the restoration of what I would call a viable political system in South Korea so that we do not have a repetition of what happened in Vietnam and Cambodia and during 1946–48 China, where we gave more and better arms. We lost in those countries because we have a political system that just does not work—no private will stand up and fight for that system. I would recommend the restoration of minimal civil liberties and limited freedom of the press. I would restore paragraph 4.A–D of the armistice agreement which the United States signed in 1953—we still have our signatures on it. We have said we are not abiding by it, but that does not mean that we are not violating it every day. We are. That is the part of the agreement that says that we and the communists will bring in no further arms or troops to the Korean peninsula, and it establishes some sort of supervision therefore.

I advocate making a four-power entente on Korea; that is, some sort of restored four-power communication, not necessarily of a conference table variety because that may not be immediately practical. This is a matter of far higher priority than we are now giving it; its first order of business should be the mutual reduction of arms to both sides of the Korean peninsula.

I would advocate making the Korean peninsula, if at all possible, at this late date, a free nuclear zone. We are heavily derelict in not having done this in the past few years. I think it is probably the area that, of all areas, most needs and calls for a nuclear free zone. I think we should cease the sale or gift of any arms to South Korea that have greater potential power than those we know are possessed by North Korea. We are nevertheless selling them for example, Phantom jet bombers that have a combat radius three to five times as great as those of the MIGs which oppose them in North Korea.

I think we should probe more closely for the DPRK's position. We should see its officials somewhat more often than we do; we should allow trade with North Korea; we should gradually move towards recognition of Pyongyang. We should also urge Japan to do the same thing, and of course, we should continue our efforts to have Moscow and Peking recognize the Seoul regime. In other words, we should try to pursue further the application to the Korean situation of the "two Germanies" solution.

I would like to clarify what I said earlier about democracy. What I did point out was that in the past—and I do not think it is at all idealized in the past—the Koreans had in their system a system of balances involving the censorate and other organs that permitted and encouraged criticism of the monarch and of government policy. That system, which Koreans once had as native people, they no longer have today in either the North or South. That is a shame. Not that you don't have American democracy—that is not what I said—but that you do not have the expression of governmental criticism which was your own tradition before you even heard of the U.S. That is entirely different from the point Mr. Lee made. As you know, under Emergency Decree #9, no system of criticism of the government is permitted, and anyone who thinks or says that there is criticism of the government is out of his mind. At the present time, South Korea has only one freedom— that is the freedom to do what the government wants the people to do.

I see no reason why a man who was paid by the Japanese to prevent the liberation of Korea should sit on the throne in Seoul and shut every other Korean citizen up. It does not matter, Mr. Lee, what intention of American aid is or was; what matters is the result. Aid has unintended results and one is fully justified in criticizing the intended as well as the unintended. On the subject of corruption, I would certainly agree that corruption is widely shared by all kinds of nations including our own, but I note that there has recently been a tendency for corruption to be imported into the U.S. from Korea, rather than the opposite. Dr. Simon made the point about internal politics being more dependent on internal elites rather than on the inputs from outside. I would say that the elites we have now are, in essence, elites created by the operation of American policy that I was describing. These are not people who had ever held an elite position in Korean society before. As a matter of fact, if you see the character of the population that has fled or come over to the U.S., you will find among it the members of really old Korean families who have found that they no longer play the elite roles they once expected to play inside their own country.

In regards to Dr. Oliver, I do not think that the four powers should necessarily impose a solution. Quite the contrary; I think they should arrange between themselves a backing away from the Korean peninsula. I would like to see a greater "hands off" policy on Korea so that it can become a more neutralized place where Koreans can talk to each other above the chatter of American and Soviet-made machine guns. I do not think that nature is taking its course; American policy has been interfering radically. I wish we could get back to some sort of nature in order to bring a solution to Korea.

Finally, in regard to Dr. Jo's question about four-power guarantee, it is true that the great powers and the Korean people are not anxious to restart some sort of four-power communication in Korea. What is driving us there is the fact that if we do not do that, we are going to have an explosion in Korea for a number of reasons. One is that we have more arms there than in any other similar territory in the entire world. Secondly, no two people are more hostile to each other than any other two peoples in the world, including the Israelis and the Arabs. Finally, power is so concentrated in the hands of Kim Il-sung and Park Chung-hee that the psychological effects of that degree of concentration of power on the human soul will be shattering and is extremely dangerous. These two men are now ruthless, brutal, and unrestrained—and the operation of power in their hands is simply not something we can suffer world peace to beat in the long run.

AUDIENCE: I did not hear the phrase "cheap labor" used all day. But this pool of cheap labor—which means a great advantage to Americans, and particularly to the Japanese capitalists who are 80 percent of the investors in South Korea—have no voice. We church people got in trouble because we happened to be working with young people, who are a source of cheap labor, and teaching them something about dignity and human rights—which is the reason we were quieted and I was expelled. Why don't you consider this cheap labor market as a part of the basic U.S. policy, a quick-kill capitalist investment, not a long-term investment? Why doesn't Professor Bearwald consider this basic to American-Japanese policies in South Korea?

BAERWALD: I think this Father has raised a very important issue. I know that, for example, at the time the treaty re-establishing diplomatic relations between Korea and Japan was being debated, one of the issues that the opposition parties raised was the danger to the trade union movement in Japan that might be occasioned by virtue of the fact that Japanese enterprises would be able to go to Korea to utilize non-unionized, or as you put it, cheap labor for the purposes of manufacturing goods that could be made in Japan by unionized labor, or at least labor that had somewhat higher wages. The Japanese recognize this. By the same token, one must realize that there are Japanese enterprises that are indeed looking for a quick-kill in terms of making profits, and looking for the kind of situation that still seems to prevail in Korea where unionization is not permitted, which does afford an opportunity that is almost irresistable. The Japanese are not alone in being greedy. People all over the world exhibit that tendency, including ourselves. We must not look upon this as a problem in the context of either Japan, China, Korea, or Asia in general, but as a worldwide phenomenon. That it plays a direct role in explaining the support for President Park's government, I have some doubts. But that is a separate issue.

LEE: On the question of political corruption being imported from the U.S. or exported to the U.S., let me just say that when the Lord created us we were created as sinners....

AUDIENCE: Which does not mean that we have to go on sinning!

Part III

OTHER ASIAN SIDES' PERCEPTIONS OF AMERICA'S ROLE

Prospects for Détente in Asia

Bernd Kaufmann

If we analyze development in Asia—by this I mean mainly Eastern and Southeastern Asia and the territory bordering the Pacific—since the end of the Second World War, it is not difficult to see that this continent needs a much higher degree of détente and security; it needs in fact, a radical change in its international relations.

As a citizen of a country that made an active contribution to the staging of the Conference on Security and Cooperation in Europe, I can permit myself to give my personal opinions on détente in Asia, mainly because we in the German Democratic Republic believe that peace is an indivisible entity. The securing of peace is the most important factor in the relations of any country; détente and security are the basic requirements for the development of any kind of political, economic or cultural cooperation between nations. Thus the resolutions taken at Helsinki will not only be important for us Europeans. They also show the peoples of other continents the way to eliminate tension and secure peace. The setting up of a stable peace order in Asia, therefore, demands not only the willingness of the countries in that region to cooperate in this great task, but also the institutionalization of détente and security on the Asian continent. Peace is the right of all the peoples of this earth; détente must be reinforced and extended to all continents. In the GDR, therefore, we consider it our duty to make some attempt to help change the international situation, so that the hopes and desires of all the peoples of the world can be realized. We have no illusions about the possibilities and the limitations that exist. We will have many obstacles to overcome; a long and difficult road lies before us.

More than two thousand million of the four thousand million people on this earth live in Asia. Some 40 percent of these live in the People's Republic of China alone. The Asian nations had the oldest developed cultures known to mankind. The continent of Asia is faced

313

with diverse and extraordinarily complicated problems. The fact alone that since 1945 Asia has seen almost fifty local wars and armed conflicts is proof enough of this. The great powers were, to differing extents, either involved in these wars or took part in them.

The Vietnam War, which for the American people was completely senseless, is an obvious example of such intervention. One of the facts that emerges from all this is that the Soviet Union, the People's Republic of China, Japan and the United States of America, because of their political influence and their economic and military strength, and all the countries of Asia bear a heavy responsibility for future development in Asia. The Soviet Union is the only one of the great powers in Asia to make any concrete efforts to shoulder this responsibility with her proposal for setting up a collective security system in Asia, which she first made in 1969. Since then this proposal has repeatedly been expressed in more detail as a long-term program, for example in speeches made by Leonid Brezhnev in March 1972 at the 15th Congress of the Soviet Trade Unions and at Alma Ata in August 1973, and in the statements of I. Alexandrov on the principles of setting up collective security in Asia. This Soviet proposal, which is part of their active Asian policy, also stems from the fact that the Soviet Union belongs geographically, historically, economically, politically and culturally not only to Europe but also to Asia. Of the 22.4 million square kilometers of the total area of the territory of the Soviet Union, 16.8 million square kilometers lie in Asia. This poses problems of peaceful coexistence and of the development of inter-state relations with the Asian countries and problems of national security, problems that can only be settled in conjunction with the governments of the Asian countries. We must not forget, of course, that during the Second World War the Soviet Union took an active part in Asian-Pacific acts of war.

The Soviet proposal of setting up an all-Asian security system, which was considerably influenced by the success of the Helsinki Conference, is based on the fact that the maximal development of all-Asian economic, scientific, technical and cultural cooperation will take a central place in an all-Asian security policy.

But collective security and lasting cooperation will only be achieved in Asia if they are handled as *an all-Asian problem,* with all necessary consideration of regional and sub-regional specifics and long-standing problems, and despite the possibility of regional solutions for certain concrete questions. *All the Asian countries* (which in this article does not include the Near and Middle East) must, of course, take an active part in this security system. This concerns the People's Republic of China in particular. It is obvious from these simple facts that the insinuation that with this proposal the Soviet Union is carrying out encirclement strategy against the People's Republic of China cannot stand up to any serious examination. Equal participation gives all the Asian countries without exception the guarantee that an all-Asian security system does not give one-sided advantages to anyone nor does it work to the disadvantage of any one country or group of countries in Asia. The present situation demands that the United States should certainly be a party to any security system in Asia and that she should give guarantees that would be binding under international law.

Bilateral agreements and regional political and economic mergers, which are already in existence or are in the process of being formulated, can become firm foundations for setting up an all-Asian security system provided that they do not violate the interests of other countries. A comprehensive program of concrete measures must be worked out, a program that will cover essential areas of political, social and cultural life, economic cooperation and military détente.

The indispensable basic principles of a security system, which are binding for all countries and groups of countries, include:

—refraining from the threat or use of force in relations between nations;
—respecting the sovereignty and the integrity of states;
—inviolability of frontiers;
—non-intervention in the internal affairs of other countries;
—development of economic and other cooperation on the basis of equal rights and mutual advantage;
—sovereign power and disposal over all the natural resources of the country;
—peaceful settlement of all international disputes.

In such a case the Asian security system would be based on the principles of peaceful coexistence already valid for East-West relations, the Charter and other resolutions of the U.N., on the principles formulated at Bandung with the participation of the Asian peoples themselves, and on the Pancha-Shila policy of the 1950s.

If we talk about the prospects for détente in Asia, we must first of all consider that with today's new dimensions in world politics, realistic possibilities exist for achieving this. Since the beginning of the 1970s, we have been at a stage of gradual, complicated and to some extent very inconsistent and involved transition from confrontation to détente. The most important feature of this stage of development is that the principles of peaceful coexistence in political relations between states of differing social orders are becoming more and more firmly established. The Soviet-American Agreements, the European treaties and the Final Act of the Conference on Security and Cooperation in Europe can be quoted here as examples. In these and other agreements such principles as sovereign equality and respect for the rights inherent in sovereignty, refraining from the threat or use of force, inviolability of frontiers and the territorial integrity of states, peaceful settlement of disputes and non-intervention in the internal affairs of states, and equal rights and the right of self-determination of peoples have been declared as being the basic principles for forming relations between capitalist and socialist countries. The economy will, to a greater and greater extent, play an important stabilizing and stimulating role in politics by means of qualitatively new economic relations between these countries.

The change from bilateral to multilateral agreements is a second feature of this development; this is shown by the Final Act of Helsinki. But this must not limit the importance of bilateral relations between countries. The multi-lateralism of international relations and the increased merging of the political and economic interests of states are preparing the ground by setting up today regional security systems to serve the cause of détente and peace, and at the same time are making these systems more and more necessary. We therefore can hardly assume that such countries as Japan, for example, on a long-term basis would be able to meet her enormous demand for raw materials through exploitation of conflicts of interests and antagonism between the People's Republic of China, the U.S.S.R., and other countries.

If we examine the reasons for the transition from confrontation to détente, it is easy to see that changes in the international balance of power play an important role in this process. In addition, in the last few years especially, the political and economic interdependence of all parts of the international system has increased considerably, and at the same time, ideological differences have continued to grow and will go on doing so in the future. The mutual dependence of states of the two socio-economic orders, which exists to some degree, and the resultant "globalization" of the world's present political and economic problems and conflict situations are two reasons for worldwide implementation of a policy of peaceful coexistence. The recognition of the parity of opposing groupings of military forces has changed military planning and strategic thinking. At present the foreign policies of the leading Western countries are taking a more realistic line; at the same time the increasing activities of the opponents of détente should not be underestimated.

The leading Western countries have acknowledged a number of qualitative changes in international relations; attempts are being made to more or less adapt to these changes in the balance of power between the two social systems. It is my opinion that in this respect present American foreign policy, to some extent, does take the interests of the Soviet Union and other socialist countries into consideration. At the same time, however, due to an overestimation of the so-called multipolarity of the world, a useless attempt is still being made to base U.S. foreign policy on exploitation of conflicts, both regional and global, and of the opposing political, economic and military interests of other countries. Thus the important position of the People's Republic of China in U.S. foreign policy will not be as much in evidence in relations between the two countries; on the contrary this will be inferred from their efforts to maintain a world-wide balance of forces in order to protect their own global interests. Although the United States can have no real interest in military conflicts between the Soviet Union and the People's Republic of China, since these would constitute an incalculable risk for the national security of the U.S.A. because of the danger of a nuclear confrontation, attempts are being made to exploit Sino-Soviet conflicts to achieve certain aims of American foreign policy. It is obvious that this policy is ultimately unrealistic. It is based on subjective factors—i.e., those that will change sooner or later, such as the extremely anti-Soviet policy being pursued at present by the Chinese leaders with Mao Tse-tung at their head—and not, in spite of the "cultural revolution," the Sino-Soviet border conflicts and the mounting anti-Sovietism, on objective and unchanging factors such as the common interests of the peoples of the Soviet Union and the People's Republic of China in basic questions of social development in the two countries.

To sum up, it must be said that new aspects of world politics can, and must, be realized to a considerably increased extent as far as Asia is concerned; this demands a serious appraisal of the balance of forces in the Asian-Pacific area and mutual regard for the national interests of all Asian and Pacific countries, including the U.S.A. This would create in Asia, as in other regions (and branches of world politics), favorable conditions for implementing the principles of coexistence on an unlimited scale in the practical politics of countries of differing social orders, for developing a comprehensive system of political discussion, and for creating the opportunity of controlling crises.

The overall situation and general tendencies in political development in Asia are distinguished by a number of new trends and processes, which create favorable conditions for the gradual guaranteeing of détente and security and the institutionalization of these within an all-Asian security system. The historic victory of the national liberation movements of the peoples of Vietnam, Cambodia and Laos made radical changes in the balance of forces, particularly in Southeast Asia. The struggle of the other peoples and countries for their national independence, their national sovereignty, self-determination and sovereign power of disposal over all their natural resources is gaining new impetus. The military presence and the political influence of the U.S.A. in Southeast Asia has been, in part, considerably reduced. SEATO has entered the last stages of its existence, an existence that has been in question for some years now. The so-called U.S. military line of defense, except in the case of South Korea, had to be withdrawn as far as the Pacific Islands.

The new Pacific Doctrine is, in my opinion, an attempt by the Ford

Administration to adapt their Asian policy to the above-mentioned changes in order to prevent, with as little cost to themselves as possible, any further infringement on U.S. influence, particularly in the Eastern Asian and Pacific region, and to maintain a balance of power in this area by means of their "Island Strategy." This would apparently be a continuation of Nixon's Guam Doctrine, whereby the dispute between the U.S.A., the U.S.S.R. and the People's Republic of China would be switched to the Eastern Asian and Pacific region, and the anti-Soviet policy of the leaders of the People's Republic of China would be used more directly. Japan's role as the main partner of the U.S.A. in Asia would gain in importance, and economic cooperation with the countries in this area would be considerably extended. Although the Pacific Doctrine, which has been formulated only very vaguely, contains some realistic points and, for example, does not completely oppose the Soviet proposal for setting up a collective security system in Asia, we must not, however, overlook the fact that the U.S.A. is concerned with reinforcing her reduced military presence in Eastern Asia and her political position in the region. An apparently new combination of countries would be formed on the basis of traditional bloc politics but these countries are actually in opposition to the majority of Asian countries. In connection with this, Japan and the People's Republic of China have been given equal priority in the Doctrine; on the other hand, however, the legitimate security interests of the Soviet Union have been completely neglected.

Another new trend in Asia is that since the beginning of the 1970s, the Southeast Asian countries of the ASEAN bloc have begun to review their past relations with the U.S.A., to lay more emphasis on their own interests, to normalize their relations with the socialist countries and, in doing so, to adopt the principle of peaceful coexistence. They have begun to place their relations with each other on a higher political and economic level. They are trying to neutralize Southeast Asia and to set up more harmonious relations with the great powers. The already well-known Malaysian plan for neutralizing Southeast Asia has obviously been based on the fact that a neutralization of this area would be impracticable without the acceptance of the U.S.A., the People's Republic of China, and Japan and the support of the U.S.S.R. This concept of neutralization is also included in the demand made by India and Sri Lanka to make the Indian Ocean a peace zone. They also demanded that any further development of the island Diego Garcia as a military base be prevented.

With these proposals the above-mentioned countries intervened officially in the discussions, which have already begun, on the reforming of international relations in Asia. These discussions, in spite of many problems, include positive starting points for a constructive security policy, which will serve the cause of peace, and correspond with the intentions behind the Soviet proposal for setting up a collective security system in Asia, as do, strictly speaking, various other basic elements of the policies of the Asian countries. The end of the Vietnam War and the victory of the Indochinese peoples gave great encouragement to the struggle of many countries for national independence, the securing of their economic and political independence, power of disposal over their natural resources, a new international economic order, socio-economic changes and the vanquishing of the legacy of colonialism. The careful normalization of the relations of the countries on the Indian subcontinent, which began with the Simla Agreement of 1972, also favors détente in the situation in Asia.

Vietnam, which will be unified as a socialist state in 1976, in the future will play a central role as a factor of peace in Indochina and Southeast Asia, and together with Laos and Cambodia will have a strong influence on future political development in Southeast Asia. Vietnam's willingness to develop equal relations with all its neighboring countries in Southeast Asia will lead to a qualitatively new establishment of the policy of peaceful coexistence in the relations between Asian countries, and it will have a positive influence on policies of détente and security in Asia.

Vietnam's capability for coexistence can today no longer be doubted even by the leading powers of the West. In my opinion, the American veto against the acceptance of the Democratic Republic of Vietnam and the Republic of South Vietnam into the United Nations only goes to show that the U.S.A. has not found as yet any realistic concept on which to base their attitude towards Vietnam. The Democratic Republic of Vietnam, on the other hand, has been willing since 1973 to establish normal equal relations with other countries, including the United States, on the basis of the Paris Agreement of January 27, 1973. Pham Van Dong, the Prime Minister of the Democratic Republic of Vietnam, reaffirmed this position on September 2, 1975, making reference to the five principles of peaceful coexistence. One of the requirements for this is the willingness of the U.S.A. to fulfill Article 21 of the Paris Agreement, which includes the United States' obligation to make some contribution towards healing the wounds of war and towards postwar development in the whole of Indochina. The communiqué concerning the stay of Dr. Henry Kissinger, the U.S. Secretary of State, in Hanoi from February 10–13, 1973, was also signed in this spirit. The guarantee of détente and security for Southeast Asia is an essential element of Vietnamese politics. According to the view of the Vietnamese, problems of long standing can be solved in a spirit of good neighborliness. The introduction of steps towards normalization of relations towards France, and the methods for establishing political and economic relations with Japan are proof of this. Development of economic relations based on mutual advantage will no doubt play an important role in Vietnam's relations with countries in the West.

In connection with the problem of achieving détente and guaranteeing security in Asia, the Korean Question, i.e., the continued presence of American troops in South Korea and future establishment of relations between the Korean People's Democratic Republic and South Korea, poses an important problem—a problem that must be solved gradually. The Korean People's Democratic Republic is of the view that a peaceful solution to the complex problems that exist between the Korean People's Democratic Republic and South Korea must first and foremost be found by the Korean peoples themselves, without foreign intervention. In this spirit the Korean People's Democratic Republic made a great number of proposals that could have made some contribution to reducing the conflict and lessening tension. These proposals concerned the withdrawal of all foreign U.N. troops stationed in South Korea, the reduction of troops and of arms expenditures, the conclusion of a peace treaty with the U.S.A., and political, economic and cultural exchanges between the Korean People's Democratic Republic and South Korea, and so on. It is particularly interesting that the Korean People's Democratic Republic is prepared to replace the cease-fire, which has been in existence since 1953, with a peace treaty to be signed with the United States and, on this basis, to conduct their relations with South Korea on peaceful lines. This means that a realistic U.S. policy on the Korean Question could, in the future, lead to détente in the situation on the Korean peninsula.

In our judgment of the prospects for détente in Asia we must not, of course, overlook the fact that one essential feature of the situation in the Asian-Pacific region is that fundamental interests and political concepts of four great powers—the U.S.S.R., the People's Republic of China, the U.S.A., and Japan—overlap there. The politics of the Chinese leadership and the further development of American-Chinese relations are, therefore, of particular interest in this.

The Chinese leadership has succeeded in establishing the People's Republic of China as an Asian great power. The People's Republic of China has entered into official relations with most Asian countries and the U.S.A., with relatively close adhesion to the demands of the Chinese. This meant either moderation or temporary restraint of considerable tension in relations between the People's Republic of China and a great number of other Asian countries and the U.S.A.— tension that was either of historical origin or was brought about during the U.S. policy of containment, which was directed against the People's Republic of China. At first glance it seems that this has made a considerable contribution to détente and the securing of peace in Asia. In their policies toward China, a great number of the Asian countries doubtless were, and still are, geared towards these worthy aims, which reflect the basic desires of the Asian peoples, including the Chinese.

Sober consideration of Asian policies and of the political aims ef the present Chinese leadership shows, however, that these expectations have not been fulfilled. The fact is that the leaders of the People's Republic of China are becoming the opponents of real détente in Asia. Their policy is aimed at preventing the equal participation of all Asian countries in the development of international relations, up to now leaving the Soviet Union, India, and the Mongolian People's Republic, for no apparent reason, out of the group of Asian countries, with whom the Chinese leaders have normalized or extended their relations. The Chinese leaders are trying, by means of bilateral treaty connections with other Asian countries, to establish coalitions of countries that are directed against third parties. The Chinese have formally adopted principles of peaceful coexistence in all inter-state agreements on the establishing of international relations with other countries. At the same time, however, attempts, which are contrary to international law, were and still are being made to direct these relations against third parties and to involve the partner country in a policy that opposes the legitimate interests of another country. Thus, in these relations, the coexistence principle is being negated *de facto,* and principles such as sovereign equality of countries and non-intervention in the internal affairs of other countries are being seriously violated. The pressure being brought to bear by the Chinese on Japan in connection with the signing of a peace and friendship agreement is convincing evidence of this. It is a well-known fact that the nebulous clause on "efforts of a third power to achieve hegemony" is the main instrument of Chinese diplomacy in creating spheres of influence of an anti-Soviet character and in building up a dominating position for themselves. At present the main function of this clause is to interfere with the deepening of political, economic, scientifico-technical, cultural and other relations between Asian countries and the Soviet Union, to undermine the legitimate security interests of the Soviet Union, and to reduce the scope of Soviet politics. The Chinese are hoping in this way to limit the role and the influence of the Soviet Union in Asia. In practice, therefore, the "hegemony clause" is also used on a wide scale to repress the Soviet proposal for establishing an Asian security system and to encourage other Asian countries to adopt this line on a long-term basis. It must also be explained that this process causes China's neighbors in particular, to behave extremely warily when declaring their views on questions of détente and security in Asia out of fear of reprisals, or it makes them simply yield to the Chinese view. The governments of most Asian countries have not as yet given any official opinion regarding the question of a security system because the Chinese leadership—in contrast with its former declarations—is against such a system. And without China there cannot be a fully comprehensive collective security system in Asia.

In fact, the Chinese, to a great extent, base the development of their relations with other countries on the way these countries arrange their relations with the Soviet Union. This means that Chinese diplomacy is illegally interfering in the sovereign right of other countries to decide their own policies and is deliberately encouraging new tensions in the Asian-Pacific region. Apart from all this, the intentionally vague formulation of this clause gives the Chinese an opportunity to adapt it at will; it can be directed today at the Soviet Union, tomorrow at the United States, Japan or some other country. Direct or tacit support of these actions of the Chinese leaders must ultimately be a contradiction of the inherent security interests of the Asian peoples themselves. There can be no real détente in Asia if there is support for the present confrontation policy of the Chinese leaders, which is directed against the U.S.S.R. Détente and security can only be achieved in Asia if the Asian countries maintain equal relations with every one of the great powers.

The position of the Chinese leadership towards détente and security in Asia is a result of their universally destructive standpoint on the basic question of our time—the question of war and peace. According to the Chinese, the factors that could contribute to war on a world scale are increasing. This is a direct inversion of the actual development that has taken place.

Despite the successful conclusion of the Conference on Security and Cooperation in Helsinki, and in complete contradiction of the facts, there has been new talk of an allegedly growing danger of war, with Europe being the center of a future military confrontation between the Soviet Union and the U.S.A. The endeavors of the Chinese to reach this end by fanning the flames of political, and when possible, military provocation particularly between the main powers of the two social systems, even the Soviet Union and the U.S.A., are obvious. (Even after the shifting of the "Main Conflict" from the Sino-Soviet border, the thesis on the danger of an imminent surprise attack by the Soviet Union was published at the 10th Party Congress of the Communist Party of China in August 1973.) The Chinese leadership would like to keep China out of a conflict situation, such as in central Europe where the U.S. confronts the U.S.S.R., in order, in a historically shorter time, to lessen the strategic gap between the People's Republic of China and the two main powers and to gain for China the position as predominant world power by the weakening in the long term of their so-called enemy number 1, the Soviet Union, and enemy number 2, the U.S.A. There is, in my opinion, no doubt that this political idea and the hostility towards détente that lies behind it are aimed at destroying the existing order of international relations, are seriously endangering the principle of coexistence worked out between the two world political systems after such a tough struggle, and also conflict with the interests of American policy, where constructive relations with the Soviet Union have a part to play. The involvement of the Chinese leadership in Asia is, naturally, part of this global strategy of fomenting tension and confrontations. As a result, the fundamental reaction of the U.S.A. to this policy being followed by China must have serious consequences for the formulation and implementation of the United States' new policy.

The American-Chinese relationship is of decisive importance for the further development of the situation in Asia and for the prospects of détente on this continent. The implications of the U.S.-China policy of the 1940s, 1950s, and 1960s have been well known. The wrong assessment of the development of the internal situation and of the political forces in China prior to the foundation of the People's Republic, the Korean and the Vietnam Wars, as well as the failure of the policy of containment in the period of "Cold War," are part of the grim balance of American-China and Asia politics of the past decades.

After the enforced withdrawal of the United States from Indochina and the partial normalization of American-Chinese relations initiated by the visit of Nixon to Peking in 1972, the United States is nowadays facing the question of what direction should be taken in the further development of its relationship with the People's Republic of China. In outlining the America-China policy and in creating a novel type of "balance of power," as indicated by the Pacific Doctrine in the East Asian Pacific region, it will become apparent that an essential role will be played by the Chinese-Soviet relationship as well as by the risks to American policy resulting from the escalation of anti-Sovietism by the Chinese leaders. And this the more because, in my view, the attitude of the People's Republic of China toward the Soviet Union represents to the United States a calculation with the greatest number of unknown quantities that emanate primarily from the evolution of the internal situation in China and the resultant imponderabilities in Chinese foreign policy. The assessment of the American leadership as the "ruling clique" made in the editorial of *Renmin Ribao* of December 25, 1975, as well as the general situation surrounding the release of the Soviet helicopter team, accentuate the topicality of this question.

Even the security-political aspect has a high priority to the United States in its relations with China, when contemplated at long sight. Clearly with the understanding to counter the Chinese claim to power and to meet with the danger arising even for the United States due to the strategic armament of the People's Republic of China, the United States obviously wants to set up, together with the People's Republic of China, a network of political and economic relations that will bind the PRC more strongly to the United States.

President Ford, on the occasion of his visit to China in December 1975, felt the need to stress that the United States as before is interested in maintaining a well-balanced relationship to the U.S.S.R. and to China, and that the U.S. did not want to allow its foreign policy to be imposed on it by the People's Republic of China. In this way, President Ford apparently followed the line of American diplomacy pursued so far, which has been anxious to find effective instruments for influencing the foreign policy course of the Chinese government with a view to guaranteeing the role and function of the PRC within the U.S.-aspired system of "balance of power," known in Peking by the name "ostrich policy." To accomplish this, the United States is obviously prepared to support several claims of the Chinese leaders, *inter alia,* the participation of the PRC in establishing a new "balance of power" in the East-Asian-Pacific region.

The degree of support to be rendered for the Chinese big-power claims again is dependent upon the need to maintain the "balance" of the different political forces on a worldwide scale; here the actual course of Soviet-American détente will play a central role. This element again will add—as is shown by the previous development of American-Chinese relations—an essential proportion of instability to the U.S.-PRC relationship, and will reduce the freedom of maneuverability for Chinese policy. Now the Chinese leaders are trying to overcome this situation by confronting the American administration uncompromisingly with the alternative to alter the system of foreign policy priorities in favor of Chinese big-power politics. This makes it clear that the post-cultural revolution diplomacy of smiling has been superseded by a tougher appearance of the Chinese leaders toward the United States. As a result of this tactical modification of Chinese policy toward the U.S., the process of the further expansion of American-Chinese relations has been slowed down to a certain degree since about 1974. The aspirations of the Chinese side became clearer and more evident when the Chinese side was trying to divert the American government from the line of détente and economic cooperation with the Soviet Union, and to thwart further steps to limit strategic armament between the United States and the Soviet Union. The Chinese side wants the further expansion of political cooperation with the Ford administration to be dependent upon an opposition to the policy of détente to be shown by the U.S. in its relations with the U.S.S.R., quite openly and upon a lurch to the practices of "cold war." In this context it belongs to the projects of the Chinese leaders to make it a permanent factor of world politics that the Soviet Union and the United States will continue to move along the brink of a rocket and nuclear war, which would encourage the stabilization of the foreign policy and strategic position of the People's Republic of China whose own resources are still not sufficient enough.

The Deputy Chinese Premier Teng Hsiao-ping reaffirmed bluntly, at the welcome banquet given to President Ford, the readiness of the People's Republic of China "to ally with all suitable forces," i.e. with the inclusion of the United States, in the struggle against hegemonism imputed to the Soviet Union. The question asked by the PRC under what conditions it could enter an alliance within the "United Front," with what political forces and states with a view to enforcing its big-power political aims, as well as the definition of who was the "major enemy," or the distinction between "major enemy" and "secondary enemy," have for a long time assumed a central position in the foreign policy strategy and tactics of the Chinese leadership. There were verbal clashes about this crucial question that are being continued. Nevertheless, this question has not been definitely decided yet.

While at the Ninth Congress of the Chinese Communist Party (1969), the doctrine of a political "war on two fronts" against the United States and the Soviet Union was still proclaimed; by 1972 and later at the Tenth Party Congress (1973), the Soviet Union was declared to be the major enemy of China. The foreign policy concept of a political "war on two fronts" that gave priority to China's leadership role toward the countries of the third world and to the anti-imperialist liberation struggle was the result of an apparent compromise reached in the leadership of the PRC established at the Ninth Party Congress. It is reasonable to assume that the political power clashes in the Chinese leadership at the beginning of the 1970s, which among others led to the expulsion of Chen Po-ta (1970) and Lin Piao (1971), temporarily cleared the way for the PRC to lean more to the United States and to other leading Western powers.

In policy articles published in the journal *Hung Qi,* the concept of the "Revolutionary Line and Politics of Chairman Mao" was revived, which had above all been devised during the revolutionary liberation struggle before 1949. Essentially the idea was to explain in theory the new line of a political rapprochement to the United States and to other Western states as an objectively necessary step. In evaluating Mao's work "On the Negotiations in Chungking," it was made clear that it had been necessary and unavoidable to enter into negotiations with the enemy, i.e. with the leading Western powers (in 1945 negotiations in Chungking were conducted with the KMT-leadership), to make compromises and to conclude agreements.

In another policy article, with reference to Mao's work "On our Policy" of 1940, it was stated in general outline to distinguish between major enemy and secondary enemies and to enter into an alliance with secondary enemies within the frame of a "United Front" with a view to defeating the major enemy with all forces. The foreign policy "Proletarian Line of Chairman Mao" proclaimed in preparation for the Nixon visit to the People's Republic of China in 1971, necessarily resulted in the fact that the Soviet Union was declared to be China's major enemy in October 1972. For the first time the Soviet Union was characterized to be still more "tricky" and thus still more "dangerous" than the United States; the U.S.S.R. was mentioned in principle first before the United States and explicitly declared to be the major enemy of China.

As a result, in the tactical approach of the Chinese leaders towards the Soviet Union, a decisive change had occurred. Virtually it resulted in a shift and extension of China's struggle waged against the Soviet Union and subsequently against the other socialist states from the level of inter-state relations to the international level, or even to regional situations of conflicts and crises.

The so-called revolutionary foreign policy line of Chairman Mao, which implied China's rapprochement to the United States and to the other Western big powers, consequently can be characterized as a "One-Front-Strategy" directed exclusively against the Soviet Union and the community of socialist states. This line of policy has set itself the task to inflict on the Soviet Union an all-out political and strategic defeat by the "United Front Policy," which incorporated alternatively the forces of the so-called first and second intermediate zone ("Third World," Western Europe, Japan, Canada) and those of the "old," "decaying" imperialism (U.S.). Chinese-American rapprochement was called an "important strategic maneuver" that is oriented toward the isolation of the Soviet Union and has the task to obstruct a further development of the relations between the U.S.S.R. and the U.S. At the Tenth Party Congress of the Communist Party of China in 1973, the political "One-Front-Strategy" was further developed by making the preparations for the war against the U.S.S.R. into a topical task of the Chinese people.

In establishing the theory of the existence of the two "superpowers," the Chinese leaders had developed a tactic that made it possible for them to take advantage of the worldwide struggle between the two social systems to enforce their own selfish aims. However, the Chinese did not succeed in achieving their objectives. The U.S.S.R. and the U.S. are continuing their détente-oriented policy in a bilateral relationship despite all contradictions and obstacles. Attempts made by the Chinese leaders to seriously jeopardize the Soviet-American relations have failed. Important agreements have been signed between the Soviet Union and the United States. The Chinese attempts at an international isolation of the Soviet Union failed in the same way as attempts at undermining the peace program proclaimed by the Twenty-Fourth Congress of the Communist Party of the U.S.S.R. The international process of détente was substantively and successfully pushed ahead.

Militant anti-Sovietism pursued by the Chinese leaders is becoming increasingly at variance even with the policy pursued by certain ruling circles in the leading Western countries. The support rendered by Chinese leaders for the global interests of the United States—such as the maintenance of a political and military strength of the U.S. in Asia and Europe—has so far not even reached the aim of being recognized by the United States as a worldwide acting big power. Up to now the United States had obviously granted to the People's Republic of China the status of a big power only within the Asian region. The Chinese leadership has above all been unsuccessful so far to cause the United States to abandon its "Two-China Policy" and to renounce its military engagement on Taiwan.

As is known, the Tenth Congress of the Chinese Communist Party had ushered in a new period of severe verbal clashes on domestic issues. It became again clear that internal vibrations and clashes are immediately transmitted to foreign policy fields. There were signs that suggested a kind of return to the doctrine of a political "war on two fronts." Apart from a more critical attitude toward the United States and limited progress in the development of bilateral political relations between the People's Republic of China and the United States, there have been voices in the Chinese press since 1973 that in historical allegory cautioned against a too close rapprochement to imperialism, accorded absolute priority to the economic and scientific-technical independence of China, and gave greater importance to the aggravation of the general crisis of capitalism than they did some time before.

When comparing the foreign policy line of the Tenth Party Congress with the policy statements on foreign policy at the meeting of the 4th National People's Congress in January 1975, several new variations are discernible in the tactical field. While the Party Congress explicitly reaffirmed the political compromise reached between China and the United States, characterizing them as "revolutionary compromises," the 4th National People's Congress pointed out the fact that there are "basic divergencies of opinion" between the two states. This may be valued as a reaction to the unchanged priority accorded by the United States to its relations with the U.S.S.R. However, it may even be the position adopted by several forces who do not approve of the policy practiced above all toward the U.S. and the other leading Western countries, and who are trying to evade the danger for China of getting entangled in a state of dependence with the leading Western countries and thus stand up for a more realistic line toward the Soviet Union.

The foreign policy part in the report to the 4th National People's Congress is oriented toward the fact that China should establish herself more pronouncedly as a "Third Force," should follow a policy that approaches international issues flexibly and pragmatically, and should put forward more effectively China's potentialities as the most populous state of the globe, as a nuclear power and as a potential big power. It has become a matter of fact that the Chinese leadership well understands how to operate from its own weak position and to make gains in the political field by surprise actions. To achieve this, the Chinese leadership is trying to play off its "enemies" one against the other and to maneuver them into a conflict situation that will initially not affect China, but that makes it possible to gain a strategically advantageous position.

This old tactical principle is found in the materials of the 4th National People's Congress and manifests itself in the aspirations of the Chinese leaders to create a permanent political and military conflict situation between the Soviet Union and the U.S. For this reason the thesis is propagated that a new world war is inevitable, which would be triggered off by the United States and the U.S.S.R. as the two so-called superpowers. As to the relationship to the Soviet Union, the general orientation is still in the direction of a long-term rift. At the same time there are signs that indicate that the Chinese leadership might in the future accord greater importance to the bilateral relations with the Soviet Union, apart from the global relationship. In this context it is remarkable to see that a thesis is persistently maintained to show that the major danger to world peace had been shifted to Europe. This is in correspondence with another tactical move, by which the idea of an imminent surprise attack by the U.S.S.R. against the People's Republic of China is sometimes subdued.

A second, primarily domestically oriented line of policy appears to be of interest, too. Since about the middle of 1974, an extremely sharp attack has been launched against those forces who are trying to come to a "showdown" with the Soviet Union (or with the "Huns" as is verbally stated in a historical allegory), who behave "capitulationist" toward the U.S.S.R., who shy away from military preventive strikes, or an offensive defense, who embark upon the way of negotiations, thus weakening the central power and promote the emergence of "independent kingdoms."

In addition, it is warned not to ally too closely with internal and external bourgeoisie and it is pointed out not to lose the historical initiative. There are also statements that plead for the consolidation of one's own position by pursuing a more elastic policy. Thus, e.g. in an article of *Renmin Ribao* of November 2, 1974, it was called upon to see things not unilaterally, but in an all-sided manner and in the process of their development, to recognize the unity of contradiction and to take into account that under definite conditions it is possible to interchange the different sides of a contradiction, etc. The question of a sober evaluation of the relationship of forces between the People's Republic of China and the Soviet Union has always been an important subject of the more recent political campaigns, such as the campaign of the criticism against Lin Piao and Confucius, the movement to consolidate the dictatorship of the proletariat as well as the "Water Margin" discussion.

Foreign policy practice and a number of policy articles of the Chinese press, such as the article in *Renmin Ribao* of November 10, 1975, under the heading "An important document in opposing capitulationism—A study of Chairman Mao's brilliant work 'The Situation and Tasks in the Anti-Japanese War after the Fall of Shanghai and Taiyuan'" indicate that by considering the course and the results achieved for the PRC from the development of Chinese-American relations, the primary question now is to find out whether and under what conditions the United States and other leading Western countries should be directly incorporated into the "United Front" against the Soviet Union. In the above-mentioned article the following can be read: "Historical experience has proved that when we seek unity through stuggle we shall have unity and that when we seek unity by making concessions we shall lose unity."

With regard to the economic relations with the Western countries the question is asked: "With regard to foreign things, should one critically accept them and correctly introduce them or blindly worship them, unconditionally copy them and so forth?" All these are major questions of principle involving class struggle and the struggle between the two lines.

As a result of this discussion the Chinese leadership has obviously decided to show a tougher approach toward the United States in an attempt to pin down the U.S., as outlined at the beginning, to basic positions of Chinese foreign policy and to force it to abandon or modify its concept of the global "balance of power." This makes it clear that big-power politics pursued by the Chinese leadership has produced a certain degree of confrontation with basic foreign policy interests of the United States. It can be safely assumed that this conflict of interests will possibly be implemented in the future within the Asian region, preferably, so that serious dangers may arise to the situation in this region.

It appears as if the United States is trying to adhere to its so far held concept of incorporating China into the policy of the "balance of forces" and to the continuation of the process of détente with the Soviet Union. Nevertheless, it seems to be appropriate to put in several question marks, and it appears to be advisable to recall the warnings of the U.S.-China hands who, based on the U.S.-China policy of the 1940s and 1950s, had come to the conclusion that the United States was not in a position to master the problem of China. As a result, it appears to me that the view widely held in the American press is wrong by saying that nowadays China in Asia is much more dependent upon the U.S. than conversely the U.S. is dependent upon China. Still more questionable is the consideration arguing that the United States should begin with China a strategic cooperation in the interest of a stronger utilization of the anti-Soviet policy pursued by China.

In an article of the journal *Foreign Policy* (No. 20/1975) the view is expressed that the United States, together with the establishment of parity within the global power triangle U.S.-U.S.S.R.-PRC, should develop a policy that should recognize that China must have a legitimate interest in improving her forces of deterrence against the dangers of an alleged Soviet attack. It is pleaded to develop a closer American-Chinese bond in the Pacific region with the inclusion of Japan as a new form of containment of the Soviet Union, and it is demanded to abandon the present China policy that prohibits the transfer of defense technologies and the exchange of intelligence material. It reads further that it must be brought home to the Soviet Union that in the event of a military conflict between the Soviet Union and the People's Republic of China, the United States would stand at the side of China.

The possibility of a change of U.S.-China policy was also suggested by Secretary of State Kissinger at a press conference on December 4, 1975, in Peking when he (according to *U.S. News & World Report* of December 15, 1975) said: "Should the Chinese interpretation [of Soviet ambitions] be correct and should there be military expansion, I believe that the U.S. would see the problem quite similar. The U.S. is opposed to military expansion and . . . would resist it!"

Here, in my view, becomes discernible a second line of American-China policy. This policy implies obviously the danger to reverse the concept of the "balance of power" with the aim to exercise a stronger pressure against the Soviet Union. The United States would render more support to the big-power ambitions of China's foreign policy as the "weak side" in the triangular relationship, because China's foreign policy at present ostensibly does not constitute any threat to American interests. One is under the impression that the advocates of this line of policy want to absorb the tougher U.S. policy by the Chinese leaders by yielding to Chinese pressure and by making concessions in the field of strategic cooperation, thus ignoring existing political points of confrontation. It may be the diplomatic relations with Taiwan and the military strength on Taiwan that the United States wants to maintain for the time being because of the international prestige of the U.S after Vietnam and because of domestic considerations of opportuneness, so that the U.S. government cannot establish any diplomatic relations with the People's Republic of China.

As another motivation, it is argued that on condition that the United States would refuse the PRC the assurance of support against the Soviet Union, China might again approach the Soviet Union. No doubt, this concept of a fictitious military threat by the Soviet Union serves as a motivation. It is a fictitious concept created years ago by

Chinese leaders to be able to explain conclusively the accelerated development of relations with the countries of the Western world, a concept that nowadays substantially is given up by the Chinese side itself because of the "shift of the major hotbed of war to Europe," according to Chinese parlance.

This approach shows clearly that this was a tactical element rather than political reality suitable to be used as a basis for constructing foreign policy strategies. Furthermore, it should be considered that any kind of support to be given to the big-power ambitions of Chinese leaders would increase the area of confrontation between the United States and China within a short time especially in Asia and, in addition, would result in tensions in the relationship to the Soviet Union, which in my opinion, cannot be within the scope of interests of the United States.

It cannot be overlooked that the presently existing identity of views between the Chinese and American governments in terms of Asian affairs is not unlimited; this identity of views has come about only temporarily in several fields and especially in relation to a third power, to the Soviet Union. This refers, among others, to the temporary maintenance of U.S. military strength in the Asian-Pacific region (the Chinese side internally accentuated the aspect of temporariness), to the maintenance of the American-Japanese "Security Treaty" and in the interest of preserving the given "balance of power" in Asia, to the maintenance of the present status quo in Korea.

The United States would be ill-advised, in my view, if it based its attitude toward China primarily on the Chinese-Soviet opposition. There are a number of indications implying that the enormous escalation of the anti-Soviet policy of China is decisively linked with the person of Mao Tse-tung. After the death of Mao Tse-tung it is possible that changes in the Soviet-Chinese relationship can be brought about, which may release those forces, especially in the army, *inter alia,* who may stand up for more balanced relations with the Soviet Union. In China the general view will prevail that for reasons of comprehensive national interests it would be desirable to normalize the relations with the Soviet Union and with the other socialist states. The socialist production relations in the People's Republic of China will objectively encourage this process in the long run.

If you try to find a common denominator for the different versions of the trend of development even in American-Chinese relations it becomes obvious, in my view, that the implementation of a policy of détente and security in Asia will give all participants the best guarantee for the prospective preservation of their legitimate concerns and will bring benefit to all states concerned.

Discussion

ROBINSON: Professor Kaufmann's paper places emphasis on the need for what he calls détente between the United States and the Soviet Union, for the need for security in Asia, and the institutionalization of both détente and security. He sees that process well served by the collective security proposals forwarded by the Soviet Union. He states that all Asian countries must take part in this system, including the People's Republic of China, despite the feelings of the Chinese that they may feel encircled thereby. The means he proposes for the emplacement of such a system is the gradual building up of a series of bilateral agreements between the Soviet Union and individual states. The agreement with India is given as a felicitous example. He also adduces the Helsinki agreements as a non-Asian example. The basis for this collective security system in Asia he finds in the change in the "international relation of forces." He does not say "balance of forces," but that is probably what is meant by the changes induced by the increase in Soviet military strength throughout the world, by the increasing mutual dependence of the two global socio-economic systems, as he calls them, and by American recognition of Soviet-American strategic parity.

All of these are factual statements, but I am not sure how he moves from this set of facts to the conclusion that it is necessary to construct a new security system in Asia. Professor Kaufmann goes on to say that American policies should not attempt to exploit the Sino-Soviet conflict. This seems to be the paper's basic message and the one that I would agree with most, at least as concerns the long run. He says that such an American policy is unrealistic and is based on subjective, that is, changing factors. Here I presume that he means the declining life span of Mao Tse-tung. However, Kaufmann then says that American policy otherwise is a realistic reaction to the changing situation—he quotes the Nixon Pacific Doctrine—and approves of the American resolve to defend Taiwan. So he accepts current American policy, taking exception only to the change in Washington's policy toward China itself and to the alleged American attempt to form a new block of Asian powers to carry out American policy—a bloc supposedly composed of Japan, non-communist Southeast Asia, South Korea, and Taiwan. That, he concludes, would be a bad thing, bad also because it would wrongfully neglect legitimate Soviet interest in the Asian arena.

On the other hand, he approves of plans to neutralize Southeast Asia, at least non-communist Southeast Asia, and asserts that communist states of Southeast Asia are factors of peace in the area. I presume this means that they are territorially satiated and will henceforth practice "peaceful coexistence." This assertion, I think, needs further discussion and demonstration, for it is on this basis that he says that neutralization can be successfully carried out. He couples this, moreover, with a castigation of the United States for vetoing the North Vietnamese applications for membership in the United Nations and in not aiding North Vietnam economically. We should be aware of the reason for that veto, which was linked to the question of Korea itself, and the American policy of the admission of all divided states into the United Nations—this was not agreed to by the Soviet Union, which takes an overtly political approach. In Korea, he regards the American presence in the South as a continuing problem. I am not clear as to *why* that is a problem, but Kaufmann does say that a peaceful solution should be sought, that unification is the central task for both North and South Korea, and that the Soviet policy also moves in that direction.

The paper as a whole is not about these topics. Rather, it is about Chinese policy and Sino-American relations. Professor Kaufmann begins by saying that it is not true that the present moderation of Chinese leadership in Asia is a contribution to détente, because he regards that moderation as anti-Soviet in character. It is also anti-Indian and anti-Mongolian because it continues to interfere in the internal affairs of other countries, such as these. As an example of such interference, he quotes Chinese pressure on the Japanese government to include the anti-hegemony clause in the upcoming peace treaty between the two countries: this is taken to be anti-Sovietism. I am sure that the Chinese would agree that this is the reason for pressuring the Japanese in this regard, but I am not sure why it should be regarded as interference in the internal affairs of Japan. This is what states do in the normal course of diplomatic interchange, and China has every right to do so.

He rightly concludes, on the other hand, that the People's Republic of China bases its relations with its Asian neighbors on their own attitudes towards the Soviet Union, just as it did previously in the United States. Now, it is those countries' attitudes towards the Soviet Union that counts. And therefore he concludes that this policy is also interfering, that it is also anti-détentist, and is anti-peace. It is the syllogism that bothers me: I am not sure how he moves from one to the other. The conclusion (interference) does not follow from the premise (anti-Sovietism). Incidentally, Professor Kaufmann implicitly denies that American-Soviet détente is at least partially based on the Sino-Soviet conflict. I think it obviously is.

Then Professor Kaufmann assesses Chinese policy toward Europe as actually encouraging Soviet-American military conflict, as a means of shortening the time and closing the strategic gap between China and the Soviet Union. This is an interesting thesis and I have not heard it put in this manner before, but I rather think that if the Chinese were asked about this, they would say something different. Their assessment seems to be that there is a plain Chinese interest in supporting such institutions as NATO as a means to avoid, not to promote, war between the United States and the Soviet Union, a war that would ultimately be disastrous to China itself.

As to Sino-American relations, Professor Kaufmann warns the United States not to place too much emphasis on long-term Sino-Soviet disagreements. That is very good advice and I think we all ought to realize that the present character of American-Chinese relations represents a temporary confluence of interests. Kaufmann has one additional interesting opinion here: he says that the release of the Soviet helicopter team was decided upon within the rubric of a more "general situation"—and it is that "general situation" that he points to as a partial illustration of his thesis that Sino-Soviet relations will not continue to be as bad as they are now. I would like to know what that "general situation" is. It is a very important point, more than just a subtlety.

He also correctly assesses American policy. He says that the United States obviously wants to establish a network of political and economic relations with the People's Republic of China, in order to bind the two more closely together. This is a capsule statement of American policy as a whole with regard to China. This includes drawing China into a new Asian balance of power, as I would term it, and he is correct in seeing American support for China as dependent on the course of triangular relations of the three countries, not only with regard to Sino-American relations but also as concerns Soviet-American relations. Global politics is indeed triangular and I think Professor Kaufmann is correct to place emphasis upon that point. Moreover, he accurately concludes that there has been a cooling-down of Sino-American relations recently because of continued American détentist cooperation with Moscow. That is an illustration of the triangularity of global politics. He also understands quite well that Chinese policy is to keep the United States and the Soviet Union at odds militarily.

Rather than castigate Peking and Washington for this parallel policy toward the Soviet Union, however, I believe it is better to label it for what it is: a balance of power *policy* and *situation* among the three major world actors in which both Washington and Peking perceive their interests to be served for the foreseeable future through cooperation against a common and increasingly threatening opponent. Indeed, Professor Kaufmann himself has assented to this conclusion implicitly in his analysis of China's united front strategy, which distinguishes between primary and secondary enemies. That distinction, to me, is what a balance of power strategy policy is all about. A Chinese united front strategy is a species of a balance of power policy and should be viewed by policy-makers and analysts as just that. Kaufmann also correctly, in my opinion, quotes various Chinese party declarations and Maoist scriptures to justify this particular policy. But then he goes on to blame the Chinese for the decline in Soviet-American détentist relations by supporting the American side around the globe, a good example recently being the situation in Angola. There are many reasons why Soviet-American relations have deteriorated recently; the Chinese do not deserve all the blame.

Professor Kaufmann addresses the question of where and what evidence there is for possible Sino-Soviet détente. He points to the apparent debate in 1974 in China on this question. I would like to invite the Professor to go into some detail in his analysis of this matter, which concerns esoteric political communications in China. It is a very important point and it should be made widely known so that the United States and the Soviet Union could take it into policy consideration. If his analysis is correct, the results of this debate would seem to point to a much more balanced Chinese policy between the Soviet Union and the United States. In practice this means moving away from the American ties such as have developed in the past and that is indeed what has been happening in the last six to nine months.

Professor Kaufmann then addresses the equally important topic of Sino-American military cooperation against the Soviet Union. This is done by quoting from the well-known Pillsbury article in *Foreign Policy* magazine (Fall, 1975), which advocated a number of cooperative military measures, between Washington and Peking, many of which in fact have been established practice for several years. He does discern that there are two lines in the American government as concerns the range and extent of concession that the United States should possibly make to Peking, as a means of maintaining momentum in Sino-American relations. There are indeed two such lines, if you want to call it that: there was a debate on this issue, and on the general topic of Sino-American relations, in the American administration about a year ago. It was resolved in favor of maintaining the present American policy, particularly as concerns Taiwan. The results, for better or for worse, were seen in the general lack of results of the Ford trip to Peking. The Chinese had a debate at about the same time on this same topic, and they decided to be a little bit tougher with the Americans, to move a little bit farther away. The United States also decided to be a little bit tougher, and also to move a little farther away. The results are now to be seen. I think we are grateful to Professor Kaufmann for pointing out the Chinese side of this debate.

Finally, the Professor considers the question of Sino-Soviet military relations directly. Contrary to what Professor Kaufmann perceives, the Soviet threat to China is not a fictitious thing. It is real in terms of size and force disposition, and it is evaluated by strategists in almost every state, save perhaps the Soviet Union alone, as a real threat. The question is what to do about it, in order to lessen the probability of Sino-Soviet war and, so far as the United States is concerned, to serve American interests in promoting a multi-lateral balance of power and an emerging degree of political pluralism in the world as a whole. The Soviet leadership would adopt a policy similar to that of the United States if it were in American shoes, so I do not think it does too much good to make judgments that sound moralistic as regards American activities in this manner.

On the other hand, Professor Kaufmann is absolutely accurate, in my opinion, in his concluding remarks. He says the United States would be ill-advised if it were to base its attitude towards China primarily on continuation of Sino-Soviet opposition. There are a number of indications that the enormous escalation of the anti-Soviet policy of China is decisively linked with the person of Mao Tse-tung. That is absolutely correct in my opinion. After the death of Mao Tse-tung, it is possible that changes in Sino-Soviet relations can be brought about that may release forces, especially in the army, which may favor far more balanced relations with the Soviet Union. I think these are absolutely correct conclusions, and I would underscore them so that our general discussion might focus on this vital element. The question, of course, is *when* improvement in Sino-Soviet ties will occur, how long it will continue, and under what Sino-American circumstances it will take place. The future of Sino-Soviet relations will be determined by those three factors, as well as by the fact that it will indeed take place.

WEATHERBEE: Dr. Kaufmann is associated with the section *Asienwissenschaften* at the Humboldt University. A number of years ago, I was an exchange professor at a sister institution studying the same kinds of problems, but surveyed from a very different vantage point. I won't say that we were involved in mirror-imaging—or if it is mirror-imaging, it is the kind of mirror one finds in amusement parks where if you are fat and short, your image is tall and skinny, or if you are tall and skinny, your image is fat and short. Perhaps the same kind of phenomenon is at work here, since I must confess that I am operating from a different vantage point and am not sure whether I am going to come out tall and skinny or fat and short. But I am certainly going to come out with a different kind of conclusion than Dr. Kaufmann did.

I want to address my comments particularly to the notion of the collective system of security in Asia and the premises upon which it is supposedly founded. Those of you who are familiar with traditional Southeast Asian cultures and Southeast Asian literatures are aware of a term in literature, a form of expression, which for want of a better term we can call "verbal magic"—that is, you create a reality by simply saying it is so; if you say it, therefore it is. In a sense, the expressions since 1969 of the Soviet's collective security proposal is a form of verbal magic. No one really knows what its ends are, but it is assumed that because it is said to be a collective security system, that it is something to be considered. What I would like to do is to turn it around—look at it from the Asian perspective, look at the proposal as something being put forward by the Soviet Union. Here the question of reality must be addressed, for despite the rhetoric and the symbolic manipulation of the collective security proposal, it has not been received with approval, and it has not been accepted as a form of orderly relations by any Asian nation. The Southeast Asian states look at it with suspicion, a suspicion that is founded on the notion which Dr. Kaufmann says is not true. Nevertheless, it is their perception that collective security is essentially anti-Chinese, that it is essentially a system of isolating the People's Republic of China from the rest of Southeast Asia, from the rest of Asia. That in a sense is the Soviet collective security system. It is a dark shadow of that from which they have just escaped—an American collective security system, but designed with the same end in mind, the containment of the People's Republic of China. In this respect the Soviet Union operates at a great disadvantage, and they have very few levers in Southeast Asia. There is a Burmese saying—it is expressed in a rather indelicate fashion, and I will try to make it a little more delicate—that is, "When the Chinese urinate, we drown." In a sense this is true for all of Southeast Asia. They are terribly impressed, if not even apprehensive, about the potential power from the north. There is no way that the realistic leaders in Southeast Asia—and most of them are realists—are going to entangle themselves in a scheme or proposal that is perceived by the Chinese as being anti-Chinese. The Soviet Union has not been able to place its collective security proposals, whatever the details might turn out to be, in a neutral context vis-à-vis the People's Republic of China. Although they can say it is not anti-Chinese, although they say the Chinese are welcome to join, it is imbedded in propaganda, in an ideological and a behavioral pattern of anti-Chinese actions and attitudes. Dr. Kaufmann spoke at great length about what he called anti-Sovietism on the part of the People's Republic of China. This is paralleled by what the Chinese would call anti-PRC activities and behavior on the part of the Soviet Union. Yet there is a mirror image, however distorted it might be. As one who is a professional and is concerned with what happens in Southeast Asia, one of the aspects of what I consider to be the most unpleasant from the human point of view of the anti-PRC activities by the Soviet Union is the way the Soviet Union seeks to feed upon the fears of the Southeast Asian leadership and people, about the resident alien Chinese in their own countries.

I think there is potential for danger as the Soviet Union continues to say over and over again, publicly and privately, to the Southeast Asian leaders that the Chinese are their enemies. This is not designed, I would submit, to suggest that the Soviet Union's collective security proposal has a neutral context vis-à-vis the PRC.

A word or two about the premises upon which the Soviet policy in Southeast Asia is founded. In his paper, Dr. Kaufmann presents a lengthy description of Soviet behavior in Southeast Asia. He says that it is premised on the fact that it is certainly not perceived as such by the People's Republic of China. I believe that it was Jayne Werner who put us into a historical context about imperialism in the Asian sphere. She talked about the Portuguese and so forth. I think that much of what could be described in terms of the Soviet Union, could be geographically described as Asian, and could also be placed in the context of the operation of a pattern of territorial expansion and imperialism right up to the end of the 19th century by Russia—which the Soviet Union refuses today to accept in the terms of the Chinese submission that the Soviet Union is occupying land that was stolen from the Chinese imperialists. Of course, it would be a great advantage to the Soviet Union in this issue if détente, described as the acceptance of the status quo in terms of sovereignty, were accepted because this then would legitimize the continued Soviet occupation of Chinese land, from the Chinese point of view. I am afraid that this premise has to be looked at a little more closely. Let me just point out that economically, as far as Southeast Asia is concerned, the Soviet Union and Eastern Europe are insignificant. Less than 2 percent of the exports of the Asian countries go to the Soviet Union and East Europe. A statistically insignificant amount of their imports come from the Soviet Union. Their orientation is to Japan, the United States, and the European economic community. If there is going to be an increase in economic ties with the socialist world, with a socialist country, it is not going to go to the Soviet Union; it is going to go to China as normalized relations develop between China and the other Southeast countries. One can already see this in the Philippines trade figures. Culturally, there is no way that the Soviet Union is perceived as "Asian" in Southeast Asia. They are perceived as European; to say that the Soviet Union is culturally an Asian country is simply to fly in the face of the perception of—and I hate to use this word—"real" Asians. I would suggest that if we put this to one side, we can ask, "What are the real premises of Soviet policy in Asia?" We can better seek the answer to these premises in the context of the Soviet Union as a global power, as a great power-seeking country, very closely related to the security of different views, seeking interests now and very competitive with the People's Republic of China.

KAUFMANN: Regarding your comment on my views on perspectives of détente in Asia, I would like to stress the following aspects. Unfortunately, Mr. Weatherbee, your comment contained, it seems to me, too much propaganda. That is why I will not argue it. It appears to me extraordinary that the United States has to show its readiness, in accordance with the general trend in world politics, to insult contradictions and further differences between the two opposing world systems, even in relation to Asia, by resorting to political means. In my view, it has to be taken into account that the Soviet Union is an Asian power that has a primary interest in safeguarding the peace and maintaining security in Asia. Nobody is in the position to exclude the Soviet Union from Asia, neither the United States nor the People's Republic of China. It is noteworthy to underline that the future of U.S. policy in Asia has been relatively closely related to the good contact of the Chinese leadership to the United States. This was done, although the present Chinese leadership is unmistakably revising a policy of détente, and they are deliberately supporting the idea of playing up American stakes against Soviet interests in order to gain as much as possible.

China and Russia

Thomas Robinson

I am asked to talk about Soviet and Chinese perceptions of the American role in Asia, particularly with regard to Korea. There are six points I wish to cover, with regard to attitudes and perceptions from the Soviets and the Chinese. There is the Korean situation, and the Vietnamese situation. What is the role of America with regard to all of this?

One cannot speak of the American role in Asia without bringing in the roles of the Soviets and Chinese, concurrently, if not in a preliminary sense. What I hope to achieve here is to go through a series of over-intellectualized statements, leading to rather specific policies, and/or complex conclusions.

When we talk of conceptions, we refer, of course, to attitudes of a psychological nature or quality. Attitudes are not on an operational basis, as would be the subject of policy, which you can see in front of you. The question is in finding some operational or policy measure of the psychological (or attitudinal) phenomena. Within the role-playing interactions there are three points or factors to be taken into account: 1) policies, 2) pronouncements, and 3) actions. The interaction between states is conducive to the reciprocity in initiatory and responsive action measured by these three points. What we are dealing with here is an exceedingly complex cybernetic relationship. It is hopefully descriptive of the complex phenomena that is international politics.

As stated previously, there are three measures to this sort of thing: 1) pronouncements (past and present) which are representative of ideological statements, particularly those by Russia and China; 2) past actions, such as we have come to know them; and 3) present policies, declaratory and operational. I think we must make the distinction between the declaratory and operational aspects of policies when dealing with communist states; so we may not fall into a trap of regarding what is said as equivalent to what is done; there is this difference. Upon what are these three points dependent? How can they be made operational? Here there are at least six qualities we must talk about in order to reach some aspect towards the reality of the situation.

What are the issues concerning America's role in Asia? Is the past weighed down from previous misunderstandings, and how does this affect policies for the present and the future? We need be concerned with the international relationship of Russia, China and ourselves, on both a global and regional level. The various global situations are necessary to be able to understand our present policies with Russia and China, with regards to Korea and Vietnam, and especially with regard to the Soviet-American strategic relationship. The understanding of the regional level is also necessary as there are some countries divorced from the global level.

Another variable is international politics, yet the domestic situation is of equal importance, and complex in its own makeup. There is also the factor of changing relative power of the countries derived from the standard measures of power but relative when discussing the three states in question (China, Russia, and Korea), and the areas around them. No one knows how to measure power yet, but this does not make it any less of a reality.

Lastly, the discounting of the future. The states today act as if there were a reality in the future which is somehow imported into the present. They presume things will happen in the future that have not already occurred in the past. But there is a type of avoidance which reflects back to the state of present policies, again with avoidance towards the future, or to bring that future about to reality. In shorter terms the six qualities consist of 1) issue, 2) weight of the past, 3) global policy, 4) domestic variables, 5) relative power, and 6) the discounting of the future.

From these we will look at Soviet/Chinese perceptions of the U.S. and further investigate the role of America. First, the issue with America's role in Northeast Asia must be studied in terms of the Sino-Soviet relations and the discordancy between the two. America is still considered as a stabilizing force on the peninsula, as there is little desire on the part of China or Russia to come to conflict, which could bring one or the other or both into direct conflict with the U.S. Whether or not either of these two states would admit to the fact, the fact is that they do prefer America remaining, in one form or another. The past brings to mind the difference in relationship vis-à-vis China and Russia towards the U.S. For Russia one must think of the Cold War phenomenon as transient, or in more modern terms, what we have is détente. Now the Chinese, despite the pre-1944 era, reflect over their first and most bitter experience with the U.S.—the Korean War—and more presently, the Taiwan situation.

The Soviets tend to stand back from total support of the North

Koreans (to the point of invading the South). Détente with the U.S. is more important and the U.S. tends to link the two in causal relationship. This prevents the Soviets from what they might do otherwise, if given the situation.

With the Chinese, the operational consequences are there but for different reasons. Fear of American power (with regards to Korea) leads to a fear of a shooting war and further afflictions there.

The Soviet Union, on a global level, is maintaining a relationship of conventional and strategic parity with the U.S., while working towards strategic superiority. The Chinese tend to support the U.S. in order to work against the Soviet Union; this has particular illustration in the support of NATO. The Soviets would have and do have the tendency to press the Americans to reduce but not eliminate their forces and bases in Korea and Japan. They feel they can gain the upper hand strategically and conventionally, in competition over the U.S. In the case of the Chinese, I think it is precisely the opposite. They do not want to see a reduction or the elimination of U.S. bases, for reason of support of the U.S., given the Sino-Soviet conflict.

Domestically, the Soviets want to keep continued political stability in the country, in what now appears to be the Brezhnev succession period, to continue with the economic progress, especially in agricultural recovery. The Chinese with the Mao succession are in a parallel situation; they wish to assure economic progress on all fronts. For both, their domestic factors influence their situation and attitudes towards the American role. Relative agricultural yield equates to relative pressures produced.

In China, the leadership influences the ability to resist Kim Il-sung and his demands for more aid against the South. I should think we would have a rather interesting dysfunction in the Chinese leadership, in terms of a very weak leadership as opposed to a rather strong Chinese leadership that would not wish to render aid to Kim Il-sung, simply because of the possibility of war, and the involvements therein, due to the weak situation at home. So, on both sides of the spectrum of strong versus weak leadership in China, you will find similar policies; but somewhere on the middle road there is danger. There is the Chinese leadership situation, which was neither terribly stable nor unstable, in which some factions could press for some foreign adventure in order to make political gains at home. This is the kind of theory we have to watch for and that is the kind of situation that could influence Chinese attitudes towards the American presence and the security of Korea.

Now, the fifth factor is the relative power of these two countries. The Soviet Union is primarily concerned over China and the U.S. for global and political reasons, while China is largely concerned with the

Soviet Union. With regards to Korea, the Soviet Union has, regarding conventional weaponry, the ability to arm the North Koreans to overcome the South, if the Americans were not there to do the same (for the South). The Soviets are, or are coming into a position to interdict American supply routes to the South in case of a military conflict. In a nuclear power sense, the Soviets wish to and do promote a standoff. If there were to be a North/South war, the U.S. would not be the first to engage in nuclear weapons, even though it is our policy to threaten the use of or to use nuclear weapons against the North if they were to invade the South.

Increasing power of the Soviet Union gives them the opportunity to persuade the U.S. that it would not be a good idea to do such, and hence this is somewhat touch-and-go. The Chinese will continue to encourage the Americans to keep their bases in Japan, for anti-Soviet purposes, and to retain our security treaty with them (Japan); this is all, of course, from a power point of view. The Chinese do render military arms and assistance to North Korea so as to compete, in a balanced state, with the Soviets, and to gain influence over Pyongyang, but not to the point where Kim would believe that he could successfully invade the South.

Finally, with regards to the future. It is a bit more complex, and I have to divide this discourse into two possibilities: the first being one of continued loss of American willingness and ability to involve itself globally with the Soviet Union and China; the second alternative being a reversal of the present trend to strengthen the economy, or to work for greater military power (strength), a willingness to back the American interests with the power necessary, with whatever thoughts which are desirable. Concerning these two possible futures in Korea, there may rise different conclusions.

In the first sense, the Soviets could presume the continuation of an American decline in strength and willingness to use its power, wait for the U.S. to pull out, unilaterally, of the South, then encourage the North Korean invasion. This is, of course, the problem we are trying to avoid.

For the Chinese, there is the propensity in such a situation (of American weakness) to move to stall the Sino-Soviet problems in the post-Maoist era; therefore, they would follow the same policy as is with the Soviet Union. American weakness encourages Soviet adventurism; it also encourages Sino-Soviet rapprochement. The situation of Soviet and Chinese policies and attitudes towards America in Asia—Northeast and Southeast Asia—is contradictory, and complex. There are many variables and it is difficult to evaluate. Their perceptions are viewed in light of their own Sino-Soviet conflict, primarily, and also from the knowledge of the propensity for the Americans to advance and defend their own interests in these regions. A cyclical pattern develops because following this is the dependency upon Chinese and American developments domestically. The Soviet evaluation is dependent upon the same factors but with the addition of the factor of Soviet-American strategic nuclear relations. The cyclical patterns may explain why there is so much emphasis placed on this issue in policy-making circles within public affairs today.

Japan's Korean Policy, and Her Perceptions and Expectations Regarding America's Role in Korea

Yung H. Park

The primary purpose of this paper is to examine Japan's perceptions and expectations regarding the United States' role in Korea in the post-Vietnam period. More specifically, the paper seeks to answer the following questions: How does Japan view America's policy in Korea? What role does Japan expect the United States to play in Korea? Why such a role? How does this role fit into Japan's overall policy toward two Koreas? Do Japan's expectations differ from what the U.S. perceives to be her role? If so, how do they differ? In attempting to answer these questions, a major focus will be placed upon Japan's domestic politics and especially those elements that play key roles in the formulation of Japan's foreign policy (i.e., the ruling Liberal-Democratic Party and the business community). In the first half of the paper I shall examine Japan's Korean policy in the 1970s, for it is in the context of her own Korean policy that Japan views America's policy and role in Korea.

Japan's posture toward Korea in the early 1970s had an air of cautious optimism, which was attributable to a series of external developments affecting East Asian international relations. The 1972 Nixon-Chou meeting highlighted in a dramatic fashion the fact that Asian international politics had been undergoing major changes for several years. Although in many respects the summit meeting gave impetus to trends underway for some time, it nevertheless symbolized the beginning of a new era in Asian international relations. The *volte-face* in Washington's China policy was a major catalyst to Japan's reassessment of her own traditional orientation toward Asian communist states, which culminated in her recognition of Peking, Hanoi and Ulan Bator. Of particular importance to Japan's Korean policy was the historic initiation in 1972 of a Seoul-Pyongyang dialogue, which in turn was attributable to the thawing of tension between the two major transpacific powers. The *de facto* recognition of Pyongyang by Seoul made it possible for the former to launch an intensive diplomatic offensive that led to her entry into major world organizations (e.g., World Health Organization) and to the establishment of diplomatic relations with a large number of noncommunist nations including five Scandinavian countries that recognized Pyongyang in March 1973.

Especially significant to Japan's changing attitude toward North Korea were a series of dramatic turnabouts in Seoul's traditional foreign policy. Deviating from her version of the so-called Hallstein doctrine (severing diplomatic relations with any country recognizing North Korea), Seoul announced in July 1973, that relations with Chile, which recently recognized Pyongyang, would be maintained as a "special case." In another policy departure Seoul shifted from her policy of eschewing all relations with communist nations to one of seeking improved relations with "non-hostile" communist states, including the Soviet Union and China. In June, President Park said, also departing from his earlier position, that he would not oppose the simultaneous entry of two Koreas into the United Nations as a step toward eventual unification.[1]

These developments in Korea precipitated a significant change in the attitude toward North Korea of the Tokyo government and its two pillars—the Liberal-Democratic Party (LDP) and the business community (*zaikai*). The pre-Seoul consensus within the party quickly disintegrated, and the concept of "two Koreas" gained a strong momentum. LDPers belonging to the Society for the Study of Afro-Asian Problems (*Ajia afurika mondai kenkyukai;* commonly known as AA group), long the intraparty champion for improved relations with communist states, vigorously pushed for a change in Tokyo's posture toward North Korea. The breakdown of the party's consensus was obvious when AA members joined with the opposition parties to form a suprapartisan Dietmen's League for the Promotion of Japanese-North Korean Relations (*Nitcho yuko sokushin giin renmei*) in October 1971, and then a League mission, headed by Kuno Chuji, a leading AA member, was dispatched to North Korea in January 1972. A major outcome of this "unofficial diplomacy" was the signing in January of a Japanese-North Korean communiqué stating pledges and hopes shared by both parties. The League group and the North Koreans noted the optimism that "positive efforts by both peoples will lead to the establishment of diplomatic relations" between the two governments. The communiqué also stressed the importance of "people's diplomacy" in all areas to promote Japanese-North Korean friendship. Pledging to make efforts to improve trade ties between the two countries, both parties proposed the use of Japan's Export-Import Bank (a governmental corporation) loans and the reciprocal establishment of trade missions in both countries. In sharp denunciation of Tokyo's North Korean stand, the communiqué urged that Tokyo "abandon its unfriendly policy" toward Pyongyang.[2] Also reflecting the LDP's changing North Korean mood was the decision by leading AA members, including Utsunomiya Tokuma, to join the opposition parties to organize a National Council for the Normalization of Japanese-North Korea Relations (*Nitcho kokko seichoka kokumin kaigi*) in September 1973. Inaugurated with the backing of all the opposition parties and major labor groups, the Council called for an early recognition of North Korea and changes in Tokyo's Seoul policy in a way contributing to the peaceful unification of two Koreas.[3]

The business community's North Korean posture was most decisively affected by the changing orientation of East Asian international politics and the thawing of tension in Korea. In the wake of Nixon's China visit, Tokyo's policy toward Asian communist regimes underwent a major shift from *seikei bunri* (separation of politics and trade) to the establishment of diplomatic relations and active encouragement of trade with these countries. Assured by Peking that her economic interests in Taiwan would not be disrupted, Japan quickly proceeded to establish diplomatic relations with Peking in 1972. The business community now argued that Tokyo's new policy should apply to Japan's relations with North Korea. The formation of the Dietmen's League and the Kuno mission were largely in response to the demands of the business sector.[4] Unlike small and medium-sized firms eager to expand trade with North Korea, major industrial giants and especially those having close ties with South Korea were initially hesitant about getting on the North Korean bandwagon for fear that their interests in South Korea might suffer. The continued thawing of tension in Korea, however, changed this thinking. Industrial giants that had labored under the so-called "Four Principles of Sino-Japanese Trade" (which China had imposed on Japanese business to steer it away from its pro-Taiwan orientation), were delighted that North Korea insisted on no such restrictions vis-à-vis Japanese business firms with close ties with South Korea. They were especially attracted to the strong interest that North Korea, less concerned with a Chinese-style policy of "self-reliance," had shown in purchasing some thirty major prefabricated plants from Japan to meet the needs of her new Six-Year Economic Plan initiated in 1971. Since the export of these plants called for the use of Export-Import Bank (EIB) loans, payable on a deferred basis, one can understand the length to which interested Japanese industries (e.g., textiles, shipbuilding, electronics, automobiles, and steel) went to persuade the Tokyo government to drop its current policy of denying such loans for Japanese-North Korean trade.[5]

Taking advantage of the new mood, New-Japan Steel, Japan's largest industrial corporation, and such ambitious automakers as Toyota (which was already involved in a joint venture with a South Korean automaker) and Isuzu quickly initiated talks with the North

Korean authorities for export of their products. In October 1972, an agreement was reached between North Korea and New-Japan Steel under which the latter was to build a steel plant in North Korea. In August 1972, Toshiba, a major electronics-maker, agreed to export a massive TV picture-tube manufacturing plant to North Korea. Pyongyang's decision to buy the plant was apparently designed to meet the needs of its plan for providing home appliances to its people. The transaction was the largest ever made by a Japanese firm with North Korea and was the first electronics-related export to a communist state. It was also revealed that talks were already underway for export of other Toshiba plants manufacturing such items as refrigerators, washing machines, and radios.[6] By the end of 1972, virtually every major corporation had expressed an interest or was involved in business transactions with North Korea. While carrying on individual efforts to establish business ties with North Korea, in July 1972, leading trading firms joined their hands to create a Kyoa Bussan (Kyoa Industrial Company) to function as their "window agency" in dealing with the North Koreans and as the Japanese counterpart to a North Korea-Japan Import-Export Corporation set up by pro-Pyongyang Korean residents to represent North Korean interests. Significantly, Kyoa Bussan's shareholders included "dummies" or subsidiaries of major firms in such areas as shipbuilding, petroleum, construction equipments, textiles, steel and iron, and electronics.[7]

Zaikai's activities were not confined to immediate economic concerns. *Zaikai* leaders concluded that diplomatic normalization and improved business relations with North Korea were inseparable, and that Tokyo's policy of *seikei bunri* was the major obstacle to increased trade with North Korea. For this reason, *zaikai* leaders agreed to make greater efforts, comparable to those being made in connection with the Chinese question,[8] to facilitate a consensus within the Tokyo government and the LDP in favor of recognizing North Korea. Thus, when Pyongyang approached *zaikai* elders (e.g., Uemura Kogoro, Nagano Shigeo, Doko Toshio, and Iwasa Yoshizane) for a possible business mission to North Korea, they were most enthusiastic. The proposed mission, business leaders felt, would go a long way in improving Japanese-North Korean relations and in influencing the LDP government in the direction of establishing diplomatic relations with Pyongyang.[9] Subsequently, a decision was made to send in late 1972 a *zaikai* mission headed by Doko, a *Keidanren* vice-president and chairman of Toshiba, and composed of *zaikai* leaders representing Japan's major firms including Mitsui, Mitsubishi and Sumitomo.[10] In the words of the *Nihon keizai shimbun* often reflecting *zaikai's* thinking, "the business community's demand [for changes in Tokyo's Pyongyang policy] is so vigorous that the government will have to respond to it."[11] The major breakthrough in Japanese-North Korean trade relations came in December 1973, when the Tokyo government authorized an EIB loan, payable on a deferred basis, to be used for the export of a towel-manufacturing plant to North Korea, thus departing from its policy of *seikei bunri* and of denying any governmental loans to North Korea. Another governmental loan was later authorized for the sale of a nuts-bolts plant to North Korea. The growing governmental involvement in the Japanese-North Korean trade gave a further impetus to *zaikai's* rapidly rising expectations toward the North Korean market.[12]

The Tokyo government's North Korean posture was decisively affected by the external developments as well as the changing attitudes of the key elements of Japanese politics. While continuing to give priority to its relations with Seoul, the government made several cautious but significant changes in its North Korean policy. Going beyond its earlier policy of approving only "humanitarian and cultural contacts" with North Korea, Japan adopted an "incremental approach" under which all non-political contacts, leading ultimately to diplomatic normalization, were encouraged. Reflecting this changing governmental mood, in June 1972, Foreign Minister Ohira Masayoshi announced that his government would now endorse "economic contacts" with North Korea.[13] The forward-looking posture gained such a momentum in the government that some Foreign Ministry (*Gaimusho*) officials even proposed a governmental mission to Pyongyang. Also, a view was seriously considered within the government that in its aid policy toward Seoul the government should concentrate more on light industry and welfare-oriented programs rather than heavy industry projects, to avoid irritating North Korea unnecessarily.[14]

All sectors of the government were involved in the implementation of the incremental policy. The Justice Ministry issued entry permits to a large variety of North Korean visitors including a group of journalists and even a labor mission attending the 1973 convention of the anti-governmental Japan Teachers' Union.[15] The Postal Service Ministry proposed the establishment of telecommunications services between the two countries. The Ministry of International Trade and Industry (MITI) and *Gaimusho,* favorably responding to domestic pressures, let it be known that the government would seriously consider EIB loan requests even before the establishment of diplomatic relations.[16] The MITI, supporting the proposed establishment of trade offices in both countries, even included in its 1973 budgetary requests funds for a "private" Japanese trade office in North Korea. In December 1973, as noted earlier, the government authorized its first EIB loan after obtaining Seoul's "reluctant consent."[17]

By the end of 1973 it looked as though a consensus favoring recognition of North Korea was in the making within the government and its key domestic supporters. In 1974, however, the growing domestic support for improved relations with North Korea was dealt a fatal blow by a series of dramatic turnabouts in Tokyo-Seoul relations, a fact that demonstrated the unusually reactive and vulnerable character of Japan's North Korean policy. Tokyo-Seoul relations, which in 1973 had been strained in the wake of the Kim Tae-jung incident, experienced further setbacks in 1974. A major thorny issue involved Seoul's trial of Kim on charges of alleged violations of election laws. Tokyo considered the trial and Seoul's reluctance to permit Kim to leave the country to be a breach of an understanding between the two governments in late 1973. The Tokyo-Seoul relationship was further strained by the arrest and trial of two Japanese citizens in South Korea on charges of attempted subversion through outlawed South Korean youth organizations. The relationship was dealt a most serious blow by the alleged North Korean attempt to assassinate the South Korean President and the killing of his wife. The allegation that the assassin, a Korean resident in Japan, was an agent for the Pyongyang-controlled *Chosoren*, was aggressively pushed by Seoul in its demand that the organization be disbanded or at least be subjected to greater governmental control. To appease the Seoul government, Premier Tanaka Kakuei attended the funeral of the President's wife, and Shiina Etsusaburo, LDP Vice-President, hand-carried to Park a letter from Tanaka apologizing for Japan's "involvement" in the assassination incident and pledging his efforts to bring *Chosoren* under control.

At the peak of the strained Tokyo-Seoul relations came the controversial remarks of Foreign Minister Kimura Toshio. Challenging the pro-Seoul position supported by right-wing LDPers (e.g., Kishi Nobusuke and Shiina), Kimura, an advocate of a Tokyo-Peking détente, stated that while Japan was not yet ready for recognition of Pyongyang, North Korea did not pose a military threat to the South Koreans and hence no need for Seoul's fear of the North. He also rejected the notion that Seoul was the only legitimate government on the Korean peninsula. Also, broadening of the so-called Korean clause of the 1969 Nixon-Sato communiqué that the security of South Korea was essential to that of Japan, the Foreign Minister said that Japan now regarded the stability of the entire Korean peninsula as essential to her security.[18] While the Kimura statements pleased North Korea and her LDP supporters, they nevertheless aggravated Tokyo's relations with Seoul and infuriated the pro-Seoul elements of the LDP.[19]

Seoul's relations with Pyongyang turned bad, as the initial optimism and hope generated by the easing of tension between two Koreas evaporated by the end of 1973. In the course of a series of talks both sides quickly realized the differences separating them were as formidable as ever and thus defied easy reconciliation. Both sides progressively hardened their positions, and by early 1974 their relationship became extremely hostile again, producing small-scale armed skirmishes along the border. The Kim incident, Seoul's authoritarian measures to tighten domestic political control, the assassination attempt, and the discovery of the infamous tunnels under the DMZ, all contributed to the revival of tension between two Koreas. The latter two incidents, which caused a major stir and shock in South Korea, reinforced Seoul's claim that Pyongyang had never given up its aggressive designs toward the South.

The developments—the deterioration of Tokyo-Seoul relations and the resumption of a "cold war" between two Koreas—had most chilling effects upon Japan's emerging North Korean policy. Within the ruling party vigorous concerted efforts were made by pro-Seoul members to reverse the deteriorating Tokyo-Seoul relations, and the argument was driven home that any gestures favorable to Pyongyang would further alienate the Seoul government. In an unprecedented joint meeting of LDPers belonging to three major pro-Seoul organizations—the Japan-South Korea Legislators' Consultative Committee (*Nikkan gün konshinkai*), the Japan-South Korea Cooperative Committee (*Nikkan kyoryoku iinkai*), and the Asian Parliamentary Union (*Ajia kokkai gün rengokai*)—in September 1974, bitter criticisms were made of Kimura's "irresponsible" remarks. It was also under the pressure of these pro-Seoul LDPers that the Executive Board (*Somukai*) decided to explore ways to more effectively regulate *Chosoren's* political activities.[20] The assassination attempt, the tunnels, and Kim Il-sung's apparently belligerent utterances were vigorously cited by pro-Seoul LDPers to counter pro-Pyongyang members' arguments that North Korea was not aggressive and was seeking a peaceful unification of the peninsula.[21] It was evident that Kishi, Fukuda Takeo, Funada Naka, Shiina and other pro-Seoul elders still carried much weight in LDP politics and were a major influence in the LDP's Korean stand. Obviously to reinforce the party position that any improvement of relations with Pyongyang must come within the framework of close Tokyo-Seoul relations, Miki Takeo, the new LDP President and Premier, attended and welcomed a January 1975 meeting of Japanese and South Korean legislators where a resolution was adopted calling for a most prudent approach toward North Korea lest "the precarious balance of power in Asia" and Japanese-South Korean relations would be impaired.[22]

Zaikai's forward-looking North Korean posture and high hopes were equally dampened by the changing external developments as well as Seoul's vigorous protest. *Zaikai* leaders concluded that efforts to improve trade relations with North Korea could proceed on the basis of close Tokyo-Seoul cooperation and that the North Korean issue should not be allowed to aggravate the already strained relations with Seoul. Business leaders also came to the conclusion that Japan's forward-looking trade policy toward North Korea was not compatible with the tension in Korea. In fact, even when most Japanese business firms were rushing to the North Korean market, certain pro-Seoul companies, concerned with Seoul's reactions, abided by "voluntary restraints" in dealing with North Korea. For example, Mitsubishi Heavy Industries decided to shun getting involved in any heavy industry transactions that would help strengthen Pyongyang's military might. Mitsubishi even turned down a North Korean offer to buy a cement plant. Several reasons accounted for Mitsubishi's sensitivity to the Seoul government. Fujino Chujiro, chairman of the Mitsubishi Trading Company, was known to be on close terms with South Korea's Park. In fact, between them was an informal understanding that Mitsubishi would refrain from exporting any production facilities that would add to Pyongyang's military potentials.[23] Mitsubishi was deeply involved in the South Korean economy, holding a major share of private Japanese investments in the country.[24] Mitsubishi Heavy Industries was under contract to provide expensive equipment needed to complete the new expansion program of South Korea's largest iron and steel works in Pohang and was expecting to receive additional orders from South Korea. According to the *Nihon keizai shimbun*, Mitsubishi leaders were of the view that larger gains were expected from the South Korean market than from North Korea and that, for the time being, greater efforts be made to improve trade relations with the South. Obviously, Mitsubishi's strategy was to wait until governmental relations between Tokyo and Pyongyang had significantly improved and then embark upon an aggressive drive into the North Korean market. Mitsubishi leaders again saw wisdom in the celebrated statement by Makida Yoichiro, the late President of Mitsubishi Heavy Industries, on his company's China policy in the pre-1972 years: "Although we are not on the [China] bandwagon, we will catch up with them by jet plane."[25]

As two Koreas returned to their pre-1972 hostility, and Tokyo-Seoul relations continued to deteriorate, the caution that had characterized Mitsubishi's North Korean posture came to affect other industrial giants as well. The proposed *zaikai* mission never materialized, as interested business leaders took their names out of it. Against this background of *zaikai's* changed thinking the new Miki government decided in December 1974 not to authorize EIB loans even for the export of light industry plants to North Korea "for the time being." The government also announced that the sale of heavy industry plants would not be authorized as long as the current tension between two Koreas continued.[26] Significantly, the Miki government's "retrograde" decisions came at a time when Tokyo was liberalizing its trade restrictions vis-à-vis other communist nations in response to *zaikai's* demands. For example, only hours before its North Korean decisions the government authorized a loan for the export of a fertilizer plant to North Vietnam. Moreover, *Keidanren,* the authoritative business spokesman, indicated that it would seek additional governmental loans for the export of other plants, including steel plants, to North Vietnam.[27] As a result of the government's decisions, Japan's plant exports to North Korea and major transactions requiring the use of EIB loans came to a sudden halt, to the grave dismay of the business community.

As relations between Tokyo and Seoul deteriorated after the assassination attempt, the Tokyo government, too, adopted a noticeably cautious policy toward North Korea. While admitting that Seoul was not the only legitimate government in Korea, Tokyo went out of its way to stress that it was not considering diplomatic recognition of Pyongyang.[28] Indications are that by the end of 1974 the momentum for a Japanese-North Korean détente came to a virtual standstill, and pro-Seoul positions came to assert themselves vigorously within the government. For example, in a rebuttal to the Kimura statement that "there is no threat from the north," Defense Agency chief Yamanaka Sadanori said that "foreign governments have no right to pass judgments" on such a matter.[29] The Miki government dropped the Tanaka government's policy of authorizing EIB loans for trade with the North, as mentioned above, while promoting trade with other Asian communist nations on the basis of deferred payment. Premier Miki, who once was a leading champion of improved relations with communist nations, visibly identified himself with pro-Seoul elements of the party by attending gatherings of pro-Seoul LDPers. These actions were obviously in keeping with the policy of giving priority to the improvement of Tokyo-Seoul relations and of avoiding actions detrimental to this. In his first policy speech before the Diet in January 1975, Miki made clear his leaning toward Seoul when he announced that "Japan will further strengthen friendly relations with South Korea and with all countries in Asia."[30] In his elaboration of Miki's statement, Foreign Minister Miyazawa Kiichi said:

> In the past year or so there have been several unhappy developments in Japanese-Republic of Korea relations, but the importance of close Japanese-Republic of Korea relations in our foreign policy has not diminished at all. Our government sincerely hopes that there will be peace and stability on the Korean peninsula. Our government also intends to make greater efforts to improve friendly relations with the Republic of Korea.[31]

Also, reversing his predecessor Kimura's position of "no threat from the north," the new Foreign Minister admitted that his government was "most uneasy about the situation" on the Korean peninsula.[32]

II.

Seoul's charges of Pyongyang's aggressive intentions gained a new momentum after the communist takeovers in Indochina. The abandonment of South Vietnam by Washington came as a severe shock to the Seoul government, causing uneasiness among the South Koreans about the durability and the credibility of the American defense commitment to South Korea. Several factors contributed to Seoul's doubts and anxieties. One was the markedly decreased support of the Park government in the U.S. (especially in congressional and public opinion), which was largely attributable to Seoul's repressive domestic policy. Seoul apparently feared that, taking advantage of the post-Vietnam situation and America's changing public opinion, North Korea might mount another invasion in order to unify the country under communist rule. Kim Il-sung's belligerent rhetoric and his visit to Peking did not help mitigate widespread fears of a new attack among the South Koreans. To alleviate these fears, the U.S. took a series of measures. As early as November 1974, President Ford stopped in Seoul on his way to Vladivostok to reassure the Seoul government that Washington would honor its commitment to Seoul and had no intention of withdrawing American troops from South Korea. In his report to Congress (dated February 5, 1975) Defense Secretary James Schlesinger reiterated Ford's pledge. He said that the presence of U.S. troops in South Korea would deter North Korea from again turning to "adventurism," and that South Korea was "most essential" to the defense of America's major Asian ally, Japan.[33] Moreover, Washington increased its troop strength in South Korea from 38,000 to 42,000. Shortly after the fall of Saigon, Schlesinger announced at a hastily called news conference that the defense of Europe, South Korea and Japan was of "utmost importance" in his administration's strategic thinking. Pointing out that the plan to withdraw American troops from South Korea was "a measure of the previous administration," he indicated that specific plans for long-term stationing of American troops in South Korea were being studied. Washington officials took pains to dissociate U.S. policy from the Park government's domestic policy, but Schlesinger reaffirmed to a Senate Armed Services Committee meeting that the U.S. in any case was not prepared to permit Pyongyang to conquer South Korea. For this reason, Ford, Schlesinger and Kissinger all announced that Washington did not foreclose the option of first use of tactical nuclear weapons in the event of a new Korean war. Schlesinger also noted that one of the lessons of the Vietnamese war was that "it is necessary to go for the heart of the opponents' military power." Schlesinger's visit to Seoul in August 1975 was also designed to convince the South Koreans that his government intended to keep its commitment.[34]

The post-Indochina developments in Korea had most significant impacts upon Japan's Korean policy. Even before the collapse of the Saigon government, *Gaimusho* concluded that the National Liberation Front's victory in South Vietnam was inevitable and Japan's foreign policy should be formulated on the basis of this eventuality.[35] One key aspect of this post-Vietnam policy was to strengthen Japan's traditional ties with the U.S. and South Korea. For this reason, Tokyo welcomed Washington's renewed pledges to Seoul and Tokyo. During his Washington visit in April 1975, Foreign Minister Miyazawa told Ford and Kissinger that close American-Japanese relations and firm American commitment to Seoul were all the more important in the post-Vietnam period. In fact, the Foreign Minister was under his party's mandate to seek Washington's assurances on its commitment to Japan and South Korea. Just before he left for Washington, the LDP's three committees on foreign and security affairs (the Foreign Policy Division, the Investigative Committee on Foreign Policy, and the Investigative Committee on National Security) passed a joint resolution urging Miyazawa to stress the importance of the American-Japanese alliance during his talks with Washington officials. The Foreign Minister was also urged to tell American leaders that they should not falter in their commitment to Seoul.[36] At a Washington press conference Miyazawa reaffirmed the spirit of the 1969 Nixon-Sato communiqué stating the importance of South Korea to Japan's security. Significantly, Ford chose to reiterate America's Asian commitment in his April 10, 1975, speech before Congress while Miyazawa was still in Washington.[37] When Miki met with Ford in Washington in August 1975, Korea was again a priority item. Reflecting the LDP's dominant pro-Seoul view,[38] Miki agreed with Ford that "the Security of the Republic of Korea is essential to the maintenance of peace on the Korean peninsula, which in turn is necessary for the peace and security in East Asia, including Japan." Miki urged Ford to maintain the current American policy toward Seoul so that the delicate equilibrium in Korea would not be disturbed.[39] As Miki put it in Washington, "We trust there will be no sudden change in this U.S. policy."[40]

The American-Japanese security talks of August 1975 in Tokyo set the stage for closer security cooperation between the two countries. Korea was again a key item discussed. Acting on the Self-Defense Agency's recommendation that North Korea posed a threat to South Korea and "the possibility of limited military conflicts in Korea has increased in the post-Vietnam period," Sakata Michita, the Agency's director, formally requested to Schlesinger, of course, with his cabinet's understanding, that "American troops in South Korea be maintained on a long-term basis."[41] Sakata also reassured the Americans of "continued use of their bases" in Japan and pledged that his government would strengthen its own self-defense capabilities. With regard to "prior consultations" on military operations launched from the U.S. bases in Japan, Sakata indicated that in actual crises threatening South Korea's security, Japan would not hesitate or quibble in saying Yes. The Sakata-Schlesinger communiqué showed that an agreement had been reached between the two on the "long-term stationing of American troops" in South Korea.[42]

Japan's Korean policy was affected by the post-Indochina events in other major ways. The Tokyo government decided to speed up the process of restoring its relations with Seoul to their pre-Kim Tae-jung affair level as part of its policy of strengthening Tokyo-Seoul ties, which had the effect of reversing the Tanaka government's policy of expanding relations with both Koreas. Japan's new South Korean posture was strongly endorsed by Gaimusho, pro-Seoul LDP leaders and Dietmen (e.g., then Deputy but now Premier Fukuda Takeo, and LDP Vice-President Shiina Etsusaburo), and the business community. A major indication of LDP support for the Seoul government was the creation and activities of a Japan-South Korea Legislators' League (*Nikkan giin renmei*). Organized in June 1975 to replace *Nikkan giin konshinkai,* which was composed of South Korean and pro-Seoul LDP Dietmen, the new bi-national group, chaired by none other than Shiina, included not only LDP Dietmen numbering more than 170 but also thirty Democratic-Socialist Party (DPS) legislators. The latter's participation clearly signalled the success of Seoul's effort to woo non-LDP political forces in Japan. It also meant a widening of Seoul's appeal in the Japanese political circles. Sixty-seven LDP and DSP Dietmen took part in the organization's founding ceremony in Seoul where congratulatory messages by leaders of both governments including Miki were read. While expressing support for improvement in Seoul-Pyongyang relations in its communiqué, the League urged the U.S. to "deter communist aggression" against South Korea by "fully honoring its security commitments in East Asia." The communiqué also stressed that Japan should refrain from making "a hasty approach toward North Korea that would disrupt peace on the Korean peninsula" and "the promotion of friendly relations" between Japan and South Korea.[43]

The Japanese business community, equally affected by the post-Vietnam developments, also moved to adopt a policy of closely cooperating with South Korea. In June, Uemura Kogoro, "doyen" of the business community, headed a twenty-three man *zaikai* group at the seventh annual meeting of the Joint Japan-Republic of Korea Committee for Private Economic Cooperation (*Nikkan minkan godo keizai iinkai*) in Seoul. Significantly, the Japanese delegation, unlike its predecessors, included few proxies. Also significant was the fact that a number of Japanese corporate giants including New-Japan Steel, whose massive North Korean projects were thwarted in the wake of renewed Seoul-Pyongyang tension, did not take part in the Seoul conference. The Japanese participants promised continued economic support to the South Koreans. Specific promises included aid and loans for South Korea's fourth five-year plan to commence in 1977 as well as for the development of the heavy and chemical industries.[44]

Gaimusho also demonstrated strong support for the Seoul government. For example, speaking before a business group in June, Deputy Foreign Minister Togo Fumihiko said, in an indirect criticism of Japanese firms interested in plant exports to North Korea, that if the prevailing balance of power between two Koreas was disrupted, it would only add to the current tension on the Korean peninsula.[45] Strongest *Gaimusho* endorsement of the Seoul government came in the form of a statement by Tokyo's Seoul envoy Nishiyama Akira in July: "It is singularly important [for Japan] to deter North Korea from disrupting peace in East Asia," and "Japan should not be fooled by North Korea's propaganda."[46]

Encouraged by domestic support, the Miki government quickly moved to improve strained relations with Seoul. In implementation of this policy, Tokyo decided to put aside or remove major irritants (e.g., the Kim Tai-jung matter) to its relations with Seoul. After returning from Seoul in mid-July where an understanding was reached with South Korean leaders on the Kim affair, Miyazawa said that "Japanese-Republic of Korea relations have now returned to normalcy." Signalling the return to normalcy, a Japanese-South Korean ministerial conference was held in Seoul in September, for the first time since 1973. As Fukuda heading the Japanese delegation put it, "The world is yet to see peace and stability. In this situation a closer Japanese-Republic of Korea cooperation is all the more important," and "we hope that this conference will lay the foundation for such a relationship." Commenting on the strained interlude in Japanese-South Korean relations, Fukuda said, "The soil further firms up after a spell of rain."[47]

A number of key agreements were made at the meeting, but the Japanese ministers did not go as far as to endorse Seoul's positions and demands *in toto*. For example, rather than acceding to a Seoul demand that Japan reaffirm her anti-Pyongyang position as defined in the Nixon-Sato communiqué of 1969, Japan suggested the language used in the Ford-Miki communiqué. The Seoul demand was later replaced by an agreement that "good neighbourliness, friendship and cooperation" would contribute to "peace and stability of East Asia."[48] In their behind-the-scenes talks, however, the Japanese delegates made their serious concern with South Korean security known to the South Koreans. In the area of economics, which was uppermost in Seoul's mind, Japan promised continued cooperation and support. Reversing her earlier decision to have private organizations assume the responsibility for all aid, loans and investment activities in South Korea after 1977 (when Seoul's current five-year plan is to be completed), Japan also agreed to expand her aid and loans for the development of South Korea's heavy industry (e.g., iron and steel).[49] In the words of the *Nihon keizai shimbun* often reflecting governmental and *zaikai* thinking, Japan's decision to aid South Korean economy was based on her acceptance of Seoul's position that "the only way to stop the North Korean goal of military unification is to strengthen South Korea's national power through economic means."[50] On Japan's relations with North Korea, Seoul urged Tokyo to refrain from approaching Pyongyang too closely. Though the communiqué made no specific reference to this, Japan obviously assured South Korea that her Pyongyang posture would continue to be shaped on the basis of close Tokyo-Seoul cooperation and in a manner not disruptive to Seoul's security.[51]

III.

In the preceding pages I have discussed Japan's policy toward two Koreas and its recent shifts, with particular emphasis upon the views of the major political groups shaping Japan's policy. From this discussion a few conclusions can be drawn in the context of which Japan's current perceptions and expectations regarding America's role in Korea must be examined. First of all, Japan's domestic political considerations and economic interests have dictated that she pursue a policy of closely cooperating with the Seoul government. The LDP, while divided on the Korean issue, has continued to be influenced by a pro-Seoul majority including a variety of right-wing groups (e.g., *Seirankai* and the Fukuda faction). These LDPers have supported Seoul not only for ideological and security reasons but also out of the economic considerations that have governed the business community's attitude toward South Korea. Significantly, these groups have the closest ties with "mainstream" *zaikai* leaders. An overriding economic concern obviously involves Japan's large investments and loans to Seoul totalling more than $1.5 billion, a profitable trade with South Korea, and other functions South Korea performs for Japanese economy (e.g., cheap labor). It is for these political and economic reasons that Japan has pursued a policy of supporting Seoul's independence and viability. Thus, at the peak of the so-called war scare in South Korea in the wake of the Indochina debacle, the Tokyo government, backed by pro-Seoul LDPers and business sectors, quickly moved to reiterate its support of the Seoul government and urged the U.S. to refrain from any actions that might endanger South Korea's security or increase her sense of insecurity. Therefore, contrary to popular assumptions that Japan has been "pressured" by Washington into stressing South Korea's importance to Japan,[52] she has her own intrinsic reasons to declare South Korea to be important. In fact, available evidence suggests that the U.S. was urged by Japan to take an unequivocal position on the defense of South Korea while avoiding actions overtly hostile to North Korea. The continued U.S. commitment to Seoul and the latter's own defense capabilities are obviously deemed to be essential guarantees of Japan's interests in South Korea.

My previous discussions also show that Tokyo's North Korean posture, and that of its domestic allies, has been singularly influenced by events and developments on the Korean peninsula as well as by Seoul's attitudes. Notwithstanding her economic power, Japan has had no or little control over external developments and has been highly reticent about assuming initiatives in international politics, prompting one Japanese observer to remark that Japan's postwar foreign relations have "developed as a mere repetition of passive responses to successive events rather than as a planned policy based on carefully selected policy decisions."[53] The reactive character of Japan's foreign policy has been most conspicuous in her Korean policy. Japan's forward-looking and optimistic posture toward Pyongyang in the early 1970s was frustrated by the developments on the Korean peninsula over which she had little control, and Japan was left with no choice but to revert largely to her pre-1971 policy toward North Korea. Japanese leaders, with the exception of extreme right-wing LDPers generally supporting Seoul, deplored this particular external constraint upon Japan's North Korean policy. It was obviously decided in Tokyo that efforts should be made to reduce Japan's vulnerability in her Korean policy and to correct the unusually reactive character of her Korean policy. A new consensus in Tokyo, supported by all political elements, was that Japan should emerge from the old way of reticence and attempt to play a larger role in shaping external developments involving the Korean peninsula.

These observations about Japan's Korean policy of the 1970s have to be kept in mind as we look at Japan's perceptions and expectations regarding the United States' role in Korea.

Insofar as Japan's immediate concern in Korea is concerned (i.e., to support a viable and independent South Korea), there is a basic convergence of Japanese and American positions. Both Tokyo and Washington support the Seoul government and do not want to see that government overrun by Pyongyang. For this reason, as some Japanese observers put it, the Japanese have assumed an economic role, and the Americans a military role, in their support of South Korea. Beyond this short-range policy concern there is no firm unity of positions between Japan and the U.S. This divergence is primarily attributable to Japan's two-Korea inclination and America's one-Korea posture, which are in turn derived from their differing domestic and political considerations and external perceptions. Japan, whose foreign policy has been dictated to an extraordinary degree by economic considerations[54] (hence *zaikai's* influence in Japanese foreign policy-making), has continued to be attracted to the potentials, justifiable or not, of the North Korean market and natural resources. It is no coincidence that within the so-called ruling Japanese establishment the business community was in the forefront of the movement to improve relations with North Korea. And it is also the business sector that has been most directly and adversely affected by the return to the pre-1971 bellicosity on the

Korean peninsula, which has in turn dictated Japan's reversion to her pre-1971 North Korean posture. Well aware of the significant jump in their trade with China following the diplomatic normalization of 1972, Japanese corporate leaders who had high hopes on expanding Japanese-North Korean economic relations prior to 1974, feel that, although Pyongyang has not imposed anything comparable to China's "Four Principles of Sino-Japanese Trade," business cannot be indifferent to politics, and that improved political relations with North Korea are intimately related to increased economic activities between Japan and North Korea. In fact, North Korean leaders told LDP Dietman Tamura Hajime last July that economic and political relations were closely interrelated, and that "Japanese business should not expect to have profitable trade relations with North Korea while doing nothing to improve political relations with Pyongyang."[55] Not overlooked by Japanese business is a significant drop in the Japanese-North Korean trade following the deterioration of Tokyo-Pyongyang relations in 1974.[56] Business leaders are painfully aware that the political component of the Japanese-North Korean relationship is largely dependent upon relations between Seoul and Pyongyang as well as upon Seoul's attitudes.

The desire to improve relations with North Korea is now confined to left-wing political circles and small business firms heavily dependent on trade with Pyongyang. In fact, it enjoys significant support in both the LDP and *zaikai,* key domestic determinants of Japan's foreign policy. It was largely for this reason that such industrial giants as New-Japan Steel, with an eye on the North Korean market, "judiciously" stayed out of the 1975 meeting of *Nikkan minkan godo keizai iinkai* in Seoul. Not only pro-Pyongyang AA members but many LDPers of centrist persuasion have strongly supported improving Tokyo's relations with Pyongyang. A brief look at views of Utsunomiya Tokuma, the recognized spokesman for the AA group, is in order. His political sympathy, like that of many other AA members, clearly lies with North Korea and its ruler, Kim Il-sung. He has argued that while "Premier Kim Il-sung is committed to general relaxation of the tension" with South Korea, "President Park, driven by fear and hatred of North Korea, is pursuing a hard-line posture." The AA leader has proposed the following suggestions for relaxation of tension between two Koreas as "a preliminary step to eventual unification." In cooperation with the U.S., Japan should persuade the Park government to "restore freedom and democracy" in South Korea, but he says nothing about the authoritarian character of North Korea; Japan should move to establish diplomatic relations with Pyongyang, and make efforts to help improve relations between Pyongyang and Washington.[57] Other leading AA members, such as Tamura Hajime, chairman of AA's Korean Question Subcommittee, and Kuno Chuji, largely share Utsunomiya's views, and argue that Japanese diplomacy should help create an international environment that will make peaceful and stable relations between two Koreas possible. They see Japan's recognition of North Korea as immensely contributing to promoting this international environment.[58] Even "mainstream" LDPers not belonging to AA, such as Kitazawa Naokichi, chairman of the party's Investigative Committee on Foreign Policy, though not supportive of the North Korean regime, feel that Japan has two simultaneous tasks: improving relations with Pyongyang through increased cultural and economic contracts, and helping to create an international climate in cooperation with other powers that would stabilize the situation in Korea and promote a friendly dialogue between two Koreas.[59] While there are differences among these positions, they all agree that Japanese-North Korean relations are closely related to improvement of the international climate surrounding the Korean peninsula.

The Miki government obviously feels that improvement of Tokyo-Pyongyang relations will contribute to the creation of the favorable international environment, while the latter is essential to continued improvement of Japan's relations with North Korea and to eventual normalization of the relations. Thus, maintaining an essentially forward-looking posture toward Pyongyang, of course, within the framework of close Tokyo-Seoul cooperation,[60] the Miki government has urged the major powers and especially the U.S. to assume a larger and active role in the creation of an international environment conducive to peace and stability on the Korean peninsula. As Miki's foreign policy advisor Hirasawa Kazushige put it, "the ultimate challenge to Japanese diplomacy is to influence events away from war and toward a stable peace on the whole of the Korean peninsula."[61] While endorsing (and in fact urging) Washington's commitment to Seoul, the Japanese government has argued that the U.S. should ameliorate its "hard-line" posture toward Pyongyang and move in the direction of reducing the tension with Pyongyang as a means of stabilizing the situation in Korea. Often mentioned in private American-Japanese conversations is that Washington's North Korea posture is like Peking's hard-line posture toward Seoul and should be more like Moscow's apparently flexible policy toward Seoul (e.g., limited economic and cultural contacts between Moscow and Seoul). In fact, there is evidence that in the wake of the post-Vietnam War scare in East Asia, Japanese leaders told Ford and Kissinger that Washington was too much concerned with the short-range objective of deterring North Korea from invading the South, at the expense of long-range concerns. In other words, Tokyo's position was that Washington's South Korean policy should be such that it would not seriously interfere with the larger objective of bringing about peace and stability on the Korean peninsula. This explains why the Tokyo government, while endorsing Washington's show of support for Seoul, was less than enthusiastic about such "belligerent" statements as: "It is necessary to go for the heart of the opponents' military power," and "We will not hesitate to use tactical nuclear weapons" against North Korean aggressors. In fact, upon returning from the Miki-Ford summit talks in Washington, Foreign Minister Miyazawa told an LDP gathering that there was a difference between Japan's Korean stand based more on "long-range" considerations and America's "short-range concern." Obviously, Ford and Kissinger argued that long-range considerations should not jeopardize in any way "the immediate objectives of deterring North Korea from starting a war" and of reducing Seoul's sense of insecurity.[62] Miki also took the position that Japan and the U.S. refrain from actions and statements that would unnecessarily irritate Pyongyang. For this reason, Miki's language on the Korean question, drafted in Tokyo for inclusion in the joint Ford-Miki communiqué, merely stated, without mentioning Japan, that "the maintenance of peace on the Korean peninsula is essential to peace and stability in Asia," while Ford insisted on the reiteration of the 1969 Nixon-Sato statement. The final Ford-Miki communiqué, mentioned earlier, was based on a compromise between these two differing positions.[63] But in a private meeting with LDP foreign policy specialists Miyazawa said that as far as its basic intents were concerned, the Ford-Miki statement did not differ from the 1969 Korean clause.[64] It was also with an eye on Pyongyang that at the conclusion of the Japanese-South Korean ministerial talks last September the Japanese delegation opposed using in the joint communiqué a strong language offensive to North Korea.

As an additional measure of relaxing international tension surrounding Korea, the Miki government has concentrated on efforts to get Washington to agree to a dialogue with Pyongyang. Japan views more than ever her role as that of an intermediary between Pyongyang and Washington. Tokyo's decision to promote a dialogue between the two feuding governments may have been given a further impetus by Gaimusho's view that some sort of informal contracts between Pyongyang and Washington had already taken place and nothing constructive came out of them.[65] It is in the context of Japan's interest in a Washington-Pyongyang dialogue that the so-called "Utsunomiya mission" must be looked at. During his tour of China in July 1975, Utsunomiya took a secret trip to Pyongyang, although it is not clear if he did so at Miki's request. Utsunomiya has denied press reports that he was Miki's personal emissary. What is now known is that the LDP Dietman had lengthy talks with Kim and hand-carried the latter's personal message to Miki. It is also known that its contents were later conveyed to Ford and discussed at the Miki-Ford conference in Washington in August. While dismissing "any desire on his part to invade South Korea" and noting his "commitment to peaceful unification,"

Kim reiterated some of his familiar position on unification. Kim also stated that "it would be difficult [for him] to deal with the Park regime," although he was prepared to "negotiate with any other regime if it is democratic." Kim also warned Japan and the U.S. against "any scheme intended to maintain the two contending Koreas," for this would "only prolong tension and increase the possibility of a new war in Korea."[66] Kim also expressed a strong interest in initiating direct talks with Washington that would lead to an American-North Korean bilateral peace agreement to replace the Korean armistice agreement.[67]

Although Miki did not endorse Kim's proposals *in toto*[68] and did not expect Washington to be receptive to them, he considered them to be a sign of Pyongyang's flexible posture toward Washinton. The Japanese Premier, for this reason, urged Ford to make efforts to accommodate the spirit of Kim's gesture. As for his own policy toward North Korea, Miki argued that improvement in Japanese-North Korean relations would have a moderating effect upon Pyongyang's behavior. Pyongyang, Japan feels, must know that the Japanese government considers South Korea as vital to Japanese interests and security, and that any armed incursions into the South will run the risk of seriously damaging Pyongyang's relations with Japan. Miki may have argued that Washington should follow Tokyo's suit—encouragement of "people's diplomacy" with North Korea. Ford was sympathetic toward Miki's suggestions and did not argue against the need for a dialogue between his government and Pyongyang.[69] Ford also indicated that South Korea's sense of security was his foremost concern. Moreover, since the Korean question is "something to be solved by the Koreans themselves," Ford could not agree to Kim's suggested exclusion of the Seoul government from the proposed Washington-Pyongyang dialogue. As Kissinger put it,

> We are not opposed to North Korea as such. What we don't want to do is have bilateral talks with North Korea to the exclusion of South Korea. We don't want to have South Korea maneuvered into the position of an international pariah while we settle the future of North Korea in negotiations with other countries. We would be prepared to participate in any negotiations or in any conference whose composition was reasonably balanced that included South Korea.[70]

Miki was obviously unhappy with what he considered to be Ford's "hard-nosed" reaction to Kim's gesture. But this did not thwart Japan's interest in a Washington-Pyongyang dialogue, as shown in her activities in the U.N. Firm in the belief that settlement of "the Korean question requires an American-North Korean dialogue sooner or later," Miyazawa urged U.N. Secretary-General Kurt Waldheim to use the prestige of his office to prevail upon Washington and Pyongyang to sit down in a conference to discuss the Korean question.[71] Indications are that the Foreign Minister's urging was also prompted by Kissinger's proposal in the U.N. on a four-state parley (the U.S., China, and two Koreas) on the Korean question, as well as by the Secretary's position that Peking's and Pyongyang's rejection of his proposal was not "absolutely their last word on the subject."[72]

As for the long-range future of two Koreas there is an emerging consensus in the key circles of Japanese politics. Left-wing forces advocate a Japanese policy that will contribute to the realization of the Korean people's ultimate objective of unification. Conservative groups also speak of Japan's role in terms of the creation of an international environment promoting eventual unification of the peninsula. Miki did say, in a rebuttal to charges that he was really working for a two-Korea solution, that it was "not desirable to keep the status quo on the Korean peninsula since all Korean people long for reunification."[73] However, the new emerging consensus, supported by both left-wing and conservative elements, is in favor of the stabilization and maintenance of the status quo in Korea "for the time being." This view is particularly strong in business, LDP and bureaucratic circles. *Gaimusho* officials have indicated, somewhat in contradiction to Miki's public position, that, "for the time being," Japan's diplomacy should be more concerned with "maintaining the status quo in Korea" than with such long-range considerations as unification.[74] In the words of Ushiba Nobuhiko, a *Gaimusho* councillor and ex-Japanese envoy to Washington, "Of course, we endorse the grand ideal of unification, but it cannot be realized in the near future so long as the ideological confrontation exists between two Koreas. There is no alternative but to maintaining the status quo for a considerably long period of time."[75] It is largely for this reason that Japan has endorsed the simultaneous entry of North and South Korea into the U.N. as well as the so-called "cross recognition" formula under which Chinese and Soviet recognition of South Korea would be reciprocated by American and Japanese recognition of North Korea.

There is reason to believe that Japan's two-Koreas status quo is also influenced by her perceptions of the major powers and of the Sino-Soviet conflict. While both Moscow and Peking hammer home the theme of peaceful unification of Korea, in Tokyo's thinking, the real intentions of the two communist powers is to see the two-Koreas situation stabilized and maintained. Neither the Russians nor the Chinese place as high a priority on Korean unification as does North Korea. In fact, both powers do not want to see two Koreas unified for their own reasons. China does not want a unified Korea to fall under the "hegemony" of any of the three major powers and especially the Soviet Union. The Soviet Union has similar fears vis-à-vis other powers and especially China. Moreover, in Chinese and Soviet thinking, a Korea unified and controlled by Kim does not necessarily guarantee a friendly and cooperative policy. This view is derived from Soviet and

Chinese experience with and perceptions of Kim as an unreliable ally. As far as the Chinese are concerned, this view of Kim has been reinforced by his refusal to echo Peking's warnings against the dangers of big power (i.e., Soviet) hegemony in Asia, despite Peking's support of Kim's recent position that Pyongyang is the sole legal government on the Korean peninsula. The Russians have yet to endorse this formula, which implies rejection of a two-Koreas notion. Japan is obviously of the view that Moscow's interest in the maintenance of the Korean status quo is serious, as demonstrated in Soviet overtures to Seoul and in their endorsement of a cross-recognition suggestion. Inasmuch as the major powers place a premium on maintaining the status quo in Korea rather than bringing about a unified Korea, Japan feels that this common policy should be formalized in a big power pact as a more effective guarantee of peace and stability in Korea. In March 1975, Miki said that any Japanese plan for Pyongyang must be acceptable to both Koreas and that his government had no such plan at that time. The Premier also stated that Seoul will oppose Japanese and American recognition of Pyongyang until the two communist powers recognize Seoul. Miki was "in effect insisting on a reciprocal normalization of relations between the two Koreas and the four major powers."[76] Japan feels that neither the four power pact nor the reciprocal normalization will come into being soon. Although Moscow has hinted its endorsement of these suggestions, both China and North Korea have rejected them as perpetuating the current divided status in Korea. However, Pyongyang obviously fears that at some point in the future, the Soviet Union and even China might move to improve their relations with, and even to recognize, Seoul. This fear has been reinforced by growing Soviet-South Korean contacts, Japanese and American support of cross-recognition, and China's policy of improving relations with Japan and the U.S. It was to forestall such moves on the part of the two communist powers that in 1975 Pyongyang reverted to its earlier argument that the only "independent" state of the Korean people is the government in Pyongyang and that "the Seoul government is not an independent state but a puppet of the U.S. with no capacity for independent action."[77] For the same reason, Kim proposed a direct bilateral talk with the U.S. in his message to Miki in the summer of 1975. Moreover, North Korea bluntly warned that "socialist" states "cannot deal with puppets . . . still less recognize them."[78] More recently, during his trip to Peking, Kim obtained China's concurrence with his position that Pyongyang is the sole legal government of Korea, as noted earlier.

So long as Pyongyang remains adamant in opposing a two-Koreas formula and the Sino-Soviet split continues, Japan feels it is unlikely that reciprocal recognition of two Koreas by the four powers will come about. However, the Tokyo government appears to feel that sooner or later North Korea will come around to seeing the new political realities in East Asia and opt for a two-Koreas policy that the major powers favor. Japan's hope is that the U.S. should and can do more in facilitating this change in Pyongyang's policy. Also entertained in Japan's thinking is that if China places a high priority upon improving relations with Tokyo and Washington, as she appears to, she may also be persuaded into adopting a flexible posture toward Seoul as a gesture of goodwill toward Tokyo and Washington. Indications are that Korea is a priority item in Japan's China diplomacy. But due to other pressing matters more directly affecting Sino-Japanese relations (e.g., the proposed Sino-Japanese treaty of peace and amity, and the so-called anti-hegemony controversy), the Korean question has not been accorded adequate attention. Once these issues are settled, Japan may well take up the Korean question, and China may decide to hear what Japan has to say. Japan feels that, since China is interested in a détente with the U.S., she may also decide to remove the Korean issue as a thorny issue of Sino-American relations by agreeing to formalizing the two-Koreas status quo. To *Gaimusho's* delight, in November 1975, China did not boycott, for the first time, an international conference where South Korea was represented. The gathering was an Asian-Pacific Shipbuilders' Conference held in Tokyo and attended by eleven nations. North Korea was absent. Japanese reporters covering the meeting noted that no rude language was exchanged between the Chinese and South Korean representatives and that the conference atmosphere was most congenial.[79] With the possibility of change in China's Seoul policy in mind, Japanese leaders expect the U.S. to give greater attention to the Korean question in her dealings with China.

Tokyo also expects Washington to use its influence and make greater efforts to convince the Seoul government that improvement of relations between Pyongyang and Seoul's major allies (including Japan) will have a moderating influence upon Pyongyang's behavior and thus in the long run will contribute to the thawing of tension on the Korean peninsula. This is the position Japan has taken with Seoul all along, but she has not been very successful in persuading Seoul of the logic of her position. The Japanese have learned that their important economic role in South Korea cannot be readily converted into political leverage in dealing with the Seoul government. Largely for historical reasons, Seoul is most sensitive to and resentful of Tokyo's pressure. Knowing this, the Japanese have been reticent about taking actions that Seoul might interpret as Japan's interference with Seoul's policy. The Japanese feel that the U.S., free from these constraints, is in a far better position to prevail upon the Seoul government to show greater understanding for Japan's posture toward North Korea. In short, as Miki recently said before a Japan-American Society meeting, "Japanese-American cooperation is most essential to promoting a Seoul-Pyongyang dialogue."[80]

1. Saito Takashi, "Japan and Korean Unification," *Japan Interpreter*, vol. VIII, no. 1 (Winter, 1973), p. 31. See also *Asahi Shimbun*, 23 June, evening, 1973. (This paper will hereafter be referred to as *Asahi*.)

2. *Asahi nenkan (Asahi Almanac)*, 1973, p. 262.

3. *Asahi*, 9 September 1973.

4. *Asahi*, 24 January, evening, 1972.

5. Ibid.

6. *Asahi*, 29 August 1972.

7. *Nihon keizai shimbun*, 7 July 1972.

8. See my paper, "The Politics of Japan's China Decision," *ORBIS*, vol. XIX, no. 2 (Summer, 1975), pp. 562–590.

9. *Asahi*, 8 August 1972.

10. *Nihon keizai shimbun*, 3 September 1972.

11. *Nihon keizai shimbun*, 14 September 1973.

12. *Asahi*, 28 December 1973.

13. *Asahi*, 6 September, evening, 1972.

14. *Asahi*, 8 January, evening, 1973.

15. *Asahi*, 4 and 5 July, 1973.

16. For Ohira's remarks, see *Asahi*, 23 June, evening, 1973.

17. *Asahi*, 6 September, evening, and 28 December 1973.

18. *Japan Times*, 31 August 1974.

19. *Asahi*, 2 October, and 9 December 1974.

20. *Sekai*, no. 348 (November, 1974), p. 186 and p. 200.

21. *Sekai*, no. 353 (April, 1975,) p. 178.

22. Ibid.

23. *Nihon keizai shimbun*, 28 December, evening, 1972.

24. For its involvement in South Korea, see Nakagawa Nobuo, "Kankoku no nakano 'nihon kabushiki kaisha'," ("Japan Incorporated" in South Korea), *Sekai*, no. 338 (January, 1974), pp. 130–135.

25. *Nihon keizai shimbun*, 28 December, evening, 1972.

26. *Sekai*, no. 352 (March, 1975), p. 207.

27. *Asahi*, 3 January 1975.

28. *Sekai*, no. 348 (November, 1974), p. 183.

29. Ibid.

30. *Japan Report*, 16 January 1975, p. 3.

31. *Sekai*, no. 353 (April, 1975), p. 180.

32. *Sekai*, no. 354 (May, 1975), p. 219.

33. For summary of this report, see Kitabatake Kasumi, "Tohoku ajia ni okeru nikkanbei" (Japan, South Korea and the U.S. in East Asia), *Sekai*, no. 355 (June, 1975), pp. 47–53.

34. *Asahi*, 28 August 1975.

35. *Asahi*, 4 April 1975.

36. "Miyazawa hobei ni miru hoshu gaiko no konmei" (Conservative Diplomacy's Confusion as Revealed in Miyazawa's U.S. Visit), *Sekai*, no. 355 (June, 1975), pp. 183–84.

37. *Yomiuri shimbun*, 12 April 1975.

38. Just before Miki left for Washington, Shiina Etsusaburo urged the Premier to

handle the Korean question most prudently lest Tokyo-Seoul relations would suffer. See *Asahi,* 1 August 1975.

39. *Sekai,* no. 359 (October, 1975), p. 214.

40. Hirasawa Kazushige, "Japan's Emerging Foreign Policy," *Foreign Affairs,* vol. 54, no. 1 (October, 1975), p. 169.

41. *Asahi,* 24 August 1975.

42. *Asahi,* 30 August 1975.

43. For text of the communiqué see *Sekai,* no. 358 (September, 1975), pp. 231–233.

44. *Asahi,* 28 September 1975.

45. *Tokyo shimbun,* 6 June 1975.

46. *Asahi,* 18 July 1975.

47. *Sekai,* no. 360 (November, 1975), p. 159.

48. For text of the communiqué, see *Asahi,* 16 September 1975.

49. *Asahi,* 10, 16 and 28 September 1975.

50. *Nihon keizai shimbun,* 16 September 1975.

51. *Asahi,* 16 September 1975.

52. For a typical argument of this nature, see Jerome A. Cohen, "De-Americanizing South Korea," *Christian Science Monitor,* 10 November 1975.

53. Yamamoto Mitsuru, "Book Review of F. C. Langdon's *Japan's Foreign Policy,*" *Japan Quarterly,* vol. 22, no. 1 (January-March, 1975), p. 74.

54. For example, see Japan's policy shift from her pro-Israel to a pro-Arab posture during the oil crisis.

55. Komaki Teruo, "Nitcho boeki no kenkyo to kadai" (The Present State and Tasks of Japanese-North Korean Trade), *Sekai,* no. 360 (November, 1975), p. 129.

56. For ups and downs in Japanese-North Korean trade for 1974 and 1975, see *Far Eastern Economic Review,* vol. 90, no 51 (19 December 1975), p. 37.

57. Utsunomiya Tokuma, "Betonamu no kyuhen to chosen seisaku" (Sudden Turn of Events in Vietnam and Japan's Korean Policy), *Sekai,* no. 355 (June, 1975), pp. 44–45.

58. *Asahi,* 29 September 1975.

59. *Asahi,* 2 August 1975.

60. *Asahi,* 4 September, evening, 1975.

61. Hirasawa, p. 168.

62. *Asahi,* 15 August 1975.

63. Iwami Takao, "Miki seiken-ron" (A Study of the Miki Regime), *Chuo koron,* vol. 90, no. 12 (December, 1975), p. 96.

64. *Asahi,* 15 August 1975.

65. *Asahi,* 30 September 1975.

66. For summary of the letter, see *Asahi,* 10 August 1975.

67. *Asahi,* 2 August 1975.

68. Virtually all LDPers present at the August 2nd meeting of chairmen and vice-chairmen of the party's two foreign policy committees criticized Kim's proposal on an American-North Korean peace agreement for excluding South Korea. *Asahi,* 3 August 1975.

69. A State Department spokesman, commenting on Kim's proposal, referred to Washington's U.N. resolution on the Korean question indicating Washington's interest in meeting with North Koreans. *Asahi,* 2 August 1975.

70. *Time,* 27 October 1975, p. 27

71. *Asahi,* 17 October 1975.

72. Ibid., and *Time,* 27 October 1975, p. 37.

73. *Japan Times,* 19 June 1975.

74. Ibid.

75. *Asahi,* 24 September 1975.

76. D. S. Zagoria and Y. K. Kim, "North Korea and the Major Powers," *Asian Survey*, vol. XV, no. 12 (December, 1975), p. 1034.

77. Ibid., p. 1025.

78. Ibid.

79. *Asahi*, 22 November 1975.

80. *Sekai*, no. 361 (December, 1975), p. 198.

How Taipei Views American Policy in Asia

Douglas H. Mendel, Jr.

The biggest shock to the Republic of China was the July 15, 1971 announcement that Richard Nixon would accept Peking's invitation to visit the People's Republic of China the following February. I was in Tokyo at the time and none of the Taiwan independence groups had any comment, although all were anticommunist. The second biggest shock, possibly worse, was the Ford-Kissinger visit to Peking in December 1975, when they announced that the United States would adopt the "Japan model" for relations with the two Chinas. The U.S. consulate-general in Hong Kong had told the writer in August 1975, that a switch in U.S. relations from Taipei to Peking was likely within two or three years, but the shock of the actual statements that December was unforeseen as Taipei did not think President Ford would make any change in the China policy. The reaction from Taipei has been muted, although their distrust of Kissinger is very obvious, because they think Ford will be deterred by the 1976 presidential campaign and the popularity of Ronald Reagan—a closer friend of Taipei than Ford —in the polls.

This paper is an analysis of Taipei's views of America's Asia policy today, but it is helpful to look back over the past forty years as the writer has studied U.S.-ROC relations since 1936, and observed many inconsistencies and examples of fickle loyalty over those four decades. The entire world scene is more uncertain and confused than at any time since 1945, due to rise of the Third World, the power of nationalism over ideologies, and the growing cynicism of the American public in most institutions and perhaps even in the maintenance of security treaty commitments to non-European nations. The pro-Israeli lobby is probably the strongest in the United States, despite the lack of any formal treaty commitment to Israel, but the American public and Congress have shown far more loyalty to the Republic of China than some diplomats, especially Dr. Kissinger, and some members of Congress who put power above principles.

The fickleness of Washington toward Nationalist China can be seen in the refusal of the United States to apply serious sanctions against the Japanese invasion of Manchuria in 1931 or the mainland in 1937. The American public was in an isolationist mood and did not want to become involved in either a European or Asian war, although then as now the Americans were far more oriented toward Europe than Asia. Only when Japan secured permission from the defeated Vichy French government in 1941 to transit Northern Vietnam en route to China did Washington cancel all trade with Japan. Thus, one may say that Vietnam triggered the Pacific War, not China. There was widespread sympathy for Nationalist China in the American media of the 1930s as it seemed the underdog, but sympathy did not lead to heavy military aid although quite a few Americans followed Claire Chennault to volunteer to fight for the Nationalists. Up until Pearl Harbor, in fact, Russia provided the Nationalists with more military aid than the United States did, as several ex-Nationalist pilots reported to me flying Soviet planes and driving Soviet tanks. Moscow itself was, of course, far more afraid of Hitler than of Japan and urged the Chinese communists to join with the Kuomingtang (Nationalists) against the Japanese invaders. Both Russia and the U.S. stressed the European struggle and simply wanted to keep the Sino-Japanese war (which most Japanese navy and diplomatic veterans of the China area opposed) going to tie down Japanese forces from moving elsewhere. Even the Japanese Emperor, on the eve of Pearl Harbor, challenged his generals who predicted an early peace with Washington by citing their 1937 optimism about China when the China War was still dragging on in 1941.

Another wartime policy of Washington's was not to invade the China mainland (on the theory it was bad to fight a land war in Asia), but to defeat Japan by air and naval power. Nor did Washington ever accept the advice of General Chiang Kai-shek, seconded by ex-Ambassador Joseph Grew, who was acting Secretary of State in 1944, and by myself in Hawaii during the war, to promise to retain the Japanese imperial institution. If the allies, most of whom opposed such a concession to the unconditional surrender policy, had accepted such good advice, it is probable that Tokyo would have surrendered in late 1944, after the fall of the Tojo Cabinet, thus saving thousands of Japanese and allied lives, keeping Russia out of the war, and preventing other postwar problems. While we cannot certify that hypothesis, most of my Japanese contacts since 1945 agree with it.

Few American generals or politicians thought beyond the immediate objective of defeating Germany and Japan, and ignored the postwar problems that were caused by such shortsightedness. No preparation for the occupation of Korea, for example, and no attention paid to this writer's warnings from 1947 to 1949 that Russia would help North Korea attack the South, as she had always shown great interest in the Korean peninsula and in Manchuria and other Chinese borderlands. Nor did Washington invade Taiwan, though contingency plans were made, because Okinawa seemed a smaller island easier to capture and use as a staging area for the invasion of Kyushu in October 1945, if the war had not ended.

The 1943 Cairo Declaration promised to return to the Republic of China all lands stolen by Japan, including Taiwan, but the secret part of the 1945 Yalta Agreement promised Russia not only Japanese islands it had never before claimed, but also the old Czarist rights in Manchuria as inducement to enter the war against Japan. Actually, postwar studies showed that neither the Soviet entry in the Pacific War nor the atomic bombs were needed to defeat Japan, but Americans are always impatient for a solution to international problems and their concession of Chinese land to Russia annoyed both the Republic of China and its communist adversaries.[1] Few Americans knew the history of Russian imperialism in East Asia, and the United States had probably been the least aggressive of all world powers as it was Britain and Russia and later Japan that tried to keep the Chinese disunited for their own benefit, while the U.S. favored non-intervention. It increased aid to Chungking but sent military and diplomatic agents to the communist base headquarters at Yenan (the "Dixie Mission").[2]

After Japan's defeat, the Marshall mission was a fruitless effort to bring the two warring Chinese factions together, when neither wanted to cooperate with the other and Mao himself had predicted that the Japanese invasion would defeat the KMT, then America would defeat Japan, and the Chinese communists could take over after that. Both the Republic of China and the Chinese communists planned to resume their civil war which had never really been recessed except that the Nationalists were forced out of the populous areas of the country. Moreover, the Chinese public was weary of civil strife which had caused so much suffering since 1911, and the middle class was affected most by the postwar inflation. Washington did not really protest the military misrule of Taiwan under the horrible General Chen Yi, later executed in Taipei for trying to sell his mainland unit to the communists. By 1948, Washington wanted to wash its hands of the China issue and published a White Paper blaming the loss of the mainland on the Nationalists.

Many in Washington preferred to recognize the new Peking regime in 1949, after the Nationalists fled to Taiwan, but the Korean War saved Taiwan as it also spurred the rearmament of NATO allies and caused a two decade containment program. When the ROC moved from Nanking to Canton, before fleeing to Taiwan, the U.S. embassy stayed in Nanking while the Soviet one moved to Canton, another example of American ambiguity. As American military aid to Taipei increased after 1951, and Washington signed a security treaty with the ROC in 1954, it became clear that Washington wanted only a defensive commitment to Taiwan, not a policy to encourage a counterattack on the mainland. After the 1952 campaign slogans of "unleashing Chiang Kai-shek," Eisenhower ended the Korean War by compromise and later vetoed sending of U.S. aid to the French at Dienbienphu, while his Secretary of State John Foster Dulles forced Nationalist Foreign Minister George Yeh to sign an exchange of notes in December 1954 requiring joint agreement for any "offensive operations by either party from the territories held by the Republic of China."

Many officers of the U.S. Military Advisory Group attached to Taipei favored a more hawkish policy of mainland counterattack, while others criticized the Nationalists for asking too much military aid, and some even sympathized with the Taiwanese native complaints of the 1950s and 1960s. There were also differences inside the Republic of China government on foreign and domestic policy, but U.S. economic aid programs of $1.6 billion (ended in 1965) encouraged free enterprise, which benefitted the native businessmen. Some ROC bureaucrats complained that the wealth of Taiwan was in the hands of native business leaders, but Washington did not interfere in the internal political scene in Taiwan or in many other allied states. In 1962, Washington told its ambassador in Warsaw to assure the Chinese communist ambassador that "the United States would not support any such (mainland attack) undertaking by the Chinese Nationalists, but on the other hand would defend Taiwan if Peking mistakenly resorted to force."[3]

Washington did not accept the use of Chinese Nationalist troops in the Korean War, probably not to antagonize Peking, nor did Saigon or Washington accept more than a few political commissar advisors in the fighting there. It was clear to President Nixon before his 1968 campaign that the U.S. public was disenchanted with Vietnam, so he promised to disentangle U.S. combat forces and encourage Asian states to be more self-reliant (the "Nixon Doctrine" of 1969 was about as ambiguous in Taipei eyes as the Ford "Pacific Doctrine" of 1975).[4] Nixon, who had been considered in the 1960s as Taipei's best American friend and annual visitor, soon became its worst enemy as he was drawn into Peking's strategy of using the U.S. as a counterbalance to the Soviet threat. Allen Whiting and others always claim that the PRC was mainly responsible for the opening to the United States, not as many Americans assumed it was Nixon or Kissinger who opened the doors to mainland China. One of the writer's ex-diplomat friends who served once in Hong Kong said in 1974: "who cares about a tiny island like Taiwan when we have the doors to China open?" Nixon's visit to Peking in 1972 and the Shanghai Communiqué shocked Taipei and angered them because Nixon seemed to be suggesting that the U.S.

considered the solution of the Peking-Taipei dispute to be an internal issue of China (as the PRC always claims) and would encourage Taipei to reach a peaceful agreement with Peking. Echoes of the Marshall Mission made Taipei wonder if Nixon had only used anti-communism as a political ladder and would now desert his anti-communist friends to win the 1972 presidential election.

Later, of course, the American public lost faith in Nixon in the wake of the Watergate exposure, but Taipei was very worried about Washington's support for Peking's seating in the United Nations. It was obvious to most that after the Nixon trip to China, the U.S.-sponsored "important question" resolution on Chinese U.N. representation would fail for the first time in late 1971. When it did, the Chinese U.N. delegation walked out of the General Assembly and the communist delegation was overwhelmingly voted in. As Peking had warned Taipei frequently, could it trust its American ally? Would any politician seek votes of an American public always fond of the Chinese people and, after the traumatic experience of Vietnam, willing to support détente with both Moscow and Peking? It was clear after the Nixon visit and tours of many American media, sports, Congressional, and entertainment people that even conservative Americans felt it safe to be pro-Peking.

Washington allowed Peking to open a liaison mission in Washington not far from the Republic of China embassy, while members of the U.S. liaison office in Peking complained of not being able to mingle with the Chinese or live as they had in pre-1949 China.[5] Other Americans with less expertise in Chinese affairs were truly brainwashed by their guided tours, and any overseas Taiwanese could get red-carpet treatment although not many believed the communist propaganda about liberation of Taiwan as benefitting the Taiwanese. We should mention here that Taipei was not very happy with the American hospitality to about 10,000 Taiwanese, most of whom went to America for graduate study and remained for good jobs, some of whom were active in Taiwan independence demonstrations. When Professor Peng Mingmin, former chairman of political science at National Taiwan University but imprisoned in 1964 for trying to publish an inflammatory pamphlet, was admitted from Sweden on a visa to teach at the University of Michigan and later elsewhere, Taipei knew he had been friendly with Dr. Kissinger at Harvard and knew he would be politically active as nominal leader of the Taiwan Independence Movement (TIM) in the U.S., although by 1975 his name was dead inside the island. But Taipei knew the United States was a very open society and it could not expect Washington to deport TIM activists to Taiwan as Prime Minister Sato had done in Japan.

Taipei always disagreed with those Americans who predicted Taipei would merge with the communist mainland or would ally itself with

Russia if the U.S. dropped its security commitment. Allen Whiting and some others with both government and academic credentials predicted the merger, but after Michael Lindsay and his wife toured the mainland they changed their views and defended the Republic of China.[6] One of the most anti-KMT members of the U.S. Embassy in Taipei in August 1974, told me that "everyone in Taiwan would fight against a merger as they know it would mean the end of their prosperity and freedoms."[7] Others minimized the prospect of any Taipei-Moscow connection as James Wei, director of the Central News Agency and former Government Information Office director, told me in 1975 that the Nationalists would not even allow Russian freighters to put into Taiwan ports to frighten Peking as then Peking could claim that Taipei was moving close to the Russians and all Chinese tend to be anti-Russian. Moreover, Chiang Ching-kuo, who was imprisoned in 1927 as a hostage after his father expelled Russian advisors, would hardly trust the Russians while Moscow keeps hoping for a less anti-Soviet leadership to emerge in Peking.

In 1965, A. T. Steele found that of the 60 percent of Americans who were aware of the communist government in mainland China, only 40 percent knew another Chinese government existed in Taipei.[8] The American public, as we shall note below, is far more aware of "Free" China today and supports it more than Dr. Kissinger does in his effort to get along with big powers and ignore the smaller ones. After the Nixon visit of 1972, Taipei relaxed all its political rules and encouraged Taiwanese in Japan to take up Japanese citizenship (which it previously opposed). It also welcomed all kinds of foreigners, even those who had been to mainland China and those with a mainland visa (while Peking refuses to admit anyone with a Nationalist visa). The nature of the liberalization in Taiwan under Premier Chiang Ching-kuo (called the "hero of the native Taiwanese" by the anti-KMT embassy officer in 1974) cannot be detailed here, but anyone who contrasts the life in the mainland with the living standards in Taiwan knows they are five times higher and that consumer delights abound in Taiwan where wages, freedoms of all kinds, and political stability far exceed those in the mainland.[9]

Taipei has also successfully fought the diplomatic isolation promoted by the PRC and encouraged by the loss of its U.N. seat in 1971 by substituting unofficial relations. It opened four new consulates in the United States in 1974 for a total of fourteen, and added information offices to many of them. While the mainland regime exploits traditional Chinese culture in its acrobatic and other performance troupes abroad, while trying to stamp it out domestically, Taipei also competes on the same level and must do more to counter the use of Chinese culture by Peking. Dr. Kissinger told a Washington audience of pro-Peking traders and contact men that the U.S. "has and will continue to have an interest in a strong People's Republic of China. . . . No policy has had greater bipartisan support than normalization of relations with that country."[10] By 1975, Congress proved him wrong by strongly opposing a switch in diplomatic relations, while the American public also agreed.

In the 1974 Gallup Poll of American attitudes toward the ROC, conducted in the same month as this writer's Japan poll showing only 8 percent who favored communist control of Taiwan, 72 percent opposed Peking's conditions for normalization of relations while only 11 percent approved them, while 50 percent wanted to normalize relations with the PRC in principle. On the 1954 security treaty, which President Ford and other administration spokesmen had often reaffirmed in the months after Indochina fell in 1975, 48 percent favored it against 35 opposed.[11] In October 1975, a similar Gallup Poll showed far better knowledge of the economic and political stability in Taiwan and that government's friendship for the U.S., while 58 percent thought the Indochina collapse caused other Asian governments to question the credibility of U.S. commitments. Over 70 percent favored continued diplomatic relations with Taipei, while 53 percent had favorable impressions of Taiwan and only 27 percent had a good image of the mainland.[12] Over 61 percent favored normalization with Peking against 23 percent opposed, but when asked if they would break our ties with Taiwan, the negative reply was 70 percent to 14 percent. Such survey results, however, did not deter Dr. Kissinger and President Ford (who relies on him for most foreign policy decisions) from promising to follow the Japan formula of moving the embassy to Peking and keeping liaison offices in Taiwan.

As Assistant Secretary for East Asia and Pacific, Philip Habib commented after that announcement, "We have certain treaty obligations with Taiwan which Japan did not have, and the Chinese Communists are well aware that Washington has a treaty obligation to come to Taiwan's defense if it is attacked."[13] Few people with knowledge of international law or diplomacy could imagine a government keeping a defense commitment to a nation it did not recognize—and only the U.S. has such a commitment to the Republic of China. All other nations could use the Japan model, but the U.S. is in a special position, and Taipei strongly agreed with Habib and others who favored continued diplomatic recognition of the ROC.

Many cities of the U.S. saw Chinese student groups demonstrate against the 1975 Ford visit to mainland China, and Nationalist Foreign Minister Shen Chang-huan also called it a useless trip. But few Taipei newspapers ever thought Ford would adopt the Japan formula for PRC relations, and all the Taiwan spokesmen from government and academic circles warned Ford not to make any more concessions as the U.S.-PRC relationship since 1971 has mainly benefitted the PRC.

Nixon had affirmed after his 1972 trip that he would not abandon old friends and allies, and Taipei assumed that Ford as a Nixon appointee and anti-communist, would follow the same line. But most Washington newsmen thought Ford had little expertise in foreign affairs and relied excessively on Kissinger, whose image in Congress was very low. The House of Representatives sent a petition signed by a majority of members and seconded by twenty-nine senators to Ford before his Peking trip advising against any change in diplomatic relations.[14]

Washington had extended an Export-Import Bank loan for construction of the ten capital projects to speed the industrialization and self-reliance of the ROC, and loaned Taipei funds to build many new F-5 fighters for defense (the annual military loan program averages $80 million). U.S. forces in Taiwan, however, were cut from a 9,000 maximum during the Vietnam War to under 2,800 in 1976, and Premier Chiang said they could all be withdrawn without any problem as they are not combat forces and the ROC has 500,000 troops and 2.2 million reservists.[15] Taipei always opposed senators such as Henry Jackson or J. William Fulbright who urged a switch in diplomatic ties to Peking, but they know that the American public has always been more anti-Moscow than anti-Peking and that poses a danger if the Jackson-Fulbright mood extends throughout Congress. James Reston, who visited mainland China in mid-1971, wrote a strong criticism of Kissinger's secret diplomacy which stresses personal relations: "Enduring agreements among nations must rest on national interests and not on personalities—a rule most world leaders accept in principle but defy in practice."[16]

The American Chambers of Commerce Asian-Pacific Council met in Seoul in November 1975, to warn President Ford not to shift diplomatic links to Peking, as did the May 2, 1975, article in the *Far Eastern Economic Review* entitled "The American Conscience":

> For the Nationalists, there is no place to escape from the American frying pan— except into the fire. Speculation about a deal with the Soviets is considered unrealistic . . . the reed of American reliance is stronger than any possible trust in Moscow. Another kind of China Lobby is operating in the U.S. now, but the Nationalists still rely on friends in high places, the American disinclination to dismiss treaties as scraps of paper, and a clear willingness to fight if need be. There is not much to retreat to in Taiwan and no differences between the Taiwanese and mainlanders about the identity of the enemy.[17]

A Chinese reporter in Taipei wrote a similar article about ROC trust in the United States but it was in July 1975, long before the shock of the Ford trip to Peking:

> . . . for the more emotional young nationalists, the standard line nowadays is "The U.S. is unreliable, we have to depend on ourselves. . . ." Chiang Ching-kuo said that "Even though we emphasize self-reliance and the concept that only

those who help themselves can be helped by others, we do not exclude the opportunity of group security and defense cooperation with allies. . . ." For cool-headed officials at least, the United States is still the most important ally that Taiwan has, and an ally Taiwan has to trust.[18]

Dr. Frederick Chien, former head of the Government Information Office and now deputy foreign minister, told a Taipei seminar that "normalization of relations between the United States and the Chinese Communists is strewn with obstacles and cannot be achieved quickly . . . American policy is still concerned mainly with the Russians, so Maoist detente plays only second fiddle. . . ."[19] It may seem second to Chien, but to Peking and Moscow, the Sino-Soviet dispute is paramount and any U.S. ties to Peking are welcome there but not in Russia.

Allen S. Whiting, after his November group trip to mainland China, wrote that:

> Implicit in Teng Hsiao-ping's readiness to wait ten or 100 years for acquisition of Taiwan is the recognition that the Nationalist regime will not collapse when the United States withdraws its defense commitment. Peking lacks both the military means to invade the island successfully and the political means to win it by subversion. Nor are negotiations tempting for Taipei, at least until the post-Mao succession struggle clearly establishes a lasting leadership.[20]

This writer gave a talk on "Free" China to the Georgetown Center for Strategic Studies on January 12, 1976, and everyone in the room agreed that no such deal would ever be made, while A. M. Halpern of the George Washington University later doubted that the post-Mao struggle would produce a "lasting leadership."

Premier Chiang Ching-kuo gave an interview to the ABC-TV network's Harry Reasoner on December 22, 1975, two weeks after Reasoner had accompanied President Ford to mainland China. Chiang denied there would ever be any accommodation between the People's Republic and the Republic of China ("Today our people are all aiming at the defeat of their fourth enemy, the Chinese Communist regime"). Then Reasoner asked about the visit of Assistant Secretary Philip Habib to Taipei at the request of President Ford to reassure the Taipei government.

> The premier says that the Republic of China, as a member of the international community, of course, is susceptible to outside influence because in today's world everything is interrelated. But the most important thing for the Republic of China is its own unity and its own efforts . . . so he told Mr. Habib that the relationship between the Republic of China and the United States, as compared with the relationship between the U.S. and the communist regime in China, has one sharp contrast, one stark difference: That is to say between our two countries, we share the same philosophy, the same ideology, the same institutions, as well as the same way of life. So it's much easier to communicate between our two peoples.

When Reasoner asked if Taiwan could survive if the U.S. broke relations and recognized the mainland regime after the 1976 presidential election (obviously the Kissinger plan to adopt the "Japan model"), Chiang said that was a hypothetical question that could not be answered directly as it might happen or might not happen.

> But we can say that if it were ever to happen, it would cause serious damage not only to the Republic of China but would cause damage to the United States as well as to Asia and the entire free world. So this is something that will have very serious consequences and any decision-maker will have to think very carefully about it.[21]

The three Chinese present at my January 12th Georgetown Center talk reacted similarly as they worried about the strategic vacuum if the security treaty were rescinded and also about the possible loss of U.S. investment. Over 200 American firms now invest in Taiwan, and the Ford administration made fifty-two pledges to keep its commitments to the ROC since the Nixon trip of 1972.[22] Even some normally pro-Peking Americans stated that Washington cannot ignore 16 million people on Taiwan in dealing with mainland China. This was stated by the *New York Times,* the *Wall Street Journal,* and the *New Republic* editorially, while John Fairbank of Harvard agreed that "if the end of the security treaty meant turning Taiwan over to Peking's levelling control, many would brand it a major crime even for the 20th century."[23] Doak Barnett, Richard Moorsteen, and Morton Abramowitz, despite their hostile views of Taipei, seemed to agree that the U.S. must keep its security commitment.

Nationalist foreign minister Shen Chang-huan claimed that the visit of Philip Habib, who had opposed the Kissinger Japan model concept as impossible to implement, showed that the U.S. would maintain friendly relations with the Republic of China. He told members of the Legislative Yuan that Ford had sent Habib to Taipei to assure people of Washington's intention to continue such friendly relations. On November 13th, before Ford's trip, the Taipei foreign ministry had strongly opposed the trip or any dealings between Washington and Peking, but it seemed assured after Habib's visit. What Taipei says may not always reflect its inner fears, however, and there are differences of opinion inside any elite. The foreign ministry issued a strong statement on December 5th warning that the Ford-Kissinger statements about normalizing relations with the PRC:

> . . . give encouragement to the evil force of aggression and international adventurism which the Chinese Communist regime certainly is. In so doing, the United States is departing from its declared intent of maintaining equilibrium in Asia and assisting the free and democratic nations in a collective effort to check the forces of aggression and oppression.[24]

William Armbruster, an astute young American reporter in Taipei, wrote a fine article for the *Christian Science Monitor* in mid-December explaining the displeasure of the Taiwan people over the Ford visit to mainland China, but their relief that nothing definite by way of communiqué or a schedule for normalization had been issued. Local media gave little coverage to the Ford visit, while the *China Post* wrote that Ford's commitment to normalization represented "a danger of further appeasement measures being taken by the United States." But the same newspaper went on to assure its readers that any such normalization with Peking would meet strong opposition from the U.S. Congress and the public. The other Taipei English-language paper, the *China News* warned that war would break out in the Taiwan Straits if the U.S. recognized Peking and it angrily rejected American use of the Japanese "model." The final day of the Ford visit coincided with the opening of an election campaign for twenty-two seats in the Legislative Yuan, again increasing the number of natives in that body. One candidate told a reporter that he hoped the U.S. would move slowly toward recognizing Peking because "that would be best for both Taiwan and the United States."[25]

Another post-Ford visit article from Taipei in the *New York Times* saw no early shift in U.S. policy toward the two Chinese regimes in the wake of the trip. Comments included a high official saying that "We have not resigned ourselves to losing relations with the United States and in the coming year must step up our efforts to impress on the American people and government that we are a good friend and useful ally whose continued strength and stability is also in your national interest"; attacks on the Japan formula because only the U.S. has a defense commitment to Taiwan which would be nullified by such a step; and mention of the $3.5 billion annual trade which might suffer by a loss of diplomatic ties.[26] Some people outside the government in Taipei did not worry so much about loss of official relations, as they thought trade and security would continue under a system of liaison offices, but such people knew little of world politics.

Finally, Diane Ying, a perceptive reporter in Taipei, wrote that most people believed the U.S. would not dump Taiwan completely "out of political expediency . . . but even if that happens most people believe the Nationalists could go it alone. They have weathered many adversities and therefore developed a psychological ability to absorb shocks and they seem to feel a sense of security that even if politically isolated they can still survive and do well."[27] Miss Ying cited the Gallup Poll objection to switching relations away from Taipei as a cause of popular confidence among people in Taiwan, as well as the trade level eight times greater than U.S. trade with the PRC in 1975.

Experts disagree on the course of U.S. China policy after the 1976 elections, but most think there will not be a drastic change even then. Much will depend on mainland Chinese domestic politics and the problem of succession to Mao because, as Premier Chiang told Edward

Neilan in December 1975, "a struggle for power is inevitable after the death of any dictator ... and struggle will intensify after Mao's death."[28] The results of the 1976 American elections and the post-Mao struggle will both have an effect on Taipei but the Republic of China is confident of its self-reliance and support from the American public.

1. See, for example, John S. Service, *Lost Chance in China* (New York: Vintage-Random House, 1974); Barbara Tuchman, *Stilwell and the American Experience in China 1941–1945* (New York: Bantam Books, 1971); and the most objective, John F. Melby, *The Mandate of Heaven* (New York: Doubleday-Anchor Books, 1971).

2. See Robert Goldston, *The Rise of Red China* (Greenwich, Connecticut: Fawcett, 1967); and the writings of Col. Barrett who participated in the "Dixie Mission."

3. Kenneth Young, "American Dealings with Peking," *Foreign Affairs*, 45, 1, (October 1966), pp. 81–82.

4. For the text of President Ford's speech at the East-West Center, University of Hawaii, see the Department of State News Release, 7 December 1975, titled "President Ford's Pacific Doctrine," which the head of the Asian Peoples' Anti-Communist League immediately opposed. A group of seven members of Congress headed by Senator Charles Percy wrote a sixty-eight page report on their August trip to the mainland also opposing any switch in diplomatic relations to Peking (see *China News*, 1 November 1975).

5. See editorial praising the critical comments of Alfred Jenkins (who said his liaison life in Peking was very restricted and he couldn't talk with common people as he had in pre-1949 China) in the *China News*, 1 July 1974, which also criticized Jenkins' view that U.S.-Peking relations do not depend on the identity of PRC leaders. American Society of Newspaper Editors' mission to the mainland also produced very critical comments on the mainland cf. Taiwan (*China News*, 11 July 1975).

6. One of Michael Lindsay's many anti-PRC talks was at a Chinese student rally protesting Ford's trip, New York, 25 October 1975, as reported in the *China News*, 27 October 1975. At the February 1973 Arizona State symposium on Taiwan, he had predicted a merger between the two Chinese regimes, as did Allen Whiting and one other speaker, but everyone else denied that.

7. Interview with Sidney Goldsmith at the U.S. embassy, Taipei, 6 August 1974. Goldsmith was a specialist for six years in Taiwan internal politics and praised Chiang Ching-kuo for "giving the Taiwanese more than they expected" although that antagonized some mainlanders but pleased those who thought the Taiwanese had been discriminated against in the past.

8. A. T. Steele, *The American People and China* (New York: McGraw-Hill, 1966), pp. 257–263. The full poll results are in the appendix from pp. 252–313. Steele cited no names of his informants.

9. Conversation with Leo Goodstadt, managing editor of the *Far Eastern Economic Review*, 27 August 1975, and many other reports such as the *New York Times* article by Fox Butterfield, formerly very critical of Taipei, extremely laudatory of Premier Chiang and the stability of Taiwan, 14 October 1975.

10. *Japan Times*, 5 June 1974. Kissinger has been enchanted by his visits to mainland China, causing Taipei and Chinese students in the United States to demand his removal from office.

11. Full results in "Gallup Study of Public Attitudes toward Nations of the World," August 1974, Gallup Organization, Princeton, New Jersey.

12. Results in report of the same title as footnote #11, published October 1975, by the Gallup Organization.

13. *China News*, 18 December 1975.

14. See the *China Report,* published by the Committee for a Free China, October and November issues, 1975.

15. Premier Chiang's views detailed in the *China News,* 18 September 1975. Members of the U.S. embassy in August 1975, thought the ROC did not mean that, but the writer agrees with Premier Chiang.

16. *China News,* 26 October 1975.

17. *Far Eastern Economic Review,* 2 May 1975, pp. 29–30. The 24 January 1975 issue had an article, "Coming to Terms with Two Chinas," which thought the U.S. mood would permit a switch of relations from Taipei to Peking—those writers did not know the Gallup or Congressional temper.

18. *Mainichi Daily News,* 6 July 1975.

19. *China News,* 17 December 1975. See also the excellent article by Bill Armbruster, an American free-lance writer in Taipei with whom the writer spoke at length in August 1975, "A Gust of Liberalism," in *Far Eastern Economic Review,* 17 October 1975, pp. 35–36.

20. The *New York Times,* 30 November 1975. Also see the article by Hung-Mao Tien, "Taiwan in Transition: Prospects for Socio-political Change," *China Quarterly,* December 1975, pp. 615–644, which approves many of the recent changes but expects more in the future.

21. Chinese Information Service release of 24 December 1975. The TV interview was on 22 December.

22. Joseph Lelyveld, "A One and a Half China Policy," *New York Times Magazine,* 6 April 1975, sec. 6, p. 32.

23. "Ticklish Taiwan," *New Republic,* March 1975, p. 7, by Professor Fairbank, usually considered pro-Peking.

24. Chinese Information Service release, 5 December 1975.

25. *Christian Science Monitor,* 16 December 1975.

26. The *New York Times,* 7 December 1975.

27. *Anchorage Alaska Times,* 3 December 1975.

28. Copley News Service, 28 December 1975, as reported by the Chinese Information Service release of 29 December 1975. Congressman Edward Derwinski called for Ford to fire Secretary Kissinger because of the Japan model idea, and Admiral Elmo Zumwalt made the same suggestion at a New York Rotary Club lunch at the Commodore Hotel on 8 January 1976, when he accused Kissinger of ignoring the National Security Council and concealing Soviet violations of the Salt I agreement. Zumwalt got a standing ovation. One of the writer's friends on the State Department Policy Planning Council said he knew of Kissinger's low image in Congress (interview in Washington 13 January 1976).

*Philippine-American Relations
under the "New Society"*

Robert L. Youngblood

On Sunday, December 7, 1975, thirty-four years to the day after the bombing of Pearl Harbor, the American television viewing public was treated to a glimpse of President Ford and Henry Kissinger relaxing aboard the Philippine presidential yacht during an outing to Corregidor Island where President Ford and President Marcos commemorated the valor and sacrifice of Philippine and American forces in World War II.[1] Although the wreath laying at the Fil-American war memorial was a solemn ceremony, most of the shots of the two presidential parties tended to emphasize the intimacy and gaiety of the occasion. In one pose Marcos and Ford, themselves World War II veterans, were side-by-side over a map at the yacht's rail gazing at what appeared to be the Bataan Peninsula in the distance, presumably recounting former battles and previous glories of their two closely allied nations,[2] while in another sequence, President Ford was shown obviously enjoying the tight embrace of a beautiful Filipina as they danced to the soft rhythmic beat of a tropical dance band. Panning in another direction, the camera caught Secretary of State Kissinger (with a button popped off his *barong tagalog*) laughing and bantering with President Marcos' attractive wife, Imelda, as they danced and alternately joked with nearby newsmen and guests.[3]

The Corregidor cruise capped in the words of Philippine Secretary of Foreign Affairs, Carlos P. Romulo, "the greatest reception given any American visitor" to the Philippine Islands,[4] evidently topping the tremendous welcome extended to Douglas MacArthur during his emotional farewell visit in 1961. President Marcos called the United States the Philippines' "strongest ally" and reaffirmed his belief that Manila and Washington would remain closely linked "for a long time to come"[5] and saw to it that President and Mrs. Ford were greeted by over a million cheering Filipinos during the hour it took their motorcade to traverse the seven and a half miles between the airport and

Malacañang Palace.[6] Yet even as Marcos was rolling out the red carpet and extending hospitality to the Fords as only the Filipinos know how to do, unresolved economic, military, and political problems confronting Philippine-American relations lurked in the background. To understand the meaning of the greeting organized for the American President, one must first examine the major issues in Philippine-American relations since Philippine independence in 1946, and then consider the current needs of President Marcos' martial law regime in post-Vietnam Asia.

II.

Despite the fact that every president of the Philippines has openly acclaimed relations with the United States as the cornerstone of the Republic's foreign policy and the fact that the Philippine Congress, until its dissolution in 1972, responded favorably on all key legislative measures affecting Philippine-American relations (see Table I), a number of foreign policy issues confronting Manila and Washington have remained unresolved throughout much of the postwar period. The first major irritant was the linking by the United States Congress of $620 million in rehabilitation aid to the Philippines' acceptance of a new trade act that would allow Americans the right to own and operate public utilities and to develop natural resources in the Republic on an equal footing with Filipino citizens. Many Filipinos were not only disappointed that the amount of rehabilitation assistance was about half of what they felt had been promised by President Roosevelt as "just compensation," but they were also unhappy over the fact that the Trade Act of 1946 would require an amendment to the 1935 Constitution.[7]

With Manila in ruin and the country almost totally dislocated economically, President Roxas believed that only the United States was in a position to provide the amount of aid necessary for immediate reconstruction.[8] And under pressure from him, the Philippine Congress, after two days of acrimonious debate, passed a resolution authorizing Roxas to enter into an executive agreement with the United States on trade by just barely the necessary two-thirds of those seated. Later in another close vote, the Congress proposed the necessary constitutional amendment on parity rights for Americans be submitted to the Filipino electorate by exactly three-fourths of those seated in the Senate and two more than three-fourths of the House members seated and voting (Table I).[9] Although the amendment was accepted by a margin of eight-to-one in the plebiscite (1,696,753 to 222,665), both congressional votes raised important constitutional questions because six Democratic Alliance congressmen from Central Luzon and another House member sympathetic to them from Bulacan along with three opposition Senators were denied their seats on questionable grounds by the Liberal Party congressional leadership.[10]

Rather than general jubilation at the outcome of the plebiscite, many Filipinos were critical of the terms of the Trade Act, which they thought were an infringement of Philippine sovereignty and would continue to keep the Republic economically dependent on the United States.[11] In addition to special privileges for American investors, the legislation pegged the peso to the dollar, established fixed quotas on a number of key Philippine products, and allowed the American President certain discretionary powers in imposing further restrictions on Philippine commodities that "are coming or likely to come into substantial competition with like articles which are the product of the United States."[12] While some short-term benefits accrued to the Philippines, the long-run effect of the agreement was to retain, according to Jenkins, "a quasicolonial character" in the economic relations between Manila and Washington by encouraging the re-emergence of economic overspecialization geared to preferences on the American market.[13] The pattern of dependence even after the Trade Act's revision in 1954 (the Laurel-Langley Agreement) remained substantially unbroken as reflected in the fact that in the 1969–1971 period the Philippines still sent 41 percent of her exports to and obtained 27 percent of her imports from the United States.[14]

During the war Manuel Quezon changed his mind about the stationing of American troops and the continuation of American bases in the Philippines after independence.[15] Accordingly, following Quezon's death in 1944, President Osmeña made it plain that the Philippine government welcomed the U.S. military on its soil, and the Congress in its first postwar session gave the President the authority to negotiate a bases agreement with the United States to insure "the territorial integrity of the Philippines, the mutual protection of the Philippines and the United States, and the maintenance of peace in the Pacific."[16] After a period of negotiations handled by Vice-President Quirino, Roxas signed the Military Bases Agreement with Ambassador McNutt on March 14, 1947.

The agreement gave the United States a ninety-nine year lease on twenty-three bases throughout the Philippines and liberal jurisdictional terms over all personnel on the bases (except in cases where offenses were against Philippine security and where both conflicting parties were Filipinos) and over Americans off the bases in conflict with one another, committing offenses against U.S. security, and on official government business.[17] Although the bases arrangement seemed acceptable to Filipinos at the time, it became (and still is) a focal point of Philippine dissatisfaction with United States policy toward the Republic. First, from a strategic perspective, a number of prominent Filipinos argued that the Bases Agreement gave America an Asian outpost to protect her own security and vital interests but provided no ironclad guarantee of military response should the Philippines be attacked. Concern over America's commitment to defend the Philippines, despite assurances of Secretary of State Dulles and other American officials, led the Filipinos to sign a Mutual Defense Treaty with Washington in 1951 and join the Southeast Asian Treaty Organization in 1954.[18] It is ironic, however, that during the Garcia administration (1957–1961) nationalists who had earlier been worried about a U.S. commitment to defend the Philippines were now concerned that the Bases Agreement and other military arrangements would act as a magnet, drawing the Republic into an American conflict that otherwise might be avoided.[19]

Ownership of the bases and a series of "incidents" in and around the reservations involving Filipinos and Americans generated even more intense feelings than the question of America's intention to defend the Republic in time of war. Following the conclusion of the NATO Status of Forces Agreement with America's European allies and a bases agreement with Japan, Filipinos felt they had received much less favorable terms from the United States, and as a result, became increasingly sensitive about the meaning of the Bases Agreement to Philippine sovereignty and about conflicts over jurisdictional interpretations of criminal offenses committed on and off the reservations involving both Filipinos and Americans.[20]

In this kind of an atmosphere, a ruling by Herbert Brownell, Eisenhower's Attorney General, that the United States held title to (in contrast to sovereignty over) the military bases created a furor in the local press and among Filipino nationalists.[21] Although this matter was clarified in favor of the Philippine position in a joint statement of then Vice-President Nixon and President Magsaysay in 1956, the criminal jurisdiction problems continued to nettle Philippine-American relations.[22] Two subsequent negotiation attempts, the Pelaez-Bendetsen Talks of 1956 and the Serrano-Bohlen Talks of 1958–1959, failed to resolve the question of criminal jurisdiction.[23]

Under the liberal terms of the Bases Agreement, United States military authorities routinely claimed legal authority in criminal cases, resulting in Filipino citizens being tried in American courts and allowing U.S. servicemen to remain beyond the reach of the Philippine judicial system. The continuation of these arrangements was necessary, according to American military officials, to maintain the high morale of the U.S. forces in the Philippines and to retain the absolute loyalty of the Negritos (who felt persecuted by the lowland Filipinos) guarding the reservations.[24] Filipinos countered by pointing out that the United States did not enjoy similar privileges in Europe and Japan and that such arguments not only denigrated the Philippine court system but were in effect a *de facto* infringement of Philippine sovereignty.

Statements from American military legal officers and statistics from the U.S. Department of Defense tend to support the Filipino contention that U.S. servicemen falling under Philippine legal authority have received fair treatment. Joseph Dodd found, for instance, that "although United States military authorities voiced objections to the slow judicial process, they made no complaints about the percentage of those tried who were convicted or the type of punishments administered."[25] An analysis of Defense Department figures shows that out of a total of 1031 criminal cases involving United States personnel in the Philippine courts between 1954 and 1964 jurisdiction was either waived or charges dropped 90 percent of the time and less than 6 percent of the cases came to trial. Less than half of those tried were convicted, with most paying fines and only seven being confined.[26] The United States was nevertheless slow in responding to Philippine desires for changes in the criminal jurisdiction provisions of the agreement. It was not until the Mendez-Blair Agreement of 1965 that the Philippines obtained greater judicial authority over American servicemen accused of violating Philippine laws.[27]

United States economic and military policies contributed to the rise of a nationalist sentiment that increasingly took on an anti-American coloration in the years just prior to the declaration of martial law. Rather than develop a bold and creative program for economic recovery and military self-sufficiency, American diplomacy responded to a motley array of U.S. interests, resulting in the restoration of prewar economic and military dependence.[28] Many Filipinos were disappointed—others outraged—at these developments, for they had expected better treatment for having remained steadfast against Japanese imperialism. It especially galled them that Japan received more postwar economic assistance from the United States and obtained greater control over American bases on Japanese soil.

An analysis of the background of the data presented in Table I reveals that while legislation crucial to relations with the United States passed, the voting patterns were frequently close and the accompanying debate often heated. In addition to deep dissatisfaction over the Bell Trade Act and the parity amendment of 1946, it took the Senate over a year to approve the SEATO Treaty (by one more than the necessary two-thirds of the then twenty-two seated senators) and the Congress fought off and on with both Presidents Macapagal and Marcos over the sending of Philippine troops (PHILCAG) to Vietnam.[29] It was only after four months of bitter fighting in a special congressional session called by President Marcos in 1966 that the Congress finally voted the 35 million pesos necessary to underwrite the dispatch of 2,000 "armed noncombatants" to the war zone.[30] In contrast, on issues of military assistance, U.S. guarantee to defend the Philippines, and the need to revise the Bell Trade Act (the Laurel-Langley Agreement), the Congress acted with relative dispatch and with little acrimony.

Two opinion surveys conducted in 1960 and 1968, respectively, revealed that even as Philippine legislators generally held the United States in high esteem, more than half of those interviewed in both time periods evinced dissatisfaction with Philippine-American relations.[31] Unsettled war claims, need for more economic assistance without strings attached, and taking the Philippines for granted were among the most frequently mentioned criticisms of the U.S. On the military bases issue, the lawmakers were firmly committed to retaining U.S. forces in the Republic, but in 1968 only 31 percent were "completely in favor" of keeping U.S. troops in contrast to 78 percent in 1960 who said they would be "against" a withdrawal of American forces.[32] The continual haggling over issues of criminal jurisdiction and the intense fight over PHILCAG undoubtedly made some inroads among the more conservative elements of the Congress.

TABLE I: PHILIPPINE CONGRESSIONAL VOTES ON LEGISLATION AFFECTING RP-U.S. RELATIONS SINCE INDEPENDENCE[a]

Legislation	House[b] Yes	No	Abstained/ Absent[c]	Senate[b] Yes	No	Abstained/ Absent[c]
Resolution on Philippine Trade Act, 1946	57	19	20	15	5	4
Parity Rights Amendment, 1946	68	18	2	16	5	—
Military Asst. Agreement, 1947	52	0	34	11	1	10
Bases Agreement (Treaty), 1947	(not applicable)			18	0	3
Quirino-Foster Agreement (Treaty), 1951	(not applicable)			20	—	3
Laurel-Langley Agreement, 1955	57	2	38	19	0	5
Manila Treaty (SEATO), 1955	(not applicable)			17	0	7
Philippine Forces to Vietnam (PHILCAG), 1966	(missing data)			15	8	1

[a]Source: Milton W. Meyer, *A Diplomatic History of the Philippine Republic* (Honolulu: University of Hawaii Press, 1965), passim; and *New York Times*, 4 June 1966, p. 5:5.

[b]The 1935 Constitution limited the membership of the House of Representatives to not more than 120 and fixed the Senate at 24. The normal House membership in the early postwar period was 96, but the figures in Meyer do not always add to that figure, probably due to unfilled seats and missing data.

[c]Abstained/Absent category includes seven House members and three Senators denied their seats by a Roxas administration majority in the Congress.

Concomitant with heightened criticism of America in Congress was a rise of nationalist sentiment in the 1960s against close economic and military links with the United States, which culminated in the years just prior to martial law in a series of protest demonstrations at Malaca-ñang Palace and the American Embassy. While the United States was often a convenient whipping boy for ills in Philippine society beyond its control, a long record of American insensitivity to issues of impor-tance to Filipinos and occasional embassy gaffes provided ample meat for the nationalists. For instance, when American embassy officials, presumably Ambassador William McCormick Blair, erroneously in-dicated in 1964 that two Filipinos had tried to bomb an elementary school at Clark Air Base during a period of jurisdictional dispute over an American serviceman charged with killing a Filipino scavenging for scrap metal on the base, reaction in the press and among nationalists was swift. Ambassador Blair was immediately given the sobriquet of "Blast Blair" and featured in a Manila newspaper comic strip, and a protest rally was organized in Angles City near Clark Air Base.[33]

Conflicts like the "Blast Blair" incident and the protest rallies of the late 1960s and early 1970s increasingly forced the last two occu-pants of Malacañang to alter their public statements on relations with the United States. Whereas Presidents Roxas, Quirino, and Magsaysay could emphasize the overwhelming significance of the American con-nection, President Macapagal, and to a greater extent President Mar-cos, began to stress that the Philippines was embarked on an independent foreign policy that would include a substantial readjust-ment in relations with America based on equal partnership and Philip-pine national interests.

III.

Spokesmen for Philippine foreign policy have been discussing at least since the administration of Elpidio Quirino the need for greater independence from the United States. In recent years in response to kaleidoscopic changes in domestic and international conditions, Car-los P. Romulo has stated that the Philippines is fully engaged in design-ing its own foreign policy in terms of Filipino needs and priorities.[34] In support of this argument, the Marcos administration can point to intensified Philippine participation in ASEAN affairs,[35] an active search for new friends and markets among the communist nations of Eastern Europe, and the recent establishment of diplomatic relations with the People's Republic of China, following a state visit by President Marcos in June 1975.[36] The Philippines can likewise point to a lower percent-age of total trade with the U.S. (76.1 percent in 1946–1949 vs. 37.4 percent in 1965–1969),[37] the termination of the Laurel-Langley Trade Agreement in 1974, and renewed demands for greater Filipino control over the U.S. military bases as further indications of growing independence in foreign policy matters.

The record clearly shows that the Philippines under Marcos' leadership has moved in a number of new directions on the international scene. Yet, with regard to relations with Washington, do these shifts represent measurable distance down the road toward independence from America? A close examination of Philippine activities in ASEAN indicates that increased consultation and calls for greater unity have yet to be matched by dramatic increases in trade with other members. Between 1963 and 1967, for example, the percentage of total Philippine trade with ASEAN countries rose only 1.1 percent, from 1.8 percent to 2.9 percent of total imports and exports.[38] Although this was a 61 percent increase in trade, the volume of trade hardly represents the emergence of a significant alternative to traditional trading patterns. And while percentage of total trade with the United States has dropped since independence, most of the slack has been picked up by Japan, America's major ally in East Asia, thus keeping the Philippines well within a U.S. dominated trading orbit.[39]

Opponents of the New Society, rather than hailing Marcos' recent visit to the People's Republic of China as a great diplomatic coup, have criticized it as a shallow grandstand performance.[40] Daniel Shirmer, in testimony before Senator Inouye's Subcommittee on Appropriations, suggested that Marcos' trip to Peking was a "game of appearances" instead of a clear indication of independence on the part of Manila.[41] To bolster his argument Shirmer quotes from 1949 cables between Myron Cowen, the American ambassador to the Philippines, and Secretary of State Dean Acheson in which Cowen argues that Philippine loyalty has earned it the right "to announce its decision regarding recognition" of Peking "in advance of" the United States "should it wish to do so," for to do otherwise would suggest the absence of true Filipino independence. Acheson reassured Cowen that the State Department was sensitive to the Philippines' desire to avoid the "appearance" of following American recognition, and, accordingly, would keep Manila "fully informed in advance" of any U.S. decision on recognition.[42] Since the State Department earlier indicated it had no objection to the Philippines establishing diplomatic relations with Peking first, perhaps, suggests Shirmer, this scenario has finally been completed.

Analysts even more critical of the Marcos regime than Shirmer argue that American businesses in the Philippines, strategically located to exploit trade with China, have for some time been in favor of formal ties between Manila and Peking.[43] A key industry dominated largely by American interests that could profit from trade with China is the oil industry. A 1971 report indicated, for example, that foreign-owned oil companies controlled 79.9 percent of the sales, 97.6 percent of the income, 86.5 percent of the assets and 96.2 percent of the equity of the industry as a whole.[44] Once refining capacity is adjusted to handle the high wax content of Chinese crude, assuming of course that Marcos can continue to obtain reasonably priced Chinese oil, American-owned oil firms stand to gain substantially from this trade.[45]

To be sure, the Marcos government is attempting to expand the Philippines' markets and diplomatic contacts in ways that were only half-heartedly put forth in past administrations. But put in the context of the totality of the relations of the Republic with the United States (and to a lesser extent Japan), official statements about the new independence of Philippine foreign policy represent more of a commitment to the future than an actual achievement in the present. Even in this commitment some analysts see the heavy hand of American influence, for Marcos, just as his predecessors, according to Lela Noble, views the American connection as a necessity, although greater independence from the United States would be desirable.[46]

Although President Marcos has taken a nationalist stance in indicating the need for a thorough re-examination of the economic and military agreements with the U.S., he has been equally firm in stressing the importance of good relations with Washington. Part of Marcos' ambivalence is rooted in the need to protect the good name of the Philippine credit card in Washington and New York, for a confidential Asian Development Bank report predicts that the country's trade deficit could increase to $1,146 million in 1976, requiring the additional borrowing abroad of $2.4 to $3.0 billion. With earlier loan payments falling due in 1976, it will not be easy, according to the Bank, to finance these deficits that are expected to reach 10 percent of the projected G.N.P.[47]

Signs of ambivalence on economic matters were also visible in the Philippines' reluctance to terminate completely its preferential treatment on the American market as the end of the Laurel-Langley Agreement drew near,[48] and more recently in Manila's call for duty free treatment of certain products not covered under a generalized system of preferences passed by the U.S. Congress.[49] Evidently Marcos pushed his desire for preferential tariff treatment of important Philippine commodities such as coconut oil and mahogany during President Ford's visit, because their joint communiqué indicated a new trade agreement would be negotiated "to enhance economic cooperation between the two countries."[50]

Nationalist charges that the Philippines was rapidly becoming an economic neo-colony of America were swept aside by Marcos after the declaration of martial law as he moved swiftly to muzzle anti-American Filipino nationalism, to assure American investors their interests were safe, and to encourage greater investment by American corporations. Marcos also overturned a number of nationalist Supreme Court decisions that were detrimental to American corporate interests, and reversed all of the anti-American proposals before the Constitutional Convention in favor of American companies.[51] Backed by the advice of a group of American trained technocrats, the President chose to stake the future of Philippine economic development on massive infusions of American and other foreign investments.

The reaction of the American business community was overwhelmingly favorable, and has since September 22, 1972, been backed up by substantial amounts of additional investment in the Philippines.[52] Where estimates of total U.S. investment in the Republic ranged from $800 million to $1 billion in 1972, the figure is estimated close to $3 billion at the present time, representing roughly a 200 percent increase over the past three years.[53] This hardly matches the Marcos regime's rhetoric of increased self-reliance and greater economic independence from the United States.

But put in the context of the kind of American economic influence prior to martial law, this new infusion of American capital is even more ominous from a nationalist perspective. For instance, 39.7 percent of the total equity capital of the nine hundred largest corporations in 1970 was held by foreign investors, of which 80 percent were Americans, giving them "approximately one-third of all the total equity capital of the 900 largest corporations in the Philippines."[54] The American share of foreign investment in the Philippines, according to recent reports, continues to remain at the 80 percent level.[55] Much of the U.S. foreign investment is linked to huge multinational corporations and concentrated in key sectors of the economy such as oil, automobile production, banking, and communications. As former Senator Salonga pointed out in a 1974 speech, ten of the world's top corporations are firmly entrenched in the Philippine economy.[56]

The magnitude and kind of American investment in the Republic raises serious questions as to the government's ability to control its economic future. Two examples of the overpowering influence of American corporations in the Philippines are the oil industry and banking institutions. Claiming falling profits, the oil corporations, which are 80 percent American owned, were able to obtain three major price increases from the Marcos Administration in less than a thirty-six month period just prior to martial law, despite widespread nationalist opposition and a carefully documented report by a Senate committee chaired by Jose Diokno demonstrating that the oil industry had engaged in overpricing at each stage of production right down to local distribution.[57] Since martial law, President Marcos has decreed legislation offering attractive terms for foreign participation in oil exploration, a step that has received a positive response from the industry.[58]

The profile of American financial institutions, while large in the pre-martial law period, has increased dramatically since a 1973 decree requiring commercial banks to increase their capitalization to at least 100 million pesos and allowing for the first time foreign capital participation in those banks. The result has been a flurry of mergers that critics contend represent little more than thinly veiled foreign takeovers.[59] So far seven American banks, including Chase Manhattan, Morgan Trust, Citicorp, and Bank of America, have become part-owners (as have other foreign banks) of well known commercial banks, such as the Bank of Asia, the Traders Bank, the Bank of the Philippine Islands, and the Commercial Bank & Trust.[60] In light of foreign banks' past performance of serving the interests of global enterprises at the expense of local entrepreneurs and investors, these new mergers clearly have the potential for more rather than less American influence on Malacañang.[61]

President Marcos has other reasons for demonstrating flexibility in calling for a readjustment of economic relations with the United States. First, it is estimated that half of the Philippine national debt is underwritten by the United States, and American controlled or backed financial institutions continue to be a major source of credit for the struggling Philippine economy.[62] Second, as Table II indicates, the United States' economic assistance has continued to remain high since martial law, and in the case of certain kinds of U.S. government expenditures, increased markedly since 1972. Given the projected deficit levels for fiscal 1976, it is absolutely essential to the Marcos government that these expenditures remain at least at their present level.

As a further sign of the Philippines' growing independence from the United States, officials of the New Society like to point to statements indicating that President Marcos is demanding significant concessions from the U.S. for continued use of the military bases in the Philippines. Among the changes mentioned are provisions for more Filipino supervision of the 15,000 American troops stationed there, the payment of rents, the conversion of portions of the reservations for commercial activities, and an expansion of Philippine sovereignty over base activities presently under exclusive American jurisdiction.[63]

Encouraged by statements from officials in Washington, including President Ford himself, that the bases are vital to a U.S. defense posture in the Western Pacific, a number of Filipinos feel Marcos is in an ideal bargaining position for obtaining what he wants.[64] Yet a careful analysis of Marcos' statements over the past year suggests a shrewd balance between demanding concessions, presumably to satisfy latent nationalist opinion, and reaffirming support for continued American presence in the Republic.

Just prior to Marcos' Peking visit, for example, reportedly as a result of a slow evolution toward nonalignment, displeasure over American criticism of martial law, and recent U.S. reverses in Cambodia, Marcos requested a thorough renegotiation of the security ar-

TABLE II: U.S. GOVERNMENT EXPENDITURES AND ECONOMIC ASSISTANCE
TO THE PHILIPPINES, 1966-1976[a] (in millions of dollars)

Year	U.S. Government Expenditures to the Philippines[b]	U.S. Economic Assistance to the Philippines[c]
1966	121	—
1967	181	—
1968	182	—
1969	147	—
1970	130	25.1
1971	150	40.5
1972	203	63.4
1973	241	124.0
1974	259	63.1
1975	—	58.4
1976	—	41.5

[a] Sources: FFP Washington Report, Vol. Nos. 9 and 10, October and November, 1975.
[b] These calendar year figures include "military base expenditures, non-military base expenditures such as Special Forces, Civic Action Teams, Special Investigation Teams, and U.S. civilian expenditures such as the diplomatic mission" but not "MAP (Military Assistance Program) grants or loans, salaries or U.S. personnel not spent in the Philippines, and contracts for goods and services to suppliers outside of the Philippines." Originally compiled by the Philippine Central Bank, Manila.
[c] These fiscal year figures include monies from AID loans and grants, PL 480, Title I and II, and Peace Corps funds.

rangements with the United States.[65] He went out of his way at the same time to emphasize that "the Philippines needs the United States," and upon returning from China, underscored that any security negotiations "should not be construed as an effort to diminish" the historic relationship the Philippines has enjoyed with America.[66] And although Manila placed restrictions on refugees entering the American bases in transit to the U.S. after the collapse of the Saigon government, forcing the United States to locate its forward refugee centers on Guam and Wake, President Marcos nevertheless reaffirmed the Philippine-American alliance during Ford's visit in December 1975.

It is also interesting to note that while President Marcos, in conjunction with Prime Minister Kukrit of Thailand, pushed for the termination of SEATO, indicating in the process the "temporary character" of the American bases in the region, neither leader wanted to drop the Pacific Charter, a document appended to the 1954 agreement that calls for "common action to maintain peace and security in Southeast Asia and the Southwest Pacific."[67]

A number of informed observers feel that while part of Marcos' demands for renegotiation of the Bases Agreement is aimed at placating nationalist sentiment, the President is primarily concerned in the wake of the U.S. debacle in Vietnam about the dependability of an American defense commitment and about obtaining rental payments to offset monetary deficits brought on by the rise in oil prices, a lessening of demand for Philippine products on the world market, and the widening Muslim war in the South.[68] Others see continued American support as necessary for Marcos to remain in power, and the monetary payments for the bases as a way for the Philippine military to purchase more sophisticated and deadly arms in the U.S. than they are currently receiving under the military assistance program.[69]

Although Washington will doubtless agree to make some adjustments to the Philippines on the bases issue, American officials reportedly feel the Marcos regime needs the bases more than the United States does, and in spite of the New Society rhetoric of military independence, fundamental aspects of the Bases Agreement will remain intact.[70] Also, despite assertions as to the importance of the bases to the U.S. defense posture in the region, Manila is undoubtedly aware of pressure from anti-martial law groups to abandon them and U.S. moves to acquire a new territory in the Marianas considered crucial by the Department of Defense.[71] Accordingly, top advisors to President Ford have indicated the U.S. is unwilling to meet all of the Philippines' demands but that America is prepared to give Marcos "a cosmetic form of sovereignty that would improve his standing among third-world nations of Asia."[72]

Regardless of whether Marcos obtains the concessions he desires from the United States in the present bases negotiations, most of the empirical data indicates greater reliance on the U.S., rather than less, since the inauguration of the New Society. This can be dramatically demonstrated by comparing American military aid to the Philippines in the three years before and the three years after the declaration of martial law (Table III). These figures are backed up by a spirit of close cooperation between the U.S. and Philippine military establishments, reaching from the colonial era through World War II and the Huk campaigns down to the present.[73] In recent months, for example, the Philippine military has attacked Filipino critics of the United States as

TABLE III: U. S. MILITARY ASSISTANCE BEFORE AND AFTER MARTIAL LAW
(in millions of dollars)

	Fiscal Years 1970–1972	Fiscal Years 1973–1975
MAP	43.9	51.7
FMS	—	15.6
Excess Defense	7.2	21.8
Ship Transfers	1.8	22.8
MAAG	4.4	4.9
Training	2.9	1.9
TOTAL	60.2	118.7

Source: The National Coordinating Committee of the Anti-Martial Law (Philippines) Movement, "The Logistics of Repression," *Philippines Information Bulletin*, 3 (July 1975), p. 5.

"left-wingers" around the President,[74] while the commander of the United States Military Advisory Group denounced as "inaccurate and baseless" Associated Press reports that uninterrupted American military aid hinged on the outcome of the bases negotiations now under way.[75]

The lavishness of the welcome organized for President Ford was undoubtedly also related to the sagging image of the Marcos regime in Washington. Since September 1972, the Marcos government has been besieged by a proliferation of anti-martial law organizations and publications in the United States and by a growing number of clergymen and scholars familiar with the political abuses and program failures of the regime testifying before various committees of the U.S. Congress. In the beginning, buoyed by almost a $1 billion trade surplus due to high prices for Philippine commodities on the world market, Marcos could afford to ignore the activities of these protest groups, who were often forced to count their victories in terms of signatures on petitions and the number of times Imelda was unable to see the American president during her frequent visits to Washington.[76] Yet in time the cumulative impact of the anti-martial law forces began to be felt in hearings before the U.S. Congress in the summer and fall of 1975 and contributed to the passage of the Abourezk-McGovern amendment to a $3 billion foreign aid authorization bill. The effect of the amendment would be to curtail aid to repressive regimes that consistently violate human rights, and among the nations singled out by Senator McGovern during the debate on the floor was the Philippines.[77]

A key figure in the hearings was Primitivo Mijares, a former high ranking official in the Marcos government, who sought political asylum in the United States in February 1975. Before his defection Mijares was an advisor to the President, chairman of the Media Advisory Council, a columnist for the *Daily Express,* and president of the National Press Club in 1973–74.[78] Because of these and other activities, he reportedly had twenty-four hour access to Malacañang, and was in a position to know the decision-making process in the inner chambers of the Presidential Palace. Thus Mijares' claims that he assisted Governor Benjamin Romualdez, the brother-in-law of Marcos, rig two national referendums in 1973, and that the government was becoming more corrupt and repressive were very damaging, especially since they substantiated long-standing charges by anti-martial law forces both in and outside of the Philippines.[79]

The veracity of Mijares' statements and the extent to which Marcos is willing to go to protect Manila's good name in Washington were underscored by alleged attempts to keep Mijares from testifying on human rights violations in the Philippines before a House subcommittee chaired by Congressman Donald Fraser. Two days before the scheduled hearing, Marcos reportedly telephoned to ask Mijares not to testify, and later through an aide, offered a $50,000 bribe for his silence.[80] Documents uncovered by *Washington Post* columnist Jack Anderson showed that the "money actually was deposited in a San Francisco branch of Lloyds Bank of California in the names of Primitivo Mijares and Ambassador Trinidad Alconcel, the Philippines' consul general" on June 17, 1975.[81] Mijares could not withdraw the money without the countersignature of Alconcel, and the Ambassador had Mijares' name removed from the account the day after he testified, June 18th.[82] Later Mijares was allegedly offered $100,000 to retract his testimony, repudiate the Anderson articles, and leave for Australia.[83]

In a long telegram to Anderson, President Marcos countered that the $50,000 was seed money for Mijares to start a newspaper in California and payment for information that Mijares had obtained about an alleged assassination plot by Philippine exiles and CIA agents.[84] He further pointed out that the traceable bank transactions of Ambassador Alconcel were evidence against the bribery charge and stated that the $100,000 was an attempt on the part of Mijares, according to information he had obtained from his top aide Dr. Guillermo de Vega, at "plain and simple blackmail."[85] Mijares responded by challenging Alconcel and others involved in the case to waive their diplomatic immunity and join him in taking a polygraph test and testifying before Congress. The offer was rebuffed "on principle" by the Philippine Embassy.[86]

Regardless of where the truth lies in this sordid affair, it did nothing to improve Marcos' image in the United States and may have had a decisive effect on the passage of the Abourezk-McGovern amendment. Given the current economic and social problems in the Philippines, the Marcos government can ill afford a drastic curtailment of American economic and military assistance. With ongoing Muslim conflicts, a rising military budget, and a growing trade deficit, assistance from the U.S. is essential at least for the near future.

IV.

While every American president visiting the Philippines has received a warm *official* reception, none has been welcomed as extravagantly as President Ford. Part of the warmth and intimacy of the visit is clearly attributable to the long-standing good relations between Manila and Washington and a Philippine cultural imperative to spare little in entertaining an honored guest. Yet the lavishness of the reception for President Ford went beyond a simple reaffirmation of ties with the United States and a routine expression of the Filipinos' highly developed sense of hospitality. Why? Primarily because the Philippines, despite the expiration of the Laurel-Langley Trade Agreement and the termination of SEATO, is more dependent economically and militarily on the United States now than it was in the years immediately preceding the declaration of martial law. Figures show American investment and economic and military aid have increased substantially during the past three years, and the Philippine government continues to seek additional credit and improved trade concessions in the United States.

At least one analyst has argued that independence in Philippine foreign policy has usually meant taking forthright action within an Asian context without tampering with the fundamentals of relations with the United States.[87] Certainly the rhetoric of Manila's independent foreign policy has yet to be matched with significant substantive achievements in weakening the Philippines' dependence on America. But at the same time it is a mistake to assume that the search for new markets in Eastern Europe and increased diplomatic activity in Asia are not honest attempts to readjust Philippine international relations in a post-Vietnam Asia. Filipinos for some time have wanted an independent foreign policy, and, indeed, much of the nationalist turbulence of the late 1960s and early 1970s was aimed at attaining that goal. The dilemma facing policy-makers in Manila is whether the Republic can achieve an independent foreign policy within the context of greater reliance on the United States.

It is equally shortsighted for the United States to think that "cosmetic" adjustments to the Military Bases Agreement will more than temporarily satisfy the Philippines although Manila undoubtedly can be brought to terms if it wants American aid and investment to continue unimpeded. The future of good Philippine-American relations, however, will depend in large measure on the ability of decision-makers in Washington making substantive concession on questions of Philippine sovereignty and honestly assisting the Philippines in its quest for true independence. To do less will not only be interpreted as a sign of heavy-handed neo-colonial manipulation by nationalists and the radical left but also as an indication of perennial American ingratitude for steadfast Filipino loyalty and friendship by more moderate elements within the society.

*Portions of this paper originally appeared in my paper "Public Attitudes and Philippine Foreign Policy," presented at the annual meeting of the Western Conference of the Association for Asian Studies, Boulder, Colorado, 10–11 October 1975.

1. CBS Evening News with Dan Rather, 7 December 1975.

2. President Marcos is the Philippines' most decorated hero of World War II. A favorable account of his many exploits against the Japanese is contained in Hartzell Spence's biography, *Marcos of the Philippines* (New York: The World Publishing Company, 1969).

3. The good natured repartee between the Philippine First Lady and Secretary Kissinger is captured in "Kissinger a Racist? Ask FL," *The Manila Journal,* 14–20 December 1975, pp. 1, 16.

4. The *Phoenix Gazette,* 6 December 1975.

5. Ibid.

6. Ibid.

7. Milton W. Meyer, *A Diplomatic History of the Philippine Republic* (Honolulu: The University of Hawaii Press, 1965), p. 9.

8. U.S. Department of State, Public Services Division, "The Philippines, 1954," *Background* (Washington, D.C.: U.S. Government Printing Office, 1954), p. 5, and Meyer, op. cit., p. 3.

9. Meyer, op. cit., pp. 14, 50.

10. A. V. H. Hartendorp, *History of Industry and Trade of the Philippines,* Vol. 1 (Manila: American Chamber of Commerce of the Philippines, Inc., 1958), p. 229, and Benedict J. Kerkvliet, "Elite Resistance to Local Initiatives for Political Change: Central Luzon in the 1940s," a paper prepared for the Western Conference of the Association for Asian Studies, Boulder, Colorado, 10–11 October 1975, pp. 29–30.

11. For the Filipino reaction to the trade legislation, consult Shirley Jenkins, *American Economic Policy Toward the Philippines* (Stanford, California: Stanford University Press, 1954), Chap. 7.

12. Philippine Trade Act of 1946 (Chapter 244, Public Law No. 371, Title V, Section 504), cited in ibid., p. 66.

13. Jenkins, op. cit., pp. 64–66.

14. Donald Sherk, "Post-Vietnam Asia," *Pacific Community* 2 (January 1974), p. 245, cited in Mark Selden, "American Global Enterprise and Asia," *Bulletin of Concerned Asian Scholars* (April–June 1975), p. 22.

15. Joseph W. Dodd, *Criminal Jurisdiction Under the United States-Philippine Military Bases Agreement* (The Hague: Martinus Nijhoff, 1968), pp. 22–24.

16. Republic of the Philippines, *Official Gazette,* XLI:8 (November 1945), 952, cited in Meyer, op. cit., p. 16.

17. A detailed analysis of the jurisdictional terms of the Bases Agreement is contained in Dodd, op. cit.

18. Russell H. Fifield, *The Diplomacy of Southeast Asia 1945–1958* (New York: Harper & Row, Inc., 1958), Chap. 4.

19. George E. Taylor, *The Philippines and the United States: Problems of Partnership* (New York: Frederick A. Praeger, Inc., 1964), p. 242.

20. Dodd, op. cit., p. 51.

21. Ibid., pp. 86–88, and Meyer, op. cit., pp. 173–181.

22. Republic of the Philippines, Department of Foreign Affairs, "The Military

Bases Renegotiation Talks: Joint Statement of President Ramon Magsaysay and U.S. Vice-President Richard Nixon," *Department of Foreign Affairs Review* II (August 1956), 53.

23. Dodd, op. cit., pp. 88–100.

24. Dodd, op. cit., Chap. 4. It should be pointed out that very few Filipinos have in fact been tried in the American courts. Also it is ironic that although the criminal jurisdiction question has been a major irritant in RP-U.S. relations, American military authorities have claimed that the " 'exercise of jurisdiction by Philippine authorities over our personnel has favorably affected the morale and discipline of our forces.' " p. 54.

25. Ibid., p. 53.

26. Computed from U. S. Department of Defense figures contained in ibid., p. 52.

27. Ibid., pp. 100–123.

28. Taylor, op. cit., pp. 114–115.

29. Meyer, op. cit., p.238, and Diosdado Macapagal, *A Stone for the Edifice* (Quezon City: Mac Publishing House, 1968), p. 336.

30. *New York Times,* 4 June 1966, p. 5:5, and David Wurfel, "The Philippines: Intensified Dialog," *Asian Survey,* 7 (January 1967), 46.

31. Lloyd A. Free, *A Compilation of Attitudes of Philippine Legislators* (Princeton, N.J.: The Institute for International Social Research, 1966), and *International Attitudes in Four Asian Democracies* (Princeton, N.J.: The Institute for International Social Research, 1969).

32. Some of the difference in the response patterns in the two surveys may be due to the difference in the wording of the bases question in 1960 and 1968. Another 32 percent in 1968 said "There are arguments for and against but, on balance, I am in favor."

33. Martin Meadows, "Recent Developments in Philippine-American Relations: A Case Study in Emergent Nationalism," *Asian Survey* V (June 1965), pp. 312–314.

34. Carlos P. Romulo, "Philippine Foreign Policy under the New Society," *The Fookien Times Yearbook, 1974,* pp. 72, 76–77.

35. *Far Eastern Economic Review,* 21 November 1975, p. 51.

36. *New York Times,* 10 June 1975, p. 3.

37. Computed from The Center for Strategic and International Studies, *U.S.-Philippines Economic Relations,* Special Report Series: No. 12 (Washington, D.C.: Georgetown University, 1971), Table 7, p. 57.

38. Computed from Estrella D. Solidum, *Towards a Southeast Asian Community* (Quezon City: University of the Philippines Press, 1974), Table XI, pp. 164–165.

39. Mark Selden, op. cit., p. 22.

40. Senator Jovito R. Salonga, "The Need for Enlightenment on RP's Policy Towards China," excerpts from a speech given to the Rotary Club of Cubao, Quezon City, *The Philippine Times,* 1–15 October and 16–31 October 1975.

41. Testimony cited in *The Philippine Times,* 16–30 September 1975, p. 5.

42. Ibid.

43. William J. Pomeroy, *An American Made Tragedy, Neo-Colonialism & Dictatorship in the Philippines* (New York: International Publishers Co., Inc., 1974), p. 66.

44. Corporate Information Center of the National Council of Churches of Christ in the U.S.A., *The Philippines: American Corporations, Martial Law, and Underdevelopment* (New York: IDOC-North America, Inc., 1973), p. 58.

45. *The Philippine Times,* 16–31 December 1974, p. 4.

46. Lela G. Noble, "The National Interest and the National Image: Philippine Policy in Asia," *Asian Survey,* 13 (June 1973), 560–576.

47. *The Philippine Times,* 1–15 January 1976, p. 3.

48. U.S.-Philippines Economic Relations, op. cit., pp. 115–116.

49. *The Philippine Times,* 1–15 June 1975, pp. 2, 14.

50. *The Philippine Times,* 16–31 December 1975, p. 8.

51. *The Philippines: American Corporations, Martial Law, and Underdevelopment,* op. cit., p. 30.

52. Peter R. Kann, "Philippines Without Democracy," *Foreign Affairs*, 52 (April 1974), 612–632.

53. *The Philippines: American Corporations, Martial Law, and Underdevelopment*, op. cit., p. 11, and *The Philippine Times*, 16–31 August 1975, p. 8.

54. *The Philippines: American Corporations, Martial Law, and Underdevelopment*, op. cit., p. 11.

55. *The Philippine Times*, 16–31 August 1975, p. 8.

56. Senator Jovito R. Salonga, "Multinational Corporations and National Development," a lecture delivered at the Institute of Social Work and Community Development, University of the Philippines, Diliman, Quezon City, 20 September 1974, reprinted in *The Philippine Times*, 1–15 March 1975, p. 6.

57. Robert B. Stauffer, "The Political Economy of a Coup: Transnational Linkages and Philippine Political Response," *Journal of Peace Research* 10 (1974), p. 167.

58. *The Philippines: American Corporations, Martial Law, and Underdevelopment*, op. cit., pp. 58–60.

59. Mark Selden, op. cit., p. 29.

60. Ibid., and Salonga, "Multinational Corporations," and *The Philippine Times*, 1–15 March 1975, p. 20.

61. Mark Selden, op. cit., p. 29, and Salvador Araneta, "A Re-Examination of Policies Governing Philippine American Relations," in *American Policies as They Affect Philippine Economy*. Report No. 18, Institute of Economic Studies and Social Action, Araneta University, January 1967, pp. 31–53.

62. Mark Selden, op. cit., p. 29.

63. *New York Times*, 7 December 1975, and Terry J. O'Rear, "U.S. Bases in the Philippines: Are They Leaving Or Is Their Rent Increasing?" *Pahayag* 29 (May 1975, pp. 2–5.

64. *The Manila Journal*, 7–13 December 1975, p. 4.

65. *The Philippine Times*, 1–15 May and 1–15 June 1975, passim.

66. *The Philippine Times*, 1–15 July, p. 2. Reprinted from the Philippine Airline Press Service, the Philippine Consulate General in Chicago and the Philippine News Agency (PNA).

67. *The Philippine Times*, 1–15 August, p. 19.

68. Sheldon W. Simon, "The Problems of Asian Security with a Communist Indochina," *International Perspectives* (July-August 1975), O'Rear, op. cit., and *The Philippine Times*, 1–15 May 1975, p. 16.

69. The National Coordinating Committee of the Anti-Martial Law (Philippines) Movement, "The Logistics of Repression," *Philippines Information Bulletin* 3 (July 1975), passim.

70. *The Philippine Times*, 1–15 May 1975, p. 16.

71. Michael P. Onorato, "Lose a War, Gain a Colony: Vietnam, The United States, and the Commonwealth of the Northern Marianas," a paper delivered at the annual meeting of the Western Conference of the Association for Asian Studies, Boulder, Colorado, 10–11 October 1975.

72. *New York Times*, 7 December 1975, p. 25.

73. For a personal account of an American officer who assisted Ramon Magsaysay in the Huk campaigns in the 1950s, see Edward G. Landsdale, *In the Midst of Wars* (New York: Harper & Row, Publishers, 1972).

74. *The Philippine Times*, 1–15 January 1975, pp. 8, 10.

75. *The Philippine Times*, 1–15 December 1975, p. 21.

76. *The Philippine Times*, 1–15 February 1975, p. 4.

77. Serverina Rivera, "Human Rights Victory," *FFP Washington Report*, 1 (November 1975), 1–2, and *The Philippine Times*, 16–30 November 1975, pp. 1, 26–27.

78. *The Philippine Times*, 1–15 March 1975, pp. 1, 11, and 1–15 July 1975, pp. 8, 18.

79. Ibid.

80. Jack Anderson, "Marcos Made an Offer That His Former Aide Refused," *The Washington Post,* 2 July 1975, reprinted in *The Philippine Times,* 16–31 July 1975, p. 5.

81. Ibid.

82. Ibid.

83. Two additional Jack Anderson articles are reprinted in *The Philippine Times,* 1–15 August 1975, pp. 5, 20.

84. Ibid., p. 5.

85. Ibid.

86. Ibid., p. 20.

87. Noble, op. cit., pp. 572–573.

Discussion

SIMON: Professor Park documents and analyzes Japan's shift toward Korea between 1929 and 1975, in effect, delineating three separate orientations, coming full circle to the present time. Somewhat paradoxically, in the aftermath of the Indochina War, instead of attempting to withdraw from the American relationship, Japan has actually urged the United States on to a closer security role in Northeast Asia, and has promised a greater Japanese contribution to that role within the parameters of the Japanese constitution.

At this time and for the foreseeable future, I would contend that neither Japan, the United States, the PRC, nor the U.S.S.R. is interested in seeing any change in the status quo on the Korean peninsula, because of the unpredictability of a unified Korea in Northeast Asia, and perhaps more importantly because short-range reunification could only come about through revolution and/or war. If such an event would transpire, there would be intense pressure on both the Soviet Union and China to become involved in order to pre-empt the other. Hence the possibility of a Sino-Soviet war, which is a confrontation that all four powers in Northeast Asia want to avoid.

Regarding Professor Mendel's presentation, the one comment that I have has to do with the likelihood of the maintenance of the status quo on Taiwan. My own projection would be as follows: for the foreseeable future, indeed I would go on to say indefinitely, the status quo might well be maintained as long as each actor sticks to the 1972 communiqué, that all Chinese on both sides of the straits would agree that Taiwan is a part of China. However, if in the future a Republic of Taiwan were declared, then problems would arise, because the PRC would be faced with an international law situation in which, if it did not do anything, it would in effect recognize the independence, the non-PRC nature of the island. The United States, however, would have the option of withdrawing its security protection from Taiwan, because this security relationship was signed with the Republic of China and not the Republic of Taiwan. Hence I would maintain that if the policy is to maintain an independent Taiwan, the best thing to do is to do nothing.

Moving on to Professor Youngblood's presentation, it strikes me that President Marcos is trying to pursue what may be contradictory goals. On the one hand he is pursuing political nationalism and Southeast Asian regionalism (through the Association of Southeast Asian Nations), and on the other hand he justifies martial law by the improvement of economic conditions within the Philippines. I notice here a parallel with what Mrs. Gandhi is trying to do in India right now—justifying the state of emergency through the better living conditions of the Indian population. The realization of economic growth is premised, as Professor Youngblood points out, on the maintenance of U.S. bases for employment, and on American and Japanese capital for industrial growth. The U.S. desires, vis-à-vis the Philippines, can probably be summed up in four different categories. One is the maintenance of the Philippines' independence, insofar as that would be threatened by an outside aggressor. But if one looks at the situation in the Philippines, there is no outside aggressor about to threaten their independence. The second U.S. goal is the strengthening of ASEAN. Insofar as that is accomplished, the U.S. role within Southeast Asia would be, and I think should be, reduced. The third U.S. interest is, of course, access to trade and investment. The fourth I think is a temporary one—that is the maintenance of military bases on Subic and Clark, but only probably for another five or ten years until mid-Pacific locations are fully ready, after which, access to locations in Southeast Asia and perhaps even Northeast Asia would be required by U.S. military planners only on an emergency basis.

MENDEL: I agree with my friend Sheldon Simon that it would be best for the immediate future to retain the status quo in Taiwan, although a friend of mine in the Consulate in Hong Kong thought it would be desirable, before the U.S. embassies switched to Peking, to switch the name of the government in Taipei. That would be extremely difficult, at least until the mainland political instability and post-Mao succession problem is clearer. Also Peking would be very much annoyed if Taipei tried to make a separatist movement. I have studied public opinion in Japan and it does not favor U.S. defense of South Korea in the event of a North Korean attack. This is a reflection of Japanese hostility toward the use of violence in any form whether it is left-wing violence of students or whether it is any sort of terrorism or assassination.

PORTER: There seems to be some very large lessons growing out of the American experience in Vietnam, Laos and Cambodia that have been shortchanged in this conference. This is a reassessment of America's role in Asia. Surely, the twenty to twenty-five years of America being in Vietnam, and the sacrifice of some 50,000 American lives, $180,000,000,000 and 1,500,000 Vietnamese should have more impact than has been reflected in the discussion thus far. I would like to briefly raise a couple of points in this regard. One is that the old nostrums, the old conventional wisdom about American security has collapsed around us in Indochina and in the Far East generally. We have always been told that the United States security interests in this part of the world are based on the need for access to the trade, investment, raw materials, etc. We have always been told that one danger the U.S. faces is being isolated from the countries of the area, that we will be cut off from fruitful intercourse in these countries, and thereby we will withdraw further into a shell. Now we suddenly find that we have been defeated in our efforts to maintain the kind of government we wanted to maintain in the three capitals of Indochina. In the case of both Cambodia and Vietnam, we are intentionally isolating ourselves. But both of these governments, particularly Vietnam, are willing to have relationships with the U.S. The U.S. now is taking the position that we want to let the dust settle, or that we want to make demands on these governments to meet U.S. conditions for their policies before we will have any kind of trade or normal relations with them. As I mentioned before, the Vietnamese are particularly interested in economic relationships with the U.S., and the U.S. could have a very significant economic role in that part of the world. What I am pointing to here is that the old rationalization for American political military intervention in the Far East turns out to be devoid of any real meaning at all; it was a hoax. One of the lessons of our involvement in that part of the world should be to be very careful about taking seriously what our leaders tell us about why we must continue to support one government over another, and why we must have security ties, etc.

The second point is something with which my paper dealt. One of the lessons of Vietnam, Cambodia and Laos surely is that the U.S. cannot continue to support elites in such a way that is against the interests and aspirations of the vast majority of the people in those countries, without almost (and certainly in the long run) being defeated and coming to grief. There were statistics this morning about South Korea that I have never heard and that I find astounding, such as the number of school children who have to go without lunch. This is just one small indication of the kind of thing that we have to make the basis for American foreign policy. This gets back to the main theme of whether American definitions of security in the past have worked. Basing the policy on the concept of security, which is based on the idea of the U.S. maximizing its power in a particular part of the world, is going to fail. The U.S. is going to be defeated again and again—in Thailand, the Philippines, in Indonesia, and in South Korea—unless we base our policy primarily and fundamentally on the economic, social interests, and aspirations of those people for a better life.

SIMON: I was very pleased to hear Mr. Porter's statement because it seems to me it begins to create the kind of dialogue that I was a little concerned about yesterday when I chaired the afternoon's panel. One of the things that we as scholars and observers have to begin to do is ask ourselves what is the future of America's relations with the new states of Indochina and with the Democratic People's Republic of

Korea. What are the roles these States are going to play in the region? How may the U.S. engage with them in a mutually beneficial fashion? It is these kinds of questions that are absolutely crucial to the future of the politics of the region, and American foreign policy in Asia. Insofar as we engage in the old polemics and the old perspectives, either the perspective of the old right or new left, it seems to me we are not really shedding very much light on these kinds of questions. I welcome Mr. Porter's statements. I think he is absolutely right, and I would hope that at some future conference we could direct ourselves more closely to it.

TOTTEN: I was very glad to hear Sheldon Simon say this because actually in his comments he said that he could not see merit in the discussion of the unification of Korea. This whole panel more or less took the position that there is really nothing to be done. An example is Professor Robinson's position that actually the Chinese, in spite of the fact of what they say, prefer to have American troops in South Korea. Then Doug Mendel mentioned that we better not do anything about Taiwan at the present time. We have not really looked toward the future very much. Since this conference is a reassessment of what American policy is, we must be looking further ahead than just a few years. We should look to the next twenty-five years to see what kind of a world we want, and what we can do at the present time that will bring that kind of a world together. Professor Kaufmann's paper was a very good analysis in many ways, a very excellent piece of work, but really it just comes out to be a Russian attempt to isolate China and try to persuade the U.S. to go along with that—a very short-range kind of thing. It just hinted that if the U.S. did not go along, then China and the Soviet Union might get together in the future, and then the U.S. might have to look out. But all of that is on such a low level. What kind of a world are we going to create in the future? What do we have now? We are spending much too much money on arms all over the world, and the problems of food for the future and the development of international law still exist. These are all aspects of the very basis of our foreign policy and this reassessment.

WEATHERBEE: I have just a brief addition because of Professor Henderson's remark at the very end concerning what we can do in South Korea to change the situation. I can merely say that the American interference in South Korea, only if we apply that pressure in clear-cut fashion, may be tied into aid or whatever. Now the inference is what we saw last night. Why would the Ambassador of South Korea come to our dinner, and in the sweetest lullabye I have ever heard, present South Korea in such a way that the United States would not want to do anything to interfere with anything that they are doing. That seems a reverse vindication of the proposition that American pressure properly exerted on South Korea would have a beneficial effect, that in turning the conditions around to either direction both South Korea and America would have what they mutually desire.

GURTOV: With the prerogative of the chair, I would just like to throw out an idea. What always bothers me about suggestions of that kind —to reverse course and continue involvement in a new way—is that pressure creates new obligations, or at least new feelings of obligations, even if it is pressure with the best of intentions. Such pressure, presumably toward the aim of rescuing the South Korean people from their government, invariably creates new responsibilities. As someone who is committed to a foreign policy of non-intervention, it frankly frightens me.

WEATHERBEE: Since we are beginning to talk in general terms, I will confine myself to this discussion in which, despite American experience in Indochina, there is still the expectation that the U.S. both has the capabilities, and, this is more important, should use what capabilities it has to arrange the futures of Asian states. I would find myself in agreement with the last comment rather than with those who would seek, despite Vietnam, a more active American role, directly trying to arrange the future of Asian states. I would also have to associate myself with those who keep saying that we must seek the legitimate aspirations of the peoples of Asia. It strikes me that these tend to get defined by the people who are in control. Regardless of their orientations, they are the ones who define what their peoples' aspirations are. We may not want to associate ourselves with particular elites because we do not like them, or we may want to associate ourselves with other elites because we do like them. It is an impossible situation to find who in fact speaks for the people. Historically in Asia, the people who claim to speak for the people are the people who have been able to mobilize force.

KAHNG: In terms of reassessing foreign policy, I would like to suggest an idea. Korea has been a liability from the day of her birth. Now why can't we, all the scholars and the experts here, turn this liability into an asset? The human rights question is not the fundamental issue, it is only a partial issue. The fundamental issue, the central problem to all Koreans—North and South—is the problem of unification. What can we do about unification? This is, I think, the question with which we should be concerned. Another point I would like to make is that on March 25, 1974, the People's Congress of North Korea sent a letter to the Congress of the United States. The Congress of the United States ignored it, did not acknowledge it. This is unimaginable arrogance. We should recognize that we are not absolutely qualified to talk about Korea. We do not even extend the minimum decency with this kind of attitude. We are completely disqualified in the eyes of the North Koreans.

JO: This is the final session. We do not have much time to reflect and project. We have gotten the impression that we talked too much and arrived nowhere, the same as climbing a tree to catch a fish—this is a Chinese proverb. But I think discussion of this sort is the foundation of democracy. When I was formulating this topic, way before the fall of Saigon, I was thinking that there was and will be growing dissatisfaction with the status quo. It is not the question of radical change of the status quo in the South, but the question is how far are we satisfied with the status quo? If we are not satisfied with the status quo, how far can we change? The undesirability of the status quo does not mean that what we desire is something feasible. The question, then, is how to relate the desirability of the changes with the feasibility.

I would like to make two or three further points. We need to reassess some of our basic assumptions with regard to foreign policies. Professor Gurtov, Professor Kahng, talked about the value systems of the United States. Professor Kahng mentioned the psychic systems of the United States. Can we do something more than what we have done, or are our policies in the past been do-nothing policies? If so, how can we shape do-something policies with regard to what we desire and what appears to be feasible? The question of relating freedom to national interest in a country like Korea was also raised. Also, the underlying assumptions of some of the discussions seem to be that we are in the midst of carrying détente policies for our allies such as Japan, and that we should not let South Korea prevent that new détente policy. However, it seems that we failed to take into account adequately the aspirations and human needs of the people in Asia. On the other hand, because one talks about certain specific policies and how to operationalize certain policies in view of what seems to be feasible and desirable from the United States' viewpoint, does not necessarily mean that one fails to take into account the aspirations of the people. The question is how can we equate the aspirations of the Asian people with the national interest of the United States? I think the point was well taken when it was mentioned that to dichotomize realism on the one hand, idealism on the other hand, is a bit unrealistic. This is a time to discover how to bridge it as well as carry on meaningful policies.

WALKER: What aspects of the American role, in general, should we be interested in, either in the sense of projection or to make a recommendation? I think there are four concepts of American foreign policy that really define America's role in Asia and indeed in other parts of the world. First, the extent of the U.S. role; by this I mean the range of issues in which the U.S. chooses to become involved. I think running through the entire conference there has been different preference and different priority ranking for what issue of its foreign policy project the U.S. should address itself. The second concept has to do with the direction of American policy with respect to either the entire range of issues or each issue taken singly. Here I mean we should be essentially neutral, or engage in cooperative or conflictual behavior in a way that we address ourselves to the particular issue. The third aspect of American foreign policy, which I think confronts us for analysis and prescription, is the intensity with which the U.S. follows particular lines of policy. This refers to whether or not we wish to fight about it, or pursue the policy of some low level of conflict, or whether we want to engage in cooperative behavior that includes perhaps taking over some domestic functions of a particular government, helping with the economic development, and so forth. The last characteristic of American foreign policy is the style with which American foreign policy is implemented. That is to say, whether we do it with one kind of rationale—idealistic rationale, or another kind of rationale—realism. These are the aspects of American foreign policy with which we have been concerned throughout this conference.

If you do take role analysis seriously—the notion of role, the sources of a country's role, and an individual's role in the behavior space in which one operates—it can shed some light on these kinds of questions. Role analysis really means that there are fine points involved in determining a country's role. First, the systematic constraint within which a country operates. I am talking here about America's geopolitical position, the type of domestic structure we have, for example, rather than being an advanced economic country, democracy rather than dictatorship, and so forth. Second, an aspect of role analysis has to do with the impact of other countries' expectations about the way we should act; that is to say the cues that we take from them and in fact the way we behave. The third aspect of role analysis is the subjective orientations of our decision-makers. That is to say, what dispositions they bring with them to a position of political decision-making that in turn helps them to define the role that the United States follows. The fourth aspect of role analysis is the learning process that goes on over a period of time, and which has been addressed frequently in the papers that were presented at the conference. That is to say, how American decision-makers go about reconciling the expectations of other countries and their behavior and demands upon us with their own subjective preference about what they think should be done. The final aspect of role analysis that I think should concern us is the issue areas to which the roles are addressed. It is possible to talk about several American roles if our orientations are subdivided into different issues. The problem that emerges from a perspective that makes distinctions among issues is the phenomenon of role conflict; that is to say when we address ourselves to one issue, is it possible that we are contradicting our policy or behavior toward another issue? These are the aspects of role analysis that we brought to bear in making some kind of general prescriptions or projections about American policy. Basically these fit together in the following ways. The extent of America's role and the style in which it is carried out are primarly the results of systemic constraints, or international positions, if you will, the United States finds itself in and the subjective orientations of its policy-makers. On the other hand, the direction and intensity of the U.S. role in the world is a function of expectations and behavior of other actors in the international arena, the issue area to which the policymakers are addressing themselves and again their own subjective orientations.

I would like to conclude with a series of questions to which we might want to address ourselves in the remainder of discussion. The first question is, What have we learned from the socialization process that has gone on as the United States involved itself heavily in Asia over the last twenty years? In other words, as we tried to reconcile our subjective national orientations with Asian expectations and the constraints imposed upon our role in the region, what conclusions have we come to about redefining or reassessing America's role in Asia? Second, How should we respond to potential role conflicts? That is to say, how are we to respond to different and contradictory demands from the Sino-Soviet dispute? How are we to respond to what the Chinese want us to do versus the Soviet expectation of what they want us to do? And how should we respond to expectations of regimes within a particular country and the national aspirations of the majority of the people? Third, Are the systemic constraints changing on the United States so that the extent of the U.S. role should be declining or expanding? That is to say, with the passing of bipolarity and diminishing United States resources, does it mean our global and regional role should shrink particularly with respect to Asia, or are there a host of new and continuing issues that require heightened participation by the United States in this area of the world? I think panel papers have clearly suggested that there are some, including economic development, human rights, Sino-Soviet conflict, Soviet naval expansion, Korean unification, and ecological population problems. Next, Can the United States adopt a new style in addressing itself to these issues or are we to be constrained in our response by our old ways? Is our national political culture, the operational codes of our decision-makers so ingrained that we cannot respond in other than a traditional fashion as we always have? Next, What direction should we pursue and with what intensity should we address ourselves to these kinds of issues? And finally, Do we need domestic reform in the United States in order to respond effectively to the problems abroad?

Jo: Thank you very much. I am afraid Professor Walker could raise an even greater number of serious questions, but it might be advisable for us to think about some of the questions that were raised already.

Meisner: The last question raised, on the relationship between the domestic political nature of the United States and its foreign policy, is an excellent one. Again it raises this problem of idealism discussion, which is that you talk as if oftentimes choices and values having to do with foreign policies are disembodied from the state of political forces, and the pattern of development of the society. Of course, that is not true.

Winn: Yesterday there was a comment that we cannot talk about Vietnam. We have talked so long, but I think what we have here is the realization that we made some tragic errors. Given these tragic errors, we have to re-evaluate our foreign policy. You can do something by choosing among alternatives, or do nothing. The odds are that doing nothing will be a disastrous course. We have a situation of interventionism right now, although as a philosophy I do not like interventionism. Under the present situation, we must find out how to withdraw from Korea or how to change the present situation in Korea. What you get down to in the final estimation is a need for various people to sit down and say what the philosophical underpinnings of American foreign policy are.

Carrier: I think we finally are getting around to something that Professor Meisner quite correctly said we should have considered. There is an obvious interaction between our own domestic behavior and our colonial policies. I think the conference is just like the United States government. It does not confront the reality. We should begin to address ourselves to questions such as, "Was Vietnam a tragic mistake?" In one sense it was tragic in that the United States government thought that it could destroy a national liberation movement and set about to do that; but it was not a mistake in the sense that the United States intentions were very clear. If anyone reads the Pentagon Papers or any other sources that come from out of the inside of our government, they will see that this was not a mistake. We are trying to do the same thing in Korea, and probably would do it in Angola, except that it is already too late there. We have to confront that, and I do not consider that a question of rhetoric. What we have here is an obvious unwillingness by the scholarly world to take upon oneself a risk of non-conformity, of social disapprobation, of moral responsibility. This runs in conflict with the university and obviously to our government. Our foreign policy is a reflection of an unjust society at home, and until we confront that, we are talking in the wind about change.

HENDERSON: It seems to me that the case of North Korea and South Korea is significantly different in one respect. We have sent anywhere from between 40 and 160 million dollars, which our leaders have said was for the sake of protecting a Korean democracy—or dictatorship or whatever other formulations you want to use—and we have not spent one cent on doing that in North Korea. That is a considerable difference. It means that what we can do in North Korea in terms of our influence, by having some sort of expanding communication along with the fact that other nations are now recognizing Pyongyang, is quite different. The hope is that gradually this new communication input into the North Korean system will begin to have slow but gradual perceptual effects.

JO: Talking about influence or intervention abroad as a benefit not only for the United States but also for humanity as a whole, would you say that the cost/benefit analysis of our foreign policy is very often based on illusions unlike good American businessmen who estimate the cost and benefits of their enterprises?

HENDERSON: The trouble is that Korea has been seen primarily as a security issue. The benefit analysis tends to be seen only along military lines.

KENNEDY: During the last nine years or so, at the U.S. Army War College, I have witnessed a better appreciation of the political, economic, ecological, and cultural aspects of foreign policy, plus the security aspects, than I have yet to see in the civilian community which may be professional, political, or socio-economical. None have any real appreciation of the security problems in confronting communism.

JO: Is there anyone who wants to make a philosophical comment?

AUDIENCE: The United States is in many ways, as we learned through Vietnam, a paper tiger; but it is a paper tiger that has a real tiger by the tail. The tiger we have by the tail in Asia is the people of Asia. We have created a small elite in many cases, and we rule through that elite. We can't let go. Obviously in Korea we are in exactly that situation. We are talking about democratic reforms in Korea—that's crazy. We trained the police, we train the army, we train the torturers—and then we asked why the hell we do not have democratic reforms. Throughout Asia, they do not have to rely on the people of their own country—they rely on the United States.

RHEE: I want to respond to Mr. Kennedy's remarks. I can cite only a couple of problems to demonstrate where military short-sightedness had created very dangerous political problems thereby nullifying the whole consideration that would have gone into the military considerations for security. For instance, there are many statements being made by top defense officials urging Japan to rearm with nuclear weapons. Also, because of the military considerations that were so short-sighted, we had supported the colonels' junta in Athens. Now, after the Cyprus question, which had overthrown the regime of the colonels, anti-Americanism in Greece is rampant, even among those Greeks who had been pro-American. I think this is why Cleamonsworth said politics is too important to be left to military officers' judgment.

WEATHERBEE: There is a bit of confusion here. Let us not confuse national security policy-making with the military institution. After all, it is Congress that votes the money, that votes reality.

SIMON: One of the things that struck me about the last few days is the whole notion of U.S. intervention. On the one hand, there are those who argue that all U.S. intervention in the recent past has been an unmitigated disaster. There are good interventions and there are bad interventions, and we should be engaged in good interventions. Good interventions deal with such things as the aspirations of the people, human rights and economic growth. In the conference, these particular kinds of interventions, labeled good interventions, were discussed in the context of South Korea and past behavior with respect to South Vietnam, and perhaps Laos and Cambodia. They are relevant as the United States begins to engage with new kinds of economic relationships with the DRV, perhaps Laos and Cambodia, and perhaps the DPRK. But again, one has to raise the question.

WASHINGTON-SEOUL TIES AND JAPAN, THE U.S.S.R., AND CHINA

U.S. Policy in Korea

Robert A. Scalapino

Korea, together with China-Taiwan, represents the last of the un-resolved "divided states" issues. The German problem, which at one point threatened to be the most explosive, has been handled peace-fully. The fate of Vietnam has been settled by force. The Indonesian-Timor issue, if this counts, has been approached in the same manner. In point of fact, of course, a number of states remain divided in the real sense, with serious regional and ethnic problems lending them-selves to varying degrees of separatism. The status of such states as *de jure* entities, however, is well-nigh universally established. That is not true in the case of Korea, and whether one accepts or rejects the thesis that the threat of war here is real and imminent, no one can doubt that conditions on the Korean peninsula are scarcely conducive to peace and harmony.

The antecedents of the Korean problem are too well known to require any detailed recapitulation. The division of this nation was an accident, initially unintended by any of the parties concerned, at least as far as currently available records show. Once this type of ideologi-cal-political separation took place in the post-1945 world, however, there has not yet been an instance of peaceful reunification. In this sense, Korea is not unique. The issues that first emerged between Americans and Russians in late 1945, and were to remain central to the South-North discussions subsequently, revolved around a single domi-nant concern: would a unified Korea be communist or non-commu-nist? While various formulae have been advanced that appear to dodge or obscure this issue, it has always been uppermost in the minds of the parties primarily involved, and no real solution or compromise accept-able to both sides has ever been discovered.

Kim Il-sung was entirely cognizant of these facts when he sought to determine the Korean outcome by force through his invasion of the South in 1950. And despite the hopes that accompanied the opening of bilateral contacts in 1972, the same issue has remained an obstacle to meaningful progress on reunification down to the present.

Meanwhile, much has happened within both South and North Korea, and since the domestic environment within these two countries is one important determinant of attitudes and policies in the foreign policy arena, a brief summary of current trends is warranted.

The politics of South Korea might be defined as the policies of insecurity. Rightly or wrongly, Park Chung-hee drew two lessons from Vietnam. First, South Vietnam lacked the requisite unity to survive despite the fact that its people were overwhelmingly non-communist. Second, the United States proved to be an unreliable ally in this instance, and sooner or later, it would also withdraw from Korea. These conclusions, it should be asserted, fitted with Park's personal political proclivities, and with some "lessons" he had drawn from developments within Korea. Son of a peasant, trainee in a Japanese military school, and staunch Korea-centered nationalist, Park was the first wholly *Asian* leader of post-war South Korea. And while he was firmly committed to nation-building and economic modernization, his model was closer to that of the Meiji Restoration than of Western liberalism.

Furthermore, there *were* signs of growing political disunity in South Korea in the late 1960s and the early 1970s. In part, they stemmed from the disenchantment of the student-intellectual-journalist communities with Park's personality and policies; in part, from the socio-economic issues connected with the particular growth program adopted; and in part, from international concerns, including the question of relations with the North. The relatively close presidential election of 1971 between Park and Kim Tae-jung mirrored these facts.

The evidence also suggests that Park envisaged a trade-off as necessary between seeking some new arrangement with the North and containing political divisions in the South. The earlier trends toward liberalization were therefore reversed, and an enforced unity was sought, albeit one that permitted retention of an opposition party and the National Assembly. The expressed goals, as well as the institutional structure of the Republic of Korea, continue to distinguish it from the one-party dictatorship preached and practiced by the Democratic People's Republic of Korea.

A distinction should also be made in the human rights field. South Korea is not a Western-style democracy, nor has it ever been so. Today, moreover, the restraints upon intellectuals, journalists and political activists are relatively severe. At the same time, no South Korean is forced to recite the thoughts of Park Chung-hee, or to make certain that Park's picture is prominently displayed in his home. Nor is he forced to belong to party-controlled organizations that direct his every waking hour. In sum, there is a freedom of silence, and in broader terms, a freedom of privacy that only a pluralistic society can grant in any significant measure. This contrast from the lifestyle under the intensively mobilized, one-party dictatorship of the North is a major one, and often not appreciated by the outside observer.

In sum, South Korea is today a society marked by political paradoxes. The recent trend has been away from liberalism, and some of the leaders, including Park, have suggested that the Western-style democratic model is not applicable to Korea, at least at this point. Indeed, independence from the United States and other societies has been heralded as a part of the quest for an indigenous Korean system, symbolic of the always present, if sometimes latent nationalist spirit pervading the society. At the same time, the commitment remains to a pluralist, politically competitive structure. Thus, the gap between commitment and performance serves as an embarrassment that the communists of the North—free from any such commitments—duly exploit.

Let us turn to the economic front. In 1977, Seoul launches its fourth Five-Year Plan in a mood of relative optimism. The overall growth rate has averaged roughly 10 percent in the last decade, despite the Western recession and the oil crisis. Per capita G.N.P. now stands at $532 according to government figures, with total G.N.P. having risen to $18,800,000,000, three times that of the estimated G.N.P. of the DPRK. The nation expects to reach nearly 80 percent self-sufficiency in food this year, and to keep the growth rate high. Korean economic planning, modelled after that of Japan, has resulted in an export-oriented economy, with the premium upon the rapid development of higher technology products, as new markets open. This in turn has necessitated a close interaction (and growing competition) with Japan and the United States.

The economic scene is not without its problems. The extensive Japanese involvement in the Korean economy, as well as the U.S. presence, have led to charges of exploitation. Currently, it is probably more important that South Korea has increasingly moved into a position of greater competition for markets with Japan, Taiwan, and Hong Kong, and at a time when all states—including the U.S.—are adopting protectionist policies. Thus, South Korea may have too great a dependence upon foreign trade for its future economic health. Moreover, an urban-rural gap of considerable proportions continues to exist, with the results of the New Community Movement yet unclear. Inflation also remains a potentially serious problem. After these difficulties and dangers have been signalled, however, it remains a fact that on balance, the South Korean economic record of the past fifteen years has been a striking success, in contrast to the dismal performance of an earlier period. In assessing the strength of the ROK, it is a decidedly positive factor.

In foreign policy, the record is more mixed. The Republic of Korea as of 1977 had diplomatic relations with ninety-six nations, and operated 103 overseas diplomatic missions. However, its efforts to establish such ties with communist states had not yet borne fruit, and it had also been denied admission to the so-called Non-Aligned Nations Group.

More seriously, its relations with the United States and Japan were in varying degrees of trouble. With respect to ROK-U.S. relations, the human rights issue provided a rallying point for those in Congress and elsewhere to argue that American commitments to South Korea should be drastically curtailed or ended. The alleged bribery efforts of a government-connected Korean businessman added fuel to this fire, and touched a number of American public officials. On the reverse side, the reported American bugging of the presidential office in Seoul created deep resentment among many Koreans, by no means all of them supporters of Park. Beyond this, there is a growing feeling in Korean circles that in its dealings with Europe versus Asia, the United States—consciously or unconsciously—exhibits its racial priorities.

ROK-Japan relations must operate against an ex-colonial background, and one that also contains a strong measure of racial prejudice on both sides. The large influx of Japanese capital—and tourists—into Korea has been a mixed blessing. It has been critical to the economic boom, and if further evidence on this score were needed, Pyongyang's recent efforts to solicit a similar economic interaction serve as evidence. At the same time, it has induced charges of neo-colonialism, and created a number of tensions. The Kim Tai-jung kidnapping illustrated a reverse unhealthy involvement, that of South Korea in Japan. The Korean issue, indeed, has been even more highly politicized in Tokyo than in Washington, with the left strongly pro-Pyongyang, and a portion of the center opting for a more straightforward "two Koreas" policy. However, recent indications are that for the duration of Liberal Democratic Party rule at least, the security of South Korea and close ROK-Japan economic ties will be regarded as vital to the Japanese national interest. In the event of coalition government, moreover, the shift of attitudes would probably not be of major proportions, although the "two Koreas" position might become stronger.

Meanwhile, Seoul has taken a series of positions of its own in the foreign policy arena that represent a progressive stance on balance, but one dependent upon the cooperation of other nations. As noted, Seoul now accepts the principle of universal recognition, being willing to have diplomatic relations with any nation prepared to reciprocate. It has also accepted the dual recognition of South and North Korea by a growing number of states. Further, it has indicated a willingness to sit in the U.N. and its auxiliary bodies with the North pending unification. At the same time, it has insisted that any negotiations involving a formal termination of the Korean Armistice involve it, and it has strongly opposed Pyongyang's efforts to by-pass it in dealing directly with the United States.

Regarding reunification, the ROK has favored a step-by-step approach, insisting that the first steps be limited ones involving humanitarian measures, then economic interaction, and only after some experience and trust has been established, broader political and military considerations. Few if any South Korean leaders believe that the communists are prepared to settle for anything less than domination of a unified Korea. Hence, the element of trust is totally lacking at present. However, the ROK continues to urge a resumption of negotiations without conditions, a re-establishment of the hot line which was disconnected by the North at the time of the axe-murder incident in August 1976, and the signing of a non-aggression pact between the two governments.

What is the situation with respect to the North? Information concerning the domestic politics of this tightly closed society is both scanty and unreliable. The evidence, nevertheless, suggests that the succession issue is already deeply interwoven into the politics of the DPRK monocracy. While Kim Il-sung is still in his mid-60s, his health has been a subject of much speculation. Apart from Kim, moreover, the entire generation of Kapsan guerrillas who rose with him is now passing from the scene. Word has clearly been passed to all cadres to build up Kim's son, Kim Chung-il, and a cult of personality is now gradually being created around this young man.

Nepotism, going far beyond Kim's son, has become an increasingly prominent feature of Pyongyang politics. Kim's younger brother has been much less prominent recently, presumably for health reasons. But his second wife, head of the Women's Federation, is often displayed. Kim's uncle has long been prominent as a key front figure, and his cousin's husband is foreign minister. With nepotism often goes intrigue, and rumors of inner friction around the palace persist despite limited evidence.

In sum, could the political unity under an all-powerful leader that has been the DPRK's strong point for over two decades, give way to serious factionalism, especially if the leader were to suffer a serious decline in health or suddenly pass from the scene? Few elites have been kept as isolated from the rest of the world, including the communist world, as have the North Koreans. A younger group of highly indoctrinated cadres and technicians exists, but the military would appear to be critical in any post-Kim regime, just as proved to be the case in post-Mao China, and would also be true in post-Park South Korea. But whether the DPRK can make the transition from Kim without grave political instability seems doubtful. This problem has always been the Achilles' Heel of such governments, particularly when they have revolved so tightly around a single individual. Will the test come in months or years? This—together with the trauma of succession in the South—could play a significant role in South-North relations in the period ahead.

Meanwhile, in the economic arena, the crisis is now. In the recent past, the DPRK has had the dubious distinction of being the first communist nation to default involuntarily upon its international economic obligations. Hundreds of millions of dollars (some sources put the figure much higher) are owed a sizable circle of creditors, both communist and non-communist, and repayment arrangements have not yet been satisfactorily consummated. What caused the severe economic difficulties? A part of the problem stems from the sustained, heavy military expenditures extending back to 1963. After a brief dip in the early 1970s, those expenditures again rose, consuming nearly 14 percent of total G.N.P. by 1975, and remaining high thereafter. Another factor was overextended purchases in an inflationary period, in an effort to provide some sorely needed modernization of North Korea's industries, and wholly inadequate exports to meet balance of payment needs. It is quite probable that economic mismanagement at home has also been involved. North Korean authorities have spoken of serious inbalances.

The economic crunch appears to have led to one of the most bizarre scandals involving a government in recent years. North Korean embassies were discovered to have been engaged in large-scale smuggling of liquor, tobacco and drugs throughout Scandinavia. Current difficulties also led to the dispatch of Premier Park Sung-chull to Moscow in January 1977. Thus, Park made a pilgrimage which Kim Il-sung had conspicuously not taken in 1975, when his far-reaching journey took him to the PRC, East Europe (including Albania) and North Africa. Since Park's mission included economic technicians and his chief discussions were with Kosygin, it is clear that economic relations constituted the primary item on the agenda. Whether the reserved Soviet comments on the visit are also a reflection of the results is uncertain, but it would be surprising if the Soviets were prepared to be extraordinarily generous, given the recent pattern of U.S.S.R.-DPRK relations.

With the domestic scene thus troubled, North Korea, like its rival, has obtained mixed results in the international arena. Following a diplomatic offensive that began in the early 1970s, the DPRK has obtained official recognition from ninety-one countries, and now participates in ten world organizations (the ROK takes part in forty-six). Its success in gaining admission to the Non-Aligned Conferences was regarded as a triumph in Pyongyang, and at one point, it seemed likely that relations with Japan would be much improved. Early in its tenure, the Miki administration signalled its interest in a "two Koreas" policy.

The drive to separate the ROK from both Japan and the U.S. continues, but with modest results at this point. Relations with Japan remain stalemated, partly because of the unresolved debt problem, but also because the Japanese government has become increasingly apprehensive lest any actions on its part promote a shift in American policies, or weaken South Korea. In the long term, Japan will favor a "two Koreas" policy, but not at the expense of its economic interests in the South, or undertaken in such a fashion as to jeopardize the status-quo in security terms.

One of the chief DPRK objectives remains that of getting the United States to deal with it directly, by-passing the ROK. Hence, despite the earlier insistence that the Korean issue must be settled by the Korean people themselves, without outside interference, Pyongyang now insists that there should be direct negotiations for a peace treaty between it and the U.S. alone, followed by the complete withdrawal of all American forces from South Korea. Meanwhile, it seeks to establish unofficial as well as official cultural contacts with America in various ways, although its attacks on U.S. policies have not abated.

Up to date, these efforts have produced limited results. As has already been noted, moreover, relations between North Korea and the two major communist states differ, with each containing its complexities. Ties with the Soviet Union have been troubled for many years, indeed, since 1956, and in fact, the Kremlin neither likes nor trusts Kim Il-sung. At times, such as at the end of the Khrushchev era, Russian assistance to Pyongyang was cut off, and on various occasions, the North Koreans have been subjected to very cool treatment by Soviet leaders. In recent years, moreover, the Russians have winked at South Korea on more than one occasion, granting visas to South Korean athletes and maintaining certain "cultural" relations at an unobtrusive level.

There is absolutely no evidence that Moscow would be overjoyed in the event that Kim Il-sung were to preside over a unified Korea, and it is certain that they would not approve of the risk of using open force in any such attempt. On the other hand, the Soviets are restrained in their public attitudes and actions both by various East European and third world states and by the pressures of rivalry with China. To "abandon" North Korea might have repercussions elsewhere, and would certainly present Peking with a golden propaganda opportunity. Thus, Moscow supports DPRK resolutions in the United Nations, and proclaims its commitment to Kim's formulae for the "peaceful unification" of Korea, as well as his demand that all American forces be withdrawn. Considering the proximity of American nuclear weapons to Vladivostok, the latter demand may strike a responsive chord in Moscow, although to the extent that an American presence restrains both North and South Korea, and reduces the threat of conflict on the Korean peninsula, the Russians must have mixed feelings.

Is this also true of Peking? Certain American observers are convinced that the Chinese also have both a public and a private position on the Korean issue. The evidence is exceedingly hard to find.

Whereas the recent Park-Kosygin discussions were described by the Soviet media as "friendly and businesslike," most Chinese-North Korean conferences are heralded by the official Chinese media as solidarity sessions between comrades whose bonds are sealed in blood. The latter reference, of course, is to the joint struggle against "American imperialism" that led to "victory" in the "war to defend the Korean fatherland." And relations between the two peoples are defined as those between lips and teeth. Making allowance for a certain stylistic hyperbole, there can be no doubt that for many years, the Chinese have striven to keep Pyongyang on their side in the Sino-Soviet dispute, and since 1969 at least, they have generally succeeded.

Kim Il-sung first tilted sharply toward Peking in the late Khrushchev era, leading to a major crisis in relations with the Soviet Union in the 1962–64 period. Russian aid was severed, and polemics emerged to the surface. Some improvements occurred upon the advent of Brezhnev-Kosygin to power, and these were desperately needed by the North Koreans, both for economic and security reasons. However, a coolness remained, and from time to time, a genuine freeze took over. But at the height of the Cultural Revolution, relations between the Chinese and North Koreans grew very strained, with wall-poster attacks upon Kim in Peking, and some reports of border clashes. One of Chou En-lai's first acts after he regained control of the foreign ministry was to travel to Pyongyang in 1969 to restore good relations. Subsequent evidence indicates that he succeeded.

At the conclusion of his Peking visit following the collapse of South Vietnam, in April 1975, Kim signed a joint communiqué with the Chinese that represented, at least on paper, a considerable triumph. The communiqué not only gave full support to Kim's reunification proposals, but also asserted that the PRC recognized the DPRK as the sole sovereign state on the Korean peninsula. In addition, it coupled Korean reunification with the "liberation" of Taiwan. This couplet was to be repeated on a number of occasions subsequently, suggesting an agreement on mutual support. Some American sources take comfort from the fact that in this communiqué and later Chinese pronouncements, the phrase used was "peaceful reunification." They regard this as evidence of a restraint upon Kim.

Neither the PRC nor the U.S.S.R. want a conflict to erupt on the Korean peninsula at this point. It is the principle item of agreement among all of the major powers involved in the area. But it should be noted that Kim Il-sung himself has frequently used the term "peaceful reunification" in describing his own approach. Long ago, Kim opted against another Korean War *à la* 1950, and sought to apply modified Vietnam tactics, namely, to seed and feed a revolutionary movement in the South, helping to create the conditions for "liberation" in which the aid from the North could be largely camouflaged. This is a lower risk policy, and one of proven success. Thus, on this particular issue, Kim did not need to be pressured.

To be sure, it would be surprising if the Chinese did not have some private reservations about Kim and his government, and vice-versa. These are seldom absent from bilateral relations, however intimate. In all border ties, moreover, the Chinese have had a mixed impact for many centuries, with elements of cooperation and adaptation on the one hand, resistance and the quest for independence on the other, although the admixture has varied from society to society, and period to period. Inevitably, a leader in the position of Kim Il-sung would like to be able to achieve a position of rough equidistance between the PRC and the U.S.S.R., enabling him in some measure to play one off against the other, achieving maximum assistance from both. Reality always interferes with ideals, however, and Kim has been drawn into a rather sharp tilt toward Peking in recent times, after having first emerged as a protégé of the Soviets.

All bridges have not been burned in Pyongyang. Sino-North Korean communiqués on occasion pledge to uphold Marxism-Leninism and to oppose modern revisionism, but the North Koreans have declined to associate themselves with any overt attack upon the U.S.S.R. in this setting. The need for continued military and economic links with Moscow is too acute to permit this. And that need has recently grown, as we have noted. Beyond this, recent developments in China —the combination of political instability and economic troubles— must have caused apprehension in North Korea. For the time being at least, the Soviet Union is clearly the more powerful and the more stable of the DPRK's two big communist neighbors.

It would thus be unwise to ignore the possibility of the shift from time to time in the precise relations between the DPRK and each major communist power. However, it is difficult to avoid the feeling that proximity and culture combine to provide the Chinese with an advantage *if* internal Chinese conditions do not deteriorate too greatly. The closeness of the Yalu River to China's Manchurian industrial complex and the sizable Korean populations in the northeast counties that adjoin North Korea make the Korea issue a matter of urgent security concern, as the Korean War demonstrated so graphically. Thus, whenever China's relations with the Russians are greatly troubled, the disposition of the North Koreans becomes a matter of prime importance to Peking. To achieve and maintain a "sphere of influence" here is likely to be as steadfast an objective in the future as in the past.

Some of these factors, of course, also apply to the Soviet Union. The DPRK's extreme northeast border touches upon the U.S.S.R., with Vladivostok in the near vicinity. The vital centers of the Soviet Union, however, are great distances from North Korea, and the sizable Korean populations that once lived in Siberia were moved to Central

Asia in the 1930s when a major conflict with Japan was threatened. Thus, the Russians cannot feel the same degree of concern on the Korean issue in security terms as do the Chinese, although that concern could well increase as the further military and economic development of Siberia progresses. With the present older generation of North Korean leaders, however, Russia's image is badly tarnished. The Kapsan group headed by Kim Il-sung, having served loyally as a client state in Stalin's era, found themselves in a complex struggle both at home and abroad against Khrushchev. And the Russians remain both foreign and forceful.

Against this background, what are the alternatives confronting the United States in assessing its future relations with the Republic of Korea and its approach to the Korea problem? Since the legacy of the recent past is reasonably well known, only some broader interpretations will be attempted here. One of the central dilemmas confronting the United States after World War II was the question of where to establish a viable defense perimeter against what was perceived to be Soviet expansionist ambitions. In this period, the Soviet Union was only a regional power, and one vastly inferior to the United States in military or economic strength. In its efforts to construct a buffer system in depth, however, Moscow projected such strength as it had outward, depending partly upon the chaotic conditions that prevailed almost everywhere in the aftermath of a devastating war. In this process, it was bound to confront the United States.

While the American dilemma over defense perimeters was a serious one, it cannot be said that the U.S. government generally took the initiative in resolving the issue after painstaking study and debate. On the contrary, decisions were usually forced by the turn of events, coming about piece-meal and in the midst of crisis. In this manner, alternatives were often narrowed to the choice between acquiescence or military involvement.

In Europe, an early decision was made, largely by default, not to respond militarily to the Soviet extension of its control over most of Eastern Europe. In effect, this was accepted as a legitimate Soviet "sphere of influence," although some encouragement was given to "roll back" possibilities until the ill-fated Hungarian revolt. In central Europe, the situation was left ambiguous. West Berlin stood as a symbol of resistance; Austria as a "neutral" zone. The potentials for a buffer state system were allowed to come into existence, providing a part of the basis for the later détente between the U.S. and the U.S.S.R., and between West and East Europe.

In Asia, the situation has been vastly more complex for a number of reasons, cultural, developmental and geopolitical. The question of whether to make a strategic commitment to any portion of the Asian continent has plagued American policy-makers for more than three decades, and is still hotly disputed. On the one hand, the capacity of the United States to sustain any such commitment was always questioned, taking into account the various factors and costs involved. On the other hand, the viability of a simple island *cordon sanitaire* policy applied to East Asia was also questioned. Could a meaningful political-strategic equilibrium in Asia hinge upon such a division? Did the emergence of national communism change the need for, or the potentialities of such an equilibrium?

The issues indicated so briefly here have not been resolved, and there are others, including the question of the impact of another American withdrawal or defeat upon American credibility everywhere —with adversaries as well as with allies. Once again, however, events themselves have gone a certain distance in determining American strategic policies in Asia. The defeat in Indochina forced a strategic withdrawal from continental Southeast Asia, but not from the region as a whole. American sea and air power, in rather minimal amounts, remains—with bases in the Philippines employed. Here, the island *cordon sanitaire* principle is in effect, with military aid to Indonesia a natural development. In continental Southeast Asia, the American presence is now limited to the economic, political and cultural spheres.

In Northeast Asia, on the other hand, the Korean military conflict in which the United States participated ended in victory, not defeat, albeit, a limited victory. Thus, the American presence has continued in strategic as well as other forms. That presence, moreover, is still regarded by many as essential to the maintenance of peace on the Korean peninsula, and in broader terms, to the peaceful relations among the major states involved in the region, as well as the security of Japan. Yet a number of Americans seriously question either the entire Korean commitment, or the manner in which it is currently being pursued.

Some would go as far as ex-Senator Mansfield, insisting that our strategic commitments should be cut back everywhere, and that in this region of the world, we should consider ourselves a Pacific but not an Asian power—thereby limiting our strategic commitments to our own territories. Most critics would not take such an extreme position, but many would feel more comfortable if American strategic commitments were limited to Japan, and so argue on both economic-political and strategic grounds. Japan is more compatible with our values, more vital to our national interests and more defensible, they assert.

Thus a new enclave theory has emerged, namely, that Japan can be our strategic enclave in Asia, and a nation drawn into the American-West European alliance. The only problem with this theory is that the Japanese themselves reject it, as do the West Europeans. Increasingly, Japan has shown its concern about signs that the U.S. might cease to be a credible power in Asia, and particular worries have been expressed regarding American policies toward Korea and Taiwan. These are regions where both Japanese security and economic interests are deeply at stake.

This is the context in which the Carter administration will make decisions regarding American policy toward Korea. In actuality the policies thus far revealed represent a continuity with past policies far more than a divergence. The withdrawal of American ground forces on a phased basis in conjunction with a stepped-up program of assistance in modernizing and expanding ROK military forces, especially naval and air forces, was an integral part of American planning in the Nixon-Ford period. The principle of consultation with both South Korea and Japan, announced by President Carter, was also a standard part of that policy.

Nor has the United States yet departed from its call for a conference among the signatories to the Korean Armistice to reach a settlement of the outstanding issues, with the possibility of the later inclusion of the U.S.S.R. and Japan, a proposal set forth by Secretary Kissinger several times. Meanwhile, it remains U.S. policy to decline any bilateral agreements with the DPRK to which the ROK is not a party. The United States has reiterated its willingness to recognize the DPRK on a reciprocal basis if the PRC and the U.S.S.R. are prepared to recognize the ROK. It continues to support the basic formula for reunification advanced by the South Korean government, and its proposal for dual representation in the United Nations. When the North Koreans had their resolution withdrawn from the U.N. in the fall of 1976 due to the likelihood of a poor showing, the pro-South Korean resolution was also withdrawn, but the position of the two sides on the issues at stake do not appear to have changed in any significant manner.

It is also noteworthy that while the Carter administration has elected to make human rights a major foreign policy issue, and one with very considerable repercussions at this moment both in American-Soviet relations and with respect to certain "Third World" countries, Secretary Vance specifically exempted the Republic of Korea from sanctions due to overriding security considerations. In point of fact, this administration like its predecessors has been forced to recognize the complexity of the human rights issue. First, American leverage on this issue varies from state to state, but almost everywhere, it is appreciably lower than in the period when the United States was a major grant-giving agency, and with the capacity to commit or withhold its power in many areas. Second, in the case of South Korea, the very dissidents who are being repressed, with very few exceptions, do not want the United States to take the type of punitive actions against the South Korean government that might encourage the communists. They are opposed, for example, to a withdrawal of military support.

Finally, as a growing number of Americans are coming to realize, there is a difference between South and North on this issue—a vital difference from the standpoint of citizenry, as noted earlier. Thus, if human rights is to be made an issue, some more sophisticated means of measurement and the application of sanctions will be necessary, not the crude black-white standards of today. Whether any government can adequately define and apply such standards seems very doubtful. And as the actions of the Carter administration have already shown, if the exemption is to be made on security grounds alone, a charge of dual standards will certainly be advanced.

None of this is to assert that the actions of the Park government in matters of domestic political and economic policy will have no impact upon American policy. Even if the executive branch of government were to set these actions aside, Congress and the American public will react to commitments in some degree based upon their general appraisal of South Korea's political and economic health—measured against American values. The increased assertiveness of Congress in the aftermath of Watergate, moreover, will not quickly or easily dissipate. Park Chung-hee is aware of these facts, and he probably considers the alternative risks when making certain domestic decisions. As indicated earlier, Park's growing conviction at the end of the 1960s that the United States would undertake a strategic withdrawal from Asia unquestionably induced him to take anti-liberal, rather than pro-liberal risks, contrary to his policies of a few years earlier, when American credibility was much higher with South Koreans.

Setting this issue aside, what are the other major considerations with respect to U.S. policy toward Korea in the years immediately ahead? The foremost questions obviously relate to the timing and the nature of American military withdrawals, since—barring some unforeseen major crisis—such withdrawals have already been signalled. An interrelated issue is whether American policy should be fashioned and executed on a unilateral basis, irrespective of communist policy decisions, or whether it should be in some degree contingent upon reciprocal actions by the communists.

The current strength of American ground forces in Korea is approximately 37,000. Compared to the 300,000 troops maintained in Europe (and some 7,000 nuclear weapons), this is a miniscule force, and no one would argue that it constitutes a significant military component. Its purpose is clearly psychological and political—evidence of the American commitment intended to reassure the South Koreans and to deter the North Koreans. The fact that some American troops are on the DMZ, and the American military show of force that followed the bloody incident of August 1976, are illustrative of both the role and its risks.

The least American action would be represented if the U.S. first repositioned, then gradually withdrew its ground forces over the years immediately ahead, as the current South Korean military enhancement program moved to completion, but retained its technical installations, including the nuclear facilities, with the requisite number of military personnel to maintain them. It is difficult to see how such a development would greatly reduce the credibility of the American commitment, especially if the various stages were carefully coordinated with Seoul and Tokyo, although *any* withdrawal will probably have some adverse psychological impact since a climate of suspicion regarding American capacities and intentions already exists.

What are the weaknesses and strengths of such a policy? On the negative side, it will clearly not satisfy the communists. Pyongyang will continue to demand the *total* withdrawal of American forces, and presumably, it will obtain public support for that position from both the PRC and the U.S.S.R. With South and North Koreans facing each other alone along the 38th parallel, and conditions of militant hostility prevailing, moreover, it may be tempting for an incident to be provoked, merely to test American reaction under the new circumstances. Certainly, American leverage upon the situation will be reduced—leverage relating to both sides.

On the other hand, this policy of limited withdrawal removes the United States from a "front line" position and places greater responsibility on the South Korean government, the place where responsibility must ultimately rest. It also signals a fact of life, namely, the strong improbability that in the event of another open conflict, large-scale American ground forces would be used. It may be important for all parties to adjust to that fact, but with the knowledge that where American commitments hold, U.S. air and sea power will be brought to bear.

Another alternative is to withdraw all American forces, including the removal of nuclear facilities. If such an action were taken outside the context of any South-North or major power agreement, it would almost surely have a very destabilizing effect not merely upon Korea, but upon the entire Northeast Asian region. Indeed, the repercussions would probably go beyond Asia, reopening the general issue of American credibility. And if this policy were executed while the U.S. held firm to its European commitments, an additional question noted earlier would be raised among Asians, namely, whether there were not some racial factors involved. This is an issue already discussed privately in certain quarters.

Let us be specific. The impact of this policy upon both South and North Korea would in all probability *not* be conducive to constructive negotiations leading to substantive agreements. The South would feel itself in a defensive position, not so much because of the North's power, but because of its weak or uncertain international support vis-à-vis the continuing guarantees to Pyongyang from the PRC and the U.S.S.R. Thus, it would tighten internal controls even further and seek maximum military security from within its own resources. While Park made a public commitment in January 1977 to eschew the development of nuclear weapons, that matter might well be reopened if Seoul felt abandoned. And the mere continuance of the Mutual Security Treaty—*sans* all American visible support and any international agreement—would probably not suffice as a guarantee.

The North, on the other hand, might feel compelled to ride on such psychological-political momentum as the situation afforded, putting heavy pressure upon the PRC and the U.S.S.R. to give it greater support, whether for probing actions that involved military forces (raids and operations at sea) or a stronger political offensive. To the extent that the risk of American involvement in a Korean conflict appeared to have lessened, it would not be easy for either the PRC or the U.S.S.R., and particularly the former, to decline such support.

Japan, meanwhile, would almost certainly find its faith in the American defense commitment weakened, with new alternatives posed. The recent trend in some circles toward a more Asia-centered "non-alignment," but with strong nationalist overtones, would increase. But so would a disposition in other circles to strengthen Japan's own military capabilites. The resulting clash between these two positions might well immobilize Japanese defense policy, at least for a certain period. But whichever direction the ultimate policy, it would not be likely to strengthen U.S.-Japan relations.

Nor can the repercussions of such a policy on relations with the People's Republic of China and the Soviet Union be overlooked. As has already been indicated, both of these governments would feel themselves under heavier pressure to support some type of North Korean action, possibly diverse types of action. The issue of American credibility, moreover, has been as important to Peking and Moscow in their respective ways as it has been to Seoul and Tokyo.

If full U.S. military withdrawal is not to be undertaken unilaterally, what *quid pro quo* involving the DPRK and its big "allies" would be important? Three factors involving communist attitudes *and* actions would seem to be critical. First, the prior agreement of both South and North to seek a *peaceful* solution to the problem of reunification clearly needs implementation, particularly since Northern-supported covert operations continue, and hostilities erupt from time to time upon diverse initiatives. Thus, some type of formal agreement is warranted, together with a permanent commission to monitor and investigate charges, a commission consisting solely of Koreans—but with assurances by both sides that it will not be terminated in the fashion of the Red Cross and Joint Commission talks of the past. In addition, those talks—possibly with an altered format—should be resumed, with the understanding that they too will be terminated or postponed only upon mutual agreement.

Secondly, the Korean issue must be encased in some firmer international understanding and agreement. Ultimately, there should be a Four-Power guarantee of the freedom and security of both North and South Korea pending peaceful reunification, and that guarantee must be accepted by the United States, the People's Republic of China, the U.S.S.R., and Japan. This will require a series of conferences, and at some point, both Koreas must be involved.

Finally, pending any "ultimate" solution, the *de facto* situation should be recognized, with both the ROK and the DPRK being accorded formal recognition by all states, and the two Koreas being seated in the United Nations. Neither of these actions constitutes a barrier to peaceful reunification if and when the parties concerned can work out an acceptable formula. The present situation, however, is both an anomaly and unhealthy. The two Koreas are jointly recognized by a number of countries, and both accept that recognition. They jointly sit, moreover, in some of the U.N. auxiliary bodies. It is thus foolish not to universalize this situation, and the current objections of Pyongyang have no validity—particularly since it is extremely anxious to establish bilateral relations with the U.S. and Japan.

To reach agreement on these matters may be extremely difficult, but there are some matters of principle—and of future bearing on peace or war—of sufficient importance to warrant a combination of American firmness and patience.

Discussion

PALAIS: There was much in Professor Scalapino's presentation with which I could agree, and we covered so many topics that it certainly would not be wise to try to give my opinion on all of those. There are certain central areas of disagreement in terms of interpretation on which I would like to concentrate. First, I disagree on the interpretation of the nature of the Park Chung-hee regime. I regard the present regime as a much more serious political situation created by Park than has been depicted in Professor Scalapino's paper. Because of the way I view the Park Chung-hee regime, the remarks that Professor Scalapino made about the problems of maintaining the status quo in Northeast Asia and maintaining American credibility in terms of the defense of its current commitments have in fact been changed by the nature of the Park regime. Maybe it all centers around the question of status quo. I think it is a mistake to assume that there is a single status quo. We have a status quo today, we had one in 1975, 1972, 1969, 1967, 1965, 1963, 1961 . . ., in terms of what was going on inside of South Korea. Every one of those years represents a change in the domestic political situation inside Korea as created by Park himself. The changes in domestic politics in Korea have an effect on what the U.S. can do, and what it should do vis-à-vis the Korean situation; in other words, Park Chung-hee created different situations in Korea in a step-by-step fashion, most of it geared to the problem of controlling the domestic political situation in Korea itself, which has now created a situation that makes it very difficult, if not impossible, for the U.S. to maintain the same kind of commitments that it has in the past. I have spent twenty years studying the history of Korea, living in South Korea, and emotionally would like to take the position that the U.S. should maintain that commitment. But the situation is such now that we are forced into a position of re-evaluating.

I would like to focus on one question: whether or not Park Chung-hee's turn toward the right, the turn towards repression, since 1972, has been a result of the lessons he learned from Vietnam. I agree with Professor Scalapino that there are some lessons to be learned from Vietnam. It is an example of a country that was anti-communist going down to defeat; the questioning of long-term American commitment is raised. At the same time, more important than that way of looking at things is that Park Chung-hee was never really committed to any kind of competitive political system, not since 1961, when he took over power militarily; not since 1963, when he set up a force to create a civilian government.

In 1971, Kim Tae-jung came as close as anybody to replacing Park Chung-hee in a relatively open election. It might even have set a precedent. When the day comes that the Japanese can replace governments in a peaceful manner, then maybe they will have approached the stage of the South Koreans in 1971, despite centralized control over the administration, despite the lack of local elections, and despite the creation of the CIA. I think the message that was coming across in 1969 to Park was that if he continued with his commitment to his own constitution, he would not be able to run for a third term. He must get rid of that obstacle, which he indeed did. In 1971, the lesson was that if he maintained a relatively open political system, he would be defeated in the election—the same kind of message that Indira Gandhi just received in India. I think that is the main reason for the clampdown in 1972. I will not discount, however, the fact of the experience in Vietnam, which also played a factor. But I think the domestic situation in Korea is much more crucial. As time went on, I think Park increasingly tended to view himself as the indispensable leader for the Korean people. He never was committed to competitive politics. Personally, I think that it was a shame. Korea was on the verge of a breakthrough into what political scientists call the institutionalization of a stable kind of political system. If Park had taken the elder statesman approach, that of even some old genro back at the turn of the century in Japan, then he himself could have maintained some kind of a role in the future development of a Korea that would have institutionalized their politics and also solved its succession problem, which is now further away from solution than ever before.

Another factor involved in this problem is the question of disruption and Park's attitude towards internal disruption and disunity. The opposition party's program and policies were hardly different than Park's. On economic policies, for example, I'm sure that if a Kim Tae-jung regime had come into power in 1971, he would still be using advanced trained economists in the economic planning board just as Park would. His economic policies would go on the same line as far as his diplomatic policies were concerned. He was the one that called for a four-power conference in the presidential campaign of 1971. At that time what did Park say about him? He said: if you elect this man as president, he will present a weak-kneed position to the North Koreans; you can't trust him; I'm the only man that can defend South Korea against the situation. As soon as Kim Tae-jung was defeated, what happened? Park began the same kind of policies that Kim Tae-jung would have used. He began the talks with North Korea; there was not so much disunity.

Now I want to talk about the question of political repression. I regard the situation as very severe, much more severe than portrayed by Professor Scalapino, and very complex. I would tend to agree with

Professor Scalapino that the economic situation is very good despite my reservations about the distribution of wealth and the prevention of the emergence of labor unions, and freedom of negotiation, the urban-rural gap that was mentioned. Generally speaking no one can help but notice the vast improvement in the economic condition of Korea, at least since I have been there—I first went to Korea in 1957. The basic problem is political. To call the situation the freedom of silence is too mild a description for the current situation. What about the ubiquity of the CIA, the use of torture, for example, in interrogation, the complete absence of any kind of guarantee, a habeas corpus or anything of that nature, the total insecurity of the individual as he faces this kind of system, the fact that the system does not leave him alone? I don't think that the individual is left alone to keep his mouth shut. I have had the experience with some of my old graduate students where an idle comment in a restaurant is immediately transported, where information is conveyed to the CIA.

I have had people in the U.S. come to me and ask, "Should I go to Korea and ask for this person or that person; what will they do to me at the airport?" Koreans are aware of the intensity of the situation that prevails. I do not talk politics with anybody when I go to Korea. I do not want to compromise that individual. I think the situation now is worse than any time that I have been in Korea, including 1957, and this tells on people. Another thing, too, is the cross-dating of all the students I handle. It is not simply a question of setting up the troops at the front gate and not letting them out; it is the infiltration of the student community by spies and informers. As far as intellectuals are concerned, in the past year and a half, serious attacks have been launched. The tenure system has been disbanded with these five year contracts that they have now—private institutions as well as public. Who are these people who were laid off first? Anybody who was at all critical of the regime has been laid off and is currently out of a job. Faculty members with whom I have talked at various universities this past summer are quite cognizant of the situation and have a tremendous feeling of fear and insecurity. In addition, to say that the only segment of the population that is being suppressed by the regime is the students and intellectuals and the newspapermen I think is also erroneous. To be sure these people are the most courageous and the most outstanding. But the mere fact that Kim Tae-jung got over 40 percent of the vote in 1971, means that the anti-Park sentiment is much larger than simply the elite intellectual community—the people who are the most vocal.

Next, I would like to consider the question of maintaining the status quo, and the problem of credibility. As I said earlier, nothing would give me greater satisfaction than to see that the U.S. should really maintain our commitment to Korea no matter what the nature of the Park regime. But I really do not feel that is the case. One factor here is the lesson of Vietnam. In terms of American commitment to countries around the world, it is important to evaluate those regimes and those countries, to be sure in terms of the security situations but also in terms of the nature of those regimes. If the regimes become tremendously oppressive, there is a moral question involved whether the U.S. should defend regimes of that nature. Of course, we have to discuss the security question—that is a separate issue. We have to constantly re-evaluate the nature of the regime that we support. Furthermore, the question of possibilities of support is involved here, too. In my view, one of the aftermath problems of the Vietnam War is the situation that the tremendous opposition to the war generated in the U.S., due to discontent on the part of a large segment of the American population about the nature of the South Vietnamese regime. Now, in the U.S., more and more people feel that the Park regime is not one that Americans can support. I would find it difficult to advocate the defense and preservation of the Park regime to any American citizens going to Korea right now. I find it a difficult position to support. Where does the responsibility lie in a situation like this? Is it because the U.S. has become flabby in its support of its allies around the world? I say no, that is not the main reason. The current situation exists now because the Park regime has taken South Korea so far in the direction of opposition and has attributed to the destruction of the reputation of many people of the U.S. by its activities. The current situation is not a result of the flabbiness of U.S. liberals or the nature of American policy itself.

The American position in terms of credibility in support of the status quo, I believe, has been weakened by the nature of Park's policies both in terms of domestic oppression and his actions in the U.S. I take a different position than Jimmy Carter does. Jimmy Carter is continuing the line of thinking of Ford and Nixon, before we eventually have to pull out of Korea. In fact, that way of thinking is quite like Mansfield. I do not think that Mansfield cares about Korea at all. But I do not think this kind of regime can be supported. The pullback of military commitment can be used, and it has some effect on Korea in terms of moving the political aspect to a more liberal aspect—one with which the U.S. can live. From my own standpoint, I would be willing to make a long-term commitment to the defense of Korea—not a short-term one based upon the interest of the Korean people themselves.

I have not talked about the security situation involved here—those are very complex questions and I really cannot do justice to them. Generally I am in agreement with the construction that Professor Scalapino lays out. I think the crucial question has not been explored deeply enough, however. Let's put it this way. I am in favor of a phased withdrawal, in the use of pressure to induce a turnback toward a liberal and decent kind of government. Who needs American democracy? I think that it is an impossibility, that it is too much to ask. We need some kind of direction, so that the U.S. can really commit itself to the defense of the Korean people for their own sake. In this context, as we are pointing out options—and I don't think we should lose that flexibility—I don't think the U.S. should lose its complete ability to determine its options in Korea simply because Korea is anti-communist. As we are doing this, we can try to deal with some of these situations about which Professor Scalapino was talking, which is a diplomatic attempt to neutralize the Korean peninsula, working closely with the Russians and Chinese, and things of this nature. I would point out that the real question is, if we do withdraw slightly, is it possible to maintain peace on the peninsula with only the use of air and naval weaponry? Isn't the Sino-Soviet balance such that the North Koreans cannot commit aggressive warfare unless they have some type of guarantee from Russia and/or China? At the present time it doesn't look like they have it, although that is a matter for the future.

SCALAPINO: I feel that the primary difference between myself and Professor Palais is that I see the issue in considerably more complex terms than he. In a broad sense we are moving away from liberal democracy all over the world. Our choices are between what we would regard as quasi-authoritarian regimes and highly authoritarian one-party dictatorship mobilization type regimes, some of which also have certain expansionist motives.

The very fact that South Korea is prepared, for the time being at least, to live with a divided Korea, and that the North Koreans continuously talk about various forms of pressures to bring about the unification of all Korea *under their leader, Kim Il-sung,* is symbolic of the problem.

Professor Palais and I have had different experiences. I do not for a moment defend many of the political actions of the Park administration, and I too have been in Korea. Last summer I purposely spent time talking to five of the people under indictment, in their homes. I spent a considerable time with them, and what I found was a much more complex situation than Professor Palais has indicated. These are people who dislike the Park government but they do not want the kind of policies suggested by Professor Palais. They do not want policies of military withdrawal, and they are very clear about that. Furthermore, you can talk to these people, have them express their opposition, and not look over their shoulder. This was also true of many people teaching in the universities, who were not reticent in private to tell me what they felt was wrong with the administration.

I have not been in North Korea, but I would maintain that there is a significant difference between their degree of freedom and my experience in China, where I have been, and even in the Soviet Union, where the situation regarding intellectual discussion is considerably more open, and where we are beginning to get frank discussions on some issues (albeit not criticism of the Soviet regime). If we cannot make these vital distinctions, we had better not venture into the human rights issue. You cannot throw all countries into a black or white category. If we are going to make human rights an issue, we must have a fairly sophisticated, intricately graded table.

EMMERSON: I have very little to disagree with Scalapino's paper, and I would rather focus my comments on "Relations between Japan and the Koreas" in the following manner. The traditional enmity which has prevailed between Koreans and Japanese for centuries still affects present-day relations between the governments on the peninsula and Japan. Koreans still occasionally remind listeners of Hideyoshi's invasion of 1592 and their bitterness toward Japanese colonial domination which prevented normalization of relations after World War II for twenty years.

Korea remains a security problem for Japan. However, changing attitudes and situations are reflected in the wording of the so-called "Korean clauses" in communiqués issued after three meetings of presidents of the United States and prime ministers of Japan in 1969, 1975, and 1977. In 1969 Prime Minister Sato stated in a joint communiqué with President Nixon that "The security of the Republic of Korea is essential to the security of Japan." In 1975, in a subtle change of wording, Prime Minister Miki and President Ford affirmed: "the security of the Republic of Korea is essential to the maintenance of peace on the Korean peninsula, and the maintenance of peace on the Korean peninsula is necessary for the peace and security of East Asia, including Japan." A lessened degree of urgency and anxiety was expressed in the Fukuda-Carter statement of 1977: "the Prime Minister and the President noted the continuing importance of the maintenance of peace and stability on the Korean peninsula for the security of Japan and East Asia as a whole."

In 1969, while the Vietnam War still continued, it was important to the United States that Japan recognize a close link between Korean and Japanese security. The Japanese, who sought the return of Okinawa, were ready to take such a public position. Sato went even further than the communiqué in his speech to the National Press Club in Washington, giving assurances that the government of Japan would take a "forward-looking" (*mae-muki*) attitude should prior consultation by the United States result from an armed attack against the Republic of Korea. The opposition called this statement a dangerous commitment which could involve Japan in an American war. Sato explained to the Diet that if the United States, in the course of prior consultation, asked for Japanese cooperation in case of an emergency on the Korean peninsula, the answer could be either "yes" or "no." Fukuda, on March 29, 1977, told the Budget Committee of the House of Councillors that his position remained the same as that expressed in 1969 by Sato.

With respect to the issue of withdrawal of American ground troops from South Korea, the conservative wing of the Liberal Democratic Party, including such "hawks" as Kishi, Funada, Shiina, and Nadao, want the forces to stay. The leaders of the Self Defense Forces and other prominent members of the LDP, knowing that the Carter Administration was determined to carry out a phased withdrawal, have urged "caution" on the American government. Apparently during the discussions of the joint statement in Washington following the Carter-Fukuda talks in March 1977, the Japanese side tried, without success, to substitute the word "reduction" (*sakugen*) for "withdrawal" (*tettai*) in the communiqué's reference to American ground troops in the Republic of Korea.

The Japanese government is now reconciled to the eventual withdrawal of U.S. ground troops, as well as tactical nuclear weapons, from South Korea. Some politicians would prefer a "trip-wire" concept which would require a military presence but see that this is now impossible. They hope that the withdrawal will be gradual and that close consultation will be maintained by the U.S. government with both Seoul and Tokyo. An American withdrawal will not, however, result in any increase in the Self Defense Forces. Clearly the emphasis for Japan's defense establishment will be on *quality* rather than *quantity*, regardless of what the United States does in Korea. For Japan, the U.S.-Japan mutual security treaty is the important guarantee of the nation's security, not the presence of American ground forces in Korea.

The likely political trend in Japan toward the "center" will make Japanese foreign policy more rather than less cautious. Japanese leaders will probably favor a "two Koreas" policy, convinced that peaceful reunification is an unrealistic hope for the foreseeable future. They would like to see Washington open a dialogue with Pyongyang. Pressure from opposition forces for improved and expanded relations with North Korea will undoubtedly increase but the Japanese government will attempt to prevent a deterioration of economic and political relations with the Republic of Korea. Trade, investment, and economic aid are important elements in this policy. Difficult problems remain. The legacies of the Kim Tae-jung kidnapping and of the assassination of the wife of President Park have not been obliterated. By mid-May the continental shelf treaty between the two countries had not yet been ratified by the Japanese Diet. The suspicion of corruption, involving government officials and private citizens of both countries had not been dissipated and the so-called "Korean connection" remained to be thoroughly investigated. Additionally, the conflicting claims of each country over the tiny island of Takeshima, left unresolved by the normalization agreement of 1965, still plague the relationship between Seoul and Tokyo.

The prospects for the future are that within five years American ground forces and nuclear weapons will have been removed from South Korea. The U.S. commitments to both the Republic of Korea and to Japan will remain in force, but, in the case of Korea, the "trip-wire" concept will have vanished with a resulting increase in options open to the American government. Air forces will remain, for negotiation at some later stage.

The Japanese will press for direct contacts between the United States and the Democratic People's Republic of Korea and will be sensitive to signals from the north. They will continue to urge commitments from both North and South to "peaceful reunification." They recognize that any lasting solution will require negotiations in which both the People's Republic of China and the Soviet Union would participate. In the meantime the Japanese would favor recognition of the present *de facto* situation, meaning admission of both Koreas to the United Nations and recognition of both by all states.

AUDIENCE: When the American troops are entirely withdrawn from Korea within the next five years, and South Korea approaches the Soviet Union, what would North Korea do?

SYNN: If we approach the Soviet Union, Kim Il-sung and communist China might do something about it. When the American troops are entirely withdrawn from Korea, we have no choice but to approach the Soviet Union. I have not thought about the consequences.

First of all I would like to mention that I have not much disagreement with Professor Scalapino's point of view. In the conclusion of his paper, he seems to suggest that before the withdrawal of the American troops from Korea, there should be a kind of four-power guarantee. I agree with this point of view. Now I would like to say something about the Soviet interests on the Korean peninsula.

At the present moment I am doing my research at Arizona State University. There I have read the U.S. Diplomatic documents which dealt with the American and Soviet Far Eastern policies after the Second World War.

Traditionally, Imperial Russia had some interests on the Korean peninsula. But Korea is less significant to the Soviet Union than most of the Koreans would believe. During the Second World War, the Americans showed more their interests for the Korean peninsula before the Russians had any idea about the Korean problem. Since 1943, the Americans knew that they would have to take over the colonies of the now diminished Japanese Empire. From the beginning of the war, President Roosevelt did have a vague idea of trusteeship over Korea. At the Yalta Conference Roosevelt and Stalin agreed orally to a four-power trusteeship for Korea. Although there was no specific agreement between Roosevelt and Stalin at the Yalta Conference, their private decision was to have great influence toward the future of Korea. Stalin promised to enter the Pacific War against Japan, and in return the Soviet Union was to gain Russia's pre-1905 rights in Manchuria. In a broad sense we can say that the U.S. gave the northern part of Korea as the price for their (Russian) entry into the Pacific theatre against Japan.

It is interesting to note that it was the U.S. who took initiative as far as Korea was concerned. On August 8, 1945, the Soviet Union declared war on Japan. In order to prevent the Soviet occupation of all of Korea, the U.S. decided then to draw the line at the 38th parallel. In December 1945, at the Moscow Conference, Secretary Byrnes proposed to the Soviet Union a four-power trusteeship which was to last for a five year period. The Soviets accepted the American proposal. Secretary Byrnes did not know anything about Korea. When he proposed the trusteeship to Molotov, the latter pointed out that this was an unusual arrangement with no precedent, and that therefore it would be necessary to come to a detailed understanding. Secretary Byrnes proposed the trusteeship idea for political reasons at home. Generals Hodge and MacArthur opposed the idea of trusteeship over Korea. As expected, the South Koreans strongly opposed the idea. On the other hand, the Russians and North Koreans supported the trusteeship plan. I have the feeling that the Russians were sure that if the trusteeship plan was carried out, the entire Korean peninsula would be communized sooner or later.

After the failure of the U.S.-Soviet Commission, the U.S. decided to refer the Korean problem to the U.N. This was an admission by the U.S. of failure in her policy towards Korea. Naturally the Russians opposed the American proposal of referring the Korean problem to the U.N. They knew that the majority of the members in the U.N. were close to the U.S. in interests.

As early as April of 1947, the Korean problem went to stalemate. The Secretary of War, Patterson, advocated getting out of Korea at an early date. In September of 1947, the Joint Chiefs of Staff considered that, from the standpoint of military security, the U.S. had little strategic interest in maintaining the American troops and bases in Korea. Patterson argued that in the event of hostilities in the Far East, the U.S. troops in Korea would be a military liability. Even after the establishment of the Republic of Korea, the American troops were withdrawn so that there would be a minimum of bad effects.

Professor Scalapino has succinctly pointed out the U.S. policy in Korea for recent years. What I want to point out is that in early 1947, the U.S. decided to abandon Korea even before mainland China was communized. As far as Korea was concerned, the U.S. pursued a hands-off policy in 1949 and 1950. Kim Il-sung and Stalin were very sure that the U.S. would not intervene if the North Koreans invaded South Korea. But, when the Korean War broke out, the U.S. did intervene.

About the U.S. Far Eastern policy in general, ever since 1945, the American Far Eastern policy was made by George F. Kennan, John Davies, and some other influential State Department officials. Their hypothesis was that, in Asia, the Russians and the Chinese communists were working hand-in-hand, and that together they were going to expand throughout East and Southeast Asia. However, when reading through the *Foreign Relations of the U.S. (1945–1950),* I got the impression that there were no close ties between the Soviet Union and Communist China. In fact, Stalin delayed communization of China by helping Chiang Kai-shek. Mao Tse-tung communized China without Stalin's military and economic assistance. What I am trying to say is that the U.S. policy toward China or Korea was formed under the assumption that the Soviet Union and Communist China were *working hand-in-hand* with regards to Asian policy as a whole.

Specifically, during the Korean conflict, I do not think that Stalin consulted Mao prior to the outbreak of the war. It was only when the North Korean army was retreating, that Stalin asked Mao to intervene. So far as I know, if Communist China had not intervened, the Russians would have abandoned North Korea in November of 1950. In other words, Korea was not important enough to the Russians to start a general war with the U.S. And even after the Korean War, the Soviets did not make any effort to solve the Korean problem. There might be many reasons for this. The Soviet government makes public statements from time to time, stating that it supports the DPRK. This is because they do not want to lose North Korea to Communist China. The Russians do not have that much interest or stake in the Korean peninsula to raise the Korean problem to the Americans or Chinese.

At the end of his paper, Professor Scalapino suggests that before the withdrawal of U.S. troops from Korea, there should be a four-power guarantee to North and South Korea, to ensure that another war would not break out on the peninsula. I entirely agree with him. However, I would like to point out one more thing. If the U.S. withdraws troops entirely from Korea within the next five years, including its air force, I feel that South Korea would have to come to some kind of agreement with the Soviet Union. As we all know, the Soviet Union is the largest country in the world, Korea has nothing to offer in return for Soviet protection, except perhaps to fulfill the need for coaling stations or for radio stations. I feel that when the American troops are gradually withdrawn from East Asia, as they have been withdrawn from Southeast Asia, we have no choice but to turn to the Soviet Union.

SCALAPINO: I have very little disagreement with John Emmerson or Professor Synn, so I won't spend much time on their comments.

It has been suggested that in the various Japanese positions on the Korean security issue, there have been numerous differences and important nuances on Korean security in Japan, and I suspect this will continue to be the case even should the Liberal Democratic Party remain the political dominant force. It is rather difficult for the LDP to state precisely its position, not to mention the problem of coalition policy should that become a reality. However, I would submit that the general concern of the Japanese government over the Korean issue has been made quite clear.

Regarding Professor Synn's remarks, I can only say that turning to the Soviet Union may have an appeal, but that Russian bear has a very big head, one has to be aware of that.

PILLSBURY: I don't like to be on panels with Professor Scalapino, because first of all, he knows more than I do; secondly, he speaks better than I do; and thirdly, the times we have disagreed in the past in public, in the following six months to a year, I learn more, my mind changes, and I agree with him. But I have read this paper just this afternoon and learned a great deal from it. I have written down seven or eight points on which I disagree with him today.

First, in his first sentence, he misses an opportunity to comment about the possibilities of a Shanghai Communiqué type of solution to the North/South problem. In other words, in the Shanghai Communiqué, the U.S. government promised to withdraw in principle all of its military forces from Taiwan in return for a certain kind of agreement or pledge. This withdrawal was linked to peace and security in Asia, so I was surprised with this marvelous opening sentence to this forthcoming article, that Professor Scalapino neglected to take us back to the question of divided states and a possible Shanghai Communiqué type of solution.

Secondly, I missed in the paper, especially towards the very end when he discusses Kim Il-sung and the North Korean capabilities, the discussion of·what to me is the critical question about North/South relations; that is, what deters a North Korean attack? Why doesn't Kim Il-sung attack, either with a massive conventionalized attack or with much more serious probes than the things that have happened in the last four or five years? I would suggest that the answers to this question, however one answers them, affect what one would recommend in terms of U.S. policy. There is, first of all, the view that American ground forces in Korea deter Kim Il-sung. This is a prime factor. If this is the case, then moving the forces is very serious. My own suspicion is that in fact a major role is played by other factors detering Kim Il-sung, not least of which is his own judgment. This is pure speculation, that the South Korean ground forces and air forces may be adequate to repel a North Korean attack. To the question I raise, in terms of an article that deals with U.S. policy, we have to try to explain why certain things are not happening, as well as describing what has been happening in the last two to three years. I would also suspect that the Soviet-Sino relationship plays a major role in deterring Kim Il-sung. In this regard, I find that the role of China is neglected, and I think I disagree as well in Professor Scalapino's description of the Chinese role as basically unhelpful to the U.S. at this time in Korea. He mentions that apparently some people disagree with this and that the evidence is very hard to find. The only evidence I could discuss, which would be persuasive, would be that the general thrust of Chinese foreign policy in the past four or five years has been in part to act on the basis of parallel interests with the U.S. on a worldwide basis. We see the Chinese communists supporting NATO, calling for an increase in defense budgets in Western Europe. We see them encouraging East European countries to become more independent and autonomous, we see them taking action as well as payments in the Middle East. We see similar parallel interests in South Asia, and we see them in Southeast Asia. The question, then, should be raised: aren't there important parallel interests between Washington and Peking in the Korean situation?

My belief is that there are, and these come in part from the Chinese view. This again is speculation, but if North Korea were to become closely tied to the Soviet Union, this would fundamentally change the Chinese sense of threat from the Soviet Union. In the past four or five years, as we all know, the Chinese have expressed their fear of a surprise attack. If we had a large map here, we would notice, first of all, that if Soviet divisions would cross through North Korea, they could immediately enter into the empty area of Southern Manchuria and drive into Peking quite quickly. They would, in some sense, outflank the Chinese armed forces in Manchuria and on the borders. There would be a certain number of articles that prescribed Soviet deployments against China stressing that they are mostly around the two sides of Manchuria. From the Chinese point of view—and here we must also remember that the Chinese military has had a significant influence on Chinese policy in the last five years—and from a military man's point of view, North Korea is very important to the Chinese, and a war between North and South Korea would upset that kind of balance, and it would cause a shift in China's relations with the Soviet Union. I found this to be missing from the paper, we might disagree; but my impression is that this is an important element of the whole

U.S. policy problem—that is, Chinese perceptions of what could happen in the future in North/South Korea.

I also found a point of disagreement concerning the role of the Soviet Union. In discussing ex-Secretary Kissinger's proposal to have a four-power conference, Professor Scalapino suggests that there is a possibility that the Japanese and the Soviet Union could also participate at some point later on in the conference. It seems to me that a parallel interest of Peking and Washington may very well be that we cannot have the Soviets play a role in a four-power conference on Korea. This goes back again to the overall question of what is the Soviet Union up to these days in the world? As you know very well, this is a major debate in our government, a major debate in our Congress, a major debate in our academic community. One extreme view would say that the Soviets have always been paranoiac, have been afraid of invasion, from Napolean to the Nazis. Therefore, they feel they need to have a very strong military force to prevent a horrible devastation of their population from happening again, and that the U.S. should be forthcoming and generous in appreciating the Soviet psychological dilemma. Another extreme view—and here the Chinese perhaps would join in because they recently invited what is called a Committee for the Clear and Present Danger, and Admiral Zumwalt to visit them this coming month—the Chinese, in the extreme view of the U.S., would also say that the Soviets have one rather simple goal. They intend to use these military forces for political purposes. Now, depending on which point on the spectrum of what the Soviets are up to that you choose, I would suggest that your attitude towards U.S. policy in Korea is determined. Yet, in this paper there is no discussion of Soviet objectives either in the world or Northeast Asia. There is a hint that we should welcome a Soviet involvement in North/South discussions, and here I would recommend prudence and caution before advocating a Soviet role in this area.

On the question of possible cross-recognition, one has to confront the question of Soviet involvement. If the U.S. were to recognize the North, in return for Chinese recognition of the South, could the Soviets *not* be involved in this? The answer is probably "no." Those who would like to see a linkage between a cross-recognition and American withdrawal of forces—we intend to be inviting the Soviet camel into the Northeast Asian tent.

It seems to me that the Soviets have been quite active in the past ten years, in seeking naval facilities overseas in a broad circle around China, and the Chinese have been very explicit in describing this Soviet attempted encirclement of them. I have already mentioned the North Korean role in a Sino-Soviet war. I would also mention that there have been newspaper rumors of possible Soviet interests in facilities in South Korea. So I am sorry to appear before you as the

China specialist and yet talk so much about the Soviet Union. All I can say is that this is what the Chinese are talking about.

SCALAPINO: What deters a North Korean attack? I doubt that there is any single factor. Certainly increased military aid to the South is *a* factor. Another exists in the clear signals from both Moscow and Peking that they are not interested in another Korean war since they must be the principal suppliers of North Korea, and particularly the Soviet Union in military terms. I would say the American commitment is a crucial linch pin. The North might gamble on the strength of South Korea or at least it might escalate violence (since there are many steps short of an all-out war) if only South Korea were involved. Moreover, Pyongyang might get stronger permission from Peking and Moscow, or at least less resistance, if only South Korea were involved. What makes this crucial is no one wants to tangle with the U.S. even if they have doubts about its capacity at this stage in history. So I cannot believe that we are not a fairly crucial factor in this scene.

On the role of China, many Americans want desperately to believe that the Chinese are interested in helping us in Korea, or at least that they will take a parallel course because of their concern about the Soviet Union. I have looked at the evidence recently, and I would cite for all of you the most recent full statement of *Jen-min Jih-pao*, which is the official Chinese organ, of this year (February 17, 1977). It is about as hard a statement on the Korean issue as you could make. It comes out four-square for the Kim Il-sung approach to reunification, it calls for the withdrawal of all American forces immediately, it charges that American aggression has been responsible for the Korean problem, and continues to be responsible for it. One could simply not make a harder statement than this one and it comes from a very official source. If that were the only statement, one could excuse it by saying it was a pro forma. But in the last six to eight weeks there have been at least five major statements emanating from China that have done precisely the same thing, and this is not new; it has been consistent. Therefore it is wishful thinking to believe that the Chinese are interested in our staying in certain places in the world. They are all for keeping our troops and nuclear weapons in Europe, they are even in favor of us staying in Asia; they want us in Japan and they do not object at all to continued American presence in the Philippines, at this time; they always make it clear that this is temporary, but that does not mean by logic or by fact that they want us everywhere. In my opinion, Peking has worked out with Pyongyang an arrangement of support for Korean reunification in exchange for support for Chinese unification. The coupling on the Taiwan issue is now almost automatic in major pronouncements about the Korean problem, and I think we should take this seriously. I don't see how we can assume that this is all a facade and that Peking really does not mean any of it and they are secretly very anxious to have us stay.

I am not saying in the paper that this may forever be the case. The Chinese political situation is very volatile today; it is very uncertain, and a different regime might take different positions on this issue, as it might on other issues. But we should read the evidence that exists very, very carefully. Now, I happen to know, and I am not inhibited by dealing with classified materials so I can say this: there are high officials in American government who feel they have gotten signals at earlier points from the Chinese that are at least encouraging on the Korea issue. I think these could be read several different ways myself, from what I know of them. It is also true that we were encouraged at one point by Chinese action in the U.N., but again, it was a very modest action, and it has been overturned by certain events. As I said in the paper, I do not think that Peking imposes total trust in Kim Il-sung or vice-versa. But I think that the Chinese situation vis-à-vis North Korea at the moment is quite different than the Russian position. They are not the same, in my opinion.

That brings up my fourth point: What are the Soviets up to? I suppose my view is this. The Soviet Union intends to be a global power and it sees that as part of an equality with the U.S., and it believes itself capable of this. In my opinion, it will increase its power in Asia in the decade that lies ahead—its military power. If I am somewhat less than frantic about the Soviet threat, however, it is that as I looked at Soviet foreign policy in Asia, I do not regard it as totally successful. If the Soviets had the equivalent of the Senate Foreign Relations Committee, with Brezhnev on the griddle, they would assert these facts: we have made no progress in China, contrary to our hopes and expectations. Our relations with Japan are bad. We have not had good relations with North Korea for decades now. We may be about to "lose India" or so it seems. Our position in Southeast Asia hinges entirely upon our willingness to rehabilitate the Vietnamese. Where are we doing well in Asia?

I strongly doubt that military prowess makes up for Soviet political, economic, and cultural problems in Asia.

None of this means we should be oblivious to the Soviet problem. Obviously we are not and we should not be. This is going to be an issue for the rest of our lives—how we work out a *modus vivendi* with the Soviet Union that preserves two very essential premises: reciprocity and accountability. If the negotiatory process is to be accepted by the Americans over time, these are the two premises that must underride it; reciprocity and accountability in international terms. The question of how far to push human rights vis-à-vis the Soviet Union is, in my mind, a very debatable question, because I think the timing of liberalization inside Russia and the timing of the Soviet's accountability for its international behavior have to be viewed from an American perspective as evolving—and important to us—on very different time scales. When we confuse these, I am very much afraid of the consequences.

The point I would make in closing is that I do not think we can leave the Soviet Union out of the Korean question, and in my opinion, Pillsbury went full circle on this. First he suggested we ought not to bring the Soviet Union into a multi-lateral discussion regarding Korea since it might be dangerous to let the camel put his nose in the tent. My response is, the camel is already in the tent. The question is, How are you going to control him? You can't take this camel out of this tent. He is there. In the question of dual recognition, one comes flush up against that. But North Korea is still primarily sustained militarily by the Soviet Union. Hence I do not think there is any possibility, even if we wanted to, of leaving the Soviets out of a Korean solution.

AUDIENCE: In a lecture given by Dr. Jo recently here in Los Angeles, he was pessimistic about the prospects of reunification of Korea. Do you care to comment on this and also about the future of American commitment or policies toward Asia?

SCALAPINO: Let me comment on the last question first. In one sense, we are expanding in Asia rather than contracting. Our economic interaction with Asia is becoming steadily larger. It now exceeds our economic interaction with Europe. Our cultural interaction with Asia is also growing more meaningful. Even in terms of our population, under the new immigration policies, although the Asian part of America is still small, it is becoming significant in certain areas.

At the same time I think it is clear that the U.S.—and the so-called Guam or Nixon Doctrine is the first signal of this—under foreseeable circumstances is unlikely to put large ground armies into military conflict in this region. And I'm not certain, incidentally, that that applies only to Asia. It may very well apply globally.

The Guam Doctrine asserts that the premium for defense must be placed initially on the country threatened, the country with whom we have a commitment. The American nuclear umbrella and the air-sea power behind the ally will be used to try to sustain that commitment. But in the aftermath of Korea and Vietnam, I personally believe the capacity of the U.S. to fight a protracted limited war involving American ground forces in significant numbers does not really exist any longer. One is hesitant to use the word "never," because dramatic changes and conditions can produce dramatic changes in American public opinion and political mood. But, under present circumstances, I would say we are not likely to expand militarily, and thus the premium upon indigenous efforts. But at the same time, our interest and involvement in Asia, our concern, about a broad political and economic equilibrium in Asia is getting greater, if anything, as a result of our own interest.

On the question of the prospects for reunification, I hate to echo Dr. Jo's negativism, but I am afraid my view is that as long as you have such very different socio-economic systems as exist in North and South Korea, peaceful reunification is not very possible. I think any change will take a very long time. This does not mean forever. Nothing in politics is frozen, but I wouldn't hold my breath, waiting for this particular change.

JO: Since a question derives from my previous talk with regard to the prospect of reunification, I should comment briefly and then conclude this panel by way of dealing with the impacts of U.S. withdrawal. In so doing, I would like to perhaps try to change the negative image I might have inadvertently conveyed, that I am a cynic, that there is no prospect of any improvement on the Korean peninsula. It is true that the thing I did not care much about in the past administrations of the U.S. was over-emphasis on "power realism" nearing the sense of cynicism. Philosophically I believe in this idea of combining this power realism with "planetary humanism" in order to produce "corporative activism" for the solution of the Korean problem. Both Koreas should realize that there is no such thing as a real zero-sum game; this is one area the superpowers can bear witness to on the basis of their own experiences. The problem of the two Koreas, as in many instances in international relations, is a propensity to resort to mutual defections when knowingly there is far more advantage in mutual cooperation. The question is, "How can one encourage mutual cooperation instead of mutual defection in a situation like a *prisoner's* dilemma?"

Turning to the question of troop withdrawal, I was told that former Defense Secretary Laird did propose to Nixon that troops would be withdrawn by 1967, but the plan was aborted since Kissinger opposed it. And then, two years later, the Guam Doctrine was announced in 1969, and as you know, in 1970 Agnew also mentioned to the South Korean president about the withdrawal plan of troops by 1975. Now, I think we should not feel panicked with the prospect of total or abrupt troop withdrawal because I think, even in the mind of President Carter, the total abrupt withdrawal of U.S. troops from South Korea will bring drastic consequences about which he cannot assume any responsibility. So I think what might end up would be perhaps token and gradual withdrawal, in a sense, perhaps retaining air forces and naval forces, perhaps even to the degree of reducing the ground forces to about 1,000. This kind of change, in my estimation, is not a fundamental strategic change but it is only a tactical change because this is in no way tantamount to the loss of U.S. commitment.

Often in South Korea policy-makers and opinion-makers tend to analyze almost all political issues in terms of "To what extent is this going to affect our relations with the U.S.?" In sharp contrast to this "total dependence" in North Korea, they always talk about to what extent their policy is worthy of independence. So here is a contrast between total dependence and total independence, each of which is following a very extreme way of life. And I think somewhat reduced dependence on the U.S. might increase ability in crisis management in South Korea. It might also reduce the gap with the independent though almost myopic approach in North Korea. Also, as alluded in the comments made by Professor Synn, Korean-American relations were founded upon this cold war situation which took account of the Sino-Soviet alliance. But in view of the fact that the U.S. is now trying to improve relations with China, and Japan is doing the same with China, and in view of the continuing Sino-Soviet dispute, it seems to me that neither China nor Russia can support the war in Korea, even if North Korea might have a chance to win the war. Overall changes in the environment surrounding Korea seem to indicate that the status quo is not tenable in terms of long-range American interest, because the fundamental basis of that interest seems to be changing. One final note is this: according to quantum mechanics, a certain amount of uncertainty is sometimes helpful to produce or sustain stability, so all the talks of equating precariousness of Seoul as sources of instability may not necessarily be true in this case.

APPENDIX 1

The Other Sides' Views: Washington–Seoul Ties*

Yung-hwan Jo

Much has been said about America's role in Korea from the perspectives of the countries allied with the U.S., especially those in Asia. But how are the U.S.-Korea relations viewed from Socialist countries? This article deals with the image-systems and objectives of four communist polities, each of which differs in its views of American policy toward Korea. These are the People's Republic of China, the U.S.S.R., the German Democratic Republic, and Vietnam. The latter two are included for their similar "divided status" at least once even though they are not involved as much in determining policies affecting Korea as China and the Soviet Union are.

At the outset it should be noted that the perceptions and pronouncements of the decision-makers are not the same thing as the policies to be implemented. Even the policy objectives pursued in the past may not necessarily be operationalized in future policy. Besides, the views and actions of these societies are often affected not only by what we say and do but also by the global situation. The last but not the least disclaimer is that this article is prepared from the standpoint of an outsider, namely, a non-Marxist. In spite of these limitations, an article on this sort of topic might have a balancing place in the general understanding of U.S.-Korean relations. After all, more of the world's conflicts probably have had their origins in the misperception or perceptual distortion of the intention of the various sides.

In 1950, who could have visualized that the Soviet Union and China would have the almost zero-sum relations of today? The ideological orientation of Marxism-Leninism, the heritage of "Oriental" despotism, and a unified geostrategic framework covering the Eurasian heartland were all supposed to work toward cohesion between the two Communist giants. The final document issued by the European

---

*Reprinted with permission of *Pacific Community* (Tokyo).

Summit Conference, held in June 1976 in East Berlin,[1] made no reference whatsoever to "proletarian internationalism" but to a new doctrine of "national communism." This change reflects the interests differentially perceived in each socialist country. Since change in objective reality usually proceeds ahead of the corresponding change in perception, the ruling elite in these socialist countries would still share the views that: (1) the U.S. policy from its inception stood opposed to revolutionary change in China, Vietnam, and Korea; (2) "Maoism" and *juche* are Asian adaptations of Marxism-Leninism respectively to China and North Korea; and (3) the capitalist U.S. wishes to control the former "colonial" areas of the world through capital investment.

Almost all Marxists would argue that Marxism could be creatively applied to the dynamic conditions of all societies and hence the revolutionary developments in the latter cannot be analyzed in terms of strict interpretation of a set of dogma pronounced by Marx in the 19th century. Nevertheless, Kim Il-sung is about the only living leader who claims originality in his thoughts. Hence the use of "Kim Il-sung'ism" in North Korea, whereas there is no use of "Mao*ism*" (in distinction from Mao's *thought*) in China or "Hoism" in Vietnam.

II.

It is assumed here that the triangular Moscow-Peking-Washington relationship initiated by the team of Nixon-Kissinger will remain as a cornerstone of U.S. foreign policy and that real reconciliation between the Soviet Union and China is not possible under a Carter presidency of even two terms.

Let us turn first to the Soviet perception of the American presence in Korea. The Soviet Union sees no alternative but to support peaceful coexistence and détente with the U.S., although it is not willing to extend them to the realm of ideology. The Soviets are, however, adamant in resisting "coexistence" with Maoism, which is viewed as "a danger to all states, regardless of that social system."[2]

Following the conclusion of the European security conference held in Helsinki in July 1975, the Soviets shifted the campaign into high gear for the Asian collective security system, which, since its original pronouncement in 1969, has thus far failed to elicit a responsive chord in Asia. Although Outer Mongolia and Iran endorsed the Soviet proposal, no Asian states located on the periphery of China have accepted it. Neither Hanoi nor Pyongyang made any independent statements on it. In fact, only in South Korea and in Taiwan was there an expression or indication of interest in such a proposal.[3] This Asian collective system was aimed at containing China and was also a Russian attempt to be accepted as a major Asian power as the United States has been. (Soviet scholars and officials say that this security system applies to China and the U.S.)

The Soviet Union criticizes China for supporting a U.S. military presence in Asia, thus working against the national interests of other Asian countries. Today it condemns the Washington-Tokyo-Seoul ties more vehemently than China does; before 1970 Peking's condemnation was stronger than Moscow's. In fact, the "New Pacific Ocean Doctrine" put forth by Ford in December 1975, specifically spells out this tripartite partnership, support for ASEAN and normalization of relations with China as all being goals of the doctrine.[4] This doctrine calls for the continued necessity for American presence for the "stable correlation of forces in the Pacific Ocean," especially after the Vietnam fiasco. China was accused of having approved Ford's Pacific Doctrine.[5]

In 1976 the U.S.S.R. cited the proposals for limited U.S. military aid to China and for U.S. support for Japanese military build-up, respectively made by Schlesinger and Senator Bartlett of Oklahoma, as steps jeopardizing détente and increasing tension in Asia.[6]

The agreements reached in Helsinki and the proposed Asian collective security organization can be cited as evidence of the Soviet interest in and shift toward a multilateral approach to the solution of security problems, especially among the states of different socio-economic systems. It is even possible for some Soviet elite to see that the Pacific Doctrine is not diametrically opposed to the Soviet security system of Asia in that the former does not spell out the Soviet Union as a target; it was simply ignored in the Doctrine.

As to the question of Korea, what are Russia's stakes in the status quo or in change—including unification by either side? Unlike Vietnam where fear and hatred of Chinese domination has historically been great, a unified communist Korea is likely to be more closely affiliated with the Chinese than with the Soviet Union unless the post-Kim elite become obsessed with economic and technological assistance from the U.S.S.R. Also a communist Korea would mean a major defeat to the United States, and could be viewed by many in Japan as a grave threat to their country. If communization of Korea was in any way assisted by the Soviet Union, it would jeopardize the détente with the U.S. Hence the Soviet Union would not be interested in assisting the North to unify the South at the expense of its relations with the U.S. and/or Japan. On the other hand, if a unified Korea became closer to the Soviet Union, it would negate the long-sought Soviet objective of preventing a Sino-Japanese rapprochement.

In spite of their public support of the position held by the Democratic People's Republic of Korea on an American withdrawal from South Korea, the Russians privately see no advantage in such a withdrawal that would not only increase the threat of war on the peninsula, but also could easily strain Soviet-American relations if not cause confrontation and exacerbate Sino-Soviet competition.[7]

The conspicuous absence of Soviet reaction to the Kissinger proposal at the United Nations on 31 September 1976 on the phased four-party conference on Korea might signify a receptivity to the proposal for a multilateral approach to the Korean problem as much as, if not more than, the "lukewarm" reaction shown by China,[8] which is closer in terms of security to North Korea than Russia. In fact, the Soviet refusal to invite Kim Il-sung to visit Moscow in mid-1975 symbolizes the deepening suspicion of the North Korean leadership by Soviet leaders.

Lastly, the Russians seem to feel that two Koreas, as they exist today, will eventually be recognized either at the U.N. and/or outside as in the case of the two Germanys. The Soviet Union has signaled an interest in establishing some contacts with South Korea such as: (1) inviting sporting teams in the U.S.S.R. in 1973, which North Korea boycotted in protest, (2) their scholars mingling with those of South Korea outside of South Korea, and (3) even secret parley between ambassadors of the two countries. Not a remote possibility is reciprocal exchanges of recognition as suggested by Secretaries Habib and Kissinger, i.e. Peking and Moscow recognize Seoul while Washington and Tokyo do the same for Pyongyang. Here is a situation where the private wishes of the Russians could not be operationalized into a public policy in view of the resistance by North Korea and criticism by China of Brezhnev's "Two-Korea" policy.[9] In this regard the views of the East Germans run parallel with the Russians (a matter to be discussed at length below).

III.

No major event has revolutionized American assumptions of security in Asia more than the establishment of a Communist regime in China and its subsequent intervention in the Korean War against U.S. troops. Ever since, Communist China has been encircled by American allies with their air and missile bases supported by American submarines equipped with nuclear weapons. China is thus prevented from achieving territorial unification with Taiwan.

The U.S. clearly emerged as China's number one enemy, containing and threatening her. Just as the U.S. overreacted to China's new military capability, the Chinese officials overreacted to "American threats." Yet the Chinese perception of such threats appeared to be reinforced by their self-image. Because they do not see themselves to be encircling the U.S., American actions cannot be viewed as a response to a Communist threat.

Due to its ancient position in Asia, geographic propinquity, history, and cultural ties, China had many reasons to view Americans as alien meddlers and neocolonialists in Asia. China perceived any intrusions by American forces in such contiguous areas as Korea and Vietnam as a threat to its physical security. China wanted to keep hostile nations at a safe distance. Thus the geographical factor plus the fear of aggression from the "imperialist" United States on ideological grounds, explain China's major motivations behind its participation in the Korean War and its policy in the Vietnam War.

During the war between North and South Korea in 1950, it was the People's Republic of China that assisted the North, as the United States assisted the South. In fact, China's direct involvement in the Korean War and firm stand against U.S. activities in Asia have helped sustain the tie between China and North Korea; and this tie, in addition to the *juche* stance, has hindered the Soviet Union from regaining the dominant influence it once had in Pyongyang. Recently, however, over the heads of their respective allies, China and the United States have been taking a path of normalization.

This dramatic about-face in Sino-American relations was based on the growing mutual need for balance-of-power politics, as a counterweight to the Soviet Union. But from the Chinese standpoint, such a new relationship with the U.S. was perceived also to undermine the Taiwan independence movement. The official Chinese explanation of this policy shift, which was given to Chinese cadre, was that this facilitated taking advantage of newly revised analyses that named the Soviet Union, rather than the United States, as being the primary threat to the People's Republic of China. The U.S. with its threat to China receding, especially after Vietnam, can be utilized to offset the rapidly growing threat of the neighboring country.[10]

It must be added that China's limited détente with the U.S. did not represent, at least in the eyes of the Chinese, any abandonment of principle, in spite of the Russian charges to the contrary. Indeed, formation of a united front with a remote power against a neighboring primary foe has been a familiar Chinese style of behavior in ancient China and also during its civil war period. Besides, the present emphasis on détente with the United States and the preferability of American to Soviet influence in Southeast Asia tend to reflect less the communist zero-sum attitude and perhaps more the traditional Chinese point of view that the United States is less predatory than other powers. Traditionally, the closer the foreign country to China, the less the Chinese like the particular country to be entangled in penetrative foreign alliances—the military presence of a threatening foreign power in a contiguous country was always considered intolerable.[11]

The U.S. is now perceived by China to be moving toward normalization and détente with China, in spite of the former's reluctance to recognize China on a Japanese model and also to undermine the existing accommodation with the Soviet Union. The reasons are as follows:

(1) Inside the United States, there is an interesting consensus among the more liberal and conservative elements on the American

political scene, which, both for their own reasons, support improved relations with China. The amalgamation of these forces indeed creates an unusual and powerful impetus to promote relations with China. A stronger China could be tantamount to having China share the U.S. defense burden vis-à-vis the U.S.S.R. Hence, liberals who want a cut in the defense budget and conservatives who are against lowering the U.S. vigilance against the Russians are in agreement in wishing to increase China's defense capability against the Soviet Union.

(2) Not only is there a move in the United States leadership to improve relations with China, but also on China's counterpart there is a ready audience seeking to improve Chinese-American relations. This has been apparent in my preliminary study of Chinese Communist publications over the past two and one-half years.

(3) Both China and the United States desire to see NATO grow stronger. NATO is in a more effective position to reduce Soviet power worldwide than any other group.

(4) China is in need of "passive defense capabilities" such as satellite cameras and underwater listening devices that can be used in both military and civilian applications. Only the United States and Japan can provide this technology.

However, the foundation of the emerging détente between China and the United States would be shattered if not for the Chinese belief and anxiousness that the U.S. remain a credible power in Asia, including the Korean peninsula. Hence, the new phase of Sino-American relations is about the most important determinant for China's policy toward Korea.

As assailed by the Soviets, the Chinese have been receptive to the main trend of the "new" U.S. policy such as enunciated in the Pacific Doctrine. And the goals of their policy consist of Sino-American détente as well as acceptance of U.S. military presence on the Asia mainland with 38,000 U.S. troops in Korea. Such advocates of this policy as A. D. Barnett, former Secretary of Defense Schlesinger and Secretary Kissinger are all adamant on these points. Schlesinger, a darling of the Chinese officials for his anti-Soviet stand in 1975, even threatened to use atomic weapons against North Korea, an ally closer to China than to the Soviet Union.

The American role in Korea has thus become a test case of China's new strategy. The Chinese representatives at the U.N. have publicly supported the position of North Korea regarding its demand for U.S. troop withdrawal from South Korea, and even charged that the Soviet position is supportive of the Seoul government. At the U.N. debate on Korea in 1975, Yakov A. Malik changed the Korean people's slogan "*independent* and peaceful reunification" into "peaceful and *democratic* reunification."[12] (Emphasis added.) While the latter slogan is compatible with the position of South Korea, which has the majority of the

Korean population and which prefers the solution of the Korean question with the consent and guarantee of the four powers concerned rather than bilaterally with North Korea alone, the Chinese would privately entertain doubts about the prospects of solving the security or unification problems by the Koreans themselves, when the Chinese have not yet been able to resolve their own Taiwan problem *independently*. It appears that the Chinese stand on the stationing of American GIs in Korea has tended to soften in recent years and especially when their position is not publicly compared with the Soviet stand at a place like the U.N.

Just as Schlesinger, in the aftermath of the Vietnam fiasco, warned North Korea against attacking the South, it was Kissinger who warned the U.S.S.R. openly for the first time against assaulting the People's Republic of China. Kissinger's repeated declaration of support for China in October 1976, including the possibility of sales of arms to China, was apparently triggered by the political upheaval in the Peking government. However the desirability of providing China with some passive defense technology was already being discussed with the governments of Seoul and Tokyo in the early part of 1976.[13] To the degree that Sino-American détente moves in the direction of consulting Seoul and Tokyo, Chinese support for Pyongyang would not be operationalized into policy in spite of its public support of the latter. The Chinese stakes in North Korea against the U.S.S.R. must be measured against their stakes in cooperating with the U.S. and Japan to contain the Soviets. Pyongyang cannot "have its cake and eat it too" in that it cannot convince its allies to help it reunify Korea while soliciting their support in normalizing its relations with Washington and Tokyo.

Compared to the Soviet Union, China has been more openly supportive of Pyongyang and more openly critical of Seoul. It had appeared to be more willing to make concessions to North Korea within the limit of not jeopardizing Sino-American relations. It is interesting to note that the Chinese reaction to the West-drafted U.N. resolution on Korea was milder in 1976 than in 1975.[14] Unlike 1975, the Chinese foreign minister, Chiao Kuan-hua, attacked neither the Seoul government nor the Kissinger draft resolution on Korea. China, too, cannot afford to support any military action by Pyongyang that could not only involve it in a confrontation with the U.S. and Japan, but also that might excite Japan into rearmament. The latter is an eventuality that China fears, though to a lesser degree than the Soviets.

Turning to the future American role in Korea, much of it will be based on Sino-Soviet relations. The discord between the two affects Soviet and Chinese attitudes, statements, and actions particularly towards the U.S. including its relations with Korea. Likewise it tends to make both feel less threatened by the status quo in South Korea. For both, the American presence can be a stabilizing force on the peninsula in that the U.S. withdrawal might not only force them to confront the U.S. but also would promote further conflict between themselves.[15] Hence, contrary to their public statements, Moscow and Peking are less interested in advocating the U.S. withdrawal from South Korea, and the last thing they want at this time is a recurrence of a conflict in Korea.

IV.

Of all the Socialist countries no country is more obsessed with hatred for Americans than the Democratic People's Republic of Korea (DPRK). Since America's role in South Korea most directly affects North Korea, the focus of this article should be on North Korea's views and policies.

In sharp contrast to the South, North Korea is probably the land least influenced by the outside world and had been locked against Americans for half a century until the early 1970s. Reunification by independent means is being pounded into peoples' brains as the most cherished national goal along with U.S. "imperialism" as the main source of sufferings in Korea. Here children are taught to sing a song called, "We Will Mutilate Any American Soldiers We Catch Today."

Harrison E. Salisbury of *The New York Times* compared his visit to Pyongyang in 1972 with Hanoi in the follow manner:

> Not once in Hanoi had I ever been hectored by a Vietnamese about the conduct of the United States. Not once had a North Vietnamese come up to tell me that 'all Americans are liars.' Not once had it been suggested that I might be in danger if I walked in Hanoi's streets as an American. And, in fact, I had walked all over Hanoi without guide, censor or guard, simply by myself, at a time when American bombing raids over the capitol were a daily occurrence.[16]

Kim Il-sung told Salisbury that "the most important thing in our preparation for war is to educate all the people to hate U.S. imperialism."[17]

From the DPRK's perspective, the nationalist revolution has proceeded rapidly in the northern part of the country, and the entire peninsula would have become a socialist Korea had it not been for U.S. intervention in 1945 to abort the democratic revolution and in 1953 to abort the socialist revolution. Professor Fred J. Carrier, when visiting the DPRK in 1973, was asked why Americans who led the anti-Vietnam War movement are not more active in regards to Korea; he said he found it difficult to explain.[18]

Pyongyang has viewed the U.S. military bases in Korea and elsewhere in Asia as sowing seeds of discontent among Asians making good relations with the U.S. impossible. The Pacific Doctrine, which was implicitly supported by China, was perceived by the North Koreans as nothing more than a substitution of the bankrupt "Nixon

Doctrine" of aggression and a counterrevolutionary strategy designed to prop up the tottering system of aggression.[19] Even the Russians would not see it in such totally negative terms.

The success of a military coup in South Korea, and the increasing Japanese involvement in the latter's economy were viewed as a part of America's aggressive policy toward the peninsula. These events plus the changing nature of the external environment such as Russia's policy of "co-existence to détente" and China's emerging relations with the U.S.—all of these are perceived by the North Koreans to have increased the outgroup threat to their security and/or to have perpetuated the division of Korea.

Even though it is difficult to imagine how seriously Kim Il-sung is concerned about an unprovoked American or Republic of Korea attack upon the DPRK, the top leadership has been going to considerable lengths to contrive an image of imminent American attack leading inevitably to the final liberation of the South.[20]

The years 1967 to 1970 is the period of maximum North Korean militancy, not only in terms of defense spending but also in terms of the number of armed violations and guerrilla incidents.[21] The North Koreans apparently have attempted systematically to take advantage of the American preoccupation with the Vietnam War. At those times, when the U.S. threat is perceived to be receding, militancy of calls to war seem to have become more pronounced in North Korea.

In late 1970 the Fifth Congress of the Korean Workers Party signaled a shift from the heretofore held strategy of militant national liberation to the new strategy of the people's democratic revolution. This was followed by the North-South talks and there has been a noticeable increase in North Korean militancy in the two economically bad years of 1974 and 1975, coupled with the increases in the defense budget.

In 1974, Pyongyang made attempts to initiate a *direct* dialogue with the U.S. by repeating the idea of replacing the 1953 armistice agreement with a peace agreement. Renewal of these attempts are related to its perception of the South being vulnerable as a non-participant of the armistice agreement.[22] (According to their scenario, the impacts of direct negotiation if not détente with the U.S. will be extended to the South, which in turn would pressure the latter to acquiesce in the U.S. withdrawal. This will leave both Koreas with no alternative but to opt for an independent solution between themselves, a precondition for a confederation.) The former U.S. Ambassador to the United Nations, William Scranton, indicated the preference of the Soviet Union and China for a multilateral conference on Korea as proposed by Kissinger over the bilateral approach proposed by North Korea. Even the latter is rumored to have realized the futility of their bilateral solution.[23]

In the 1960s, Kim's policy of ambivalent neutrality toward Moscow and Peking provided him not only with a certain maneuverability but also with the diminished cumulative support from both. In the 1970s, especially following the debacle of Indochina, Kim cannot even be certain about obtaining Sino-Soviet commitment to this persistent idea of *"one* confederate *Korea."* Japan and the U.S. have supported the Seoul idea of "two Koreas." Since the stakes of the Russians and the Chinese in improving relations with the former are so great, as North Korea rightly fears, this will make the two communist giants not only unwilling to provide support for a war in Korea but even push one or both of them to eventually adopt a "two Korea" policy. This nightmarish fear of North Korea was somewhat alleviated in April 1975, when the joint Sino-North Korea communiqué referred to the DPRK as "The sole legitimate sovereign state of the Korean nation,"[24] thus cutting off any future Chinese move in the direction of "two Koreas." The Russians have not followed suit. (Careful analysis of the above communiqué reveals a conflict of interest on both sides, although it is easy for China, which is still divided, to support the idea of a unified Korea.)

North Korea's efforts to isolate South Korea diplomatically have not been successful. An increasing number of countries would extend recognition to both Koreas, thus making Pyongyang's resistance to the admission of both to the U.N. increasingly difficult, as in the case of dealings between its allies and South Korea. As small powers learn to cut across the old alliance system and deal independently with the larger powers, to extend cross recognition by the great powers of the two Koreas will not be too remote in the future. The cross pressures stemming from the changing international environment and the urging of its allies plus its own learning process will eventually contribute to a fundamental reorientation process of North Korean strategy.

It may be worthwhile to add a note on the recent development on the part of *chochonryon,* a pro-North Korean residents' organization in Japan, which, in the eyes of the DPRK, collaborated militarily and economically with South Korea and the United States. Japan was criticized for supporting the "two Korea plot," and also for agreeing to comply with Washington's request for the introduction of nuclear weapons into Japan in the event of the development of an emergency situation in Korea.[25] In an extensive interview I had in June 1976 with Oh Chung-tae, head of the *Chominryon* formed with the dissidents of the *Chochonryon,* he indicated that one of the catalysts that alienated him from the pro-North Korean organization was his lingering doubts about Pyongyang's myopic view of U.S.-Korean relations, doubts that were later confirmed by his recent visit to South Korea. It is possible that the suspicion, if not paranoiac fear, on the part of the Korean communists, and the human tendency to buttress their own perceptions with a healthy dose of communist dogma probably led them and Mr. Oh to believe what they say publicly about the U.S.

As evidenced by those Koreans in Japan who, in spite of their allegiance to Pyongyang, could not avoid the penetration of influence by bourgeois society, the more the North Koreans interact with the international community, the smaller a perceptual gap they are likely to have toward the United States. (See the Figure in the following pages.) This should result in them attaining at least the Chinese level of external behavior in a decade and the Eastern European and Russian level in another decade.

It was North Korea that initiated bringing up the Korean question again at the 31st General Assembly of the United Nations, but in September of 1976, North Korea surprised its allies as well as its adversaries by retracting her demand for another U.N. confrontation on the question. Various interpretations and speculations have been made on this, namely: (1) a palace struggle is being waged over leadership succession, (2) a diplomatic rebuff for the Pyongyang government at the nonaligned summit in Sri Lanka, (3) cooler attitudes by the new Chinese Communist Chairman Hua Kuo-feng regarding the North Korean positions on unification efforts and on the U.N., and (4) erosion of support on the part of Yugoslavia and Rumania to say nothing of the U.S.S.R. on these issues.[26]

The worldwide reaction to the Panmunjom incident of 18 August 1976, which resulted in the deaths of two American servicemen, could be the catalyst for the U.N. shift. But it has now been revealed that the U.S. then had information about the smuggling activities of the North Korean diplomats in Scandinavia and was prepared to discuss these embarrassing matters at the forthcoming U.N. debate. The threat of such scandal prompted the abrupt withdrawal of North Korea from the debates.[27]

V.

How can one, without being subjective, assess the implications of these turns of events for Pyongyang as far as U.S.-Korean relations are concerned?

First it may be of some use to refer to the views expressed on the subject by East Germans and Vietnamese for the purpose of comparison.

The Democratic Republic of Vietnam (DRV) shares many of the views of Pyongyang with respect to the U.S. presence in Korea, on independent reunification of Korea, on the third world, and on the Pacific Doctrine. It agrees with the DPRK in perceiving the U.S. as no longer being the number one world power and having been surpassed by the U.S.S.R. in many areas.[28] But Vietnam shows a more pragmatic, less ideological coloration compared to Pyongyang. Hanoi would have no qualm in receiving aid or credits from the capitalist world, although Pyongyang was forced by necessity to develop a similar attitude vis-à-vis Japan and European countries. Compared to North Korea, Vietnamese interest in normalizing relations in trade, travel and diplomacy with the outside world is far stronger, although still limited in scope. In establishing diplomatic relations with the U.S., it anticipates a more cautious approach and yet is not afraid of even the C.I.A. penetration.[29]

Another kind of possibility, which is unthinkable to North Korea, is being seriously considered by Hanoi; that is, the possibility of a joint venture with U.S. oil companies for off-shore drilling.[30]

As for the East Germans, American movies are shown to them and American tourists are allowed to enter daily—utterly unthinkable to the North Koreans. (I was privileged to be the first American to lecture for a week at one of their universities in November 1975. During the more than two weeks that I spent in North Korea, I was never asked to give any lectures; rather I was being lectured most of my stay in February 1974.) Even if the different nature of the East-West confrontation between the two Germanys and the two Koreas is taken into account, one cannot help being struck with the marked contrast.

In East Germany it is difficult to ascertain a fierce sense of xenophobia, chauvinism, personality cult of the leader, such as that so evident in North Korea. There is daily traffic between the two sectors on many levels, far fewer misconceptions regarding the other Germany and a clear priority for peace and prosperity over reunification. East Germans are more reconciled to the reality of the division and less interested in reunification efforts than West Germans. Although Koreans on both sides attach greater value to the ultimate unification, it is the North that is more adamant on a unified Korea whereas the South insists on the acceptance of two Koreas and peace as a precondition to unification. In fact, I was privately warned in East Germany not to judge socialism by North Korean behavior, which was described as that of a "socialist Prussia."

VI.

In summary, my analysis on the difference in point of view about the U.S. role in Korea can be assigned numerical values as shown in the following three scales.

Clearly the DPRK is by far the least knowledgeable about the affairs of the United States. The perceptual gap of the CPR and the DRV cluster together at a half point level, and the USSR and GDR cluster at an even lesser point. The perceptual gap of the GDR is lowest of all.

SCALE I: PERCEPTUAL GAP (knowledge)

	Highest				Lowest	
	5	4	3	2	1	0
USSR					1.2	
GDR					1.0	
CPR				1.9		
DRV				2		
DPRK		4				

SCALE II: ANTI-AMERICAN SENTIMENT

	Highest				Lowest	
	5	4	3	2	1	0
USSR					1.3	
GDR					1.5	
CPR			2.5			
DRV		3.5				
DPRK	5					

SCALE III: AGREEMENT WITH DPRK UNIFICATION POSITION

	Highest				Lowest	
	5	4	3	2	1	0
USSR				2.3		
GDR			2.5			
CPR			3			
DRV		3.5				

In terms of anti-American sentiment, the DPRK ranks highest. The CPR and the DRV are a little apart because the Chinese have been more successful diplomatically with the U.S., although the DRV is also making efforts in this direction. The USSR and the GDR are old hands at détente.

Agreement with the DPRK's position on unification is very close among all these communist countries. The Chinese and the Vietnamese, who have slightly greater perceptual gaps of the U.S. and more anti-American sentiment, feel more strongly than the others.

Are these three scales causally related? The following composite rank-order figure for the three scales answers in the strong affirmative. That is, the rank correlation between perceptual gap, anti-American sentiment, and agreement with the DPRK position is very high; only the USSR and GDR ranks reverse themselves across scales.

The U.S.S.R., China, and East Germany regard aggression from the North as likely as suppression of a national liberation movement in the South by the Seoul government, while North Korea alone (Hanoi with some reservation) regards the latter a reality and the former a figment of imagination.

THE COMPOSITE FIGURE OF THE THREE SCALES

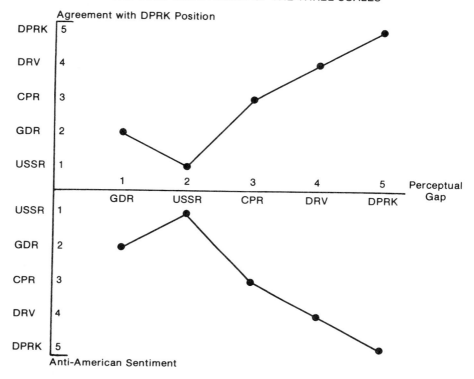

Note: The numbers on the axes are ordinal rank and not interval scales.[31]

North Korea argues that a peace treaty with the U.S. should supersede the 1953 armistice and that a precondition of détente and independence is withdrawal of all U.S. forces. But China is apprehensive about the U.S. military withdrawal from the Korean peninsula, a tactic that is being labeled by the Soviet Union as an "anti-socialistic policy." Nevertheless, both Pyongyang and Peking (with reservations) are more inclined toward a bilateral approach to the solution of security problems whereas Moscow, East Berlin and Hanoi (with reservations) prefer "multi-lateralism."

Vietnam is as much interested as North Korea in fostering the development of independence from the U.S.S.R. and China, but the former is far more flexible in its foreign policy and willing to normalize relations with the U.S. This reflects the fact that Pyongyang understands far less than Hanoi, East Berlin, or Moscow regarding the intricacies of the new American policy in Asia.

The most myopic view of U.S.-Korean relations is held by North Korea, and the crucial question is how to encourage North Korea (via remote control?) to think more like the German Democratic Republic, the Soviet Union, the People's Republic of China, and the Democratic Republic of Vietnam without offending North Korea's sensibilities.

The *juche* ideology of North Korea is being twittered at by the U.S.S.R. and the G.D.R. Even China and Vietnam would look upon the behavioral manifestation of it with cynicism. By now the personality cult of Kim Il-sung and the elevation of his son, Kim Chung-il, as a possible successor are sources of private ridicule by almost all elites in these countries. (At a recent meeting in the New York area, a North Korean official reportedly responded to the criticism of this nepotism by stating that the automatic succession of the Junior Kim is a "fabrication of imperialists' propaganda and that one of the generals" has an equal if not better chance to succeed Kim Il-sung.)[32]

All of these developments plus economic difficulties, succession struggles and diplomatic embarrassments seem to have turned the North Korean polity inward-looking for a while. Any unwarranted threat by an outsider at this time might have a very dysfunctional effect upon Pyongyang's policy decisions toward both South Korea and the United States.

VII.

What are the future implications of the other sides' views for Washington, Seoul, and Japan?

All the noticeable trends in the data collected for this article suggest that the support of North Korea within the other side's camp is by far less than the support of South Korea in this side of the camp, even if one takes into account the negative impacts of "Koreagate" on Washington. Neither China nor the Soviet Union is likely to assist the North in a war as they did during the Korean War. The Sino-Soviet alliance was fragile from the beginning and now is dead for all practical purposes as is the idea of the monolithic communist strategy, which, according to the recently declassified U.S. documents, hardly existed during the Korean War, or even before or after.

Under these circumstances, even if a conventional and nuclear vacuum is created in South Korea in four to five years, when President Carter plans to complete withdrawal of U.S. ground troops, such a vacuum cannot be as inviting to North Korea as that which existed in Korea prior to 1950. In the first place, American naval and sea power, both conventional and nuclear, will remain in and around South Korea (they are viewed by China as restraining the U.S.S.R.), and an anticipated future inferiority in modern aircraft and missiles in the absence of American troops will be made up by U.S. assistance in modernizing the defense capability of South Korea. President Park Chung Hee is probably right in stating recently that South Korea today can defend itself against a North Korean attack staged without the support of China and the Soviet Union.[33] Two years ago he told an American correspondent that by 1979 or 1980 South Korea's armed forces would be sufficiently modernized to be able to defend itself against such an attack without U.S. air and sea support.[34] For these reasons, the phased withdrawal of U.S. troops should not be that alarming to South Koreans and Japanese. After all, thanks to the Indochina debacle, ironic as it may sound, averting another war in Korea has become a more important priority for the U.S., if not for Japan, than before the debacle.

Alarmists and opponents of American withdrawal warn of Japan being forced to increase its air and naval power and to consider nuclear weaponry. But such a consequence, though welcome to the U.S., is likely to accrue only in the event of abrupt withdrawal. The Carter Administration cannot afford to take this latter option for fear of its contrasting impacts on the minds of the South Korean people and Kim Il-sung, not to mention Japan.[35]

The fact that none of the four major powers, i.e., the U.S.S.R., U.S.A., China, and Japan, would welcome any change in the strategic balance around Korea should be an assurance for the security of South Korea, but that is not sufficient for the needs of the war-allergic people in Seoul. Yet the South Korean security has not been enhanced by the kidnapping of Kim Doe-jung, repressive measures toward dissidents, and the "Koreagate" scandal. In fact, it can be argued that the "mistakes" committed by North Korea such as digging tunnels across the DMZ, unprovoked assault on U.S. guards at Panmunjom, and its propensity to take risks against the South have contributed more to the security of South Korea by way of alerting the peoples there and the U.S. to the precarious state of Seoul.

In the long run, as long as Seoul retains its credibility in the eyes of the American and Japanese peoples by avoiding a regressive trend in political development, even without a parallel progression of economic development, the Soviet Union and China will eventually come to support "the two Koreas first approach" of Seoul, which is now being endorsed by the U.S. and Japan. Since the U.S.S.R. has already expressed its interests in establishing limited contacts with Seoul by allowing its naturalized citizens of Korean origin to visit South Korea, in addition to those interactions listed above, South Korea has been hastening to seize such opportunities by exploring commercial contests etc.; there was even a hint dropped about the possibility of leasing Cheju Island to the Russians as a fueling station. Such a leaning towards Russia sans China policy would complicate, if not foreclose, future relations with China. In view of the emerging rapprochement between China and the U.S., the latter two could do as much, if not more, for Seoul, than the two disputing Communist giants could do for North Korea. After normalization of Sino-American relations, China could come close to the Seoul position of "two Koreas" first, and "gradualistic approach toward unification" next.

*This is a reorganized and updated version of the paper delivered at the U.S.-Korean Conference, Western Michigan University, November 4–6, 1976. Thanks are due to my colleagues, Sheldon W. Simson and Stephen G. Walker for their comments and also to Sarah Veblen for proofreading and typing the manuscript.

1. *New York Times,* 1 July 1976.

2. *Yearbook on International Communist Affairs* (Stanford, California: Hoover Institute Press, 1976), p. 82.

3. Jae Kyu Park and S. Han, ed., *East Asia and the Major Powers* (Seoul: Kyong Nam University Press, 1975), p. 99; Yung-hwan Jo, ed., *Taiwan's Future?* (Hong Kong: Union Research Institute, 1974), p. 6.

4. *Foreign Broadcast Information Service* (FBIS), III, 9 December 1975, B 1–4.

5. *FBIS,* III, 24 December 1975, Cl.

6. *FBIS,* III, 24 April, 7 May, 20 May, 2 June 1976.

7. Robert A. Scalapino, *Asia and the Road Ahead* (Berkeley: University of California Press, 1975), pp. 176–78.

8. *The Korea Herald,* 12 October 1976.

9. My own contacts with the Russians bear this out. Also, witness Scalapino, *loc. cit.*

10. See *Confidential Document: Outline of Education on Situation for Company* (Lien Tui Hsing Shih Chiao Yu Ti Kang), Published in Taiwan, 1974.

11. Norton Ginsberg, "On the Chinese Perception of a World Order," *China in Crisis,* Vol. Two, ed. by Tang Tsou (Chicago: University of Chicago Press, 1968), p. 87.

12. *FBIS,* IV, 5 November 1975, A2.

13. *The Joong-ang Daily News,* 27 April 1976.

14. *The Korea Herald,* 7 October 1976.

15. This idea was discussed with Dr. Thomas Robinson at our 1976 symposium on "A Reassessment of America's Role in Asia." Consult this forthcoming book.

16. Quoted from his *To Peking and Beyond* (New York: Capricorn Books, 1973), p. 204.

17. Quoted in Kim Il-sung, *For the Unification of Korea* (Montreal: Spark Publication, 1976), p. 18.

18. See his papers in the *Symposium.*

19. *FBIS,* 10 December 1975.

20. Robert A. Scalapino and C. Lee, *Communism in Korea, Part II* (Berkeley: University of California Press, 1972), p. 948.

21. See various tables cited in D. S. Zagoria and Y. K. Kim, "North Korea and the Major Powers," *Asian Survey,* December 1975, Vol. XV, No. 12, pp. 1018–1026.

22. See Young C. Kim, "The DPRK in 1975," *Asian Survey,* January 1976, pp. 87–88.

23. Quoted in *The Washington Observer,* 1 September 1976.

24. *Korean Central News Agency,* 26 April 1976, *Kita-Chosen Kenkyu,* I(11), April 1975.

25. *Nodong Shinmun,* 10 March and 19 April 1976.

26. *Asahi Shinbun,* 10 June and 10 October 1976.

27. *Dong-a Ilbo,* 23 October 1976.

28. *FBIS,* Vol. IV, No. 114, 11 June 1976.

29.   Cited in Nguyen Khac Vien, *Tradition and Revolution in Vietnam* (Washington, D.C.: Indochina Resource Center, 1974), p. 150; also see the Year Book, *op. cit.*, p. 405.

30.   *Far Eastern Economic Review*, 12 December 1975.

31.   For a correlation coefficient that summarizes the relationships between the three scales and their statistical significance, consult H. M. Blalock, *Social Statistics* (New York: McGraw-Hill Book Co., Inc., 1960), Chapter 18, Section 3.

32.   As relayed during the discussion at the Association for Asian Studies Meeting, March 25–27, 1977.

33.   Republic of Korea, U.N. Observer Office *Press Release*, No. 20/77, 25 April 1977.

34.   Cited in an interview with Richard Halloran, *The New York Times*, 21 August 1975.

35.   See Drew Middleton, "Korean Withdrawal Debate Warms," *The Arizona Republic*, 8 April 1977.

Bio-Data of Participants

HANS BAERWALD. A Professor of Political Science at UCLA and currently chairman of the Japan Seminar in Los Angeles. Author of *Japan Parliament* (Cambridge) and others.

PETER BERTON. Professor and Coordinator of the East Asian Regional Studies Program in the School of International Relations at USC. Editor of *Studies in Comparative Communism* and *Far Eastern and Russian Research Series*.

FRED J. CARRIER. History Professor, Villanova University. Co-chairman of the American-Korean Friendship and Information Center, New York, an organization with close affiliations with the North Korean government. He has also authored *North Korean Journey: The Revolution Against Colonialism*.

PHAN THIEN CHAU. Chairman, Department of Political Science, Rider College. Chairman, Viet Nam Studies Committee, Association for Asian Studies, 1975–76. Author of *Vietnamese Communism* and numerous articles on Vietnam.

SOON SUNG CHO. Professor of Political Science at the University of Missouri-Columbia, after an intermittent teaching career at Japanese and Korean universities. This scholar is author of *Korea in World Politics* (Berkeley).

JOHN K. EMMERSON. Senior Research Fellow at the Center for Research in International Studies at Stanford University. Former Foreign Service Officer with specialty in Japan.

MELVIN GURTOV. Professor and former chairman of the Department of Political Science at the University of California-Riverside. Formerly a member of the Pentagon Papers Task Force, 1967, while on the staff of the Rand Corporation. Author of articles and books on Southeast Asia and China.

PYONG-CHOON HAHM. Until recently, Ambassador of the Republic of Korea to the United States since 1973. Previously served as Special Assistant to the President from 1970–1973. After graduating from Harvard Law School, he taught law at Yonsei University, and was research scholar for Yale Law School.

GREGORY HENDERSON. Former Cultural Attaché of the U.S. embassy in Korea. Author of *Korea: the Politics of the Vortex*. Professor at Fletcher

School of Law and Diplomacy, Tufts University, and recently was awarded Visiting Knight Professor of Humanities chair at Case Western Reserve University.

YUNG-HWAN JO.   Director of the Center for Asian Studies and Professor of Political Science at Arizona State University. Editor of *Asian Forum* (quarterly). Taught in Japan and Taiwan on Fulbright, and visited China and North Korea, and recently lectured in East Germany. Edited *Taiwan's Future?*.

ANTHONY KAHNG.   Associate Professor of Organizational and Social Sciences at the New Jersey Institute of Technology. After graduating from Yale Law School, he has taught labor law and legal problems of Asian-Americans.

BERND KAUFMANN.   An East German expert on American foreign policy in Asia. While working in Peking as the First Secretary, Embassy of the German Democratic Republic, he visited both North Korea and North Vietnam. For the past few years Dr. Kaufmann has been on the faculty of Section Asienwissenschaften, der Humboldt-Universität zu Berlin. His areas of publication and research are on Chinese foreign policy.

WILLIAM V. KENNEDY.   A military writer currently assigned to the U.S. Army War College as a Military Operations Research Analyst.

CHANG SOO LEE.   Director and Assistant Professor in the Center for Asian-American Studies, University of Southern California.

SCOTT G. McNALL.   Chairman and Professor in the Department of Sociology, University of Kansas. Director of the National Security Seminar. He is the author of several books and articles in the field of military sociology.

MITCH MEISNER.   Lecturer in Chinese Politics, University of California-Santa Cruz. He visited China in 1972 as a member of the second delegation of the Committee of Concerned Asian Scholars. One of his primary interests is in American relations with China and Vietnam.

DOUGLAS MENDEL, JR.   Professor of Political Science at the University of Wisconsin-Milwaukee. Author of books on Japanese and American foreign policy as well as Formosan nationalism. He is also Far Eastern Representative for the Roper Public Opinion Research Center at Williams College.

ROBERT T. OLIVER.   Advisor to the late President Syngman Rhee from 1942–1960. He has authored more than thirty books—six of which deal with Korea and Asia. The Research Professor Emeritus of International Speech at Pennsylvania State University.

JAMES B. PALAIS.   Professor of Korean History, Institute of Comparative and Foreign Area Studies at University of Washington.

YUNG H. PARK.   Professor of Political Science at California State University-Humboldt. Co-author of *Area Handbook for the Republic of Korea* and articles on Japan-Korea relations.

GUY J. PAUKER.   A Senior Staff member of the Rand Corporation and specialist in Southeast Asia and security policies.

DOUGLAS PIKE.   A member of the Policy Planning Staff of Henry Kissinger's Secretariat in the Department of State. He authored *Viet Cong* and is generally considered to be the U.S. government's chief expert on the Indochinese communist movement.

MICHAEL PILLSBURY.   China specialist for the Rand Corporation, and former Assistant Political Affairs Officer at the United Nations Secretariat.

DANIEL GARETH PORTER.   Director, Indochina Resource Center, Washington, D.C. He has done field research for his Ph.D. (Cornell) in South Vietnam in 1971 and returned to North Vietnam in December 1974-January 1975. He is a well-known critic of U.S. involvement in Vietnam and has a list of publications dealing with this subject.

DENNIS M. RAY.   Professor of Government at California State University at Los Angeles. His area of research and publications covers Chinese political economy and the U.S.-Asian relations.

T. C. RHEE.   Professor of History at the University of Dayton. He frequently lectures on a wide-range of East Asian subjects—but mostly on foreign relations of China, Japan, and Korea. Several of his works have been published in Belgium, Holland, Britain, Germany, Argentina, Israel, and the United States.

THOMAS ROBINSON.   Associate Professor in the Institute for Comparative and Foreign Area Studies at the University of Washington. He formerly worked for the Rand Corporation and for the Council on Foreign Relations. Specialist of Sino-Soviet affairs with publications including future studies of China.

ROBERT SCALAPINO.   Professor of Political Science and Director of the Institute of East Asian Studies at University of California-Berkeley. Editor of *Asian Survey,* and author of many books on China, Japan, Korea, and the communist movement in East Asia.

SHELDON SIMON.   Chairman and Professor in the Department of Political Science, Arizona State University. Author of books and articles on international relations and regional security of Asia.

SEUNG KWON SYNN.   Chairman of the Political Science Department, Chung-Ang University. Harvard Ph.D. in Soviet Studies.

GEORGE OAKLEY TOTTEN III.   Director of the East Asian Studies Center and Professor of Political Science at University of Southern California. Taught at universities in both the U.S. and Japan. Author of books and articles on left-wing movements in modern Japan.

STEPHEN G. WALKER.   Assistant Professor and Graduate Advisor in the Department of Political Science, Arizona State University. His research interests include comparative and American foreign policy.

DONALD E. WEATHERBEE.   Currently on leave from the University of South Carolina where he holds the Donald S. Russell Professorship of Contemporary Foreign Policy. He is presently the Henry L. Stimson Professor of Political Science at the U.S. Army War College. He is a frequent lecturer in the U.S. and abroad in the area of Southeast Asian politics and international relations. He has an extensive list of publications in this field.

JAYNE WERNER.   Currently a lecturer in the Department of Government, University of Arizona. She has visited North Vietnam in 1973 and 1975. Specialist of internal and external relations of Vietnam.

GREGORY WINN.   Recently returned from Korea on a Fulbright research grant and currently affiliated with University of Southern California.

ROBERT L. YOUNGBLOOD.   Assistant Professor of Political Science, Arizona State University. His research interests include Southeast Asia and the Philippines.

Index

Index